Yale Linguistic Series, 9

BEGINNING CEBUANO

Part I

by John U. Wolff

New Haven and London, Yale University Press

Second printing, August 1967.
Set in IBM Documentary and
printed in the United States of America by
The Murray Printing Co., Forge Village, Mass.

Library of Congress catalog card number: 65–22474

This work was developed pursuant to a contract
between the United States Office of Education
and Yale University and is published with permission
of the United States Office of Education,
Department of Health, Education, and Welfare.

PREFACE

Beginning Cebuano, Part One, is the first of two volumes of a basic elementary course. It presents the broad outlines of the grammatical structure and illustrates this structure with conversations and exercises. Part Two, to appear shortly, fills detail into the outline, provides further conversations and exercises and presents readings in a variety of styles. These lessons present the first texts ever to be published of normal, colloquial Cebuano (as opposed to the formal and ornate written style usual in Cebuano publications).

These materials are intended for missionaries, diplomats, students, and others who desire or need an active knowledge of Cebuano. Accordingly, emphasis is given to the constructions and expressions which are of frequent, everyday occurrence and which make up the backbone of every normal Cebuano conversation. The exercises and conversations focus on bringing the learner to using these forms actively and with a ready fluency. More formal styles of Cebuano are not ignored, however. The learner is introduced to these through the reading selections.

These lessons could not have been compiled without the help of a great number of people. First and foremost, my thanks are due to the Filipino staff which did the actual preparation of the exercises and conversations and devoted their full interest and energy to their completion. They are too numerous to list by name. However, I owe especial acknowledgments to my wife, Ida Operario Wolff, who worked devotedly on these lessons for the past four years and has edited the Cebuano portions with great care and perspicacity. Her careful judgments and acute comments have enabled me to eliminate numerous errors which, as a non-native speaker, I would otherwise have allowed to slip in. Thanks are due to Carol Robinson and Selene Fung for their skillful illustrations.

I also have a special debt of gratitude to the personnel of the Yale University Press for their professional skill and patience. I would like to mention in particular Elinor C. Horne, who examined every word in the manuscript with minute attention and made comments on literally every page. Through her helpful prodding and criticisms I was able to give the manuscript a new and much improved shape. The analysis and the determination of the form of the lessons is my own, however, and I alone bear the responsibility for errors and omissions.

The research reported here was performed pursuant to a contract between Yale University and the United States Office of Education, Department of Health, Education, and Welfare. To the personnel of both institutions I am grateful for having made this project possible. Finally, thanks are due to the Southeast Asia Program, Cornell University, for supplying funds for typing and editorial assistance.

J. U. W.

Ithaca, New York
March 1966

CONTENTS

PREFACE v
LIST OF PATTERN PRACTICES xiii
INTRODUCTION xv
1. Cebuano Bisayan xv
2. Aim of the Course xv
3. Achievement xvi
4. General Remarks to the Student xvi
5. Classroom Procedure xviii
6. Disposition of the Class xxi
7. Cebuano Pronunciation xxii
LESSON 1. GREETINGS 1
Basic Sentences, Part 1 1
Commentary to Basic Sentences 6
Pronunciation Exercises 7
Grammatical Section 10
1 A. Demonstratives and deictics 10
1 B. Personal pronouns 14
1 C. Ang, y, and the nominative pronouns 15
1 D. Particles 15
1 E. How to say 'It is late' 16
1 F. Linkers 16
Pattern Practices and Exercises 16
Conversation 25
LESSON 2. VISITING 27
Basic Sentences, Part 1 27
Basic Sentences, Part 2 31
Commentary to Basic Sentences 40
Grammatical Section 41
2 A. Deictics and interrogative deictics 41
2 B. Negatives 43
2 C. Suffix -a 44
2 D. Maqú 44
2 E. Preposed genitives 45
Pattern Practices and Exercises 46
Conversation 59
LESSON 3. LOOKING FOR A ROOM 61
Basic Sentences, Part 1 61
Basic Sentences, Part 2 70
Basic Sentences, Part 3 80
Commentary to Basic Sentences 89
Grammatical Section 91
3 A. Existential sentences 91
3 B. Subject and predicate 93

LESSON 3. LOOKING FOR A ROOM [continued]
3 C. Word order 96
3 D. Háqin, ása, and diqín 98
3 E. Linking of prepositives 99
3 F. Long and short forms of words; contractions 99
Pattern Practices and Exercises 103
Conversation 121

LESSON 4. GOING TO THE BEACH 123
Basic Sentences, Part 1 123
Basic Sentences, Part 2 133
Commentary to Basic Sentences 141
Grammatical Section 142
4 A. Verbs: Active 142
4 B. Real active vs. unreal active verb forms 142
4 C. 'There are many' and 'there are few' 144
4 D. Kanúsqa vs. anúsqa 'when?' 144
4 E. The symbol -N- 144
4 F. Indirect questions 145
Pattern Practices and Exercises 145
Reading 154
Conversation 156

LESSON 5. A CONVERSATION WITH VILLAGERS 158
Basic Sentences, Part 1 158
Basic Sentences, Part 2 166
Commentary to Basic Sentences 174
Grammatical Section 174
5 A. Exclamatory sentences 174
5 B. Ug meaning 'have' 175
5 C. Volitional, durative, and potential forms 176
5 D. Agents and goals 181
Pattern Practices and Exercises 182
Reading 211
Conversation 212

LESSON 6. SHOPPING 214
Basic Sentences, Part 1 214
Basic Sentences, Part 2 221
Commentary to Basic Sentences 226
Grammatical Section 227
6 A. Direct passive verb forms 227
6 B. Genitives 232
6 C. More on goals 234
6 D. Order of agent and subject with passive verbs 234
Pattern Practices and Exercises 237
Reading 263
Conversation 264

LESSON 7. REVIEW 266
Reading 266
Pattern Practices and Exercises 269

LESSON 8. ABOARD SHIP 284
Basic Sentences, Part 1 284
Basic Sentences, Part 2 291
Basic Sentences, Part 3 296
Commentary to Basic Sentences 304
Grammatical Section 305
8 A. Local passives 305
8 B. Local passives contrasted with direct passives 308
8 C. Agents and goals 311
8 D. Linking with ug 312
Pattern Practices and Exercises 312
Reading 323
Conversation 324

LESSON 9. A VISIT TO PULAMBATO 326
Basic Sentences, Part 1 326
Basic Sentences, Part 2 332
Basic Sentences, Part 3 337
Commentary to Basic Sentences 344
Grammatical Section 345
9 A. Use of ta, kitá, etc. for first person singular 345
9 B. Abstract forms 346
9 C. Expressions of manner 348
9 D. Exclamations of manner 349
Pattern Practices and Exercises 349
Reading 362
Conversation 365

LESSON 10. OCCUPATIONS IN THE BARRIO 367
Basic Sentences, Part 1 367
Basic Sentences, Part 2 375
Commentary to Basic Sentences 382
Grammatical Section 383
10 A. The instrumental passive 383
10 B. Local and instrumental passives with verbs of conveyance 385
10 C. Verbs meaning both 'put' and 'go' 387
Pattern Practices and Exercises 388
Reading 405
Conversation 407

LESSON 11. AMUSEMENTS IN THE BARRIO 409
Basic Sentences, Part 1 409
Basic Sentences, Part 2 417
Basic Sentences, Part 3 428
Commentary on Basic Sentences 434
Grammatical Section 436
11 A. The derivative verb prefix paN- 436
11 B. The derivative verb prefix ka- 438
11 C. Imperative verb forms 439
11 D. Obligatory use of the potentials 441
Pattern Practices and Exercises 441
Reading 457
Conversation 459

LESSON 12. IN THE BOOKSTORE 461
Basic Sentences, Part 1 461
Basic Sentences, Part 2 466
Basic Sentences, Part 3 472
Commentary to Basic Sentences 476
Grammatical Section 477
12A. Summary of passive verb forms 477
12B. Forms with the base únsa 'what?' 478
12C. The derivational verb prefix pa- 479
12D. Linking of díliq and waláq 481
12E. Complements 481
12F. Exclamatory sentences with pagka- and -a 483
12G. Postpositive particles 483
Pattern Practices and Exercises 486
Reading 508
Conversation 509

LESSON 13. AT SCHOOL 511
Basic Sentences, Part 1 511
Basic Sentences, Part 2 515
Commentary to Basic Sentences 521
Grammatical Section 521
13A. Obligatory use of the passive 521
13B. Obligatory use of the active 523
13C. Bísan kínsa 'Anyone' 524
13D. Meanings of active and passive verb forms: review 524
13E. Kitá, kamí, kamú, silá, si/ni X 527
13F. Use of the subjunctive passive and unreal active 527
13G. Particles lang and diqáy 527
Pattern Practices and Exercises 530
Reading 547
Conversation 548

LESSON 14. SICK IN BED 549
Basic Sentences, Part 1 549
Basic Sentences, Part 2 553
Commentary to Basic Sentences 560
Grammatical Section 561
14A. Other ways of expressing manner 561
14B. Naga-/maga- /ga- 562
14C. Doubled verb roots 562
14D. Measurements and amounts 563
14E. The accidental passive -an / -i 563
14F. Verbs with direct and instrumental passives 564
14G. More postpositive particles: man, ra 566
Pattern Practices and Exercises 570
Reading 587
Conversation 589

LESSON 15. REVIEW 591
Reading 591
Pattern Practices and Exercises 594

KEY TO THE EXERCISES 621
CEBUANO-ENGLISH GLOSSARY 649
INDEX 681

LIST OF PATTERN PRACTICES

Pattern Practice	Subject Matter	
PP-A	Nominative Forms	16
PP-B	Deictics and Interrogatives	46
PP-C	Preposed Genitives	56
PP-D	Existential Sentences	106
PP-E	Word Order	112
PP-F	Use of Y	115
PP-G	Active Verbs	147
PP-H	Changing Existential Sentences into Sentences with Ug	191
PP-I	Exclamatory Sentences	186
PP-J	Difference in Meaning between Volitional, Durative, and Potential Forms	198
PP-K	Goals	202
PP-L	Agents	205
PP-M	Use of Agent and Subject—Direct Passive Only	245
PP-N	Genitives	252
PP-O	Use of Agent and Subject	353
PP-P	Use of Agent and Subject	397
PP-Q	Direct vs. Local (No Transformations)	313
PP-R	Local vs. Instrumental (No Transformations)	388
PP-S	Transformation of Active to Passive	278
PP-T	Direct vs. Local (Transformation of Active to Passive)	441
PP-V	Direct vs. Local vs. Instrumental (Change of Emphasis)	595
PP-Y	Díliq vs. Waláq—Direct Passive	275
PP-BB	Giqúnsa vs. Unsáqun	492
PP-CC	Change of Singular to Plural	449
PP-DD	Direct, Local and Instrumental of Causatives	493
PP-EE	Transforming Statements into Negative Existential Sentences	538
PP-FF	Expressions of Manner	574
PP-GG	Transformation into Accidental Passive	579

INTRODUCTION

1. Cebuano Bisayan

These lessons provide learning materials for Cebuano Bisayan. This language is also called Visayan, Bisayan, Cebuan, or Sugbuhanon. Since the terms Visayan or Bisayan are also applied to other languages or dialects spoken in the Visayas (the islands of the central Philippines), we prefer to call this language Cebuano. In Cebuano the language is called binisayáq or sinibuwanú. In 1960 there were around seven and a half million native speakers of Cebuano (nearly a third of the total population of the Philippines — more native speakers than of any other language in the Philippines). Cebuano is spoken in Cebu, Bohol, the western half of Leyte, Negros Oriental and other islands in this neighborhood, northern and eastern coasts of Mindanao, and various other places in Bukidnon, Agusan, Surigao, Davao, Cotabato, and Zamboanga del Sur. It is also widely spoken as a second language in contiguous areas. There are differences in the Cebuano used in various places, but as spoken in Negros, Cebu, most of Leyte, and Mindanao (except Surigao and Agusan), Cebuano has only slight variations and is considered standard. It is this Cebuano which is presented here. In Surigao, Bohol and other places where it is different, most people know how to speak and understand standard Cebuano as well as their local dialect.

2. Aim of the Course

The aim of language learning is to use the language like a native speaker. A learner cannot, of course, duplicate in a few months the experiences of a whole childhood of a native speaker—especially since as an adult he is not so pliable as a child and thus not so amenable to new habits. However, he can learn to communicate. This means not only that the student can learn to understand everything and say what he wants to say himself, but, more important, that he can get to know the subtleties and nuances which express people's attitudes and feelings: Is it a joke or is it serious? Does the person mean what he says, or is he just being polite? Is he keeping his distance, or is he making overtures of friendship? Is he satisfied, or is he resentful? And so on. These attitudes are expressed by language (as well as by other behavior), and the foreigner must learn not only to recognize the signals, but also to use the signals to convey his own feelings to others.

In this course we aim primarily to give you a feeling for the important—that is, frequently used—aspects of Cebuano grammatical structure and develop your ability to use these automatically and correctly. With an automatic control of grammar you will be on the road to complete understanding and full expression of these signals for conveying attitudes and feelings.

We also aim to present a picture of Cebuano life and attitudes. The situations depicted in the lessons are typical: the things said are the typical things said in the situation and the responses are typical responses. The exercises drill you in these behavioral patterns as well as in the grammatical patterns, for you will best learn to recognize language signals after you learn how people regard situations and how they tend to respond.

3. Achievement

Lessons 1-15 cover the basic principles without which it is impossible to form correct sentences or understand normal Cebuano. Lessons 16-21 describe and exercise frequently used constructions and inflections, a knowledge of which is necessary to express oneself clearly and fully. Lessons 22-25 deal with constructions which are not basic to conversation, but are important for full expression and for comprehension of written materials. Some detailed points of grammar are not covered, but these are not of frequent occurrence in daily conversation.

Lessons 1-15 can be completed in 350 classroom hours by rapid learners who come to class well prepared. The entire course can be completed in approximately 600 classroom hours by fast, well prepared students. Slower or less diligent students will take proportionately more time.

4. General Remarks to the Student

You should keep in mind that your goal is to attain a command of Cebuano as near to that of the native speaker as possible. How does one go about achieving this goal? The method on which our course is modeled and the procedures to be followed are described in Section 5 below. These are the methods employed with proven success at the leading language training centers of the United States. Before publication the lessons of this book were used with excellent results by more than two hundred Americans. In some cases people who had been studying Cebuano for five years or more by other methods with little success became excellent speakers of Cebuano after working through this course.

Why must we parrot our informant?

It is precisely by repetition that you come to understand a foreign language. When you first hear a foreign utterance, it is just a jumble of sounds to you, and you pay no further attention. However, if you are to repeat this jumble of sounds, you must observe every minute aspect of it;* you learn to fix your attention on the elements that are significant, which, if you were just listening passively, you might never notice.

Mimicking has another purpose as well: when you repeat and imitate, the patterns of the language become impressed on your mind. One or two repetitions

---

* What seems minute and unimportant to the foreigner may actually differentiate one utterance from another. We must assume that any element of which the native speaker is aware is important for the meaning. For us there is a clear difference between nitrate and night rate, though they have very similar sounds. For a foreigner the difference might well go unnoticed unless his attention were drawn to it.

will not make the pattern a part of you, but in these lessons, all of the important intonational and grammatical patterns are repeated several thousand times, and they will become so much a part of you that you will form sentences just like those of a native speaker, without thinking about how to express the idea. The largest proportion of class time is given to plain repetitions, to the point that you do not think about what you are doing; the response comes out automatically.

Language learning, then, is a matter of habit formation. For this reason, little class time is to be devoted to grammatical explanations. Automatic responses are developed not by talking about them or examining their content but by constantly practicing them. (The foreigner may be told that after I we use am instead of is, but only after he has practiced saying I am many times will he say am without thinking.) To be sure, if you know the explanation you are in a better position to develop an automatic response; and grammatical discussion, with exercises to clarify it, are a useful part of the course. But explanation alone will not achieve automatic control of the patterns.

Do we have to memorize sentences?

You cannot avoid memorizing sentences—though for many people this process is tedious and distasteful. To achieve an active knowledge of Cebuano, you must memorize something—either sentences or individual words. You can easily see which is better if you take the case of the Cebuano learning English. Suppose he is to learn the word around. There is no Cebuano equivalent to around. Even if the Cebuano student were given a complicated explanation of around there is little chance that he would understand how to use it. But if he has memorized the sentence "I am just looking around," he knows at least one meaning of it; if he has also learned the sentence "Stop sitting around; do something," he probably also has developed a good feeling for around in this meaning (and probably an idea of how to use the word stop and the other words as well). Much of the meaning of English speech resides in common words like around, the, is, would, get, well, and so forth, all of which defy lucid explanation but which can be grasped through well chosen examples. It is the same with Cebuano. That is why you are asked to memorize sentences. The sentences illustrate the common elements that cannot be defined meaningfully. If you memorize faithfully, you will be able to come out with normal, well-formed sentences, using these very elements instinctively.

Do we need to use English in class?

The answer to this question is never—except perhaps for a small proportion of the time devoted to grammatical explanations. These lessons are so designed that English need not be used at all from the first day. Remember, you learn a language by hearing it and imitating it, not by talking about it. Therefore, FROM THE FIRST DAY DRILL HOURS MUST BE CONDUCTED EXCLUSIVELY IN CEBUANO.

A special time may be set aside for grammatical explanations and questions in English, if there is someone available who can profitably lead such a period. The time should not exceed one-fourth of the total classroom hours. The rest of the time should be devoted to speaking Cebuano and hearing it spoken.

Should the informant speak more slowly than normal?

The answer to this question is decidedly not. ALWAYS USE NORMAL SPEED. Do not ask your informant to slow down his speech for you. You can learn to understand normal speech only by hearing normal speech. Learning a slow, artificial speech such as is never heard outside the classroom is obviously a hindrance rather than a steppingstone to understanding normal speech. Slow, deliberate pronunciations involve distortions that do not occur in normal speech; and these distortions are all you will learn if your informant does not use normal speech with you. You will never hear little elements of normal speech which may be pregnant with meaning.

Does it sound funny?

When you first try imitating the sounds of a new language, they sound funny and embarrass you. But you must bear in mind that these are part of the language, and within a couple of days it will sound all right to you. Let this be your guide: if your pronunciation sounds funny to you and your informant accepts it, chances are it is right. If it does not sound funny to you, you are probably speaking with a strong foreign accent. (The situation is complicated, to be sure, by the fact that your informant may be too polite to correct you, or may not understand that it is his task to hold you to high standards.)

What does the informant do?

The informant provides the model which you imitate and shows you the right way to say something when you have said it wrong. Note the term informant applies to your Cebuano instructor. He has no function other than to show you how to speak. Do not expect him to teach you—that is, to answer your questions, understand your difficulties, or devise methods for making the repetition easier. If you expect this, you will be sacrificing your chance to hear and speak Cebuano. THE MOMENT YOU SPEAK ENGLISH YOUR PROGRESS STOPS. EVERY MOMENT YOU ARE HEARING AND SPEAKING CEBUANO YOU ARE MAKING PROGRESS. Furthermore, if you expect your informant to teach you, you will be disappointed. Even an expert rarely will know how to answer you profitably. Try instead to get your answers from the book. In the beginning you will have many questions; these questions get answered, one by one, as you go along. In the end there will be few, if any, unsolved problems.

The best solution to the problem of wasting time speaking English is: get an informant who speaks no English. Many students have successfully used these lessons with monolingual informants. The informant must be taught (through an interpreter) to correct you; in fact, you must insist that he correct you. He must understand that he is not making you lose status if he corrects you. And you yourself must cheerfully accept corrections. When he corrects you, say what he wanted you to say and let it go at that. Do not look puzzled (even if you are); do not argue; above all, do not show anger or disappointment; try instead to look enlightened and happy upon receiving corrections. If your informant still refuses to correct you—or if he insists on speaking English—fire him.

Train your informant.

Before you begin your lessons, go through mock classroom situations to show the informant what to do before you begin your lessons. This will enable you to set up a routine and develop proper teaching habits beforehand, so that once you have begun your routine, you will rarely need to break in on your informant to correct his teaching methods. If he is monolingual, you will need an interpreter to help you train him properly, but once you have started your routine, you will manage to understand each other without an interpreter.

5. Classroom Procedure

Each lesson consists of (1) basic sentences to be memorized, followed by questions, matching exercises, and commentary to the basic sentences; (2) grammatical explanations; and (3) exercises. The exercises consist of pattern practices, grammatical exercises, intonational exercises, and readings. Five of the lessons are review lessons, with readings and exercises of the same type as those in the other lessons.

All basic sentences, pattern practices, and intonational exercises have been recorded on tapes, for supplementary study and practice outside of the classroom.

A. Basic sentences

The informant selects a certain portion of the lesson for each day's assignment. (Rapid learners can cover one part of a lesson in four classroom hours.)

1. The informant reads the sentences one at a time. The students repeat in unison after each sentence.
2. The informant reads each sentence for each student. (Take one sentence and go around the room; take the next sentence and go around the room; etc.) The student repeats what the informant said. The informant corrects the student. The student repeats the informant's correction.

Overnight, the students memorize the sentences practiced in class. The following day they are examined orally:

1. Students cover the Cebuano.
2. The informant gives a number and calls on the student.
3. The student says the Cebuano sentence corresponding to the number.
4. The informant gives the correct answer (even if the student answered correctly).
5. The student repeats the informant's model.

A good procedure for memorizing at home is to cover the Cebuano, give the Cebuano from the English translation, and then listen to the tape to see if you said the sentence correctly with the right intonation.

The purpose of the basic sentences is to give the student a treasury of constructions, intonations, usages, and ways of expression to act as a basis for understanding the grammar and upon which he can expand to produce his own utterances. You will find that if you have done an adequate job of memorizing the sentences and practicing the intonations, you will gradually become able to speak smoothly without thinking, and your intonations and turns of expression will be like those used by native speakers.

The basic sentences not only exemplify normal responses to common situations; they have a wider application as a springboard for further conversation. For example, the informant may ask questions similar to those given at the end of each lesson, which are based on the basic sentences or which require a response eliciting the basic sentence (or a variation of it). Or, the informant may outline a situation parallel to that of the lesson and assign members of the class to take roles. (If this technique is used, there must be constant rotation so that no member of the class is left unoccupied.)

It is important to remember that these other uses of the basic sentences do not substitute for memorization and testing, which are the first order of the day and are the foundation upon which you learn to speak.

B. Questions and matching exercises

These are designed to give you practice using the vocabulary and expressions of the lesson. You can derive the most profit from these if you use them as a springboard for expanding on what you have learned, by experimenting with variations on a sentence you know, using the words you know in a new context, and so on. For advanced students the matching questions may be used for their own sake and also may serve as a basis for further conversation. Many of the matching exercises show normal responses to questions and yet are imaginative answers, not necessarily the predicted responses.

The questions can profitably be answered in written form and corrected by the informant. This procedure gives you a chance to study your errors at leisure and gain a better idea of what you still do not understand or mistakes you tend to make.

C. Pattern practices

The pattern practices are designed to teach the grammatical rules and to develop automatic habits for applying them. Each pattern practice is divided into steps of successive difficulty. The first step is always easy and involves simple substitution of one word. The final step is more difficult and may involve a number of complicated changes, such as one would be obliged to make in ordinary conversation.

The pattern practices appear after each grammatical section and provide exercise on the material presented in the section. They should be performed immediately after the grammatical explanation. (If the pattern practice is done first, the students tend to ask questions and break up the continuity which is necessary to develop an automatic response.)

The pattern practices should be done orally, with normal speed and normal intonation, and the students should not refer to their books. The pace must be kept rapid; otherwise the students will forget the sentence. The steps in each pattern practice should be followed in order: Step I, Step II, etc.

First, the informant should write the Cebuano and its English translation on the blackboard. He reads the Cebuano sentence and has the students repeat. He reads the cue and has the students repeat the sentence with the change suggested by the cue. He repeats for the students only if the change was not proper, or there was incorrect pronunciation or intonation, and has the students repeat the corrected form after him. He then gives the next cue, and proceeds throughout as above. When several answers are possible, he should accept any correct one without comment. If he himself gives the answer, he should choose one correct answer and make no comment.

After a certain amount of unison answering, the informant may then skip around calling on individual students. In no case, however, should the class know who is going to be called next. He should also remember to keep the pace rapid so that the students will not forget the sentence.

If a pattern practice is too long, there is no harm in stopping in the middle. When the practice is resumed, the informant should review some of the earlier steps so that the students will not plunge into something very difficult without adequate preparation.

When the class experiences difficulty, the informant may go back to an earlier step and try to cover the ground again until he feels that they have mastered the principles. Under no circumstances should he move ahead when a large percentage of the class is unable to give the answer automatically. (An exception to this is certain of the pattern practices, particularly a number of the more difficult steps of PP-M through PP-DD, giving processes that are difficult to make automatic. Here, the informant should not insist on the impossible, but should be satisfied with a less than automatic reaction in the beginning.) An intelligent informant should also be able to make up intermediate exercises on the spot, as a bridge to those sentences which are too difficult.

When the material is too easy, the informant should not waste time following each step through to the bitter end. Once it is clear that the students have mastered the material and can answer automatically, he should abandon that step and move directly to the next.

The informant should avoid overtiring the students. In general a half hour of pattern practices is the most they can take at a stretch. If the informant notices that the students are listless or having difficulty because of fatigue, the class should move to another type of occupation or take a break.

Students are easily discouraged if the exercises are too hard for them. The teacher should by no means push them if it turns out that they are unable to handle the material. If the students show signs of discouragement, he should stop and give them an easy exercise to restore their self-confidence.

The pattern practices are adapted to self-study. The tapes on which the pattern practices are recorded have blank intervals after the cues, so that the student has time to supply the answer; he then checks this against the correct, recorded answer. If he is not using the tapes, he should take a piece of paper and cover the sentence below the cue. When he has made the substitution he moves the paper down a space to see if his answer is proper. With difficult pattern practices, it is always a good idea to review at home on one's own.

D. Grammatical exercises

The grammatical exercises are to be done orally in class; also, some of them should be practiced at home every night. Responses should consist of complete sentences—not isolated answers. These exercises are designed to reinforce an understanding of the explanations and eventually develop automatic responses. (The vocabulary of the exercises and pattern practices is confined to that of the basic sentences.)

E. Intonational exercises

The intonational exercises emphasize correct production of the intonational patterns. The informant may give a few sentences as examples, having the student repeat his model, and then the students should say some of the sentences without the model. Each time the student says a sentence, the informant should repeat it correctly (whether or not the student said it right).

F. Readings

The readings within the lessons (called pagbása) are designed to show uses of certain inflectional forms or particles in a context, and to provide exercise on the vocabulary of the basic sentences; they may be used as a basis for conversation.

Other reading selections have been prepared and are to appear in Part Two. Their purpose is to give the student a survey of Cebuano styles other than the informal colloquial style presented in the lessons of basic sentences, and also to build his vocabulary. They may be used independently or in conjunction with the basic sentences at any point after Lesson 12.

6. Disposition of the Class

Length. Classes should not last more than 45 minutes to an hour. After this time the students should be given a short break, and after two classes a longer recess is necessary.

Schedule of an ordinary day. It is not recommended that classes be held for more than five hours a day. For most students, four hours with an equal amount of study time at home give the best results.

First hour: Quick repetition of sentences memorized for that day; test of memorization; begin sentences to be memorized for the following day.

Second hour: Continue new sentences; do matching exercises, questions.

Third hour: Grammatical explanation, exercises, or pattern practices.

Fourth hour: Pattern practice and/or grammatical exercises and/or free conversation based on the basic sentences.

Fifth hour: If given, the fifth hour should be of the same character as the fourth.

After the students begin the separate section of readings, the procedure described in the introduction to that section may replace one or two of these hours.

Size of the class. The optimum class size is four or five students. This is a sufficient number for competition but not too large to prevent the informant from engaging every member of the class constantly. Ideally they should be grouped according to their aptitude. Poor students become discouraged if they are forced to compete with good students; good students, on the other hand, tend to lose interest if not allowed to exercise their abilities to the utmost. The informant should sit as close as possible to each student so that he can be heard clearly.

Discipline. There must be an established routine, and attendance must be regular if progress is to be made.

Above all: STICK TO CEBUANO.

7. Cebuano Pronunciation

Every language has its own set of sounds which is different from that of every other language. No two languages are the same in every detail of their sound systems. Thus when one learns a new language, he must form the habit of making new sounds and using them automatically. The habit is not formed without conscious effort. The student learns new sounds by a zeroing-in process: he listens to an utterance; imitates it; has it repeated again; and imitates again, trying to come closer. The habit of making new sounds develops as he repeats the process hundreds of times, up to the point that he himself knows—without comparing what he has said with a native speaker's model—whether or not it sounds right. Good pronunciation results from an awareness of what the sounds of the language are like and constant practice in making them correctly.

In Lesson 1, there are hints and exercises on making Cebuano sounds which English does not have. Other Cebuano sounds are more like English sounds, though still different enough to make it important for you to imitate your informant carefully.

A. Stress and Intonation

In Cebuano words containing more than one vowel,* one of the vowels is louder than all the others in the word: these have STRESS (are STRESSED). Stress is indicated with the symbol ´ placed over the vowel. In lútuq 'cook,' for example, the first u is louder than the second u; in lutúq 'cooked,' the second u is louder than the first u.

---

* The Cebuano vowels are a, i, and u.

Cebuano sentences have rises and falls of pitch. These are indicated, in the basic sentence sections and occasionally elsewhere, by solid lines drawn above the sentence. The pitch is high where the line is high and low where the line is low. Thus in the first basic sentence,

Maqáyu. 'Hello.'

ma has the lowest pitch; qa has a higher pitch; and yu is lower than qa but higher than ma. Of course these rises and falls are relative to each other within a single utterance; they are not absolute. A speaker with a high voice will say everything at a higher absolute pitch than a speaker with a low voice. But no matter what the quality of the speaker's voice, in the utterance maqáyu 'hello,' ma will be lower than qa or yu; qa will be higher than ma or yu; and yu will be intermediate between the two.

The pitches shape themselves into regular contours—that is, the sequences of rises and falls are repeated in certain patterns. The particular contour pattern varies according to the meaning of the sentence. In greetings, for example, the sequence 'beginning low—high on the penult (next-to-last vowel)—slight drop on the final vowel' is frequent; in questions a sharp rise on the final vowel is common; and so forth.*

We refer to these intonations by sequences of the numbers 1, 2, 3, or 4. The highest number represents the highest pitch, the lowest number the lowest. In any utterance the highest pitch is represented by 4 and the lowest pitch is represented by 1, 2, or 3, depending on the interval between the pitch extremes of the contour pattern. Thus the pattern of our example maqáyu 'hello' is designated by the sequence 243. The symbol 1 is used only when a greater interval between the highest pitch and the lowest pitch contrasts with a smaller interval between the highest pitch and the lowest pitch. An example of such a contrast is the following pair: the first has a pattern symbolized 214; the second, a pattern symbolized 324.

---

*In this respect Cebuano is not unlike English. Certain patterns appear regularly in certain English questions: for example, a question that anticipates a 'yes' or 'no' answer ends on a rise, while a question asking for information ('what?' 'why?' etc.) ends on a low pitch; another set of patterns is used for commands; and so forth. Thus the utterance

No?

is a question (anticipating confirmation) with a rise in pitch. With a sharp fall it is a statement:

No.

With a fall, but not so sharp, it is a statement which is to be qualified:

No, . . . (No, but . . .)

Ákuq ni 'Is this mine?'

Ákuq ni. 'This is mine.'

Long sentences are usually broken by pauses. Places where such pauses are usual are indicated by the symbol # in the intonation line and by punctuation marks in the alphabetic representation.

B. Vowels and Diphthongs

Cebuano has three vowel sounds, represented here by the symbols i, a, and u, and five diphthongs, represented by iy, ay, uy, iw, and aw. The description below gives the nearest English equivalent to each Cebuano sound:

i like i in bit; when long or doubled, like i in bid.*
a like a in father.
u like oo in look; when long or doubled, like oo in good.*
iy like ey in key.
ay like igh in sight; when long or doubled (aay), like igh in sigh.*
uy like oi in foist.
iw This sound has no equivalent in English. It is composed of i (as in bit) followed by u (like oo in look).
aw This sound has no equivalent in English.† It is composed of a (as in father) followed by u (like oo in look).

In general, Cebuano vowels differ from English vowels in the following ways: (1) Cebuano i and u may end a word; the comparable English sounds may not.‡ (2) Cebuano vowels are shorter than English vowels, except that in the sequence stressed-vowel + consonant + vowel, the stressed vowel is longer than vowels in the other positions: e.g. in lútuq 'cook' the first u is longer than the second u and longer than either u in lutúq 'cooked.' (A vowel written as double is a

* The i of bit is shorter than the i of bid. (To get an idea of the difference say bit, bid without interruption several times; then say bid, bit several times in that order.) Similarly, oo is shorter in look than in good, and igh is shorter in sight than in sigh.

† However, speakers from the Northeastern United States pronounce out with a vowel sound very close to Cebuano aw. To learn to make the Cebuano sound, contrast English loud against a Cebuano speaker's láwud 'sea.' Contrast English cow against a Cebuano speaker's táwu 'man.'

‡ English speakers tend to substitute the English sound ay (as in bay) for Cebuano i at the end of a word. Contrast Cebuano bi 'give me' with English bay: in English the tongue moves forward and upward as the ay is being pronounced, while in Cebuano the tongue does not move as the i is being pronounced. Similarly, English speakers tend to substitute ow (as in know) for Cebuano u at the end of a word. Contrast Cebuano nu 'that's so, isn't it?' with English know: in English, the tongue moves forward and upward as the ow of know is being pronounced, but in Cebuano the tongue does not move during the articulation of u.

lengthened variety of a single vowel: e.g. in nakasáaq 'sinned' the aa has the same quality as the two preceding a's but is held longer.) (3) Cebuano vowels are not weakened (or centralized) in unstressed position like, for example, the second a in English drama, which is different in pronunciation from the first a. In Cebuano the three a's of salámat 'thanks' are pronounced alike.

C. Consonants

Here is a table of the Cebuano consonant symbols:

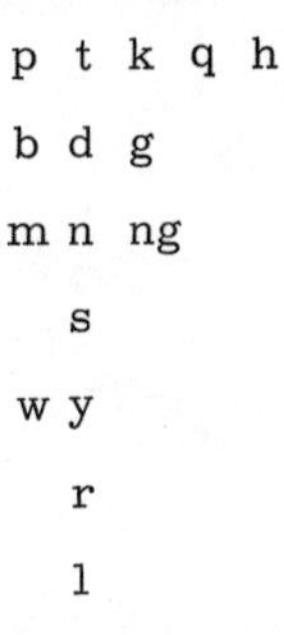

p	t	k	q	h
b	d	g		
m	n	ng		
	s			
w	y			
	r			
	l			

In general these sounds are like the English counterparts,* with the following exceptions:

- p like p in spin (i.e. no puff of air after p, as there is in pin).
- t like t in stop (i.e. no puff of air after t, as there is in top); also, t is pronounced with the tongue tip pressed against the inside of the upper teeth—not as in English where the tongue tip is further back.
- k like k in skip (i.e. no puff of air after k as in keep).
- d like d in dog but with the tip of the tongue as for t.
- n like n in no but with the tip of the tongue as for t, d.
- ng like ng in sing.
- l like l in clean (i.e. with the tip of the tongue pressed against the roof of the mouth just in back of the upper teeth).
- r After a consonant or at the end of a word, like English r in roll (except that the tongue is never curled back). Initially and between vowels, like tt in pretty.
- q A stopping of the breath (glottal stop), as represented by the hyphen in English oh-oh (exclamation of surprise or warning, as for example when one has dropped something).

See the comments and exercises for some of these sounds in Lesson 1, page 7.

---

*Except that Cebuano q has no English counterpart.

LESSON 1. GREETINGS

Sagquluhúnun (Basic Sentences)

John and Vincent visit Mr. Abaya.	Si Huwán ug si Ínting mibisíta ni Místir Abáya.
1. Hello! (Lit. Good.) †	*1. Maqáyu.
good	maqáyu
[linker between maqáyu and búntag]	nga
morning	búntag
2. Good morning.	*2. Maqáyung búntag.
what?	únsa
[question particle after interrogative]	man
[subject marker]	y
ours	átuq
3. What can I do for you? (Lit. What is ours?)	*3. Únsa may átuq?
is there, are there	náqa
[question particle]	ba
[particle preceding names]	si
4. Is Mr. Abaya there?	*4. Náqa ba si Místir Abáya?
is here, are here	níqa
[particle used on giving information]	man
5. Yes, he is. (Lit. He is here.)	5. Níqa man.
6. Come on in. (Lit. Just come in.)	6. Dayún lang.

* An asterisk preceding a Cebuano sentence indicates that there is a note on it in the Commentary to Basic Sentences.

† The translations give English equivalents. Literal meanings, when different, are placed in parentheses.

ah [pause before speaking]	aa
Ting [short for Ínting]	Ting
how are? how is?	kumústa
7. Ah, Ting! How are you?	7. Aa, Ting! # Kumústa?
good	maqáyu
[particle used on giving information]	man
8. Good!	8. Maqáyu man.
is here, are here	níqa
we	mi
here	dínhi
because	kay
is here, are here	níqa
[existential particle]	y
my	ákuq
[linker between ákuq and amígu]	nga
friend	amígu
9. We came here to see you (Lit. We are here) because (I) have a friend here (to introduce to you).	*9. Níqa mi dínhi kay níqay ákung ... amígu.
this	kiní
[particle preceding personal names and titles when used as subject]	si
10. This is Mr. Gamelo.	*10. Kiní si Místir Gamílu.
how is? how are?	kumústa
you	ka
11. How are you, Mr. Gamelo?	11. Kumústa ka Místir Gamílu?
12. Good morning, Mr. Abaya.	12. Maqáyung búntag Místir Abáya.
[hesitation word]	kiníng
[word used to fill in]	kuqán
[term of address for female same age as or younger than speaker]	Day

to be got for	ikúhaq
I, me	ku
[particle preceding goal]	ug
beer	bir
13. Er, what's-your-name—Miss Beer! Get me some beer.	*13. Kinîng, kuqán—Day. Bir. Ikúhaq kug bir.
[pause before speaking]	aa
don't!	ayáw
now	na
just	lang
14. No thank you! (Lit. Ah, just don't now.)	*14. Aa, ayáw na lang.
because	kay
am (is, are) in a hurry	nagdalîq
[particle giving reason]	man
I	ku
15. Because I'm in a hurry.	*15. Kay nagdalîq man ku.
I	ákuq
just	lang
will leave	ibîlin
this	ni
[linker between ni and amîgu]	nga
my	ákuq
[linker between ákuq and amîgu]	nga
friend	amîgu
here	dînhi
16. I'll just leave my friend here. (Lit. . . . this my friend . . .)	*16. Ákuq lang ibîlin ning . . . ákung amîgu dînhi.
do something before someone else	magquná
just	lang
I	ku
of him	nîya

17. Good-by. (Lit. I'll just go ahead of him.)
17. Magquná lang ku nīya.

over there [future] — ádtu
now — na
I — ku

18. I'll be going now. (Lit. I will be over there now.)
*18. Ádtu na ku.

yes — uu
go on, continue — sīgi
thanks — salámat

19. O.K. Good-by. Thanks.
19. Uu, sīgi. Salámat.

[future] [not near person spoken to] — arī
now — na
I — ku

20. I'm going now. (Lit. I will be over here now.)
20. Arī na ku.

yes — uu

21. O.K.
21. Uu.

what? — únsa
[question particle after interrogative] — man
[subject marker] — y
our — átuq

22. What will you have, Mr. Gamelo? (Lit. What is ours?)
22. Únsa may átuq Mīstir Gamīlu?

Coca-Cola — kukakúla
just — lang

23. Just Coca-Cola.
23. Kukakúla lang.

oh — uh
noon — údtu
already, by now — na
[particle used upon giving new fact] — man

[particle used upon discovering something]	diqáy
very	kaqáyu
24. Oh, it's very late! (Lit. It is very late by now, I see.)	24. Uh, údtu na man diqáy kaqáyu.
over there	ádtu
[particle used to indicate the least undesirable of limited choices]	na lang
I	ku
much, many	dághan
[linker between dághan and salámat]	nga
thanks	salámat
25. I'll just be going now. Thank you very much, Mr. Abaya.	25. Ádtu na lang ku. Dághang salámat Místir Abáya.
you're welcome	way sapayán
come back again	balikbálik
26. You're welcome! Come again.	26. Way sapayán. Balikbálik.

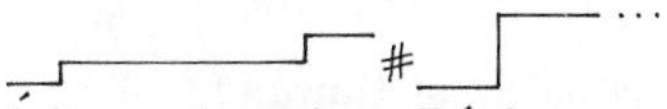

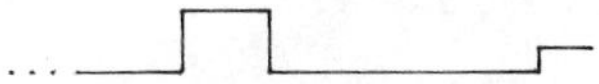

Pangutána (Matching)

(1) Match the letter response with the question.
(2) Cover the right column and answer the questions in the left column.
(3) Cover the left column and make up the questions which evoke the responses in the right column.

1. Maqáyung búntag.	a. Maqáyu man.
2. Náqa ba si Huwán?	b. Uu. Sígi.
3. Ádtu na ku.	c. Kumústa ka Místir Abáya?
4. Únsa may átuq?	d. Kumústa ka Místir Gamílu?
5. Gabíqi na man kaqáyu. (Gabíqi 'evening')	e. Maqáyung búntag.
6. Salámat.	f. Níqa man.
7. Kumústa si Mísis Abáya?	g. Maqáyung údtu.
	h. Aa, ayáw na lang! Kay nagdalíq man ku.

8. Maqáyung údtu.
9. Kinî si Mîstir Abáya.
10. Nîqa mi dînhi kay nîqa si Mîstir Gamîlu.

i. Way sapayán.
j. Ádtu na ku.

Mangá Pangutána (Questions)

1. Nîqa ba si Luqîs?
2. Únsa may átuq?
3. Nîqa ba ang îmung amîgu?
4. Náqa ba si Tátay mu?
5. Kumústa ka?
6. Nîqa ba siyá dînhi?
7. Nîqa ba si Huwán?
8. Way kukakúla?
9. Ádtu ka na ba?
10. Nagdalîq ka ba?
11. Gabîqi na ba kaqáyu?
12. Údtu na ba?

mu	your, you
îmu	your
ka	you
ang	[subject marker]
tátay	daddy
gabîqi	evening

Commentary to Basic Sentences

1.1* It is customary to call out maqáyu when coming to the door instead of knocking. This is short for maqáyung búntag 'good morning,' maqáyung gabîqi 'good evening,' etc.

1.2 Note that a is dropped from nga after a word ending with a vowel.

1.3 Note that n drops from man before the particle y.

1.3 For use of man see grammatical section, 1 D.†

---

* The reference 1.1 means Lesson 1, basic sentence 1.

† References containing numbers followed by letters are to the grammatical sections: 1 D means Lesson 1, section D, p. 15 below.

1.4 Náqa and ba are explained in the grammatical section. Si precedes personal names used as subject (1 C).

1.9 Mi and ákuq are explained in the grammatical section (1 B).

1.9 The y is a particle meaning 'has' or 'there is (are).' This particle is explained in Lesson 3 (3 A 1).

1.9 Ákung is from ákuq + nga. Ákuq drops q before nga, and nga drops a after a word ending in a vowel. See the note to 1.2 above.

1.10 Kiní is explained in the grammatical section (1 A 1).

1.13 Day is the appellation of a woman or girl the same age as or younger than the speaker. Here Mr. Abaya is using Day to call his maid. (He cannot remember her name.)
Ku is the nominative form listed in 1 B.

1.14 Ayáw is the negative for imperative forms.

1.14–15 Inting's refusal would be impolite in a more formal circumstance: his excuse that he is in a hurry could not be accepted. Inting and Mr. Abaya are close friends, however, and so they speak informally. The politest response to such an invitation is to accept; if that is not possible, say that it would not be good for you to drink at this time.

1.16 Ning is from ni + nga by the rule given in 1.2 above. For ákung see the comment to 1.9 above.

1.18 This is the normal way of saying good-by upon leaving someone behind.

1.18 Note that the words referring to place in Cebuano also have a time meaning. Here ádtu 'over there' has a future meaning. See grammatical section, 1 A 2.

Linitukán (Pronunciation)

1. P, T, K These sounds are pronounced with no explosion of breath following them. Practice them by holding the back of your hand to your mouth and saying ta in such a way that no air hits your hand. Do the same for pa, ka.

2. T, D, N For Cebuano T, D, and N (as contrasted with English T, D, N) the tongue touches the back of the upper teeth: tátay 'Dad,' day 'Miss,' náqa 'is there.' (Remember also that with t there is no explosion of breath.)

3. Q (glottal stop) This sound is made by momentarily stopping the air passage at the glottis or Adam's apple, as between the oh's in the English expression of mild alarm oh-oh! [oq-o], used for example when you have dropped something and in the informal negative hm-mm. (A glottal stop occurs also in New York pronunciations of bottle [boq-l], little [liq-l], etc.)

4. NG Ng represents the last sound of English sing, going. The pronunciation exercises will give you practice in making this sound at

the beginning of the word, a position it does not occupy in English.

5. Stress — The stress mark (´) appears over a vowel which is louder and in some cases longer than the other vowels in a word. (It is longer when it is followed by a single consonant and is not the last vowel in the word.) Stress occurs on either of the last two syllables of a word.

6. Intonation — The lines above the basic sentences correspond to rises and falls in pitch of the speaker's voice. (Note that there is no pause before a term of address: in the examples, Místir Abáya and Day.)

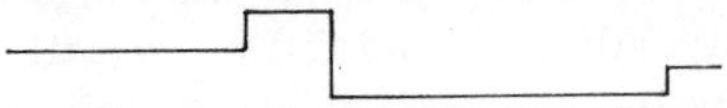

Maqáyung búntag Místir Abáya. 'Good morning, Mr. Abaya.'

Ikúhaq kug bir Day. 'Get me some beer, Miss.'

Ihirsísyu sa Paglitúk (Pronunciation Exercises)

The following exercises will give the student practice in pronouncing Q (glottal stop: 3 in the preceding section) and in word stress (5 in the preceding section). The informant should demonstrate the contrast by pronouncing both words of the pair; then he should say one of them, and ask the student to identify it. The student should keep coming back to this exercise until he has learned to recognize and pronounce the sounds without difficulty.

I. Examples of q at the end of a word contrasting with its absence.

A.	1. tulúq tulú	2. ubúq ubú	3. daluqdalúq daludalú	4. balíq balí
	tulú tulúq	ubú ubúq	daludalú daluqdalúq	balí balíq
B.	5. bangáq bangá	6. ámuq ámu	7. súkaq súka	8. bátaq báta
	bangá bangáq	ámu ámuq	súka súkaq	báta bátaq
C.	síbuq síbu	timúq timú	mahímuq mahímu	ikúq ikú
	sákuq sáku	báhuq báhu	balúq balú	kútuq kútu
	kútuq kútu	pilúq pilú	tiyúq tiyú	waláq walá
	unáq uná	búqbuq búbuq	dúqduq dúduq	tukúq tukú

puyúq	bagaqbagáq	kisiqkisîq	butúq
puyú	bagabagá	kisikisî	butú
daluqdalúq	sîpaq	bukáq	pangáyuq
daludalú	sîpa	buká	pangáyu

II. Examples of q in the middle of a word contrasting with its absence.

kaqáyu	maqáyu	dáqan	suqúd
káyu	máyu	daan	suud
búwak	nîya	luwág	túu
buqák	níqa	luqág	túqu
sáqag	dagáqang	táwun	sáwup
saag	dagáng	taqún	saqúp

III. Examples of words with q after consonants contrasting with words having no q in that position.

bátqa	súkqa	bátqang	bágqu
báta	súka	bátang	bágu
búnqi	látqa	tágqas	dagqanáy
búni	láta	tágas	daganáy

IV. Examples of contrasting stresses (several syllables).

táqas	kúhit	báhuq	túluq
taqás	kuhît	bahúq	tulúq
ámuq	súlud	lútuq	sanggîqun
amúq	sulúd	lutúq	sanggiqún
pilîqun	bágaq	dakuqdákuq	súluq
piliqún	bagáq	dakuqdakúq	sulúq
dágan	káhaq	bîyaq	agíqan
dagán	kaháq	biyáq	agiqán

V. Words contrasting q and t in final position.

dukút	bakát	balát	gipîlit	kálut
dukúq	bakáq	baláq	gipîliq	káluq
gidútdut	gipatúlut	ámut	ikút	balút
gidúqduq	gipatúluq	ámuq	ikúq	balúq
káwat	îgut	hugút	tigpilît	kítkit
káwaq	îguq	hugúq	tigpilíq	kíqkiq

VI. Words contrasting q and k in final position.

tiyúq	halúq	natáqtaq	báqbaq
tiyúk	halúk	natáktak	bákbak

tagúq	buhúq	dúqduq	támbuq
tagúk	buhúk	dúkduk	támbuk
nadúgmuq	gihúqhuq	háwaq	ámbaq
nadúgmuk	gihúkhuk	háwak	ámbak
lutúq	pilúq	gisúqsuq	búqbuq
lutúk	pilúk	gisúksuk	búkbuk

Practice the following exercise by reading across in rows. Only the last column necessarily contains real words. The students may keep coming back to this exercise until they have learned to recognize and pronounce the sounds without difficulty.

oq-o	túq-o	lutúq-o	lutúq	lútuq
oq-o	túq-o	lutúq-o	lútuq-o	lútuq
aq-o	wáq-o	waq		
aq-o	káq-o	sukáq-o	súkaq-o	súkaq
aq-o	káq-o	sukáq-o	sukáq	súkaq
iq-o	díq-o	diq		
iq-o	líq-o	dilíq-o	díliq-o	díliq
mánga	mangá	mangánu	m-ngánu	ngánu
sínga	singá	singábil	s-ngábil	ngábil
túnga	tungá	tungábil	t-ngábil	ngábil
mángi	mangí	mangípun	m-ngípun	ngípun
síngi	singí	singípun	s-ngípun	ngípun
mángu	mangú	mangút	mangútngut	ngútngut
sínga	singá	singári	singarí	ngarí
síngil	singíl	singilít	s-ngilít	ngilít

Grammatical Section

1 A 1. Demonstratives

Note the word ni in 1.16* and kiní in 1.10, both meaning 'this.' For English 'this,' 'that,' 'these,' and 'those,' there are a number of words in Cebuano, as shown in the following reference chart. Look up each demonstrative on the chart as you come to it in your lessons or in your readings.

---

* The reference 1.16 means Lesson 1, basic sentence 16.

Demonstratives

		Nominative		Genitive-Dative	
		Full form	Short form	Full form	Short form
'This'	near speaker but not near person spoken to	{kirí, karí}*	ri	{niqîri, niqári}	{íri, ári, ri}
'This'	near speaker and person spoken to	{kiní, kanî}	ni	{niqîni, niqáni}	{îni, áni, ni}
'That'	near person spoken to but not near speaker†	kanáq	naq	niqánaq	ánaq
'That'	not near person spoken to or speaker	kádtu	tu	niqádtu	ádtu

The forms in this lesson are all nominatives. The difference between nominative and genitive-dative will be discussed later.

In the genitive-dative column, any of the short forms in the right-hand column can substitute for any of the full forms in the left-hand column. In the nominative column, any short form can substitute for any full form except in one case (to be discussed in Lesson 3, 3 B 4).

Examples:

Ákuq kirí; ímu kanáq. 'This (near me) is mine. That (near you) is yours.'
Átuq kiníng báya. 'This house is ours.'
Kínsa kádtung kukakúla? 'Whose Coca-Cola is that (over there)?'

Pattern Practice PP-A below; Exercises 1.I, 1.V, 1.VI below.‡

1 A 2. Deictics (place words)

For the deictics (words meaning 'here,' 'there') the positions relative to the speaker and hearer correspond to those for the demonstratives.

Deictics with time meaning. Deictics which have a time meaning (past, present, or future) have two uses: (1) They precede the words or phrases they modify; or (2) they mean 'is (are, was, were, will be) here or there.' The following reference chart shows the deictics with time meanings. Refer to it as you come to deictics in your lessons or readings.

---

* The forms enclosed in braces {} are all interchangeable with one another.

† Kanáq and the other words in this row are also used for 'that' not near person spoken to or speaker, if it is not far away from either.

‡ The following exercises in Lessons 3, 5, 6, and 7 review this section: 3.I, 5.I A, 6.I B, 7.III. Do these exercises when you have learned the basic sentences for these lessons.

Deictics with Time Meanings

		Demonstrative	Present	Past*	Future
'Here'	near speaker, far from hearer	{kirí karí}	{díqa adíqa}	dirí	arí
'Here'	near speaker and hearer	{kiní kaní}	{níqa aníqa}	dínhi	ánhi
'There'	near hearer far from speaker†	kanáq	{náqa anáqa}	{dínhaq diháq}	ánhaq
'There'	far from speaker, far from hearer	kádtu	{túqa atúqa}	dídtu	ádtu

Deictics with no time meaning. Deictics with no time meaning follow the words or phrases they modify. The reference chart below shows these deictics. (Without time meanings, the deictics beginning with d and those beginning with ng—shown in the far right columns of the chart—are used interchangeably.)

Deictics with No Time Meaning

		Demonstrative	Deictics	
			With d	With ng
'Here'	near speaker, far from hearer	kirí	dirí	ngarí
'Here'	near speaker and hearer	kiní	dínhi	ngánhi
'There'	near hearer, far from speaker	kanáq	{diháq dínhaq}	ngánhaq
'There'	far from speaker, far from hearer	kádtu	dídtu	ngádtu

Note that the deictics beginning with d (dirí, dínhi, etc.) occur both with and without a time meaning. (They are listed in both charts above.) With a time meaning, they precede the word they modify, or else they mean 'was (were) here,' 'was (were) there.' Without time meaning, they follow the word or phrase they modify.

---

* The past deictics also occur with no time meaning, as shown in the following chart. (Also, in section 16 C 1 of Lesson 16, we will see an additional meaning of the deictics with d.)

† Remember that kanáq, náqa, etc., are also used for something not near the hearer and speaker if it is not too far away: 1 A 1 above.

1 A 2 a. Deictics with present meaning

The forms adíqa, aníqa, anáqa, and atúqa mean 'be here (there) at the present time.' Díqa, níqa, náqa, and túqa, shortenings of these, are the forms most commonly used. They precede the words or phrases they modify, or else they mean 'am (is, are) here or there.'

Díqa si Místir Abáya. 'Mr. Abaya is here (where I am, but not where you are).' (This is said, for example, on the telephone.)

Níqa si Místir Abáya sa Sibú. 'Mr. Abaya is here in Cebu.'

Náqa ba si Místir Abáya? 'Is Mr. Abaya there?' (This is said, for example, to the maid while the inquirer is at the door.)

Túqa si Místir Abáya sa Amiriká. 'Mr. Abaya is in America.' (The speaker is not in America.)

Exercises 1.I and 1.IV; Exercises 2.IC (when the basic sentences of Lesson 2 have been learned).

1 A 2 b. The d deictics (dirí, dínhi, dínhaq, diháq, dídtu)

Past meaning. The d deictics with past meaning precede the words or phrases they modify and mean 'was (were) here or there.'

Dirí si Ínting sa Sibú. 'Ínting was here in Cebu.' [This is said in a letter or over the telephone—dirí 'was here' modifies sa Sibú 'in Cebu.']

Dínhi si Místir Abáya gahápun. 'Mr. Abaya was here yesterday.'

{Diháq / Dínhaq} ba si Místir Abáya? 'Was Mr. Abaya there?'

Dídtu silá sa Sibú gahápun. 'They were in Cebu yesterday.'

Niqádtung Dumínggu dínhi si Huwán sa baláy. 'John was here at the house last Sunday.'

No time meaning. When they follow the word or phrase they modify, dirí, dínhi, dínhaq (diháq), and dídtu have no time meaning.

Díqa dirí ang kukakúla. 'The Coca-Cola is over here.' [Dirí 'here' modifies díqa 'is here'; it follows díqa, and so has no time meaning.]

Níqa mi dínhi. (1.9) 'We are here.'

Ánhaq ang bir diháq kanímu. 'Keep the beer.' (Lit. Let the beer be there where you are.)

Dághan kaqáyung táwu dídtu. 'There are (were, will be) many people there.' [Dídtu 'there' modifies dághan kaqáyung táwu 'there are (were, will be) many people.' It follows the phrase it modifies, and therefore has no time meaning.]

Exercise 1.III; Exercise 2.I A (after you have learned the basic sentences of Lesson 2).

1 A 2 c. Deictics with future meaning

The deictics with future meaning are arí, ánhi, ánhaq, ádtu. They precede the words or phrases they modify and also occur in the meaning 'will be here (there).'

Arí na ku. 'I am on my way.' (Lit. 'I will be here where you are not.')

Ánhi siyá sa Sibú. 'He is coming to Cebu.' [Speaker and hearer are in Cebu.]

Ánhaq ba ku? 'Shall I go there (where you are)?'

Ádtu ba siyá sa Sibú? 'Is he going to Cebu?' (Neither speaker nor hearer is in Cebu.)

Exercises 1.II and 2.I B.

1 A 2 d. Deictics beginning with ng

The deictics with ng are given in the chart of section 1 A (above, p. 12 for reference purposes. When these words follow the word or phrase they modify, the deictics with d can always substitute for those with ng, and vice versa. (See Lesson 2, 2 A 1, for further discussion and exemplification of this point.)*

1 B. Personal pronouns

1. The following chart, showing the personal pronouns, is for reference purposes. It will help you understand the forms as they appear in the lessons.

Personal Pronouns

	Nominative		Genitive		Dative		Preposed genitive
	Full form	Short form	Full form	Short form	Full form	Short form	
1st Singular 'I, me'	akú	ku	nákuq	ku	kanákuq	nákuq	ákuq
2d Singular 'you'	ikáw	ka	nímu	mu	kanímu	nímu	ímu
3d Singular 'he, him; she, her'	siyá	—	níya	—	kaníya	níya	íya
1st Inclusive† 'we, us'	kitá	ta	nátuq	ta	kanátuq	nátuq	átuq
1st Exclusive† 'we, us'	kamí	mi	námuq	—	kanámuq	námuq	ámuq
2d Plural 'you'	kamú	mu	nínyu	—	kanínyu	nínyu	ínyu
3d Plural 'they'	silá	—	níla	—	kaníla	níla	íla
Particle before names	si	—	{ni‡ / ng}	—	kang	{ni‡ / ng}	—

The rules for using these forms are taken up in the succeeding lessons.

---

* The following exercises from Lessons 2, 3, 6, and 7 apply to the deictics: 2.III C, 2.IV, 3.I B, 6.I A, 7.I. Do these exercises when reviewing this section after you have memorized the basic sentences of those lessons.

† Inclusive means 'including the person spoken to' (e.g. you and I). Exclusive means 'excluding the person addressed' (e.g. he and I but not you).

‡ Pronounced ni after consonants, ng after vowels.

2. Kamī vs. kitá. Kamī (mi, etc.) means 'we' or 'us' if the person spoken to is not included.

Ádtu na mi. 'We're going [but not you].'
Duhá kamī. 'There are two of us [excluding you].'
Ikúhaq mig bir. 'Get us [e.g. him and me] some beer.'

Kitá (ta, etc.) means 'we' or 'us' if the person spoken to is included:

Ādtu na ta? 'Shall we go?'
Nīqa na kitá sa Sibú. 'Now we are in Cebu.'

The following exercises refer to this section: 1.VII, 3.I C, 7.II, 7.IX. Do them after you have memorized the basic sentences for the lessons.

1C. Ang, y, and the nominative pronouns

Ang and y are SUBJECT MARKERS: the word or phrase following them is a SUBJECT. The nominative of the pronouns (listed in the chart 1 B above) also occur as subjects, without markers. We will discuss the subject construction—its meaning and place in the sentence—in Lesson 3 (3 B). In the following sentences the subject is underlined:

Kinī si Mīstir Gamīlu. (1.10) 'This is Mr. Gamelo.'
Kinī ang ákung amīgu. 'This is my friend.'
Nīqa mi dīnhi. (1.9) 'We are here.'
Nīqa dīnhi si Mīstir Gamīlu. 'Mr. Gamelo is here.'
Ikúhaq kug bir. (1.12) 'Get me some beer.'
Ikúhag bir si Mīstir Gamīlu. 'Get Mr. Gamelo some beer.'
Únsa may atuq? (1.3) 'What will you have? (What is ours?)'

Pattern Practice PP-A.

1D. Particles

1. The particles si, ang, and y appear before the subject and mark the following word or phrase as the subject (above, 1 C). Si is used before personal names. (The use of y and ang is taken up in 3 B 5.)

2. Question particles. Questions are usually marked with one of the following particles (we will study their position in the sentence in Lesson 3):

Ba: used (optionally) if there is no question word (e.g. word meaning 'who,' 'which,' 'what,' 'where').

Man: used (optionally) if there is a question word.

Náqa ba si Mīstir Abáya? } 'Is Mr. Abaya there?'
Náqa si Místir Abáya? }

Únsa may átuq? } 'What is ours?'
Únsay átuq? }

3. Particles in statements. The particle man is used in short statements or short answers which supply information:

Nīqa man. (1.5) 'He is here' (in answer to the question Náqa ba si Mīstir Abáya? 'Is Mr. Abaya there?').
Maqáyu man (1.8) 'Good' (in answer to the question Kumústa? 'How are you?').

The particle man also means 'because':

Kay nagdalīq man ku. (1.15) 'Because I am in a hurry.'

The particle diqáy shows that the speaker has received new information:

Nīqa ka man diqáy. 'Oh, so you're here!'
Hápun na man diqáy. 'Oh, why it's late now!'

1 E. How to say 'It is late'

'It is late' is expressed by mentioning the time of day: búntag 'morning,' údtu 'noon,' palís 'early afternoon,' hápun 'late afternoon or early evening,' and gabíqi 'night.'

If it is morning and you want to say 'It is late,' you say údtu na (literally, 'It is already noon'). If it is early afternoon and you want to say 'It is late,' you say hápun na (literally, 'It is already late afternoon'). If it is evening and you want to say 'It is late,' you say gabíqi na (literally, 'It is already night').

1 F. Linkers

The particle nga is a linker. (There are also other linkers which we will come across in later lessons.) Note that it is pronounced ng after a vowel:

maqáyu + nga + búntag = maqáyung búntag. (1.12) 'Good morning.'

Note also that nga causes the final q and n to drop from words preceding it:

ni + nga + ákuq + nga + amígu = ning ákung amígu (1.16) 'this friend of mine'

Ákuq + man + nga + amígu = Ákuq mang amígu. 'Because it was my friend.'

Linkers mark words or phrases which are in construction with each other: That is, they show that the word or phrase before the linker modifies the word or phrase after it or is in apposition to it. In the following example, the linker nga joins the demonstrative and the noun which is in apposition to it:

demonstrative	linker	noun
ni	ng	amígu (1.16) 'this friend'

In the following example, nga stands between a noun and a preposed genitive which modifies it:

preposed genitive	linker	noun
áku	ng	amígu (1.9 and 1.16) 'my friend'

In the following example, nga stands between a noun and an adjective which modifies it:

adjective	linker	noun
maqáyu	ng	búntag (1.12) 'good morning'

Pattern Practices

PP-A Nominative forms (1 A 1, 1 B, 1 C)

Step I. Various subjects

'He is here.'

Níqa siyá dínhi.	(si Huwán)
Níqa si Huwán dínhi.	(silá)
Níqa silá dínhi.	(ang ákung amígu)
Níqa ang ákung amígu dínhi.	(kamí)
Níqa kamí dínhi.	(ta)
Níqa ta dínhi.	(mu)

Níqa mu dínhi. (kiní)

Níqa kiní dínhi. (si Ínting)

Níqa si Ínting dínhi. (ang ákung bir)

Níqa ang ákung bir dínhi. (ang kukakúla)

Níqa ang kukakúla dínhi. (si Gamílu)

Níqa si Gamílu dínhi. (mi)

Níqa mi dínhi. (ku)

Níqa ku dínhi. (si Místir Abáya)

Níqas Místir Abáya dínhi. (kitá)

Níqa kitá dínhi. (kamú)

Níqa kamú dínhi.

Step II. Various demonstrative subjects

'I will leave my friend here.'

Ibílin ku kiníng ákung amígu dínhi. (kanáq)

Ibílin ku kanáng ákung amígu dínhi. (karí)

Ibílin ku karíng ákung amígu dínhi. (ni)

Ibílin ku ning ákung amígu dínhi. (kádtu)

Ibílin ku kádtung ákung amígu dínhi. (ri)

Ibílin ku ring ákung amígu dínhi. (kaní)

Ibílin ku kaníng ákung amígu dínhi. (tu)

Ibílin ku tung ákung amígu dínhi. (naq)

Ibílin ku nang ákung amígu dínhi. (kirí)

Ibílin ku kiríng ákung amígu dínhi.

Step III. Deictic predicates (1 A 2)

'He is here.'

Díqa siyá dirí. (náqa, diháq)

Náqa siyá diháq. (túqa, dídtu)

Túqa siyá dídtu. (níqa, dínhi)

Níqa siyá dínhi. (ádtu, dídtu)

Ádtu siyá dídtu. (arí, dirí)

Arí siya dirí. (ánhi, dínhi)

Ánhi siyá dínhi. (adíqa, dirí)

Adíqa siya dirí. (aníqa, dínhi)

Aníqa siyá dínhi. (anáqa, dínhaq)

Anáqa siyá dínhaq. (atúqa, dídtu)

Atúqa siyá dídtu. (ánhaq, dínhaq)

Ánhaq siyá dínhaq.

Step IV. Deictic predicates

'He is here in Cebu.'

Níqa siyá dínhis Sibú. (túqa)

Túqa siyá dídtus Sibú. (náqa)

Náqa siyá {dínhas / dihás} Sibú. (díqa)

Díqa siyá dirís Sibú. (ári)

Arí siyá dirís Sibú. (ánhi)

Ánhi siyá dínhis Sibú. (ánhaq)

Ánhaq siyá {dínhas / dihás} Sibú. (ádtu)

Ádtu siyá dídtus Sibú. (atúqa)

Atúqa siyá dídtus Sibú. (anáqa)

Anáqa siyá {dihás / dínhas} Sibú. (aníqa)

Aniqa siyá dínhis Sibú. (adíqa)

Adíqa siyá díris Sibú.

Step V. Various subjects and predicates

'This book is mine.'

Ákuq kíning líbru. (kanáng lamísa)

Ákuq kanáng lamísa. (ibílin ku)

Ibílin ku kanáng lamísa. (si Hwan)

Ibílin ku si Hwan. (mu kiní)

Mu kiní si Hwan. (ang ákung amígu)

Mu kiní ang ákung amígu. (ang ákung bir)

Mu kiní ang ákung bir. (ánhaq ibílin)

Ánhaq ibílin ang ákung bir. (kádtung dídtu)

Kádtung dídtu ang ákung bir. (kiní)

Kiní ang ákung bir. (si Místir Gamílu)

Kiní si Místir Gamílu. (ang íyang kukakúla)

Kiní ang íyang kukakúla. (mu kanáq)

Mu kanáq ang íyang kukakúla. (si Ínting)

Mu kanáq si Ínting. (dínhi)

Dínhi si Ínting. (ádtu dídtu)

Ádtu dídtu si Ínting.	(náqa diháq)
Náqa diháq si Ínting.	(si Místir Abáya)
Náqa diháq si Místir Abáya.	(níqa man)
Níqa man si Místir Abáya.	(ang kukakúla)
Níqa man ang kukakúla.	(ibílin ta)
Ibílin ta ang kukakúla.	(si Hwan)
Ibílin ta si Hwan.	(nagdalíq)
Nagdalíq si Hwan.	(magquná lang)
Magquná lang si Hwan.	(ádtu na)
Ádtu na si Hwan.	

Exercises

I. Insert the correct present deictic into the blank (díqa, níqa, náqa, or túqa). (1 A 2 a)

1. Ang bir __________ na dirí.
2. __________ na ba diháq ang kukakúla?
3. Si Místir Bílu __________ dídtu sa Dábaw.
4. Si Místir Gamílu __________ dínhi sa Súgbu.
5. __________ dídtu sa Amiriká si Místir Abáya.
6. Ang líbru __________ dirí kanákuq.
7. __________ dínhi ang átung amígu.
8. Ang líbru __________ diháq kanímu.
9. __________ ba dínhi si Místir Abáya?
10. __________ dirí ang líbru sa ka Místir Bílu (at Mr. Vilo's place).
11. Si Místir Abáya __________ dídtu sa ka Ínting (at Inting's place).
12. __________ na ba dínhi ang líbru?
13. __________ dirí ang bir sa ámuq.
14. __________ ba diháq ang ákung kukakúla?
15. __________ ba dínhaq sa ínyu si Ínting?

II. Insert the correct future deictic into the blank (arí, ánhi, ánhaq, or ádtu). (1 A 2 c)

1. __________ si Hwan dínhaq sa Nígrus.
2. __________ dirí ang kukakúla.
3. __________ ba dínhi nátuq ímna ang bir? 'Shall we drink the beer here?'

4. ___________ ku diháq sa ínyu úgmaq. 'I will come to your place to-morrow.'

5. ___________ ku mukáqun dídtu sa ámuq. 'I will eat at our place.'

6. ___________ lang dínhaq kanínyu ang líbru.

7. Ang bir ___________ dídtu ibílin.

8. ___________ dínhi ibílin ang kukakúla.

9. ___________ dínhi sa ámuq úgmaq.

10. ___________ ba dirí ibílin ang líbru?

11. ___________ dídtu mukáqun si Místir Abáya.

12. ___________ ba dídtu nátuq ibílin si Místir Bílu?

13. ___________ ku dirí mukáqun sa ámuq.

14. ___________ ku dídtu sa ka Místir Abáya muqinúm ug bir.

III. Insert the correct form of the deictics with d into the blank (dirí, dínhi, dínhaq, and dídtu). (1 A 2 b)

1. Ang bir díqa na ___________.

2. Náqa ba ___________ ang kukakúla?

3. Si Místir Bílu túqa ___________ sa Dábaw.

4. Si Místir Gamílu níqa ___________ sa Súgbu.

5. Túqa ___________ sa Amiriká si Místir Abáya.

6. Ang líbru díqa ___________ kanákuq.

7. Níqa ___________ ang átung amígu.

8. Ang líbru náqa ___________ kanímu.

9. Níqa ba ___________ si Místir Abáya?

10. Díqa ___________ ang líbru sa ka Místir Bílu.

11. Si Místir Abáya túqa ___________ sa ka Ínting.

12. Níqa na ba ___________ ang líbru?

13. Díqa ___________ ang bir sa ámuq.

14. Náqa ba ___________ ang ákung kukakúla?

15. Ang bir túqa ___________ ibílin ni Místir Abáya.

16. Ánhi ba ___________ nátuq ang líbru?

17. Ang líbru ádtu ___________ ibílin sa ka Místir Bílu.

18. Ang átung amígu ánhaq ___________ mukáqun.

19. Ánhi ___________ sa ámuq úgmaq.

20. Arí ba ___________ ibílin ang líbru?

21. Ádtu ___________ mukáqun si Místir Abáya.

ABCDEFGHIJKLMNOPQRSTU
C
B
A
A

22. Ádtu ba ____________ nátuq ibílin si Místir Bilu?

23. Arí ku ____________ mukáqun sa ámuq.

24. Ádtu ku ____________ sa ka Místir Abáya muqinúm ug bir.

25. Ang bir ug líbru ánhi ____________ sa ámuq ibílin.

IV. Refer to the picture on page 21 and fill in the blanks with the correct forms of the present and d deictics (níqa, náqa, etc., and dirí, dínhi, etc.) or with the correct combination of them. The capital letters preceding each sentence refer to the person speaking and the person spoken to: C-A means, for example, that C says the sentence to A. (1 A 2 a)

1. (C-A) ____________ ang pawntinpín ____________ sa ímung lamísa. (is)
2. (C-B) Ang tísaq ____________ ____________ sa blákburd.
3. (C-AB) ____________ ba ____________ kanínyu ang líbru ug ang kukakúla?
4. (C-B) ____________ ang pawntinpín sa lamísang A.
5. (C-D) ____________ ba ____________ ang líbru sa ímung lamísa?
6. (B-C) ____________ sa ákung lamísa ang líbru.
7. (D-C) ____________ sa lamísang B ang lápis.
8. (C-A) ____________ ba sa ímung lamísa ang kukakúla?
9. (D-C) Ang kukakúla ____________ ____________ sa lamísang A.
10. (A-B) ____________ ba ____________ ang bir sa ímung lamísa?
11. (C-A) ____________ sa ákung lamísa ang bir.
12. (B-D) Ang ákung pawntinpín ____________ ____________ sa lamísang A.
13. (D-C) Ang ákung lápis ____________ ____________ sa lamísang B.
14. (B-A) ____________ ____________ sa blákburd ang tísaq.
15. (B-D) ____________ ____________ sa ákung lamísa ang ímung lápis.

Before doing exercises V, VI, and VII, you may review PP-A, steps I and II.

V. Fill the blank with the correct demonstrative—kirí, kiní, kanáq, and kádtu—or with the short forms which may substitute for them—ri, ni, naq, or tu. (1 A 1)

1. Ibílin lang dínhi ____________ ng ímung amígu.
2. ____________ ng kukakúla dídtu párang Místir Abáya.
3. ____________ ng kukakúla dirí pára kanímu.
4. Ibílin lang dínhaq ____________ ng ímung bir.
5. ____________ ng ímung líbru ibílin dirí.
6. Dídtu ____________ ng átung amígu si Místir Bílu.
7. ____________ ng líbru dirí pára kanímu.

8. Ímna dínhi ____________ ng kukakúla. 'Drink that Coca-Cola here.'
9. ____________ ng líbru diháq párang Místir Gamílu.
10. Ánhaq lang dínhaq ____________ ng ákung líbru. 'Leave that book of mine there.'
11. Arí lang dirí ____________ ng ímung bir.
12. ____________ ng bir dínhi lang ímna. 'Drink that beer here.'
13. ____________ ng kukakúla dirí pára sa átung amígu.
14. ____________ ng ákung bir dínhaq lang kanímu.
15. ____________ ng ímung líbru dirí lang sa ámuq.

VI. Refer to the picture on page 21 and fill in the blanks with the proper form of the demonstrative (kirí, kiní, kanáq, or kádtu). The letters before each sentence indicate the person speaking and the person spoken to. (1 A 1)

1. (C-A) Kuháqa ____________ ng bir sa lamísa. (kuháqa 'come or go (and) get')
2. (C-D) Ibílin lang ____________ ng bir sa lamísa.
3. (A-C) Kuháqa ____________ ng kukakúla.
4. (C-A) Ibílin lang ____________ ng pawntinpín.
5. (A-BD) ____________ ng kukakúla pára sa átung maqístra. (maqístra 'teacher')
6. (B-A) Ímu ba ____________ ng lápis dirí sa ákung lamísa? 'Is this pencil here on my table yours?'
7. (A-B) Ákuq ____________ ng lápis diháq sa ímung lamísa.
8. (C-ADB) ____________ ng tísaq ákung isulát sa blákburd. 'I will write with this chalk on the blackboard.'
9. (C-B) Isulát ____________ ng lápis sa ímung papíl. 'Write with that pencil on your paper.'
10. (B-A) Kuháqa ____________ ng ímung lápis sa ákung lamísa. 'Come get this pencil from my table.'
11. (C-AD) ____________ ng líbru sa lamísang B pára kanínyu.
12. (C-ADB) ____________ ng bir sa lamísa pára sa átung amígung si Místir Abáya.
13. (A-C) Ákung kuháqun ____________ ng bir sa ímung lamísa. 'I will go get that beer from your table.'
14. (C-B) Kuháqa ____________ ng tísaq sa blákburd. 'Come get this chalk from the blackboard.'
15. (C-A) ____________ ng kukakúla ákung ímnun dínhi.

VII. A. Insert kamí or kitá in the blanks. (1 B)

1. Ádtu na ____________. 'We are going now.'

2. Ikúhaq ___________g bir.

3. Magquná lang ___________ nímu.

B. Refer to the picture on page 21 and insert kamí or kitá in the blanks.

4. (C-D) Ádtu na ___________ sa lamísa.

5. (AB-C) Díqa ___________ sa ámung lamísa.

6. (D-AB) Mangá tinúnqan ___________. 'We are students.'

7. (A-C) Ádtu na ___________ Mam. 'We are going now, Ma'am.'

8. (B-AD) Arí ___________ magsulát sa ákung lamísa. 'Let us write here at my desk.'

9. (ADB-C) Bínli ___________ ug bir. 'Leave some beer for us.'

10. (A-DB) Manginúm ___________ ug kukakúla. 'Let's drink some Coca-Cola.'

11. (D-B) Ádtu na lang ___________ sa átuq manginúm ug bir. 'Let's just drink beer at home.'

12. (DB-A) Ádtu na lang ___________ manginúm ug bir sa ámuq. 'We'll just drink beer at home.'

13. (C-ADB) Magsulát ___________ sa blákburd. 'Let's write on the blackboard.'

14. (ABD-C) Magbása ba ___________? 'Shall we read?'

15. (AD-CB) ___________ mangá amíga ni Místir Abáya.

VIII. Mangá Paglitúk (Intonations)

A. An intonation is a contour of rising or falling pitch in the tone of voice that accompanies the pronunciation of a sentence. The following intonation, consisting of a rise in pitch and then a slight drop (symbolized 243, on a 4-tone scale of normal pitches in the individual speaker's voice ranging from the lowest, 1, to the highest, 4) is used for greetings and other social formulas. Listen to the informant and then repeat the sentences. Then, see if you can reproduce them without your informant as a model.

1. Maqáyu	1.1
2. Maqáyung búntag.	1.2
3. Way sapayán.	1.26
4. Balikbálik.	1.26
5. Arí na ku.	1.20

B. The following intonation, consisting of a steady rise (symbolized 234), is used for commands and for statements without emotional overtones. Listen to your informant and repeat; then see if you can reproduce them without the model.

1. Dayún lang.	1.6

2.	Maqáyu man.	1.8
3.	Maqáyung búntag Místir Abáya.	1.12
4.	Ayáw na lang.	1.14
5.	Ádtu na ku.	1.18
6.	Kukakúla lang.	1.23
7.	Ádtu na lang ku.	1.25
8.	Níqa man.	1.5
9.	Sigí.	1.19
10.	Ikúhaq kug bir.	1.13
11.	Dághang salámat.	1.25
12.	Kumústa ka Místir Gamílu.	1.11

Observe that the 234 intonation, used with normal statements and commands, is quite unlike the intonation (a falling one) that normally accompanies the equivalent English sentences. Intonation patterns are an integral segment of our speech habits, and it will take rigorous effort to form new, separate habits for speaking Cebuano.

IX. Sultiqánay (Conversation)

Listen to the following conversation without looking at it. Then answer the true-false questions below.

Si Ínting mibisíta kang Dyuu.

A. Maqáyu. (nagtúktuk)

B. Maqáyung gabíqi.

A. Maqáyung gabíqi.

B. Dayún Dung. Únsa may átuq?

A. Níqa ba si Dyuu?

B. Níqa man, dayún lang.

* * *

C. Ting! Kumústa ka man?

A. Maqáyu man. Ikáw kumústa?

C. Maqáyu man sad.

A. Aa Dyuu, ákuq lang ibílin ning ímung líbru. Ádtu na lang ku, kay nagdalíq man ku.

C. Ádtu na ka?

A. Uu, ádtu na ku. Díqa ra ímung líbru uh, salámat ha?

C. Uu. Salámat.

A. Arí na ku. Magquná lang ku nímu.

C. Sigí. Balikbálik.

Tubagá ang musunúd sa <u>hústu</u> u <u>díliq hústu</u> (true-false questions).

1. Si Dyuu náqa diháq.
2. Waq dídtu si Dyuu.
3. Túqa si Ínting kay túqay íyang amígu dídtu.
4. Maqáyu si Ínting.
5. Túqa si Ínting dídtu kay íyang ibílin ang líbrung Dyuu.
6. Nagdalíq si Dyuu.
7. Gibílin ni Ínting ang íyang amígu.
8. Magquná si Ínting kang Dyuu.

LESSON 2. VISITING

Sagquluhúnun (Basic Sentences)

First Part	Únang Báhin
hello (for telephone only)	hilúu
who?	kínsa
this	ni

1. Hello, who is this?	1. Hilúu, kínsa ni?
ah (pause before speaking)	aa
is (are) at	níqa
[question particle]	ba
[name particle]	si
Dr. Fernandez	Dúktur Pirnándis
	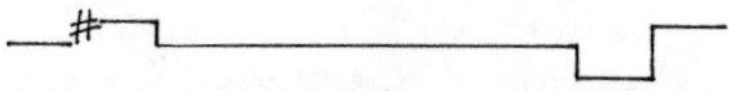
2. Is Dr. Fernandez there (lit. here)?	*2. Aa, níqa ba si Dúktur Pirnándis?
went out	nilakáw
[particle used on giving information]	man
that one	tu

3. He (lit. That one) went out.	3. Nilakáw man tu.
who?	kínsa
this	ni
[linker between <u>ni</u> and <u>nagtawág</u>]	nga
calling	nagtawág
	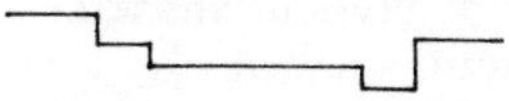
4. Who is this calling?	4. Kínsa ning nagtawág?
this	kiní
[name particle]	si

5. This is Dodong Gamelo.	5. Kiní si Dúdung Gamílu.
tell him	íngna
just	lang
that [linker between <u>íngna</u> and the rest of the sentence]	nga

will be where hearer is	ánhaq
we	mi
there where hearer is	dínhaq
6. Just tell him that we'll be over (lit. that we will be over there).	6. Íngna lang nga ánhaq mi dínhaq.
driver	dráybir
toward	padulúng
[question particle]	ba
that	naq
to	sa
Banawa	Banáwaq
7. Driver, do you go to Banawa? (Lit. Driver, does that go to Banawa?)	*7. Draybír, padúung ba naq sa Banáwaq.
no	díliq
[form of address for male of same age and sex as speaker]	Bay
for, to	pára sa
this	ni
Lahug	Lahúg
8. No, I go (lit. this goes) to Lahug.	*8. Díliq Bay. Pára ni sa Lahúg.
what?	únsa
[question particle following question word]	man
[particle following question when the interlocutor gave an unsatisfactory answer]	diqáy
[linker between únsa and dyip]	nga
jeep	dyip
our, us	ámuq
[linker between ámuq and sákyan]	nga
get on (a vehicle)	sákyan
toward	padulúng sa
Banawa	Banáwaq
9. Then what jeep do we get to go to Banawa? (Lit. What	*9. Únsa man diqáy dyip ámung

jeep is it then which we ride to Banawa?)	sákyan padúung sa Banáwaq?
look for	pangítaq
just	lang
you (plural)	mu
[particle preceding goal of action]	ug
for, to	pára sa
Capitol	Kapitúl
10. Just look for one for the Capitol.	10. Pangítaq lang mug pára sa Kapitúl.
driver	dráybir
toward	padulúng sa
[question particle]	ba
that	naq
Banawa	Banáwaq
11. Driver, do you go to Banawa? (Lit. Is that one toward Banawa?)	*11. Draybír, padúung ba naq sa Banáwaq?
there	ádtu
to	sa
Capitol	Kapitúl
12. It goes to the Capitol. (Lit. It will be there at the Capitol.)	12. Ádtu sa Kapitúl.
will take	muhatúd
[question particle]	ba
this	ni
there	ngádtu
to	sa
——'s house	ka
13. Will you take us to Dr. Fernandez' house? (Lit. Will this take us to Dr. Fernandez'?)	13. Muhatúd ba ni ngádtu sa ka Dúktur Pirnándis?
how many?	pilá
[question particle following interrogative]	man

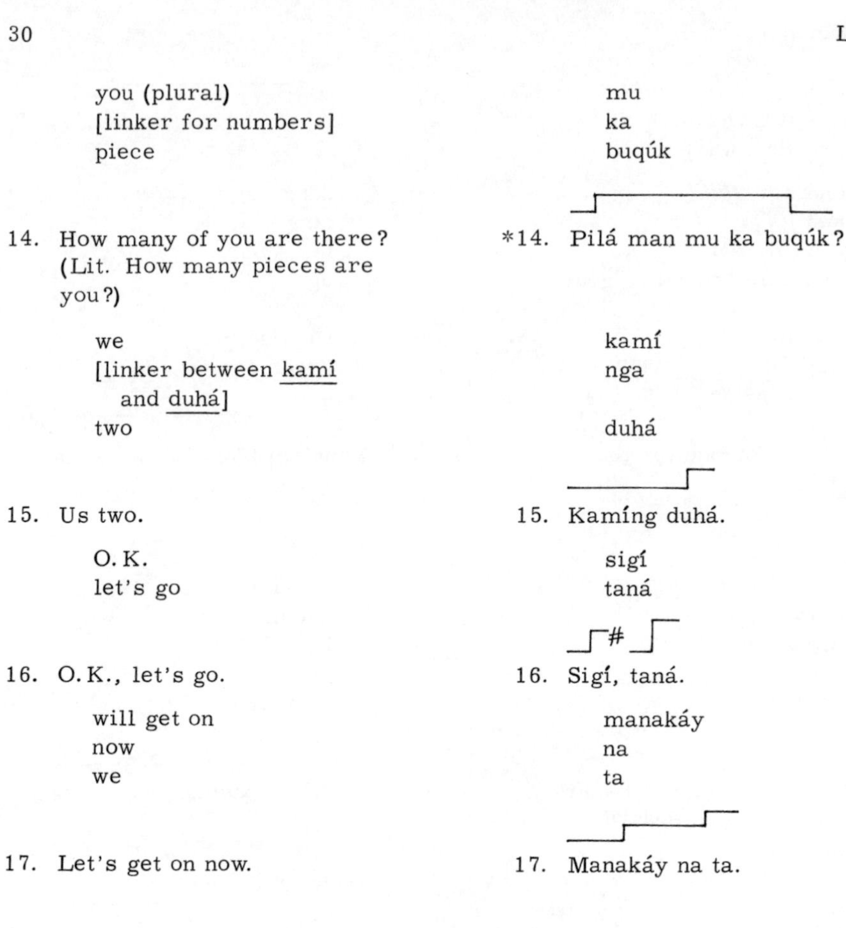

you (plural)	mu
[linker for numbers]	ka
piece	buqúk
14. How many of you are there? (Lit. How many pieces are you?)	*14. Pilá man mu ka buqúk?
we	kamí
[linker between kamí and duhá]	nga
two	duhá
15. Us two.	15. Kamíng duhá.
O. K.	sigí
let's go	taná
16. O. K., let's go.	16. Sigí, taná.
will get on	manakáy
now	na
we	ta
17. Let's get on now.	17. Manakáy na ta.

Mangá Pangutána (Questions)

Únang Báhin (First Part)

1. Náqa na ba si Dúktur Pirnándis?
2. Kínsa si Dúktur Pirnándis?
3. Ádtu ka sa Banáwaq Bay?
4. Únsa man ni?
5. Pára sa Lahúg na ba nang dyip?
6. Dínhaq na ba si Dúdung?
7. Kiní si Místir Abáya, ádtu ba sa Banáwaq?
8. Níqa na ba ang dráybir sa dyip?
9. Muhatúd ka ba sa Kapitúl Ting?
10. Manakáy na ta?
11. Nilakáw ba dáyun si Duktúr? (dáyun 'immediately')
12. Ibílin ku ba si Dúdung sa Banáwaq? ('Shall I leave . . . ?')

13. Únsa mang dyípay ámung sákyan?
14. Ḍuhá bay musakáy?
15. Ádtu na ta Bay?
16. Kiníng—níqa na ba ang ákung amígu?
17. Kínsa ang nagtawág ug dyip?
18. Pilá ang manakáy?

Mangá Pangutána (Matching)

Follow the instructions given for the matching exercises in Lesson 1, page 5.

1. Kínsa ang nagtawág ni Dúktur Pirnándis?
2. Kínsa ang nilakáw padulúng sa Lahúg?
3. Pilá man ka buqúk ang musakáy?
4. Únsa may átung sákyan?
5. Dínhaq na ba ang ímung amígu?
6. Níqa na ba si Dúdung?
7. Kiníng dyip padulúng ba sa Banáwaq?
8. Nilakáw na ba ang dráybir?
9. Díliq ba lang ta manakáy?

a. Kamíng duhá. Ádtu mi sa Banáwaq.
b. Dyip na lang.
c. Si Dúdung Gamílu ang nagtawág sa dúktur.
d. Si Místir Abáya ang nilakáw padulúng sa Lahúg.
e. Ang dráybir? Úqu. Nilakáw na.
f. Manakáy. Dyip ang átung sákyan.
g. Waláq pa si Dúdung. Ádtu pa siyá sa Banáwaq.
h. Ang ákung amígu? Waláq pa siyá dirí.
i. Díliq Bay. Ádtu ni sa Lahúg.

Sagquluhúnun (Basic Sentences)

Second Part	Ikaduháng Báhin
[particle preceding subject if there is a nominal predicate]	maqú
[question particle]	ba
this	ni
[subject marker]	y
their	íla
[linker between íla and baláy]	nga
house	baláy

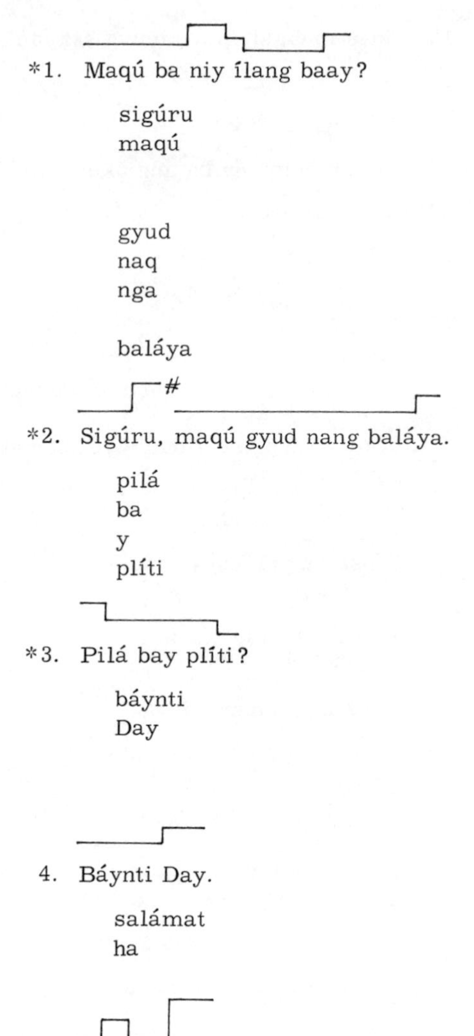

1. Is this their house?	*1. Maqú ba niy ílang baay?
certain, sure	sigúru
[particle preceding subject if there is a nominal predicate]	maqú
for sure	gyud
that	naq
[linker between <u>naq</u> and <u>baláya</u>]	nga
house	baláya
2. That's the house for sure.	*2. Sigúru, maqú gyud nang baláya.
how much?	pilá
[question particle]	ba
[subject marker]	y
fare	plíti
3. How much is the fare?	*3. Pilá bay plíti?
twenty	báynti
[term of address for female same age as or younger than speaker]	Day
4. Twenty, Miss.	4. Báynti Day.
thanks	salámat
O.K.? ('Do you understand?')	ha
5. Thanks.	*5. Salámat ha.
thanks	salámat
also	pud
6. You're welcome. (Lit. Thank you, too.)	6. Salámat pud.
come in	dayún
7. Come in.	7. Dayún.
where?	háqin
[question particle after interrogative]	man
[particle preceding names]	si

is (are) here	níqa
[question particle]	ba
8. Where is Dr. Fernandez?	8. Háqin man si Dúktur Pirnándis?
Is he here?	Níqa ba?
[pause before speaking]	aa
he is there	túqa
at	sa
upstairs	táqas
9. He is (there) upstairs.	9. Aa, túqa sa táqas.
wait a minute	isáq pa
I	ákuq
[linker between ákuq and táwgun]	nga
will call	táwgun
10. Wait a minute. I'll call him.	10. Isáq pa. Ákung táwgun.
just now	karún pa
you	ka
have arrived	muqabút
11. Have you just arrived?	*11. Karún ka pa muqabút?
just now	karún pa
for certain	gyud
12. Just this minute.	12. Karún pa gyud.
are here	níqa
we	mi
here	dínhi
because	kay
here	níqa
because	man gud
[existential particle]	y
wife	asáwa
my	nákuq
from	gíkan sa
America	Amiriká
13. We came here because my wife is here from America.	*13. Níqa mi dínhi, kay níqa

. . . man guy asáwa nákuq gíkan

. . . sa Amiriká.

want	gústu
I	nákuq
[linker between gústu and the rest of the sentence]	nga
introduce	ipaqilaqíla
to you	nímu

14. I would like to introduce her to you. — *14. Gústu nákung ipaqilaqíla nímu.

[particle after receipt of new information]	diqáy

15. Oh, really! — 15. Diqáy!

how is (are)?	kumústa
you	ka

16. How are you? — 16. Kumústa ka?

didn't	waláq
you (all)	mu
have difficulty	maglisúd
to come	pagqánhi
to this place	ngánhi

17. Did you have any difficulty in coming here? (Lit. You had no difficulty . . .) — *17. Waq mu maglisúd pagqánhi . . . ngánhi?

did not	waq
[particle contradicting what is said]	man
very much	kaqáyu
we	mi
have difficulty	maglisúd

18. We did not have much difficulty. — 18. Waq man kaqáyu mi maglisúd.

(A little boy comes in.) — (Misulúd ang usá ka bátaq.)

who?	kínsa

[subject marker]	y
your	ímu
[linker between ímu and ngálan]	nga
name	ngálan
[term of address for male same age as or younger than speaker]	Dung

19. What is your name, boy?	*19. Kínsay ímung ngálan Dung?

ran away	midágan
[particle with information given]	man

20. Oh, he ran away.	20. Midágan man.

ran away	midágan
[particle with information given]	man
[subject marker]	ang
fool	túntu
ignoramus	ignuránti

21. That ignorant fool, he ran away.	*21. Midágan mang túntu, ignuránti.

[term of address for males same age as or younger than the speaker]	Dung
will take	dádqun
you	ka
we	námuq
to	sa
America	Amiriká

22. Son, we'll take you to America.	22. Dung, dádqun ka námuq sa ... Amiriká.

not want	díliq
I	ku
[particle indicating rejection of what interlocutor said]	uy

23. I don't want to!	23. Díliq ku uy!

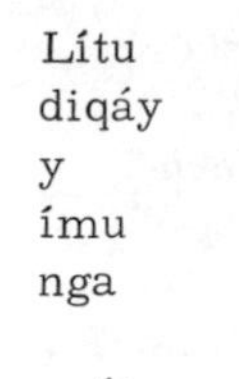

[man's name]	Lítu
[particle]	diqáy
[subject marker]	y
your	ímu
[linker between ímu and ngálan]	nga
name	ngálan

24. Oh, so your name is Lito? — *24. Lítu diqáy ímung ngálan?

hey (calling out impolitely)	uy
[a name, Dolores]	Lúling
come here (to inferior)	mariká

25. Hey, Loling, come here! — *25. Uy Lulíng, mariká!

bring	pagdalá
here	dirí
[particle before goal of action: 'some']	ug
beer	bir

26. Bring some beer. (Lit. Bring some beer here.) — 26. Pagdalá diríg bir.

no more	waláq na
[particles indicating an apologetic tone]	ra ba
[existential particle: 'there is']	y
beer	bir
Sir	Nyur

27. There is no more beer, Sir. — 27. Waq na ra bay bir Nyur.

never mind	ságdi
[particles indicating best of limited choices available]	na lang
Doctor [as a title]	Duktúr

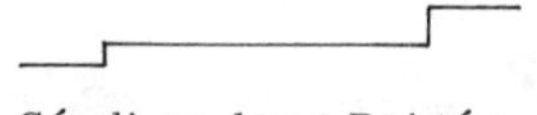

28. Never mind, Doctor. — 28. Ságdi na lang Duktúr.

thanks	salámat
the only worthwhile thing	na lang

29. Thanks very much, Doctor. — 29. Salámat na lang Duktúr.

over there	ádtu
[particles meaning the best of limited choices available]	na lang
we	mi
because	kay
afternoon	hápun
already	na
because	man

30\. We'd better go now because it's late. (Lit. We will be just over there now because it's already afternoon.)

30\. Ádtu na lang mi kay hápun ... na man.

here	ánhi
merely	lang
we	ta
eat supper	manihápun

31\. Have your supper here with us. (Lit. Let's just eat supper here.)

31\. Ánhi lang ta manihápun.

thanks	salámat
[particles meaning best of limited choices available]	na lang
very much	kaqáyu

32\. Thanks very much.

32\. Salámat na lang kaqáyu.

have promised	nakasáqad
because	man
we	mi
that [linker between nakasáqad and the rest of the sentence]	nga
over there	ádtu
will eat supper	manihápun
at	sa
———'s place	ka
Mr. Abaya	Místir Abáya

33\. We have promised that we would eat supper at Mr. Abaya's.

33\. Nakasáqad man ming ádtu ... manihápun sa ka Místir Abáya.

go	ádtu

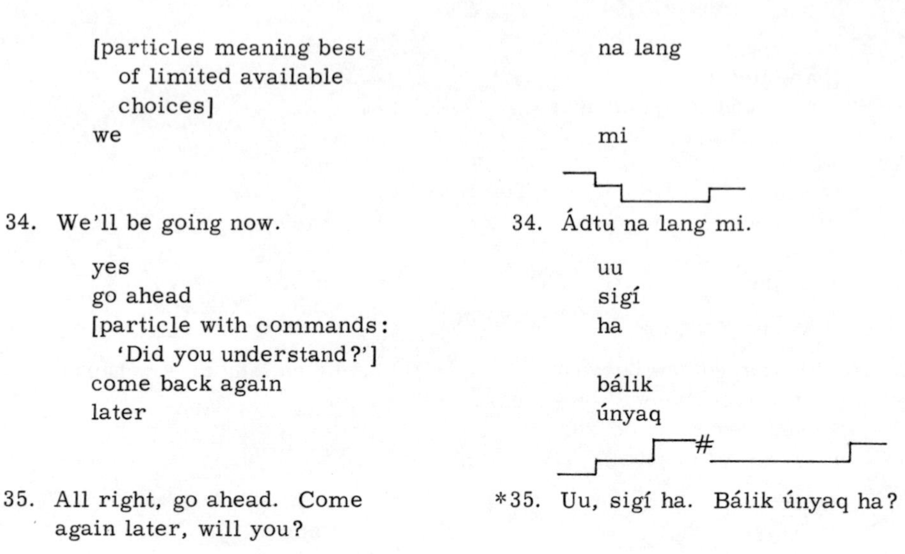

[particles meaning best of limited available choices] — na lang
we — mi

34. We'll be going now. — 34. Ádtu na lang mi.

yes — uu
go ahead — sigí
[particle with commands: 'Did you understand?'] — ha
come back again — bálik
later — únyaq

35. All right, go ahead. Come again later, will you? — *35. Uu, sigí ha. Bálik únyaq ha?

Mangá Pangutána (Questions)

Ikaduháng Báhin (Second Part)

1. Maqú ba ni ang baláy ni Dúktur Pirnándis?
2. Pilá ba ang plíti padulúng sa Banáwaq?
3. Báynti ba ang plíti ngádtu sa ka Dúktur Pirnándis?
4. Karún ka pa muqabút?
5. Gíkan ka pa ba sa Amiriká?
6. Waq mu maglisúd pagqádtu ngádtu sa ka Dyuu?
7. Gústu ba nímung ipaqilaqíla ang ímung asáwa?
8. Kínsay ímung ngálan?
9. Lítu diqáy ímung ngálan?
10. Náqa bay bir diháq?
11. Ánhi ba ta maniqúdtu?
12. Muqádtu na ba mu?
13. Nakasáqad ba mu nga muqádtu mu dídtu?
14. Díliq mu mubálik dínhi?
15. Sigúru ka bang báynti ang plíti?
16. Pilá may ílang baláy?
17. Milakáw ba ang íyang asáwa?
18. Nakasáqad ka bang mubálik?
19. Háqin man si Lúling?

20. Midágan ba si Místir Abáya?
21. Pilá bay manihápun dínhi?
22. Ádtu diqáy silá manakáy?
23. Dádqun ba nímu ang dráybir?
24. Díliq ba mi amígu?
25. Pára bang Dúktur Pirnándis ang kukakúla?
26. Ibílin mu ba ang plíti?
27. Nagdalíq ba diqáy ka?
28. Túqa ba sa Amiriká si Huwán?
29. Kamí ra bang duhá ang manakáy?
30. Gidalá ba ni Ínting ang duhá?
31. Díliq ba mu maglisúd?
32. Muhatúd ba ug amígu si Místir Abáya?

Mangá Pangutána (Matching)

1. Kínsa ba ang nagtawág?
2. Karún pa siyá muqabút?
3. Kínsay íyang ngálan?
4. Milakáw ba siyá?
5. Piláy plíti sa Banáwaq?
6. Maqáyung hápun.
7. Salámat ha.
8. Kínsay ímung asáwa?
9. Ása ka padulúng?
10. Gíkan ka pa sa Amiriká?
11. Kínsay maniqúdtu dínhi?
12. Háqin man si Mísis Abáya?

a. Salámat pud.
b. Ang ákung asáwa? Si Náti.
c. Túqa siyá sa táqas.
d. Kamíng duhá ang maniqúdtu dínhi.
e. Maqáyu. Dayún.
f. Si Dyuu ang nagtawág.
g. Waláq pa siyá mulakáw.
h. Ang íyang ngálan Ída.
i. Sa Banáwaq? Báynti.
j. Ngádtu sa Kapitúl.
k. Uu, gíkan pa gyud ku dídtu.
l. Karún pa gyud.

Mangá Pangutána (Additional Matching Questions)

1. Kínsa ang muhatúd ni Dúktur Pirnándis?
2. Díliq ba mu musakáy?

a. Díliq ku siyá amígu.
b. Ang íyang dráybir si Tásyu.

3. Kiní ba si Ínting?
4. Únsa may íyang gústu?
5. Kapitúl na ba kiní?
6. Pilá man mung maniqúdtu?
7. Nilakáw ba si Huwán?
8. Amígu mu ba siyá?
9. Arí na ku ha?
10. Túqa na ba ang plíti?

c. Túqa na.
d. Waláq, túqa siyá sa táqas.
e. Uu, sigí.
f. Uu, Kapitúl na kiní.
g. Uu, musakáy mi.
h. Duhá kamíng maniqúdtu.
i. Gústu siyág kukakúla.
j. Díliq. Si Tásyu ni. Túqa ra si Ínting.

Commentary to Basic Sentences

2 a 2* níqa — When speaking on the telephone or writing letters the speaker may consider himself to be close to the listener. Thus we have níqa 'is here' rather than náqa 'is there.'

2 a 7 ba — The word order of ba and naq is discussed in the grammatical section of Lesson 3 (3 C).

2 a 8 Bay — Bay is used only by males to address other males of the same age as the speaker. Females and males call males of the same age as or younger than themselves Dung. Males and females call females the same age as or younger than themselves Day.

2 a 9 padúung — Note the dropping of the l between two u's, resulting in a long vowel. In northern areas (including Cebu City) l usually drops between two u's, two a's, an a and a u, or a u and an a (south of Cebu City the l is not dropped). There is always a stress on the first part of a long vowel. (This dropping of l is discussed in detail in Lesson 17, Part Two.)

2 a 11 — Note the shift of accent when the word dráybir is called out. (Cf. Lúling—Lulíng in 2 b 25.)

2 a 14 ka — This is a linker between numerals and nouns. The position of man and mu is discussed in the grammatical section of Lesson 3 (3 C).

2 b 1† baay — Note the dropping of the l in baláy. See the note to padúung in 2 a 9.

y — This y sound after i is difficult for Americans to hear. Maqú is explained in the grammatical section (2 D).

---

* The notation 2 a 2 means Lesson 2, first section of basic sentences, sentence 2.

† The letter b in the notation 2 b 1 means basic sentences, second section.

2 b 2	The -a of baláya is discussed in the grammatical section (2 C).
2 b 3 ba	When this particle is used with interrogatives, it means almost the same thing as man with interrogatives except that it shows a little impatience.
2 b 5 ha	This particle, used at the end of a command, asks whether the listener has no objection. It is used after salámat 'thanks' with the same feeling to make sure the hearer understands. (See 2 b 35.)
2 b 11	The pa of karún pa makes karún 'now' mean 'just now'; gíkan 'from' + pa = gíkan pa 'just came from'; kanúsqa 'when' + pa = kanúsqa pa 'when did [it] first happen?'
2 b 13	The d in gud drops before y.
2 b 14	Note that gústu 'want' is connected to the rest by a linker nga. The appearance of nákuq before the linker is discussed in the grammatical section of Lesson 3 (3 C). Note also that the q of nákuq is dropped before the linker.
2 b 14 ipaqilaqíla	The word for 'her' is not expressed here, but it could have been, with siyá: Gústu nákuq siyáng ipaqilaqíla nímu, or gústu nákung ipaqilaqíla siyá nímu.
2 b 17 ngánhi	The use of the deictic with initial ng is discussed in the grammatical section (2 A 1).
2 b 19 Dung	This term of address refers to boys or men the same age as or younger than the speaker. The equivalent reference to girls and women is Day. A synonym for Dung, equally common, is Duq. See the note to 2 a 8.
2 b 19 kínsa	The literal Cebuano rendition of 'What is your name?' is 'Who is your name?'
2 b 21	The combination man plus ang fuses into mang. In this situation Dr. Fernandez is not being kind to Lito in calling him túntu or ignuránti.
2 b 24	The subject marker y drops after the y of diqáy.
2 b 25	Note the shift of the accent when the name Lúling is called out. Mariká 'Come here' is used to summon persons inferior in age or social status.
2 b 35 ha	See the note to 2 b 5.

Grammatical Section

2 A. Deictics and interrogative deictics

2 A 1. The deictics beginning with ng

The deictics with ng (listed in the second chart of 1 A 2, p. 12) occur after words or phrases to modify them. These deictics have locational meanings corresponding to those of the deictics beginning with d:

ngarí (corresponding to dirí)
ngánhi (corresponding to dínhi)
ngánhaq (corresponding to diháq)
ngádtu (corresponding to dídtu)

A common use of the ng deictics is to follow and modify words showing motion to a place ('go,' 'bring,' 'come,' and so forth):

1. Kiníng dyip padulúng ngádtu sa Banáwaq. 'This jeep is going to Banawa.'
2. Pagdalá ngaríg bir Day. 'Bring some beer (here), Miss.'
3. Gadalá siyá ngánhig bir. 'He is bringing some beer here.'
4. Magdalá ku ngánhag bir. 'I will bring beer to where you are.'

The deictics with d occur wherever the deictics with ng occur, and thus they also modify words or phrases showing motion to a place. (This usage, though common, is not considered 'correct' by purists: cf. English 'It's me.')

1 a. Kiníng dyip padulúng dídtu sa Banáwaq. 'This jeep is going to Banawa.'
2 a. Pagdalá diríg bir Day. (2 b 26) 'Bring some beer (here).'
3 a. Gadalá siyá dínhig bir. 'He is bringing some beer here.'
4 a. Magdalá ku diháq bir. 'I will bring beer to where you are.'

Deictics in ng follow, and modify, words and phrases with other meanings also. In such usages, they are interchangeable with the deictics in d; moreover, both are considered equally correct and are equally common.

5. Níqa si Dúktur Pirnándis {ngánhi / dínhi}. 'Dr. Fernandez is here.'
6. Ákuq lang ibílin ning ákung amígu {dínhi / ngánhi}. 'I will just leave my friend here.'
7. Díqa {ngarí / dirí} ang bir kanákuq. 'The beer is here with me.'
8. Túqa na siyá {ngádtu / dídtu}. 'He is over there now.'

Exercises 2.II; Pattern practice PP-B.

2 A 2. The interrogative deictics

The interrogative deictics (words meaning 'where?') have past, present, or future meaning, like other deictics with time meaning. (See the first chart in 1 A 2, p. 12.)

Interrogative Deictics

	Present	Past	Future
Interrogative deictic	háqin	diqín	ása
Deictics with the same temporal meaning as the interrogative deictic	díqa níqa náqa túqa	dirí dínhi diháq dídtu	arí ánhi ánhaq ádtu

To state this another way,

Díqa, níqa, náqa, and túqa answer the question háqin?
Dídtu, dínhi, dirí, and dínhaq (diháq) answer the question diqín?
Ádtu, ánhi, arí and ánhaq answer the question ása?

1. Háqin man si Dúktur Pirnándis? 'Where is Dr. Fernandez?' [Answer: Níqa man. 'He is here.']
2. Diqín man si Lítu? 'Where was Lito?' [Answer: Dídtu siyá sa Amiriká. Karún pa siyá muqabút dínhi. 'He was in America. He has just arrived here.']
3. Ása man ni padulúng? 'Where is this jeep headed for?' [Answer: Ádtu ni padulúng sa Kapitúl. 'It (lit. this) is going toward the Capitol.']

Exercises 2.III A, 2.III B, 2.III C, 2.IV; Pattern practice PP-B-I.

2 B. Negatives

In Cebuano there are three negatives: waláq (short form waq), díliq (short form diq), and ayáw (short form ay).

Ayáw is used in negative imperatives; it means 'don't.'

a. Ayáw pagdalág bir. 'Don't bring beer.'

Ayáw also occurs in refusals, in this expression:

b. Ayáw na lang. 'No, thanks.' [Note the intonation.] The same sentence with the short form of ayáw is: b(1). Ay na lang.

Díliq is used to negate nouns, pronouns, and adjectives. (Nouns refer to persons, places, or things; the pronouns are the forms listed in the charts of 1 A and 1 B; adjectives describe qualities. More rigorous definitions of these terms will be given later.)

c. Díliq Lítu ang íyang ngálan. 'His name is not Lito.'
d. Díliq kanáq maqú ang muqádtu sa Banáwaq. 'That is not the one that goes to Banawa.'
e. Díliq maqáyu ang dyip nga ákung gisákyan ngánhi. 'The jeep I rode coming here was no good.'

Díliq also negates verbs when the action referred to is in the future ('will not'), is possible ('cannot'), or is habitual ('isn't/doesn't [etc.]'):

f. Díliq ka padúung sa Banáwaq. 'You're not going to go to Banawa.'
g. Díliq siyá muqádtu sa siní. 'He's not going to go to the show.'
h. Díliq siyá makabinisayáq. 'He can't speak Visayan.'
i. Díliq naq muqádtung dyip sa Banáwaq. 'That jeep doesn't go to Banawa.'

Also, díliq is the negative used with gústu 'want' and kinahánglan 'need':

k. Díliq ku gústu makigkítaq kaníya, pirú miqánhi man núqun siyá. 'I didn't want to see him but he came anyway.'
j. Díliq siyá gústung ipaqilaqíla nímu. 'He doesn't want to be introduced to you.'

Waláq is the negative when the action referred to is past time (did, has done, had done) or continuing time (is or was or will be [do]ing):

l. Waq mu maglisúd pagqánhi ngánhi? (2 b 17) 'Didn't you have a hard time coming here?'
m. Waq siyá muqádtu sa siní. 'He didn't go to the movies.' (Cf. g above.)
n. Waq na magqulán. 'It's not raining any more.'
o. Waq ka tugnawá? 'Don't you feel cold?'*

Waláq also negates the deictics in present or past meaning:

p. Waq siyá dídtu sa baay. 'He {was not / is not} at home.'
q. Waq dirí ang kukakúla. 'The Coca-Cola is not here.'

Examples p and q above show waláq (waq) modifying d deictics. Since the d deictics are used interchangeably with the ng deictics, examples p and q can also have ng deictics:

p (1). Waq siyá ngádtu sa baay. 'He was not (is not) at home.'
q (1). Waq ngarí ang kukakúla. 'The Coca-Cola is not here.'

(A third usage of waláq is described below, Lesson 3, 3 A 1.) Exercises 2.V A, 2.V B, 2.V C (also, for later use, 3.I D, 3.IV C, 4.I C, 4.I D, 4.I F, 5.I C, 5.I D, 5.I F, 6.I C, 6.I E, 6.IV D, 7.IV, when you have learned the basic sentences of the relevant lessons).

2 C. Suffix -a

A noun suffixed with -a and preceded by a demonstrative means 'a particular one [of several].' (The stress falls on the vowel before the -a.)

Maqú gyud nang baláya. (2 b 2) 'It is that house there for sure.' [There are several houses, and the one the speaker is pointing to is the one.]
Kiníng dyípay átung sákyan. 'This is the jeep we get on.' [There are several jeeps and this is the one we choose. If there is only one jeep, or if you are not talking about one particular jeep of several, you say the sentence below:
Átung sákyan kiníng dyip. 'We'll get on this jeep.']

Exercises 2.VI, 2.VII.

2 D. Maqú 'is (are, was, etc.) the one' (short forms maw, mu, muqú)

2 D 1. Maqú in sentences with noun or pronoun subject and predicate

The particle maqú (or its short colloquial forms maw, muqú, mu) is used—optionally—in sentences consisting of two parts, X and Y, each of which is either (1) a word or phrase preceded by the subject marker (ang, si, y) or (2) a nominative pronoun. Sentences with maqú mean 'X is the one which is Y.' The following sentence consists of the two parts kiní 'this,' y ílang baay 'their house,' and maqú 'is the one':

---

* English adjectives or adverbs sometimes correspond to Cebuano verbs. Tugnawá, corresponding to English cold, is one of these.

a. Maqú kiníy ílang baay. 'This is their house.' Compare the same sentence with maqú omitted:
a (1). Kiníy ílang baay. 'This is their house.'
b. Maqú kiní si Místir Gamílu. 'This is Mr. Gamelo.' Without maqú:
b (1). Kiní si Místir Gamílu. (1.10) 'This is Mr. Gamelo.'

2 D 2. Maqú in sentences consisting only of noun or pronoun predicate

Maqú is used (also optionally) in sentences composed only of pronouns or of phrases preceded by a subject marker. Such sentences mean 'X is the one':

Maqú gyud nang baláya. 'That house is the one for sure.'

2 E. Preposed genitives

Look at the chart in 1 B 1 (page 14). The forms in the column on the right side are PREPOSED GENITIVES—that is, genitives that are placed before what they modify. They have three uses.

(1) Preposed genitives are used before nouns (linked with nga) meaning 'my (your, his, etc.) [noun]':

Kiní ang ákung amígu si Místir Gamílu. 'This is my friend Mr. Gamelo.'

(Note that the q of ákuq is dropped before nga; also, when nga is attached to the preceding word, the a is dropped.)

Maqú ba niy ílang baay? (2 b 1) 'Is this their house?'
Kínsay ímung ngálan Dung? (2 b 19) 'What is your name, Boy?'

(2) Preposed genitives are also used with passive verbs to indicate the doer of the action. (Passive verbs and rules for the preposed genitive in conjunction with them are discussed in detail later. For the present, study these sentences in their entirety without analyzing.)

Ákuq lang ibílin ning ákung amígu dínhi. (1.16) 'I will just leave my friend here.'
Únsa man diqáyng dyip ámung sákyan padúung sa Banáwaq? (2 a 9) 'Then what jeep is it that we get to go to Banawa?'

(3) Preposed genitives are used in the meaning 'be mine (yours, his, hers, ours, theirs),' either present (is, are) or past (was, were):

Ámuq kanáng baláya. 'That house is ours.'
Ákuq kirí; ímu kanáq. 'This is mine; that is yours.'

(1 a) They are used as subjects (after the subject markers ang or y) to mean 'yours (his, hers, etc.) is . . . ':

Únsa may átuq? 'What shall we have?' (Lit. 'Ours is what?')

(1 b) Preposed genitives also occur in certain idioms:

(1) The plural forms (íla, 'their,' ámuq 'our,' átuq 'our,' and ínyu 'your') are used to mean 'at the home of':

Ádtu ku sa ílang Dúktur Pirnándis. 'I am going to Dr. Fernandez' house.' (Lit. 'I am going to the their of Dr. Fernandez.') (ílang = íla ni)
Ádtu ku manihápun sa ámuq. 'I will eat supper at home (lit. at ours).'

(2) The form akuq 'I' has this special use:

Ákuq na ni ha? 'May I keep this?' (Lit. 'This is mine now, O.K.?')

2 E 1. Kang with personal names

'Belong to X' where X is a personal name is expressed by kang preceding the name.

Kang Mîstir Gamîlu kinîng báya. 'This house belongs to Mr. Gamelo.'

2 E 1 a. Ka with personal names

Ka plus X, where X is a personal name, means 'at X's place':

Nakasáqad man ming ádtu manihápun sa ka Mîstir Abáya. (2 b 33) 'We promised that we would eat supper at Mr. Abaya's.'

Exercise 2.VII, Pattern practice PP-C.

Pattern Practices and Exercises

PP-B Deictics and interrogatives

Step I. (Háqin vs. diqîn vs. ása: 2 A 2.) Ask the question for which the answer is given.

'He is there.'
'Where is he?'

1. a. Túqa siyá dîdtu.
   b. Háqin man siyá?
2. a. Ádtu siyá dîdtu.
   b. Ása man siyá?
3. a. Dîdtu siyá sa înyu.
   b. Diqîn man siyá?
4. a. Nîqa siyá dînhi.
   b. Háqin man siyá?
5. a. Dînhaq siyá sa dyip.
   b. Diqîn man siyá?
6. a. Ánhaq siya sa baay ni Dúktur Pirnándis.
   b. Ása man siyá?
7. a. Arî siyá dirî.
   b. Ása man siyá?
8. a. Túqa siyá sa Kapitúl.
   b. Háqin man siyá?
9. a. Dîdtu siyá sa Banáwaq.
   b. Diqîn man siyá?
10. a. Diháq siyá sa baay.
    b. Diqîn man siyá?

11. a. Ádtu siyá sa Amiriká.
    b. Ása man siyá?

12. a. Náqa siyá sa ka Místir Abáya.
    b. Háqin man siyá?

13. a. Dínhaq siyá sa ka Ínting.
    b. Diqín man siyá?

Step II. (Ngarí vs. ngádtu vs. ngánhaq vs. ngánhi: 2 A 1.)

'He is here in Cebu.'

Níqa siyá ngánhis Sibu.	(túqa)
Túqa siyá ngádtus Sibú.	(náqa)
Náqa siyá ngánhas Sibú.	(ádtu)
Ádtu siyá ngádtus Sibú.	(díqa)
Díqa siyá ngarís Sibú.	(arí)
Arí siyá ngarís Sibú.	(ánhi)
Ánhi siyá ngánhis Sibú.	(ánhaq)
Ánhaq siyá ngánhas Sibú.	(ádtu)
Ádtu siyá ngádtus Sibú.	(adíqa)
Adíqa siyá ngarís Sibú.	(aníqa)
Aníqa siyá ngánhis Sibú.	(anáqa)
Anáqa siyá ngánhas Sibú.	(atúqa)
Atúqa siyá ngádtus Sibú.	

Step III. (Níqa vs. náqa vs. túqa vs. díqa; dirí vs. dínhi vs. dínhaq vs. dídtu.)

'He is there.'

Náqa siyá diháq.	(ádtu)
Ádtu siyá dídtu.	(díqa)
Díqa siyá dirí.	(ánhi)
Ánhi siyá dínhi.	(ánhaq)
Ánhaq siyá dínhaq.	(arí)
Arí siyá dirí.	(níqa)
Níqa siyá dínhi.	(náqa)
Náqa siyá dínhaq.	(túqa)
Túqa siyá dídtu.	(arí)
Arí siyá dirí.	(ánhi)
Ánhi siyá dínhi.	(ánhaq)
Ánhaq siyá dínhaq.	(ádtu)

Ádtu siyá dīdtu. (dīqa)

Dīqa siyá dirī. (níqa)

Nīqa siyá dīnhi. (náqa)

Náqa siyá dīnhaq. (túqa)

Túqa siyá dīdtu.

Step IV. (Nīqa vs. náqa vs. túqa vs. dīqa; dirī vs. dīnhi vs. dīnhaq vs. dīdtu; and ngarī vs. ngánhi vs. ngánhaq vs. ngádtu: 1 A 2 and 2 A 1.)

'He is there.'

Náqa siyá diháq. (dīdtu)

Túqa siyá dīdtu. (dīqa)

Dīqa siyá dirī. (túqa)

Túqa siyá dīdtu. (ádtu)

Ádtu siyá dīdtu. (ngádtu)

Ádtu siyá ngádtu. (dīnhi)

Ánhi siyá dīnhi. (nīqa)

Nīqa siyá dīnhi. (dirī)

Dīqa siyá dirī. (arī)

Ári siyá dirī. (ngarī)

Arī siyá ngarī. (ánhi)

Ánhi siyá ngánhi. (náqa)

Náqa siyá ngánhaq. (ánhaq)

Ánhaq siyá ngánhaq.

Step V. (Changing subject and deictic predicates.)

'John is over there.'

Náqa si Hwan diháq. (ang lībru)

Náqa ang lībru diháq. (túqa)

Túqa ang lībru dīdtu. (silá)

Túqa silá dīdtu. (si Ínting)

Túqa si Ínting dīdtu. (nīqa)

Nīqa si Ínting dīnhi. (ang ákung amīgu)

Nīqa ang ákung amīgu dīnhi. (siyá)

Nīqa siyá dīnhi. (ádtu)

Ádtu siyá dīdtu. (si Mīstir Abáya)

Ádtu si Mīstir Abáya dīdtu. (mu)

Ádtu mu dīdtu.	(ánhaq)
Ánhaq mu {dīnhaq / diháq}.	(ka)
Ánhaq ka {dīnhaq / diháq}.	(ang mga bir)
Ánhaq ang mga bir dīnhaq.	(kitá)
Ánhaq kitá dínhaq.	(nīqa)
Nīqa kitá dīnhi.	(mi)
Nīqa mi dīnhi.	(ang kukakúla)
Nīqa ang kukakúla dīnhi.	(si Mīstir Gamīlu)
Nīqa si Mīstir Gamīlu dīnhi.	(túqa)
Túqa si Mīstir Gamīlu dīdtu.	(si Hwan)
Túqa si Hwan dīdtu.	(ádtu)
Ádtu si Hwan dīdtu.	(ang dráybir)
Ádtu ang dráybir dīdtu.	(siyá)
Ádtu siyá dīdtu.	(ánhi)
Ánhi siyá dīnhi.	(ang bátaq)
Ánhi ang bátaq dīnhi.	

I. Deictics (see 1 A 2 and subsections). PP-A-V may be reviewed before this exercise is taken up.

A. dirī, dīnhi, dīdtu

1. Díqa__________sa ámuq ang īmung asáwa.
2. Ádtu padulúng ang dyip__________sa Kapitúl.
3. Nīqa ba__________si Ída?
4. Ádtu pagdalá ug kukakúla__________sa ka Dyuu.
5. Sigúru ka ba nga ánhi__________mi manakáy?

B. ádtu, arī, ánhi, ánhaq

1. __________dirī sa ámuq ang paniqúdtu ('lunch').
2. __________lang ka dīnhaq muqinúm ('will drink') ug bir.
3. Gústu ni Dyuu__________dīnhi sa ámuq.
4. __________ba ni dídtu sa Lahúg? (to jeep driver)
5. Ang asáwa ni Mīstir Abrigána__________dīnhi maniqúdtu.
6. __________siyá dīdtu sa Manīlaq. (place far from persons speaking and spoken to)

7. __________únyaq dirī sa ámung baláy.
8. __________ku ngádtu sa ka Dyuu. 'I'll be going to Joe's place.'
9. __________ta ngánhi maniqúdtu. 'Let's eat here.'
10. __________lang mi muqinúm ('will drink') ug kukakúla ngánhaq sa ínyu.

C. túqa, náqa, nīqa, dīqa

1. Ang asáwa ni Dyuu__________dīnhi.
2. __________na dīnhi ang dyip gīkan sa Kapitúl. (near person spoken to)
3. __________dirī kanákuq ang lībru.
4. __________ba diháq si Huwán?
5. __________siyá dīdtu sa īlang Dúktur Pirnándis.
6. Ang bátaq__________dirī maniqúdtu sa ámuq.
7. Ang báynti sintábus ('cents')__________dīdtu sa ákung asáwa.
8. Ang kukakúla__________diháq.

II. Insert one of the following in the blank: ngarī, ngánhi, ngánhaq, or ngádtu. (2 A 1)

1. Padúung ba kinīng dyip__________sa Banáwaq?
2. Íngna lang nga ánhaq mi__________.
3. Karún ka pa muqabút__________?
4. Maglisúd mi pagqádtu__________.
5. Ánhi siyá__________magtawág ug dyip.
6. Si Mīstir Abáya ang muhatúd nátuq__________sa Banáwaq.
7. Si Dúktur Pirnándis muqabút karún__________. 'Dr. Fernandez is about to come now (lit. will be here any minute).'
8. Ári mi__________.
9. Ádtu ba mu__________?
10. Padúung na ang dyip__________sa Banáwaq.
11. Ánhaq ba ta__________magtawág ug dyip?
12. Ánhi lang mi__________manakáy.
13. Arī ku__________muqinúm ug kukakúla.
14. Ánhaq mi__________sa ka Dúktur Pirnándis.
15. Ádtu ba mu__________sa Banáwaq?

III. Deictics

A. Insert one of the following in the blank: háqin, ása, or diqín. (2 A 2)

1. __________man si Ínting? Náqa ba?
2. __________man gīkan ang īmung asáwa?

3. __________ni padúung?
4. __________si Místir Abáya karún? Waq ba siyá dínhi?
5. __________man mu ganíha? (ganíha 'before')
6. __________ku man ibílin ang bir? 'Where shall I leave the beer?'
7. __________ka muqinúm ug kukakúla kagahápun? (kagahápun 'yesterday')
8. __________tung ímung dyip karún? Díliq ba nang náqa diháq ímu?
9. __________man gíkan kádtung dyípa?
10. __________ang ímung asáwa karún? Ngánung waq siyá dínhi?
11. __________man siyá magtawág ug dyip? 'Where should she call a jeep?'
12. __________man kitá manakáy?
13. __________ang baláy ni Dúktur Pirnándis?
14. __________man gíkan si Místir Abáya Day?
15. __________man mu gahápun?

B. Find Cebuano questions which can be answered by the following statements. Use ása, háqin, or diqín. (1 A 2, 2 A 2)

1. Dídtu siyá sa Banáwaq.
2. Ánhi siyá maniqúdtu dínhi.
3. Níqa siyá dínhi.
4. Túqa silá sa Manílaq.
5. Ádtu mi padúung sa Kapitúl Day.
6. Níqa dínhi si Místir Abáya.
7. Náqa diháq ang baláy ni Ínting.
8. Si Místir Bílu níqa sa Súgbu.
9. Díqa siyá dirí sa ámuq Mis.
10. Ánhi ta dínhi manakáy ug dyip Day.
11. Arí mi dirí Day.
12. Dirí siyá muqinúm ug kukakúla.
13. Díqa dirí si Místir Bílu sa ámuq.
14. Gíkan si Místir Abáya sa Amiriká.
15. Si Ínting túqa sa Kapitúl.

C. Answer the following questions using deictics. (1 A 2, 2 A 2)

1. Diqín ka man manihápun Ting?
2. Ása ka man maniqúdtu Duktúr?
3. Háqin man si Tátay nímu Day?

4. Ásа man ning dyípa padúung Dung?
5. Diqín man mu gíkan Misís?
6. Ása man ta manakáy?
7. Háqin man ang baláy ni Dúktur Pirnándis Day?
8. Diqín nímu ibílin ang bir Ting?
9. Ása ba mu karún?
10. Háqin ang ákung kukakúla Day?
11. Diqín man gíkan kiníng dyípa?
12. Ása man ta manihápun Ting?
13. Háqin si Místir Abáya Day?
14. Diqín man ka ug bir? 'Where did you get beer?'
15. Háqin ba tung átung dráybir?
16. Diqín ka maniqúdtu?
17. Háqin si Gamílu?
18. Ása man ang ímung asáwa manihápun karún?
19. Diqín man ka muqinúm ug kukakúla?
20. Ása man ta magtawág ug dyip?

IV. Refer to the picture on page 53 and insert the proper deictic in the blank. (The letters refer to the speaker and the person spoken to.) (1 A 2, 2 A 2)

1. (A-C) __________lang ka manihápun.
2. (D-A) __________ang lítsi__________sa kusína.
3. (D-B) __________na ba diháq ang paan?
4. (B-D) __________man__________sa lamísa.
5. (B-D) Waq man__________ang súdqan.
6. (B-A) __________ba__________y básu nímu?
7. (A-B) __________man.
8. (A-D) Ikúhaq__________g plátu si Ínting.
9. (B-A) __________ba ang kutsílyu?
10. (A-B) __________ __________sa kusína ang kutsílyu.
11. (D-AB) __________ __________sa kusína ang kutsílyu.
12. (A-D) __________bay paan párang Ínting?
13. (D-A) __________man. __________ __________sa kusína.
14. (C-AB) __________na lang ku__________muqinúm sa ámuq.
15. (AB-C) __________lang dirí káqun.

D
B
C
A

V. Negatives (2 B)

A. Insert walág, díliq or ayáw in the blank.

1. Gústu ka bag bir? __________na lang.
2. __________kaqáyu maqáyu ang panihápun. 'Dinner was not very good.'
3. __________kiní si Tásyu. Kádtu man.
4. __________ku makabinisayáq. 'I cannot speak Visayan.'
5. __________ku gústu manihápun sa ámuq.
6. __________si Lúling ang ákung gitawág. 'Loling was not the one I called.'
7. __________ku maglisúd pagqánhi dínhi. 'I did not have trouble in coming here.'
8. __________ra ba siyá dínhi. Milakáw man tu.
9. __________na lang ku musakáy. 'I won't get on.'
10. __________na lang kug ikúhag bir Day.
11. __________ka ba magtawág ug dyip dídtu? 'Did you not call . . . ?'
12. __________na lang nang kukakúla. Bir na lang.
13. __________dídtu si Místir Abáya sa ámuq.
14. __________ba muqabút si Gamílu karún? 'Isn't it time for Gamelo to arrive now?' (Lit. 'Isn't Gamelo going to arrive now?')
15. __________na pagqánhi ngánhi. 'Don't come here any more.'
16. __________pagqádtu dídtu. 'Don't go there.'
17. __________ba naq si Gamílu?
18. __________ba dínhi si Ínting?
19. __________dirí ug panihápun. Ádtu lang dídtu.
20. __________ba si Místir Abáya kádtu? 'Wasn't that Mr. Abaya?'

B. Walág, díliq, ayáw

1. __________siyá musakáy sa dyip. 'He won't . . .'
2. __________pagqinúm ('drink') ug bir. 'Don't . . .'
3. __________si Dúktur Pirnándis maniqúdtu dínhi. 'He did not . . .'
4. __________ning dyípa ang padulúng sa Kapitúl. 'This is not the jeep going to the Capitol.'
5. __________siyá dirí. 'He is not here.'
6. Si Pídru__________ku amígu. 'Pedro is not my friend.'
7. __________bir ang íyang ímnun. 'He won't be drinking beer.'
8. __________nay bir dirí.

9. Si Ída__________níya asáwa.

10. __________pagqánhi dínhi. 'Don't . . .'

C. Answer the following questions using waláq, díliq, or ayáw.

1. Gústu ka ba manihápun run?
2. Níqa ba si Dúktur Pirnándis?
3. Makabinisayáq ka na ba?
4. Padulúng ba ni sa Lahúg?
5. Dídtu ka ba maniqúdtu sa ílang Tásyu?
6. Náqa ba si Místir Abáya?
7. Náqa ba diháq ang bir?
8. Muqinúm ka bag bir?
9. Dínhaq ba tung átung amígu sa ka Ínting?
10. Banáwaq ba ni Bay?
11. Gústu ka bag kukakúla?
12. Padulúng ka ba ngádtu?
13. Níqa ba ang ímung asáwa?
14. Náqa ba karún si Tásyu sa Banáwaq?
15. Kukakúla ba ni Day?

VI. Insert the suffix -a wherever possible in the following sentences. (2 C)

1. Kínsa man ning baláy?
2. Únsa diqáyng dyip ang pára sa Banáwaq?
3. Kínsa man ning dráybir?
4. Maqáyu nang bir ímnun?
5. Kínsay mukáqun ning kánqun? 'Who will eat this rice?'
6. Kínsang Pirnándis ang dúktur?
7. Háqin man nang bátaq karún?
8. Kánqun ku ba nang paan?
9. Karíng súdqan kánqun ku ba?
10. Kanáng básu kang Místir Abáya.
11. Kiríng kutsílyu kang Lúling.
12. Kiníng lítsi párang Místir Bílu.
13. Ámuq kanáng lamísa.
14. Háqin man ánang plátu ang ímu?
15. Kínsang Dúdung ang miqabút, si Gamílu u si Ínting?

PP-C Preposed genitives (2 E)

Step I. (Preposed genitives used alone as predicates)

'Is that yours?'

Ímu ba kanáq? (ákuq)

Ákuq ba kanáq? (íla)

Íla ba kanáq? (kanáng báya)

Íla ba kanáng báya? (ámuq)

Ámuq ba kanáng báya? (kádtung dyip)

Ámuq ba kádtung dyip? (íya)

Íya ba kádtung dyip? (kiníng líbru)

Íya ba kiníng líbru? (ínyu)

Ínyu ba kiníng líbru? (ámuq)

Ámuq ba kiníng líbru? (kirí)

Ámuq ba kirí? (átuq)

Átuq ba kirí? (kanáng kwártu)

Átuq ba kanáng kwártu?

Step II. (Preposed genitives before nouns)

'This is my friend.'

Kiní ang ákung amígu. (átuq)

Kiní ang átung amígu. (íla)

Kiní ang ílang amígu. (báay)

Kiní ang ílang baay. (ámuq)

Kiní ang ámung baay. (ínyu)

Kiní ang ínyung baay. (dyip)

Kiní ang ínyung dyip. (íya)

Kiní ang íyang dyip. (ímu)

Kiní ang ímung dyip. (átuq)

Kiní ang átung dyip. (kukakúla)

Kiní ang átung kukakúla. (íla)

Kiní ang ílang kukakúla. (ákuq)

Kiní ang ákung kukakúla. (bisíta)

Kiní ang ákung bisíta. (íya)

Kiní ang íyang bisíta.

Step III. (Transforming preposed genitives from position before pronoun to the predicate)

'Is this house theirs?'

1. a. Kiní bay ílang baay?
   b. Íla ba kiníng baay?

2. a. Kanáq bay ínyung dyip?
   b. Ínyu ba kanáng dyip?

3. a. Kádtu bay íyang amígu?
   b. Íya ba kádtung amígu?

4. a. Kirí bay ímung líbru?
   b. Ímu ba kiríng líbru?

5. a. Kanáq bay ákung lamísa?
   b. Ákuq ba kanáng lamísa?

6. a. Kádtu bay ílang kwártu?
   b. Íla ba kádtung kwártu?

7. a. Kiní bay átung bisíta?
   b. Átuq ba kiníng bisíta?

VII. Translate the following into Cebuano. (2 E)

1. This is mine.
2. Is this yours?
3. I am going to John's house.
4. Let's eat supper at our house.
5. My wife is at Dr. Fernandez'.
6. That house is ours.
7. That jeep is theirs.
8. This loaf of bread is mine. (loaf of bread: paan)
9. Is that their glass?
10. This is Tasyo's milk.
11. My friend is at Mr. Gamelo's.
12. Is this your Coke?
13. That beer is yours.
14. I will eat my dinner at Mr. Abaya's.
15. This jeep is Dr. Fernandez'.

VIII. Kínsa, únsa (see second comment to 2 b 19 in Commentary to Basic Sentences).

1. __________y ímung ngálan?
2. __________ng dyípa ang padulúng sa Banáwaq?

3. __________y ngálan sa bátaq?
4. __________y ĭmung ĭmnun?
5. __________y átuq?
6. __________ba ang asáwa ni Hwan?
7. __________y átung paniqúdtu? 'What will we have for lunch?' (Lit. 'What is our lunch?')

IX. Mangá paglitúk (intonations)

1. Informant reads the first few sentences with the intonation indicated.
2. The student repeats after the informant.
3. The student reads the rest of the sentences with the correct intonation without benefit of the informant's model.
4. The informant repeats with correct intonation each sentence the student has read incorrectly.

A. Review of <u>234</u> statement or command (Exercise 1.VIII B).

1.	Ádtu sa Kapitúl.	(2 a 12)
2.	Manakáy na ta.	(2 a 17)
3.	Báynti Day.	(2 b 4)
4.	Kumústa ka?	(2 b 16)
5.	Íngna lang.	(2 a 6)
6.	Dayún.	(2 b 7)
7.	Karún pa gyud.	(2 b 12)
8.	Pagdalá dirĭg bir.	(2 b 26)
9.	Ságdi na lang Duktúr.	(2 b 28)
10.	Ádtu na lang mi.	(2 b 30)
11.	Kay hápun na man.	(2 b 30)
12.	Wánqa ra bay bir Nyur.	(2 b 27)
13.	Waq man kaqáyu maglisúd.	(2 b 18)
14.	Midágan man.	(2 b 20)
15.	Karún pa gyud.	(2 b 12)
16.	Kamĭng duhá.	(2 a 15)

B. Questions are pronounced with rising pitch, like statements (see the examples in the exercise just above), except that the rise in questions is much sharper than that in statements. The rising contour of questions is symbolized <u>124</u>.

1. Karún ka pa muqabút? (2 b 11)
2. Waq mu maglisúd pagqánhi? (2 b 17)
3. Lítu diqáy ímung ngálan? (2 b 24)
4. Sigí ha? (2 b 35)

X. Sultiqánay (Conversation) Listen to the following conversation without looking at the text; then answer the true-false questions:

Únang Báhin (Part 1)

Mutsátsa: Únsay átuq Day?

Pírla: Mu ba ning baay ni Dúktur Pirnándis?

Mutsátsa: Uu, Dayún lang Day.

Pírla: Háqin man si Dúktur Pirnándis? Níqa ba?

Mutsátsa: Uu. Níqa man. Túqas táqas.

Pírla: Íngna lang ang Dúktur nga níqa ku.

Mutsátsa: Kínsay ímung ngálan Day.

Pírla: Akú si Mis Pírla Sántus. Gipaqilaqíla akú níya sa dídtu pa siyá sa Amiriká.

Mutsátsa: Saq pa. Ákung táwgun.

Ikaduháng Báhin (Part 2)

Dúktur Pirnándis: Uh! Mis Sántus. Níqa ka man diqáy. Kumústa ka man?

Pírla: Maay man Duktúr. Ikáw kumústa?

Dúktur Pirnándis: Maqáyu sad. Naglisúd ka ba pagqánhi ngánhi?

Pírla: Uu Duktúr. Kay way dyip nga muhatúd ngánhi.

Dúktur Pirnándis: Únsa man diqáy ímung gisákyan ngánhi?

Pírla: Táksi lang.

Tubagág hústug díliq (True-false questions)

Únang Báhin

1. Túqa si Pírla sa ka Dúktur Pirnándis.
2. Waq dídtu si Dúktur Pirnándis. Nilakáw.
3. Túqa ang dúktur sa táqas.
4. Waq pa si Mis Sántus ipaqilaqíla sa dúktur.
5. Dídtu si Dúktur Pirnándis sa Amiriká sa gipaqilaqíla si Pírla níya.

Ikaduháng Báhin

6. Díliq maqáyu si Pírla, pirú ang dúktur maqáyu man.
7. Waq maglisúd si Pírla pagqádtu ngádtu.
8. Dyip nga muhatúd sa Kapitúl ang gisákyan ni Pírla.
9. Kay waláq may dyip padúung ngádtu, naglakáw na lang si Pírla.
10. Midágan si Pírla kay misulúd si Dúktur Pirnándis.

LESSON 3. LOOKING FOR A ROOM

Sagquluhúnun (Basic Sentences)

First Part	Únang Báhin
Miss Wilby and Miss Santos go house hunting in Banawa.	Si Mis Wílbi ug si Mis Sántus nangítag sakqanán sa Banáwaq.
Perla (name of woman)	Pírla
where?	ása
[question particle after interrogative]	man
that (far from speaker and hearer)	tu
[linker between tu and baay]	nga
house	baay
of	ni
Mrs.	Mísis
Abellana	Abilyána
1. Perla, where is that house of Mrs. Abellana's?	*1. Pírlá, ása man tung baay ni Mísis Abilyána?
ah (acknowledging a fact known previously)	aa
that (far from speaker and hearer)	kádtu
[linker between kádtu and abángan]	nga
person from whom to be rented	abángan
by us	nátuq
[particle preceding goal]	sa
house	baláy
2. Ah, the one we are going to rent the house from?	*2. Aa, kádtung abángan nátus baláy?
3. Yes.	3. Uu.
is there [present deictic]	túqa

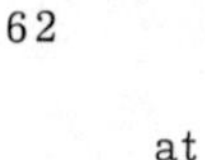

at	sa
Banawa	Banáwaq
	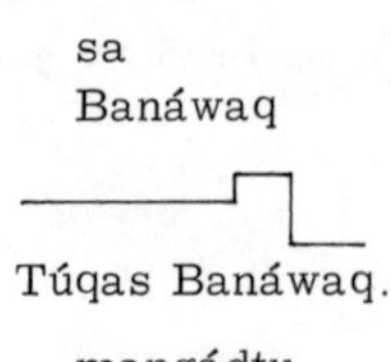
4. It is (there) in Banawa.	4. Túqas Banáwaq.
will go (plural)	mangádtu
we	ta
now	run
5. Shall we go now?	5. Mangádtu ta run?
6. O.K.	6. Sigí.
then, after that, next	únyaq
how will?	unsáqun
[question particle after interrogative]	man
go	pagqádtu
to	sa
Banawa	Banáwaq
	#
7. Then, how do (we) go to Banawa? (Lit. How to go to Banawa?)	7. Únyaq, unsáqun man pagqádtus 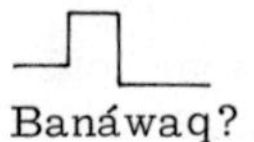 Banáwaq?
ah (pause before speaking)	aa
will ask	mangutána
we	ta
	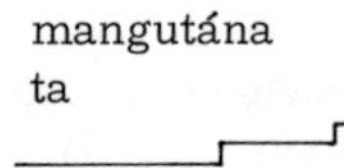 #
8. Ah, let's ask.	8. Aa, mangutána ta.
there is (present deictic)	náqa
[existential particle]	y
person	táwu
[particle for pointing to something]	ay
ask him	pangutánqa
	#
9. There's a man. Ask him.	9. Náqay táwu ay, pangutánqa.
ah (pause before speaking)	aa
I	akú
[subject marker]	y
will ask	mangutána
	#
10. Who, me? (Lit. Shall I be the one to ask?)	10. Aa, akúy mangutána?

11. Yes.	11. Uu.
good	maqáyu
[linker between maqáyu and búntag]	nga
morning	búntag
[term of address for male older than speaker]	Nuy
12. Good morning, Sir.	*12. Maqáyung búntag Nuy.
good	máyu
13. Good morning.	13. Máyu.
can	mahímuq
[question particle]	ba
[linker between mahímuq and the rest of the sentence]	nga
ask	mangutána
14. May I ask a question?	14. Mahímuq bang mangutána?
yes	uu
can	mahímuq
very	kaqáyu
15. Yes. Surely. (Lit. Yes. It is very possible.)	15. Uu. # Mahímuq kaqáyu.
where?	ása
[question particle after interrogative]	man
we	ta
get on	musakáy
if	ug
go	muqádtu
to	sa
Banawa	Banáwaq
16. Where do we get the jeep to Banawa? (Lit. Where do we get on if we go to Banawa?)	16. Ása man ta musakáy ug ... muqádtu tas Banáwaq?
umm (pause before speaking)	aa
go	mangádtu
you (plural)	mu
to	sa

17. Umm, you are going to Banawa?	*17. Aa, mangádtu mus Banáwaq?
18. Yes.	18. Uu.
that (not far away)	kanáq
[linker between kanáq and iskína]	nga
corner	iskína
there	ngánhaq
[particle asking if interlocutor understood]	nu
[particle meaning 'is the one']	maqú
[particle with statement giving information]	man
that (not far away)	naq
corner	iskína
of	sa
Pelaez (name of street in Cebu City)	Piláyis
Pedro del Rosario (usually called P. del Rosario) (name of a street in Cebu City)	Pidíl Rusáryu
19. Mmm, that corner there, that's the corner of Pelaez and P. del Rosario.	19. Aa, kanáng iskína ngánhaq nu, ... maqú man nang iskínas Piláyis ... Pidíl Rusáryu.
20. Yes.	20. Uu.
follow	subáya
just	lang
that (not far away)	naq
you (plural)	nínyu
that (not far away)	kanáq
[linker between kanáq and dálan]	nga
street	dálan
Pelaez	Piláyis

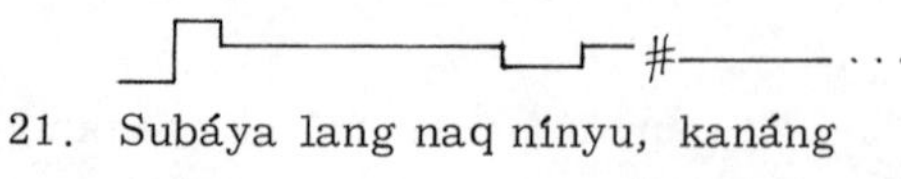

21. Just follow that street—Pelaez Street. (Lit. Just follow that—that Pelaez Street.)

21. Subáya lang naq nínyu, kanáng

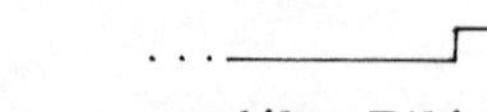

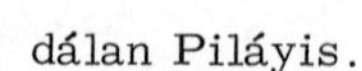

dálan Piláyis.

go down	dúlhug
there	ngádtu
a little bit	ug gamáy

22. Go down a bit. — 22. Dúlhug ngádtug gamáy.

upon reaching (future)	inigqabút
you (plural)	nínyu
at	sa
Sanciangko (name of street in Cebu City)	Sansyángku
turn	likúq
to	sa
right	tuqú

23. When you reach Sanciangko, turn right. — 23. Inigqabút nínyus Sansyángku, # likúq sa tuqú.

ah (preceding 'is that so?')	aa
so	diqáy

24. Ah, is that so? — 24. Aa, diqáy.

upon reaching	inigqabút
you (plural)	nínyu
the	sa
corner	iskína
Juan Luna (name of street in Cebu City)	Huwán Lúna
there	ánhaq
there	dínhaq
stop	muhúnung
[subject marker]	ang
[plural marker for nouns]	mangá
jeeps	dyip

25. When you get to the corner of Juan Luna and Sanciangko, the jeeps stop there. — *25. Inigqabút nínyus iskína Huwán ... # ... Lúna Sansyángku, ánhaq ... dínhaq muhúnung ang mangá ... dyip.

there are (there exist)	dúna
[existential particle]	y

[plural marker for nouns]	mangá
jeeps	dyip
there	ngánhaq
headed for	padúung sa
26. There are jeeps there headed for Banawa.	26. Dúnay mangá dyip ngánhaq ... padúung sa Banáwaq.
oh (particle before a statement conceding a point)	aa
many	dághan
[particle of agreement: that's right]	túqud
[linker between <u>dághan</u> and <u>mangági</u>]	nga
pass	mangági
there	diháq
27. Oh, that's right. Lots (of them) go by that way.	*27. Aa, dághan túqung mangági ... diháq.
ah (pause before speaking)	aa
many	dághan
[linker between <u>dághan</u> and <u>salámat</u>]	nga
thanks	salámat
[term of address for male older than speaker]	Nuy
[interrogative asking whether speaker is understood]	ha

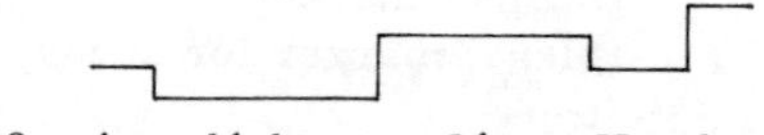

28. Thank you very much, Sir. (Lit. Many thanks, Sir.)	28. Aa, dághang salámat Nuy ha.
yes	uu
go ahead	sigí
29. Uh-huh, you're welcome. (Lit. Yes, go ahead.)	*29. Uu, sigí.
over here (toward speaker)	arí
now	na
we	mi

30. We're going now. (Lit. We are over here now.)	30. Arí na mi.
31. Don't mention it.	31. Waláy sapayán.
ask	pangutánqa
that (near hearer)	naq
[linker netween naq and dyip]	nga
jeep	dyip
[particle following a statement pointing to something the speaker sees but the hearer does not]	uh
	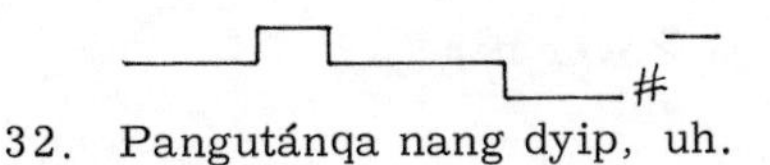
32. Ask him! (Lit. Ask that jeep.)	32. Pangutánqa nang dyip, uh.
there is (there exist)	náqa
[existential particle]	y
driver	dráybir
33. There is the driver.	33. Náqay dráybir.
ask him	pangutánqa
whether	ug
[particle meaning 'is the one']	maqú
[question particle]	ba
this	ni
[subject marker]	ang
for	pára sa
34. Ask him if this is the one which goes to Banawa.	34. Pangutánqa ug maqú ba ni ang ... páras Banáwaq.
ah [particle preceding a statement meaning 'so that's the way it is']	aa
[particle meaning 'is the one']	maqú
this	ni
let's get on	sakáy
we (inclusive)	ta
	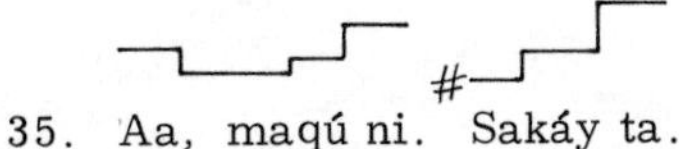
35. Ah, this is it. Let's get on.	35. Aa, maqú ni. Sakáy ta.

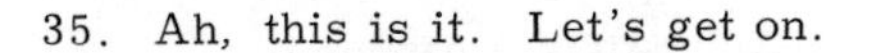

is there (present deictic)	náqa
[existential particle]	y
sign	márka
[linker between márka and Banáwaq]	nga

36. There is a sign Banawa. — 36. Náqay márkang Banáwaq.

that is so	túqud
isn't it?	nu
there is	náqa

37. So there is, isn't there? — 37. Túqud nu, náqa.

over here	ánhi
us	ta
here	dínhi
get off	manáqug

38. Let's get off here. — 38. Ánhi ta dínhi manáqug.

already	na
because	man
this	ni

39. This is Banawa now. (Lit. Because this is Banawa now.) — 39. Banáwaq na man ni.

stop	pára
[term of address for male younger than speaker]	Dung
over here	ánhi
only	ra
we	mi
here	dínhi

40. Stop, boy! We'll get off here, boy. — 40. Pára Dung. Ánhi ra mi dínhi Dung.

come on!	taná
is the one	maw (short for maqú)
this	ni
[subject marker]	ang
house	baláy
of	ni
Mrs. Abellana	Mísis Abilyána

41. Come on, this is Mrs. Abellana's house.	*41. Taná, maw ning baláy ni Mísis Abilyána.
yes	uu
that (not far away)	kanáq, naq
is the one	maw (short for maqú)
[linker between kanáq and ikaduhá]	nga
second one	ikaduhá
42. Yes, that's the one. The second one.	42. Uu, kanáq. Maw naq, kanáng ikaduhá.
is there (present deictic)	náqa
probably	tingáli
she	siyá
now	run
don't you think	nu
43. She's probably there now, don't you think?	*43. Náqa tingáli siyá run, nu?
44. I hope so.	44. Básin pa.

Mangá Pangutána (Questions)

Únang Báhin

1. Kiní na ba ang baay ni Mísis Abilyána?
2. Abángan ba nátuq kádtung baláy ni Pírla?
3. Ása ka Pirlá?
4. Díliq ba ta run mangádtu sa Banáwaq?
5. Ása man ta mangutána sa baláy ni Mísis Abilyána?
6. Kínsa man ruy mangutána ánang táwu?
7. Ása man mi musakáy pára sa Banáwaq Nuy?
8. Mangutána mi Nuy mahímuq ba?
9. Díliq ba kamú mangádtu sa Lahúg?
10. Banáwaq ka Nuy? (Ádtu ka ba sa Banáwaq?)

11. Kun muqádtu ku sa Lahúg ása man ku mangítag dyip nga sákyan?
12. Ádtu kamú sa iskína Huwán Lúna Sansyángku?
13. Muhúnung ba ning dyip sa Piláyis?
14. Túqa sa Pidíl Rusáryu ang baláy mu Pirlá?
15. Unsáqun man nímu pagqádtu sa Banáwaq?
16. Ánhaq ka ra sa iskína sa Piláyis Sansyángku Nuy?
17. Ádtu kamú dúlhug sa Huwán Lúna Pirlá?
18. Ánhi ra kamú dínhi Dung?
19. Dághan bang dyip dínhi Nuy?
20. Náqa bay márkang Banáwaq?

Mangá Pangutána (Matching)

Únang Báhin

1. Únsay átuq Nuy?
2. Ása ta Pirlá?
3. Maqú na ba ni ang baláy ni Mísis Abilyána?
4. Unsáqun man nátuq pagqádtu sa Banáwaq?
5. Ádtu ka sa Pidíl Rusáryu Dung?
6. Inigqabút sa iskína likúq sa tuqú?
7. Dínhi ka lang Pirlá? 'Are you getting off here, Perla?'
8. Abángan ba nímu ang baláy?
9. Musakáy na ba ta?

(a) Ug muqádtu ta sa Banáwaq musakáy tag dyip.
(b) Úqu. Únsa may átuq Nuy?
(c) Ádtu ta sa Lahúg Misís.
(d) Gústu ku musakáy pára sa Piláyis.
(e) Úqu Misís. Úqu. Magquná lang ku nímu ha?
(f) Úqu. Musakáy na ta kay údtu na.
(g) Díliq Nuy. Ádtu ku sa Huwán Lúna.
(h) Úqu Dung. Unyáq dúlhug ug gamáy.
(i) Úqu. Abángan ku.

Sagquluhúnun (Basic Sentences)

Second Part	Ikaduháng Báhin
good	máyu
1. Good morning.	1. Máyu.

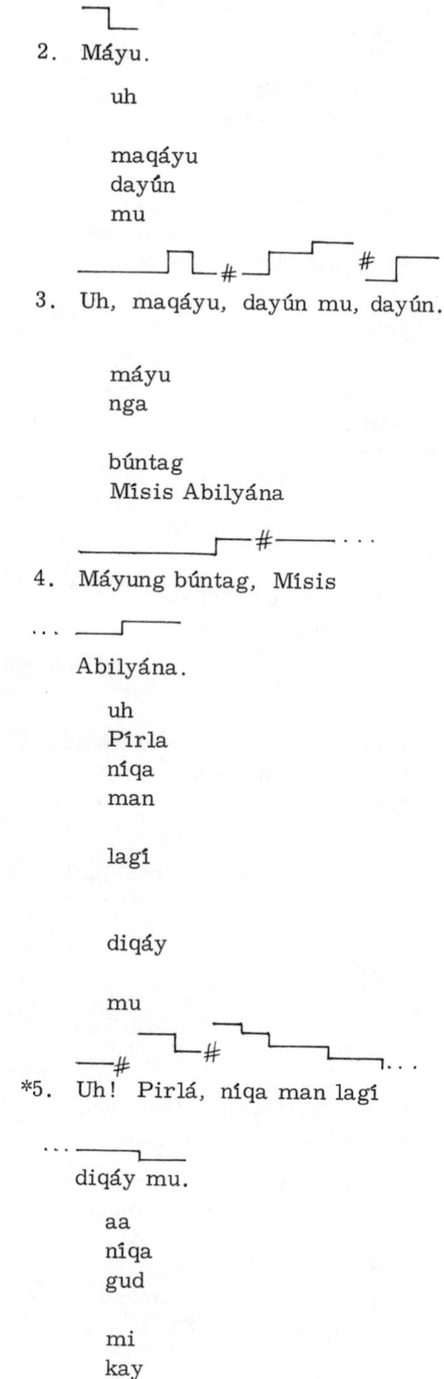

2. Good morning.	2. Máyu.
oh (surprise at seeing someone)	uh
good morning	maqáyu
come in	dayún
you (plural)	mu
3. Oh! Good morning. Come in, come in.	3. Uh, maqáyu, dayún mu, dayún.
good	máyu
[linker between máyu and búntag]	nga
morning	búntag
Mrs. Abellana	Mísis Abilyána
4. Good morning, Mrs. Abellana.	4. Máyung búntag, Mísis ... Abilyána.
oh (expressing surprise)	uh
Perla	Pírla
here	níqa
[particle with statement giving information]	man
[particle expressing that something is contrary to speaker's expectation]	lagí
[particle used on acquisition of new information]	diqáy
you (plural)	mu
5. Oh! Perla, you're here after all.	*5. Uh! Pirlá, níqa man lagí ... diqáy mu.
ah (pause before speaking)	aa
here	níqa
[particle introducing an explanation]	gud
we	mi
because	kay
I	ákuq
[linker between ákuq and gidalá]	nga

brought	gidalá
[particle preceding name]	si
Miss Wilby	Mis Wílbi
toward here	ngánhi

6. May I introduce Miss Wilby? (Lit. Ah, we're here because I brought Miss Wilby here.)

*6. Aa níqa gud mi kay ákung ... gidalá si Mis Wílbi ngánhi.

because	kay
will rent	muqábang
she says	nu
she	siyá
[particle preceding grammatical goal]	ug
room	kwártu
in	sa
your	ímu
[linker between ímu and baláy]	nga
house	baláy

7. (Because) she says she would like to rent a room in your house.

*7. Kay muqábang nu siyág ... kwártus ímung baláy.

oh (pause before speaking)	uu
come here	dalíq
you (plural)	mu
toward here	ngarí
to	sa
inside	suud

8. Oh! Come on in. (Lit. Oh, come in here to the inside.)

8. Uu, # dalíq mu ngarís suud.

sit down	língkud
for now, for the moment	saq
you (plural)	mu
for a second	kadyút
[particle with commands: 'Is it all right?']	ha

9. Sit down a moment, (for a second) won't you?

9. Língkud saq mu kadyút ha?

ah (pause before speaking)	aa
is the one	maqú

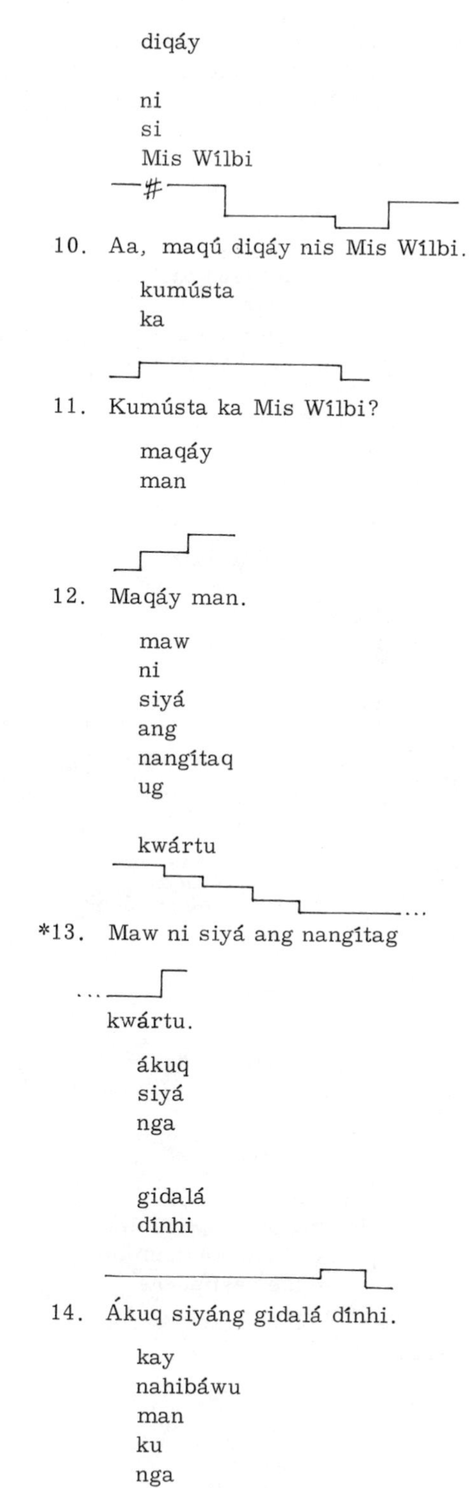

[particle used on acquiring new information] — diqáy
this — ni
[particle preceding names] — si
Miss Wilby — Mis Wílbi

10. Ah, so this is Miss Wilby. — 10. Aa, maqú diqáy nis Mis Wílbi.

how are — kumústa
you — ka

11. How are you, Miss Wilby? — 11. Kumústa ka Mis Wílbi?

good — maqáy
[particle with statement giving information] — man

12. I'm fine. (Lit. Good.) — 12. Maqáy man.

is the one — maw
this — ni
she — siyá
[subject marker] — ang
is looking for — nangítaq
[particle preceding grammatical goal] — ug
room — kwártu

13. She's the one who is looking for a room. (Lit. This she is the one . . .) — *13. Maw ni siyá ang nangítag . . . kwártu.

I — ákuq
her — siyá
[linker between ákuq and gidalá] — nga
brought — gidalá
here — dínhi

14. I brought her here. — 14. Ákuq siyáng gidalá dínhi.

because — kay
know — nahibáwu
because — man
I — ku
that (linker between nahibáwu and what follows) — nga

there is, there exists	náqa
[existential particle]	y
room	kwártu
in	sa
your	ínyu
[linker between ínyu and baláy]	nga
house	baláy
[linker between baláy and paqabángan]	nga
thing to be rented	paqabángan

15. Because I know there's a room for rent in your house.

15. Kay nahibáwu man ku nga ... náqay kwártus ínyung baayng ... paqabángan.

furthermore	nyaq
likes	gústu
she	siyá
[linker between gústu and the rest of the sentence]	nga
take a look	mutánqaw
now	run

16. Also, she would like to look at it now.

*16. Nyaq, gústu siyáng mutánqaw ... run.

ah	aa
is that so?	diqáy

17. Ah, is that so?

17. Aa, diqáy?

may	mahímu
[interrogative particle]	ba
[linker between mahímu and the rest of the sentence]	nga
look	mutánqaw
we	mi
now	run

18. May we look at it now?

18. Mahímu bang mutánqaw mi ... run?

yes	uu
there are, there exist	dúna
[existential particle]	y
two	duhá
[numeral linker]	ka
[counter]	buqúk
room	kwártu
[linker between kwártu and paqabángan]	nga
thing to be rented out	paqabángan

19. Yes, there are two rooms for rent. — *19. Uu, dúnay duhá ka buqúk kwártung paqabángan.

one	usá
at	sa
upstairs	táqas

20. One (is) upstairs. — 20. Usás táqas.

is here	níqa
also	sad
[existential particle]	y
one	usá
at	sa
downstairs	ubús

21. There's also one downstairs here. — 21. Níqa say usás ubús.

you	ikáw
just	lang
[subject marker]	y
select	magpíliq
which (of several)	háqin
this	íni
[linker between íni and duhá]	nga
two	duhá
[subject marker]	ang
you	ímu
[linker between ímu and gústu]	nga
desire	gústu

22. You choose which of these two you like. (Lit. You just be the one to choose which of these two you like.) — *22. Ikáw lay magpíliq háqin íning duhá ang ímung gústu.

ah [pause indicating that the thing under consideration is of no consequence]	aa
for	pára
me	nákuq
anywhere	bísan ug ása
merely	lang

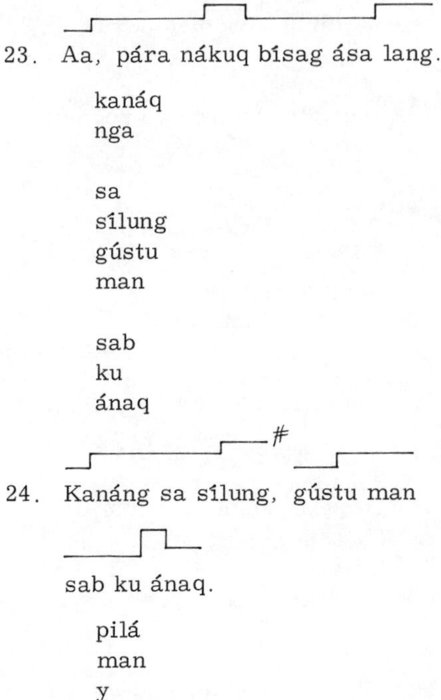

23. Oh, for me either one will do.	23. Aa, pára nákuq bísag ása lang.

that (just mentioned)	kanáq
[linker between kanáq and sa sílung]	nga
at	sa
downstairs	sílung
like	gústu
[particle with statement giving information]	man
also	sab
I	ku
that (just mentioned)	ánaq

24. I like the one downstairs. (Lit. The one downstairs, I also like that one.)	24. Kanáng sa sílung, gústu man sab ku ánaq.

how much?	pilá
[interrogative particle]	man
[subject marker]	y
thing to be paid	bayranán
that (just mentioned)	ánaq
for	sa
every	káda
month	búwan

25. How much is the monthly rent? (Lit. How much is the payment for that every month?)	25. Pilá may bayranán ánaq sa ... káda búwan?

well [pause word]	aw
that (previously there)	kádtu
[linker between kádtu and úna]	nga
previous	úna
[linker between úna and nagqabáng]	nga
was renting	nagqabáng
here	ngánhi
were paying	nagbayád

they — silá
[particle preceding grammatical goal] — ug
forty — kwarínta
pesos — písus
every — matág
month — búlan

26. Well, the previous tenants paid forty pesos a month. (Lit. Those that were renting here previously—they were paying forty pesos a month.)

*26. Aw, kádtung únang nagqabáng ngánhi, nagbayád silág kwarínta písus matág búlan.

free — líbri
you understand (with an explanation) — man gud
[subject marker] — ang
light — sugáq
and — ug
water — túbig

27. You see, light and water are free.

*27. Líbri man gung sugáq ug túbig.

rather expensive — mahalmahál
[particle meaning 'for sure'] — dyud
that (previously mentioned) — naq
by a little bit — ug dyútay

28. That's really rather expensive. (Lit. That's really rather expensive by a little bit.)

28. Mahalmahál dyud nag dyútay.

not any more — diq na
that (previously mentioned) — naq
thing that can be bargained — mahángyuq

29. Can't you make the price any lower? (Lit. Can that not be bargained over any more?)

*29. Diq na naq mahángyuq?

not — díliq
probably — tingáli
because — kay
there is, there exist — náqa
[particle used with statement giving reason] — man

[existential particle]	y
light	sugáq
and	ug
water	túbig
[linker between túbig and bayranán]	nga
thing to be paid for	bayranán

30. Probably not, because there is the light and water to be paid for.

*30. Díliq tingáli kay náqa may sugáq ug túbig nga bayranán.

yes	uu
good	maqáyu
also	sad
that (previously mentioned)	naq
[linker between naq and kwartúha]	nga
particular room	kwartúha
because	kay
its own	kaqugalíngun
[subject marker]	ang
toilet	kasílyas

31. Also [lit. yes], that room is good too, because it has its own toilet.

*31. Uu, maqáyu sad nang kwartúha ... kay kaqugalíngun ang kasílyas.

Mangá Pangutána (Questions)

Ikaduháng Báhin

1. Pilá man ang bayranán sa sugáq ug túbig?
2. May kaqugalíngun bang kasílyas kanáng mangá kwartúha?
3. Kiní ba siyá ang muqábang ug kwártu?
4. Ngánung mahál mag dyútay ang ábang?
5. Tingálig waláq siyá run sa baláy nu?
6. Kamú ba ang muqábang sa baláy ni Mísis Abáya?
7. Ngánung gidalá pa man nímu si Mis Wílbi?
8. Kiní ba si Mis Wílbi?
9. Ása man ta, sa suud?
10. Kínsa man diqáy ang mangítag kwártu nga paqabángan?

11. Dúna bay paqabángan nga kwártu?
12. Díliq na ba lang mu mutánqaw sa kwártu?
13. Pilá ka kwártu ang paqabángan Misis?
14. Díliq ka ba magpíliq, gamáy ra ba nang kwártu?
15. Háqin may ímu, ang sa sílung?
16. Pilá may bayranán káda búwan ánang kwártu sa sílung?
17. Líbri ba ang sugáq ug ang túbig ánang kwarínta písus?
18. Kínsa ang nagbayád ug kwarínta písus matág búlan sa baláy?
19. Díliq na gyud naq mahángyuq Dung?
20. Pilá ka buqúk ang kasílyas sa baláy mu Pirlá?

Mangá Pangutána (Matching)

Ikaduháng Báhin

1. Ngánung mahalmahál man ning kwártu sa sílung? 'Why is this room downstairs more expensive?'
2. Kaqugalíngun ba ang kasílyas sa matág kwártu?
3. Kínsa man ang nagbayád sa bayranán sa túbig?
4. Mahángyuq pa ba ni Nuy?
5. Piláy bayranán sa únang búwan?
6. Sa káda búwan piláy bayranán sa sugáq ug túbig?
7. Sa duhá ka kwártu háqi* ang ímung gústu?
8. Gústu ka bang mutánqaw sa kwártu?
9. May paqabángan ka bang kwártu Misis?

(a) Úqu kun mahímung mutánqaw.
(b) Ang bayranán sa sugáq ug túbig sa káda búwan dyis písus.
(c) Dúna. Gústu ka bang mutánqaw?
(d) Gústu ku ang kwártu sa sílung.
(e) Uu, matág kwártu náqay kaqugalíngung kasílyas.
(f) Kwarínta písus sa únang búwan.
(g) Díliq na gyud mahímuq Dung.
(h) Gamáy ra man gud kádtung sa táqas.
(i) Kádtung nagqabáng sa kwártu maqúy nagbayád.

---

*Háqi is a colloquial form for háqin.

Sagquluhúnun (Basic Sentences)

Third Part	Ikatulúng Báhin
oh	uy
there are, there exist	dúna
[particle used on giving information]	man
[particle used on receiving information]	diqáy
we	ta
[existential particle]	y
[plural marker]	mangá
guests	bisíta
Ma (term of address for one's mother)	Ma
1. Oh, so we have visitors, Ma!	1. Uy, dúna man diqáy tay mangá bisíta Ma!
come here	dalíq
[particle used to soften commands]	ra gud
a moment	kadiyút
[shortened nickname for the woman's name Inday]	Day
2. Come here a moment, Day.	2. Dalíq ra gud kadiyút Day.
is the one	mu (short for maqú)
this	ni
she	siyá
[particle preceding name]	si
Miss Wilby	Mis Wílbi
who (linker between Mis Wílbi and muqábang)	nga
will rent	muqábang
[particle preceding grammatical goal]	sa
one	usá
of	sa
[plural marker]	mangá
rooms	kwártu
3. This (lit. This she) is Miss	*3. Mu ni siyá si Mis Wílbi, nga

Wilby, who is going to rent one of the rooms.	... muqábang sa usá sa mangá ... kwártu.
the one	mu
this	ni
[woman's nickname]	Índay
4. Miss Wilby, this is Inday.	4. Mis Wílbi, mu ni si Índay.
how are	kumústa
you	ka
5. How are you, Inday?	5. Kumústa ka Indáy?
ah (pause before speaking)	aa
good	maqáy
[particle with statement giving information]	man
6. I'm fine. (Lit. I am good.)	6. Aa, maqáy man.
you	kamú
[interrogative particle]	ba
[linker between kamú and duhá]	nga
two	duhá
[particle used on acquiring new information]	diqáy
[subject particle]	y
will rent	muqábang
[particle preceding goal]	sa
room	kwártu
7. So you two are the ones who are renting the rooms.	*7. Kamú bang duhá diqáy ... muqábang sa kwártu?
no	díliq
me	akú
[particle: 'nothing but']	ra
8. No. Just me.	8. Díliq. Akú ra.
(Inday leaves.)	(Milakáw si Índay.)
that (one previously there)	kádtu

[linker between kádtu and anák]	nga
my	ákuq
[linker between ákuq and anák]	nga
daughter	anák
there	túqa
is living	magpuyúq
at	sa
upstairs	táqas

9. That was my daughter. She lives upstairs. (Lit. That daughter of mine lives upstairs there.)

*9. Kádtung ákung anák, # túqa ... magpuyúq sa táqas.

has	dúna
she	siyá
[existential particle]	y
four	upát
[numeral linker]	ka
[counter]	buqúk
[plural marker]	mangá
children	bátaq

10. She has four children.

10. Dúna siyáy upát ka buqúk ... mangá bátaq.

not	diq
you	ka
[particle meaning 'would it be possible that . . .?']	kaháq
later on	unyáq
consider bothersome	samúkan
[goal marker]	sa
[plural marker]	mangá
children	bátaq

11. Won't the children bother you? (Lit. Won't you perhaps consider the children bothersome later?)

11. Diq ka kaháq únyaq samúkans ... mangá bátaq?

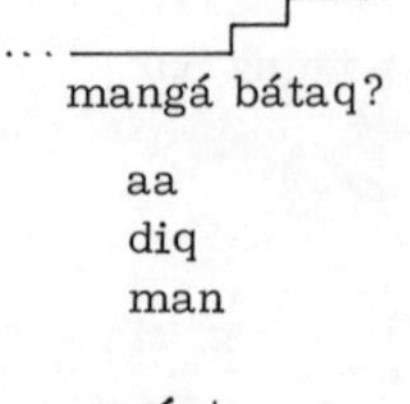

ah (pause before speaking)	aa
not	diq
[particle contradicting interlocutor]	man
like	gústu

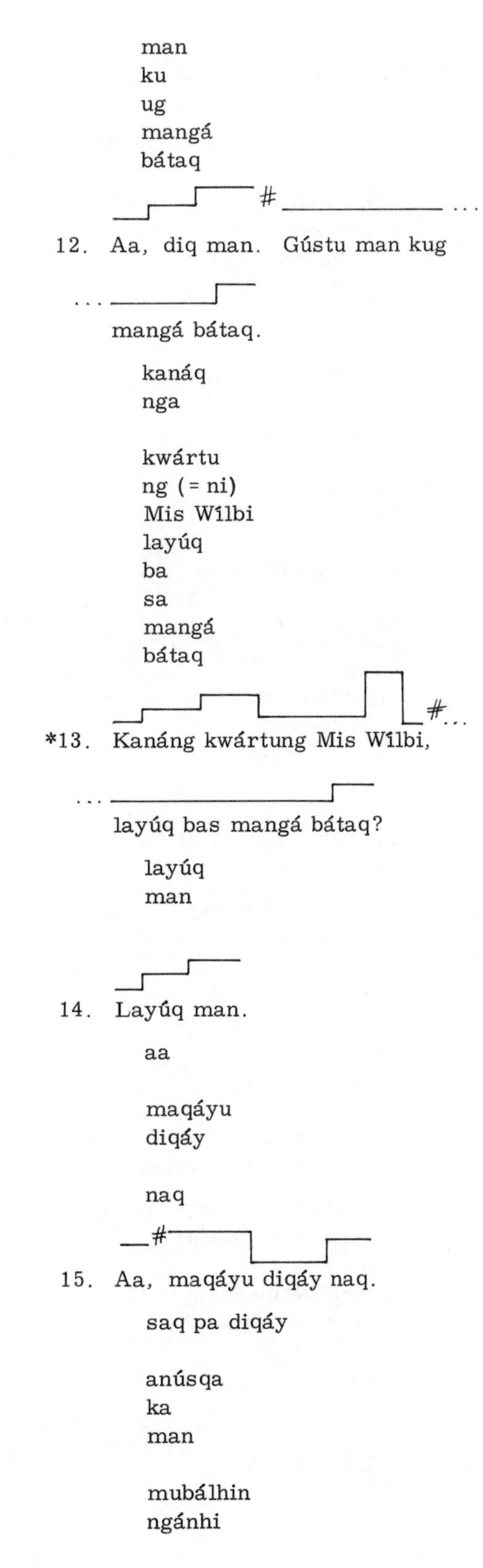

contrary to what you think	man
I	ku
[particle preceding goal]	ug
[plural marker]	mangá
children	bátaq

12. Oh no. I like children. — 12. Aa, diq man. Gústu man kug mangá bátaq.

that (previously mentioned)	kanáq
[linker between kanáq and kwártu]	nga
room	kwártu
[genitive preceding names]	ng (= ni)
Miss Wilby	Mis Wílbi
far	layúq
[interrogative particle]	ba
from	sa
[plural marker]	mangá
children	bátaq

13. Is Miss Wilby's room far from the children's? (Lit. That room of Miss Wilby's—is it far from the children?) — *13. Kanáng kwártung Mis Wílbi, layúq bas mangá bátaq?

far	layúq
[particle used with statement giving information]	man

14. It's far away. — 14. Layúq man.

Oh (particle before a statement conceding a point)	aa
good	maqáyu
[particle used on receiving new information]	diqáy
that (previously mentioned)	naq

15. Oh, that's good. — 15. Aa, maqáyu diqáy naq.

excuse me (interrupting the conversation)	saq pa diqáy
when?	anúsqa
you	ka
[question particle after interrogatives]	man
move in	mubálhin
here	ngánhi

16. Excuse me, when do you move in?	16. Saq pa diqáy, anúsqa ka man mubálhin ngánhi?
this coming [date, etc.]	karún
[linker between karún and primíru]	nga
first	primíru
of	sa
next	sunúd
month	búwan
if	ug
possible	mahĩmuq
17. The first day [lit. This coming first day] of next month, if possible.	17. Karúng primĩru sa sunúd búwan ug mahĩmuq.

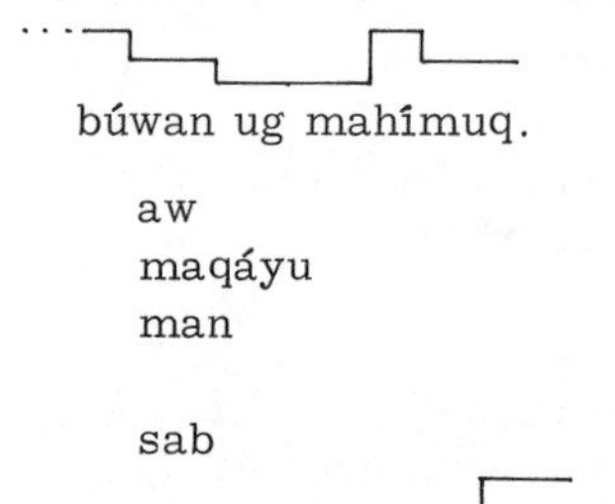

ah (pause before speaking)	aw
good	maqáyu
[particle used upon giving information]	man
too	sab
18. Oh, that's fine. (Lit. Ah, it is good, too.)	*18. Aw, maqáyu man sab.
[particle to change trend of conversation]	na
go	ádtu
[particle meaning best choice available]	na lang
we	mi
19. Well, we're going now. (Lit. We might as well go.)	19. Na, ádtu na lang mi.
[particle to change trend of conversation]	na
go	ádtu
[particle meaning best choice available]	na lang
we	ta
Perla	Pírla
20. Let's go, Perla.	20. Na, ádtu na lang ta Pirlá.

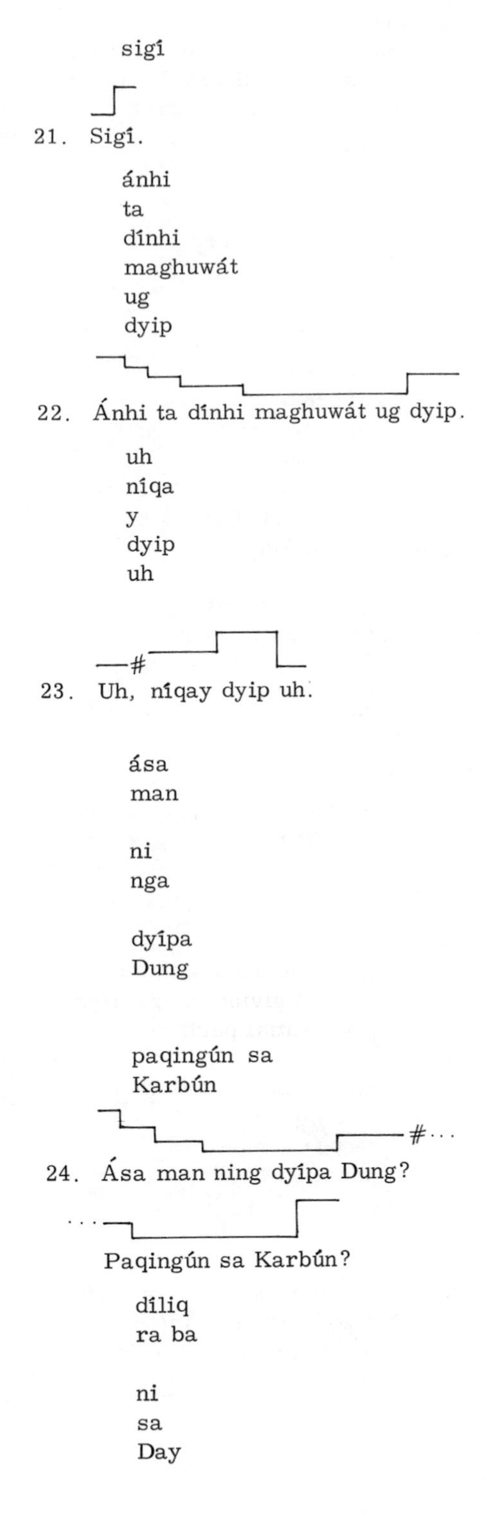

go ahead	sigî

21. So long. (Lit. Go ahead.) — 21. Sigî.

here	ánhi
us	ta
here	dînhi
should wait	maghuwát
[particle preceding goal]	ug
jeep	dyip

22. Let's wait for a jeep here. — 22. Ánhi ta dínhi maghuwát ug dyip.

oh [pause before speaking]	uh
here	níqa
[existential particle]	y
jeep	dyip
[pointer for something the interlocutor does not see]	uh

23. Oh, here comes a jeep. (Lit. Oh, there is a jeep here.) — 23. Uh, nîqay dyip uh.

where?	ása
[question particle after interrogative]	man
this	ni
[linker between ni and dyîpa]	nga
particular jeep	dyîpa
[form of address for males same age as or younger than speaker]	Dung
head for	paqingún sa
Carbon (market in Cebu City)	Karbún

24. Where does this jeep go, boy? To Carbon? (Lit. Where is this jeep going? Headed for Carbon?) — 24. Ása man ning dyípa Dung? Paqingún sa Karbún?

not	dîliq
[particle expressing apology]	ra ba
this	ni
for	sa
[form of address for females same age as or younger than speaker]	Day

25. Sorry, I don't go to Carbon, Miss. (Lit. Sorry, this is not for Carbon, Miss.)	25. Díliq ra ba nis Karbún Day.
go	muqádtu
I	ku
to	sa
Calamba (street in Cebu City)	Kalámba
26. I go to Calamba.	26. Muqádtu kus Kalámba.
furthermore	nyaq
where?	ása
[question particle after interrogatives]	man
[particle with interrogative, requesting clarification]	diqáy
we	ta
get on (plural)	manakáy
[particle preceding goal]	ug
jeep	dyip
for	pára sa
Carbon	Karbún
27. Then where do we get a jeep for Carbon?	27. Nyaq, # ása man diqáy ta ... manakáyg dyip páras Karbún?
here	níqa
[particle used with statement giving information]	man
[existential particle]	y
lots	dághan
[linker between dághan and dyip]	nga
jeep	dyip
pass by	muqági
here	dínhi
28. Well, there are lots of jeeps that go by here. (Lit. Umm, here are lots of jeeps that go by here.)	28. Aa, # níqa may dághang dyip ... muqági dínhi.
but	pirú
not	díliq
I	ku
go	muqádtu
to	sa

29. But I don't go to Carbon.	29. Pirú díliq ku muqádtus Karbún.
look for	pangítaq
merely	lang
you (plural)	mu
[particle preceding goal]	ug
another	láqin
30. Take a different one. (Lit. Just look for another one.)	30. Pangítaq lang mug láqin.
[particle drawing hearer's attention]	uh
here	níqa
[existential particle]	y
another	láqin
[form of address for males same age as or younger than speaker]	Dung
31. Oh, here comes another one. Carbon, boy?	31. Uh! níqay láqin, Karbún ... Dung?
one	usá
[particles: 'only X left now']	na lang
[particle of apology]	ra ba
[existential particle]	y
place	lugár
here	dirí
32. Sorry, there is room for only one here.	32. Usá na lang ra bay lugár dirí.
well	na
you	ikáw
[particle indicating the best available choice]	na lang
[subject marker]	y
get on	musakáy
33. O.K. You (just) get on, Perla.	33. Na, ikáw na lay musakáy ... Pirlá.
will wait	maghuwát
just	lang

I	ku
[particle preceding goal]	ug
anóther	lágin

34. I'll (just) wait for another one. — 34. Maghuwát lang kug láqin.

good-by	sigí
[particle asking for agreement]	ha
will do [something] before [someone else]	magquná
just	lang
I	ku
you	nímu

35. Well—good-by. I'll (just) go ahead of you. — 35. Aa, sigí ha. Magquná lang ku nímu.

Mangá Pangutána (Questions)

Ikatulúng Báhin

1. Dúna tay mangá bisíta Ma?
2. Si Mis Wílbi ba ang muqábang sa usá sa átung mangá kwártu Ma?
3. Upát na ka buqúk ang bátaq sa ímung anák?
4. Túqa ba magpuyúq ang ímung anák sa táqas?
5. Si Mis Wílbi diq ba gústug mangá bátaq?
6. Layúq bas kwártu sa mangá bátaq ang kwártu ni Mis Wílbi?
7. Mubálhin ka ba dáyun karún?
8. Karúng sunúd búwan ka pa mubálhin?
9. Ásа man kamú maghuwát ug sakyanán?
10. Ánhi ra kamú dínhi Day?
11. Ásа man ni paqingúng dyípa Dung?
12. Muqádtu ba ning dyípa sa Kalámba Day?
13. Ásа man mi manakáy páras Karbún Dung?
14. Dághan ba dínhing dyip nga muqági páras Kalámba Dung?
15. Dúna pa bay dyip nga muqági páras Karbún Day?
16. May lugár pa ba diháq Dung?

17. Usá ra ba ang musakáy?
18. Unyáq maghuwát ka na lang ug láqin Pirlá?
19. Ásа man ta manakáyg dyip?
20. Ása na man kamú Pirlá?

Mangá Pangutána (Matching)

Ikatulúng Báhin

1. Kínsay átung bisíta Ma?
2. Níqa ba ang ímung anák Mísis Abilyána?
3. Ikáw Pirlá, gústu ka bag mangá bátaq?
4. Ikáw ba diqáy ang muqábang ug kwártu?
5. Ang ímung bátaq dúna na bay anák?
6. Samúkan ka bag mangá bátaq Mis Wílbi?
7. Únsa mang dyípa átung sákyan?
8. May dyip bang muqági páras Karbún?
9. Pilá ka búwan ka na dínhi Pirlá?

(a) Kanáng dyip nga páras Kalámba.
(b) Uu. Upát na ka buqúk ang íyang anák.
(c) Usá pa lang ka búwan Misís.
(d) Silá si Pírla ug si Mis Wílbi.
(e) Uu. Dúnay dághan dínhing muqági.
(f) Diq gyud ku gústug mangá bátaq Misís.
(g) Samúkan kun dághan naq silá.
(h) Úqu. Akú.
(i) Úqu. Túqa siyá magpuyúq sa táqas.

Commentary to Basic Sentences

3 a 1 ni — Either ni or ng could be used here. (Cf. chart, I B, p. 14).

3 a 2 s — The use of s for sa is explained in 3 F 2.

3 a 12 Nuy — Nuy is short for Mánuy, term of address for one's elder brother. Nuy is also a respectful term of address for a man older than the speaker. The short form Nang (short for Manáng 'elder sister') is a respectful term for women older than the speaker.

3 a 17 mangádtu — Mangádtu and muqádtu are almost the same, except that mangádtu is used only with plural subjects, while muqádtu is used with both singular and plural subjects. (Cf. 5 C 4 and 11 A 1.)

3 a 25 mangá — The plural marker mangá is optional with all plural nouns.

3 a 27	túqung	Note that túqud plus the linker nga gives túqung. (Túqud is stressed tuqúd by some speakers.)
3 a 29	Uu, sigí	This is an informal way of saying 'You're welcome.' In flavor it is like English 'uh-huh' or 'mmm-hmm' in reply to 'Thanks.'
3 a 41	maw	Maw (also pronounced mu) is short for maqú.
3 a 43	nu	The particle nu asks the hearer to agree: 'isn't it?' 'doesn't it?' etc.
	run	Short for karún 'now.'
3 b 5	lagí	The nuance this particle adds is that Mrs. Abellana had been thinking they would not come.
3 b 6	gud	The use of this particle means that the speaker is explaining something in anticipation of a question by the interlocutor.
3 b 7	ug	Here, ug is a particle preceding and marking the grammatical goal. The goal construction usually means 'person or thing affected by the action of the verb.' In this sentence kwártu 'room' is the goal of the action of the verb muqábang 'rent' and accordingly is marked by ug. (The goal construction is discussed in detail in Lesson 5.)
3 b 7	nu	Short for kunú 'he or she says.'
3 b 13	ug	See comment to 3 b 7 above.
		Perla says this sentence to Mrs. Abellana. Note ni siyá 'this she.' A demonstrative is used in combination with personal pronouns in constructions having maqú (or one of its short forms) 'is the one.'
3 b 16	nyaq	Short for únyaq 'the next thing.'
	nga	The nga is explained in the grammatical section, 3 E.
3 b 19	buqúk	Buqúk 'piece' is commonly used in number expressions.
3 b 22	lay	Lang plus y gives lay.
3 b 26	kádtu	Kádtu (tu, etc.) basically means 'that (remote in distance from speaker and hearer).' It is also used to mean 'that (which is remote in time).'
	matág	Matág and káda 'each, every' have the same meaning.
	ug	See comment to 3 b 7 above.
3 b 27	gung	Gud plus ang gives gung.
3 b 29	na	Here, the meaning of diq na is that the thing referred to is not in the same class as other things. 'Can this not be in a class of things that can be bargained for?'
3 b 30	may	Man plus y gives may.
	bayranán	Sugáq ug túbig nga bayranán 'water and light to be paid for.'

3 b 31	Uu	Miss Wilby says 'yes' here because she wants to establish good feelings after she has been arguing with Mrs. Abellana about the price. By uu she means 'Yes, you are right, and I am in agreement.' It is usual in the Philippines to make a show of agreement after a disagreement, to smooth over ruffled feelings.
3 c 3	mu	Mu is short for maqú (cf. 3 a 41).
	ni siyá	See the note to 3 b 13 above.
	sa	The particle sa marks the goal construction just as ug does. (See the comment to 3 b 7 above.)
3 c 7	y	Note that y before muqábang is absorbed by the preceding diqáy. Without diqáy this sentence would read: Kamú bang duháy muqábang sa kwártu?
3 c 9	kadtú	Kádtu is used here because Índay has left.
3 c 13	ng	This is the ng which equals ni (cf. chart, 1 B).
3 c 18	sab	Sab means 'too.' Here Mrs. Abellana, by saying 'that is good, too,' pretends something else is good, just to be pleasant.

Grammatical Section

3 A 1. Existential sentences

Existential sentences mean 'there is (are, was, will be, etc.) [the existent]. The EXISTENT is either a noun or a verb, and is introduced by one of the following:

(1) may 'there is (was, will be, etc.)' (no place meaning)

(2) adúna (or dúna) plus y 'there is (was, will be, etc.)' (no place meaning)

(3) a present-time deictic plus y (with place meaning)

(4) a past-time deictic plus y (with place meaning)

(5) waláq plus y 'there is (was, will be, etc.) (no place meaning)

The present-time deictics are díqa, níqa, náqa, and túqa; the past-time deictics are those beginning with d.* (Refer to the chart in 1 A 2, p. 12). In examples a–k below, the existent is bir 'beer':

a. May bir. 'There's beer.'
b. Adúnay bir. 'There's beer.'
c. Díqay bir. 'There's beer here (where I am).'
d. Níqay bir. 'There's beer here (where we are).'
e. Náqay bir. 'There's beer there (where you are).'
f. Túqay bir. 'There's beer (over there).'
g. Diríy bir. 'There was beer here (where I am).'

---

* The díqa that is short for adíqa is of course not a past-time form.

h. Dínhiy bir. 'There was beer here (where we are).'
i. Dínhay (or Diháy) bir. 'There was beer there (where you are).'
j. Dídtuy bir. 'There was beer there.'
k. Way (or Waláy) bir. 'There's no beer.'
l. Duháy dráybir. 'There are (were, will be) two drivers.'
m. Usá na lang ra bay lugár dirí. (3 c 32) 'Sorry, there is room for only one here.'

The following sentences are among the other existential sentences you have learned:

n. Níqay ákung amígu. (1.9) 'There's a friend of mine here.'
o. Náqay táwu ay. (3 a 9) 'There's a man over there.'
p. Náqay dráybir. (3 a 33) 'There's a driver.'
q. Dúnay mangá dyip ngánhaq padúung sa Banáwaq. (3 a 26) 'There are jeeps there headed for Banawa.'

3 A 2 a. Náqa in the same meaning as dúna

In 3 A 1 above we said dúna (or adúna) is without place meaning and is used for present, past, or future time ('there is, are, was, were, will be'). Náqa is used without place meaning, like dúna; but in contrast to dúna, it refers only to present time ('there is, there are').

Náqay kwártung paqabángan sa ínyung baláy. (3 b 15) 'There is a room for rent in your house.'

(Náqa is also used with place meaning: see examples e and o of 3 A 1 above.)

Diháq (or dínhaq) is used without place meaning, like dúna; but in contrast to dúna, diháq specifies past time ('there was, there were').

Dínhay bir. 'There was beer.'

(Diháq dínhaq is also used with place meaning: see example i of 3 A 1 above.)

3 A 2 b. Náqa, diháq, dúna, and waláq as sentences by themselves

Náqa, dínhaq (diháq), dúna, and waláq occur as sentences by themselves, with these meanings:

náqa	'There is, there are'
dínhaq (diháq)	'There was, there were'
dúna	'There is (are), there was (were), there will be'
waláq	'There isn't (aren't), there wasn't (weren't), there won't be'

May 'there is (are, was, etc.),' on the other hand, does not occur as a sentence by itself. For example, in answer to the question

Náqa bay bir? 'Is there any beer?'

one can say

Dúna. 'There is.' or
Náqa. 'There is.' or
Waláq. 'There isn't.'

In answer to the question

Dínhaq bay bir? 'Was there any beer?'

one can say

Dúna. 'There was.' or
Dínhaq. 'There was.' or
Waláq. 'There wasn't.'

3 A 3. Subject of existential sentences

Existential sentences occur also with subjects (a subject is a nominative pronoun, or a word or phrase preceded by si or ang). The existent is the word or phrase that follows y or may. Existential sentences with subjects correspond to English sentences with the verb 'have (=possess).' The time meaning depends on whether the sentence contains a deictic, or dúna 'has, have, had, will have,' or a numeral: if dúna or a numeral, the time meaning is past, present, or future; if a deictic, it is the deictic that determines the time reference. In the following examples the subject is underlined:

Dúna siyáy upát ka buqúk bátaq. (3 c 10) 'She has [had] four children.' (Lit. She, there are [there were] four pieces children.')

Náqa muy kwártung paqabángan. 'You have a room for rent.' (Lit. You, there is a room for rent.')

Dinhay bir si Lúling. 'Loling had beer.'

May bir si Lúling. 'Loling has [had] beer.'

If the existential sentence contains the negative word waláq (waq) the meaning is negative, with past, present, or future time meaning:

Waláy bir si Lúling. 'Loling has no beer.' (Lit. 'Loling, there is no beer.')

Waq na ra ba tay bir Nyur. (2 b 27) 'We don't have any more beer, Sir.'

3 B. Subject and predicate

The predicate is the main part of the sentence: it tells what something or somebody is (or was, or will be); or it tells what somebody or something does (did, will do, has done, etc.); or it tells what happened (happens, etc.) to somebody or something. In the following examples, the predicate is underlined twice:

a. Nangítag kwártu si Mis Wílbi. 'Miss Wilby is looking for a room.' [Nangítag kwártu 'looking for a room' tells what Miss Wilby is doing.]
b. Ákung gidalá si Mis Wílbi ngánhi. (3 b 6) 'I brought Miss Wilby here.' [Ákung gidalá 'I brought' tells what happened to Miss Wilby.]
c. Pangutánqa nang dyip. (3 a 32) 'Ask him (lit. 'Ask that jeep'). [Pangutánqa 'ask him' tells what should happen to that jeep.]
d. Kiní si Místir Gamílu. 'This is Mr. Gamelo.' [Kiní 'this' tells what Mr. Gamelo is.]
e. Si Mis Wílbi ang nangítag kwártu. 'Miss Wilby is the one who is looking for a room.' [Mis Wílbi tells who the one looking for a room is.]
f. Akúy mangutána. (3 a 10) 'Let me ask (lit. I am the one who should ask'). [Akú tells who the one who should ask is.]

Subjects (nominatives, or words or phrases preceded by si, ang, or y*) tell who is (or was, or will be) the predicate, or it tells who did (does, will do) the predicate, or it tells who the predicate happened (happens, will happen) to. In the following examples the subject is underlined once, the predicate twice (this is the procedure for the rest of this lesson).

---

* The subject marker y is not the same thing as the existential marker y in existential sentences (3 A 1).

a (1). Nangítag kwártu si Mis Wílbi. 'Miss Wilby is looking for a room.' [Mis Wílbi, the subject, tells who did the predicate, nangítag kwártu 'looked for a room.']

b (1). Ákung gidalá si Mis Wílbi ngánhi. (3 b 6) 'I brought Miss Wilby here.' [It is the subject, 'Miss Wilby,' that the predicate, 'I brought,' happens to.]

c (1). Pangutánqa nang dyip. (3 a 32) 'Ask that jeep.' [Nang dyip is the thing pangutánqa should happen to.]

d (1). Kiní si Místir Gamílu. 'This is Mr. Gamelo.' [Mr. Gamelo, the subject, is the one who is kiní 'this.']

e (1). Si Mis Wílbi ang nangítag kwártu. 'Miss Wilby is the one looking for a room.' [The subject, ang nangítag kwártu 'the one looking for a room,' is the person who is Miss Wilby, the predicate.]

If a sentence contains an interrogative (kínsa 'who?,' únsa 'what?,' pilá 'how many?,' or unsáqun or giqúnsa 'how?'), the interrogative or a phrase containing the interrogative is the predicate.

g. Kinsay ímung ngálan? 'What is your name?'

h. Unsa may átuq? 'What shall we have?'

i. Pilá ka táwuy nangítag kwártu? 'How many people are looking for a room?'

3 B 1. Sentences consisting of two subject-like constituents

Some sentences are composed of two constituents each having the make-up of a subject—that is, each is either a nominative pronoun or a word or phrase preceded by si, ang, or y. In sentences of this type, the first constituent is the predicate and the second is the subject:

a. Akúy mangutána. (3 a 10) 'Let me ask.'

b. Si Mis Wílbi ang nangítag kwártu. 'Miss Wilby is the one looking for a room.'

c. Maw ni siya ang nangítag kwártu. (3 b 13) 'She is the one looking for a room.'

3 B 2. Sentences with verbs as subjects

In the examples of 3 B 1, the subject of each is a verb preceded by ang or y, and the predicate is a nominative pronoun or a name preceded by si. This construction emphasizes the subject in a special way: '[subject] is the one who [verb]' or 'it is [subject] who [verb].' By contrast, sentences having the verb as the predicate place only normal emphasis on the subject.

a. Akúy mangutána. (3 a 10) 'Let me ask.' (Lit. 'It is I who should ask.')

a (1). Mangutána akú. 'I will ask.'

b. Si Mis Wílbi ang nangítag kwártu. 'Miss Wilby is the one looking for a room.'

b (1). Nangítag kwártu si Mis Wílbi. 'Miss Wilby is looking for a room.'

c. Kamú bang duhá diqáy ang muqábang sa kwártu? (see 3 c 7) 'So you two are the ones who are going to rent the room?'

c (1). Muqábang ba diqáy sa kwártu kamúng duhá? 'So you two are going to rent the room?'

Any sentence consisting of a subject and a predicate (unless the predicate is an interrogative) can be transformed in this way, to shift the emphasis.

a. Mangutána akú. 'I'll ask.'
a (1). Akúy mangutána. 'Let me ask.'
b. Dúna siyáy* upát ka buqúk bátaq. 'She has four children.'
b (1). Siyá ang dúnay upát ka buqúk bátaq. 'She is the one who has four children.'

Exercise 3.III.

3 B 3. Sentences consisting of a predicate by itself with no subject

Cebuano major sentences all contain a predicate, but the subject is optional. Thus the predicates of the examples in 3 B 1 and 3 B 2 above can all be used by themselves as a complete sentence:

a. Nangítag kwártu. '(He) is looking for a room.'
b. Ákung gidalá. 'I brought (her).'
c. Pangutánqa. 'Ask (him).'
d. Kiní. 'This (is the one).'
e. Si Mis Wílbi. 'Miss Wilby (is the one).'

3 B 4. Long forms as predicates

When a pronoun is used as a predicate, it must occur in its long form. The same is true of the demonstratives, except that if there is a form maqú in the sentence, demonstratives may appear in the short form.

Ikáw [not ka] ba ang adúnay upát ka buqúk anák? 'Are you the one who has four children?'

Akú [not ku] ang muqábang sa usá sa mangá kwártu. (3 c 3) 'I am the one who wants to rent one of the rooms.'

Kiní [not ni] ang ímung sákyan ngádtu. 'This is what you take to get there.' (Lit. 'This is what you ride going there.')

Compare the following sentence containing mu (for maqú), where a demonstrative appears in either the long or the short form:

Mu ni [or kiní] ang ímung sákyan ngádtu. 'This is what you take going there.'

3 B 5. Use of y as subject marker

In sentences composed of two subject-like constituents (see 3 B 1 above), the subject may be marked by y instead of ang. That is, if the predicate is a word or phrase preceded by ang or si, the subject is preceded by either ang or y. There is no difference in meaning; but the y marking is more common.

Akúy mangutána. (3 a 10) or [less commonly] Akú ang mangutána 'Let me ask.'

Mu man nay iskína. (3 a 19) or [less commonly] Mu man naq ang iskína. 'That is the corner.'

Si Mis Wílbiy mangutána. or [less commonly] Si Mis Wílbi ang mangutána. 'Let Miss Wilby ask.'

If kínsa 'who?' or únsa 'what?' is the predicate, y (rather than ang) is usual:

Kínsay ímung ngálan? 'What (lit. Who) is your name?'

Únsa may átuq? 'What shall we have?' (Lit. 'What is ours?')

If the predicate is not a noun or kínsa or únsa, the subject is preceded by ang and not by y.

---

*See 3 C 3 d below for the word order.

3 C. Word Order

3 C 1. Subject and predicate with no pronouns

When neither subject nor predicate is a pronoun, the most common order is predicate-subject.

a. Muqábang si Mis Wílbi sa usá sa mangá kwártu. 'Miss Wilby will rent one of the rooms.'

b. Náqa ba si Dúktur Pirnándis? 'Is Dr. Fernandez there?'

c. Kínsay ímung ngálan Dung? 'What (lit. Who) is your name, son?'

d. Ánhaq ngánhaq muhúnung ang mangá dyip. 'The jeeps stop there.'

If the predicate is not an interrogative (únsa 'what?,' kínsa 'who?,' etc.), the order subject-predicate also occurs. Sentence (a) just above, for example, could appear as:

a (1). Si Mis Wílbi muqábang sa usá sa mangá kwártu.

Sentence b can also have its subject and predicate transposed; but sentence c cannot, as the predicate is an interrogative. (The order predicate-subject is more frequent.)

3 C 2. Postpositives

The POSTPOSITIVES are the short forms of the pronouns (see the chart in 1 B, p. 14), the short forms of the demonstratives (chart 1 A 1, p. 12), and certain short words which convey the speaker's attitude.* Postpositives follow the first word of the predicate. In the following examples, the postpositives are the words that are not underlined:

Ákuq lang ibílin ning ákung amígu dínhi. 'I will just leave my friend here.'

Ikáw lay magpíliq. 'You be the one to choose.'

Pilá may bayranán ánaq? 'How much does that cost?'

Mahalmahál dyud naq ug dyútay. 'That is a bit more expensive.'

Kamú ba diqáyng duhá ang muqábang sa kwártu? [Here the postpositive diqáy has a linker attached.] 'So you two are the ones who are going to rent the room?

If the predicate consists of several words and there are several postpositives, one or more of the postpositives may follow the last word of the predicate. The sentence just above may also be said:

---

* The postpositive words that have appeared in the basic sentences of Lessons 1, 2, and 3 are as follows. (The glosses are not definitions; they give no more than a hint of the meanings of these words.) Ba [question particle], diqáy [new information], dyud, gyud, gayúd 'for sure,' gud [explanation], kaháq 'perhaps,' kaqáyu 'very,' kunú 'he says,' lagí 'nevertheless,' lang 'just,' man 'contrary to what you say,' pa 'still,' na 'already,' ra 'only,' sab, sad, 'also,' saq 'for the moment,' túqud 'so it is.'

Kamú bang duhá diqáy ang muqábang sa kwártu? 'So you two are the ones who are going to rent the room.'

3 C 3. Attraction of postpositives to other words

3 C 3 a. To prepositives

Certain words modify predicates by preceding the entire predicate: these are PREPOSITIVES. The prepositives we have had so far are mahímuq 'can,' gústu 'like,' kinahánglan 'need,' ayáw 'don't,' díliq (diq) 'no' or 'not,' and waláq (waq) 'no' or 'not.' The deictics with place meaning (first chart in 1 A 2, p. 12), the interrogative deictics (chart 2 A 2, p. 42), and words meaning 'when?' (anúsqa and kanúsqa, 4 D) are also prepositives.

The prepositive may be linked to the predicate. If linking occurs, mahímuq, gústu, and kinahánglan are linked with nga; díliq (diq) and waláq (waq) are linked with nga (under some conditions; see Lesson 12, 12 D); ayáw is linked with ug (3 E 1, 8 D).

When a predicate is modified by both a prepositive and one or more post-positives, the latter are ATTRACTED to the prepositive: that is, they shift to the position right after the prepositive, so that they now precede the predicate. If there is linking of the prepositive, the postpositives are placed in between the prepositive and the linker.

a. Diq na naq mahángyuq? (3 b 29) 'Can't you make the price any lower?' [Diq is a prepositive; na and naq (postpositives) are attracted to diq.]
b. Mahímuq bang mangutána? (3 a 14) 'May I ask a question?' [Mahímuq is a prepositive linked with nga (in the alternant ng here); ba, a postpositive attracted to mahímuq, precedes the linker ng of mahímuq.]
c. Gústu ming mutánqaw run. 'We'd like to look now.' [Gústu is a prepositive linked with nga. Mi is a postpositive attracted to gustu, preceding ng, the linker for gústu.]

3 C 3 b. Attraction to maqú

Postpositives are also attracted to maqú 'is the one' (or its short forms).

Maqú man naq ang iskínas Piláyis Pidíl Rusáryu. (3 a 19) 'That is the corner of Pelaez and P. del Rosario.' [Man and naq are postpositives attracted to maqú.]

3 C 3 c. Attraction to other time and place words

The postpositives are also attracted to time and place words that precede the predicate.

Ásа man ta musakáy? 'Where shall we get on?' [Man and ta, postpositives, are attracted to ása 'where? (future),' a word referring to place.]

Ánhi ra mi manáqug dínhi. 'This is where we get off.' [The postpositives ra and mi are attracted to ánhi 'here (future).']

3 C 3 d. Attraction to the deictics or adúna in existential sentences

The postpositives are attracted to the deictics or to dúna (adúna) 'there is (was, etc.)' in existential sentences. (They are not attracted to may 'there is (was, etc.)': see 3 C 3 d (1) below.) The postpositives precede the y of existential sentences.

Náqa may sugáq ug túbig. (3 b 30) 'For there is light and water.' [Náqa is a deictic; man (in the alternant ma) is a postpositive and comes between náqa and the y of the existential sentence.]

Dúna na man diqáy tay mangá bisíta Ma. (3 c 1) 'Oh, we have visitors, Ma.' [The postpositives na, man, diqáy, and ta follow dúna immediately and precede the y of the existential sentence.]

3 C 3 d (1). Word order with may 'there is (are, etc.)'

May 'there is (are, etc.)' does not attract the postpositives. Compare the following sentences with the sentences of 3 C 3 d above.

May sugáq ug túbig man. 'For there is light and water.'

May mangá bisíta na man diqáy ta Ma. 'Oh, we have visitors, Ma!'

3 C 4. Long forms of pronouns and demonstratives

The long forms of the demonstratives and the pronouns (see charts 1 A 1 and 1 B, pp. 12, 14) usually occur in the same position as the short forms (cf. 3 C 2).

Nagbayád silág kwarínta písus matág búlan. (3 b 26) 'They used to pay forty pesos a month.' [Silá, a long pronoun, follows the first word of the predicate, nagbayád.]

Gústu siyáng mutánqaw run. (3 b 16) 'She would like to look at it now.' [Siyá, a long pronoun, follows the prepositive qualifier gústu 'want,' intervening between it and its linker ng.]

For word order, do PP-D, E. When you have finished the appropriate lessons, do Exercises 3.IV A, 3.IV B, 3.IV C, 3.IV D; 4.I E, 4.I F; 5.I E, 5.I F; 6.I F.

3 D. Háqin (háqi), ása, and diqín meaning 'which (of several)?'

Háqin (and its alternant háqi) and ása are used—interchangeably with each other—to mean 'which (of several)?'

Ikáw lay magpíliq ása (or háqin) íning duhá ang ímung gústu. (3 b 22) 'You choose which of these two you want.'

In a similar construction, háqin and ása are used—like demonstratives kiní 'this,' etc.—in phrases with noun plus suffix -a (see Lesson 2, p. 44), meaning 'which [noun] (of several)?' In this usage háqin and ása are linked to the noun with nga.

Ásang (or Háqing) baláya ang íla? 'Which house is theirs?'

Háqing (or Ásang) kwartúha ang paqabángan? 'Which of the rooms is for rent?'

3 D 1. Diqín meaning 'which (of several places)?'

Diqín is used to mean 'which (of several places)?'

Diqín ang ímu? 'Where are you going?' (Lit. 'Which place is yours?')

Diqín is used in phrases with nouns, to mean 'which [place] (of several)?' This construction takes either of two forms, used interchangeably:

(a) diqín + linker nga + noun + suffix -a

(b) diqín + noun

Examples:

Diqín dapít [or, Diqíng dapíta] sa Burumíyu ang ímu? 'What part of Borromeo are you going to?' (Lit. 'Which place on Borromeo is yours?')

Diqín man lugár [or Diqín mang lugára] ang hunúngan sa dyip? 'Which place is the one the jeeps stop at?'

3 D 2. Diqín introducing a clause

Diqín also means 'where' to introduce a clause that modifies a noun.

Nangítaq kug kwártu diqín díliq akú samúkun sa mangá bátaq. 'I am looking for a room where I won't be disturbed by children.' [Diqín 'where' introduces the clause díliq akú samúkun sa mangá bátaq.]

3 E. Linking of the prepositives

The prepositives mahímuq 'can,' gústu 'want,' and kinahánglan 'need' are linked with nga to the predicate. If there are postpositives, the linker follows the postpositives.

Mahímuq báng mutánqaw mi run? 'May we look now?' [Ng (alternant of nga) links mahímuq, a prepositive, to mutánqaw, the predicate. Ng follows the postpositive ba.]

Gústu siyáng mutánqaw run. (3 b 16) 'She wants to look now.'

3 E 1. Linking of ayáw 'don't'

Ayáw 'don't' is not linked at all to verb forms having the prefix pag-; to verbs with any other affix,* it is linked optionally (the sentence may be said with or without ug with no difference in meaning); and to verbs having no affixes, it is regularly linked. The linker occurring with ayáw is ug.

Ayáw mug sakáy. 'Don't get on.' [Ayáw is linked to the verb sakáy with ug (in its alternant form g) because sakáy has no affix.]

Ayáw mu pagsakáy. 'Don't get on.' [Ayáw is not linked to pagsakáy because there is a prefix pag-.]

Ayáw mu katúlug. or Ayáw mug katúlug. 'Don't go to sleep.' [Ayáw is either linked or not linked to katúlug, because katúlug has a prefix ka-.]

3 F 1. Long and short forms of words

When a word has both a long form and a short form, the short form is most common in rapid speech. (The tendency in writing, on the other hand, is to use long forms.) The short forms of the pronouns (chart, 1 B, p. 14) are examples. Many of the postpositives and other frequently used words have long and short forms: for example, run (short for karún) 'now,' nyaq (short for únyaq) 'later,' and gyud or dyud (short for gayúd) 'for certain.' From now on, the lessons give the rapid speech forms—the ones used in normal everyday speech.

---

*Affixes are forms which are not words by themselves but are added to other words to derive new ones. An affix added to the beginning of a word is a PREFIX; one added to the end is a SUFFIX. The prefix pag-, for example, is added to sakáy 'ride' to make a new word pagsakáy 'ride.' (In the Glossary the listing is by words without affixes.)

3 F 2. Contractions

Contractions are a common feature of rapid speech forms. The markers (words that show grammatical relations: nga, ug, ang, sa, si, and ni) are contracted as follows:

After a vowel (a, i, u) or w or y,

ug becomes g;
nga becomes ng;
ang becomes ng;
sa becomes s;
si becomes s;
ni becomes ng.

In the following examples, the full form is shown first, with the contracted form—the usual pronunciation—directly below it.

Ayáw mu ug sakáy. 'Don't get on.'
Ayáw mug sakáy.

kiní nga baláya 'this house'
kiníng baláya

Kiní ang baláy. 'This is the house.'
Kiníng baláy.

Dídtu sa baláy. 'It was at the house.'
Dídtus baláy.

Maqú kiní si Mis Wílbi. 'This is Miss Wilby.'
Maqú kinís Mis Wílbi.

ang baláy ni Pírla 'Perla's house'
ang baláyng Pírla

These contractions also take place after words ending in n and q, and in addition the n or q drops out.

Si Pírla dághan ug kwárta. 'Perla has a lot of money.'
Si Pírla dághag kwárta.

Dághan nga kwárta. 'There was a lot of money.'
Dághang kwárta.

Dághan ang kwárta. 'There was a lot of money.' (Lit. The money was much.)
Dághang kwárta.

ang kadaghánan sa manga táwu. 'most of the people'
ang kadaghánas manga táwu.

The same contractions occur after postpositives; in addition, the final consonant of the postpositive drops out.

Ákuq man gud nga ibílin. 'Because I'll leave it.'
Ákuq man gung ibílin.

Ákuq sad nga amígu 'my friend, too'
Ákuq sang amígu

Si Pírla mangítaq gyud ug baláy. 'Perla will be sure to look for a house.'
Si Pírla mangítaq gyug baláy.

NOW PLAYING:
STARRING THE
SOCIETY BAKERS
A
C
D

A
B
C
D
ARIA~

Of these contractions, only those with nga and ug are used in writing. (The others are spoken but not written.) You have seen many instances of these contractions in the basic sentences. For example:

Aa, kádtung [short for kádtu nga] abángan nátus [short for nátuq sa] baláy? (3 a 2) 'Oh, the one we will rent the house from?'

Muqábang ni siyág [short for siya ug] kwártus [short for kwártu sa] ímung baláy. (3 b 7) 'She wants to rent a room in your house.'

Biság [short for bisán ug] ása lang. (3 b 23) 'Anywhere will do.'

Aa, dághan túqung [short for túqud nga] mangági diháq. (3 a 27) 'Oh yes, there are many that go by there.'

3 F 3. Contraction with y

When y (either the existential particle or the subject marker) comes after words ending in n or q, the n or q drops.

Únsa may [contracted from man plus y] átuq? 'What shall we have?'

Waláy [contracted from waláq plus y] sapayán. 'You're welcome.'

Postpositives also drop their final consonant before y:

Níqa say [contracted from sab plus y] usás ubús. (3 b 21) 'There is also one here downstairs.'

Ikáw lay [contracted from lang plus y] magpíliq. (3 b 22) 'You choose.'

(These contractions, as contrasted with the ones described in 3 F 2 above, are obligatory.*)

3 F 4. Rapid forms of other words

Other words also have short forms. Maqáyu 'good' is pronounced máyu or maay in rapid speech; maqú 'is the one' is pronounced maw or mu.

Taná. Maw ning baláy ni Mísis Abilyána. (3 a 41) 'Let's go. This is Mrs. Abellana's house now.'

Pattern Practices and Exercises

I A. Tanqáwa ang laráwan A. Gíkan sa mangá púlung: kiní, kirí, kádtu, ug kanáq, pilíqa ang hústung púlung ug isulát sa lunáq. Ang kumbinasyún sa mangá titík nagpasabút sa nagsúlti, ug sa gisultíhan (1 A 1). (Choose kiní, kirí, kádtu, or kanáq.)

1. (CD-A) Padúung ba ________ sa Banáwaq?
2. (A-CD) Diq ra ba. Pára man ________ sa Lahúg.
3. (A-CD) ________ ng usá maqúy páras Banáwaq.
   'That other one is the one for Banawa.'
4. (C-A) ________ bang duqúl sa sinihán maqúy páras Banáwaq?
   'That one near the movie house?'
5. (A-CD) Uu, maqú ________ ang pára sa Banáwaq.
6. (A-CD) ________ ng ákung dyip díliq na muqádtu kay údtu na man.

---

*In very fancy written forms and in some dialects (in Leyte, for example,) ing is substituted for y and contractions are not made.

7. (C-D) Tána kay díliq ________ maqú ang átung sákyan.
'Let's go, for this is not the one we're taking.'

8. (D-C) ________ diqáy nga usá ang páras Banáwaq?

9. (A-D) Maqú tingáli ________ . Pangutánqa lang nínyu.

10. (CD-A) Mulárga ba ________ dáyun ngádtus Banáwaq?

11. (A-CD) Ngánung ________ mang ákung dyip ang ínyung sákyan?
(ngánu 'why')

12. (A-CD) Díliq ba muqádtu sa Banáwaq ________ ng dyip nga duqúl sa sinihán?

13. (C-A) Díliq, kay pára kunú ________ sa Lahúg.

14. (A-CD) Aa, diqáy. Usáhay muqádtu sab ________ sa Banáwaq.

15. (CD-A) ________ muqádtu ba usáb usáhay sa Lahúg?

I B. Tanqáwa ang laráwan B. Butangí ang lunáq sa hústung púlung. Pilíqa ang ímung tubág gíkan sa mangá musunúd nga mangá púlung: arí, dirí, ánhi, dínhi, ánhaq, diháq, túqa, náqa, níqa, díqa, ádtu, dídtu, ngádtu, ngánhi, ngarí (1 A 2).

1. (B-A) ____________ mi manáqug sa íla ka Mísis Abilyána.

2. (A-B) Aa, ____________ diqáy mu sa ka Mísis Abilyána?

3. (C-B) Díliq kaqáyu maqáyu ning daan ____________ nu?
(daan 'road')

4. (B-C) Kiní ra man tingáli ____________ng dapíta ang díliq maqáyu.

5. (C-B) Níndut ba kaháq ____________ sa ka Mísis Abilyána?

6. (B-C) ____________ na kanáq nátuq mahibáwqi inigqabút nátuq ____________ . 'We will find out about it there.'

7. (A-C) Ngánu man diqáy Day, ____________ ka mupuyúq sa ka Mísis Abilyána? (ngánu 'why?')

8. (C-A) Uu, muqábang úntaq kug kwártu ____________ sa ílang baay.
'Yes, I would like to rent a room in their house.'

9. (A-BC) Maqáyu ____________ s íla kay míngaw nga dápit.

10. (B-C) Maqú na ni ____________ ang Banáwaq.

11. (B-A) ____________ kamí manáqug duqúl niqádtung dakúng káhuy.
(káhuy 'tree')

12. (B-C) Taná, ____________ lang ta ____________ manáqug.

13. (C-B) Háqin man niqánaq ____________ ang baay ni Mísis Abilyána?

14. (B-C) Karí ____________ ng dapít sa walá maqúy íla.
(walá 'left'; tuqú 'right')

15. (C-B) ____________ ba kaháq ____________ karún si Mísis Abilyána?

16. (B-C) Uu, ____________ naq siyá ____________ sa tanáng úras.

17. (D-C) Maqáyu kay niqánhi mu ____________ sa ámuq.

18. (B-D) __________ mi __________ kay mutánqaw mi sa kwártu.
19. (D-BC) __________ mu __________ sa sulúd arún makītaq nīnyu ang kwártu.
20. __________ gud mi kay ákung gidalá si Mis Wīlbi.

I C. Isulát sa lunáq ang hústung púlung. Pilīqa ang hústung tubág gīkan sa mangá púlung kamí, kitá (mi ug ta) (1 B 2).

1. Taná, manakáy na __________ sa dyip.
2. Pīrla, mangádtu ba __________ sa baláy ni Mīsis Abilyána?
3. Pára Dung. Ánhi lang __________ manáqug dīnhi.
4. Nīqa __________ dīnhi kay gústu __________ ng mutánqaw sa kwártung paqabángan.
5. Dīliq __________ ng duhá ang muqábang sa kwártu. Si Mis Wīlbi ra.
6. Taná. Manánqaw __________ sa mangá kwártu. 'Let's look at the room.'
7. Uy Ma, dúna man diqáy __________ y bisīta!
8. Maqáyu ni nga kwártu kay kaqugalīngun ang bányu ug kasīlyas. Diq na __________ kinahánglan pang mugawás. 'We don't have to go outside.'
9. Na, ádtu na lang __________ Mīsis Abilyána. 'Good-by.'
10. Taná Pirlá, ádtu na lang __________ .
11. Magpaqábut __________ nīmu sa sunúd búwan. 'We shall be expecting you next month.'
12. Ánhi __________ dīnhi magpaqábut ug dyip. 'Let's wait for a jeep here.'
13. Mangītaq lang __________ ug láqing dyip kay dīliq man kádtu muqádtus Kárbun.
14. Duhá __________ ng musakáy. Dúna bay lugár pára námung duhá?
15. Dīliq __________ makasakáyng duhá, Mis Wīlbi, kay usá ra man ang lugár.

I D. Butangī ang lunáq sa hústung púlung. Pilīqa ang hústung tubág gīkan sa mangá púlung waláq, dīliq, ayáw (2 B).

1. __________ na lang ku tagáqi ug bir kay nagdalīq man ku. 'Don't give me any beer, because I'm in a hurry.'
2. Ádtu na lang ku Mīstir Abáya, dághang salámat. __________ y sapayán. Balikbálik.
3. __________ mi diháq musakáy. __________ man kanáq páras Banáwaq. 'We didn't get on there. It wasn't going to Banawa.'
4. Maqáyu dīnhis sīlung kay __________ y sábaq.
5. __________ siyá tagáqi ug kwártung duqúl sa mangá bátaq. 'Don't give him . . .'

6. ____________ ka ba kahäq únyaq samúkans mangá bátaq? 'Won't you be bothered by the children?'

7. Aa, ____________ man, kay gústu man kug mangá bátaq.

8. ______________ pagsakáy ug dyip nga páras Mabúlu kung ádtu ka padúung sa Banáwaq. 'Don't get on a jeep for . . .'

9. ____________ y dyip nga padúung sa Banáwaq nga muhúnung dínhing dapíta.

10. ____________ ba mu gústung maniqúdtu dínhi sa ámuq?

11. Náqa ba si Místir Abáya? ____________ ra ba dirí.

12. ____________ na ba mahángyuq ang ábang sa kwártu?

13. ____________ ba diqáy kamúng duhá ang muqábang sa kwártu?

14. Ngánung ____________ man ka makaqánhi dáyun? 'Why couldn't you come right away?'

15. ____________ pa dínhi si Índay.

16. Unsáqun man nákuq pagsakáy nga ____________ na may lugár diháq sa dyip? 'How can I get on when there's no more room in the jeep?'

17. ____________ mung duhá makasakáy kay usá na lang ang lugár dirí.

18. ____________ na bay láqing dyip nga muqági dínhi?

19. Sigí lang. ____________ na lang ku musakáy.

20. ____________ na lang ku tagáqig kukakúla kay díqa nay ákuq. 'Don't give me . . .'

21. ____________ ba diháq nímu ang ákung líbru?

22. ______________ ka ba magdalá ug bir ngádtu sa ka Místir Abáya? 'Didn't you bring any beer to Mr. Abaya's?'

23. Dídtu ba si Místir Abáya sa ínyu? ____________ kay ____________ man siyá kaqádtu.

24. Gidalá ba nímu si Mis Wílbi? ____________.

25. ______________ man ni muqádtus Kárbun Day. 'This doesn't go to Carbon.'

PP-D Existential sentences (3 A 1)

Step I. (Changing predicates)

'Perla has a visitor.'

Dúnay bisíta si Pírla.	(náqa)
Náqay bisíta si Pírla.	(dínhaq)
Dínhay bisíta si Pírla.	(waláq)
Waláy bisíta si Pírla.	(may)

May bisîta si Pîrla.	(dúna)
Dúnay bisîta si Pîrla.	(náqa)
Náqay bisîta si Pîrla.	(waláq)
Waláy bisîta si Pírla.	(kaqúban)
Waláy kaqúban si Pírla.	(dînhaq)
Dînhay kaqúban si Pîrla.	(náqa)
Náqay kaqúban si Pîrla.	(dîqa)
Dîqay kaqúban si Pírla.	(waláq)
Waláy kaqúban si Pírla.	(túqa)
Túqay kaqúban si Pîrla.	(nîqa)
Nîqay kaqúban si Pîrla.	(may)
May kaqúban si Pîrla.	

Step II. (Changing subjects and predicates)

'John has a child.'

Náqay anák si Hwan.	(dúna man gud)
Dúna man guy anák si Hwan.	(waláq ra ba)
Waláq ra bay anák si Hwan.	(si Pîrla)
Waláq ra bay anák si Pîrla.	(si Índay)
Waláq ra bay anák si Índay.	(dúna)
Dúnay anák si Índay.	(dúna ra ba)
Dúna ra bay anák si Índay.	(dúna man gud)
Dúna man guy anák si Índay.	(si Nîda)
Dúna man guy anák si Nîda.	(waláq man gud)
Waláq man guy anák si Nîda.	(ang ákung apú)
Waláq man guy anák ang ákung apú.	(waláq man sad)
Waláq man say anák ang ákung apú.	(dúna man sad)
Dúna man say anák ang ákung apú.	(si Hwan)
Dúna man say anák si Hwan.	(waláq man sad)
Waláq man say anák si Hwan.	(dúna man sad)
Dúna man say anák si Hwan.	(ang táwu)
Dúna man say anák ang táwu.	(dúna ra ba sad)
Dúna ra ba say anák ang táwu.	(kinîng ámung amígu)
Dúna ra ba say anák kinîng ámung amígu.	(dúna man gud)
Dúna man guy anák kinîng ámung amígu.	(dúna ra ba)

Dúna ra bay anák kiníng ámung amígu.	(kádtung íyang apú)
Dúna ra bay anák kádtung íyang apú.	(túqa ra ba)
Túqa ra bay anák kádtung íyang apú.	

Step III. (Word order of subject and predicate, without may) (3 C 3 d)

'John has a friend.'

Dúnay amígu si Hwan.	(akú)
Dúna akúy amígu.	(si Pírla)
Dúnay amígu si Pírla.	(siyá)
Dúna siyáy amígu.	(si Lítu)
Dúnay amígu si Lítu.	(waláq)
Waláy amígu si Lítu.	(akú)
Waláq akúy amígu.	(si Manáng)
Waláy amígu si Manáng.	(naq siyá)
Waláq naq siyáy amígu.	(si Lína)
Waláy amígu si Lína.	(náqa)
Náqay amígu si Lína.	(siyá)
Náqa siyáy amígu.	(si Mísis Abáya)
Náqay amígu si Mísis Abáya.	(kamí)
Náqa kamíy amígu.	(ang babáyi)
Náqay amígu ang babáyi.	

Step IV. (Long subjects and postpositive subjects)

'Do you have a jeep?'

Dúna ka bay dyip?	(si Lína)
Dúna bay dyip si Lína?	(siyá)
Dúna ba siyáy dyip?	(ka)
Dúna ka bay dyip?	(silá)
Dúna ba siláy dyip?	(waláq)
Waláq ba siláy dyip?	(siyá)
Waláq ba siyáy dyip?	(ka)
Waláq ka bay dyip?	(ságing)
Waláq ka bay ságing?	(si Lína)
Waláq bay ságing si Lína?	(siyá)
Waláq ba siyáy ságing?	(silá)
Waláq ba siláy ságing?	(dúna)

Dúna ba siláy ságing?	(ka)
Dúna ka bay ságing?	(silá)
Dúna ba siláy ságing?	

Step V. (Word order with <u>may</u>)

'Pedro has a jeep.'

May dyip si Pídru.	(siyá)
May dyip siyá.	(dúna)
Dúna siyáy dyip.	(silá)
Dúna siláy dyip.	(may)
May dyip silá.	(náqa)
Náqa siláy dyip.	(akú)
Náqa akúy dyip.	(may)
May dyip akú.	(kamí)
May dyip kamí.	(dúna)
Dúna kamíy dyip.	(dínhaq)
Dínhaq kamíy dyip.	(akú)
Dínhaq akúy dyip.	(may)
May dyip akú.	(si Pídru)
May dyip si Pídru.	(waláq)
Waláy dyip si Pídru.	(kitá)
Waláq kitáy dyip.	(may)
May dyip kitá.	(dúna)
Dúna kitáy dyip.	(si Pírla)
Dúnay dyip si Pírla.	(siyá)
Dúna siyáy dyip.	(may)
May dyip siyá.	

Step VI. (Combination of Steps III and V)

'Perla has a house.'

Dúnay baláy si Pírla.	(siyá)
Dúna siyáy baláy.	(dínhaq)
Dínhaq siyáy baláy.	(náqa)
Náqa siyáy baláy.	(si Lítu)
Náqay baláy si Lítu.	(níqa)
Níqay baláy si Lítu.	(may)

May baláy si Lítu.	(kukakúla)
May kukakúla si Lítu.	(dínhaq)
Dínhay kukakúla si Lítu.	(dúna)
Dúnay kukakúla si Lítu.	(bátaq)
Dúnay bátaq si Lítu.	(siyá)
Dúna siyáy bátaq.	(may)
May bátaq siyá.	(akú)
May bátaq akú.	(díqa)
Díqa akúy bátaq.	(bir)
Díqa akúy bir.	(túqa)
Túqa akúy bir.	(may)
May bir akú.	(dúna)
Dúna akúy bir.	(kamí)
Dúna kamíy bir.	(túbig)
Dúna kamíy túbig.	(may)
May túbig kamí.	(si Lína)
May túbig si Lína.	(waláq)
Waláy túbig si Lína.	(bisíta)
Waláy bisíta si Lína.	(dúna)
Dúnay bisíta si Lína.	(may)
May bisíta si Lína.	

Step VII. (Make statement into negative)

1. a. May kwárta ra ba ku.
   b. Waláq ra ba kuy kwárta.

2. a. May dyip man diqáy ka.
   b. Waláq man diqáy kay dyip.

3. a. May sugáq man.
   b. Waláq may sugáq.

4. a. May amígu ka ba?
   b. Waláq ka bay amígu?

5. a. May kaqugalíngun bang kasílyas?
   b. Waláq bay kaqugalíngung kasílyas?

6. a. May kwártu bang paqabángan áning baláya?
   b. Waláq bay kwártung paqabángan áning baláya?

7. a. May bisíta man diqáy ta Ma.
   b. Waláq man diqáy tay bisíta Ma.

8. a. May kwártus ínyung baláyng paqabángan.
   b. Waláy kwártus ínyung baláyng paqabángan.

9. a. May kwártu sad mis ubús.
   b. Waláq sad miy kwártus ubús.

10. a. May dághan ra ba siyáng bátaq.
    b. Waláq ra ba siyáy dághang bátaq.

Step VIII. Do Step VII again, this time saying b before a.

Step IX. (Make questions into negative)

1. a. May baláy ba gud kamú dídtu?
   b. Waláq ba gud kamúy baláy dídtu?

2. a. May bisíta diqáy si Pírla karún?
   b. Waláq diqáy bisíta si Pírla karún?

3. a. May amígu ba sab diqáy ka?
   b. Waláq ba sab diqáy kay amígu?

4. a. May dyip ba úntaq dínhi ganína?
   b. Waláq ba úntay dyip dínhi ganína?

5. a. May kwárta ba gud diqáy kamú?
   b. Waláq ba gud diqáy kamúy kwárta?

6. a. May kasílyas ba diqáy ang ímung kwártu?
   b. Waláq ba diqáy kasílyas ang ímung kwártu?

7. a. May dyip ba lagí kunú páras Lahúg?
   b. Waláq ba lagí kunúy dyip páras Lahúg?

8. a. May táwu ba kaháq diháq sa íla?
   b. Waláq ba kaháy táwu diháq sa íla?

9. a. May lugár pa ba kaháq sa dyip?
   b. Waláq pa ba kaháy lugár sa dyip?

10. a. May bisíta na ba sab túqud siyá?
    b. Waláq na ba sab túquy bisíta siyá?

Step X. Do Step IX again, saying first b and then a.

II. Existential Sentences

Hubára ngádtu sa Sinibuwanú ang musunúd nga mangá túdling púlung (3 A 1).

1. There's no beer here.
2. There's a man over there.
3. Do you have any beer?
4. There was someone who called you on the phone. (someone who called you on the phone: nagtawág nímu sa tilipunú)
5. I have two children.

6. There was a man here who was looking for you. (who was looking for you: nga nangítaq nímu)
7. There are jeeps there headed for Banawa.
8. I know there's a room for rent in your house.
9. There are no jeeps for Banawa.
10. There are jeeps now, but there weren't any before. (before: ganína)
11. There are many jeeps at that corner. (at that corner: niqánang iskináha)
12. Are there any children in your house?
13. There was a boy at Dr. Fernandez'.
14. There is also a room for rent downstairs.
15. Is there a room for rent in your house?

PP-E Word order (3 C)

Step I. (Predicate followed by subject, no attraction; change only the subject)

'Perla will rent a house here.'

Muqábang si Pírlag baay dínhi.	(siyá)
Muqábang siyág baay dínhi.	(ang táwu)
Muqábang ang táwug baay dínhi.	(si Mis Wílbi)
Muqábang si Mis Wílbig baay dínhi.	(silá)
Muqábang silág baay dínhi.	(kádtu)
Muqábang kádtug baay dínhi.	(ang babáyi)
Muqábang ang babáyig baay dínhi.	(kamí)
Muqábang kamíg baay dínhi.	(kanáq)
Muqábang kanág baay dínhi.	(ang Amirkánu)
Muqábang ang Amirkánug baay dínhi.	(akú)
Muqábang akúg baay dínhi.	(ang dráybir)
Muqábang ang dráybir ug baay dínhi.	(ka)
Muqábang kag baay dínhi.	(kitá)
Muqábang kitág baay dínhi.	(ang bána)
Muqábang ang bánag baay dínhi.	(tu)
Muqábang tug baay dínhi.	(kamú)
Muqábang kamúg baay dínhi.	(ang asáwa)
Muqábang ang asáwag baay dínhi.	(mi)

Muqábang mig baay dínhi.	(ang anák)
Muqábang ang anák ug baay dínhi.	

Step II. (Sentence with prepositive qualifier; change subject only)

'Miss Wilby will not go to Carbon.'

Díliq muqádtu si Mis Wílbis Kárbun.	(kú)
Díliq ku muqádtus Kárbun.	(silá)
Díliq silá muqádtus Kárbun.	(si Pírla)
Díliq muqádtu si Pírlas Kárbun.	(ta)
Díliq ta muqádtus Kárbun.	(ang bátaq)
Díliq muqádtu ang bátas Kárbun.	(tu)
Díliq tu muqádtus Kárbun.	(mi)
Díliq mi muqádtus Kárbun.	(ang asáwa)
Díliq muqádtu ang asáwas Kárbun.	(mu)
Díliq mu muqádtus Kárbun.	(si Mísis Abilyána)
Díliq muqádtu si Mísis Abilyánas Kárbun.	(ang dyip)
Díliq muqádtu ang dyip sa Kárbun.	(naq)
Díliq naq muqádtus Kárbun.	(ni)
Díliq ni muqádtus Kárbun.	(ang bána)
Díliq muqádtu ang bánas Kárbun.	(ang bísita)
Díliq muqádtu ang bisítas Kárbun.	(si Máma)
Díliq muqádtu si Mámas Kárbun.	(kamí)
Díliq kamí muqádtus Kárbun.	(kádtu)
Díliq kádtu muqádtus Kárbun.	(kanáq)
Díliq kanáq muqádtus Kárbun.	

Step III. (Sentence with prepositive and postpositive qualifier; change subject only)

'Mrs. Abellana will just eat her supper here, O.K.?'

Ánhi lang manihápun si Mísis Abilyána ha?	(mi)
Ánhi lang mi manihápun ha?	(silá)
Ánhi lang silá manihápun ha?	(si Máma)
Ánhi lang manihápun si Máma ha?	(ku)
Ánhi lang ku manihápun ha?	(ta)
Ánhi lang ta manihápun ha?	(ang táwu)
Ánhi lang manihápun ang táwu ha?	(mu)

Ánhi lang mu manihápun ha?	(ang bisíta)
Ánhi lang manihápun ang bisíta ha?	(siyá)
Ánhi lang siyá manihápun ha?	(ang dráybir)
Ánhi lang manihápun ang dráybir ha?	(si Pírla)
Ánhi lang manihápun si Pírla ha?	(ni)
Ánhi lang ni manihápun ha?	(tu)
Ánhi lang tu manihápun ha?	(si Mis Wílbi)
Ánhi lang manihápun si Mis Wílbi ha?	(ang bátaq)
Ánhi lang manihápun ang bátaq ha?	(naq)
Ánhi lang naq manihápun ha?	(kamí)
Ánhi lang kamí manihápun ha?	(kitá)
Ánhi lang kitá manihápun ha?	(kamú)
Ánhi lang kamú manihápun ha?	

Step IV. (Same as Step III)

'She brought Perla there.'

Íyang gidalá si Pírla dídtu.	(siyá)
Íya siyáng gidalá dídtu.	(kamí)
Íya kamíng gidalá dídtu.	(si Mis Wílbi)
Íyang gidalá si Mis Wílbi dídtu.	(ang babáyi)
Íyang gidalá ang babáyi dídtu.	(akú)
Íya akúng gidalá dídtu.	(kanáq)
Íya kanáng gidalá dídtu.	(silá)
Íya siláng gidalá dídtu.	(ang dyip)
Íyang gidalá ang dyip dídtu.	(kiní)
Íya kiníng gidalá dídtu.	(ang kwárta)
Íyang gidalá ang kwárta dídtu.	(kitá)
Íya kitáng gidalá dídtu.	(ikáw)
Íya ikáwng gidalá dídtu.	(ang táwu)
Íyang gidalá ang táwu dídtu.	(si Místir Pirnándis)
Íyang gidalá si Místir Pirnándis dídtu.	(kamú)
Íya kamúng gidalá dídtu.	(ang larávan)
Íyang gidalá ang larávan dídtu.	(si Lítu)
Íyang gidalá si Lítu dídtu.	(ang líbru)
Íyang gidalá ang líbru dídtu.	(kádtu)
Íya kádtung gidalá dídtu.	

Step V. (Same as Step III)

'I'll just leave this friend of mine here.'

Ákuq na lang ibílin ning ákung amígu dínhi.	(siyá)
Ákuq na lang siyáng ibílin dínhi.	(si Pírla)
Ákuq na lang ibílin si Pírla dínhi.	(kamú)
Ákuq na lang kamúng ibílin dínhi.	(si Nánay)
Ákuq na lang ibílin si Nánay dínhi.	(naq)
Ákuq na lang nang ibílin dínhi.	(si Nína)
Ákuq na lang ibílin si Nína dínhi.	(tu siyá)
Ákuq na lang tu siyáng ibílin dínhi.	(si Mánang)
Ákuq na lang ibílin si Mánang dínhi.	(tu)
Ákuq na lang tung ibílin dínhi.	(si Mis Wílbi)
Ákuq na lang ibílin si Mis Wílbi dínhi.	(naq siyá)
Ákuq na lang naq siyáng ibílin dínhi.	(ang ákung amígu)
Ákuq na lang ibílin ang ákung amígu dínhi.	(kádtu)
Ákuq na lang kádtung ibílin dínhi.	(ang líbru)
Ákuq na lang ibílin ang líbru dínhi.	(kanáq)
Ákuq na lang kanáng ibílin dínhi.	

PP-F Use of y (3 B 5)

Step I. (Change of ang to y; change of y to ang)

'I will leave my friend.'

Ibílin ku ang ákung amígu.	(mu siyá)
Mu siyáy ákung amígu.	(pangutánqa)
Pangutánqa ang ákung amígu.	(si Pírla)
Si Pírlay ákung amígu.	(kanáq siyá)
Kanáq siyáy ákung amígu.	(íngna)
Íngnang ákung amígu.	(si Dyuu)
Si Dyuuy ákung amígu.	(tigúwang)
Tigúwang ang ákung amígu.	(kiní siyá)
Kiní siyáy ákung amígu.	(midágan)
Midágan ang ákung amígu.	(kádtu siyá)
Kádtu siyáy ákung amígu.	(musakáy)
Musakáy ang ákung amígu.	(si Pídru)
Si Pídruy ákung amígu.	(mupíliq)

Mupíliq ang ákung amígu.	(kirí siyá)
Kirí siyáy ákung amígu.	(muqinúm)
Muqinúm ang ákung amígu.	(si Lína)
Si Línay ákung amígu.	(mutawág)
Mutawág ang ákung amígu.	(mu kádtu)
Mu kádtuy ákung amígu.	(pangitáqa)
Pangitáqa ang ákung amígu.	(mu kanáq)
Mu kanáy ákung amígu.	(maghuwát)
Maghuwát ang ákung amígu.	(si Hwan)
Si Hway ákung amígu.	(milakáw)
Milakáw ang ákung amígu.	(si Místir Gamílu)
Si Místir Gamíluy ákung amígu.	(musaká)
Musaká ang ákung amígu.	(kanáng táwu)
Kanáng táwuy ákung amígu.	(maqáyu)
Maqáyu ang ákung amígu.	(si Lítu)
Si Lítuy ákung amígu.	(mitawág)
Mitawág ang ákung amígu.	

Step II. (Same as Step I: predicates with postpositive particles)

'I brought my wife.'

Gidalá ku ang asáwa nákuq.	(kiní gud)
Kiní guy asáwa nákuq.	(pangutánqun níya)
Pangutánqun níya ang asáwa nákuq.	(ikáw lang)
Ikáw lay asáwa nákuq.	(musakáy kaháq)
Musakáy kaháq ang asáwa nákuq?	(kiní gyud)
Kiní gyuy asáwa nákuq.	(nahibáwu sab)
Nahibáwu sab ang asáwa nákuq.	(siyá ra)
Siyá ray asáwa nákuq.	(muqádtu diqáy)
Muqádtu diqáy ang asawa nákuq.	(siyá túqud)
Siyá túquy asáwa nákuq.	(milakáw ba)
Milakáw ba ang asáwa nákuq.	(kiní pa)
Kiní pay asáwa nákuq.	(mutánqaw sad)
Mutánqaw sad ang asáwa nákuq.	(ikáw kunú)
Ikáw kunúy asáwa nákuq.	(muqinúm pa)
Muqinúm pa ang asáwa nákuq.	(kádtu pa)

Kádtu pay asáwa nákuq.	(mubálhin lagí)
Mubálhin lagí ang asáwa nákuq.	(kanáq gyud)
Kanáq gyuy asáwa nákuq.	(maghuwát sab)
Maghuwát sab ang asáwa nákuq.	(siyá man)
Siyá may asáwa nákuq.	(muqádtu ba)
Muqádtu ba ang asáwa nákuq?	(kádtu man)
Kádtu may asáwa nákuq.	(magpíliq diqáy)
Magpíliq diqáyng asáwa nákuq.	(kínsa kaháq)
Kínsa kaháy asáwa nákuq?	(midágan ba)
Midágan bang asáwa nakuq?	(kínsa gud)
Kínsa guy asáwa nákuq?	(nagtawág túqud)
Nagtawág túqud ang asáwa nákuq.	(kiní ra)
Kiní ray asáwa nákuq.	(muqági man)
Muqági man ang asáwa nákuq.	(kádtu gyud)
Kádtu gyuy asáwa nákuq.	

III. Change the subject into the predicate (3 B 2)

Mangá Pananglítan ('examples'):

a. Si Láyda ang íyang ibílin dínhi.

Tubág: Íyang ibílin si Láyda dínhi.

b. Ibílin ka níya sa baay.

Tubág: Ikáw ang ibílin níya sa baay. (Cf. 3 B 4 on changing ka to ikáw.)

1. Kukakúla ang ímnun námuq. 'Coca-Cola is what we'll drink.'
2. Dyip padúung sa Banáwaq ang átung sákyan.
3. Ákung anák ang nagpuyúq sa táqas.
4. Muqábang siyá sa kwártu sa sílung.
5. Nangítaq siláng duhá nímu.
6. Kwártu nga míngaw ang íyang abángan.
7. Dádqun ka níya sa Amiriká. (3 B 4)
8. Muqádtu sa Banáwaq ang dyip nga gamáy.
9. Si Pírla ang giqubán ni Mis Wílbi ngádtus Banáwaq.
10. Láqin nga dyip ang átung pangitáqun.
11. Nagtawág nímu ganíha ni si Místir Gamílu.
12. Gidalá níya ngánhi ang íyang asáwa.
13. Siyá ang mutawág ug dyip páras Banáwaq.

14. Mubáyad ni siyág kwarínta písus nga ábang.

15. Dádqun ka níya sa Banáwaq.

IV A. Insert into the sentences the words in parentheses, and make any necessary changes (3 C 2, 3 C 3).

Pananglítan ('example'):

a. Ikáy muqábang sa usáng kwártu? (ba diqáy)

Tubág: Ikáw ba diqáy muqábang sa usáng kwártu?

1. Díliq pára sa Banáwaq. (man ni)
2. Gústu ug mangá bátaq. (man sab ku)
3. Way dyip pára sa Kárbun kay údtu. (na ra ba, na man gud)
4. Maqú kiní si Mis Wílbi? (ba diqáy)
5. Ákuq nga abángan ning kwartúha? (na ba lang kaháq)
6. Díliq mi magdúgay kay údtu na. (na lang, man gud)
7. Pangutánqa ang dráybir kun maqú kiní ang pára sa Banáwaq. (na ba)
   (Hint: remember ba is a question particle.)
8. Díliq ku muqubán sa Amiriká. (lagí)
9. Ása ta manakáy ug dyip? (man diqáy)
10. Waq muqánhi. (túqud naq siyá)
11. Díliq mahángyuq ang ábang. (na ra ba gyud)
12. Kádtung dyip duqúl sa tindáhan muqádtu sa Banáwaq? (ba kaháq)
13. Díliq kaháq samúkan sa mangá bátaq? (ka ba)
14. Piláy bayranán sa káda búwan? (man)
15. Ikáw ang muqábang sa kwártu? (ba lang diqáy)

IV B. (Cf. 3 C 3 a.)

Pananglítan ('example'):

a. Muqábang kaháq ka íning kwartúhang gamáy ra man kaqáyu ni? (gústu)

Tubág: Gústu kaháq kang muqábang íning kwartúhang gamáy ra man kaqáyu ni?

1. Muqádtu na lang ku kay údtu na man. (kinahánglan)
2. Musakáy úntaq ku ug dyip páras Kárbun. (gústu)
3. Ang ímung sákyan nga dyip dúna gyuy márkang Banáwaq. (kinahánglan)
4. Mubálhin ka ngánhi sa primíru sa sunúd nga búwan. (kinahánglan)
5. Muqábang úntaq kug kwártu dínhi. (gústu)

6. Díliq ku muqinúm ug bir. (gústu)
7. Makaqubán silá nákuq sa Kárbun. (díliq)
8. Muqábang ba ku niqíning kwártu sa sílung? (mahímuq)
9. Sakáy mu niqánang dyip nga páras Lahúg. (ayáw)
10. Dádqun ku si Lítu sa Amiriká. (kinahánglan)

IV C. Make the following sentences negative (2 B, 3 C 3 a). (Do not do this exercise until you have completed PP-E. You may review some of PP-E before beginning this exercise.)

Pananglítan ('example'):

a. Maqú ba naq ang páras Banáwaq?

Tubág: Diq ba naq maqú ang páras Banáwaq?

1. Muqádtu ra ba ni sa Kárbun Day.
2. Ánhi diqáy ka dínhi maghuwát ug dyip?
3. Gústu man gud ku ug mangá bátaq.
4. Dúna ba siyáy mangá anák?
5. Túqa siyá magpuyúq sa táqas.
6. Kamú bang duhá diqáy ang muqábang sa kwártu?
7. Ang únang nagqabáng ngánhi nagbáyad siyá káda búwan. (Change nagbáyad to magbáyad.)
8. Gústu man ku sa kwártus táqas.
9. Mahímuq ba diqáy mutánqaw sa kwártu karún?
10. Nahibáwu ka ba nga dúna kuy kwártung gipaqabángan? (Change nahibáwu to mahibáwu.)
11. Maqú ba ni siyá ang nangítaq ug baláy?
12. Náqa man tingáli si Mísis Abilyána.
13. Maqú ba kanáq ang baláy ni Mísis Abilyána?
14. Huwatá lang ku dídtus tindáhan ha? (huwatá 'wait for,' imperative)
15. Mangádtu mus Banáwaq?

IV D. Replace the underlined words with the words in parentheses. (Cf. 3 C and subsections.) (Do not do this exercise until after PP-E.)

Pananglítan ('example'):

a. Díliq na lang muqánhi si Tibúrsyu. (siyá)

Tubág: Díliq na lang siyá muqánhi.

b. Gústu bang muqinúm ang bátaq? (ka)

Tubág: Gústu ka bang muqinúm?

c. Ánhi lang manihápun si Mis Wílbi. (ka)

Tubág: Ánhi ka lang manihápun.

1. Dídtu sa Kárbun ang tigúwang gahápun. (siyá)
2. Kinahánglan báyran ni Mis Wílbi ang kwártung giqabángan. (nímu)
3. Níqa man diqáy dínhi ang ákung amígu. (ka)
4. Mahímung abángan ang baay sa mangá Amirkánu. (níla)
5. Dúna man diqáy dalá ('you brought') ang táwu. (ka)
6. Díliq mubáyad si Pírla sa íyang útang. (siyá) (útang 'debt')
7. Íla bang dádqun ang mangá bátaq sa lúngsud? (mi) (lúngsud 'town')
8. Ayáw patanqáwa ang mutsátsa sa síni. (siyá) (patanqáwa 'send to the show')
9. Waláq musakáy sa dyip ang Amirkána. (ku)
10. Ánhaq lang manáqug ang mangá táwu sa iskína. (mi)
11. Íyang dádqun si Lítu sa Amiriká. (ka)
12. Waq na ra bay bir si Dúktur Pirnándis. (ka)
13. Mahímuq bang mutánqaw ang mangá babáyi sa síni? (mi)
14. Waláq pangitáqa si Huwána gahápun. (ku)
15. Ánhi ang mangá táwu manihápun karúng gabíqi. (mu)

V A. Review of 234 command or statement intonation.

1.	Aa, mangutána ta.	(3 a 8)
2.	Uu, sigí.	(3 a 29)
3.	Sakáy ta.	(3 a 35)
4.	Náqay márkang Banáwaq.	(3 a 36)
5.	Básin pa.	(3 a 44)
6.	Uh, dalíq mu ngarís suud.	(3 b 8)
7.	Maqáy man.	(3 b 12)
8.	Aw, kádtung únang nagqabáng ngánhi.	(3 b 26)
9.	Aa, maqáy man.	(3 c 6)
10.	Aa, diq man.	(3 c 12)
11.	Layúq man.	(3 c 14)
12.	Aw, maqáyu man sab.	(3 c 18)
13.	Muqádtu kus Kalámba.	(3 c 26)
14.	Maghuwát lang kug láqin.	(3 c 34)

V B. Another type of statement intonation has a drop on the second-to-last syllable and a rise on the end (symbolized as 423). Pronounce the following with 423 intonations.

1. Náqay dráybir. (3 a 33)
2. Maw ni siyá ang nangítag kwártu. (3 b 13)
3. Aa, maqú diqáy nis Mis Wílbi. (3 b 10)
4. Níqa say usás ubús. (3 b 21)
5. Líbri man gung sugáq ug túbig. (3 b 27)
6. Maqáyu diqáy naq. (3 c 15)
7. Na ádtu na lang mi. (3 c 19)

VI. Sultiqánay (Conversation).
New word: míngaw 'quiet, lonely'

A: Maqáyung búntag Nuy.

B: Maqáyung búntag.

A: Mahímuq bang mangutána?

B: Mahímuq kaqáyu. Únsa man?

A: Mangádtu úntaq mi sa Lahúg. Ása man mi musakáyg dyip padúung ngádtu?

B: Aa, ádtu diqáy mu sa Lahúg? Subáya lang nínyu ning dálan Pidíl Rusáryu ug pagqabút nínyus ikatulúng iskína, maqú na kanáq ang iskína Hakusalím ug Pidíl Rusáryu. Ánhaq dínhaq muhúnung ang mangá dyip padúung sa Lahúg.

A: Aa, diqáy. Salámat Nuy ha?

* * *

C: Uh. Pirlá, níqa man lagí diqáy mu.

A: Níqa mi kay nangítaq man gud ni si Mis Wílbi ug kwártu.

C: Aa, maqú diqáy ni siyá ang nangítag kwártu? Únsa man ang íyang gústu, ang sa sílung u ang sa táqas ba?

A: Gústu siyá ug kwártung míngaw.

C: Míngaw man kiníng kwártu sa sílung, kay túqa man sa táqas magpuyúq ang mangá bátaq.

A: Ang sa sílung na lang ang íyang abángan. Pilá man ang bayranán káda búlan?

C: Kwarínta písus kay dúna may kaqugalíngung kasílyas.

A: Díliq na ba naq mahángyuq?

C: Díliq na gyud Day.

Tubagág hústu u díliq:

1. Mangádtu silá si A sa Banáwaq.
2. Waq may dyip pára sa Lahúg.
3. Manakáy silá si A ug dyip.
4. Ánhaq sa iskína muhúnung ang dyip.

* * *

5. Si Pírla ang nangítag kwártu.
6. Díliq siyá gústug kwártung míngaw.
7. Ang mangá bátaq túqa magpuyúq sa sílung.
8. Muqábang siyá sa kwártu sa sílung.
9. Way kasílyas ang kwártu sa sílung.
10. Díliq diqáy mahángyuq ang kwártu.

LESSON 4. GOING TO THE BEACH

Sagquluhúnun (Basic Sentences)

First Part	Únang Báhin
how late!	kadúgay
[particle exclaiming over something the speaker has noticed]	gud
you	nímu
Merlie	Mírli
1. How late you are, Merlie!	1. Kadúgay gud nímu Mírlí!
let's go	taná
get on	musakáy
we	ta
[particle preceding goal]	ug
bus	traak
Talisay (town on shore near Cebu City)	Talísay
2. Come on. Let's take a bus to Talisay (lit. Let's get on a bus. Let's go to Talisay).	*2. Taná. Musakáy tag traak. Ádtu tas Talísay.
will go	muqádtu
still, in addition	pa
[particle with advice]	ra ba
us	ta
to	sa
Go Chan (a building in Cebu)	Gútsan
3. We still have to go to the Go Chan, you know (before we can get a bus to Talisay). (Upon arriving at the Go Chan)	3. Muqádtu pa ra ba tas Gútsan. (Pagqabút níla sa Gútsan)
not	diq
yet	pa
[particle with advice]	ra ba
full	punúq
this	ni

[linker for ni and traak]	nga
bus	traak
[exclamation on first noticing something]	daq
4. This bus isn't full yet.	*4. Aa, diq pa ra ba punúq ning ... traak daq!
will be a long time	madúgay
on this one	íni
5. We'll have to wait a long time. (Lit. We will be a long time on this one.)	5. Madúgay ta íni.
long time	dúgay
very	kaqáy (short for kaqáyu)
[linker for dúgay and the rest of the phrase]	nga
can leave	kalárga
on this	íni
6. It will be a long time before this one leaves (lit. before we can leave on this one).	*6. Dúgay kaqáy tang kalárga íni.
come on	taa (short for talá)
there (future)	ádtu
the other side	píkas
let's watch for	magbántay

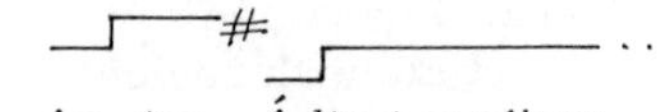

7. Come on. Let's wait on the other side (lit. Let's watch for [a bus] on the other side).	7. Aa, taa. Ádtu tas píkas ... magbántay.
we	átuq
[linker for átuq and tanqáwun]	nga
look	tanqáwun
if	ug
can get on	makasakáy
[question particle]	ba
bus or jeep not running on schedule	píkqap

8. Let's see if we can catch one of the irregular trips.

8. Átung tanqáwun ug makasakáy ... ba tas píkqap.

here there's a . . .	níqa
[existential particle]	y
jeep	dyip
we	átuq
this one	ni
[linker for <u>átuq</u> and <u>pangutánqun</u>]	nga
ask	pangutánqun

9. Ah, here's a jeep. Let's ask him (lit. this one).

9. Aa, níqay dyip. Átuq ning ... pangutánqun.

headed toward	padúung
probably	tingáli
Tabunok (town on the way to Talisay)	Tabunúk

10. This one is probably going to Tabunok.

10. Padúung tingáli ni sa Tabunúk.

will take	muhatúd
perhaps	kaháq
he	ni siyá
us	nátuq
to	sa

11. I wonder if he will take us to Talisay.

*11. Muhatúd ba kaháq ni siyá ... nátuq sa Talísay.

you	ka
us (not you)	námuq
[term of address used by males to males of the same age]	Bay

12. Will you take us to Talisay?

12. Muhatúd ka námuq sa Talísay ... Bay?

four	upát
[linker for <u>upát</u> and <u>buqúk</u>]	ka

[a counter: lit. piece]	buqúk
13. There are four of us.	13. Upát mi ka buqúk Bay.
yes	uu
go ahead	sigí
get in	sakáy
you (plural)	mu
14. Yes. Go ahead, get in.	14. Uu. Sigí. Sakáy mu.
where to?	ása
[question particle after interrogative]	man
we	ta
go	ádtu (short for muqádtu)
15. Where are we going?	15. Ása man ta ádtu?
which (of several)?	ása
[linker for ása and lugár]	nga
place	lugár
Pook (a place in Talisay)	Púquk
16. What part of Talisay are we going to—Pook?	*16. Ása man tang lugára sa Talísay muqádtu—sa Púquk?
far	layúq
very much	kaqáy
[linker for naq and Púquk]	nga
[exclamation of annoyance]	uy
17. Pook (lit. That Pook) is a very long way.	17. Layúq kaqáy nang Púquk uy.
besides	gawás pa
when we come back	inigbálik
we	nátuq
will have a hard time	maglisúd
[particle preceding infinitive]	ug
get a ride	sakáy

18. Besides, when we come back we will have a hard time getting a ride.

*18. Gawás pa, inigbálik nátuq, maglisúd tag sakáy.

because	kay
if	ug
already	na
difficult	lisúd
to get a ride	pagsakáy
[particle preceding infinitive]	ug
return	bálik

19. Because it will be hard to get a ride back from there. (Lit. Because if we are already there, it will be very hard to get a ride back.)

*19. Kay ug túqa na ta dídtu, lisúd kaqáyu pagsakáyg bálik.

merely, simply	lang
us	ta
Yarrow (name of a resort at Talisay)	Yáru
get off	manáqug*

20. Let's just get off at the Yarrow.

*20. Ádtu lang ta sa Yáru manáqug.

then	unyáq
will walk	mulakáw
merely, simply	lang
we	ta
[particle preceding goal]	ug
little bit	dyútay
[existential particle]	y
beautiful	níndut
[linker for níndut and kaliguqánan]	nga
place to go swimming	kaliguqánan†

---

* Listed in the Glossary under the heading *náqug.

† Listed in the Glossary under díguq.

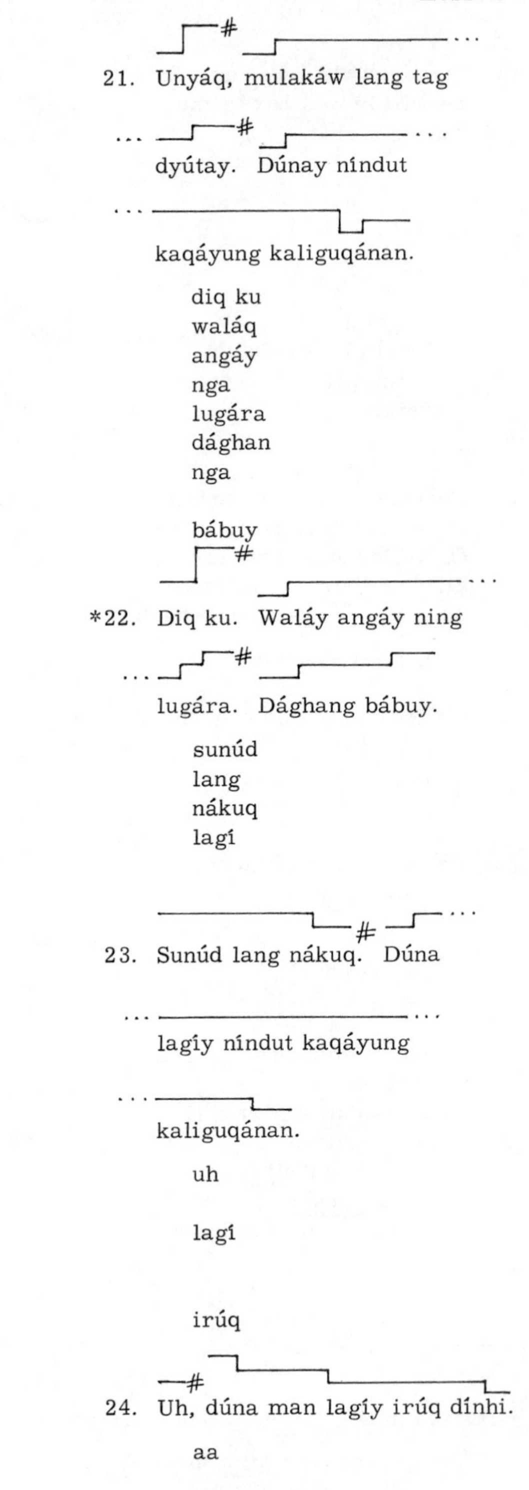

21. Then we'll walk a little. There's a good place for swimming.

21. Unyáq, mulakáw lang tag dyútay. Dúnay níndut kaqáyung kaliguqánan.

I don't want to	diq ku
there is no	waláq
suitableness	angáy
[linker for ni and lugára]	nga
particular place	lugára
many	dághan
[linker for dághan and bábuy]	nga
pig	bábuy

22. I don't want to. I don't like this place (lit. This place has no suitability). There are too many pigs.

*22. Diq ku. Waláy angáy ning lugára. Dághang bábuy.

follow	sunúd
merely, simply	lang
me	nákuq
anyway (though you disbelieve it)	lagí

23. Just follow me. There's a good place to go swimming, believe me.

23. Sunúd lang nákuq. Dúna lagíy níndut kaqáyung kaliguqánan.

[expression of surprise at seeing something]	uh
[particle expressing insistence on a contrary point of view]	lagí
dogs	irúq

24. But there are dogs here.

24. Uh, dúna man lagíy irúq dínhi.

[expression contradicting what preceded]	aa
those	kanáq
[linker for kanáq and irúq]	nga

[plural marker]	mangá
particular dog	irúqa
stray	laqág
inhabiting this place	tagadínhi

25. Heck. Those are stray dogs. They're not from around here. (Lit. Those dogs—those are strays. Those are not from here.)

*25. Aa, kanáng mangá irúqa mangá laqág naq. Díliq naq ... tagadínhi.

eat (plural)	nangáqun (listed under káqun)
merely	lang
those ones	naq
[particle preceding goal]	sa
[plural marker]	mangá
leftovers, food scraps	súbra
of	sa
people who go swimming	nangalíguq (listed under díguq)

26. They are merely eating the scraps of the people who are swimming.

*26. Nangáqun lang naq dínhaq ... sa mangá súbra sa nangalíguq.

there (pointing)	uh
see	nakakitáq
you	ka
that (not far)	ánaq
[linker for ánaq and taytáyan]	nga
bridge	taytáyan
go along or over	ági (short for muqági)

27. Oh, do you see that bridge? Let's cross there.

27. Uh, nakakitáq ka ánang ... taytáyan? Ánhaq ta diháq ági.

then, at that (future) time	unyáq
when we arrive	inigqabút
[particle preceding goal]	sa
other side	píkas
[plural marker]	mangá
little houses	baybáay (= balaybálay)

[linker for baybáay and gágmay]	nga
small (plural)	gágmay

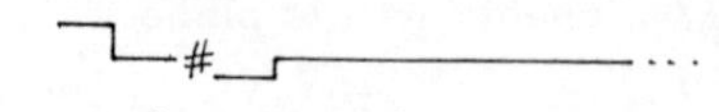

28. On the other side, there are some small shacks. (Lit. Then, when we get to the other side, there will be very many small shacks.)	*28. Unyáq inigqabút nátuq sa píkas dúnay dághan kaqáyung mangá baybáayng gágmay.
stays	gapuyúq (short for nagpuyúq)
[linker for gapuyúq and tigúwang]	nga
old man	tigúwang
29. There is an old man staying there.	29. Náqay gapuyúq diháng tigúwang.
that (just mentioned)	kanáq
[linker for kanáq and tiguwánga]	nga
old man	tigúwang
my	ákuq
that one (he) (just mentioned)	naq
[linker for ákuq and súkiq]	nga
steady customer; person steadily patronized	súkiq
30. That old man—he is the one I usually rent a shack from (lit. that is the one I usually patronize).	*30. Kanáng tiguwánga—ákuq nang súkiq.
am afraid (of something in the future)	mahádluk
[particle of contradiction]	man
I	ku
[linker for mahádluk and the rest of the phrase]	nga
go over	muqági
rickety (lit. shake, wobble)	gaqigutqigút (short for nagqigutqigút)
because	man

31. But I'm scared to cross that bridge. It's rickety.	*31. Mahádluk man kung muqági ánang taytayána; gaqigutqigút man naq.
give me	ambí
[linker for naq and butáng]	nga
your	ímu
[linker for ímu and butáng]	nga
[plural marker]	mangá
things	butáng
give me	bi
because	kay
I	akú
[subject marker]	y
will carry	dalá (short for magdalá)
32. Here, give me your things. Let me carry them (lit. Because I will be the one to carry them).	32. Ambí nang ímung mangá butáng bi, kay akúy dalá.
next thing	unyáq
go	lakáw
[linker preceding word expressing manner]	ug
fast	kusúg
so that	arún
will fall	mahúug (listed under húlug)
33. And walk fast so that you won't fall.	33. Unyáq lakáw ug kusúg arún díliq ka mahúug.

Mangá Pangutána

Únang Báhin

1. Diqín ka man Mirlí? Ngánung nadúgay man ka?
2. Únsa mang tráka átung sákyan?
3. Madúgay ba tu si Dyuu?

4. Háqin man si Huwán magbántayg traak?
5. Kínsa pay waláq makasakáy?
6. Kínsa may átung pangutánqun?
7. Díliq kaháq ta maglisúd pagsakáy inigbálik nátuq?
8. Dághan bang dyip muqádtu ngádtus Púquk?
9. Únsa may sákyan nátuq inigbálik?
10. Ádtu ba ta dídtus píkas?
11. Dúna ba guy kaliguqánan sa Yáru?
12. Ádtu pa diqáy ta sa Gútsan musakáy?
13. Punúq na ba nang tráka Dyuu?
14. Háqin mang lugára nang níndut nga kaliguqánan?
15. Diq ka mahádluk muqági ánang gaqigutqigút nga taytáyan?
16. Únsa man nang ímung dalá Mirl?
17. Kanáng tigúwang sa may taytáyan, tagadínhi ba naq?
18. May mangá laqág ba dínhing irúq?
19. May gapuyúq ba ánang baybáay?
20. Muhatúd ka ba námuq sa Dyuns Abinyú Bay?

Mangá Pangutána (Matching)

Únang Báhin

1. Ása man ta musakáyg traak?
2. Únsa may átung sákyan—kanáng náqa diháng traak?
3. Kamúng upát ang musakáy Bay?
4. Ása man diqáy ta mangalíguq—sa Púquk?
5. Kínsa pa may waláq kasakáy?
6. Ása man mu manáqug Bay?
7. Kínsa man nang tiguwánga?
8. Únsa man nang gikaqún sa mangá irúq?
9. Ása pa gud ta Dyuu?

(a) Maqú nay gapuyúq sa usá sa mangá baybáay diháq—ákuq nang súkiq.

(b) Ádtu lang ta sa Talísay kay díliq ta únyaq maglisúd pagbálik.

(c) Ang mangá súbra naq sa nangalíguq.

(d) Ádtu sa Gútsan kay waq may traak dínhing muqádtu dídtu.

(e) Uu, apán ihatúd mi sa Dyuns Abinyú.

(f) Ádtu lang mi manáqug sa Yáru Bay.

(g) Mulakáw pa tag gamáy úsaq ta muqabút sa níndut nga kaliguqánan.

(h) Pikqap na lang kay dúgay kaqáyu nang traak mulárga.

(i) Si Mírli na lang kay naglisúd sa íyang dalá.

Sagquluhúnun (Basic Sentences)

Second Part	Ikaduháng Báhin
can rest	makapahúlay
us	mi
in this	íni
[linker for íni and lugár]	nga
your	ímu
[linker for ímu and lugár]	nga
[term of address for males older than speaker]	Nuy
34. May we rest in this place of yours, Sir?	34. Makapahúlay ba mi íning ímung lugár Nuy?
yes	uu
go ahead	sigí
choose (imperative)	píliq
merely	lang
you (plural)	mu
there (near hearer)	diháq
whichever	bisán ug sáqa (= bisán ug háqin)
of those	ánaq
[linker for ánaq and lantáya]	nga
bamboo table	lántay
35. Yes, go ahead. Just pick any of those bamboo tables.	*35. Uu, sigí. Píliq lang mu diháq biság sáqa ánang lantáya.
not	diq
many	dághan
[particle meaning 'there are' after adjective]	ug
people	táwu
[linker for run and adláwa]	nga
day	ádlaw
today	rung adláwa (short for karúng adláwa)

36. I see there aren't many people today.	*36. Diq man diqáy run dághag táwung adláwa.
[exclamation of contradiction]	aa
there were (no place meaning)	dínhaq
this morning	ganíhang búntag
but	pirú
went home (plural)	namaqúliq (listed under uliq)
already	na
37. There were many this morning, but they have gone home now.	*37. Aa, dínhay dághan ganíhang búntag, pirú namaqúliq na man.
[exclamation of displeasure]	matáy
seems	mu ra (short for maqú ra)
[linker for mu ra and the rest of the phrase]	ug
feel cold	gitúgnaw
[particle giving new information]	man
go home	paqúliq (short for mupaqúliq; listed under ulíq)
38. Boy! I feel cold (lit. I seem to be cold). Let's go home.	38. Matáy, mu rag gitúgnaw man ku. Paqúliq ta.
me	akú
too	sab
[exclamation upon finding out something]	daq
39. Me too!	39. Akú sab daq!
anyway	tutál
will start to rain	muquwán
probably	tingáli

40. Anyway, it probably is going to rain.

*40. Tutál, muquwán tingáli.

let's hurry — magdalíq
instead — núqun
come on — taná
because — kay
probably — tingáli
[linker for tingáli and the following phrase] — ug
will be overtaken by night — magabhiqán

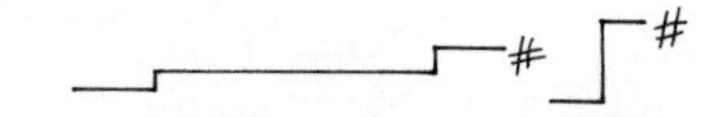

41. We'd better hurry up. Let's go, because it's getting dark (lit. because we'll probably be overtaken by night).

41. Magdalíq núqun ta. Taná. Kay tingálig magabhiqán ta.

Lord! — Sus
one who dislikes something — laqáyan
without a doubt — gyud
I — ku
[linker for laqáyan and muqági] — nga
will go past — muqági
[linker for íni and lugára] — nga
[particle indicating annoyance or dislike] — uy
smelly — bahúq

42. Lord! How I hate to go by this place—it smells.

42. Sus, laqáyan gyud kung muqági íning lugára uy, bahúq.

[particle drawing hearer's attention to something he does not see] — uh
there's . . . here — níqa
let's get on — manakáy

43. Oh, here comes a bus. Let's get on this one.

43. Uh, níqay traak. Manakáy ta íni.

[exclamation of contradiction] — aa
let's not — diq lang ta
that one (not distant) — ánaq

44. Let's not take that one. (Lit. Ah, let's not that one.)	*44. Aa, diq lang ta ánaq.
thing to be chosen	pilíqun
us	nátuq
the kind that	naq
[linker for naq and mudirítsu]	nga
goes directly	mudirítsu
45. Let's pick one that goes directly to Cebu. (Lit. Let's pick that one going directly to Cebu.)	45. Pilíqun nátuq nang mudirítsus ... Sibú.
goes	ádtu
[linker for ni and tráka]	nga
Tangke (part of Talisay)	Tángki
[term used by males to address males of same age]	Bay
46. Say, is this truck going to Tangke (Bay)?	*46. Aa, ádtu ba ning tráka sa ... Tángki Bay?
no	díliq
goes directly	dirítsu (short for mudirítsu)
47. No. It's (Lit. This is) going directly to Cebu.	47. Díliq. Dirítsu nis Sibú.

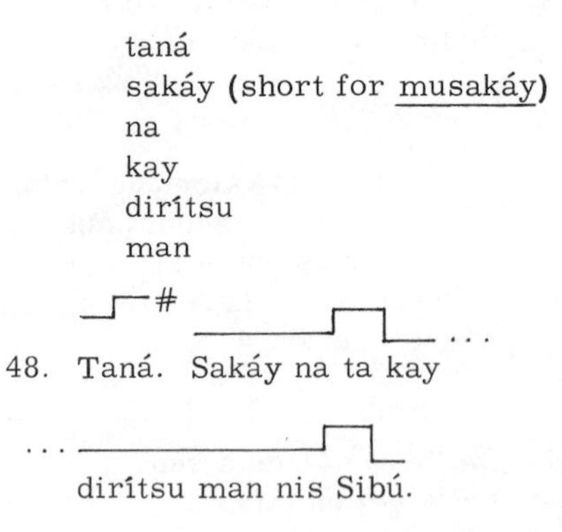

let's go	taná
let's get on	sakáy (short for musakáy)
now	na
because	kay
goes directly	dirítsu
because	man
48. Come. Let's get on. It's going straight to Cebu.	48. Taná. Sakáy na ta kay ... dirítsu man nis Sibú.

49. Will you take us to Jones Avenue, driver?

49. Muhatúd ka námuq sa Dyuns Abinyú Bay?

[exclamation contradicting what was said] — aa
goes — ádtu
only (and no more) — ra
as far as — kútub sa
Lane (name of a theater) — Liin

50. But I only go as far as the Go Chan Building and the Lane Theater.

50. Aa, ádtu ra ni kútub sa Gútsan ug sa Liin.

(Upon arriving at the Lane.)

(Pagqabút nila sa Liin.)

it is going to rain — muquwán
now — na
[expression upon finding out something] — daq

51. Come on. It's beginning to rain now.

51. Taná. Muquwán na daq.

over here — arí
at — sa
restaurant — ristáwran
take shelter (plural) — mamasílung (listed under sílung)

52. Over here to the restaurant. Let's take shelter.

52. Arí tas ristáwran. Mamasílung ta.

hurry — dalíq
Merl (way of addressing Merlie) — Mirl
run — dágan

53. Hurry, Merl! Run!

53. Dalíq Mirl! Dágan!

will get wet — mabasáq
you — ka
next thing — nyaq (short for únyaq)

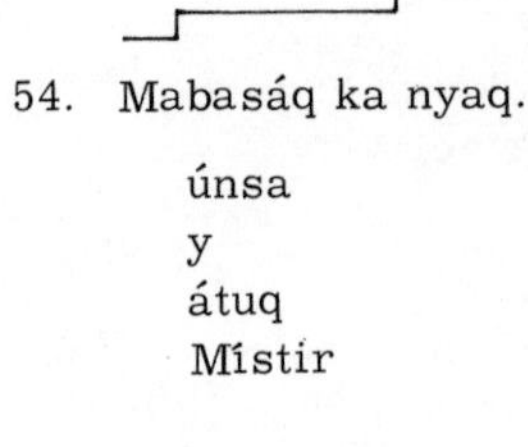

54. You're going to get wet. — 54. Mabasáq ka nyaq.

what?	únsa
[subject marker]	y
ours	átuq
Sir (term of address for male of high station)	Místir

55. What would you like, Sir? (Lit. What is ours, Sir?) — 55. Únsa may átuq Místir?

mixture of ice cream and fruit	haluqháluq
merely	lang
ours	ámuq

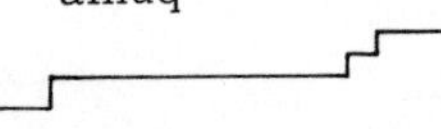

56. We'll just have halo-halo. (Lit. Just halo-halo is what we'll have.) — 56. Haluqháluq lay ámuq.

four	upát
[linker for upát and básu]	ka
glass	básu

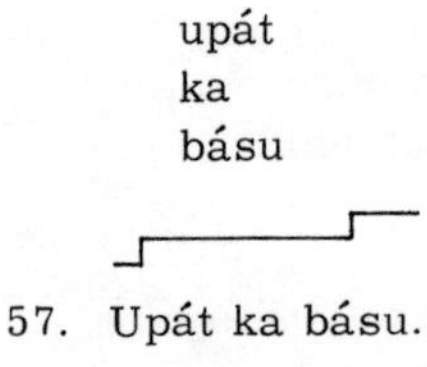

57. (We'll have) four glasses. — 57. Upát ka básu.

what?	unsálan
that (mentioned before)	naq
[linker for naq and haluqháluq]	nga

58. What is halo-halo? (Lit. What is that halo-halo?) — *58. Unsálan man nang haluqháluq?

[exclamation dismissing something as foolish]	adáa
ice cream	áyskrim
[particle of explanation]	gud
next	unyáq
mixed	gisáktan (listed under sakút)
[particle preceding goal]	ug
[plural marker]	mangá
fruit	prútas

59. It's ice cream mixed with fruits. (Lit. Why, it's ice cream. Then it's mixed with fruit.) — 59. Adáa. Áyskrim gud. Unyáq gisáktag mangá prútas.

my!	uy
nice	nĺndut
for sure	gyud
that (thing previously mentioned)	naq
60. My, that was really good.	60. Uy. Nĺndut gyud naq.
how much?	pilá
thing to be paid	bayranán
61. How much is the bill?	61. Pilá may bayranán?
never mind	ayáw lang
I	akú
just (the only one of several)	lang
pay	báyad (short for mubáyad)

62. Never mind. Let me pay. (Lit. I'll be the one to pay.)	62. Ayáw lang. Akú lay báyad.
all right (pause before introducing new topic)	na
here	ánhi
just, merely	lang
part from each other	magbúlag
63. All right. Let's say good-by here. (Lit. Let's just part from each other here.)	63. Na, ánhi lang ta dínhi ... magbúlag.
will see each other	magkítaq
tomorrow	úgmaq
64. See you tomorrow. (Lit. We'll see each other tomorrow.)	64. Magkítaq ta úgmaq.

Mangá Pangutána

Ikaduháng Báhin

1. Makapahúlay ba ta ánang lantáya diháq?
2. Díliq dághan ang nangalíguq ganíhang búntag Nuy nu?
3. Ganíha ra bang namaqúliq ang nangalíguq?

4. Matáy, waq ka tugnawá Dyuu?
5. Diq ba mu ra mag muquwán Mirl?
6. Diq ka ba laqáyan muqági íning lugára Dyuu?
7. Gústu ka bang magabhiqán dínhi?
8. Ngánung bahúq man ning lugára dínhi?
9. Ádtu mung upát sa Tángki Bay?
10. Dirítsu ba nis Sibú Bay?
11. Ásang lugára sa Dyuns Abinyú mu manáqug Bay?
12. Diq ba lang ta mamasílung?
13. Waláq ka ba mabasáq Mirl?
14. Ása man ta magkítaq—sa ristáwran?
15. Pilá ka básung haluqháluq Mistír?
16. Áyskrim ba nang haluqháluq?
17. Dághan bang prútas ang iságul ánang haluqháluq?
18. Gisáktan ba nímug prútas ning áyskrim Bay?
19. Níndut bang kaligúqan ning lugára Nuy?
20. Magbúwag na ba ta dínhi?

Mangá Pangutána (Matching)

Ikaduháng Báhin

1. Dirítsu ba ning tráka sa Talísay Dung?
2. Dághan bang nangalíguq rung adláwa Nuy?
3. Gitúgnaw ka ba Mirl?
4. Muqági ba ta ánang taytáyan?
5. Ása man ta mamasílung?
6. Únsay ínyu Mistír?
7. Pilá tu ka básu Mistír?
8. Únsa may gisákut* ánang haluqháluq?
9. Nabasáq ba si Mírli?

(a) Ay áyskrim gud naq gisáktag mangá prútas.
(b) Díqay ristáwran. Arí ta mamasílung.
(c) Upát lang Bay.
(d) Dághan, apán namaqúliq na.
(e) Díliq. Muqági pa ni sa Tabunúk.
(f) Waláq. Kay mipasílung siyá.
(g) Haluqháluq lay ámuq.
(h) Uu, ánhaq ta diháq muqági padúung sa kaliguqánan.
(i) Waláq núqun kay nagdagán man ku ganíha.

* Gisákut 'thing mixed in.'

Commentary to Basic Sentences

4 a 2	musakáy	The meanings of musakáy and manakáy are the same, except that manakáy is used only for plural, whereas musakáy is used for either singular or plural.
4 a 4		The reason the speaker uses ra ba (particle with advice) is that he is advising everybody to get on this bus.
4 a 6	nga	Nga links the prepositive (dúgay) to the rest of the sentence (3 E).
4 a 6	kalárga	Short for makalárga. (Cf. the tables in 4 A below and the comments in 4 B 1.)
4 a 11	ni siyá	The demonstrative is used together with pronouns or names mentioned previously in the context. (The choice of ni or naq or tu, of course, depends upon the distance in time or space.)
4 a 16	(word order)	Note that man and ta are attracted to ása. (Cf. 3 C 3 c.)
4 a 18	ug sakáy	This form is an infinitive (to be described in detail in a later lesson).
4 a 19	pagsakáy	Infinitive form.
4 a 19	ug bálik	Infinitive form.
4 a 20	manáqug	The unreal active of a base kanáqug: 4 B 2 below.
4 a 22	dághang bábuy	This sentence type is explained in 4 C.
4 a 25	irúqa	For -a, see 2 C, p. 44.
4 a 26	nangáqun, nangalíguq	Unreal forms of the bases of pangáqun and pangalíguq: charts, 4 A and 4 E, below.
4 a 28	gágmay	This has the same meaning as gamáy, except that it is used only for plural.
4 a 30	naq	The demonstrative may be used in place of the pronoun if the person has been mentioned before.
4 a 31	mahádluk	Unreal active of a base kahádluk: chart, 4 A.
4 b 35	lántay	Lántay is a bamboo platform raised about two feet from the ground. People lie on it, sit on it, or eat at it.
4 b 35	sáqa	A dialectal form for háqin.
4 b 36	run . . . nga	Run is used with time words to mean 'this day (week, month, etc.).' It is linked with nga. (Note that it is separated by several words from adláwa 'day.')
4 b 37	ganíha	Used with words referring to time of day to mean 'this (past) morning (evening, etc.).' In this meaning it is linked with nga.
4 b 40	muquwán	Note that muquwán means 'start to rain' and nagquwán means 'it is raining.'

4 b 44	diq	This means both 'let's not do' and 'I don't like.'
4 b 44	diq lang	Lang is used with díliq to make it more polite.
4 b 46	Tángki	Some buses take the circuitous route back to Cebu via Tangke, and some go direct.
4 b 58	unsálan	A dialectal form of únsa.

Grammatical Section

4 A. Verbs: Active

Cebuano VERB FORMS consist of a BASE alone or a BASE plus one or more affixes. The base contains the denotative meaning (run, eat, ride, etc.); the affixes, if any, give the form a particular grammatical function. Affixes of one large and important category are the ACTIVE PREFIXES; these are shown in the following chart.

Active Verb Prefixes*

	Real	Unreal
Volitional	{ni- mi-}	mu-
Durative	{ga- nag- naga-}	{mag- maga-}
Potential	{ka- naka-}	{ka- maka-}
Bases with paN-† prefix	naN-	maN-
Bases with ka-	na-	ma-

The active form of a verb is used when the performer of the action is one of the nominative forms shown in the chart of 1 A and 1 B (pp. 11, 14) or is a word or phrase preceded by ang.

4 B. Real active vs. unreal active verb forms

4 B 1. Real

The REAL ACTIVE FORM describes affirmative actions or conditions that have already happened, and actions in progress (or conditions existing) at the time the speaker speaks. (Real forms are not used in negative sentences with waláq 'not': these must have an unreal form. See 4 B 2 d below.)

---

* Any of the alternative prefixes enclosed in braces may be used interchangeably with the others, with virtually no difference in meaning.

† For the symbol -N- see 4 E, below, pp. 144.

Midágan ang túntu. (2 b 21) 'The fool ran away.' [Midágan is a real volitional form.]
Nakasáqad man ming ádtu mi manihápun run. (2 b 33) 'We have promised that we would eat supper there.' [Nakasáqad is a real potential form.]
Kádtung únang nagqabáng ngánhi nagbayád silág kwarínta. (3 b 26) 'The previous tenants paid forty pesos a month.' [Nagqabáng and nagbayád are real durative forms.]
Nangáqun lang naq dínhaq sa mangá súbra sa nangalíguq. (4 a 26) 'They are merely eating the leftovers of the people who are swimming.' [Nangáqun and nangalíguq are real forms, from bases containing the prefix paN-.]
Uh, nakakitáq ka ánang taytáyan? (4 a 27) 'Oh, do you see that bridge?' [Nakakitáq is a real potential form.]

4 B 2. Unreal

The five uses of unreal active verb forms are described below.

(a) The unreal refers to actions that have not yet taken place or conditions that have not yet come into being. These include actions or conditions with FUTURE meaning ('someone will do X' or 'X will happen') or with HORTATORY meaning (let's [do]' or 'someone should [do]'):

Mu ni siyá si Mis Wílbi nga muqábang sa usá sa mangá kwártu. (3 c 3) 'This is Miss Wilby. She is going to rent one of the rooms.' [Muqábang is an unreal volitional form, here with future meaning.]
Mangutána ta. (3 a 8) 'Let's ask.' [Mangutána is an unreal form (from a base pangutána containing the paN-prefix), here with hortatory meaning.]
Maghuwát lang kug láqin. (3 c 34) 'I will just wait for another one.' [Maghuwát is an unreal durative form, here with future meaning.]
Ikáw lay magpíliq. (3 b 22) 'You choose.' [Magpíliq is an unreal durative form, here with hortatory meaning.]

(b) The unreal describes habitual or customary actions:

Dághan túqung mangági diháq. (3 a 27) 'Many go by there.'

(c) The unreal is used after the prepositives mahímuq 'can' and gústu 'want.'

Gústu siyáng mutánqaw run. (3 b 16) 'She would like to look at it now.'
Mahímuq bang mangutána? (3 a 14) 'May I ask a question?'

(d) The unreal form is used in negative active sentences (remember that real forms are used only for affirmative: 4 B 1 above). Unreal forms with the negative díliq 'not' refer to future time or habitual (customary) actions; those with waláq 'not' refer to past time.

Díliq ku musugút. 'I will not agree (to do it).'
Waq mi maglisúd. 'We did not have a hard time.'

(e) The unreal potential means 'be able to' and refers to past, present, or future time:

Átung tanqáwun ug makasakáy ba tas píkqap. (4 a 8) 'Let us see if we can catch one of the irregular trips.'
Sa panahún sa mangá Katsílaq, kasagáran sa mangá táwu díliq makasulát. 'During the Spanish times [when the Philippines were under Spanish domination], most of the people did not know how to write.'

The differences in meaning between volitional, durative, and potential forms are described in Lesson 5.)

Pattern Practice PP-G; Exercises 4.II, 5.IV, 6.II B.

4 C. 'There are many' and 'there are few'

The expressions dághan nga X and dyútay nga X mean 'there are many X's' and 'there are few X's' respectively:

Dághang bábuy. (4 a 22) 'There are many pigs.'
Dyútay ra kaqáyung ságing. 'There are very few bananas.'

4 D. Kanúsqa vs. anúsqa 'when?'

Kanúsqa 'when?' is used with either real (past time) or unreal (future or habitual) active forms; anúsqa 'when?' is used with unreal actives only:

Anúsqa ka man mubálik sa ínyu? or
Kanúsqa ka man mubálik sa ínyu? 'When will you go back to your place?'
Kanúsqa [but not anúsqa] ka pa man miqabút? 'When did you arrive?'

4 E. The symbol -N-

The symbol -N- in paN-,* naN-, and maN- represents a nasal sound (m, n, ng) which combines with the sound after it—the first sound of the base form to which it is prefixed—in certain regular ways, as follows:

When the first sound of the base is—	-N- plus the first sound of the base produces—
p or b	m
t or d or s	n
k or ng	ng
a vowel	ng plus the vowel
l	ngl or nl
Some other consonant, or a cluster of more than one consonant	ng plus the consonant or consonant cluster

Examples:

prefix		base		
paN-	+	putúl	=	pamutúl 'cut'
paN-	+	báhin	=	pamáhin 'divide'
paN-	+	tábang	=	panábang 'help'
paN-	+	dágan	=	panágan 'run'
paN-	+	sulát	=	panulát 'write'
paN-	+	kúhaq	=	pangúhaq 'get, obtain'
paN-	+	ngálan	=	pangálan 'name'

* The prefix paN- is of a different type than the active prefixes: it is attached directly to verb bases, forming new bases to which further affixes may be added. This process and the effect on the meaning is described in detail in Lesson 11; until then it will be useful for you to observe the ways in which various elements in Cebuano verb forms are put together.

paN-	+	inúm	=	panginúm 'drink'
paN-	+	lútuq	=	panglútuq or panlútuq 'cook'
paN-	+	hísgut	=	panghísgut 'discuss'
paN-	+	galíng	=	panggalíng 'grind'
paN-	+	warawára	=	pangwarawára 'wave'
paN-	+	náytklab	=	pangnáytklab 'go to a night club'
paN-	+	máymay	=	pangmáymay 'regret'

4F. Indirect questions

Indirect questions are questions quoted after words meaning ask, wonder, doubt, know, tell, etc. (I asked him how old he was; he told me what his name was.) Cebuano indirect questions are introduced by the particles kung, kun, or ug, and except for this introductory particle, they have the same components as direct questions.

Nangutána siyá ug muqánhi ka ba. 'He asked if you were coming.'
Nangutána siyá kun ása siyá makasakáyg dyip. 'He asked where he could catch a jeep.'
Waláq siyá magsúlti ug anúsqa siyá muqánhi. 'He did not say when he would come.'

Pattern Practices and Exercises

IA. (Review) Basing your completions on the picture on page 146, insert one of the following into the blanks in the sentences below: arí, ádtu, ánhi, dínhi, ánhaq, diháq, dínhaq, dirí, dídtu, ngádtu, ngánhi, ngarí. (1 A 2 and subsections)

1. (C-D) Nuy, muqígut man diqáy tung taytayána__________.
2. (A-B) Paqabúta ku kay muqánhaq ku__________. 'Wait for me . . . '
3. (A-B) Mangádtu ta__________ sa baybáay ha?
4. (C-D) Náqa bay táwu__________s ímung balaybálay?
5. (D-C) Waláq na. __________y dághang táwu ganíhang búntag, pirú nanglákaw na.
6. (C-BA)__________ ta áring balaybaláya kay waláq nay táwu__________.
7. (D-C) Kádtung mangá táwung__________ __________s dágat nangalíguq. __________silá ganínas ákung balaybálay.
8. (F-B) Dúna bay makáqun__________ánang ímung gidalá?
9. (B-F) Unyáq na lang mi muqánhaq__________ kay __________ pa mi __________ sa baybáay.
10. (C-D) Taná Nuy, __________tas dágat.
11. (D-C) Kanáng ínyung dalá__________ása man diqáy naq nínyu ibutáng?
12. (C-D) __________lang nátuq__________sa lántay ibutáng ang átung dalá.
13. (D-C) Dúna man guy irúq__________. Tingálig kánqun nyaq naq.

A
B
C
D
E
F

14. (E-F) kádtu prútas nga átung dalá átung dádqun __________.
15. (F-E) _________ ta _________s dágat mangáqun?

IB. (PP-B of Lesson 2 may be practiced before this exercise.) Answer the following, using deictics in your answers. (1 A 2 and subsections; 2 A 2)

1. Ásā padúung ning tráka?
2. Háqin man siyá run?
3. Uy, ása man diqáy ta mangalíguq?
4. Ásā mang lugára dínhi ang díliq bahúq?
5. Nuy, ása man mi pahúway?
6. Háqin man nang níndut nga kaliguqánan?
7. Diqín man mu maghulát ug sakyanán?
8. Diqín mang ristawrána mu mupahúway?
9. Ásā pa man tung dyip nga átung sákyan?
10. Diqín ka man nga nabasáq ka man?
11. Háqin man tung bag?
12. Ásā na man tung ákung mangá dalá?
13. Háqin man tung súkiq nákung tigúwang?
14. Diqín man mu mangalíguq?
15. Háqin man ang Talísay?

PP-G Active verbs (4 A)

Step I. (Substituting verb)

'They will get on a bus.'

Musakáy silág traak.	(nagsakáy)
Nagsakáy silág traak.	(magsakáy)
Magsakáy silág traak.	(nakasakáy)
Nakasakáy silág traak.	(makasakáy)
Makasakáy silág traak.	(manakáy)
Manakáy silág traak.	(gasakáy)
Gasakáy silág traak.	(nagbántay)
Nagbántay silág traak.	(magbántay)
Magbántay silág traak.	(nakabántay)
Nakabántay silág traak.	(makabántay)
Makabántay silág traak.	(mibántay)
Mibántay silág traak.	(mamántay)

Mamántay silág traak. (namántay)

Namántay silág traak.

Step II. (Real vs. unreal)

'He saw that bridge yesterday.'

Nakakitáq siyá ánang taytáyan gahápun. (úgmaq)

Makakitáq siyá ánang taytáyan úgmaq. (mangítaq)

Mangítaq siyá ánang taytáyan úgmaq. (karún)

{Mangítaq / Nangítaq} siya ánang taytáyan karún. (ganína)

Nangítaq siyá ánang taytáyan ganína. (úgmaq)

Mangítaq siyá ánang taytáyan úgmaq. (muqági)

Muqági siyá ánang taytáyan úgmaq. (karún)

{Muqági / Niqági} siyá ánang taytáyan karún. (ganína)

Niqági siyá ánang taytáyan ganína. (nakaqagí)

Nakaqagí siyá ánang taytáyan ganína. (gahápun)

Nakaqagí siyá ánang taytáyan gahápun. (úgmaq)

Makaqagí siyá ánang taytáyan úgmaq. (silá)

Makaqagí silá ánang taytáyan úgmaq. (mangádtu)

Mangádtu silá ánang taytáyan úgmaq. (karún)

Mangádtu silá ánang taytáyan karún. (gahápun)

Nangádtu silá ánang taytáyan gahápun. (ganína)

Nangádtu silá ánang taytáyan ganína. (mitánqaw)

Mitánqaw silá ánang taytáyan ganína. (úgmaq)

Mutánqaw silá ánang taytáyan úgmaq. (makatánqaw)

Makatánqaw silá ánang taytáyan úgmaq. (gahápun)

Nakatánqaw silá ánang taytáyan gahápun. (ganína)

Nakatánqaw silá ánang taytáyan ganína. (karún)

Makatánqaw silá ánang taytáyan karún.

Step III. (Verbs with and without <u>waláq</u> and <u>díliq</u>)

'Juan was able to get a jeep.'

Nakasakáyg dyip si Hwan. (waláq)

Waláq makasakáyg dyip si Hwan. (díliq)

Díliq makasakáyg dyip si Hwan. ('he can')

Makasakáyg dyip si Hwan. (makapalít)

Makapalít ug dyip si Hwan. (waláq)

Waláq makapalít ug dyip si Hwan.	(díliq)
Díliq makapalít ug dyip si Hwan.	('he can')
Makapalít ug dyip si Hwan.	('he has')
Nakapalít ug dyip si Hwan.	(mipalít)
Mipalít ug dyip si Hwan.	(waláq)
Waláq mupalít ug dyip si Hwan.	(díliq)
Díliq mupalít ug dyip si Hwan.	('he was buying')
Nagpalít ug dyip si Hwan.	(waláq)
Waláq magpalít ug dyip si Hwan.	(díliq)
Díliq magpalít ug dyip si Hwan.	('he will be buying')
Magpalít ug dyip si Hwan.	(nakakitáq)
Nakakitáq ug dyip si Hwan.	(waláq)
Waláq makakitáq ug dyip si Hwan.	(díliq)
Díliq makakitáq ug dyip si Hwan.	('he can')
Makakitáq ug dyip si Hwan.	('he has')
Nakakitáq ug dyip si Hwan.	

Step IV. (Verbs with and without _waláq_ and _díliq_, with subject _siyá_)

'He has eaten some bread.'

Nakakaqún siyág paan.	(waláq)
Waláq siyá makakaqúg paan.	(díliq)
Díliq siyá makakaqúg paan.	('he can')
Makakaqún siyág paan.	(mikáqun)
Mikáqun siyág paan.	(waláq)
Waláq siyá mukáqug paan.	(díliq)
Díliq siyá mukáqug paan.	('he will')
Mukáqun siyág paan.	(nagkaqún)
Nagkaqún siyág paan.	(waláq)
Waláq siyá magkaqúg paan.	(nagdalá)
Nagdalá siyág paan.	(waláq)
Waláq siyá magdalág paan.	(díliq)
Díliq siyá magdalág paan.	(nakadalá)
Nakadalá siyág paan.	(waláq)
Waláq siyá makadalág paan.	(díliq)
Díliq siyá makadalág paan.	(nagkúhaq)
Nagkúhaq siyág paan.	(waláq)
Waláq siyá magkúhag paan.	(díliq)

Díliq siyá magkúhag paan.	(nakakuháq)
Nakakuháq siyág paan.	(waláq)
Waláq siyá makakuhág paan.	(díliq)
Díliq siyá makakuhág paan.	('he can')
Makakuháq siyág paan.	('he has')
Nakakuháq siyág paan.	

IC. (Before performing this exercise, do steps III and IV of PP-G, p. 148f.) Answer the following questions in the negative. Change <u>na</u> to <u>pa</u> and <u>pa</u> to <u>na</u>. (2 B)

1. Nagquwán pa ba?
2. Manakáy ta ánang trákang punúq na man naq?
3. Mahímuq bang akúy mudalá sa ímung mangá dalá?
4. Mukáqun ka bag áyskrim?
5. Nakakaqún ka na bag haluqháluq?
6. Gitúgnaw ka na ba? (If you use the verb, change it to <u>tugnawá</u>.)
7. Náqa na ba ang ákung súking tigúwang?
8. Níqa bas Yáru nang átung pangitáqun?
9. Magdalá pa ba kug túbig?
10. Mahádluk ka bang muqágis taytáyan?
11. Dúgay pa bang mulárga ang dyip?
12. Gústu ka na bang mupaqúliq?
13. Akú lay báyad ha?
14. Makapahúlay ba ta dínhis ínyung baybáay?
15. Ádtu na ta ha, kay gitúgnaw na ku.

ID. Ibutáng sa lunáq ang mangá púlung <u>díliq</u>, <u>waláq</u>, u <u>ayáw</u>. (2 B)

1. _________ pagsakáy ánang traak kay _________ naq muqádtus Talísay. 'Don't get on that bus because it doesn't go to Talisay.'
2. __________ ta kasakáy ánaq kay __________ nay lugár. 'We can't get on that one because there's no more room.'
3. __________ ba ta maglisúd ug sakáy pagbálik? 'Won't we have a hard time getting a ride back?'
4. __________ bay irúq dínhi? 'Aren't there any dogs here?'
5. __________ silá mabasáq sa ulán. 'They didn't get wet in the rain.'
6. __________ kamí mabasáq kay mamasílung mi inigqulán. 'We won't get wet because we'll take shelter when it rains.'
7. __________ na lang mug pamasílung kay __________ nay ulán. 'Don't take shelter because it's not raining any more.'

8. ________ mi makahátag ug haluqháluq kay ________ na may áyskrim. 'We can't serve halo-halo because there's no more ice cream.'

9. Ang haluqháluq _________ ba mahál?

10. Kun __________ siyá gústug haluqháluq___________g hatági. 'If he doesn't want halo-halo don't give him any.'

11. Ikáw, _________ pagbáyad ha. Kamí lang. 'Don't pay—let us.'

12. _________ diqáy ni muqádtus Dyuns Abinyú Bay?

13. _________ ni muqádtu kay ánhi ra ni sa Liin.

14. Ug _________ ka muhatúd, _________ na lang. 'If you don't want to take us, never mind.'

15. _________ mi manáqug dínhi kay layúq pang Dyuns Abinyú. 'We won't get off here because Jones Avenue is still far away.'

IE. (PP-E of Lesson III may be reviewed before this exercise is begun.) Rewrite the following sentences, inserting the words in parentheses. (3 C 3 and subsections)

1. Mangádtu mi sa Talísay. (díliq)
2. Tanqáwun nátug makasakáy pa ba ta. (kinahánglan)
3. Mirlí, mulárga ba ta dáyun? (díliq)
4. Mangalíguq ta dínhi. (ánhi)
5. Mamaqúliq pa ba ta? (anúsqa)
6. Dágan lang sa taytáyan. (ayáw)
7. Súkiq ku nang tiguwánga. (díliq)
8. Mamahúlay ta dínhis baybáay. (kinahánglan)
9. Diq na ta pahatúd sa Dyuns Abinyú. (kinahánglan)
10. Magkítaq ta pagqusáb. (anúsqa)
11. Mubálik ku dáyun sa Sibú. (gústu)
12. Magbántay tag traak dínhi. (ánhi)
13. Muqádtu ba ni sa Púquk Bay? (díliq)
14. Mamahúlay mu dínhis baybáay? (ánhi)
15. Káqun lang sa haluqháluq. (ayáw)

IF. (PP-E may be reviewed before this exercise is begun.) Make the following sentences negative. (2 B, 3 C 3 a)

1. Sakáy na mu kay dághan nang táwu. 'Get on (the bus) because there are many people.' (Change na to úsaq.)
2. Ádtu ba nis Yáru? (Change ádtu to muqádtu.)
3. Nakakitáq ka niqánang taytáyan? (Change nakakitáq to makakitáq: 4 B 2 d.)
4. Ánhaq ta diháq ági. (Change ági to muqági.)

5. Mahádluk ra ba kung muqági ánang taytayána.
6. Lakáw ug kusúg arún diq ka mahúlug. 'Walk quickly so you won't fall.'
7. Akúy mudalá sa ímung butáng.
8. Makapahúlay ba ta dínhis balaybálay?
9. Gitúgnaw man ku karún. (Change gitúgnaw to tugnawá.)
10. Dághan ganínang mangá táwu.
11. Miqulán ba ganína? 'Did it rain a while ago?' (Cf. 4 B 2 d.)
12. Nabasáq ba si Mírli sa ulán? (Change nabasáq to mabasáq.)
13. Mudirítsu sa Sibú kiníng tráka.
14. Miqádtu na ba ni sa Tángki Bay? (Change na to pa.)
15. Musakáy na ta kay dirítsu man nis Sibú. (Change na to pa.)

II. Pilíqa ang hústung púrma sa bírbu nga náqa sa sulúd sa parentheses. (4 B and subsections)

1. (Nadúgay, Madúgay) mi kay waq mi (makasakáy, nakasakáy) dáyun. 'We are late because we couldn't get on (a jeep) right away.'
2. Kun waq pa (mapunúq, napunúq) ang traak díliq úntaq mi (nadúgay, madúgay). 'If the bus hadn't been full, we wouldn't have been late.'
3. (Magdalíq, Nagdalíq) ta kay kagabhiqán unyáq ta. 'Let's hurry or we won't get there before night (lit. we'll be overtaken by night).'
4. (Mipaqúliq, Mupaqúliq) na ang mangá táwu nga dínhi ganíha. 'The people who were here before went home.'
5. (Mamahúway, Namahúway) mi sa baybáay pagqádtu námuq sa Púquk. 'We rested in the shack when we went to Pook.'
6. Ang mangá táwung (nangalíguq, mangalíguq) dínhi sa búntag (namaqúliq, mamaqúliq) na. 'The people who were swimming here this morning have gone home now.'
7. Si Mírli (nangutána, mangutána) ug ása silá (malíguq, nalíguq). 'Merlie is asking where they are going to swim.'
8. Pagqabút námuq (nanglákaw, manglákaw) na ang mangá táwu. 'When we arrived, the people had already gone away.'
9. (Nakakaqún, Makakaqún) ka na bag haluqháluq? 'Have you ever eaten halo-halo?'
10. (Mupaqúliq, Mipaqúliq) na ta kay gabíqi na. 'Let's go home; (because) it's dark now.'
11. Kanáng dyip (magpaqingún, nagpaqingún) dínhi maqúy átung sákyan. 'The jeep coming here is the one we should get on.'
12. (Nagdalá, Magdalá) mig makáqun pagqádtu námuq sa Talísay. 'We took food along when we went to Talisay.'
13. Inigqabút nátuq sa Púquk (malíguq, nalíguq) ta dáyun. 'When we get to Pook, let's go in right away.'

14. (Mabasáq, Nabasáq) siyá kay (nagqulán, magqulán) man. 'She got wet because it was raining.'

15. (Muqági, Miqági) pa ba nis Tángki Bay? 'Is this (bus) going by Tangke first (before going to Cebu)?'

16. Kadtúng (nagqabáng, magqabáng) dínhi (magbayád, nagbayád) tug kwarínta písus.

17. (Mahibáwu, Nahibáwu) ka bag ása ang ílang Mísis Abilyána?

18. (Makahángyuq, Nakahángyuq) ba mi niqánang abangán?

19. (Magpíliq, Nagpíliq) silág kwártung dakúq. 'They are going to pick a large room.'

20. Ang (magpuyúq, nagpuyúq) sa táqas maqúy ákung anák.

21. (Nadúgay, Madúgay) si Mírli pagqabút.

22. (Magpaqábut, Nagpaqábut) silá ug sakyanán sa Liin sa miqáging Dumínggu. 'They waited for transportation at the Lane last Sunday.'

23. (Mubálik, Mibálik) ba dáyun ning tráka Bay?

24. (Mitánqaw, Mutánqaw) kug níndut ba ang Yáru. 'I want to see if Yarrow is nice.'

25. Ang píkqap (makalárga, nakalárga) dáyun kay dalíq rang (napunúq, mapunúq) ug sumasákay. 'The bus left right away because it was quickly filled with passengers.'

III A. Ibúngat ang mangá musunúd nga mangá túdling púlung sa hústung paníngug. (Review of 234 command or statement intonation: p. 24.)

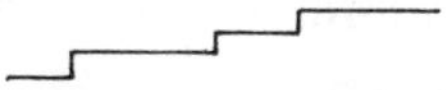

1.	Musakáy tag traak.	(4.2)
2.	Ádtu tas Talísay.	(4.2)
3.	Aa, ayáw na lang.	(1.14)
4.	Diq pa ra ba punúq ning traak daq.	(4.4)
5.	Madúgay ta íni.	(4.5)
6.	Dúgay kaqáy tang kalárga íni.	(4.6)
7.	Ádtu tas píkas magbántay.	(4.7)
8.	Waq man kaqáyu mi maglisúd.	(2 b 18)
9.	Átung tanqáwun ug makasakáy ba tag píkqap.	(4.8)
10.	Aa, níqay dyip.	(4.9)

III B. Review of 423 statement intonations: cf. 3.V B, p. 121.

1.	Padúung tingáli nis Tabunúk.	(4.10)
2.	Ákuq lang ibílin ning ákung amígu dínhi.	(1.16)

3. Ánhaq ta diháq ági. (4.27)
4. Dúnay dághan kaqáyung mangá baybáayng gágmay. (4.28)
5. Dung, dádqun ka námuq sa Amiriká. (2 b 22)
6. Náqay gapuyúq diháng tigúwang. (4.29)
7. Ákuq nang súkiq. (4.30)
8. Maw ni siyá ang nangítag kwártu. (3 b 13)
9. Pilíqun nátuq nang mudirítsus Sibú. (4.45)
10. Níqa say usá sa ubús. (3 b 21)
11. Díliq. Dirítsu nis Sibú. (4.47)
12. Unyáq gisáktag mangá prútas. (4.59)
13. Líbri man gung sugáq ug túbig. (3 b 27)
14. Níndut gyud naq. (4.60)
15. Mu ni si Índay. (3 c 4)

III C. The intonation symbolized 423 (a drop on the penult and a rise on the end) is also used for questions. Pronounce the following sentences with 423 intonation.

1. Únsa may átuq? (1.3)
2. Ása man ta musakáy ug muqádtu tas Banáwaq? (3 a 16)
3. Ása man ta ádtu? (4.15)
4. Ása man tang lugára sa Talísay muqádtu? (4.16)
5. Ása man tung baay ni Mísis Abilyána? (3 a 1)
6. Unsálan man nang haluqháluq? (4.58)
7. Pilá may bayranán ánaq sa káda búwan? (3 b 25)
8. Pilá may bayranán? (4.61)

IV A. Pagbása (Reading)

1. Retell the story in your own words.
2. Answer the questions.
3. Do Exercise IV C on the verbs of the story.

Pagsakáys Dyip (Riding the Jeep)

Mis Wílbi: Pirlá, muqádtu ka run sa ka Dúktur Pirnándis?

Pírla: Díliq ku muqádtu kay muqabút si Kulása run.

Mis Wílbi: Ánhi lang ka dínhi kay mulakáw kus Magalyánis. Ása man ku musakáy?

Pírla: Ádtu sa iskína Sansyángku Piláys ka musakáy. Maghuwát lang ku nímu dínhi.

Mis Wílbi: Ádtu na ku. Mubálik lang ku dáyun.

Pírla: Sigí, magdalíq tingáli ka. ('You probably should hurry.') Díliq nyaq ka makasakáyg dyip.

(Taqudtaqúd)

Pírla: Uh, níqa ka na man lagí. ('Why, you're back again!') Waláq diqáy ka makaqádtu* sa Magalyánis?

Mis Wílbi: Waláq ku makaqádtu* kay waláq ku makasakáys dyip. Dághan kaqáyung táwu.

Pírla: Maqáyu rang waláq ka mudayún kay waláq ka makadalág báyads dyip. (dayún 'go ahead and . . .)

Mis Wílbi: Pastilán, túqud nu? Magqúnsa na lang úntaq kug nakadayún kug sakáy? ('What would I have done if I had gone ahead and got on?')

Pírla: Maqáy ra gyung waláq ka makasakáy.

IV B. Mangá Pangutána

1. Muqádtu ba si Pírla sa ka Duktur Pirnándis? Ug díliq, ngánu man?
2. Kínsa may muqabút karún?
3. Ása man si Mis Wílbi padúung?
4. Muqádtu ba sad si Pírla sa Magalyánis?
5. Ása man si Pírla maghuwát?
6. Madúgay ba si Mis Wílbi ngádtu?
7. Ngánung kinahánglan man si Mis Wílbing magdalíq?
8. Ngánung mibálik man dáyun si Mis Wílbi?
9. Nakasakáy ba siyá?
10. Ngánu mang maqáyu rang waláq siyá makasakáy?

IV C. Exercise on actives (4 A). (To follow PP-G.) Insert prefixes and suffixes.

Pagsakáys Dyip

Mis Wílbi: Pirlá, (ádtu) ka run sa ka Dúktur Pirnándis?

Pírla: Díliq ku (ádtu) kay (abút) si Kulása run.

Mis Wílbi: Ánhi lang ka dínhi kay (lakáw) kus Magalyánis. Ása man ku (sakáy)?

---

* Muqádtu is also possible in this context.

Pírla: Ádtu sa iskína Sansyángku Piláys ka (sakáy). (Huwát) lang ku nímu dínhi.

Mis Wílbi: Ádtu na ku. (Bálik) lang ku dáyun.

Pírla: Sigí, (dalíq) tingáli ka. ('You probably should hurry.') Díliq nyaq ka (sakáy) ug dyip.

(Taqudtaqúd)

Pírla: Uh, níqa ka na man lagí. ('Why, you're back again!') Waláq diqáy ka (ádtu) sa Magalyánis?

Mis Wílbi: Waláq ku (ádtu) kay waláq ku (sakáy) sa dyip. Dághan kaqáyung táwu.

Pírla: Maqáyu rang waláq ka (dayún) kay waláq ka (dalá) ug báyads dyip.

Mis Wílbi: Pastilán, túqud nu? Magqúnsa na lang úntaq ku ug (dayún) pa kug sakáy. ('What would I have done if I had gone ahead and got on?')

Pírla: Maqáy ra gyung waláq ka (sakáy).

V. Sultiqánay (Conversation)

Si Dyuu ug si Pídru Nalíguq sa Talísay

A: Dalíq na Dyuu. Muqádtu pa ra ba tas Gútsan.

B: Ánhi lang ta sa Dyuns sakáyg dyip pára sa Talísay Dru.

A: Na, sigí. Ása man tang dapíta sa Talísay malíguq?

B: Ádtu lang tas Púquk.

A: Unyáq díliq tingáli ta kasakáyg dyip inigpaqúliq kay dyútay ra mang dyip ngádtus Púquk.

B: Hústu túqud nu. Ádtu na lang tas Yáru.

1. Si Pídru ug si Dyuu dídtu sa Dyuns musakáy ug dyip.
2. Ádtu silá malíguq sa Púquk.
3. Díliq silá malíguq sa Púquk kay díliq tingáli silá makasakáy inigpaqúliq.
4. Si Dyuu ug si Pídru ádtu na lang sa Yáru malíguq.

(Sa dídtu na silá sa Yáru)

A: Dyuu, ádtu ta dídtu mamahúway ádtung baybáay.

B: Diq ku gústu kay mangági pa ta sa taytáyan.

A: Ngánu, mahádluk ka ba muqági?

B: Uu, gaqigutqigút man naq.

A: Aa, diq ka mahúug. Lakáw lag kusúg.

B: Na sigí. (Nagdagán)
Kínsa may tagqíya ánaq, Pidrú?

A: Si Nuy Ántuy. Túqa ra ay! Ákuq naq siyáng súkiq.

5. Mangági pa silág taytáyan ug ádtu silá mamahúway sa súking Pídru.
6. Waláq kaqáyu magqigutqigút ang taytáyan.
7. Nahúug silá pagqági nila sa taytáyan.
8. Súkiq ni Pídru si Nuy Ántuy.

A: Taná Dyuu. Mamaqúliq na ta. Gitúgnaw na ku.

B: Maqáyu sab kay mu rag muqulán.

A: Níqay traak nga muqági sa Tabunúk. Manakáy ta áni.

B: Karí lang díqang dyip nga dirítsu sa Sibúy átung sákyan.

A: Sigí ug muhatúd siyá dirítsu sa Dyuns Abinyú.

B: Uu. Tutál duhá man ta ka buqúk.

9. Si Pídru gitúgnaw sa íyang pagkalíguq.
10. Gitúgnaw silá kay nagqulán.
11. Gústu siláng musakáy dirítsu sa Dyuns.

LESSON 5. A CONVERSATION WITH VILLAGERS

Sagquluhúnun (Basic Sentences)

First Part	Únang Báhin
Miss Wilby goes to Miss Santos' town, Pulambato.	Miqádtu si Mis Wílbi sa ílang Mis Sántus sa Pulambatú.
how nice!	kaníndut
[marker for noun after an exclamatory word]	sa
your place	ínyu
Perla	Pírla
[exclamation upon finding out something]	uy
quiet, silent	hílum
very	kaqáyu
1. How nice your place is Perla. (It is) very quiet!	*1. Kaníndut ngánhis ínyu Pirlá uy, hílum kaqáyu.

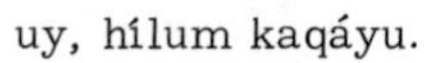

that's the way it is	mu gyud
Sunday	Dumínggu
because	man

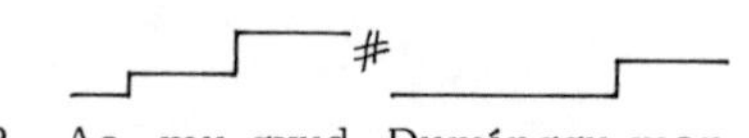

2. Ah, naturally, because it's Sunday.	*2. Aa, mu gyud, Dumínggu man.
there is here	níqa
[existential particle]	y
old man	tigúwang
[pointer for something not seen by person spoken to]	uh
3. Ah, here comes an old man.	3. Aa, níqay tigúwang uh.
[term of address to male older than speaker]	Nuy
[masculine name]	Tibúq (short for Tiburcio)
come here	dalíq
[particle making command more polite]	ra gud

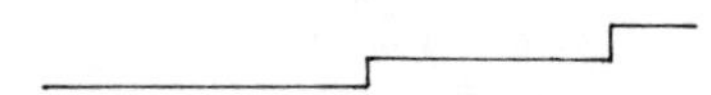

4. Tibo (lit. Noy Tibo), please come here. — 4. Nuy Tibúq, dalíq ra gud.

5. Good morning, Tibo (lit. Noy Tibo). — 5. Maqáyung búntag Nuy Tibúq.

this is	kiní
my	ákuq
[linker between ákuq and kaqúban]	nga
companion	kaqúban.

6. This is Miss Wilby, my friend (lit. my companion). — 6. Kiní si Mis Wílbi, ákung ... kaqúban.

how are you?	kumústa
[form of address to male older than speaker; used only to country people]	Iyúq

7. How are you? (How are you, Uncle?) — 7. Kumústa Iyúq?

is the one	mu
[subject marker]	y
most	labí
[linker between labí and tigúwang]	nga
old (in age)	tigúwang
person	táwu
in	sa
[linker between ámuq and lúngsud]	nga
town	lúngsud

8. This is Tibo. He is the oldest person in our town. (Lit. This Noy Tibo, he is . . .) — 8. Kiní si Nuy Tibúq, mu niy ... labíng tigúwang táwu sa ámung ... lúngsud.

is that so?	mu ba

9. Ah, is that so?	9. Aa, mu ba?
how much?	pilá
now (as contrasted with formerly)	na
[question particle after interrogative]	man
[following interrogative for clarifying some information]	diqáy
age	idád
your	nímu
[form of address for male older than speaker; used only to country people]	Iyúq
10. How old are you now? (Lit. Then, how much is your age now, Iyo?)	10. Pilá na man diqáy idád nímu Iyúq?
now	karún
around	mga
ninety-eight	nubintayqútsu
already	na
now	run (short for karún)
11. Ah, now? I am (already) about ninety-eight years old now.	*11. Aa, karún? Mga nubintayqútsu na ku run.
what! you don't say!	ha
my!	sus
how big!	kadakúq
now	na
[particle with exclamation over something the speaker has noticed]	gud
you	nímu
[particle meaning 'have' which follows an adjective]	ug
age	idád
12. What! Ninety-eight! My! What a ripe old age! (Lit. What a big age you have!)	*12. Ha? Nubintayqútsu! Sus, kadakúq na gud nímug idád!

how old!	katigúwang
now (as contrasted with formerly)	na
[particle with newly acquired information]	diqáy

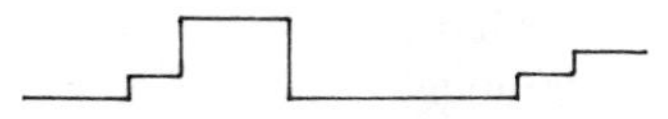

13. How old you are!	13. Katigúwang na diqáy nímu!
how (in the past)?	giqúnsa
[question particle after interrogative]	man
reach (a place or time)	pagqabút
particular age	idára
14. How did you reach that age?	14. Giqúnsa man nímu pagqabút ... ánang idára?
easy	sayún
very	ra
15. Ah, that's very easy.	15. Aa, sayún ra naq.
drink	inúm
merely	lang
[particle preceding goal]	ug
a	usá
[linker for usá and hungút]	ka
bowl made of coconut shell	húngut
(palm) toddy	tubáq
every	káda
day	ádlaw
16. I just drink a bowl of toddy every day.	*16. Inúm lang kug usá ka húngut ... tubáq káda ádlaw.

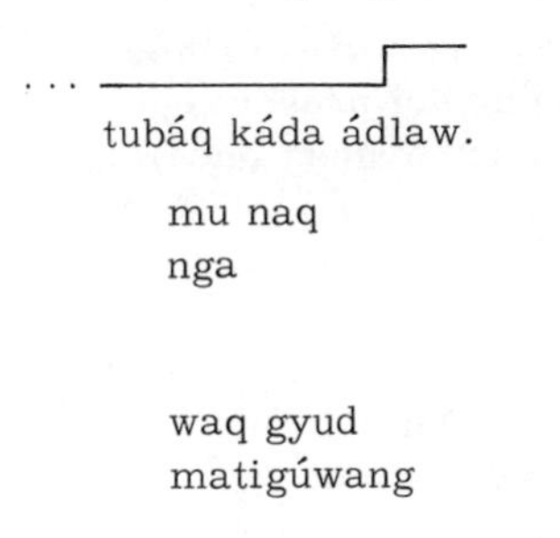

that is why	mu naq
[linker between mu naq and the rest of the sentence]	nga
never	waq gyud
become old	matigúwang
17. That is why I never did get old.	17. Mu nang waq gyud ku ... matigúwang.

that and no more	mu ra
[particle with newly acquired information]	diqáy
how easy!	kasayún
[particle: 'contrary to what I had previously thought']	aq

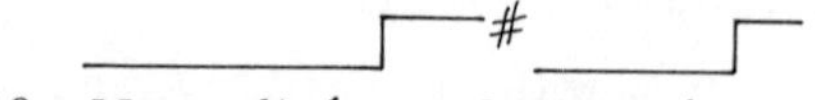

18. So, is that all? Heck, how easy!

18. Mu ra diqáy naq? Kasayún aq!

for sure	dyud (= gyud)
[existential particle]	y
children	anák

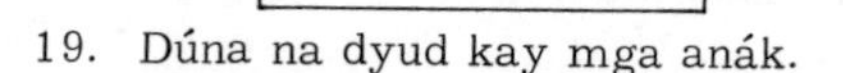

19. No doubt you have children.

19. Dúna na dyud kay mga anák.

four	upát
[numeral linker]	ka
[numeral counter]	buqúk

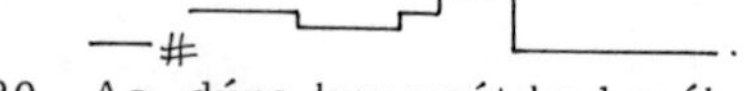

20. Umm, I have four children.

20. Aa, dúna kuy upát ka buqúk ... anák.

furthermore	unyáq
no doubt	gyud
also	sad
grandchildren	apú

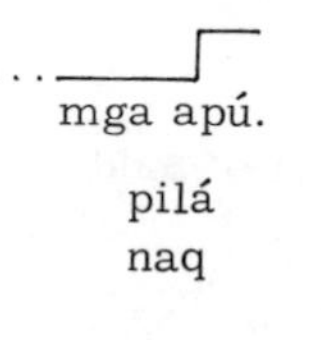

21. Also, no doubt you've got grandchildren, too.

21. Unyáq, dúna gyud sad kay ... mga apú.

how many?	pilá
that (referring to something not present but recently mentioned)	naq
they	silá

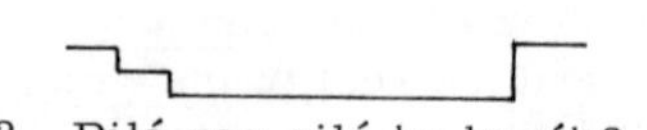

22. How many of them are there? (Lit. How many pieces are those they?)

22. Pilá naq silá ka buqúk?

many	dághan
no longer	diq na
even	gániq
can count	makaqiháp

23. Oh, there are many. I cannot even count them any more.

23. Aa, dúnay dághan. Diq na gániq ku makaqiháp.

that is so	bítaw
because	kay
have grandchildren	nangapú
already	na
even	gániq
probably	tingáli
grandchildren	apú

24. Yes, because even your grandchildren probably already have grandchildren.

24. Bítaw, kay nangapú na gániq tingáli ang ímung mga apú.

excuse me (interrupting conversation)	isáq pa diqáy
American	Amirkána
[form of address for woman same age as or younger than the speaker]	Day
is that not so?	nu

25. Excuse me. You're an American, aren't you?

25. Isáq pa diqáy, Amirkána ka Day nu?

of course	aw
yes	uu
American	Amirkána

26. Why, yes. I'm an American.

26. Aw uu. Amirkána.

you (plural)	mu
coconut	lubí
in	sa
your	ínyu
[linker between ínyu and dápit]	nga
place	dápit

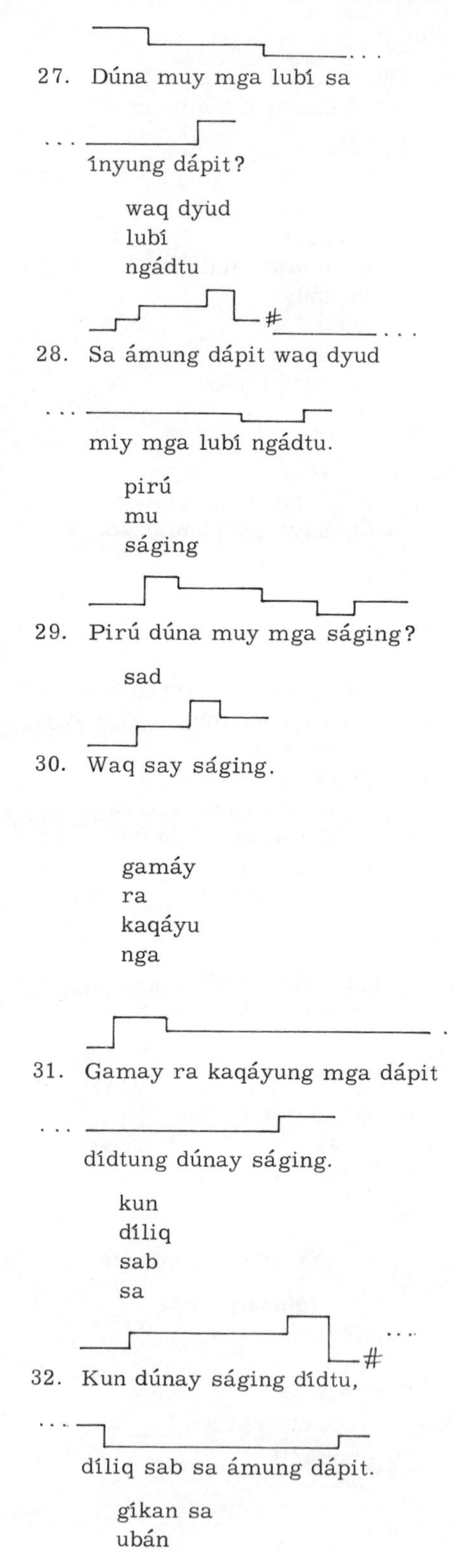

27. Do you have coconuts where you come from? (Lit. Do you have coconuts in your place?)	27. Dúna muy mga lubí sa ... ínyung dápit?
there aren't any at all	waq dyúd
coconuts	lubí
there	ngádtu
28. In my country, we have no coconuts at all.	28. Sa ámung dápit waq dyud ... miy mga lubí ngádtu.
but	pirú
you	mu
bananas	ságing
29. But do you have bananas?	29. Pirú dúna muy mga ságing?
also	sad
30. No. We don't have bananas either (lit. There are no bananas either).	30. Waq say ságing.
few	gamáy
very	ra
very	kaqáyu
[linker between dápit and dúnay ságing]	nga
31. There are only very few places there that have bananas.	31. Gamay ra kaqáyung mga dápit ... dídtung dúnay ságing.
if	kun
not	díliq
too	sab
from	sa
32. If there are bananas there, they are not home grown (lit. from our place) either.	32. Kun dúnay ságing dídtu, ... díliq sab sa ámung dápit.
come from	gíkan sa
other	ubán

[linker between ubán and lúngsud]	nga
town, country	lúngsud
are brought	gidáa
merely	lang
there	ngádtu

33. They are just brought there from other countries (towns).

*33. Gikan sa ubáng mga lúngsud, ... gidáa lang ngádtu.

very few	dyútay ra
they	silá
[particle meaning 'have' following an adjective]	ug
bananas	ságing
(to himself)	(sa íyang kaqugalíngun)

34. Ah, is that so? They (the people in America) have very few bananas.

*34. Aa, diqáy? Dyútay ra diqáy ... silág mga ságing.

Mga Pangutána

Únang Báhin

1. Kanáq bang baláy nga níndut maqúy ínyu Pirlá?
2. Kínsa man naq siyáng tiguwánga?
3. Ikáw ba si Iyúq Tibúq?
4. Kínsa man ning ímung kaqúban Pirlá?
5. Siyá ba ang labíng tigúwang dínhis ínyung lúngsud?
6. Pilá na may ímung idád Nuy Tibúq?
7. Nangapú ka na ba Nuy?
8. Unsáqun man pagqabút ánang idára Nuy?
9. Pilá ka húngut tubáq ang ímung maqinúm sa usá ka ádlaw?
10. Ug gústu kung matigúwang Nuy, unsáqun man nákuq?
11. Sayún ra ba pagqabút sa idád nga nubintayqútsu Nuy?
12. Pilá na ka buqúk ang ímung apú?
13. Amirkána kíning ímung ubán Pírla nu?
14. May lubí ba usáb sa Amiriká?

15. Dághan bang ságing sa ínyung dápit Mis Wílbi?
16. Diqíng lungsúra gíkan ang ságing?
17. Nangapú na sab ang ímung mga anák Nuy?
18. Diqín mang dapíta sa Amiriká ang dúnay dághang lubí?
19. Ngánung hílum man dínhi sa ínyu kun Dumínggu?
20. Ánhi ka ba dínhi mabúntag Nuy?

Pangutána (Matching)

Únang Báhin

1. Níqa ba ngánhi magpuyúq si Nuy Tibúq?
2. Hílum man lagí diqáy kaqáyu dínhi Pirlá.
3. Miqádtu na ba si Mis Wílbi sa Pulambatú?
4. Pilá na may idád mu karún Nuy Tibúq?
5. Dúna na bay asáwa ang tanán mung anák Nuy?
6. Díqin man gíkan kanáng tubáq Nuy?
7. Dághan ka na sab ug mga apú Nuy?
8. Amirkána ka Mis nu?
9. Dághan bag ságing sa ínyung dápit Day?

(a) Uu, may asáwa na siláng tanán.
(b) Sa ámuq? Díliq.
(c) Sus dághan. Diq na gániq ku makaqiháp kaníla.
(d) Waq na. Túqa na sa Sibú.
(e) Sus Day, tigúwang na ku kaqáyu. Nubintayqútsu na.
(f) Úqu ug misyunáryu* usáb.
(g) Mu gyud naq básta Dumínggu.
(h) Úqu. Kaqádtu nag kásqa.†
(i) Aa, kanáng tubáq gíkan sa lubí.

Sagquluhúnun (Basic Sentences)

Second Part	Ikaduháng Báhin
excuse me (interrupting a conversation)	taym pa
35. Excuse me. or Wait a second.	35. Taym pa.

---

* Misyunáryu 'missionary.'

† Ug kásqa 'one time.'

what is it that . . . ?	únsa man naq
[linker between naq and nadungúg]	nga
I	ákuq
[linker between ákuq and nadungúg]	nga
heard	nadungúg
36. What is it that I heard . . .	36. Únsa man nang ákung nadungúg,
that (linker between nadungúg and the rest of the sentence)	nga
when	kun
are asleep	natúug
we	mi
you (plural)	kamú
in	sa
are awake	magmatá
37. . . . that when we are asleep here, you in America are awake?	37. nga kun matúug mi ngánhi, kamú ngádtus Amiriká, magmatá?
and	ug
for example	pananglĩtan
when	ug
are awake	magmatá
are asleep	mangatúug
also (at the same time)	sab
38. And for example, when we are awake here, you are asleep there.	38. Ug pananglĩtag magmatá mi ngánhi, mangatúug sab mu dĩdtu.
39. Why is that? (Lit. What's that?)	39. Únsa man naq?
[word used to fill in when one cannot find the right word]	kuqán
because	man gud
that (just referred to)	naq

[form of address to male older than speaker]	Nuy 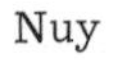
	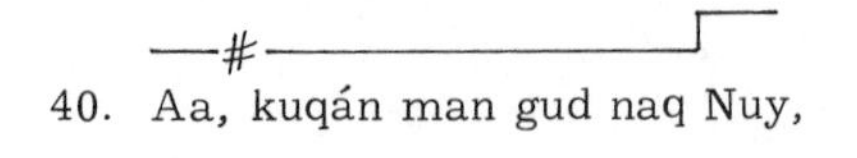
40. Ah . . . that is because . . . you know . . .	40. Aa, kuqán man gud naq Nuy,
it's like this	kiní gud
if, provided that	básta
night	gabíqi
	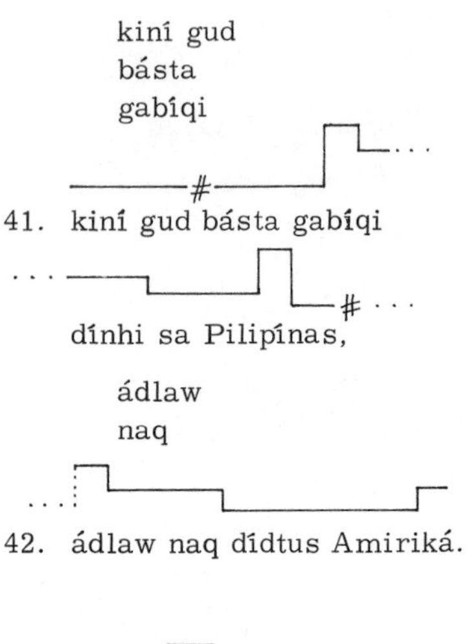
41. . . . it's like this. If it's night here in the Philippines . . .	41. kiní gud básta gabíqi dínhi sa Pilipínas,
day	ádlaw
that	naq
42. . . . it's daytime in America (lit. that's daytime there in America).	42. ádlaw naq dídtus Amiriká.
	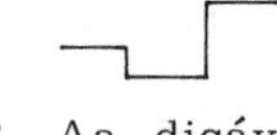
43. Oh, so that's it!	43. Aa, diqáy.
[particle used to change subject or introduce new one]	únyaq
because	kay
long	dúgay
because	man 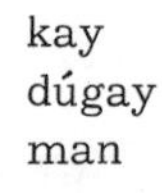
	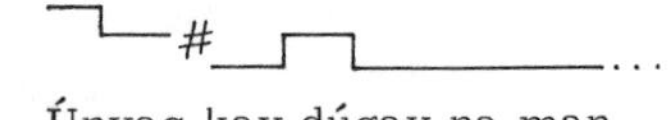
44. And then, since you have been here in the Philippines for a long time by now . . .	44. Únyaq kay dúgay na man ka dínhis Pilipínas,
if	ug
wants to marry	mangasáwa
[linker between mangasáwa and Pilipínu]	nga
Filipino	Pilipínu
will accept	musugút
by any chance	kaháq
you	ka
	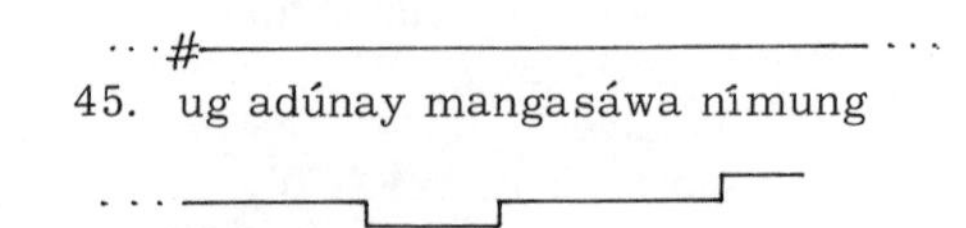
45. . . . if there is a Filipino who wants to marry you, would you by any chance accept?	45. ug adúnay mangasáwa nímung Pilipínu musugút kaháq ka?

of course	aw
would accept	musugút
if	ug
there's (no place meaning)	náqa
propose, ask a favor	muhángyuq

46. Of course I would accept if someone proposed (lit. if there is someone who proposes).

46. Aw, musugút ug náqay muhángyuq.

because	kay
not yet	waq pa
[question particles indicating disbelief]	ba gud
[particle used upon receiving new information]	diqáy

47. You mean to say (lit. Because) there hasn't been anyone yet?

47. Kay waq pa ba gud diqáy?

not yet	waq pa
at all	dyud
poor me	intáwun

48. Nobody at all yet (lit. Nobody at all yet Noy!); poor me.

48. Waq pa dyud intáwun Nuy.

always	kanúnay
this one	ni
[linker between kanúnay and nagpaqábut]	nga
waiting in expectation	nagpaqábut

49. But I am always waiting. (Lit. But this one is always waiting.)

*49. Píru kanúnay ning nagpaqábut.

come	ádtu
later on	nyaq
to	sa
house	baay
[particle used after commands to ask whether listener will comply]	ha

50. Come to the house later on, won't you?

50. Ádtu nyaq sa baay ha?

was invited	giqimbitár
[particle of contradiction]	man
I	ku
[particle preceding agent; = ni]	ng
their place	íla
[particle preceding infinitive]	ug
lunch	paniqúdtu

51. Er, Perla invited me to her (lit. their) place for lunch.

*51. Aa, giqimbitár man kung Pírla ngádtu sa ílag paniqúdtu.

perhaps	tingáli
if	ug
can go	makaqádtu
your place	ínyu
lunch	paniqúdtu
will drop by	muhapít

52. But perhaps if I get a chance to go to your place after lunch, I will drop by.

52. Píru tingáli, ug makaqádtu sa ínyu gíkan sa paniqúdtu, muhapít ku.

make sure	sigurúqa
[particle with imperative: 'make sure']	bayáq
make it a point	gyud
in order that	arún
children	bátaq
and	ug
grandchildren	apú
persons to be introduced	ipaqilaqíla
by me	ku
to you	kanímu

53. Make sure you do. Make a point of it, so that I may introduce my children and my grandchildren to you.

53. Sigurúqa bayáq gyud arún ang ákung mga bátaq ug ákung mga apú, ipaqilaqíla ku kanímu.

many	dághan
[particle with advice]	ra ba
that (referring to person not present)	naq
they	silá

54. There are very many of them, you know. (You will want to meet them because there are many of them.)

54. Dághan ra ba kaqáyu naq silá.

that's right	bítaw
it's good	maqáyu naq
that (linker between maqáyu naq and the rest)	nga
can be known	maqílhan
by me	ku

55. That's right, it would be good for me to know them.

55. Bítaw, # maqáyu nang maqílhan ... ku silá.

how many?	pilá
[question particle after interrogative]	man
[following interrogative used for clarifying information]	diqáy
you	ka
[linker for numerals]	ka
days	ádlaw

56. How many days will you be here?

56. Pilá man diqáy ka ka ádlaw ... ngánhi?

about	mga
two	duhá
only	ra
probably	tingáli
[linker between duhá and ádlaw]	ka

57. Probably only about two days.

*57. Mga duhá ra tingáli ka ádlaw.

after that is finished	inigkahumán

will go back	mubálik
at once	dáyun
[particle: 'have']	ug
things to be done	buhatúnun
store	tindáhan
58. After that, I will go back to Cebu because I have many things to do at the store.	58. Inigkahumán, mubálik dáyun sa Sibú, kay dághan kug buhatúnun sa tindáhan.
when?	kanúsqa
will come back	mubálik
again	ug usáb
59. When will you come back again?	59. Kanúsqa man ka mubálik ug usáb?
not	waq
just	lang
know	kahibáwu
60. I don't know. (Lit. I just don't know.)	60. Waq lang ku kahibáwu.
when you come back	igbálik
you	nímu
bring (imperative)	pagdalá
[particle with imperative: 'make sure']	bayáq
presents	rigálu
OK [particle asking listener to comply]	ha

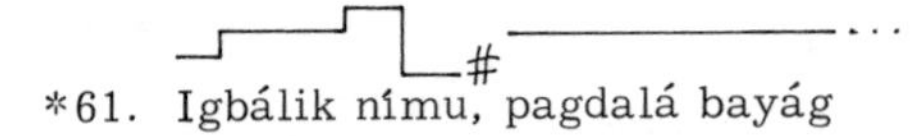

61. When you come back, be sure to bring presents, will you?	*61. Igbálik nímu, pagdalá bayág mga rigálu ha?

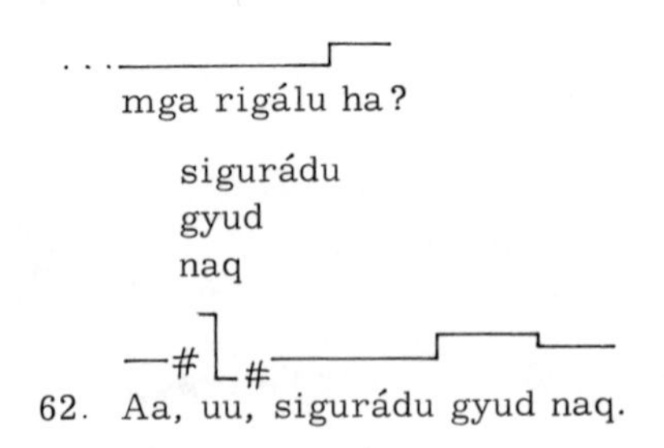

sure	sigurádu
for sure	gyud
that	naq
62. Oh yes, that's for sure.	62. Aa, uu, sigurádu gyud naq.

Mga Pangutána

Ikaduháng Báhin

1. Kun gabíqi dínhi sa Pilipínas gabíqi ba usáb sa Amiriká?
2. Magmatá na ba ka sa alás syíti sa búntag?
3. Únsay ímung nadungúg Pirlá?
4. Mangatúug na mu Nuy?
5. Dúgay ka na bang niqabút dínhis Pilipínas?
6. Giqimbitár na ba mu ni Ínting?
7. Naniqúdtu na ba mu Pirlá?
8. Kun may mangasáwa nímung Pilipínu, musugút ka ba?
9. Ása man diqáy mu maniqúdtu Ting?
10. Makaqádtu ka ba sa ámung baláy Misís?
11. Ipaqilaqíla ba akú nímus ímung mga anák Nuy?
12. Magdúgay ka ba sa Pulambatú Mis?
13. Gíkan sa Sibú, mubálik ka ba dáyun dínhi sa Pulambatú?
14. Kahibáwu na ba si Pírla kun anúsqa ku mubálik?
15. Magdalá ba kug rigálu sa ákung pagbálik?
16. Sigurádu ba gyud nga mubálik siyá karún?
17. Únsang urása mangatúug ang ímung mga bátaq?
18. Díliq na ba lang diqáy mu maniqúdtu dínhi Nuy?
19. Maqáyu bang ínyung paniqúdtu?
20. Anúsqa man ka mubálik pagqusáb?

Pangutána (Matching)

Ikaduháng Báhin

1. Naniqúdtu na ba mu Mis?
2. Makaqádtu ka ba sa tindáhan úgmaq sa búntag?
3. Naqílhan mu na bang ákung anák?
4. Mubálik ka ba dáyun sa Sibú?

(a) Uu gipaqilaqíla silá kanákuq ni Pírla.

(b) Maqú gyud naq kay gabíqi man naq sa Amiriká.

(c) Silá si Pírla ug si Mis Wílbi.

(d) Humán na* mi dídtu sa ílang Pírla.

---

* Humán na 'we have already.'

5. Tingálig díliq ka magdalág rigálu ha?
6. Ngánung mangatúug man mu sa Amiriká kun magmatá mi dínhi sa Pilipínas?
7. Natúlug na ba ang ímung apú?
8. Dúna ka pa bay asáwa Nuy?
9. Kínsa may nagqimbitár nímug paniqúdtu Nuy?

(e) Natúlug na. Túqa sa táqas.

(f) Díliq ra ba Mis kay muqádtu man ku sa Kárbun.

(g) Úqu, ug náqay traak nga mulárga karún dáyun.

(h) Waláq na intáwun.

(i) Díliq uy! Magdalá gyud kug dághang rigálu.

Commentary to Basic Sentences

5.1	ínyu	The plural forms of the pronominal genitive mean 'our (your, their) place.' (Cf. 2 E 1 a.)
5.1	kaníndut	For ka- see 5 A, p. 174.
5.2	gyud	Gyud means the same thing as dyud. The two are used interchangeably, and both are short for gayúd.
5.11	mga	This is the usual abbreviation for mangá, either as the plural or in the meaning 'approximately' (with expressions of time, it means 'approximately'). The short form will be used from now on.
5.12	ug	The ug is explained in 5 B 2, below, p. 176.
5.16	inúm	Short for muqinúm.
5.33	lúngsud	The speaker should have said násud 'country,' but since he is not too sophisticated, he used lúngsud 'place'—a more common word.
5.34	Dyútay . . . ságing	The speaker is talking to himself; this accounts for the level intonation.
5.34	ug	See 5 B.
5.49	kanúnay	Kanúnay is sometimes used as a prepositive linked with nga.
5.51	ng	This use of ng (for ni) is listed in the chart, 1 B, p. 14.
5.57	mga	Cf. comment to 5.11 above.
5.61	igbálik	The prefix ig- is short for, and interchangeable with, inig-.

Grammatical Section

5 A. Exclamatory sentences

Exclamatory sentences mean 'how . . . !' or 'what (a) . . . !' Ka- plus adjective means 'how . . . !'

Kanîndut nganhis înyu Pîrla uy! (5.1) 'How nice it is here, Perla!' (nîndut 'nice')
Katigúwang na diqáy nîmu! (5.13) 'How old you are now!'

Pattern practice PPI, steps I and II; Exercises 5.II A, 5.II B, 7.VII for 5 A and 5 A 1.

5 A 1. Definition of genitives; the use of the genitives in exclamatory sentences.

A GENITIVE is (1) a pronoun, demonstrative, or name particle in the column marked genitive of the charts in 1 A and 1 B, pp. 11, 14; or (2) a word or phrase preceded by the particle sa. The genitives are used in a number of constructions (all of them are discussed in Lesson 6). One construction in which the genitive occurs is the exclamatory sentence: in these, the genitive form is the thing exclaimed over.

a. Katigúwang na diqáy nîmu! (5.13) 'How old you are now!'

Here, nîmu 'you'—exclaimed over by katigúwang 'how old!'—is genitive. Compare the same sentence with no ka- before the adjective: the sentence is a statement, not an exclamation, and the thing about which the statement is made is nominative:

a (1). Tigúwang ka na diqáy. 'So you are old now.'

Here are some more examples:

b. Kasayún ra niqánaq! 'How easy that is!' [Niqánaq is a genitive.]
b (1). Sayún ra kanáq. 'That is easy.' (See 5.15.)
c. Kanîndut ni Pîrla! 'How beautiful Perla is!' [Ni is the genitive name marker.]
c (1). Nîndut si Pîrla. 'Perla is beautiful.'
d. Kadakúq sa îyang baay! 'How big his house is!'
d (1). Dakúq ang îyang baay. 'His house is big!'

5 B. Ug meaning 'have'

Ug means 'have (has, had, will have)' in a construction made up of adjective* plus ug plus noun or verb. In the examples below, the subject is underlined once and the predicate—consisting of adjective plus ug plus noun or verb—is underlined twice.

a. Dághan si Nuy Tibúq ug mangá anák. 'Tibo has many children.'
b. Si Pîrla nîndut ug baláy. 'Perla has a nice house.'
c. Aa, diqáy! Dyútay ra diqáy silág mangá ságing. (5.34) 'Is that so! They have few bananas.'

5 B 1. Existential sentences meaning 'have'

The above sentences of 5 B could also be said with may 'have, had' or dúna 'have, had' with no difference in meaning.

* An ADJECTIVE is a word which can take the prefix ka- in the construction described in 5 A above. In general, Cebuano adjectives, like English adjectives, indicate qualities or attributes of nouns, e.g. dakúq 'big,' nîndut 'nice,' maqáyu 'good,' etc.

a. Dúnay dághang mangá anák si Nuy Tibúq. 'Tibo has many children.'
b. Dúnay níndut nga baláy si Pírla. 'Perla has a nice house.'
c. Aa, diqáy! May dyútay ra diqáy siláng mangá ságing. 'Is that so! They have few bananas.'

Exercises 5.III A and B; Pattern practice PP-H.

5 B 2. Exclamatory sentences with ug

In exclamatory sentences containing ka- plus adjective plus genitive (described in 5 A above), the addition of ug plus noun adds the meaning 'how [adjective] [the genitive]'s [noun] is!'

a. Kadághan ni Nuy Tibúq ug mangá anák! 'How many children Tibo has!' (Lit. 'How many Tibo's children are!')
b. Kaníndut ni Pírlag baláy! 'What a nice house Perla has!'
c. Kadyútay ra diqáy nílag mangá ságing! 'How few bananas they have!'

5 B 3. Exclamations contrasted with statements

If the sentences of 5 B 2 (and others like them) had no ka- before the adjective, and had a subject instead of the genitive, they would be statements—not exclamations. Compare the examples of 5 B 2 with the examples of 5 B.

5 B 4. 'Have [a particular thing]'

For the time being you should avoid trying to express in Cebuano such English sentences as 'I have [some particular thing]' (e.g. I have the keys here.) This requires a construction that will be taken up later (16 C 2).

5 C. Differences between volitional, durative, and potential forms

Volitional verb forms are prefixed with mi- or mu-; durative forms, with nag- or mag-; and potential forms, with naka- or maka-. (Cf. chart, 4 A, p. 142 above.) The rules given below apply to verbs that can take all three.* The other forms listed in the chart of 4 A are discussed in subsequent sections.

5 C 1. Volitional (mi-/mu-) forms

(1) A volitional form prefixed with mi- (or its alternant ni-) or mu- means 'want to [do so-and-so].' Mi-/ni- is used for the real (past), and mu- for the unreal (future or after waláq 'not') (see 4 B).

a. Muqábang† ni siyág kwártus ímung baay. (3 b 7) 'She wants to rent a room in your house.'
a(1). Miqábang tu siyág kwártus ímung baay. 'She took a room in your house.'
b. Muqinúm† ku. 'I want to drink.'

---

* Some verbs do not take mi-/mu-; some do not take nag-/mag-; and some take only naka-/maka-. Verbs which do not take certain affixes are discussed in subsequent lessons.

† When a prefix ending in a vowel comes before a base beginning in a vowel, a q is automatically inserted: thus mu- plus inúm is pronounced muqinúm 'drink,' mu- plus ábang is pronounced muqábang 'rent,' and so on.

b (1). Miqinúm ku. 'I got a drink.'

(2) A volitional form is also used to refer to an action which did not last over a period of time but which happened all at one time—an action as it began or an action that was performed to its completion at one time. For verbs referring to a state or condition, a volitional form indicates that the state came into being.

c. Midágan ang túntu. (2 b 21) 'The fool ran away.'
d. Milakáw si Dúktur Pirnándis. 'Dr. Fernandez went out.'
e. Mihílak ang bátaq. 'The child burst out crying.'
f. Muhílak ang bátaq ug ímu siyáng táwgug túntu! 'The child will burst out crying if you call him a fool!'
g. Mimatá siyá pagsúud nákus kwártu. 'He woke up when I came into the room.'
h. Mumatá siyá ug musúud kas íyang kwártu. 'He will wake up if you enter his room.'

(Compare these sentences with the examples of 5 C 2 below containing durative forms.)

(3) Volitional forms prefixed with mu- but not alternatively with mi-/ni- mean '[do so-and-so] habitually or regularly.' (Remember that the meaning of habitual action is expressed by the unreal: 4 B 2 b, p. 143.)

i. Muqádtu kus Kalámba. (3 c 26) 'I go to Calamba.'
j. Maqáyu ka man diqáyng mubinisayáq! 'You really speak Visayan well!'

Which of these three meanings of the volitional [mi-, mu-] forms the speaker intends is purely a matter of context; the listener judges for himself whether to apply the meaning 'want to [do],' '[do] habitually,' or 'begin to [do].'

(4) Certain prepositives are always followed by the volitional unreal forms (forms with prefix mu-), no matter what the time meaning is and regardless of whether the meanings described above are present. Prepositives of this type that you have had so far are mahímuq 'can, may' and gústu 'want.'

k. Mahímuq ba kung muqábang sa ímung kwártu? 'May I rent your room?'
l. Gústu siyáng mutánqaw run. (3 b 16) 'She wants to look now.'
m. Gústu ka bang mulakáw? 'Do [or Did] you want to go out?'

The prepositive kinahánglan 'need' is followed either by a volitional unreal form (with prefix mu-) or by a durative unreal form (with prefix mag-), no matter what the time meaning is. The prefix mu- occurs when the meaning is 'begin to [do],' as described in (3) above. The prefix mag- occurs when the action referred to lasts over a period of time, as described in 5 C 2 (1).

n. Kinahánglan kung mulakáw run. 'I have to go out now.'
o. Kinahánglan kang maghuwát nákuq dínhi. 'You have to wait for me here.' [The action of waiting, huwát, is not instantaneous or momenary, but more extended.]

5 C 2. Durative (nag-/mag-) forms

(1) Durative forms mean 'is (was, will be) [do]ing.' These forms refer to actions which last longer than momentarily. In this meaning nag- (or its alter-

nant ga-) or mag- is prefixed to the base. (Nag-/ga- is used for the real—past or present; mag- is used for the unreal—future, or after waláq.)

c (1). Nagdagán* ang túntu. 'The fool is running around (or away).'

d (1). Túqa si Dúktur Pirnándis uh. Naglakáw paduúng sa íyang baay. 'There is Dr. Fernandez, walking toward his house.'

e (1). Sábaq kaqáyu dínhi kay naghilák man ang mangá bátaq. 'It is very noisy here because the children are crying.'

f (1). Ug túqa na mu sa traak, maghilák dyug sígi ang bátaq hástang muqabút mu sa Sibú. 'When you are on the bus, the child will keep on crying until you arrive at Cebu.'

With verbs that refer to a state or condition, the durative forms mean 'be in the state' (whereas the volitional forms mean 'come into the state': 5 C 1 (3) above).

g (1). Pagsúud nákus kwártu, nagmatá na siyá. 'When I entered the room, he was already awake.'

h (1). Ug magmatá mi ngánhi mangatúug sab mu dídtu. (5.38) 'When we are awake here, you are asleep there.'

Note also that when referring to actions which endure longer than momentarily Cebuano uses a durative, but the English equivalent is not always a progressive phrase ('be doing [so-and-so]'). For example in the following sentence ábang 'rent' is considered in Cebuano to be an extended action and so is báyad 'pay (so much for something),' and so the durative forms are used. We may translate into English, however, by using the simple past.

p. Kádtung únang nagqábang dínhi nagbáyad silág kwarínta. (3 b 26) 'Those who rented (this room) previously paid forty.'

(2) Some durative forms mean 'should or ought to [do].' In this meaning only mag- is prefixed to the base.

q. Ikáw lay magpíliq. (3 b 22) 'You choose.' (Lit. 'You are the one who should choose.')

r. Diq ka magqinúm ug tubáq. Makadáqut man naq sa láwas. 'You should not drink palm toddy. It's not good for you (lit. It ruins the body).'

Note that if there is a prepositive kinahánglan 'need,' the prefix mu- is used for action of short duration, regardless of whether there is a meaning 'should' or 'ought to.' (The prefix mag- after kinahánglan is used only for enduring action: see the statement in 5 C 1, paragraph (4).)

n. Kinahánglan kung mulakáw run. 'I have to go out now.' [The action of going out (lakáw) is considered to happen instantaneously. See also example d above.]

---

* Note that when the prefix nag-/ga- or mag- is added to dágan 'run,' the stress falls on the last syllable: nagdagán. (Compare midágan.) Many other verbs (not all) shift the stress to the last syllable after this prefix: some others are mihílak : naghilák 'cry'; miqábang : nagqabáng (also nagqábang) 'rent'; mibáyad : nagbayád (also nagbáyad) 'pay'; mikáqun : nagkaqún 'eat.'

5 C 2 a. The durative compared to the volitional

We can best understand the volitional forms referring to instantaneous actions—discussed in 5 C 1, paragraph (2)—if we compare them with the durative form meaning 'be [do]ing' discussed in 5 C 2, paragraph (1). Compare examples c, d, e, f, g, and h of 5 C 1 with c (1), d (1), e (1), f (1), g (1), and h (1) of 5 C 2. Further examples of these two usages are the following:

a. Magdalíq ta kay muquwán. 'We should hurry because it will start to rain.'
a (1). Nagdalíq mi kay nagquwán. 'We hurried because it was raining.'
b. Miqinúm siyág usá ka húngut tubáq. 'He drank up a whole coconut shell full of palm toddy.'
b (1). Nagqinúm siyág tubáq sa ákung pagkakitáq níya. 'He was drinking palm toddy when I saw him.'
c. Mitánqaw siyá kanákuq pirú waláq siyáy gisúlti. 'He looked at me, but he did not say anything.' [Mitánqaw 'looked at' here has the nuance 'took a look in the direction of.']
c (1). Nagtánqaw mig mangá ritrátu gabíqi. 'We looked at photographs last night.' [Nagtánqaw 'looked at' here has the nuance 'were examining or observing.']
d. Misakáy siyág dyip pára sa Banáwaq. 'He got on a jeep to Banawa.'
d (1). Nagsakáy siyág dyip pára sa Banáwaq pagkakitáq nákuq níya. 'He was riding a jeep to Banawa when I saw him.'

5 C 2 b. Hortatory meaning ('let's [do]')

Mag- and mu- in some sentences mean 'let's [do].'

a. Musakáy na ta! 'Let's get on now!'
b. Mulíngkúd na ta! 'Let's sit down now!'

Mu- is used for actions which happen instantaneously, as in examples a and b. Mag- is used for actions which endure longer, as in the following two examples.

c. Ánhi ta maghuwát ug dyip dínhi. 'Let's wait for a jeep here.' (Lit. 'Let's be waiting for a jeep here.')
b (1). Maglíngkud lang ta sámtang nagtánqaws mangá ritrátu. 'Let's be seated while we look at the pictures.'

5 C 3. The potential (naka-/maka-) forms

Potential forms have four meanings, as described below.

(1) 'Is (was) able to [do]; have capability of [do]ing.' Only maka- (not naka-) has this meaning (cf. 4 B 2 e).

a. Diq pa siyá makalakáw kay bátaq pa man kaqáyu. 'He cannot walk yet because he is still very young.'
b. Diq na gániq ku makaqiháp. (5 a 23) 'I cannot even count them any more.'
c. Bisán sa bátaq pa makaqiníngliš na siyá. 'Even when he was a child he was able to speak English.'

(2) 'Have an opportunity to.' Either naka- (or its alternant ka-) or maka- is used in this meaning. Naka-/ka- is the real (referring to past time: see 4 A) and maka- is the unreal (referring to future time, or occurring after waláq 'not').

d. Ug makaqádtu ku sa ínyu gíkan sa paniqúdtu muhapít ku. (5 b 52) 'If I get an opportunity to go to your place after lunch, I will drop in.'
e. Nakasakáy ku dáyun kay diq man dághang táwu. 'I managed to get on (the bus) right away because there were not many people.'
a (1). Waq gániq ku makalakáw kay síging abút ang mangá bisíta. 'I didn't even have a chance to go out because we kept having visitors.'

(3) 'Has [done].' In this meaning, maka- is used after waláq 'not'; elsewhere, naka-/ka- is used.

f. Nakasáqad man mi nga ádtu manihápun run. (2 b 33) 'We have promised that we would go to eat supper there now.'
g. Waq pa ku makapílig kwártu. 'I have not chosen a room yet.'

(4) 'Accidentally [do].' Either naka-/ka- or maka- is used in this meaning: naka-/ka- to refer to the real, maka- to the unreal. 'Accidentally' here has one of two senses. It may describe:

(i) An unintentional action:

h. Kínsay nakamánsa áni. 'Who (accidentally) stained this?'

(ii) A coincidence:

i. Nakaqábang kus kwártung giqabángan ni Prid sa úna. 'By chance, I rented the room which Fred used to rent.'

Exercises 5.V A, V B; 6.II A; Pattern practice PP-G (Lesson 4), PP-J; Reading for Lesson 5.

5 C 4. Bases with the prefix paN-

Bases containing a prefix paN-* occur with the potential prefixes (naka-/maka-) and have the usual potential meanings (for example, nakapangutána 'have asked'; makapangutána 'can ask.' The base pangutána 'ask' contains the prefix paN-.) PaN- prefixed bases do not occur with the volitional (mi-/mu-) prefixes nor (in colloquial speech) with the durative prefixes (nag-/mag-); rather, they become volitional and durative forms by replacing the paN- prefix with naN- or maN-. This amounts to saying that mi-/mu- or nag-/mag- plus paN- becomes naN- (or maN-). For example:

mi- + paN- = naN-	e.g.	mi-	+ pangutána 'ask'	= nangutána	'asked'
mu- + paN- = maN-	"	mu-	+ pangutána 'ask'	= mangutána	'will ask'
nag- + paN- = naN-	"	nag-	+ pangutána 'ask'	= nangutána	'is asking'
mag- + paN- = maN-	"	mag-	+ pangutána 'ask'	= mangutána	'will be asking'

a. Mangádtu mu sa Banáwaq? (3 a 17) 'Do you want to go to Banawa?' [This is mu- meaning 'want to [do]' plus pangádtu 'go' (plural).]
b. Ása man ta manakáy ug muqádtu tas Banáwaq? 'Where do we get (a jeep) if we go to Banawa?' [Mu- '[do] habitually' plus panakáy 'get on' (plural).]

---

* The symbol -N- (4 E, above, p. 144) stands for a nasal sound whose pronunciation depends on the initial sound of the base to which paN- is attached.

c. Mahímuq bang mangutána? (3 a 14) 'May I ask a question?' [mu- used after the prepositive mahímuq 'can' plus pangutána 'ask.']
d. Nangapú na gániq tingáli ang ímung mangá apú. (5 a 24) 'Your children probably already have grandchildren.' [Nag-, indicating that the action lasted longer than momentarily, plus pangapú 'have grandchildren.']
e. Akúy mangutána? (3 a 10) 'Who, me?' (Lit. 'Shall I be the one to ask?') [Mu- 'let's' plus pangutána 'ask.']
f. Mangasáwa gyud ka Ting, kay guwanggúwang ka na man. 'You should get married, Ting, because you're getting old.' [Mag- 'should [do]' plus pangasáwa 'take a wife.']
g. Waq pa gániq ku makapangutána, gitubág na. 'I didn't even get a chance to ask, before it was answered.' [Maka- 'have a chance to do' plus pangutána 'ask.']

5 D 1. Agents

The AGENT in a Cebuano sentence is the one who does the action of the verb. (In the examples below, the agents are underlined.)

a. Midágan ang túntu. (2 b 21) 'The fool ran away.'

If the sentence contains an active verb as predicate (an active verb is a verb form containing one of the active prefixes listed in 4 A, above, p.142), the agent is the grammatical subject of the sentence.* The agents underlined in examples b through f are subjects:

b. Nangapú na gániq tingáli ang ímung mga apú. (5 a 24) 'Even your grandchildren probably have grandchildren now.'
c. Muqábang si Mis Wílbi sa usá sa mga kwártu. 'Miss Wilby wants to rent one of the rooms.'
d. Mangítaq tag dyip. 'Let's look for a jeep.'
e. Nagbáyad silág kwarínta. 'They paid forty (pesos).'
f. Maghulát ku nímu. 'I shall wait for you.'

If the sentence contains an active verb as subject, the agent is the predicate, as shown by the underlined portions of examples a (1) through e (1):

a (1). Ang túntu ang midágan. 'The fool is the one who ran away.'
c (1). Si Mis Wílbi ang muqábang sa usá sa mangá kwártu. 'Miss Wilby is the one who wants to rent one of the rooms.'
d (1). Kitáy mangítag dyip. 'We are the ones who should look for a jeep.'
e (1). Siláy nagbáyad ug kwarínta. 'They are the ones who paid forty (pesos).'

5 D 2. Goals

The GOAL of a verb† is the thing or person acted upon by the verb. In the examples below, the goals are underlined.

---

* The grammatical subject of a Cebuano sentence is (a) a word or phrase preceded by ang, y, or si, or (b) one of the nominative pronouns or demonstratives listed in the charts of 1 A 1 and 1 B, pp. 11, 14.

† Grammatically, a goal is (a) a dative form—that is, a pronoun, a name particle, or a demonstrative as listed in the dative column in the charts of 1 A 1 and 1 B, pp. 11, 14; or (b) a word or phrase preceded by the particle ug or sa.

a. Waq pa ba guy nihángyuq kanímu? 'You mean to say no one has asked you yet?' [Kanímu 'you,' the one acted upon by nihángyuq 'asked,' is dative and therefore the goal. Nímu, the short dative, could be substituted.]
b. Nagpaqábut siyá kang (or ni or ng) Pídru. 'He is waiting for Pedro.'
c. Muqábang si Mis Wílbi sa usá sa mangá kwártu. (3 c 3) 'Miss Wilby will rent one of the rooms.'

If the goal is marked by sa, it is specific (i.e. it means 'the [noun]' or 'the one who [does]'). If the goal is marked by ug, it is not specific (i.e. 'it means 'a [noun]' or 'one who [does],' or 'some [nouns]' or 'some ones who [do]').

d. Maghuwát lang ku sa dyip nga muqádtus Banáwaq. 'I will wait for the jeep which goes to Banawa.'
d (1). Maghuwát lang kug dyip nga muqádtus Banáwaq. 'I will wait for a jeep which goes to Banawa.'
e. Muqábang ni siyág kwártus ímung baay. (3 b 7) 'She wants to rent a room in your house.'
e (1). Muqábang ni siyá sa kwártus ímung baay. 'She wants to rent the room in your house.'
f. Muqinúm kug tubáq. 'I want to drink some palm toddy.'
f (1). Muqinúm kus tubáng náqa diháq sa lamísa. 'I want to drink the palm toddy which is on the table.'
g. Muqádtu kug layúq. 'I'm going to a faraway place.'
g (1). Muqádtu kus Banáwaq. 'I'm going to Banawa.'
h. Ákuq siyáng gipaqilaqíla sa tigúwang. 'I introduced him to the old man.'
h (1). Ákuq siyáng gipaqilaqíla ug tigúwang. 'I introduced him to an old man.'

Not all sentences with verbs need goals. The following sentence is complete, although there is no goal:

i. Maghuwát lang ku. 'I'll be waiting.'

Pattern Practices and Exercises

IA. Insert the proper deictic or demonstrative in the blanks. (1 A 1, 1 A 2) This exercise is a conversation between Perla and Miss Wilby, who are standing in front of the church.

1. Kaníndut __________ sa ínyu uy, míngaw kaqáyu.
2. Básta Dumínggu míngaw __________ sa ámuq.
3. Dághan pa ba ang táwu __________ sa simbahán? (simbahán 'church')
4. Ang mga bátaq na lang ang nahibilín kay __________ man silá __________ magqiskúyla káda Dumínggu. (magqiskúyla 'go to school')

(Miss Wilby sees Tibo approaching.)

5. Kínsa man __________ ng táwu nga nagpadúung __________?
6. Maqú __________ si Iyúq Tibúq.
7. Saq pa kay átung táwgun siyá __________.
8. Iyúq Tibúq, dalíq ra gud __________.

9. __________ si Iyúq Tibúq. Maqú __________ ang labíng tigúwang táwu __________ sa ámung lúngsud.

10. Karún ka pa ba makaqánhi __________ sa ámuq?

11. Únsa man __________ ng __________ sa ímung kamút Iyúq?

12. __________ Day? Guná man __________. (Guná: a short, blunt bolo, or single-edged knife.)

13. "Giqúnsa man nímu paggámit sa guná?" "Aa, sayún ra __________."

14. __________ ka ba gíkan sa Amiriká?

15. Gíkan gyud siyá __________ sa Amiriká kay Amirikána man __________ si Mis Wílbi.

IB. Answer the following questions, using deictics in your answers. (1 A 2, 2 A 2)

1. Ása man ta maghuwát ug dyip nga páras Banáwaq?
2. Háqin man diqáy ang baláy ni Mísis Abilyána?
3. Diqín si Mis Wílbi mamisíta niqádtung Dumínggu?
4. Háqin man ang íla ka Pírla?
5. Díliq ka muqádtus ámuq? Ása ka man diqáy?
6. Waq dirí ang ákung lápis. Háqin man kaháq tu?
7. Diqín gud nímu ibílin si Místir Gamílu?
8. Ása man diqáy kiníng dyip?
9. Ása man mu magkúhag ságing?
10. Muqádtu ku sa ínyu apán háqin man dapít ang ínyung baláy?
11. Ása man ta muqági padúung sa ínyu?
12. Diqín ka makasakáy ug dyip páras Lahúg?
13. Háqin man ka karún magqabáng ug kwártu?
14. Ása man naq nímu ibutáng ímung líbru?
15. Diqín man gíkan si Iyúq Tibúq?

IC. (1) Answer in the negative. (2 B)

1. Muqádtu ka ba sa Pulambatú úgmaq?
'Are you going to Pulambato tomorrow?'

2. Gaqigutqigút ba kanáng taytáyan?
'Is that bridge rickety?'

3. Magkúhaq pa ba ku ug bir pára nímu?
'Shall I get you some beer, too?'

4. Manakáy ba ta sa bísag únsang dyip?
'Shall we get on any jeep?'

5. Ang sa táqas ba nga kwártuy ímung abángan?
'Is it the room upstairs you are going to rent?'

6. Muqinúm ka bag tubáq káda ádlaw?
   'Do you drink palm toddy every day?'

7. Muqádtu ka ba sa íla ka Iyúq Tibúq?
   'Are you going to Tibo's?'

8. Dúna na bay mihángyuq pagpangasáwa nímu?
   'Has anyone asked you to marry him yet?'

9. Níndut ba ang ínyung baláy?
   'Is your house beautiful?'

10. Gústu ka bang ibílin dínhi sa ka Dúktur Pirnándis?'
    'Do you want to be left here at Dr. Fernandez' place?'

11. Dúna pa ba tay kukakúla dínhi?
    'Do we have any more Coca-Cola here?'

12. Magquná na ba lang ku nímu?
    'Shall I just go ahead of you?'

13. Nanakáy ba mu sa dyip nga padúung sa Lahúg?
    'Did you get on the jeep going to Lahug?'

14. Nagpuyúq ka ba dínhis ka Mísis Abilyána?
    'Do you live here at Mrs. Abellana's place?'

15. Mubálik ka ba dáyun ngánhis Pulambatú?

IC. (2) Make the questions of I C (1) negative. (2 B, 3 C 2, 4 B 2 c)

ID. Ibutáng sa lunáq ang mga púlung nga díliq, waláq, ug ayáw.

1. __________ ku makaqánhi dáyun sa únang Dumínggu ('last Sunday') kay dúna man kuy bisíta.

2. __________ ku makaqánhi sa ínyu dáyun karúng gabíqi kay muqádtu pa ku sa ka Pírla.

3. __________ pagsakáy niqádtung dyip kay __________ kanáq pára sa Banáwaq. 'Don't get on that jeep . . . '

4. Ngánung __________ man nímu imbitahá si Mis Wílbi ngánhi sa átuq? 'Why didn't you invite Miss Wilby . . . ?'

5. __________ ku maniqúdtu dínhi kay muqádtu ku sa ka Místir Abáya.

6. __________ na lang kug ikúhag bir kay __________ man ku muqinúm niqánaq. 'Don't go to the trouble of getting me any beer, because I don't drink it.'

7. __________ ku makahátag ug bir nímu kay __________ na man tay bir.

8. Ngánung __________ ka man muqubán kang Pírla ngádtu sa Pulambatú ganíhang búntag?

9. Ngánung __________ ka man musugút kung Pilipínu ang mangasáwa nímu?

10. Kung dúnay bisíta __________ pagsábaq. 'If we have visitors don't make any noise.'

11. _________ diqáy ni muqádtu sa Banáwaq? 'Oh! Don't you go to Banawa?'

12. __________ na lag pangutána sa tigúwang kay díqa nay dyip páras Banáwaq. 'Don't bother asking the old man . . . '

13. _________ kamí makaqádtu sa Banáwaq kay waláy dyip. 'We could not . . . '

14. Dídtu sa ámuq _________ gayúy ságing.

15. _________ pa gyud intáwuy mihángyuq nákuq pagpangasáwa.

IE. Rewrite the following sentences with the words in parentheses. (3C 3a)

1.	Mangutána ku?	(díliq)
2.	Musakáy na ba ta ug muqádtu tas Banáwaq?	(kinahánglan)
3.	Mis Wílbi, mangádtu ba mus Banáwaq?	(gústu)
4.	Tigúwang man diqáy ka kaqáyu.	(díliq)
5.	Kaqiháp ra ba kus ákung mga apú.	(díliq)
6.	Maghuwát lang tag dyip.	(ánhi)
7.	Pangítaq lang mug láqin Day.	(dídtu)
8.	Ang kwártu ba ni ni Mis Wílbi?	(maqú)
9.	Muqábang ka sa usá ka kwártu?	(anúsqa)
10.	Samúkan kaháq ka unyáq sa mga bátaq?	(díliq)
11.	Pára ba ni sa Kárbun Day?	(díliq)
12.	Maqílhan gyud nákuq naq silá.	(kinahánglan)
13.	Matúug na lang mi.	(ánhi)
14.	Mubálik dáyun ku sa Sibú.	(gústu)
15.	Mubálik ka ba sa Amiriká?	(kanúsqa)

IF. Make the following sentences negative. (2B, 3C 3a)

1. Miqádtu ra ba si Mis Wílbi sa ílang Mis Sántus sa Pulambatú.
2. Átuq lang táwgun kanáng tigúwang. (Change átuq to nátuq.)
3. Ákuq mang kaqúban kiní si Mis Wílbi, Nuy Tibúq.
4. Si Nuy Tibúq ra ba ang labíng tigúwang táwu sa lúngsud.
5. Dúgay na man ku dínhis Pilipínas.
6. Si Nuy Tibúq man tingáli kanáng nagpadulúng ngánhi.
7. Karún, makabinisayáq na gyud ka. (Change na to pa.)
8. Dúna na gyud kay mga apú Iyúq.
9. Inigbálik nímu pagdalá bayág mga rigálu ha?
'When you come back be sure to bring presents, will you?'
10. Nangítaq gayúd si Mis Wílbi ug baláy.

11. Mahímu bang mangutána Iyúq?
12. Subáya lang nínyu kanáng dálan Piláyis.
13. Dúna may mga dyip ngánhang padúung sa Banáwaq.
14. Musugút lang ku ug náqay muhángyuq.
15. Dúna ra bay mga lubí sa ámung dápit.

PP-I Exclamatory sentences (5 A)

Step I. (No pronouns or demonstratives)

'Your house is beautiful, Perla.'
'How beautiful your house is, Perla!'

1. a. Níndut ang baláy mu Pirlá.
   b. Kaníndut sa baláy mu Pirlá!
2. a. Tigúwang na diqáy si Nuy Tibúq.
   b. Katigúwang na diqáy ni Nuy Tibúq!
3. a. Dághan na ang anák ni Índay uy.
   b. Kadághan na sa anák ni Índay uy!
4. a. Dakúq ang lúngsud nga Pulambatú.
   b. Kadakúq sa lúngsud nga Pulambatú!
5. a. Dyútay ra ang ságing dídtu sa ámuq.
   b. Kadyútay ra sa ságing dídtu sa ámuq!
6. a. Dakúq na diqáy ang idád ni Nuy Tibúq.
   b. Kadakúq na diqáy sa idád ni Nuy Tibúq!
7. a. Hílum ang lúngsud básta Dumínggu.
   b. Kahílum sa lúngsud básta Dumínggu!
8. a. Sayún ra ang pagqádtus Pulambatú.
   b. Kasayún ra sa pagqádtus Pulambatú!
9. a. Gamáy ra diqáy ang mangá dápit dínhi.
   b. Kagamáy ra diqáy sa mangá dápit dínhi!
10. a. Dághan ang ákung buhatúnun sa tindáhan.
    b. Kadághan sa ákung buhatúnun sa tindáhan!
11. a. Layúq diqáy ang ímung kwártu sa mangá bátaq.
    b. Kalayúq diqáy sa ímung kwártu sa mangá bátaq!
12. a. Dághan ang dyip nga muqági dínhi.
    b. Kadághan sa dyip nga muqági dínhi!
13. a. Sayún ra ang pagqabút sa idád nga nubintayqútsu.
    b. Kasayún ra sa pagqabút sa idád nga nubintayqútsu!
14. a. Dakúq diqáy ang baláy níla ni Pírla uy.
    b. Kadakúq diqáy sa baláy níla ni Pírla uy!
15. a. Dyútay ra ang muqági nga dyip dínhi.
    b. Kadyútay ra sa muqági nga dyip dínhi!
16. a. Tigúwang na ang anák ni Iyúq Tibúq.
    b. Katigúwang na sa anák ni Iyúq Tibúq!

17. a. Dághan ang apú ni Iyúq Tibúq.
    b. Kadághan sa apú ni Iyúq Tibúq!

18. a. Ignuránti diqáy kaqáyu si Lítu uy.
    b. Kaqignuránti diqáy kaqáyu ni Lítu uy!

19. a. Lisúd ang ámung pagqánhi ngánhi.
    b. Kalisúd sa ámung pagqánhi ngánhi!

Step II. (With pronouns and demonstratives)

'My! That's easy.'
'My! How easy that is.'

1. a. Sus! Sayún ra kanáq.
   b. Sus! Kasayún ra ánaq!

2. a. Ignuránti kádtung tawhána.
   b. Kaqignuránti ádtung tawhána!

3. a. Gamáy ra kiníng ákung bir.
   b. Kagamáy ra íning ákung bir!

4. a. Uy, dághan kanáng ímung mangá apú.
   b. Uy, kadághan ánang ímung mangá apú!

5. a. Dághan kiníng ákung buhatúnun dínhi.
   b. Kadághan íning ákung buhatúnun dínhi!

6. a. Uy, dághan na kiní.
   b. Uy, kadághan na íni!

7. a. Layúq nang ímung kwártu sa sábaq.
   b. Kalayúq ánang ímung kwártu sa sábaq!

8. a. Níndut tung anák ni Dúktur Pirnándis nu?
   b. Kaníndut ádtung anák ni Dúktur Pirnándis nu?

9. a. Tigúwang na diqáy ka.
   b. Katigúwang na diqáy nímu!

10. a. Uy, dakúq nang ílang baay.
    b. Uy, kadakúq ánang ílang baay!

11. a. Gamáy pa ka Litú uy.
    b. Kagamáy pa nímu Litú uy!

12. a. Layúq ning ínyung baay sa ámuq.
    b. Kalayúq íning ínyung baay sa ámuq!

13. a. Dyútay ra ning ságing nga ákung dalá.
    b. Kadyútay ra íning ságing nga ákung dalá!

14. a. Tigúwang na kaqáyu siyá nu?
    b. Katigúwang na kaqáyu níya nu?

15. a. Layúq pa tung ílang baláy uy.
    b. Kalayúq pa ádtung ílang baláy uy!

16. a. Dakúq na ka Litú.
    b. Kadakúq na nímu Litú!

17. a. Níndut nang ímung líbru.
    b. Kaníndut ánang ímung líbru!

18. a. Hílum kiníng ámung lúngsud.
    b. Kahílum íning ámung lúngsud!

19. a. Dághan mung niqánhi nu?
    b. Kadághan nínyung niqánhi nu?

20. a. Dakúq kádtung ámung baláy sa Banáwaq.
    b. Kadakúq ádtung ámung baláy sa Banáwaq!

Step III. (Exclamatory sentences having ug (no pronouns, demonstratives, or particles))

'My! Tibo has lots of money.'
'My! What a lot of money Tibo has!'

1. a. Sus! Dághag kwárta si Nuy Tibúq.
   b. Sus! Kadághag kwártang Nuy Tibúq!

2. a. Níndut ug baay si Pírla.
   b. Kaníndut ug baay ni Pírla!

3. a. Dághan si Lítug líbru.
   b. Kadághan ni Lítug líbru!

4. a. Dakúq na si Nuy Tibúg idád.
   b. Kadakúq na ni Nuy Tibúg idád!

5. a. Dakúg baláy si Dúktur Pirnándis.
   b. Kadakúg baláy ni Dúktur Pirnándis!

6. a. Layús Pírlag baláys Kárbun uy.
   b. Kalayúng Pírlag baláys Kárbun uy!

7. a. Dyútay pas Lítug kwárta.
   b. Kadyútay pang Lítug kwárta!

8. a. Tigúwang nas Pírlag amahán.
   b. Katigúwang nang Pírlag amahán!

9. a. Hílum si Mis Wíbig kwártu.
   b. Kahílum ni Mis Wíbig kwártu!

10. a. Dághan si Índayg bir.
    b. Kadághan ni Índayg bir!

11. a. Níndut si Lítag baláy.
    b. Kaníndut ni Lítag baláy!

12. a. Sayún si Dúdung ug trabáhu.
    b. Kasayún ni Dúdung ug trabáhu!

13. a. Dakúq si Balúduyg baláy sa Manílaq.
    b. Kadakúq ni Balúduyg baláy sa Manílaq!

14. a. Dyútay si Lítug kwárta.
    b. Kadyútay ni Lítug kwárta!

15. a. Níndut si Índayg kwártu.
    b. Kaníndut ni Índayg kwártu!

16. a. Dághan si Ústing ug bábuy.
    b. Kadághan ni Ústing ug bábuy!

17. a. Layúq si Mírlig kaliguqánan.
    b. Kalayúq ni Mírlig kaliguqánan!

18. a. Basáq si Dúdung ug sinínaq.
    b. Kabasáq ni Dúdung ug sinínaq!

19. a. Lamíq si Índayg haluqháluq.
    b. Kalamíq ni Índayg haluqháluq!

20. a. Dághan si Dúdung ug mangá irúq.
    b. Kadághan ni Dúdung ug mangá irúq!

Step IV. (Sentences having ug with particles, pronouns, and demonstratives)

'My! He certainly has a big house.'
'My! What a big house he has!'

1. a. Sus! Dakúq diqáy siyág baláy.
   b. Sus! Kadakúq diqáy níyag baláy.

2. a. Uy, níndut ra ba gyud diqáy siyág kaliguqánan.
   b. Uy, kaníndut ra ba gyud diqáy níyag kaliguqánan!

3. a. Sus, dághan na hinúqun kitág buhatúnun.
   b. Sus, kadághan na hinúqun nátug buhatúnun!

4. a. Lisúd ra ba siyág trabáhu karún uy.
   b. Kalisúd ra ba níyag trabáhu karún uy!

5. a. Hílum sab si Pírlag kwártu.
   b. Kahílum sab ni Pírlag kwártu!

6. a. Dághan ra ba silág kukakúla.
   b. Kadághan ra ba nílag kukakúla!

7. a. Dághan sab diqáy si Lítug tindáhan.
   b. Kadághan sab diqáy ni Lítug tindáhan!

8. a. Lamíq ra ba úntaq mig haluqháluq.
   b. Kalamíq ra ba úntaq námug haluqháluq!

9. a. Layúq diqáy silág baláy sa ámuq.
   b. Kalayúq diqáy nílag baláy sa ámuq!

10. a. Dyútay na lang ra ba kamíg kwárta uy.
    b. Kadyútay na lang ra ba námug kwárta uy!

11. a. Níndut diqáy kaqáyu siyág irúq.
    b. Kaníndut diqáy kaqáyu níyag irúq!

12. a. Basáq diqáy kiníng ímung lingkuránan.
    b. Kabasáq diqáy íning ímung lingkuránan!

13. a. Dághan diqáyg amígu kiní si Nuy Tibúq.
    b. Kadághan diqáyg amígu íning Nuy Tibúq!

14. a. Dakúq na ra ba diqáyg idád si Pírla.
    b. Kadakúq na ra ba diqáyg idád ni Pírla!

15. a. Hílum úntaq kaqáyu siyág amíga.
    b. Kahílum úntaq kaqáyu níyag amíga!

16. a. Sayún ra diqáy kaqáyu si Lítug búhat.
    b. Kasayún ra diqáy kaqáyu ni Lítug búhat.

17. a. Níndut gyud diqáy kádtu si Pírlag baláy.
    b. Kaníndut gyud diqáy ádtu ni Pírlag baláy!

18. a. Lamíq diqáy si Lítug haluqháluq.
    b. Kalamíq diqáy ni Lítug haluqháluq!

19. a. Tigúwang na man gud siyág inahán uy.
    b. Katigúwang na man gud níyag inahán uy!

20. a. Dakúq diqáy kaqáyu si Dúdung ug baláy.
    b. Kadakúq diqáy kaqáyu ni Dúdung ug baláy!

II A. Make the following statements into exclamatory sentences. (5 A, 5 A 1)

Statement: Níndut gyud ang ínyung baay Pirlá.
Exclamatory: Kaníndut gyud sa ínyung baay Pirlá!

1. Míngaw diqáy dínhi sa Pulambatú uy.
2. Níndut kiníng kwártu sa sílung.
3. Dághan túqud ang dyip dínhi.
4. Dághan na ang ímung mga apú.
5. Dúgay na diqáy ka dínhi sa Pilipínas.
6. Dyútay lang diqáy ang ságing dídtu sa ínyu nu.
7. Ignuránti si Lítu.
8. Sayún ra kanáq.
9. Tigúwang ka na diqáy.
10. Míngaw dídtu sa ka Mísis Abilyána.
11. Layúq tung Púquk kaligúqan.
12. Lisúd ang agiqánan paqingún sa Púquk.
13. Bahúq kiníng dapíta.
14. Lamíq diqáy ang haluqháluq.
15. Dalíq siláng nahumág kalíguq.

II B. Make the following exclamatory sentences into statements. (5 A, 5 A 1)

Exclamatory: Katigúwang na diqáy ni Íyuq Tibúq!
Statement: Tigúwang na diqáy si Íyuq Tibúq.

1. Kadakúq niqíning ínyung tindáhan!
2. Kadághan niqánaq níyag mga anák!
3. Kaníndut niqíning mga ságing!
4. Kadyútay sa mga Amirkánu dínhi sa Pilipínas!

5. Kasayún niqíning pagtulúnqang sagqulúhun!

6. Katigúwang niqánang Nuy Tibúq!

7. Kaqignuránti niqíning ímung apú Nuy Tibúq!

8. Kahílum ngádtu sa lúngsud ni Pírla!

9. Kamíngaw ngádtus ámung lugár!

10. Kadúgay níyang muqabút gíkan sa ámuq! 'What a long (time) it took him to get here from our house!'

PP-H Changing existential sentences into sentences with ug. (5 B)

Step I. (Sentences with may 'have' and subjects of more than one word)

'Tibo has many grandchildren.'

1. a. May dághang apú si Nuy Tibúq.
   b. Dághag apú si Nuy Tibúq.

2. a. May níndut nga baay si Pírla.
   b. Níndut ug baay si Pírla.

3. a. May dyútayng kwárta si Místir Abáya.
   b. Dyútayg kwárta si Místir Abáya.

4. a. May dághang lubí sa Pulambatú.
   b. Dághag lubí sa Pulambatú.

5. a. May buqútang anák si Mísis Pirnándis.
   b. Buqútag anák si Mísis Pirnándis.

6. a. May dakúng baay si Hwan.
   b. Dakúg baay si Hwan.

7. a. May níndut nga sinínaq si Pírla.
   b. Níndut ug sinínaq si Pírla.

8. a. May dyútayng lubí sa Amiriká.
   b. Dyútayg lubí sa Amiriká.

9. a. May dághang anák ang íyang amígu.
   b. Dághag anák ang íyang amígu.

10. a. May dághang apú ang anák ni Nuy Tibúq.
    b. Dághag apú ang anák ni Nuy Tibúq.

11. a. May gamáyng baay si Pírla sa Sibú.
    b. Gamáyg baay si Pírla sa Sibú.

12. a. May maqáyung kwártung paqabángan si Mísis Pirnándis.
    b. Maqáyug kwártung paqabángan si Mísis Pirnándis.

13. a. May bágqung baay si Mísis Abilyána.
    b. Bágqug baay si Mísis Abilyána.

14. a. May samukáng anák si Mísis Pirnándis.
    b. Samukág anák si Mísis Pirnándis.

15. a. May gamáyng simbahán ang Pulambatú.
    b. Gamáyg simbahán ang Pulambatú.

16. a. May dághang bábuy sa Púquk.
    b. Dághag bábuy sa Púquk.

17. a. May dághang baybáayng gágmay sa Púquk.
    b. Dághag baybáayng gágmay sa Púquk.

18. a. May nindut nga simbahán ang Pulambatú.
    b. Níndut ug simbahán ang Pulambatú.

19. a. May dághang kwárta si Ída.
    b. Dághag kwárta si Ída.

20. a. May maqáyung amígu si Gamílu.
    b. Maqáyug amígu si Gamílu.

Step II. (Sentences with positive existential predicates and subjects of more than one word)

'My big sister has plenty of bananas.'

1. a. Dúnay dághang ságing si Manáng.
   b. Dághag ságing si Manáng.

2. a. Dínhay dághang bir sa kusína.
   b. Dághag bir sa kusína.

3. a. May níndut nga baay si Pírla.
   b. Níndut ug baay si Pírla.

4. a. Túqay gágmayng baybáay sa Púquk.
   b. Gágmayg baybáay ang Púquk.

5. a. Náqay samukáng mga bátaq si Mísis Kapangpángan.
   b. Samukág mga bátaq si Mísis Kapangpángan.

6. a. Adúnay dághang anák si Nuy Tibúq.
   b. Dághag anák si Nuy Tibúq.

7. a. May dághang bábuy sa Púquk.
   b. Dághag bábuy sa Púquk.

8. a. Adúnay gágmayng baybáay ang tigúwang.
   b. Gágmayg baybáay ang tigúwang.

9. a. Túqay dakúng simbahán sa Pulambatú.
   b. Dakúg simbahán ang Pulambatú.

10. a. Dínhay dághang kwárta ang pitáka.
    b. Dághag kwárta ang pitáka.

11. a. May dyútayng kwárta ang tigúwang.
    b. Dyútayg kwárta ang tigúwang.

12. a. Dúnay níndut nga bag si Ída.
    b. Níndut ug bag si Ída.

13. a. May dakúng simbahán ang ílang dápit.
    b. Dakúg simbahán ang ílang dápit.

14. a. Náqay dághang apú si Nuy Tibúq.
    b. Dághag apú si Nuy Tibúq.

15. a. Dúnay dyútayng lubí sa Amiriká.
    b. Dyútayg lubí sa Amiriká.

16. a. Adúnay níndut nga baay si Hwan.
    b. Níndut ug baay si Hwan.

17. a. Dídtuy dághang prútas sa tindáhan.
    b. Dághag prútas sa tindáhan.

18. a. May buqútang anák si Místir Istúrku.
    b. Buqútag anák si Místir Istúrku.

19. a. Dúnay dághang dyip sa Gútsan.
    b. Dághag dyip sa Gútsan.

20. a. Túqay dághang táwu sa Kárbun.
    b. Dághag táwu sa Kárbun.

Step III. (Sentences with may 'have' with one-word subjects)

'He has a nice house.'

1. a. May níndut siyáng baláy.
   b. Níndut siyág baláy.

2. a. May buqútan akúng anák.
   b. Buqútan akúg anák.

3. a. May dyútay kung kwárta.
   b. Dyútay kug kwárta.

4. a. May níndut kang siními̇naq.
   b. Níndut kag siními̇naq.

5. a. May dághan siyáng anák.
   b. Dághan siyág anák.

6. a. May maqáyu kung amígu.
   b. Maqáyu kug amígu.

7. a. May samukán siyáng anák.
   b. Samukán siyág anák.

8. a. May dyútay siláng ságing.
   b. Dyútay silág ságing.

9. a. May tigúwang siyáng amígu.
   b. Tigúwang siyág amígu.

10. a. May gamáy kamíng kwártu sa baay.
    b. Gamáy kamíg kwártu sa baay.

11. a. May buqútan siláng dúktur.
    b. Buqútan silág dúktur.

12. a. May dághan siyáng gása.
    b. Dághan siyág gása.

13. a. May dyútay siláng bisíta.
    b. Dyútay silág bisíta.

14. a. May níndut siyáng siníinaq.
    b. Níndut siyág siníinaq.

15. a. May gamáy siyáng irúq.
    b. Gamáy siyág irúq.

16. a. May dághan kitáng líbru.
    b. Dághan kitág líbru.

17. a. May dátuq ('rich') akúng amígu.
    b. Dátuq akúg amígu.

18. a. May buqútan akúng mutsátsa ('maid').
    b. Buqútan akúg mutsátsa.

19. a. May sabaqán siyáng bátaq.
    b. Sabaqán siyág bátaq.

20. a. May dághan akúng aríyus.
    b. Dághan akúg aríyus.

Step IV. (Sentences with may 'have' or with other positive existential predicates and subjects of one or more words)

'He has a small dog.'

1. a. May gamáy siyáng irúq.
   b. Gamáy siyág irúq.

2. a. Dúnay dághang apú si Nuy Tibúq.
   b. Dághag apú si Nuy Tibúq.

3. a. Dúna man gud siláy dyútayng lántay.
   b. Dyútay man gud silág lántay.

4. a. May níndut man gung sinínaq si Pírla.
   b. Níndut man gug sinínaq si Pírla.

5. a. Dúna ra bay bágqung ('new') dyip si Mis Wílbi.
   b. Bágqu ra bag dyip si Mis Wílbi.

6. a. Dúna lagíy dághang ságing sa tindáhan.
   b. Dághan lagíg ságing sa tindáhan.

7. a. May dakúq kaqáyu kamíng baay.
   b. Dakúq kaqáyu kamíg baay.

8. a. Túqa may dyútayng lubí sa Amiriká.
   b. Dyútay mag lubí sa Amiriká.

9. a. Dídtuy dághang ságing sa Pulambatú.
   b. Dághag ságing sa Pulambatú.

10. a. Dúna diqáy siláy níndut nga dyip.
    b. Níndut diqáy silág dyip.

11. a. Dídtu kunúy maqáyung kaliguqánan sa Púquk.
    b. Maqáyu kunúg kaliguqánan sa Púquk.

12. a. Dínhay dághang baybáay ang tigúwang.
    b. Dághag baybáay ang tigúwang.

13. a. Dúna kuy dyútayng mga anák.
    b. Dyútay akúg mga anák.

14. a. May dághan ra ba siyáng mga bisíta.
    b. Dághan ra ba siyág mga bisíta.

15. a. Dínhay buqútang mutsátsa si Mísis Pirnándis.
    b. Buqútag mutsátsa si Mísis Pirnándis.

Step V. (Same as Step IV)

'Because he has many friends.'

1. a. Dúna man gud siyáy dághang amígu.
   b. Dághan man gud siyág amígu.

2. a. Dúna ba guy dághang dyip sa Gútsan run?
   b. Dághan ba gug dyip sa Gútsan run?

3. a. Dúna man siláy dakúng baay.
   b. Dakúq man silág baay.

4. a. Náqa man miy dyútayng kwárta.
   b. Dyútay man mig kwárta.

5. a. Náqa ba siyáy bágqung sinínaq?
   b. Bágqu ba siyág sinínaq?

6. a. Dúna man siláy buqútang anák.
   b. Buqútan man silág anák.

7. a. Dúna ba muy dághang lubí dídtu?
   b. Dághan ba mug lubí dídtu?

8. a. Túqa lagíy dághang gása ang babáyi.
   b. Dághan lagíg gása ang babáyi.

9. a. Dídtu ra bay dághang bisíta sa upisína.
   b. Dághan ra bag bisíta sa upisína.

10. a. Náqa pay dághang kwárta si Nuy Tibúq.
    b. Dághan pag kwárta si Nuy Tibúq.

11. a. Dúna pa siyáy dyútayng kwárta.
    b. Dyútay pa siyág kwárta.

12. a. Náqa na siláy níndut nga baay.
    b. Níndut na silág baay.

13. a. Dínhi man lagíy dághang bisíta si Hwan ganína.
    b. Dághan man lagíg bisíta si Hwan ganína.

14. a. Dúna man siyáy buqútang amígu.
    b. Buqútan man siyág amígu.

15. a. Náqa may buqútang mutsátsa si Gamílu.
    b. Buqútan mag mutsátsa si Gamílu.

Step VI. (Same as Step IV but with negative existential predicates)

'He doesn't have enough money.'

1. a. Waláq siyáy dághang kwárta.
   b. Díliq siyá dághag kwárta.

2. a. Waláy dághang apú si Nuy Tibúq.
   b. Díliq dághag apú si Nuy Tibúq.

3. a. Waláy gágmayng baay ang Púquk.
   b. Díliq gágmayg baay ang Púquk.

4. a. Waláq siláy buqútang anák.
   b. Díliq silá buqútag anák.

5. a. Waláq kamíy dághang ságing.
   b. Díliq kamí dághag ságing.

6. a. Waláq lagíy samukáng anák si Místir Abáya.
   b. Díliq lagí samukág anák si Místir Abáya.

7. a. Waláq man guy maqáyung kaliguqánan ang Talísay.
   b. Díliq man gud maqáyug kaliguqánan ang Talísay.

8. a. Waláq diqáy siláy gágmayng lántay.
   b. Díliq diqáy silá gágmayg lántay.

9. a. Waláq ra ba akúy dakúng baay.
   b. Díliq ra ba akú dakúg baay.

10. a. Waláq man guy dakúng baay si Dyuu.
    b. Díliq man gud dakúg baay si Dyuu.

11. a. Waláq man diqáy buqútang anák si Lulú.
    b. Díliq man diqáy buqútag anák si Lulú.

12. a. Waláq pa man kamíy níndut nga baay.
    b. Díliq pa man kamí níndut ug baay.

13. a. Waláq pa kamúy dakúng tindáhan.
    b. Díliq pa kamú dakúg tindáhan.

14. a. Waláq gyuy níndut nga sinínaq si Íli.
    b. Díliq gyud níndut ug sinínaq si Íli.

15. a. Waláq pay dakúng tindáhan ang Pulambatú.
    b. Díliq pa dakúg tindáhan ang Pulambatú.

16. a. Waláq diqáy siláy gamáyng simbahán.
    b. Díliq diqáy silá gamáyg simbahán.

17. a. Waláy gamáyng lamísa si Ída.
    b. Díliq gamáyg lamísa si Ída.

18. a. Waláy maqáyung líbru si Ústing.
    b. Díliq maqáyug líbru si Ústing.

19. a. Waláq kay maqáyung sinínaq.
    b. Díliq ka maqáyug sinínaq.

20. a. Waláq kuy samukáng bátaq.
    b. Díliq ku samukág bátaq.

Step VII. (Do Step VI again, saying b first instead of a)

III A. Úsba kiníng mga túdling púlung nga existential ngádtu sa mga túdling púlung nga mugámit ug ug.

Pananglítan: May dakúng dyip si Nuy Prid.
Tubág: Dakúq si Nuy Prid ug dyip.

1. Dúna na ba si Pírlay dághang anák?
2. Ang ákung kaqúban adúnay níndut gyung baláy.
3. May dyútay kung kwárta páras ábang.
4. Dúna siyáy gamáyng baay dídtus Sibú.
5. May dághang apú man diqáy si Nuy Tibúq.
6. May buqútang anák si Místir Abáya? (buqútan 'well behaved')
7. Dúna bay dághang dyip nga muqági dínhi?
8. May mga sabaqán (noisy) mung mga bátaq dínhi?
9. May maqáyung higála si Pírla.
10. Dúnay míngaw nga kwártu dídtus sílung.
11. Waláq ka pa bay dághang kaqíla? (kaqíla 'acquaintance')
12. Waláq kuy dátung ('rich') amahán ('father').
13. Dúna bay dakúng baay si Dúktur Pirnándis?
14. Waláq siláy dághang ságing sa íla.
15. Dúna kuy dághang buluhatún sa tindáhan.

III B. Úsba ang musunúd nga mga túdling púlung nga dúnay ug ngádtu sa túdling púlung nga existential.

1. Dyútay na ba lag ságing dídtu sa ínyu?
2. Dághan ba mug mga bátaq dínhi?
3. Dakúq na ba diqáy kag idád?
4. Níndut bag tíngug si Pírla?
5. Dághan diqáy kag mga higála dínhi?
6. Díliq ka ba dakúg tíngug? (dakúg tíngug 'loud voice')
7. Dakúg baláy si Iyúq Tibúq sa Pulambatú.
8. Dághan kaqáyu siyág mga apú.
9. Gamáy rag simbahán ang Pulambatú.
10. Gamáy ra ba ug kwártu dínhi sa ámuq.
11. Maqáyug mga kwártu dídtu sa táqas.
12. Níndut ug simbahán dídtu sa íla ka Pírla.
13. Dyútay rag Amirikánu dínhi sa Sibú.
14. Díliq dághag lubí dídtu sa ámuq.
15. Ngánung dághan man kag daláng gása?

IV. (Pattern Practice PP-G may be practiced before this exercise is performed.) Pilíqa ang hústung púrma nga náqa sa sulúd sa ( ). (4 B and subsections)

1. Ádtu na lang ta kay (nagsáqad, magsáqad) man tang (manihápun, nanihápun) sa ka Dúktur Pirnándis. 'Let's go, because we promised we would eat supper at Dr. Fernandez'.'
2. Mahímuq bang (mangutána, nangutána) kun ása ta (musakáy, misakáy) ug dyip nga (miqádtu, muqádtu) sa Banáwaq? (Kun introduces an indirect question here.) 'May I ask where we get a jeep that goes to Banawa?'
3. Waláq ku (makahapít, nakahapít) sa ínyu kay (mibálik, mubálik) ku dáyun sa Sibú. 'I couldn't drop in at your place because I went right back to Cebu.'
4. (Manakáy, Nanakáy) na tag dyip. 'Let's get on a jeep now.'
5. Gahápun (nagqiháp, magqiháp) ang bátaq sa íyang túdluq. 'The child was counting its toes yesterday.'
6. (Nahímu, Mahímu) bang (misakáy, musakáy) sa ínyung dyip? 'May we get on your jeep?'
7. (Namálhin, Mamálhin) mi sa Banáwaq inigkahumán sa ámung baláy dídtu. 'When our house is finished, we will move to Banawa.'
8. Si Huwán (nagdalá, magdalá) ug mga bisíta sa ámung baay. 'John brought visitors to our house.'
9. Ang apú ni Nuy Tibúq (muqádtu, miqádtu) dídtu sa ámung lungsud. 'Tibo's grandson will go to our town.'
10. (Nagtawág, Magtawág) pa ku ni Iyúq ug tartanílya kay (muqádtu, miqádtu) siyá sa Kárbun. 'I still have to call a rig for the old man because he is going to Carbon.'
11. (Mibálik, Mubálik) mi dínhi úgmaq sa hápun. 'We will come back here tomorrow afternoon.'
12. Maqáyung (magdalíq, nagdalíq) ta arún (muqabút, miqabút) sa átuq nga díliq pa gabíqi. 'We should hurry in order to get home before dark.'
13. (Mangádtu, Nangádtu) na ta sa Kalámba. 'Let's go to Calamba now.'
14. Kínsa tung (nagtawág, magtawág) kanákuq? 'Who is that calling me?'
15. Si Pídru waláq (misakáy, musakáy) sa dyip nga padulúng sa Kárbun.

PP-J Difference in meaning between volitional, durative, and potential (5 C)

Step I.

'He was able to drink water.'

Nakaqinúm siyág túbig.	(muqinúm)
Muqinúm siyág túbig.	(miqinúm)
Miqinúm siyág túbig.	(makaqinúm)
Makaqinúm siyág túbig.	(nagqinúm)
Nagqinúm siyág túbig.	(magqinúm)

Magqinúm siyág túbig.	(nakadalá)
Nakadalá siyág túbig.	(makadalá)
Makadalá siyág túbig.	(nagdalá)
Nagdalá siyág túbig.	(magdalá)
Magdalá siyág túbig.	(mihatúd)
Mihatúd siyág túbig.	(muhatúd)
Muhatúd siyág túbig.	(nakahatúd)
Nakahatúd siyág túbig.	(makahatúd)
Makahatúd siyág túbig.	(naghatúd)
Naghatúd siyág túbig.	(maghatúd)
Maghatúd siyág túbig.	

Step II.

'The boy cried.'

Mihílak ang bátaq.	(was crying: hílak)
Naghilák ang bátaq.	(was running: dágan)
Nagdagán ang bátaq.	(ran away)
Midágan ang bátaq.	(got on: sakáy)
Misakáy ang bátaq.	(was able to get on)
Nakasakáy ang bátaq.	(woke up: matá)
Mimatá / Nimatá } ang bátaq	(was able to wake up)
Nakamatá ang bátaq.	(is awake)
Nagmatá ang bátaq.	(went away: lakáw)
Milakáw ang bátaq.	(is walking)
Naglakáw ang bátaq.	(was able to go away)
Nakalakáw ang bátaq.	(was drinking: inúm)
Nagqinúm ang bátaq.	(drank)
Miqinúm ang bátaq.	(was able to drink)
Nakaqinúm ang bátaq.	(is or was counting: iháp)
Nagqiháp ang bátaq.	(counted)
Miqiháp ang bátaq.	(was able to count)
Nakaqiháp ang bátaq.	

Step III.

'Perla cannot choose a room.'

Díliq makapílig kwártu si Pírla. (She won't choose)

Díliq mupílig kwártu si Pírla. (She won't promise: sáqad)

Díliq musáqad ug kwártu si Pírla. (She can't promise)

Díliq makasáqad ug kwártu si Pírla. (She doesn't want to rent: ábang)

Díliq muqábang ug kwártu si Pírla. (Waláq)

Waláq muqábang ug kwártu si Pírla. (She's not renting)

Waláq magqabáng ug kwártu si Pírla. (She wasn't able to rent)

Waláq makaqábang ug kwártu si Pírla. (She won't live: puyúq)

Díliq mupuyúg kwártu si Pírla. (She can't live)

Díliq makapuyúg kwártu si Pírla. (Waláq)

Waláq makapuyúg kwártu si Pírla. (She's not living)

Waláq magpuyúg kwártu si Pírla. (She won't ask for: hángyuq)

Díliq muhángyug kwártu si Pírla. (She can't ask for)

Díliq makahángyug kwártu si Pírla. (She's not asking for)

Waláq maghángyug kwártu si Pírla. (She won't move out: bálhin)

Díliq mubálhig kwártu si Pírla. (She can't move out)

Díliq makabálhig kwártu si Pírla. (She won't look for: mangítaq)

Díliq mangítag kwártu si Pírla. (She can't look for)

Díliq makapangítag kwártu si Pírla. (She wasn't able to look for)

Waláq makapangítag kwártu si Pírla.

Step IV. (Combination of I, II, III)

'He will get on a jeep.'

Musakáy siyág dyip.	(nakasakáy)
Nakasakáy siyág dyip.	(was riding)
Nagsakáy siyág dyip.	(He won't get on or ride on)
Díliq siyá musakáyg dyip.	(waláq)
Waláq siyá musakáyg dyip.	(He is not riding)
Waláq siyá magsakáyg dyip.	(He is riding)
Nagsakáy siyág dyip.	(He's renting)
Nagqábang siyág dyip.	(He wants to rent)
Muqábang siyág dyip.	(He rented)
Miqábang siyág dyip.	(He was able to rent)
Nakaqábang siyág dyip.	(He won't rent)
Díliq siyá muqábag dyip.	(He's not renting)
Waláq siyá magqábag dyip.	(He can't rent)

Díliq siyá makaqábag dyip.	(He can't choose: <u>píliq</u>)
Díliq siyá makapílig dyip.	(He chose)
Nagpíliq siyág dyip.	(He was able to choose)
Nakapíliq siyág dyip.	(mupíliq)
Mupíliq siyág dyip.	(He won't choose)
Díliq siyá {magpíliq / mupílig} dyip.	(He wasn't able to choose)
Waláq siyá makapílig dyip.	(He couldn't buy: <u>palít</u>)
Waláq siyá makapalít ug dyip.	(He will buy)
{Magpalít / Mupalít} siyág dyip.	(He bought)
{Nipalít / Mipalít} siyág dyip.	(He was able to buy)
Nakapalít siyág dyip.	(He can't buy)
Díliq siyá makapalít ug dyip.	(He didn't buy)
Waláq siyá {magpalít / mupalít} ug dyip.	

V A. Pilíqa ang hústung púrma. (Choose the proper form) (5 C and subsections)

1. (Muqábang, Magqábang) mig baláy dínhi sa sunúd búwan. 'We want to rent a house here next month.'
2. Ádtu tas píkas (magbántay, mubántay) ug dyip. 'Let's wait for a jeep across the street.'
3. Gústu kung (mutánqaw, magtánqaw) sa baybáay. 'I would like to see the shack.'
4. (Muhatúd, Maghatúd) ka ba námuq sa Dyuns Abinyú? 'Will you take us to Jones Avenue?'
5. (Magsígi, Musígi) ba lang tag paqábut hángtud magabíqi? 'Shall we just keep on waiting until night falls?'
6. (Muláqag, Magláqag) nang mga irúqa dínhi káda Dumínggu. 'Those dogs wander around here every Sunday.'
7. (Mikáqun, Nagkaqún) nang mga irúqa sa súbra pagqabút námuq. 'Those dogs were eating the leftovers when we arrived.'
8. (Mibálik, Nagbálik) dáyun ang ámung gisákyan. 'The one we were riding on came back right away.'
9. (Nagqigutqigút, Muqigutqígut) ang taytáyan pagqági nákuq gahápun. 'The bridge was creaking when I went over it yesterday.'
10. (Milakáw, Naglakáw) ra ba ang tigúwang gabántay sa baybáay. 'The old man who watches the shack has gone.'
11. (Mudalá, Magdalá) kug makáqun nátuq dídtu.

12. Inigkahumán nátug kalíguq (mupaqúliq, magpaqúliq) ba ta dáyun? 'When we finish swimming, shall we go home right away?'

13. (Miqulán, Nagqulán) gahápun pagqádtu námuq sa Púquk. 'It was raining yesterday when we went to Pook.'

14. Díliq silá gústung (magpuyúq, mupuyúq) dínhi.

15. Gústu ku (muqádtu, magqádtu) sa Banáwaq.

V B. Pilíqa ang hústung púrma. (Choose the proper form.) Pilíqa gayúd ang potential kun mahímuq. (5 C and subsections)

1. (Mukáqun, Makakaqún) ka na bag haluqháluq? 'Do you want to eat halo-halo now?'

2. (Musúbay, Makasúbay) ba ta sa dálan Piláys? 'Shall we follow Pelaez Street?'

3. (Maghatúd, Makahatúd) ka ba námuq sa Dyuns Abinyú? 'Can you take us to Jones Avenue?'

4. Ang bátaq (musaká, makasaká) sa táqas. 'The child can climb to the top.'

5. (Muhúnung, Makahúnung) na ba ang traak? 'Is the truck going to stop now?'

6. (Makabántay, Magbántay) kanáng tiguwánga sa baybáay. 'That old man will watch the shack.'

7. (Makalíngkud, Mulíngkud) ba mi sa ímung lántay? 'May we sit on your bench?'

8. (Makaqabút, Muqabút) ta dáyun sa Sibú ug (makasakáy, magsakáy) ta dáyun. 'We will get to Cebu quickly if we can get a ride right away.'

9. Kínsa may (makabayád, mubáyad) sa áyskrim? 'Who's going to pay for the ice cream?'

10. (Makasakáy, Musakáy) pa kaháq kitá niqárung urása? 'Can we still get (a bus) at this hour?'

11. (Magqánhi, Makaqánhi) ka gyud kay waq ka nay trabáhu.

12. (Makahatúd, Maghatúd) ka kaháq námuq dídtu Dung?

13. Nuy, (makapangutána, mangutána) ba ku ug háqin si Pírla (magpuyúq, makapuyúq)?

14. Dalíq dirí kay (magsakáy, makasakáy) tingáli ta ug dyip.

PP-K Goals (5 D)

Step I. (Supply various goals)

'So you're the one who's going to rent the room.'

Ikáw diqáy muqábang sa kwártu?	(ug baay)
Ikáw diqáy muqábang ug baay?	(nangítaq)
Ikáw diqáy nangítag baay?	(ni Mis Wílbi)
Ikáw diqáy nangítaq ni Mis Wílbi?	(níya)

Ikáw diqáy nangítaq níya?	(sa dyip)
Ikáw diqáy nangítas dyip?	(musakáy)
Ikáw diqáy musakáys dyip?	(áni)
Ikáw diqáy musakáy áni?	(nagqimbitár)
Ikáw diqáy nagqimbitár áni?	(ni Místir Gamílu)
Ikáw diqáy nagqimbitár ni Místir Gamílu?	(ni Nuy Tibúq)
Ikáw diqáy nagqimbitár ni Nuy Tibúq?	(sa táwu)
Ikáw diqáy nagqimbitár sa táwu?	(nagtawág)
Ikáw diqáy nagtawág sa táwu?	(níla)
Ikáw diqáy nagtawág níla?	(ni Pírla)
Ikáw diqáy nagtawág ni Pírla?	(mihánggyuq)
Ikáw diqáy mihángyuq ni Pírla?	(ug dyip)
Ikáw diqáy mihángyug dyip?	(sa bátaq)
Ikáw diqáy mihángyuq sa bátaq?	(nakasáqad)
Ikáw diqáy nakasáqad sa bátaq?	(ug bisíta)
Ikáw diqáy nakasáqad ug bisíta?	

Step II. (Supply various goals; sa and ug phrases only.)

'Where can we get on a jeep?'

Ása man ta makasakáyg dyip?	(the jeep)
Ása man ta makasakáy sa dyip?	(a bus)
Ása man ta makasakáyg traak?	(the bus)
Ása man ta makasakáy sa traak?	(maghuwát)
Ása man ta maghuwát sa traak?	(the child)
Ása man ta maghuwát sa bátaq?	(a child)
Ása man ta maghuwát ug bátaq?	(the man)
Ása man ta maghuwát sa táwu?	(a man)
Ása man ta maghuwát ug táwu?	(magtawág)
Ása man ta magtawág ug táwu?	(the woman)
Ása man ta magtawág sa babáyi?	(a woman)
Ása man ta magtawág ug babáyi?	(the old man)
Ása man ta magtawág sa tigúwang?	(an old man)
Ása man ta magtawág ug tigúwang?	(makakitáq)
Ása man ta makakitág tigúwang?	(the house)
Ása man ta makakitás baay?	(a house)

Ásа man ta makakitág baay?	(the room)
Ása man ta makakitás kwártu?	(a room)
Ása man ta makakitág kwártu?	(muqábang)
Ása man ta muqábag kwártu?	

Step III. (Supply various goals: pronouns, proper nouns)

'I will never pay her.'

Díliq gyud ku mubáyad níya.	(that)
Díliq gyud ku mubáyad ánaq.	(them)
Díliq gyud ku mubáyad níla.	(this)
Díliq gyud ku mubáyad {áni / íni}.	(this man [this him])
Díliq gyud ku mubáyad áni níya.	(Miss Wilby)
Díliq gyud ku mubáyad ni Mis Wílbi.	(that one)
Díliq gyud ku mubáyad {ádtu / ánaq}.	(Perla)
Díliq gyud ku mubáyad ni Pírla.	(him)
Díliq gyud ku mubáyad níya.	(Mr. Gamelo)
Díliq gyud ku mubáyad ni Místir Gamílu.	(you)
Díliq gyud ku mubáyad nímu.	(this one)
Díliq gyud ku mubáyad {íri / íni}.	(this woman [this her])
Díliq gyud ku mubáyad {íri / íni} níya.	(Mrs. Abellana)
Díliq gyud ku mubáyad ni Mísis Abilyána.	(that man [that him])
Díliq gyud ku mubáyad {ánaq / ádtu} níya.	(Noy Tibo)
Díliq gyud ku mubáyad ni Nuy Tibúq.	(you, plural)
Díliq gyud ku mubáyad nínyu.	(that woman [that her])
Díliq gyud ku mubáyad {ádtu / ánaq} níya.	(Dr. Fernandez)
Díliq gyud ku mubáyad ni Dúktur Pirnándis.	(those people [those them])
Díliq gyud ku mubáyad {ádtu / ánaq} níla.	

Step IV. (Combination of II and III)

'I want to bring a book.'

Gústu kung magdalág líbru.	(the book)
Gústu kung magdalás líbru.	(a pencil)
Gústu kung magdalág lápis.	(the pencil)
Gústu kung magdalás lápis.	(makapíliq)
Gústu kung makapílis lápis.	(that one)
Gústu kung makapíliq {ánaq / ádtu}.	(a house)
Gústu kung makapílig baay.	(this one)
Gústu kung makapíliq íri.	(muhángyuq)
Gústu kung muhángyuq íri.	(Miss Wilby)
Gústu kung muhángyuq ni Mis Wílbi.	(her)
Gústu kung muhángyuq níya.	(a jeep)
Gústu kung muhángyug dyip.	(muqábang)
Gústu kung muqábang ug dyip.	(the house)
Gústu kung muqábang sa baay.	(that one)
Gústu kung muqábang {ádtu / ánaq}.	(a room)
Gústu kung muqábang ug kwártu.	(makakitáq)
Gústu kung makakitág kwártu.	(that man [that him])
Gústu kung makakitáq ánaq níya.	(Perla)
Gústu kung makakitáq ni Pírla.	(the woman)
Gústu kung makakitáq sa babáyi.	

PP-L Agents (5 D)

Step I. (Supply various agents)

'I'm just going to drink a glass of water.'

Muqinúm lang kug usá ka básung túbig.	(si Iyúq Tibúq)
Muqinúm lang si Iyúq Tibúg usá ka básung túbig.	(siyá)
Muqinúm lang siyág usá ka básung túbig.	(silá)
Muqinúm lang silág usá ka básung túbig.	(ang bátaq)
Muqinúm lang ang bátag usá ka básung túbig.	(kamí)
Muqinúm lang kamíg usá ka básung túbig.	(si Pírla)
Muqinúm lang si Pírlag usá ka básung túbig.	(si Mis Wílbi)
Muqinúm lang si Mis Wílbig usá ka básung túbig.	(ang tigúwang)
Muqinúm lang ang tigúwag usá ka básung túbig.	(ta)
Muqinúm lang tag usá ka básung túbig.	(ni)

Muqinúm lang nig usá ka básung túbig. (kádtu)

Muqinúm lang kádtug usá ka básung túbig. (ang asáwa)

Muqinúm lang ang asáwag usá ka básung túbig. (si Pírla)

Muqinúm lang si Pírlag usá ka básung túbig. (ang bátaq)

Muqinúm lang ang bátag usá ka básung túbig. (mi)

Muqinúm lang mig usá ka básung túbig. (ri)

Muqinúm lang rig usá ka básung túbig. (si Mísis Abilyána)

Muqinúm lang si Mísis Abilyánag usá ka básung túbig. (ang babáyi)

Muqinúm lang ang babáyig usá ka básung túbig. (si Místir Gamílu)

Muqinúm lang si Místir Gamílug usá ka básung túbig.

Step II. (Supply various subjects)

'Miss Wilby will go to sleep now.'

Matúlug na si Mis Wílbi karún. (he)

Matúlug na siyá karún. (the dog)

Matúlug na ang irúq karún. (that one)

Matúlug na {kanáq / kádtu} karún. (Nuy Tibúq)

Matúlug na si Nuy Tibúq karún. (we [not you])

Matúlug na {kamí / mi} karún. (Perla)

Matúlug na si Pírla karún. (I)

Matúlug na {akú / ku} karún. (you, singular)

Matúlug ka na karún. (the man)

Matúlug na ang táwu karún. (she)

Matúlug na siyá karún. (we [including you])

Matúlug na {kitá / ta} karún. (that one)

Matúlug na {kanáq / naq} karún. (this)

Matúlug na {kirí / ri} karún. (Mrs. Abellana)

Matúlug na si Mísis Abilyána karún. (the wife)

Matúlug na ang asáwa karún. (Mr. Gamelo)

Matúlug na si Místir Gamílu karún. (the boy)

Matúlug na ang bátaq karún. (the man)

Matúlug na ang táwu karún. (they)

Matúlug na silá karún.

Step III. (Same as II but alternating the long and short forms of the pronouns)

'I cannot go to the store any more.'

Diq na ku kaqádtus tindáhan. (John)

Diq na kaqádtus tindáhan si Hwan. (we [not you])

Diq na mi kaqádtus tindáhan. (the driver)

Diq na kaqádtus tindáhan ang dráybir. (they)

Diq na silá kaqádtus tindáhan. (the wife)

Diq na kaqádtus tindáhan ang asáwa. (that one)

Diq na $\left\{\begin{matrix}\text{tu}\\ \text{naq}\end{matrix}\right\}$ kaqádtus tindáhan. (the man)

Diq na kaqádtus tindáhan ang táwu. (she)

Diq na siyá kaqádtus tindáhan. (Miss Wilby)

Diq na kaqádtus tindáhan si Mis Wílbi. (you)

Diq na ka kaqádtus tindáhan. (Perla)

Diq na kaqádtus tindáhan si Pírla. (we [including you])

Diq na ta kaqádtus tindáhan. (Noy Tibo)

Diq na kaqádtus tindáhan si Nuy Tibúq. (you, plural)

Diq na mu kaqádtus tindáhan. (the old man)

Diq na kaqádtus tindáhan ang tigúwang. (this one)

Diq na ni kaqádtus tindáhan. (Mrs. Abellana)

Diq na kaqádtus tindáhan si Mísis Abilyána. (that one)

Diq na $\left\{\begin{matrix}\text{naq}\\ \text{tu}\end{matrix}\right\}$ kaqádtus tindáhan. (Dr. Fernandez)

Diq na kaqádtus tindáhan si Dúktur Pirnándis.

VI A. Choose the proper form.

1. Mahímuq bang mutánqaw (ug, sa) ínyung kwártu?
2. Kiní (ni, si) Mírli ang nangítaq (níya, siyá).
3. Gústu gyud (ku, nákuq)ng mutánqaw ug baybáay.
4. Magdalá (siyá, níya) (ang, ug) pagkáqun.
5. Nangáqun (kanáq, ánaq)ng mga irúq (ádtu, kádtu)ng mga súbras mga. nangalíguq.
6. Kun (nínyu, kamú) malíguq, (silá, níla) manglíngkud lang.
7. Ang gapuyúq (kiní, niqíni)ng baláya milakáw.

8. Nangítaq (silá, níla) (ug, sa) kapahuláyan ('place to rest').

9. Maqú kiní (si, ni) Mis Wílbi. Gústu (siyá, níya) muqábang sa usáng kwártu.

10. Mahímuq bang mutánqaw ku (ang, sa) ínyung kwártung paqabángan?

11. Kun natúug (nínyu, kamú) dídtu sa ínyu nagmatá (kamí, námuq) dínhi sa ámuq.

12. (Si, Ni) Máma nímu níqa ba?

13. Ug dúnay maghángyuq (kanímu, ikáw) musugút kaháq (nímu, ka)?

14. Magquná lang (akú, nákuq) (kang Huwán, si Huwán). Ibílin ku lang si Huwán dínhi.

15. Kiní (si, ni) Nuy Tibúq maqúy labíng tigúwang dínhi sa ámung lúngsud.

VI B. Pilíqa ang hústung púrma. (3 A 3 and 5 A 1)

1. Dúna ba (kamú, nínyu)y mga bátaq dínhi?

2. Kahadlukán gud (ka, nímu) nga diq ka man muqágis taytáyan. (hadlukán 'easily frightened')

3. Dúna ba (kamú, nínyu)y mga lubí dídtus ínyu?

4. Kaníndut gud (siyá, níya)g baay!

5. May apú na ba (si, ni) Nuy Tibúg?

6. Kadághan gud (nímu, ikáw)g apú!

VII A. Choose the correct form of the pronoun shown in parentheses in the nominative. (3 A 3, 5 A 1, 5 D 1, 5 D 2)

Panánglit: Waq pa ba diqáy mihángyuq _________? (ka)
Tubág: Waq pa ba diqáy mihángyuq nímu? or Waq pa ba diqáy mihángyuq kanímu?

1. Musugút _________ ba kun dúnay muhángyuq _________? (ikáw)

2. Waq ba _________ maglisúd pagqánhi dínhi? (kamú)

3. Pirlá, mangádtu ba _________ karún sa Pulambatú? (kitá)

4. Dúna ba _________ y mga bátaq sa ínyu? (kamú)

5. Kaníndut gud _________ ng (kiní) ímung gása pára _________. (akú)

6. Muqubán _________ (ikáw) ba _________ (kamí) ngádtu sa Amiriká?

7. Waláq ra ba _________ y bir Nyur. (kitá)

8. Ayáw na lang kug tagáqi ug bir kay nagdalíq man _________. (akú)

9. Dúna na tingáli apú _________ (si) Nuy Tibúq.

10. Ádtu na lang _________ kay údtu na. (kamí)

11. Kadakúq _________ng líbru ni Pírla. (kiní)

12. Kadághan gud _________ng ímung dalá nga mga gása. (kanáq)

13. Nangítaq si Pírla _________ (si Mis Wílbi).

14. Nubintayqútsu na diqáy si Iyúq Tibúq. Katigúwang na diqáy __________ nu? (si Iyúq)

15. Magquná na lang ku __________ ha? (si Huwán)

VII B. Choose the correct form of the pronoun shown in parentheses in the nominative. (2 E, 3 A 3, 5 A 1, 5 D 1, and 5 D 2)

1. Dúna bay mga lubí sa __________ng dápit? (kamú)
2. Ákung gidalá __________ng ákung amígu. (kiní)
3. Upát na ka buqúk ang __________ng anák. (siyá)
4. Giqimbitár ku ni Pírla ngádtu sa __________ ug paniqúdtu. (silá)
5. Waq pa intáwuy mihángyuq __________ (si Pilár) píru kanúnay __________ ng nagpaqábut (kanáq).
6. Míngaw kaqáyu dínhi sa __________, nu? (kamú)
7. Kiní si Índay dúna ni __________y upát ka buqúk anák. (siyá)
8. Dayún lang. Únsa may __________? (kitá)
9. Ása man __________ manakáy ug dyip páras Kárbun? (kitá)
10. __________ lay magpíliq kung háqin ang ímung gústu. (ikáw)

VIII A. Intonation (Follow procedure outlined in Lesson 1, p. 24.) (423 question)

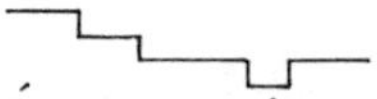

1.	Únsa may átuq?	1.3
2.	Ánhi lang ta manihápun?	2 b 31
3.	Únsa man naq?	5.39
4.	Pilá may bayranán ánaq sa káda búwan?	3 b 25
5.	Ása man ta musakáy ug muqádtu tas Banáwaq?	3 a 16
6.	Pilá na man diqáy idád nímu Iyúq?	5.10
7.	Únsa may ámung sákyan?	
8.	Pilá man mu ka buqúk?	
9.	Giqúnsa man nímu pagqabút ánang idára?	5.14
10.	Ása man ning dyípa Dung?	3 c 24
11.	Únsa may átuq Místir Gamílu?	1.22
12.	Únsa man nang ákung nadungúg?	5.36
13.	Pilá man diqáy ka ka ádlaw ngánhi?	5.56
14.	Dúna na dyud kay mga anák?	5.19
15.	Dúna gyud sad kay mga apú?	5.21

VIII B. (234 statement or command)

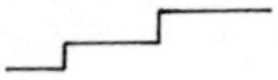

1. Aa mu gyud. 5.2
2. Ayáw na lang. 1.14
3. Aa, sayún ra naq. 5.15
4. Waq man ku maglisúd. 2.18
5. Dayún lang. 1.6
6. Gamáy ra kaqáyung mga dápit dídtung dúnay ságing. 5.31
7. Pagdalá diríg bir. 2.26
8. Maqáyu man. 1.8
9. Mga duhá ra tingáli ka ádlaw. 5.57
10. Ságdi na lang duktúr. 2.28
11. Maghuwát lang kug láqin. 3 c 34
12. Aa, dúnay dághan. 5.23

VIII C. Another question intonation consists of a fall in pitch ending with a rise on the final syllable (this final pitch is higher than that of the beginning syllable). Such an intonation is symbolized 324.

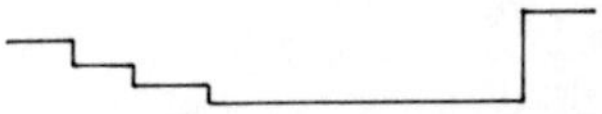

1. Náqa ba si Místir Abáya? 1.4
2. Níqa ba si Dúktur Pirnándis? 2.2
3. Kínsa ning nagtawág? 2.4
4. Dúna muy mga lubí sa ínyung dápit? 5.27
5. Diq ka kaháq unyáq samúkans mga bátaq? 3 c 11
6. Waq pa ba gud diqáy? 5.47
7. Ádtu nyaq sa baay ha? 5.50
8. Kínsa ni?
9. Kínsay ímung ngálan Dung? 2 b 19
10. Língkud saq mu ha? 3 b 9

VIII D. (423 statement)

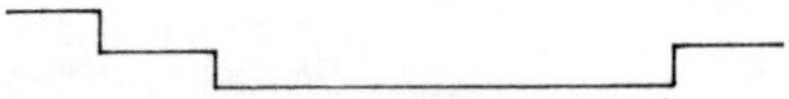

1. Mu nang waq gyud ku matigúwang. 5.17
2. Kiní si Místir Gamílu. 1.10
3. Ánhi lang ta manihápun. 2 b 31
4. Ádlaw naq dídtus Amiriká. 5.42

5. Ánhaq muhúnung ang mga dyip. 3 a 25
6. Gústu siyáng muqábang ug kwártu.
7. Líbri man gung sugáq ug túbig. 3 b 27
8. Dúna siyáy bátaq.
9. Maqáyu diqáy naq. 3 c 15
10. Mu ni si Índay. 3 c 4
11. Ákuq siyáng ibílin dínhi.

IX A. Pagbása (Reading)

1. Retell the story in Cebuano in your own words.
2. Have the informant make up questions similar to those of the reading to Lesson 4, p. 155, and answer them.
3. Do the exercise on verbs, IX B, p. 212.

Si Mis Wílbi ug si Pírla miqádtu sa Magalyánis

Pírla: Magdalíq ta kay muqádtu pa man tingáli tas Banáwaq humán tag ádtus Magalyánis.

Mis Wílbi: Isáq pa, muqinúm pa kug túbig. Ikáw lay maghuwát ug dyip kay mubálik pa kus kwártu. Magkúhaq kug plíti.

Pírla: Maghuwát kug dyip, kanáng muqági sa Kulún kay manáqug tas Liin.

Mis Wílbi: Ngánung ádtu man tas Liin muhúnung nga ádtu man tas Magalyánis?

Pírla: Ságdi lang ('Never mind') duqúl ra man ang Magalyánis gíkan sa Liin. Mudúlhug tag dyútay unyáq mulikúq, Magalyánis na. Ug diq gud ka, magsakáy ta. ('If you don't want to, let's ride.) (Sa dídtu nas Liin)

Mis Wílbi: Uy! níqa na man tas Liin. Únsa, manglíngkud pa ta gihápun dínhi? Taná.

Pírla: Isáq pa, waláq pa muhúnung ang dyip. Maglakáw lang ta ngádtus Magalyánis.

Mis Wílbi: Uu sigí, mutánqaw lang tas balígyaq ('things for sale'). Waláq man ku makadalág kwárta.

Pírla: Taym pa, musulúd saq ku áring tindáhan. Ádtu lang ka maghuwát sa sunúd tindáhan.
(Taqudtaqúd sa sulúds tindáhan, gisamúkan si Mis Wílbi sa usá ka táwu.)

Mis Wílbi: Uy! ngánu gung magsámuk ka nákuq? Tábiq, muqági ku.
(Sa íyang kaqugalíngun ['to herself'])
Uh, magqúnsa man run ku áni? Akú na man lang usá. Básin ug naghuwát dídtus Pírla ug díliq musunúd tung táwung misámuk nákuq.

Pírla: Ngánung nagdalíq ka? Naqúnsa ka? Mu ra ka mag nakakitáq ug únsa. 'You look as if you've seen something.'

Mis Wílbi: Dínhaq man guy táwung nagsámuk. Mubálik pa úntaq ku. Makabalík pa kaháq ku u diq na ba lang?

Pírla: Ay na lang. Diq na ka makahímuq. Nagdalíq ra ba ta, (makahímuq 'can')

IX B. Exercise on the actives. Supply affixes. (5 C)

Si Mis Wílbi ug si Pírla (ádtu) sa Magalyánis.

Pírla: (Dalíq) ta kay (ádtu) pa man tingáli tas Banáwaq humán tag ádtus Magalyánis.

Mis Wílbi: Isáq pa, (inúm) pa kug túbig. Ikáw lay (huwát) ug dyip kay (bálik) pa kus kwártu. (kúhaq) kug plíti.

Pírla: (Huwát) kug dyip, kanáng (ági) sa Kulún kay (kanáqug) tas Liin.

Mis Wílbi: Ngánung ádtu man tas Liin (húnung) nga ádtu man tas Magalyánis?

Pírla: Ságdi lang, duqúl ra man ang Magalyánis gíkan sa Liin. (Dúlhug) tag dyútay unyáq (likúq), Magalyánis na. Ug diq gud ka, (sakáy) ta. ['If you don't want to, let's ride.'] (Sa dídtu nas Liin)

Mis Wílbi: Uy! níqa na man tas Liin. Únsa, (panglíngkud) pa ta gihápun dínhi? Taná.

Pírla: Isáq pa, waláq pa (húnung) ang dyip. (Lakáw) lang ta ngádtus Magalyánis.

Mis Wílbi: Uu sigí (tánqaw) lang tas balígyaq ['things for sale']. Waláq man ku (dalá)g kwárta.

Pírla: Taym pa, (sulúd) saq ku áring tindáhan. Ádtu lang ka (huwát) sa sunúd tindáhan.
(Taqudtaqúd sa salúds tindáhan, gisamúkan si Miss Wílbi sa usá ka táwu.)

Mis Wílbi: Uy! ngánu gung (sámuk) ka nákuq? Tábiq (ági) ku.
(Sa íyang kaqugalíngun ['to herself'])
Uh. magqúnsa man run ku áni? Akú na man lang usá. Básin ug (huwát) dídtus Pírla ug díliq (sunúd) tung táwung (sámuk) nákuq.

Pírla: Ngánung (dalíq) ka? Naqúnsa ka? Mu ra ka mag (kitáq) ug únsa. ['What's the matter with you? You look as if you've seen something.']

Mis Wílbi: Dínhaq man guy táwung (sámuk). (Bálik) pa úntaq ku, (bálik) pa kaháq ku u diq na ba lang?

Pírla: Ay na lang. Diq na ka makahímuq. (Dalíq) ra ba ta. [makahímuq 'can']

X. Sultiqánay

Si Mis Wílbi ug si Mis Sántus túqas Pulambatú.

Únang Báhin

A. Pirlá, kínsa man nang táwung nagpadulúng ngánhi? Tigúwang na man kaqáyu nang tanqáwun.

B. Aa, kanáq. Kanáq si Nuy Tibúq. Mu naq siyáy labíng tigúwang táwu dínhis Pulambatú.

A. Kanáng mga bátang ubán níya—íya ba nang mga apú?

B. Díliq, kay tigúwang na ang íyang mga apú. Nangapú na gániq silá.

A. Táwga ra siyá.

B. Nuy Tibúq. Dalíq ra gud. Gústu kung ipaqilaqíla nímu si Mis Wílbi.

Hústu ug díliq:

1. Ang táwung nagpadulúng ngánhi díliq kaqáyu tigúwang tanqáwun.
2. Túqa silá sa Pulambatú.
3. Si Nuy Tibúq ang labíng tigúwang táwus Pulambatú.
4. Tigúwang kaqáyung tanqáwun kádtung nagqubán ni Nuy Tibúq.
5. Nahibalú si Pírla kun piláy idád ni Nuy Tibúq. Nubintayqútsu kunú.
6. Tigúwang na ang apú ni Nuy Tibúq.

Ikaduháng Báhin

C. Kumústa ka Day.

B. Maqáyu man Iyúq. Dúna kuy pangutána nímu. Mahímuq bang mangutána?

C. Uu. Mahímuq kaqáyu.

B. Piláy idád nímu run Iyúq?

C. Akú? Dakúq na akú kaqáyug idád. Diq na maqiháp ang ákung idád. Kiníng ákung asáwa run, ikatulú na ni nákung asáwa.

B. Giqúnsa man nímu Nuy pagqabút niqánang idára?

C. Sayún ra naq Day. Inúm lang kug usá ka húngut tubáq káda búntag. Mu nang waq matigúwang.

Hústu ug díliq:

7. Dúna si Mis Wílbiy pangutánang Nuy Tibúq.
8. Miqingún si Nuy Tibúq nga nubintayqútsu na ang íyang idád.
9. Duháy asáwang Nuy Tibúq.
10. Nakaqabút si Nuy Tibúq ug dakúng idád kay káda búntag siyá muqinúm ug lítsi.
11. Waq gyud muqinúm ug tubáq si Nuy Tibúq.
12. Miqingún si Mis Wílbi nga gústu siyág tubáq.

LESSON 6. SHOPPING

Sagquluhúnun (Basic Sentences)

First Part	Únang Báhin
Miss Wilby goes shopping.	Namalît si Mis Wîlby.
store	tindáhan
of	sa
jewelry	aláhas
[linker between aláhas and kinhasún]	nga
sea shells	kinhasún
will enter	musúud

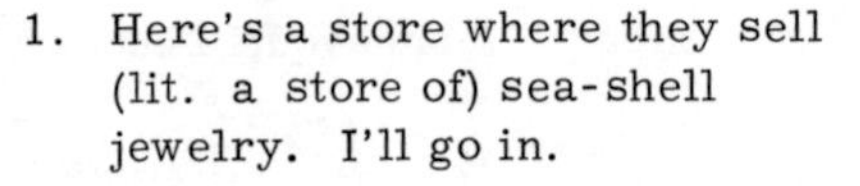

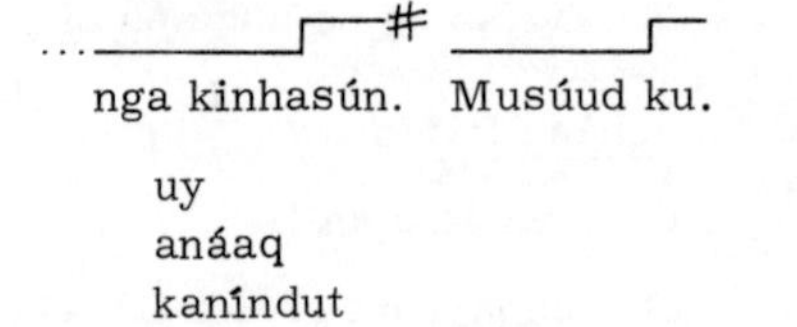

1. Here's a store where they sell (lit. a store of) sea-shell jewelry. I'll go in.	1. Díqay tindáhan sa mga aláhas nga kinhasún. Musúud ku.
oh!	uy
[expression of surprise]	anáaq
how pretty!	kanîndut
[linker between niqáni and arîyus]	nga
earrings	arîyus

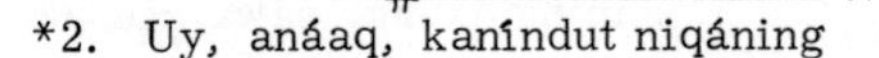

2. Oh, how beautiful these earrings are!	*2. Uy, anáaq, kanîndut niqáning mga arîyus!
how much apiece?	tagpîla
3. Miss, how much are these (apiece)?	*3. Day, tagpîla man ni?
three	tris
pesos	pîsus
pair	par
4. Three pesos a pair.	4. Tris pîsus ang par.
for example; suppose that . . .	pananglîtan
if	ug

buy	mupalīt
[particle preceding goal]	ug
dozen	dusīna
how much?	pilá
5. Suppose I buy a dozen, how much would it be?	*5. Panangl̄itag mupalīt kug ... usá ka dusīna, # pilá man?
can give	makahátag
price	prīsyu
[linker between prīsyu and ispisyál]	nga
special	ispisyál
fifteen	kīnsi
dozen	dusīna
6. Um, that one? We can give (you) a special price: fifteen pesos a dozen.	*6. Aa, kanáq? # Makahátag mig ... prīsyung ispisyál. # Kīnsi ... pīsus ang dusīna.
because	kay
American woman	Amirkána
because	man
7. Because you're an American.	7. Kay Amirkána man ka.
not	diq
[question particle]	ba
possible	mahīmuq
if	ug
ten	dyis
just . . . now	na lang
8. Can't we make it ten? (Lit. Is it not possible if just ten now?)	8. Diq ba mahīmug dyis na lang?
twelve	dúsi
just exactly	ra
for sure	gyud
final price	ultimúng prīsyu
9. Twelve is definitely the lowest price.	9. Dúsi ra gyuy ultimúng prīsyu.

for sure	gyud
[particle upon receiving information]	diqáy
can be	mahímuq
[linker between mahímuq and dyis]	nga

10. So we really cannot make it ten? — 10. Diq ba gyud diqáy mahímung dyis?

just a second	úsaq pa
by us	átuq
[linker between átuq and pangutánqun]	nga
person to be asked	pangutánqun
Chinaman (the manager)	Ínsik

11. Wait, I'll ask the manager. (Lit. Just a second, because we will ask the Chinaman.) — 11. Úsaq pa kay átung pangutánqun ang Ínsik.

tell him	íngna
that [linker between íngna and the rest of the sentence]	nga
no more than	ra
offer	hángyuq

12. Tell him I'll offer no more than ten. (Lit. No more than ten is my offer.) — 12. Íngna nga dyis ray ákung hángyuq.

[particle asking interlocutor's agreement]	ha

13. Umm, I'll ask him, shall I? — *13. Aa, ákung pangutánqun siyá ha?

as it turns out	diqáy
can be done	mahímuq
below	ubús sa
no more	waq na
profit	ganánsya
[linker between ganánsya and mahímuq]	nga
can be made	mahímuq

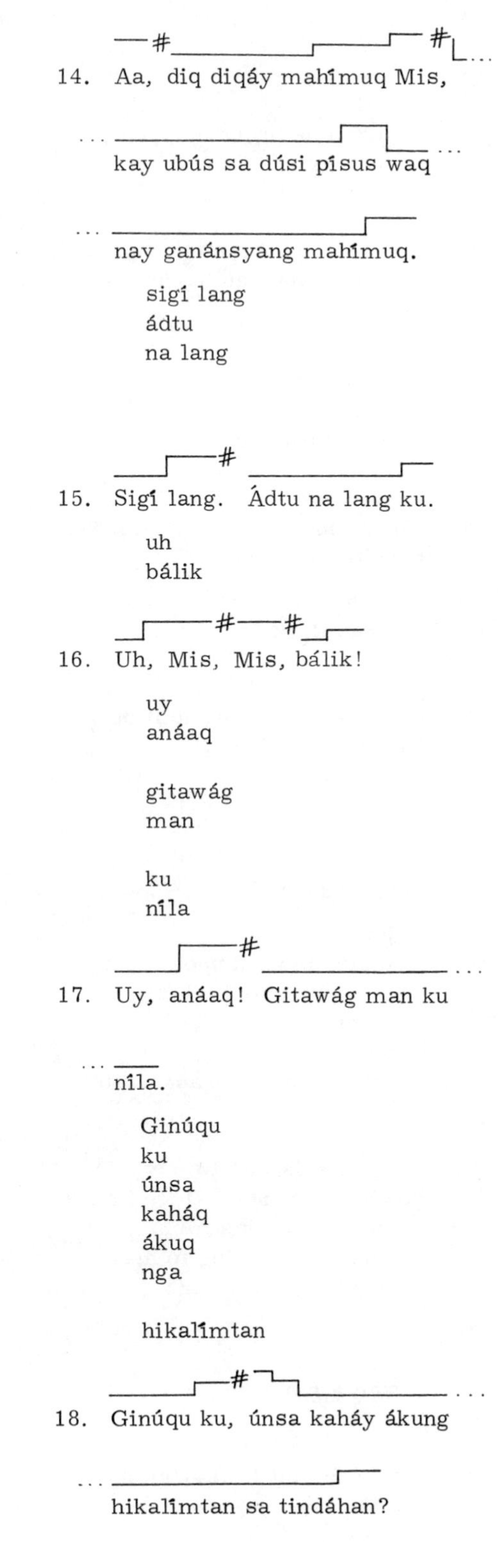

14. Mm, it can't be done, Miss, because below twelve pesos we make no profit (lit. there is no profit any longer that can be made).

14. Aa, diq diqáy mahímuq Mis, kay ubús sa dúsi písus waq nay ganánsyang mahímuq.

never mind	sigí lang
go	ádtu
[particle marking least undesirable of limited choices]	na lang

15. Never mind. I'll just go now.

15. Sigí lang. Ádtu na lang ku.

oh	uh
come back	bálik

16. Oh, Miss, Miss, come back!

16. Uh, Mis, Mis, bálik!

oh	uy
[expression of worried surprise]	anáaq
being called	gitawág
[particle upon receiving new information]	man
I	ku
by them	níla

17. O, dear! They're calling me.

17. Uy, anáaq! Gitawág man ku níla.

Lord	Ginúqu
my	ku
what?	únsa
can it be?	kaháq
by me	ákuq
[linker between ákuq and hikalímtan]	nga
accidentally forgotten	hikalímtan

18. My Lord, what can I have forgotten in the store?

18. Ginúqu ku, únsa kaháy ákung hikalímtan sa tindáhan?

can	mahímuq
now	na
buy	palitún
[particle preceding goal]	ug
ten	dyis

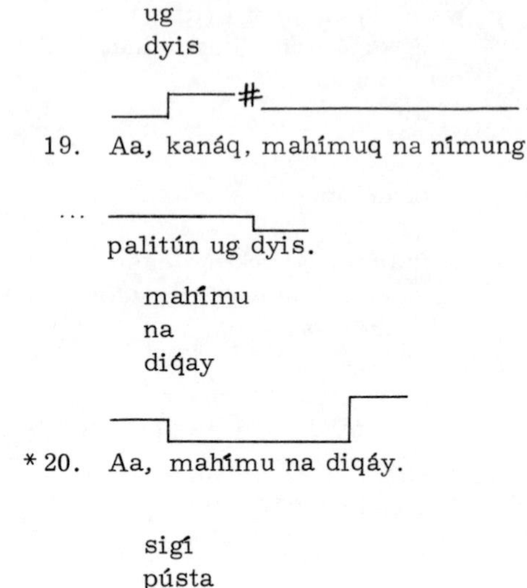

19. You can buy it for ten. (Lit. Ah, that—you can buy for ten now.)	19. Aa, kanáq, mahímuq na nímung palitún ug dyis.
it is possible	mahímu
now	na
as it turns out	diqay
20. Oh, I can? (Lit. Ah, so it is possible!)	*20. Aa, mahímu na diqáy.
go ahead	sigí
wrap it	pústa
21. Go ahead then. Wrap it up; I'll take (lit. buy) it.	21. Na sigí. Pústa kay ákung palitún.
22. Many thanks.	22. Dághang salámat.
no	waq
[particle used upon giving information]	man
other	láqin
twenty	báynti
thing to make change with	ikasinsíyu
23. All I have is this twenty. Do you have change? (Lit. I have no other than this twenty. Do you have something to make change?)	23. Waq man kuy láqin áning báynti. Dúna ba muy ikasinsíyu?
wait a moment	úsaq pa
24. Wait a moment. Let's take a look.	*24. Úsaq pa. Átung tanqáwun.
here it is	níqa
as it turns out	diqáy

25. Mm, here it is.	25. Aa, níqa diqáy.
26. Thank you. Good-by. (Lit. I'm going now).	26. Salámat ha. # Ádtu na ku.
oh type of small crab are being sold	uy kaság gipamalîgyaq
27. Oh, there are crabs for sale here!	27. Uy, # dîqay kaság nga ... gipamalígyaq!
how much apiece? [term of address for woman older than speaker; used only in addressing country people].	tagpíla Iyáq
28. How much are those crabs? (Lit. How much those crabs apiece, Iya?)	28. Tagpîla man nang kaság Iyáq?
thirty each centavos per piece	tagtráynta sintábus ang buqúk
29. Thirty centavos apiece.	29. Tagtráynta sintábus ang buqúk.
fresh	lábqas
30. Are they fresh? (Lit. Are those fresh?)	30. Lábqas ba kanáq?
alive those (just mentioned) they	búhiq naq silá
31. Fresh—they're alive! (Lit. Fresh, those, they are alive!)	31. Lábqas, # búhiq naq silá.
how? by me kill	unsáqun nákuq pagpatáy
32. How do I kill them?	32. Unsáqun man nákuq pagpatáy?
very easy	sayún ra

33. Oh, that's very easy! — 33. Aa, sayún ra naq!

cook it	lutúqa
will die	matáy
for sure	ra
be assured	bítaw

34. Cook them. Don't worry. They'll die for sure. — *34. Lutúqa, matáy ra bítaw naq.

my!	sus
how pitiful	kamakalulúquy
though (particle asking agreement to a fact exclaimed about)	ba
also	usáb

35. My, isn't that cruel! (Lit. My, how pitiful also, isn't it!) — *35. Sus, kamakalulúquy ba usáb!

Mga Pangutána

Únang Báhin

1. Tagpíla man ning aríyus nga kinhasún Day?
2. Pilá ka dusína ang ímung palitún Day?
3. Tris písus ang par?
4. Mahímuq ba nga dyis na lang ang usá ka dusína?
5. Diq ba mahímung ímu únang pangutánqun ang Ínsik?
6. May hikalímtan ba kaháq ku sa tindáhan?
7. Ngánung ímu man kung gitawág Day?
8. Palitún ba nímug dyis ang dusína sa aríyus Day?
9. Makasinsíyu ba mug bayntihún? (bayntihún 'twenty-peso bill')
10. Waq ka bay láqing kwárta Day?
11. Balígyaq ba nang kaság Iyáq?
12. Búhiq pa ba naq Iyáq?
13. Sayún ra bang pátyun nang kaság Iyáq?
14. Mupalít ka ba Day?
15. Pilá man ka buqúk ang ímung palitún?
16. Kanáng tindáhan diháq may balígyaq bang aláhas nga kinhasún?

17. Kun mupalít kug usá ka dusína, pilá man?

18. Pilá ka par ang ímung palitún Dung?

19. Pilá may hángyuq mu Day?

20. Palitún ba tu ni nímug dyis Day? (tu 'did you say?'—i.e. 'did you say that you would buy this for ten?')

Mga Pangutána (Matching)

Únang Báhin

1. Tindáhan man naq sa mga aláhas kinhasún, nu?
2. Tagpíla man ang par sa aríyus Day?
3. Pilá man kanáng giqingún mung prísyu ispisyál?
4. Diq ba mahímug dyis na lang ang dusína?
5. Palitún ba ni nímu Day?
6. Gitawág man ku nímu, dúna ba kuy hikalímtan?
7. May ikasinsíyu ka ba sa báynti písus?
8. Tagpíla man ang buqúk sa ímung kaság Yaq?
9. Búhiq pa ba nang kaság mu Yaq?

a. Aa, díliq kay waq nay ganánsyang mahímuq.
b. Waláq man. Gitawág ka lang nákuq kay mahímuq kunú sa dyis ang dusína sa mga aríyus.
c. Úqu Day, búhiq pa. Tanqáwa ra gud.
d. Úqu, dághan ra ba kaqáyung níndut diháq.
e. Kanáq diháng aríyus? Tris písus ang par.
f. Díliq lang; diq man kaháq* mahímuq sa dyis ang dusína.
g. Ang prísyu ispisyál, kínsi písus.
h. Waq ra ba Day.
i. Kiníng gágmay—tagdyis ang buqúk.

Sagquluhúnun (Basic Sentences)

Second Part	Ikaduháng Báhin
here, give me	ambí
let buy	papalitá
me	ku
[particle preceding goal]	ug
half	tungáq
of	sa
dozen	dusína

---

* Man kaháq 'you said that . . .'

36. Here. Let me have half a dozen. (Lit. Here, Iya. Let me buy half a dozen.)	*36. Ambî Iyáq.# Papalitá kug tungáq sa dusîna.
one-eighty	únu utsînta.
37. Those (what you have there)? One-eighty.	37. Kanáq?# Únu utsînta.
one-twenty	únu báynti
enough	hústu
38. One-twenty. Is (that) enough?	38. Únu báynti,# hústu ba?
give me	tagáqi ku
just	lang
[particle preceding goal]	ug
one-fifty	únu singkwînta
39. How about one-fifty? (Lit. Umm, just give me one-fifty.)	39. Aa,# tagáqi lang kug únu singkwînta.
all right	sigî
40. Yes, all right, one-fifty.	40. Uu sigî,# únu singkwînta.
five	sîngku
change it	suklîqi
[particle with statement drawing interlocutor's attention to something he doesn't see]	uh
41. Here's five (lit. There is my five here). Change it. Here.	41. Dîqay ákung sîngku,# suklîqi uh.
no	waq
[particle contradicting hearer's assumption]	man
change	sinsîyu
for	pára

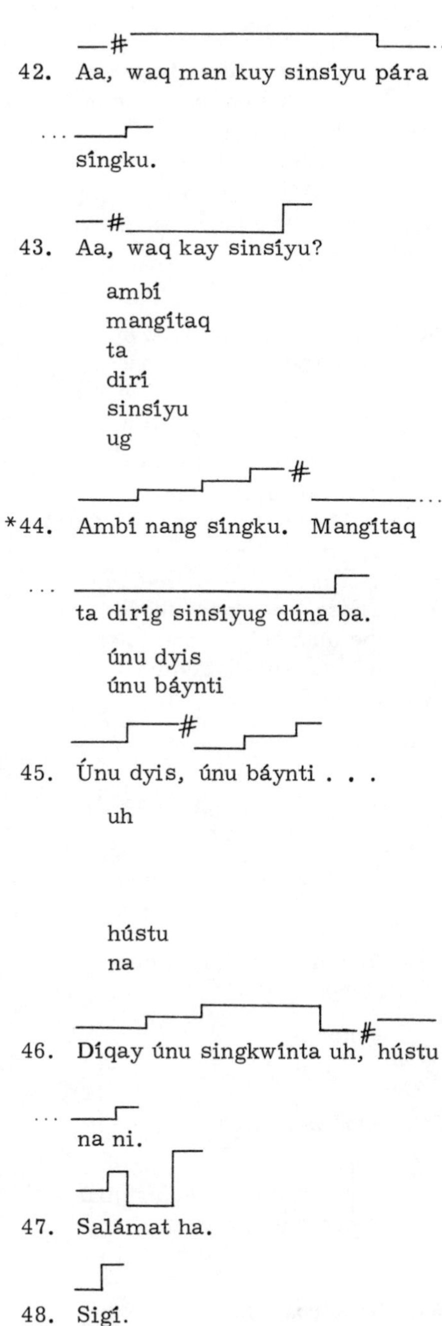

42. Hm. I have no change for a five.	42. Aa, waq man kuy sinsíyu pára síngku.
43. Oh, you have no change?	43. Aa, waq kay sinsíyu?
let me have	ambí
look for	mangítaq
we	ta
here	dirí
change	sinsíyu
if	ug
44. Let me have that five. I'll see if I have any change (lit. we'll look here for change, if there is any).	*44. Ambí nang síngku. Mangítaq ta dirig sinsíyug dúna ba.
one-ten	únu dyis
one-twenty	únu báynti
45. One-ten, one-twenty . . .	45. Únu dyis, únu báynti . . .
[particle drawing interlocutor's attention to something he doesn't notice]	uh
correct	hústu
now	na
46. Here, here's one-fifty. That (lit. This) is correct now.	46. Díqay únu singkwínta uh, hústu na ni.
47. Thank you.	47. Salámat ha.
48. Uh-huh.	48. Sigí.
for	pára sa
Mabolo (part of Cebu City)	Mabúlu
49. Sir, where do I get a jeep for Mabolo?	49. Nuy, ása man ku musakáyg dyip páras Mabúlu?

look at	tanqáwa
[particle after imperatives to to soften the command]	ra
that one (not far)	naq
[linker between naq and nagbalígyaq]	nga
selling	nagbalígyaq
hat	káluq

50. Do you see (lit. look at) that man selling hats there?

*50. Tanqáwa ra nang nagbalígyaq ... dihág mga káluq.

front	atubángan
probably	tingáli
Mabolo (part of Cebu City)	Mabúlu

51. Those jeeps over there [near the man selling hats] across the way—probably those go to Mabolo.

51. Kanáng mga dyip dínhaq sa ... atubángan, tingáli ádtu naq ... sa Mabúlu.

52. Thank you, sir.

52. Salámat Nuy ha?

53. Driver, does this (jeep) go to Mabolo?

53. Dung, ádtu ba nis Mabúlu?

no	díliq

54. Mm, no, Miss.

54. Aa, díliq Mis.

go	lakáw
[particle preceding goal]	sa
one side (of two)	píkas

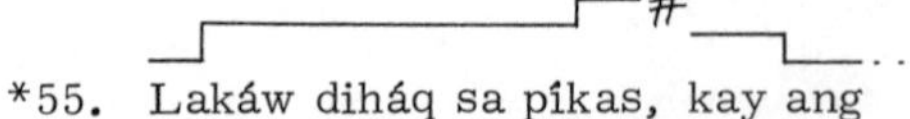

55. Go across the street; the jeeps there go to Mabolo (lit. because the jeeps that are there are the ones that go to Mabolo).

*55. Lakáw diháq sa píkas, kay ang ... dyip nga túqa dídtu, maqúy ... muqádtus Mabúlu.

Lahug (part of Cebu City)	Lahúg
56. The ones here go to Lahug. (Lit. Because those ones that are here go to Lahug.)	*56. Ang kanáng nîqa dînhi muqádtu man sa Lahúg.
57. Oh, they do? Thank you.	57. Aa, sa Lahúg diqáy? Salámat ha?

Mga Pangutána

Ikaduháng Báhin

1. Tungáq ras dusîna Day?
2. Únu utsînta ang tungás dusîna?
3. May ikasúkliq ka sa sîngku pîsus Iyáq?
4. Ásа man ku makasakáyg dyip páras Mabúlu Nuy?
5. Kanáng mga dyip sa îyang atubángan diq kaháq naq páras Mabúlu?
6. Dung, pára bas Mabúlu kanáng dyîpa?
7. Kanáng dyip nga náqas pîkas, maqú ba nang padulúng sa Mabúlu?
8. Tagpîla man nang kálung balîgyaq nîmu Nuy?
9. Sigúru ka kaháq ánaq Dung?
10. Tungáq ras dusîna ang îmu Day?
11. Pilá tu Iyáq, únu báynti?
12. May ikasinsîyu ka ba sa sîngku Day?
13. Háqi man ánaq Nuy, dághan man naq siláng nagbalîgyag káluq?
14. Kanáng sa atubángan Nuy, dîliq ba naq muhatúd sa Mabúlu?
15. Kanáng dyip nga náqas pîkas Dung?
16. Kiníng dyîpa muqádtu bas Lahúg?
17. Maqú tung túqang dyîpa Nuy páras Lahúg?
18. Mabúlu ni Dung?
19. Musakáy ka pára Lahúg Nuy?

Mga Pangutána (Matching)

Ikaduháng Báhin

1. Balígyaq ba nang mga kaság Iyáq?
2. Pilá may îmu Day?
3. Tagpíla man ang dusína Day?
4. Dúna ka bay sinsíyu sa síngku písus Bay?
5. Ása man ku makasakáyg dyip páras Mabúlu Nuy?
6. Sa Mabúlu ba ning dyípa Bay?
7. Ása man diqáy ka Day?
8. Waq ka bay láqing kwárta Day?
9. Ánhi ba ta musakáy páras Mabúlu Dung?

a. Úqu Day. Musakáy ka?
b. Waláq ra ba Bay.
c. Dínhaq ánang atubángan sa nagbalígyag mga káluq.
d. Úqu Day, palít ka?
e. Waq ra ba kuy láqing sinsíyu Iyáq.
f. Tungáq lang sa dusína Iyáq.
g. Tris saysínta Nang.
h. Sa Mabúlu untáq Dung, kun dúnay kasákyan.
i. Díliq Bay, pára nis Lahúg.

Commentary to Basic Sentences

6.2	kaníndut	An exclamatory form; see 5 A, above, p. 174.
6.3	tagpíla	The prefix tag- before numerals means '[so much] apiece.'
6.5	ka	Numerals are linked with ka.
6.6	kínsi	The numbers of Spanish origin are used for quoting prices and telling age and time.
6.13	siyá	Siyá here is not attracted to ákuq: it is a full form of the pronoun, for which attraction is optional (3 C 4).
6.20	mahímu	Mahímu has the same meaning as mahímuq; both forms occur frequently.
6.24	átuq	Either átuq or ta 'we' [inclusive] is used (instead of ákuq or ku) if the person spoken to is also involved in, or has an interest in, the action (even though only the speaker is performing the action).
6.34	lutúqa	An imperative form. (These are taken up in Lesson 11.)
6.35	Kamakalulúquy	Ka- prefixed to an adjective makalulúquy 'pitiful': see 5 A, p. 174.
6.44	ta	Cf. comment to sentence 6.24 above.
6.50		Note that a verb preceded by a demonstrative means 'this or that one who [does]': here, nang nagbalígyaq means 'that one who is selling.'

6.50 tanqáwa — An imperative form.

6.55 — A verb preceded by ang or y means 'the one who [does].'

6.56 ang kanáq — Ang before a demonstrative means 'the one (of several choices).'

Grammatical Section

6 A. Direct passive verb forms

The term DIRECT PASSIVE refers to verb forms which have certain affixes (in contrast to the active verbs examined in Lessons 4 and 5 and instrumental and local passives to be examined in succeeding lessons).* The following chart shows all affixes of the direct passive verb occurring in colloquial speech. (The constructions and meanings of the direct passive are specified in 6 A 1 ff.)

Direct Passive Verb Affixes

	Real	Unreal	Subjunctive
Nonpotential	gi-	-un	-a
Potential	na-	ma-	ma-

Examples of verbs containing these affixes are as follows:

Ákung palitún ang aríyus. (See 6 a 21) 'I will buy the earrings.'

Lutúqa ang kaság. Matáy ra bítaw maq. (6 a 34) 'Cook the crabs. Don't worry, they'll die.'

Ákung gidalá si Mis Wílbi ngáhi. (3 b 6) 'I brought Miss Wilby here.'

6 A 1 a. Sentences containing direct passives

In this section we study a new construction, the direct passive. The direct passive construction is parallel to the active construction we have studied previously. Actives and direct passives are analogous to English actives and passives in the sense that it is possible to translate Cebuano actives and passives with English actives and passives respectively (though there is by no means a one-to-one correspondence in their usage):

Active:

a. Mipalít si Mis Wílbig aríyus. 'Miss Wilby bought some earrings.'

Passive:

b. Gipalít ni Mis Wílbi ang aríyus. 'The earrings were bought by Miss Wilby.'

---

* Not all verbs take direct passive affixes; some take only active affixes, and some take other passive affixes but not the direct passive ones. (We have to learn each verb individually.) See 5 C 3 and 6 A 4 below.

The Cebuano direct passive is more commonly used than the active (by contrast with English, where the passive is not frequent). Most Cebuano direct passives correspond in actual usage to English actives—for example, b above means 'Miss Wilby bought the earrings'—and by the same token, English actives often have to be translated with direct passives in Cebuano. (Also, there are constructions in which the direct passive is obligatory in Cebuano—we shall detail them in Lesson 13—whereas in English there are no such constructions.)

6 A 1 b. Grammatical differences between active and passive

Sentences containing any type of passive verb differ grammatically from sentences containing active verbs. The passive sentence pattern is as follows:

1. The agent—the one who performs the action of the verb—is either genitive (not nominative as in sentences with active verbs) or else is preceded by sa, and corresponds to English 'by' phrases: 'by me,' etc. In the following examples the agent is underlined:

a. Ákung, gidáa si Mis Wílbi ngánhi. (3 b 6) 'I brought Miss Wilby here.' (Lit. 'Miss Wilby was brought here by me.')
b. Anáaq. Gitawág man ku sa babáyi. 'Heavens, the woman is calling me.' (Lit. 'I am being called by the woman.')
c. Gipalít ni Mis Wílbi ang kaság. 'Miss Wilby bought the crabs.' (Lit. 'The crabs were bought by Miss Wilby.')

2. The verb form has a passive verb affix. (The direct passive affixes are listed above in 6 A, p. 227.)

3. The RECIPIENT (the one acted upon by the action of the verb) is nominative, is preceded by ang or y, or is not marked. (The recipient is the subject of the sentence if the passive verb is in the predicate; it is the predicate if the passive verb is in the subject.) In the following sentences the recipients are underlined:

a. Ákung gidáa si Mis Wílbi ngánhi. (3 b 6) 'I brought Miss Wilby here.'
b. Anáaq. Gitawág man ku sa babáyi. 'Heavens, the woman is calling me.'
c. Gipalít ni Mis Wílbi ang kaság. 'Miss Wilby bought the crabs.'
a (1). Si Mis Wílbiy ákung gidáa ngánhi. 'Miss Wilby is the one I brought here.'
b (1). Anáaq. Akú man ang gitawág sa babáyi. 'Heavens. I am the one the woman is calling.'
c (1). Ang gipalít ni Mis Wílbi, kaság. 'What Miss Wilby bought was crabs.'

Sentences containing active verbs differ grammatically from sentences containing passives. The active sentence pattern is as follows. (These statements review 5 D 1, p. 181.)

1. The agent is either nominative, or is preceded by ang or y, or is unmarked. (The agent is the subject of the sentence if the active verb is in the predicate; it is the predicate if the active verb is the subject.) The agent is underlined in the following examples:

a (2). Nagdáa ku kang Mis Wílbi ngánhi. 'I was bringing Miss Wilby here.'
b (2). Nagtawág ang babáyi nákuq. 'The woman was calling me.'
c (2). Nagpalít si Mis Wílbi ug kaság. 'Miss Wilby was buying crabs.'
a (3). Akúy nagdáa kang Mis Wílbi ngánhi. 'I was the one who was bringing Miss Wilby here.'
b (3). Ang babáyi ang nagtawág nákuq. 'It was the woman who called me.'
c (3). Si Mis Wílbi ang nagpalít ug kaság. 'It was Miss Wilby who was buying crabs.'

2. The verb form has an active verb affix.

3. The recipient (the one acted upon by the action of the verb) is the goal (a dative, or a word or phrase preceded by ug or sa). In the following examples the recipient (goal of the active verb) is underlined:

a (2). Nagdáa ku kang Mis Wílbi ngánhi. 'I was bringing Miss Wilby here.'
b (2). Nagtawág ang babáyi nákuq. 'The woman was calling me.'
c (2). Nagpalít si Mis Wílbi ug kaság. 'Miss Wilby was buying crabs.'

6 A 1 c. Conversion of actives to direct passives

The nominative recipient in a direct passive sentence corresponds to the goal recipient in an active sentence; the genitive agent of a direct passive sentence corresponds to the nominative agent of an active sentence. In the following examples, the first sentence of each pair is an active sentence and the second is a direct passive sentence:

a. Mupalít silá sa kaság. 'They want to buy the crabs.'
a (1). Palitún níla ang kaság. 'They'll take (buy) the crabs.'
b. Makadáa ba ang bátaq niqánaq? 'Can the child carry that?'
b (1). Madáa ba kanáq sa bátaq? 'Can the child carry that?'
c. Mangutána siya sa Ínsik. 'She will ask the manager.'
c (1). Íyang pangutánqun ang Ínsik. 'She will ask the manager.'

PP-S in Lesson 7, p. 278.

6 A 1 d. Active and direct passive verbs in verb phrases modifying nouns

The active verb is used when the person or thing the verb modifies is the agent:

Mu ni si Mis Wílbing muqábang ug kwártu dínhi. 'This is Miss Wilby, who wants to rent a room here.' [The verb muqábang 'wants to rent' modifies Mis Wílbi, the agent: muqábang is active.]

Lítu ang ngaan sa bátang midágan. 'Lito is the name of the child who ran away.' [The verb midágan 'ran away' modifies bátaq 'child,' the agent: midágan is active.]

The direct passive is used when the person or thing the verb modifies is the recipient:

Kanáng bátang ímung dádqun sa Amiriká, kínsay íyang ngálan? 'What is the name of the child you are going to take to America?' [The verb dádqun 'will be brought' modifies bátaq 'child,' the recipient: dádqun is passive.]

Háqin man ang aríyus nga ímung gipalít ganíha? 'Where are the earrings which you bought a while ago?' [The verb gipalít 'was bought' modifies aríyus 'earrings,' the recipient: gipalít is passive.]

Here are some examples which contrast active and passive verbs in phrases modifying nouns (the first sentence of each pair has an active form, the second has a passive; the verbs are underlined):

a. Mu ni si Mis Wílbing nagdáa kang Pírla ngánhi. 'This is Miss Wilby, who brought Perla here.'
a (1). Mu ni si Pírlang gidáa ni Mis Wílbi ngánhi. 'This is Perla, who was brought here by Miss Wilby.'
b. Kínsa man nang táwung nangutána nímu? 'Who was that man asking you questions?'

b. Kínsa man nang táwung nangutána nímu? 'Who was that man asking you questions?'

b (1). Kínsa man nang táwung ímung gipangutána? 'Who was that man you asked?'

c. Ang táwung ákung gisunúd waq makasakáy. 'The man I followed couldn't get on (the bus).'

c (1). Ang táwung nagsunúd nákuq waq makasakáy. 'The man who followed me could not get on.'

d. Tigúwang kaqáyu kanáng babáying nagqinúm ug tubáq. 'That woman drinking palm toddy is very old.'

d (1). Ang tubang giqinúm sa babáyi mu nay gíkan sa lubíng Tásyu. 'The palm toddy which the woman is drinking is the toddy from Tacio's tree.'

6 A 1 e. When to choose active or passive if both are possible

There are some constructions in which only an active or only a passive occurs. (Some of these have just been discussed.) However, in many cases there is a choice of which to use (just as in English we may say either Mozart wrote that symphony or That symphony was written by Mozart). In Cebuano, the active is used to tell what somebody or something DOES; the passive is used to tell what HAPPENS TO somebody or something. The difference is one of emphasis: attention is directed by active sentences to the action itself; by passive sentences, to the person or thing it happens to. This factor accounts for the high frequency of passive sentences in Cebuano as contrasted with English. In the following examples, the active is used in the first sentence of each pair, the passive in the second:

a. Magdáa gyud kag rigálu inigqádtu nímu sa ka Pírla. 'Be sure to bring presents when you go to Perla's.' [Here the emphasis is on what you should do.]

a (1). Dádqun ba nímu ang rigálu? 'Are you going to take the present with you?' [The important thing is not what you are going to do, but what is going to happen to the present.]

b. Túqa silá uh. Nagtawág silá nákuq. 'There they are. They are calling me.' [This might be a response to a question about where they are and what they are doing.]

b (1). Anáaq. Gitawág man ku níla. (6 a 17) 'Oh, dear, they're calling me.' [Miss Wilby is thinking about what is happening to her, rather than what they are doing.]

c. Mupalít ka ba íning aríyus Day? 'Do you want to buy these earrings, Miss?' [The seller is asking the lady what she would like to do.]

c (1). Mahímuq na nímung palitúg dyis. (6 a 19) 'You can buy it for ten now.' [The salesgirl is considering not what you can do, but rather what might happen to the article under discussion.]

d. Magpíliq ta úsaq ta mupalít. 'We should choose, before we buy.' [We are considering what we should do, not what should happen to something.]

d (1). Pilíqun nátuq kanáng mudirítsus Sibú. 'Let's choose one that goes directly to Cebu.' [We are considering the thing to be chosen, not what we should do.]

e. Akú sad. Nangítaq sad kug kwártu. 'Me, too. I'm looking for a room too.' [Somebody else is looking for a room, and so am I.]

e(1). Gipangítaq ku sad siyá. 'I am also looking for him.' [I am looking for him, too, in addition to someone else.]

f. Maglútuq pa ku sa kaság úsaq ku mulakáw. 'I still have to cook the crabs, before I go out.'

f(1). Ang kaság Day. Lutúqun ku ba? 'The crabs, Ma'am. Shall I cook them?' [The maid, who has been told to cook some other things, is now asking about the crabs—if they are to be cooked too; she is not asking what she is to do.]

The difference in meaning between the active and passive will become completely clear to you as you gather experience using it. Meanwhile, the best general rule is to use a passive whenever possible. (English speakers learning Cebuano tend to use the active too much.)

6 A 2. Contraction

With the adding of suffixes (those of 6 A above and others you have not learned yet) many words drop the vowel of the last syllable of the base (the syllable before the suffix).* For example, ingún 'say' plus -a gives íngna 'tell him' (with the u of the final syllable of the base dropped):

Íngna siyáng ánhaq mi dínhaq. 'Tell him that we are coming.'

Tawág 'call' plus -un gives táwgun 'will call' (with the a of the final syllable dropped):

Isáq pa. Ákuq siyáng táwgun. 'Just a second. I'll call him.'

In some cases, when vowels are dropped, the consonants of the base are metathesized (reversed in order) or changed altogether (these changes, too, must be learned individually for each verb). E.g. putús 'wrap up' plus -a gives pústa 'wrap it up' (with the u of the final syllable of the base dropped and the t and s metathesized):

Pústa kay ákung palitún. (6 a 21) 'Wrap it up. I'll take it.'

Dalá 'take' plus -un gives dádqun 'take it' (with the a of the final syllable of the base dropped, l changed to d, and q added):

Dádqun ka námuq sa Amiriká. (2 b 22) 'We will take you to America.'

6 A 3. Use of the real, unreal, and subjunctive forms in passive sentences

The real and the unreal in the passive have the same uses as in the active (above, 4 B 1, pp. 142–143), with the exception described below in 6 A 3 c.

6 A 3 a. Real form

The real describes actions or conditions that have already taken place, and actions taking place or existing at the time the speaker speaks:

Ákung gidalá si Mis Wílbi ngánhi. (3 b 6) 'I brought Miss Wilby here.'

Uy, anáaq, gitawág man ku níla. (6 a 17) 'Goodness, they are calling me.'

6 A 3 b. Unreal form

1. The unreal describes actions that have not yet taken place or conditions that have not yet come into existence:

---

* Not all words drop vowels; only some do. Each form must be learned individually.

Átung pangutánqun̄ ang Ínsik. (6 a 11) 'Let us ask the manager.'
Dung, dádqun ka námuq sa Amiriká. (2 b 22) 'Son, we will take you to America.'

2. The unreal describes actions performed regularly or habitually:
Maqú ra nay íyang palitún ug muqádtu siyá sa tindáhan.
'That is the only thing she buys when she goes to the store.'

3. The unreal is used after the prepositives mahímuq (mahímu) 'can,' gústu 'want,' díliq (diq) 'not,' kinahánglan 'must' (as well as others to be introduced later):
Mahímuq naq nímung palitún ug dyis. (6 a 19) 'You can buy it for ten.'

6 A 3 c. Uses of the subjunctive form

The subjunctive has two uses:
1. After waláq (waq) 'not' (and other prepositives to be introduced later):
Waq pa nákuq lutúqa ang kaság. 'I have not cooked the crabs yet.'
Waláq pa ba nímu dádqa si Mis Wílbi ngánhi? 'Haven't you brought Miss Wilby here yet?'

2. The subjunctive form is also used as the passive imperative (i.e., to express a command):
Lutúqa. Matáy ra bítaw naq. (6 a 34) 'Cook it (lit. let it be cooked). Don't worry. It will die.'
Ámbi, Iyáq, papalitá kug tungáq sa dusína. (6 b 36) 'Let me have (lit. Let me be caused to buy) half a dozen.'
Tanqáwa ra nang nagbalígyaq dihág mga káluq. (6 b 50) 'Do you see (lit. Let be seen) that man selling hats there?'

Exercise 6.III A.

6 A 4. Potentials of the direct passives

The potential forms of the direct passives are shown in the chart in 6 A (above, p. 227). They are used in the same meanings as the potentials of the actives (5 C 3, above, p. 179):
a. 'Have the ability to [do so-and-so]'
Diq na naq mahángyuq? (3 b 29) 'Can't it be bargained over?'
b. 'Have the opportunity to [do so-and-so]'
Waq ku na mapalít ang kaság kay waq na kuy úras. 'I did not get to buy the crabs, because I had no more time.'
c. 'Have [done so-and-so]'
Nalútuq na ba nímu ang kaság Iyáq? 'Have you cooked the crabs yet?'
d. 'Accidentally [do so-and-so]'
Nadalá ku ang putús ni Mis Wílbi sa baay. 'I took Miss Wilby's package home by mistake.'

6 B. Summary of the uses of the genitive

For the genitive forms of the pronouns and of personal names refer to the charts of 1 A and 1 B, pages 11, 14. Other words and phrases are made genitive by placing sa before them.
The genitive is used:

1. In exclamatory sentences as the thing exclaimed over (cf. 5 A 1, above, p. 175).

Kanîndut niqáning mga arîyus! (6 a 2) 'How beautiful these earrings are!'

2. In construction with a noun to indicate possession (6 B 1 below).

3. As the agent of a passive verb (6 B 2 below). (Do not confuse the short form of the dative with the genitive, though they have the same shape. The dative and the genitive have different uses.)

4. In expressions referring to time or place (6 B 5 below).

In the chart of 1 B (p. 14) there is a special column marked preposed genitive: These forms precede the word or phrase they are in construction with and are linked to it with nga (2 E 1, 2 E 2). The other genitives, by contrast, follow the word of phrase they are in construction with, except when they are attracted to a prepositive (3 C 3 a). The two types of genitives are used interchangeably, with the exceptions noted below (6 B 1, footnote; 6 B 3, 6 B 4).

6 B 1. Genitive indicating possession

Genitive forms in construction with nouns show possession. (The nouns are underlined twice, the genitives once.)

a. Pilá man diqáy idád nîmu Iyúq? (5.10) 'How old are you?' (Lit. 'How much is your age?')
b. Mu ni si Mis Wîlbi ang kaqúban nákuq. 'This is Miss Wilby, my friend.'

The preposed genitive is also used to indicate possession;* the above two sentences can also have preposed forms:

a (1). Pilá man diqáy îmung idád Iyúq? 'How old are you?' (Lit. 'What is your age?')
b (1). Mu ni si Mis Wîlbi ang ákung kaqúban. 'This is Miss Wilby, my friend.'

6 B 2. Genitive as agent of passive verbs

The genitive is used for the agent of a passive verb.

a. Uy anáaq, gitawág man ku nîla. (6.17) 'Oh dear, they are calling me.' [The agent nîla 'by them' is genitive, and the verb is passive.]
b. Dádqun námuq si Lítu sa Amiriká. (2 b 22) 'We will take Lito to America.'

---

* If an adjective plus nga precedes the noun, only a regular genitive—not a preposed genitive—is used after the adjective. (Cf. parallel rules in 6 B 3 below, where the preposed genitive also is not used.) The genitive is optionally attracted to the adjective.

c. Siyá ang ákung amígu. 'He is my friend.'
c (1). Siyá ang suqúd kung amígu. 'He is my close friend.'
d. Gitánqaw námuq ang îlang baláy. 'We looked at their house.'
d (1). Gitánqaw námuq ang nindut nîlang baláy. 'We looked at their beautiful house.'

The preposed genitive may substitute for the regular genitive form in passive sentences if there is no prepositive (e.g. íla for níla, ámuq for námuq, etc.). Sentences a and b just above could alternatively be said as follows:

a (1). Íla man kung gitawág. 'They are calling me.'

b (1). Ámung dádqun si Lítu sa Amiriká. 'We shall take Lito to America.'

6 B 3. Preposed genitive not used after certain prepositives

Regular genitives (but not preposed genitives) serve as agents in passive sentences that contain the following prepositives: gústu 'want,' díliq 'not,' or waláq 'not' (as well as other prepositives we shall study later):

Sigí pústa. Gústu naq nákung palitún. 'All right, wrap it up. I want to buy it.'

Waláq ku siyá pangutánqa. 'I did not ask him.'

Díliq níya íngnun si Dúktur Pirnándis nga ádtu siyá dídtu. 'He won't tell Dr. Fernandez that he is going there.'

Pattern practice PP-N, Steps VIII and IX.

6 B 4. Genitives with exclamatory sentences

Regular genitives (but not preposed genitives) are used in exclamatory sentences (see 5 A 1, p. 175, and examples).

Kaníndut nímug baláy! 'What a nice house you have!'

(In this sentence the preposed genitive ímu would not occur.)

6 B 5. Genitive for expressions of place and time

The genitive is used to mean 'at, in, on [a noun referring to a place or time].' When the noun refers to a time, the genitive marker sa is optional.

Niqádtung Bírnis dídtu akú sa Lahúg. '[On] last Friday I was in Lahug.'

Kiní si Nuy Tibúq. Mu niy labíng tigúwang táwu sa ámung lúngsud. (5 a 8) 'This is Tibo. He's the oldest person in our town.'

Diháq niqánang dapíta waq gyuy mga lubí. 'There are no coconuts in that place.'

Sa sunúd na lang búwan kitá magkítaq. or Sunúd na lang búwan kitá magkítaq. 'We'll just see each other next month.'

6 C. More on goals

The goal construction occurs with passive verbs as well as with active ones. The goal of a passive verb is the recipient of the action (see 5 D 2 and 6 A 1 b). (In grammatical form, goals are either the dative forms of the charts in 1 A and 1 B, pp. 11, 14, or nouns preceded by ug or sa.)

Mahímuq na nímung palitún ug dyis. (6.21) 'You can buy it for ten.'

Ámbi Iyáq. Papalitá kug tungáq sa dusína. (6.36) 'Here. Let me have half a dozen.'

Gústu nákung ipaqilaqíla nímu ang ákung asáwa. 'I'd like to introduce my wife to you.' [Ipaqilaqíla 'be introduced to' is an instrumental passive, a type to be presented in a later lesson.]

6 D. Order of agent and subject with passive verbs

In passive sentences the word order of the agent (genitive) and the recipient (subject) is on the whole not set: either the agent precedes the recipient or the recipient precedes the agent.

Gipalít ni Mis Wílbi ang kaság. or Gipalít ang kaság ni Mis Wílbi.
'Miss Wilby bought the crabs.'

Shorter forms tend to precede longer forms.

Gipalít nákuq ang kaság. 'I bought the crabs.' [It would be unusual, though not incorrect, to have nákuq after ang kaság.]

In passive sentences having a pronoun for both agent and recipient, the word order is not free. Furthermore, of the various possible combinations of the alternative pronoun forms, only certain combinations actually occur. These combinations and word orders are as follows:

1. Any nominative form recipient may be followed by a full genitive agent.
2. Any full genitive agent may be followed by any full nominative recipient (though this combination is common only with the nominatives siyá 'he' and silá 'they').
3. Short genitive agents may be followed by full nominative recipients.

All these combinations are exemplified by the following sentences. The forms in parentheses are alternatives which, though common in writing, are not frequent in speech.

1. Nominative followed by full genitive:

		recipient (nominative)	agent (genitive)	
a.	Gitawág man	ku (akú)	nímu.	'You are calling me.'
b.	Gitawág man	ku (akú)	níya.	'He is calling me.'
c.	Gitawág man	ku (akú)	nínyu.	'You (plural) are calling me.'
d.	Gitawág man	ku (akú)	níla.	'They are calling me.'
e.	Gitawág man	ka (ikáw)	nákuq.	'I am calling you.'
f.	Gitawág man	ka (ikáw)	níya.	'He is calling you.'
g.	Gitawág man	ka (ikáw)	námuq.	'We are calling you.'
h.	Gitawág man	ka (ikáw)	níla.	'They are calling you.'
i.	Gitawág man	siyá	nákuq.	'I am calling him.'
j.	Gitawág man	siyá	nímu.	'You are calling him.'
k.	Gitawág man	siyá	níya.	'He is calling him.'
l.	Gitawág man	siyá	nátuq.	'We are calling him.'
m.	Gitawág man	siyá	námuq.	'We (not you) are calling him.'
n.	Gitawág man	siyá	nínyu.	'You (plural) are calling him.'
o.	Gitawág man	siyá	níla.	'They are calling him.'
p.	Gitawág man	ta (kitá)	níya.	'He is calling us.'
q.	Gitawág man	ta (kitá)	níla.	'They are calling us.'
r.	Gitawág man	mi (kamí)	nímu.	'You are calling us.'
s.	Gitawág man	mi (kamí)	níya.	'He is calling us (not you).'
t.	Gitawág man	mi (kamí)	nínyu.	'You (plural) are calling us.'
u.	Gitawág man	mi (kamí)	níla.	'They are calling us (not you).'
v.	Gitawág man	silá	nákuq.	'I am calling them.'
w.	Gitawág man	silá	nímu.	'You are calling them.'
x.	Gitawág man	silá	níya.	'He is calling them.'
y.	Gitawág man	silá	nátuq.	'We are calling them.'
z.	Gitawág man	silá	námuq.	'We (not you) are calling them.'
a[1].	Gitawág man	silá	nínyu.	'You (plural) are calling them.'
b[1].	Gitawág man	silá	níla.	'They are calling them.'

1. Nominative followed by full genitive: [continued]

	recipient (nominative)	agent (genitive)	
c^1. Gitawág man	mu	nákuq.	'I am calling you (plural).'
d^1. Gitawág man	mu	nîya.	'He is calling you (plural).'
e^1. Gitawág man	mu	námuq.	'We are calling you (plural).'
f^1. Gitawág man	mu	nîla.	'They are calling you (plural).'

2. Full genitive followed by full nominative:

	agent (genitive)	recipient (nominative)	
i (1). Gitawág man	nákuq	siyá.	'I am calling him.'
j (1). Gitawág man	nímu	siyá.	'You are calling him.'
k (1). Gitawág man	níya	siyá.	'He is calling him.'
l (1). Gitawág man	nátuq	siyá.	'We are calling him.'
m (1). Gitawág man	námuq	siyá.	'We (not you) are calling him.'
n (1). Gitawág man	nínyu	siyá.	'You (plural) are calling him.'
o (1). Gitawág man	níla	siyá.	'They are calling him.'
v (1). Gitawág man	nákuq	silá.	'I am calling them.'
w (1). Gitawág man	nímu	silá.	'You are calling them.'
x (1). Gitawág man	níya	silá.	'He is calling them.'
y (1). Gitawág man	nátuq	silá.	'We are calling them.'
z (1). Gitawág man	námuq	silá.	'We (not you) are calling them.'
a^1(1). Gitawág man	nínyu	silá.	'You (plural) are calling them.'
b^1(1). Gitawág man	níla	silá.	'They are calling them.'

3. Short genitive followed by full nominative:

		agent (genitive)		recipient (nominative)	
e (1).	Gitawág	ku	man	ikáw.	'I am calling you.'
i (2).	Gitawág	ku	man	siyá.	'I am calling him.'
c^1(1).	Gitawág	ku	man	mu or kamú.	'I am calling you (plural).'
v (2).	Gitawág	ku	man	silá.	'I am calling them.'
a (1).	Gitawág	mu	man	akú.	'You are calling me.'
j (2).	Gitawág	mu	man	siyá.	'You are calling him.'
r (1).	Gitawág	mu	man	kamí.	'You are calling us.'
w (2).	Gitawág	mu	man	silá.	'You are calling them.'
e (2).	Gitawág	ta	man	ka (ikáw).	'I* am calling you.'
l (2).	Gitawág	ta	man	siyá.	'We are calling him.'
c^1(2).	Gitawág	ta	man	mu (kamú).	'I* am calling you (plural).'
y (2).	Gitawág	ta	man	silá.	'We are calling them.'

---

* The meaning 'I' for ta is explained below in 9 A.

6 D 1. Position of ku, mu, ta when genitive

Note then when ku, mu, and ta are genitive—that is, when they are short forms of nákuq, nímu, and nátuq respectively—they follow the prepositive if there is one; otherwise, they follow the first word of the predicate.

a. Gitawág ku man siyá. 'I am calling him.' [Ku 'by me,' a short genitive, immediately follows the first word of the predicate, gitawág 'is being called.']

b. Diq ta na lang siyá táwgun. 'We won't bother calling him.' [Ta 'by us,' a short genitive, follows the prepositive diq 'not.']

c. Gústu mu ba siyáng táwgun? Do you wish to call him?' [Mu 'by you,' a short form of the genitive, immediately follows the prepositive gústu 'want to.']

(See also the examples under 3 of the preceding section.)

By contrast, when ku, mu, and ta are nominative—that is, when they are short for akú, kamú, and kitá respectively—they do not follow the first word of the predicate immediately if there is another postpositive qualifier.

a(1). Gitawág man ku níya. 'He is calling me.' (Ku 'me,' a short nominative, follows the postpositive man.)

b(1). Diq na lang ta níya táwgun. 'He won't bother calling us.' (Ta 'us,' a short nominative, follows the postpositives na and lang.)

c(1). Gústu ba mu níyang táwgun? 'Does he wish to call you?' (Mu 'you (plural)' is a short nominative and follows the postpositive ba.)

(See also the examples under 1 of the preceding section.)

Pattern practices PP-U and PP-N; Exercises 6.IVA, 7.XC.

Pattern Practices and Exercises

I A. (Deictics) Ibutáng sa lunáq ang hústung púrma sa deictic. (Tanqáwa ang laráwan) (1 A 2 and subsections)

1. (B-A) Uy, ____________y kaság nga gipamalígyaq.
2. (B-A) Uu, sigí, ____________ na lang ku mupalít.
3. (A-B) ____________ pa may dághan sa iláwum (iláwum 'underneath').
4. (A-B) ____________ ka man gíkan nu, Mis Wílbi [pointing across the street]? 'You came from over there?'
5. (B-A) Uu, ____________ man úntaq ku mupalít sa úbas (úbas 'grapes'). 'I want to buy some grapes here.'
6. (A-B) Mahímu bang ____________ ka lang mupalít káda ádlaw?
7. (B-A) Úqu lábqas ning mga kaság ____________.
8. (A-B) Salámat. ____________, Mis Wílbi, giputús na.
9. (B-C) Kádtung tindáhans káwung ____________ ____________?
10. (C-B) Kanáng dyip ____________ muqádtu tingáli sa Mabúlu.
11. (C-B) ____________ ka ba ganína Mis Wílbi?
12. (B-C) Uu, ____________ ku. Nagpalít kug kaság.
13. (C-B) May palitún ka ba ____________ sa tindáhan sa káluq?
14. (A-B) Ug ____________ ka mupalít úgmaq, bínlan tikáw ug kaság. '. . . I will set aside some crabs for you.'
15. (B-A) Sigí. ____________ na lang ku mupalít nímu.

SAPÁTUS
BÚLAK
A
B
C

IB. (Demonstratives) Ibutáng sa lunáq ang hústung púrma sa demonstrative. (Tanqáwa ang laráwan.) (I A 1)

1. (B-A) Lábqas ba __________ng mga kaság Iyáq?
2. (A-B) Uu, lábqas kaqáyu __________.
3. (B-A) Tagpíla man __________ng mga kaság Iyáq?
4. (B-A) Ug __________ng túqa dídtu, pilá man?
5. (B-A) Sus, kamahál pud __________. Pirú __________ng díqa dirí barátu. 'My, how expensive those are! But those that are here are cheap.'
6. (A-B) Mahál gyud __________ng náqa diháq kay lábqas man kaqáyu.
7. (B-A) Mahímuq bang mahángyuq __________ng náqa diháq?
8. (B-A) __________ diríng gamáy, tagpíla man pud?
9. (A-B) Mas barátu __________, tagkínsi sintábus.
10. (B-A) Uu sigí, tagáqi kug limá ka buqúk __________ng dágkung kaság nga náqa diháq.
11. (B-C) Nuy Pulís, ása padúung __________ng dyip?
12. (C-B) __________ng dyip padúung __________ sa Mabúlu.
13. (B-C) Sákyan ku __________ inigkahumán nákuq dínhi.
14. (B-C) Nuy Pulís, únsang urása mulárga __________ng dyip? 'What time is that jeep leaving?'
15. (B-C) Díliq ba diqáy __________ muqádtu sa Banáwaq?

IC. Answer in the negative. (2 B)

1. Dúna ka bay balígyang kaság Dung?
2. Mahángyuq ba kiníg dyis písus?
3. Barátu ba ang mga aláhas dídtus tindáhan?
4. Dúna bay mga dyip dínhing páras Mabúlu?
5. Itawág ta ba kag dyip karún? 'Shall I call a jeep for you now?'
6. Nangítaq ka bag mga káluq Day?
7. Naglakáw ka ba lang pagqánhi nímu?
8. Ikúhaq ku pa ba ikáwg láqing kaság?
9. Magdalá ba ku ngánhig dághang kinhasún pára nímu?
10. Musakáy ka bag dyip ngádtus ínyu?
11. Háqin man si Pírla? Muqubán ba siyá nímu?
12. Dúna pa ba kitáy ganánsya kung ihátag nátug dyis ang dusína sa aláhas?
13. Makasúkliq ka ba niqíning ákung báynti?
14. Gitagáqan mu na ba kug súkliq?

15. Kahibáwu ka bag unsáqun paglútuq íning mga kaság? 'Do you know how to cook these crabs?'

ID. Rewrite the following sentences with the word in parentheses inserted. (3 C 3 a, 6 B 3)

Panánglitan: Muqábang kaháq ka íning kwartúhang gamáy ra man kaqáyu ni? (gústu)

Tubag: Gústu kaháq kang muqábang íning kwartúhang gamáy ra man kaqáyu ni?

1. Musúud úntaq ku ánang tindáhan sa mga aláhas nga kinhasún. (gústu)
2. Átuq na lang pangutánqun ang Ínsik kun mahímu ba nig dyis. (díliq)
3. Mupalít úntaq ku niqánang kaság pirú diq na man lábqas kaqáyu. (gústu)
4. Mangítaq gyud kug sinsíyu dirí arún ákung mapalít nang kaság. (kinahánglan)
5. Mupalít úntaq kug usá ka dusína niqíning mga aríyus. (gústu)
6. Aa, kiní ba ang dyip páras Mabúlu? (maqú)
7. Musakáy dáyun ku páras Mabúlu. (kinahánglan)
8. Kanáq man gud ang muqádtus Mabúlu. (maqú)
9. Mubálik dáyun kus Sibú kay dághan pa ra ba kug buhatúnun sa tindáhan. (kinahánglan)
10. Muqádtu úntaq kus ínyu pirú giqimbitár man ku ni Pírla ngádtus íla. (gústu)
11. Ákuq úntang ipaqilaqíla nímu ang ákung anák. (gústu)
12. Muhapít kus ínyu gíkan sa ílang Pírla. (mahímu)
13. Ipaqilaqíla man gud úntaq nákuq kanímu ang ákung mga bátaq ug ákung mga apú. (gústu)
14. Hílum kaqáyu run ngánhis ámuq. (díliq)
15. Manihápun na lang ta sa ka Nuy Tibúq. (ádtu)

IE. Make the following sentences negative. (2 B, 3 C 3 a, 6 B 3)

1. Mahímuq bang dyis písus na lang ni?
2. Makahángyuq pa man ka. (Change pa to na.)
3. Ákuq siyáng pangutánqun.
4. Madalá gyud tingáli nig dyis Mis. 'You can probably get this for ten.'
5. Musúud ku dínhi.
6. May láqin pa ku niqáning báynti. (Change pa to na.)
7. Muqádtu ra ba nis Lahúg Mis.

8. Lakáw diháq sa píkas kay anáqa diháq ang mga dyip páras Mabúlu. 'Go across the street, because that's where the jeeps for Mabolo are.'
9. Tanqáwa nang nagbalîgyaq dihág káluq.
10. May ikasinsíyu ku niqánang îmung kwárta Mis.
11. Mamatáy naq dáyun ug lutúqun.
12. Búhiq pa naq silá Day. (Change pa to na.)
13. Âkuq na lang ning ipamalîgyaq.
14. Lakáw Mis.
15. Bálik na ngarî Mis.

II A. (Review of actives) This exercise may be preceded by PP-J of Lesson 5. Pilîqa ang hústung púrma sa mga bîrbu (nag-/mag-, mi-/mu-, naka-/maka-). Gamîta ang potential kun mahîmuq. (5 C and subsections)

Panánglitan: Tanqáwa ra nang (mibalîgyaq, nagbalîgyaq) ug káwuq diháq.

Tubág: Tanqáwa ra nang nagbalîgyag káwuq diháq.

1. (Mubisîta, Magbisîta) ku nînyu úgmaq. 'I will visit you tomorrow.'
2. Dîliq ka dînhi (magsakáy, makasakáy) ug dyip padúung sa Mabúlu kay waq may dyip nga muqági. 'You can't get a jeep to Mabolo here, because there are none going that way.'
3. Dîliq ku (magqádtu, makaqádtu) sa tindáhan kay (maglútuq, makalútuq) pa ku ug ságing. 'I can't go to the store because I still have to cook some bananas.'
4. Kung waq pa ku (makasáqad, musáqad) nga muqádtu sa ka Mîstir Abáya, ánhi gyud úntaq kus înyu (manihápun, nanihápun). 'If I hadn't promised that I would go to Mr. Abaya's, I would eat here at your place.'
5. (Nagqádtu, Nakaqádtu) ka na ba sa Pulambatú karúng bágqu? 'Have you gone to Pulambato lately?'
6. Kanúnay gyud naq siyáng (mupalît, nagpalît) ug kaság. 'She always buys crabs.'
7. Háqin na man ang babáying (nakahángyuq, naghángyuq) nga dyis na lang kinî? 'Where is the woman that was offering ten (pesos) for this?'
8. (Nagdalá, Midalá) ka bag kaság ngádtu sa Mabúlu? 'Did you bring crabs with you to Mabolo?'
9. Dîdtu ku magpalît áni sa babáying (nagbalîgyaq, mibalîgyaq) ug kaság. 'I bought this from the woman selling crabs.'
10. Kînsa kádtung (nangutána, mangutána) kun tagpîla ang dusîna sa káluq?
11. (Naglútuq, Milútuq) ka na ba sa kaság nga ákung gipalît? 'Are you cooking the crabs I bought now?'
12. Únsay îmung hunaqhúnaq? (Mupalît, Magpalît) ka ba niqîning ákung gibalîgyang aláhas? (hunaqhúnaq "thought")

13. Ngánung díliq ka man (muqádtu, magqádtu) sa ámuq?

14. Údtu na ku kaqáyung (nagmatá, magmatá) kaganíhang búntag. 'I woke up very late this morning.'

15. Ása man ta (makasakáy, nakasakáy) ug dyip?

II B. (This exercise may be preceded by PP-G.) Pilíqa ang hústung púrma sa mga bírbu nga náqa sa ( ). (4 B and subsections)

1. (Nagqingún, Magqingún) man siyáng waláq siyá (makaqádtu, nakaqádtu). 'He said that he had not gone there.'

2. Kun (misúlti, musúlti) si Husí nímu, ayáwg tubagá. 'If José talks to you, don't answer him.'

3. Ug mahímuq, (muqábang, miqábang) na lang mig baay. 'If possible, we'll just rent a house.'

4. Mis Wílbi, mahímuq kang (magpíliq, nagpíliq) sa aláhas nga ímung gústu. 'Miss Wilby, you may choose the jewelry you like.'

5. Pagkakitáq nákuq ni Místir Abáya (magsakáy, nagsakáy) siyág dyip pára sa Mabúlu. 'When I saw Mr. Abaya, he was riding to Mabolo in a jeep.'

6. Níndut (mipíliq, mupíliq) si Husíg aríyus. 'Joe chooses beautiful earrings.'

7. (Mupalít, Mipalít) si Huwán ug káluq dínhaq sa tindáhan kagahápun. 'John bought a hat in the store yesterday.'

8. Kun (makabalígyaq, nakabalígyaq) kag dághang ságing (makapaqúliq, nakapaqúliq) ka na. 'When you have sold a lot of bananas, you may go home.'

9. Mahímung (naglútuq, maglútuq) na ku sa kaság. 'I can cook the crabs now.'

10. (Mipaqúliq, Mupaqúliq) ang apú ni Nuy Tibúq sa Banáwaq inigkahumág panihápun. 'Tibo's grandson will go home to Banawa as soon as he has eaten supper.'

11. Ug maqáyu ang tyímpu sunúd ádlaw (muqádtu, miqádtu) ku sa Kárbun. 'If the weather is good the following day [i.e. the day after some other future day], I will go to Carbon.'

12. Díliq si Husí (maglútuq, naglútuq) ug bábuy. 'José will not be cooking pork.'

13. (Magdalá, Nagdalá) ka bag gása ngádtu sa Pulambatú gahápun? 'Did you take presents to Pulambato yesterday?'

14. (Makasakáy, Nakasakáy) na ang mga táwug dyip. 'The people have gotten on a jeep.'

15. Nanáqug siyá ug (mitánqaw, mutánqaw) sa mga táwung nangági. 'He got off and he looked at the people going by.'

III A. Ibutáng sa lunáq ang hústung púrma sa <u>direct passive</u>. Gamîta ang <u>non-potential</u>). (6 A 3) (Use nonpotentials)

1. Waláq ku (lútuq) ang mga kinhasún. 'I didn't cook the shellfish.'
2. (Palît) úntaq ni Mis Wîlbi ang arîyus nga gibalîgyaq sa táwu. 'Miss Wilby would have bought the earrings that the man was selling.'
3. Nasukúq si Huwán kay (kúhaq) ni Husî ang îyang papîl. 'John became angry because José took his paper.'
4. (Tawág) lang nátuq siyá sa îlang baay. 'We'll just call (telephone) him at their house.'
5. Maqáyu kay (dalá) nîmu ang Amirkánu dînhi. 'It's good that you brought the American along.'
6. Sigî na, (lútuq) na ang kaság kay gigútum na ku. 'Go ahead. Cook the crabs now. I'm hungry.'
7. Waq ba nîmu (dalá) ang îmung lîbru? 'Didn't you bring your book?'
8. Miqádtu ku nîya ug ákung (pangutána) báhin sa trabáhu. 'I went to him and asked him about the work.'
9. Anîqa ka ra man diqáy. (Tawág) ka na úntaq nákuq. 'Oh, here you are. I was about to call you.'
10. Hulát úsaq kay (putús) pa ang ákung gipamalît. 'Just a minute. My purchases are still being wrapped.'
11. (Pangutána) ba nîmu ang Însik kun mahángyuq pa ba kinîng mga aláhas? 'Did you ask the Chinaman if one can bargain for this jewelry?'
12. Barátu ang prísyu niqánang kalúqa nga îmung (palît). 'The price of that hat you bought was low.'
13. Ngánung îmu mang (inúm) ang ákung kukakúla? 'Why did you drink my Coca-Cola?'
14. Únsa man ang îmung (dalá) ngádtu sa ka Mîsis Abilyána kun muqádtu ka? 'What will you bring when you go to Mrs. Abellana's?'
15. Ákung (bisîta) úgmaq ang ákung kaqîla dîdtu sa Mabúlu. 'I am going to visit my friend in Mabolo tomorrow.'
16. Muqádtu gayúd ku bîsag waláq ku (imbitár). 'I will surely go even though I have not been invited.'
17. Ayáw kanág (palît) kay baratuhún kaqáyu naq. 'Don't buy that because it is of a cheap quality.'
18. Waq nay ságing kay (kúhaq) ang tanán ni Pipîng. 'There are no more bananas because Peping took them all.'
19. Maqú kanáq ang dyip nga îmung (tawág). 'That's the jeep you called.'
20. (Hángyuq) ni Mis Wîlbig tagdyîs ang mga kaság nga gibalîgyaq ni Iyáq Tiráy. 'Miss Wilby offered ten (centavos) apiece for the crabs Tiray sold.'

III B. (Potential and nonpotential form of the direct passives) Ibutáng sa lunáq ang hústung púrma sa <u>direct passive</u> (potential or nonpotential). (6 A 1)

Panangl\u00edtan: (Lútuq) ba kiníng kaság? 'Can these crabs be cooked?'

Tubág: <u>Malútuq</u> ba kiníng kaság?

1. (Dalá) mu na ba ang bátaq sa duktúr? 'Have you taken the child to the doctor yet?'
2. Díliq ka gústu ni Pídru? Muqánhi ra ba tu kay (imbitár) nákuq ngánhig paniqúdtu. 'You don't like Pedro? He's coming here anyway. I invited him to come here for lunch.'
3. Tabángi ra gud ku, kay díliq nákuq (kúhaq) ang unúd sa kaság. 'Will you please help me? I can't get the crab meat out.'
4. Pangutánqa si Lína kung (lútuq) na ba níya ang kaság. 'Ask Lina if she has cooked the crabs yet.'
5. Tanqáwun nátuq kun (dalá) ba nímu kiníng usá ka bukág [basket] nga kinhasún. 'Let's see if you can carry this basket of sea shells.'
6. Dídtu na ku kahibáwu pagqabút nákuq sa tindáhan nga díliq diqáy ákung pitáka ['purse'] ang ákung (dalá). 'It wasn't until I reached the store that I realized that I had taken the wrong purse.'
7. Únsa man ang ímung (palít) dídtus Karbún? 'What did you buy at Carbon?'
8. (Tánqaw) ra gud si Lítu Ma, níndut kaqáyu siyáng (tánqaw) karún nu? 'Take a look at Lito, Mom. He looks very nice now, doesn't he?'
9. Díliq diqáy ni nímu (palít)? (Putús) na ra ba nákuq. 'You aren't going to buy this? I've already wrapped it.'
10. Kínsa may ímung (bisíta) dídtu sa Mabúlu? 'Who are you going to visit in Mabolo?'
11. Dakuqá ra gud ang ímung tíngug kay díliq dirí (dungúg). 'Would you please raise your voice? I can't hear.'
12. (Kúhaq) na ba nímu ang mga káluq nga átung gibílin dídtus tindáhan? 'Have you gone to get the hats we left behind in the store?'
13. Day, (ingún) si Tátay nímu nga níqa mi dínhi. 'Tell your father that we are here.'
14. (Dungúg) ba nínyu ang ákung pagqáwit sa rádyu? 'Did you hear me sing on the radio?'
15. Díliq na kanáng kaság (palít) kay díliq na man lábqas. 'You can't buy those crabs any longer because they're not fresh.'
16. (Hángyuq) pa ba nig tagdyís lang?
17. Waq ku (pangutána) ang ákung maqístra.
18. Ayáwg (bálhin) kiníng mga líbru dínhi ha?
19. Ayáw pagdúgay kay (huwát) tikáw dínhi sa tindáhan.
20. Diq man (búhat) ang ímung gisúguq nákuq. 'What you told me to do can't be done.'

PP-M Use of the agent and the subject (6 D) Direct passive only

Step I. (Changing the agent)

'I looked at the man.'

Gitánqaw ku ang táwu.	(níya)
Gitánqaw níya ang táwu.	(níla)
Gitánqaw níla ang táwu.	(nímu)
Gitánqaw nímu ang táwu.	(námuq)
Gitánqaw námuq ang táwu.	(nínyu)
Gitánqaw nínyu ang táwu.	(níla)
Gitánqaw níla ang táwu.	(níya)
Gitánqaw níya ang táwu.	(ku)
Gitánqaw ku ang táwu.	(námuq)
Gitánqaw námuq ang táwu.	(ku)
Gitánqaw ku ang táwu.	(níya)
Gitánqaw níya ang táwu.	(námuq)
Gitánqaw námuq ang táwu.	

Step II. (Changing the agent in negative sentences)

'I won't take him.'

Dîliq siyá nákuq dádqun.	(níla)
Dîliq siyá níla dádqun.	(nímu)
Dîliq siyá nímu dádqun.	(nínyu)
Dîliq siyá nínyu dádqun.	(námuq)
Dîliq siyá námuq dádqun.	(nátuq)
Dîliq siyá nátuq dádqun.	(níya)
Dîliq siyá níya dádqun.	(nákuq)
Dîliq siyá nákuq dádqun.	(níla)
Dîliq siyá níla dádqun.	(námuq)
Dîliq siyá námuq dádqun.	

Step III. (Changing the agent in negative sentences)

'He didn't wrap it.'

Waláq tu níya pústa.	(nákuq)
Waláq tu nákuq pústa.	(níla)
Waláq tu níla pústa.	(níya)
Waláq tu níya pústa.	(námuq)

Waláq tu námuq pústa.	(nínyu)
Waláq tu nînyu pústa.	(nímu)
Waláq tu nîmu pústa.	(nátuq)
Waláq tu nátuq pústa.	(lutúqa)
Waláq tu nátuq lutúqa.	(níya)
Waláq tu nîya lutúqa.	(níla)
Waláq tu nîla lutúqa.	(námuq)
Waláq tu námuq lutúqa.	(nákuq)
Waláq tu nákuq lutúqa.	(nímu)
Waláq tu nîmu lutúqa.	(nínyu)
Waláq tu nînyu lutúqa.	

Step IV. (Changing the subject)

'She will bring him.'

Dádqun siyá níya.	(tu)
Dádqun tu níya.	(mi)
Dádqun mi níya.	(silá)
Dádqun silá nîya.	(naq)
Dádqun naq níya.	(ri)
Dádqun ri níya.	(ta)
Dádqun ta níya.	(mu)
Dádqun mu níya.	(ku)
Dádqun ku níya.	(ni)
Dádqun ni níya.	(silá)
Dádqun silá nîya.	(kanáq)
Dádqun kanáq níya.	(kádtu)
Dádqun kádtu níya.	

Step V. (Changing the verb)

'I'll bring him.'

Dádqun ku siyá.	(madalá)
Madalá ku siyá.	(gidalá)
Gidalá ku siyá.	(nadalá)
Nadalá ku siyá.	(táwgun)
Táwgun ku siyá.	(gitawág)
Gitawág ku siyá.	(matawág)

Matawág ku siyá.	(natawág)
Natawág ku siyá.	

Step VI. (Changing the subject, using both long and short forms)

'He will call the driver.'

Táwgun níya ang dráybir.	(íngnun)
Íngnun níya ang dráybir.	(nátuq)
Íngnun nátuq ang dráybir.	(si Lítu)
Íngnun nátuq si Lítu.	(níla)
Íngnun níla si Lítu.	(gipangutána)
Gipangutána níla si Lítu.	(siyá)
Gipangutána níla siyá.	(pangutánqun)
Pangutánqun níla siyá.	(ang tigúwang)
Pangutánqun níla ang tigúwang.	(nákuq)
Pangutánqun nákuq ang tigúwang.	(gitawág)
Gitawág nákuq ang tigúwang.	(si Dúdung)
Gitawág nákuq si Dúdung.	(námuq)
Gitawág námuq si Dúdung.	(si Mánuy)
Gitawág námuq si Mánuy.	(huwatún)
Huwatún námuq si Mánuy.	(silá)
Huwatún námuq silá.	(níya)
Huwatún níya silá.	(gipangítaq)
Gipangítaq níya silá.	(ang irúq)
Gipangítaq níya ang irúq.	(pangitáqun)
Pangitáqun níya ang irúq.	

Step VII. (Position of long and short forms of the genitive agent) (6 D 1)

'I'll come and get the dress.'

Kuháqun ku man ang sinínaq.	(nátuq)
Kuháqun man nátuq ang sinínaq.	(ta)
Kuháqun ta man ang sinínaq.	(níla)
Kuháqun man níla ang sinínaq.	(gikúhaq)
Gikúhaq man níla ang sinínaq.	(ku)
Gikúhaq ku man ang sinínaq.	(nákuq)
Gikúhaq man nákuq ang sinínaq.	(dádqun)
Dádqun man nákuq ang sinínaq.	(ku)

Dádqun ku man ang sinínaq.	(nátuq)
Dádqun man nátuq ang sinínaq.	(ta)
Dádqun ta man ang sinínaq.	(námuq)
Dádqun man námuq ang sinínaq.	(gidalá)
Gidalá man námuq ang sinínaq.	(ku)
Gidalá ku man ang sinínaq.	

Step VIII. (Position of pronoun subject and agent contrasted with position of noun subject and agent)

'He didn't take me to the show.'

Waláq ku níya dádqas siní.	(siyá)
Waláq ku siyá dádqas siní.	(si Ínting)
Waláq ku dádqas Ínting sa siní.	(silá)
Waláq ku silá dádqas siní.	(námuq)
Waláq námuq silá dádqas siní.	(si Pípi)
Waláq námuq dádqas Pípis siní.	(níya)
Waláq níya dádqas Pípis siní.	(ang bátaq)
Waláq níya dádqa ang bátas siní.	(ku)
Waláq ku dádqa ang bátas siní.	(níla)
Waláq níla dádqa ang bátas siní.	(nákuq)
Waláq nákuq dádqa ang bátas siní.	(silá)
Waláq nákuq silá dádqas siní.	(ta)
Waláq ta silá dádqas siní.	(siyá)
Waláq ta siyá dádqas siní.	(si Pírla)
Waláq ta dádqas Pírlas siní.	(námuq)
Waláq námuq dádqas Pírlas siní.	(nátuq)
Waláq nátuq dádqas Pírlas siní.	(siyá)
Waláq nátuq siyá dádqas siní.	

Step IX. (Preposed form of agent)

'I ate the bananas.'

Ákung gikaqún ang ságing.	(ímu)
Ímung gikaqún ang ságing.	(ínyu)
Ínyung gikaqún ang ságing.	(íla)
Ílang gikaqún ang ságing.	(ámuq)
Ámung gikaqún ang ságing.	(kánqun)

Ámung kánqun ang ságing. (lutúqun)

Ámung lutúqun ang ságing. (ákuq)

Ákung lutúqun ang ságing. (íla)

Ílang lutúqun ang ságing. (íya)

Íyang lutúqun ang ságing. (ínyu)

Ínyung lutúqun ang ságing. (ímu)

Ímung lutúqun ang ságing. (átuq)

Átung lutúqun ang ságing.

Step X. (Word order)

'Are we going to look at Perla?'

Átuq bang tanqáwun si Pírla? (nátuq)

Tanqáwun ba nátuq si Pírla? (ámuq)

Ámuq bang tanqáwun si Pírla? (námuq)

Tanqáwun ba námuq si Pírla? (íla)

Íla bang tanqáwun si Pírla? (níla)

Tanqáwun ba níla si Pírla? (ínyu)

Ínyu bang tanqáwun si Pírla? (nínyu)

Tanqáwun ba nínyu si Pírla? (ákuq)

Ákuq bang tanqáwun si Pírla? (nákuq)

Tanqáwun ba nákuq si Pírla? (íya)

Íya bang tanqáwun si Pírla? (níya)

Tanqáwun ba níya si Pírla? (ku)

Tanqáwun ku ba si Pírla? (ímu)

Ímu bang tanqáwun si Pírla? (mu)

Tanqáwun mu ba si Pírla? (íla)

Íla bang tanqáwun si Pírla? (nímu)

Tanqáwun ba nímu si Pírla?

Step XI. (Word order)

'Will you tell Perla?'

Ímu bang íngnun si Pírla? (siyá)

Ímu ba siyáng íngnun? (si Tibúq)

Ímu bang íngnun si Tibúq? (ku)

Ímu ba kung íngnun? (ang bátaq)

Ímu bang íngnun ang bátaq? (silá)

Ímu ba siláng íngnun?	(ang tigúwang)
Ímu bang íngnun ang tigúwang?	(mi)
Ímu ba ming íngnun?	(si Lítu)
Ímu bang íngnun si Lítu?	(ang ákung amígu)
Ímu bang íngnun ang ákung amígu?	

Step XII. (Word order)

'I'll call Perla.'

Ákuq na lang táwgun si Pírla.	(siyá)
Ákuq na lang siyáng táwgun.	(si Mis Wílbi)
Ákuq na lang táwgun si Mis Wílbi.	(silá)
Ákuq na lang siláng táwgun.	(nákuq)
Táwgun na lang silá nákuq.	(níya)
Táwgun na lang silá níya.	(íya)
Íya na lang siláng táwgun.	(si Mis Wílbi)
Íya na lang táwgun si Mis Wílbi.	(níla)
Táwgun na lang níla si Mis Wílbi.	(námuq)
Táwgun na lang námuq si Mis Wílbi.	(ámuq)
Ámuq na lang táwgun si Mis Wílbi.	(siyá)
Ámuq na lang siyáng táwgun.	(nákuq)
Táwgun na lang siyá nákuq.	(ímu)
Ímu na lang siyáng táwgun.	(si Dína)
Ímu na lang táwgun si Dína.	(níya)
Táwgun na lang níya si Dína.	(ta)
Táwgun na lang ta níya.	(íla)
Íla na lang tang táwgun.	

Step XIII. (Word order)

'They will call Perla.'

Íla na lang táwgun si Pírla.	(siyá)
Íla na lang siyáng táwgun.	(námuq)
Táwgun na lang siyá námuq.	(ni Pídru)
Táwgun na lang siyá ni Pídru.	(nímu)
Táwgun na lang siyá nímu.	(si Pípi)
Táwgun na lang nímu si Pípi.	(ni Pírla)
Táwgun na lang ni Pírla si Pípi.	(siyá)

Táwgun na lang siyá ni Pírla.	(nákuq)
Táwgun na lang siyá nákuq.	(ákuq)
Ákuq na lang siyáng táwgun.	(si Pírla)
Ákuq na lang táwgun si Pírla.	(ni Pídru)
Táwgun na lang ni Pídru si Pírla.	(ímu)
Ímu na lang táwgun si Pírla.	(ni Maríng)
Táwgun na lang ni Maríng si Pírla.	(siyá)
Táwgun na lang siyá ni Maríng.	(íla)
Íla na lang siyáng táwgun.	(ni Manáng)
Táwgun na lang siyá ni Manáng.	(ákuq)
Ákuq na lang siyáng táwgun.	(ni Mánuy)
Táwgun na lang siyá ni Mánuy.	(íla)
Íla na lang siyáng táwgun.	(ni Manáng)
Táwgun na lang siyá ni Manáng.	(ang babáyi)
Táwgun na lang ni Manáng ang babáyi.	(kamí)
Táwgun na lang kamí ni Manáng.	(ang bátaq)
Táwgun na lang ni Manáng ang bátaq.	(ámuq)
Ámuq na lang táwgun ang bátaq.	

Step XIV. (Word order)

'Did he buy the book?'

Íya bang gipalít ang líbru?	(íla)
Íla bang gipalít ang líbru?	(níla)
Gipalít ba níla ang líbru?	(níya)
Gipalít ba níya ang líbru?	(nímu)
Gipalít ba nímu ang líbru?	(ni Lína)
Gipalít ba ni Lína ang líbru?	(nínyu)
Gipalít ba nínyu ang líbru?	(mu)
Gipalít mu ba ang líbru?	(nátuq)
Gipalít ba nátuq ang líbru?	(námuq)
Gipalít ba námuq ang líbru?	(ímu)
Ímu bang gipalít ang líbru?	(átuq)
Átuq bang gipalít ang líbru?	(ámuq)
Ámuq bang gipalít ang líbru?	(ínyu)
Ínyu bang gipalít ang líbru?	(ni Líta)
Gipalít ba ni Líta ang líbru?	

PP-N Genitives (6 B)

Step I. (Genitives with nouns) Change the regular genitive to the preposed genitive.

'How old are you?'

1. a. Pilá man diqáy idád mu Nuy?
   b. Pilá man diqáy ímung idád Nuy?

2. a. Mu kiní si Mis Wílbi ang kaqúban ku.
   b. Mu kiní si Mis Wílbi ang ákung kaqúban.

3. a. Upát na ba ang anák mu?
   b. Upát na ba ang ímung anák?

4. a. Diq na maqiháp ang mga apú ku.
   b. Diq na maqiháp ang ákung mga apú.

5. a. Uu, Amirkána ang amíga níya.
   b. Uu, Amirkána ang íyang amíga.

6. a. Dúnay mga lubí sa dápit nínyu?
   b. Dúnay mga lubí sa ínyung dápit?

7. a. Way ságing sa dápit níla, sa?
   b. Way ságing sa ílang dápit, sa?

8. a. Mu kádtung tindáhan námuq.
   b. Mu kádtung ámung tindáhan.

9. a. Kiníy lántay níya.
   b. Kiníy íyang lántay.

10. a. Dághang ságing sa dápit níla.
    b. Dághang ságing sa ílang dápit.

11. a. Dúna bay mga táwu karún sa simbahán níla?
    b. Dúna bay mga táwu karún sa ílang simbahán?

12. a. Dakúq ang baláy níya.
    b. Dakúq ang íyang baláy.

13. a. Mu kiní si Gamílung amígu ku.
    b. Mu kiní si Gamílung ákung amígu.

14. a. Kanáq ang upisína námuq.
    b. Kanáq ang ámung upisína.

15. a. Dínhi ang amahán mu gahápun.
    b. Dínhi ang ímung amahán gahápun.

16. a. Kiníy dyip níya.
    b. Kiníy íyang dyip.

17. a. Waláq dínhing dráybir nátuq.
    b. Waláq dínhing átung dráybir.

18. a. Náqa ang dyip níla.
    b. Náqa ang ílang dyip.

19. a. Kanáy kwártu níya.
    b. Kanáy íyang kwártu.

20. a. Mu kiní si Ída ang amíga níya.
    b. Mu kiní si Ída ang íyang amíga.

Step II. Change regular genitive to preposed genitive (same as Step I but with direct passive verbs).

'I'll take Lito.'

1. a. Dádqun ku si Lítu.
   b. Ákung dádqun si Lítu.

2. a. Tanqáwun níya si Ída.
   b. Íyang tanqáwun si Ída.

3. a. Kuháqun nátuq ang líbru.
   b. Átung kuháqun ang líbru.

4. a. Kánqun námuq ang haluqháluq.
   b. Ámung kánqun ang haluqháluq.

5. a. Hulatún níla si Mis Wílbi.
   b. Ílang hulatún si Mis Wílbi.

6. a. Pangitáqun níya ang íyang amíga.
   b. Íyang pangitáqun ang íyang amíga.

7. a. Pangutánqun ku si Lulú.
   b. Ákung pangutánqun si Lulú.

8. a. Táwgun ku ang anák mu, ha?
   b. Ákung táwgun ang anák mu, ha?

9. a. Hangyúqun nátuq ang prísyu sa aríyus.
   b. Átung hangyúqun ang prísyu sa aríyus.

10. a. Ilaqiláhun námuq si Místir Bílu.
    b. Ámung ilaqiláhun si Místir Bílu.

11. a. Pangitáqun nákuq ang pitákang nahibilín.
    b. Ákung pangitáqun ang pitákang nahibilín.

12. a. Ímnun níla ang bir.
    b. Ílang ímnun ang bir.

13. a. Imbitahún níla si Mánuy sa písta.
    b. Ílang imbitahún si Mánuy sa písta.

14. a. Humanún níya ang íyang trabáhu.
    b. Íyang humanún ang íyang trabáhu.

15. a. Palitún ku ang mga kaság.
    b. Ákung palitún ang mga kaság.

16. a. Pústun nákuq ang ímung gipalít.
    b. Ákung pústun ang ímung gipalít.

17. a. Lutúqun níya ang súdqan.
    b. Íyang lutúqun ang súdqan.

18. a. Lákwun nátuq ang Burumíyu ha?
    b. Átung lákwun ang Burumíyu ha?

19. a. Pangitáqun níya ang gamáyng bátaq.
    b. Íyang pangitáqun ang gamáyng bátaq.

20. a. Pilíqun ku ang níndut nga sinínaq.
    b. Ákung pilíqun ang níndut nga sinínaq.

Step III. (Same as Step II, but with postpositives)

'Shall I wait for Grandpa?'

1. a. Hulatún ku ba si Lúlu?
   b. Ákuq bang hulatún si Lúlu?

2. a. Daliqún ku ra ba ning ákung trabáhu.
   b. Ákuq ra bang daliqún ning ákung trabáhu.

3. a. Tanqáwun ta kunú nang líbru.
   b. Átuq kunúng tanqáwun nang líbru.

4. a. Pangitáqun ku man ang ákung amígu.
   b. Ákuq mang pangitáqun ang ákung amígu.

5. a. Pangutánqun mu lang nang tigúwang.
   b. Ímu lang pangutánqun nang tigúwang.

6. a. Kánqun mu ba ang haluqháluq?
   b. Ímu bang kánqun ang haluqháluq?

7. a. Dádqun ku gyud si Dúdung.
   b. Ákuq gyung dádqun si Dúdung.

8. a. Pangitáqun pa nátuq ang irúq.
   b. Átuq pang pangitáqun ang irúq.

9. a. Gihulát lagí níla si Iyúq Tibúq.
   b. Íla lagíng gihulát si Iyúq Tibúq.

10. a. Táwgun ba nínyu si Níniq?
    b. Ínyu bang táwgun si Níniq?

11. a. Palitún ta ba nang pitáka?
    b. Átuq bang palitún nang pitáka?

12. a. Giqimbitár man gud níya si Ída.
    b. Íya man gung giqimbitár si Ída.

13. a. Ilaqiláhun diqáy níya si Dyuu.
    b. Íya diqáyng ilaqiláhun si Dyuu.

14. a. Gilútuq gyud nákuq ang ísdaq.
    b. Ákuq gyung gilútuq ang ísdaq.

15. a. Gipangítaq ku lagí si Hwan.
    b. Ákuq lagíng gipangítaq si Hwan.

16. a. Hulatún gyud námuq si Pídru úgmaq.
    b. Ámuq gyung hulatún si Pídru úgmaq.

17. a. Pilíqun ku gyud ang níndut nga sinínaq.
    b. Ákuq gyung pilíqun ang níndut nga sinínaq.

18. a. Gipangítaq lang níya ang Magalyánis.
    b. Íya lang gipangítaq ang Magalyánis.

19. a. Pangutánqun mu ba si Mis Wílbi Buy?
    b. Ímu bang pangutánqun si Mis Wílbi Buy?

20. a. Pangitáqun na níya ang bag.
    b. Íya nang pangitáqun ang bag.

Step IV. Transform the preposed genitive to the regular genitive (same as Step I, reading b before a).

Step V. (Same as Step II, reading b before a)

Step VI. (Same as Step III, reading b before a)

Step VII. Change one full form of the genitive to the short form: nákuq becomes ku, nímu becomes mu, nátuq becomes ta. (6 D 1)

'I just didn't buy the bananas.'

1. a. Waláq na lang nákuq palitá ang ságing.
   b. Waláq ku na lang palitá ang ságing.

2. a. Gústu úntaq nákung tanqáwun ang ímung bag.
   b. Gústu ku úntang tanqáwun ang ímung bag.

3. a. Mahímu na naq nímung palitúg dyis.
   b. Mahímu mu na nang palitúg dyis.

4. a. Diq gyud nátuq hulatún siyá.
   b. Diq ta gyud siyá hulatún.

5. a. Kuháqun pa nákuq si Lulú.
   b. Kuháqun ku pa si Lulú.

6. a. Dínhi na lang nákuq pangitáqa si Pírla.
   b. Dínhi ku na lang pangitáqa si Pírla.

7. a. Táwgun ba nímu ang anák ku?
   b. Táwgun mu ba ang anák ku?

8. a. Nalútuq na ba nímung súdqan?
   b. Nalútuq mu na bang súdqan?

9. a. Upát na ang gibúhat nákung lamísa.
   b. Upát na ang gibúhat kung lamísa.

10. a. Diq lang nátuq dádqun ang líbru.
    b. Diq ta lang dádqun ang líbru.

11. a. Kinahánglan nákuq nang kwárta.
    b. Kinahánglan ku nang kwárta.

12. a. Gústu kiní nákung imbitahún si Pírla.
    b. Gústu ku kiníng imbitahún si Pírla.

13. a. Waq gyud nímu makúhaq ang bag?
    b. Waq mu gyud makúhaq ang bag?

14. a. Ubanán siyá nátuq sa sini.
    b. Ubanán ta siyá sa sini.

15. a. Gústu gyud nákung samúkun si Níniq.
    b. Gústu ku gyung samúkun si Níniq.

16. a. Mahímuq lagí tu nímung dádqun.
    b. Mahímuq mu lagí tung dádqun.

17. a. Palitún ba nátuq ning mga gása Dung?
    b. Palitún ta ba ning mga gása Dung?

18. a. Ímnun na nátuq nang kukakúla.
    b. Ímnun ta na nang kukakúla.

19. a. Diq na lang nákuq palitún ang líbru.
    b. Diq ku na lang palitún ang líbru.

20. a. Ngánung waq man lagí nátuq lutúqa ang mga kaság.
    b. Ngánung waq ta man lagí lutúqa ang mga kaság.

Step VIII. (Changing preposed genitive to regular genitive with prepositives) Ibutáng ang púlung sa ( ) sa musunúd nga mga túdling púlung. Himúqa ang gikinahánglang pagqusáb. (6 B 3)

'I'll buy this bag.'

1. a. Ákung palitún kiníng bag. (gústu)
   b. Gústu {kung / nákung} palitún kiníng bag.

2. a. Átung dádqun si Lítu ha? (diq)
   b. Diq {ta / nátuq} dádqun si Lítu ha?

3. a. Ílang hulatún silás Hwan. (mahímuq)
   b. Mahímuq nílang hulatún silás Hwan.

4. a. Ámung pangitáqun ang mga butáng ni Dyuu. (kinahánglan)
   b. Kinahánglan námung pangitáqun ang mga butáng ni Dyuu.

5. a. Ínyung kuháqun ang mga líbru? (gústu)
   b. Gústu nínyung kuháqun ang mga líbru?

6. a. Íyang imbitahún si Pírla sa písta. (mahímu)
   b. Mahímu níyang imbitahún si Pírla sa písta.

7. a. Ákung tanqáwun ang balígyang pitáka. (diq)
   b. Diq {ku / nákuq} tanqáwun ang balígyang pitáka.

8. a. Ímung kánqun nang haluqháluq. (kinahánglan)
   b. Kinahánglan {mung / nímung} kánqun nang haluqháluq.

9. a. Átung pangutánqun ang tigúwang. (mahímu)
   b. Mahímu {tang / nátung} pangutánqun ang tigúwang.

10. a. Ámung pilíqun ang níndut nga sinínaq. (diq)
    b. Diq námuq pilíqun ang níndut nga sinínaq.

11. a. Íyang pangutánqun ang bátaq. (kinahánglan)
    b. Kinahánglan níyang pangutánqun ang bátaq.

12. a. Átung táwgun si Ída. (diq)
    b. Diq {ta / nátuq} táwgun si Ída.

13. a. Íyang lutúqun ang mga kaság. (gústu)
    b. Gústu níyang lutúqun ang mga kaság.

14. a. Ámung pangitáqun ang babáyi. (mahímu)
    b. Mahímu námung pangitáqun ang babáyi.

15. a. Ákung hulatún si Mis Wílbi. (gústu)
    b. Gústu {kung / nákung} hulatún si Mis Wílbi.

16. a. Ílang subáyun ang dálan Piláys. (diq)
    b. Diq níla subáyun ang dálan Piláys.

17. a. Ákung palitún ang baay ni Hwan. (gústu)
    b. Gústu {kung / nákung} palitún ang baay ni Hwan.

18. a. Íyang íngnun si Dúdung. (mahímuq)
    b. Mahímuq níyang íngnun si Dúdung.

Step IX. (The same as Step VIII, but with postpositives)

'I'll just buy this bag.'

1. a. Ákuq na lang palitún kiníng bag. (díliq)
   b. Díliq {ku na lang / na lang nákuq} palitún kiníng bag.

2. a. Ímu bang pangitáqun si Mis Wílbi? (gústu)
   b. Gústu {mu bang / ba nímung} pangitáqun si Mis Wílbi?

3. a. Íya pang huwatún ang tigúwang. (mahímu)
   b. Mahímu pa níyang huwatún ang tigúwang.

4. a. Íla diqáyng ilaqiláhun si Ída. (kinahánglan)
   b. Kinahánglan diqáy nílang ilaqiláhun si Ída.

5. a. Átuq man kaháq siyáng dádqun. (díliq)
   b. Díliq {man kaháq nátuq / ta man kaháq} siyá dádqun.

6. a. Ámuq lagíng kuháqun ang mga aríyus. (kinahánglan)
   b. Kinahánglan lagí námung kuháqun ang mga aríyus.

7. a. Ákuq gyung hulatún ang bag. (gústu)
   b. Gústu {gyud nákung / ku gyung} hulatún ang bag.

8. a. Íya na lang palitún ang líbru. (díliq)
   b. Díliq na lang níya palitún ang líbru.

9. a. Átuq pa bang pangitáqun ang baay? (kinahánglan)
   b. Kinahánglan {ta pa bang / pa ba nátung} pangitáqun ang baay?

10. a. Ámuq mang pilíqun ang níndut nga dyip. (díliq)
    b. Díliq man námuq pilíqun ang níndut nga dyip.

11. a. Íla rang hangyúqug dyis ang usá ka buqúk. (mahímu)
    b. Mahímu ra nílang hangyúqug dyis ang usá ka buqúk.

12. a. Ákuq lang táwgun si Níniq. (gústu)
    b. Gústu {ku lang / lang nákung} táwgun si Níniq.

13. a. Íya nang ímnun ang bir. (díliq)
    b. Díliq na níya ímnun ang bir.

14. a. Ákuq man kanáng tanqáwun. (gústu)
    b. Gústu {ku man kanáng / man kanáq nákung} tanqáwun.

15. a. Íla ra bang daliqún ang ílang trabáhu. (kinahánglan)
    b. Kinahánglan ra ba nílang daliqún ang ílang trabáhu.

16. a. Ámuq na lang pangutánqun ang ímung amígu. (díliq)
    b. Díliq na lang námuq pangutánqun ang ímung amígu.

17. a. Átuq ba diqáyng subáyun ang Burumíyu? (mahímu)
    b. Mahímu {ba diqáy nátung / ta ba diqáyng} subáyun ang Burumíyu?

18. a. Ákuq lang pangutánqun si Iyúq Tibúq. (gústu)
    b. Gústu {ku lang / lang nákung} pangutánqun si Iyúq Tibúq.

19. a. Ákuq bang pústun ning aríyus Diná? (kinahánglan)
    b. Kinahánglan {ba nákung / ku bang} pústun ning aríyus Diná?

20. a. Íya gyud kunúng pilíqun ang buqútang babáyi. (gústu)
    b. Gústu gyud kunú níyang pilíqun ang buqútang babáyi.

IV A. (To be preceded by PP-M and PP-N) Ipunúq ang hústung púrma sa recipient ug agent. (6 D)

		Recipient	Agent
Pananglítan:	Gitawág man ________ ________.	me	they
Tubág:	Gitawág man ku níla.		

1. Gitánqaw gyud ________ ________ ganíha. you (sing.) I

		Recipient	Agent
2.	Huwatún ________ ________ dínhi.	him	I
3.	Pangitáqun gayúd ________ ________ dídtu.	us (incl.)	he
4.	Waq ________ ________ pangutánqa.	me	you (sing.)
5.	Díliq ________ ________ bisitáhun.	him	I
6.	Anáaq gitawág ________ man ________.	you (sing.)	they
7.	Dádqun tingáli ________ ________ sa Amiriká.	them	he
8.	Dúgay na ________ng gihuwát ________ dínhi.	you (sing.)	we
9.	Uy, gipangítaq bayáq ________ ________ dídtu.	you (sing.)	they
10.	Usáq pa kay táwgun pa ________ ________.	him	we (excl.)
11.	Dádqun ba ________ ________ ngádtu sa Pulambatú?	him	you (pl.)
12.	Diq ba ________ ________ dádqun sa Amiriká?	me	you (pl.)
13.	Pagdalíq na kay gihuwát bayáq ________ ________.	us (incl.)	they
14.	Maqáyu kay gihuwát ________ ________.	us (incl.)	they
15.	Imbitahún úntaq ________ ________ ngádtu sa písta sa Árgaw.	you (pl.)	we
16.	Maqáyu kay gihatúd ________ ________ ngádtu sa baay.	us (incl.)	they
17.	Waq ba ________ ________ pangutánqa?	you (sing.)	they
18.	Anhíqun ________ gyud ________ unyáq.	you (sing.)	he
19.	Giqimbitár kunú ________ ________ ngádtu sa siní.	us (excl.)	he
20.	Madungúg gyud kaqáyu ________ ________ bísag layúq ra kitá.	them	we (incl.)

IV B. Pilíqa ang túkmang puung nga náqa diháq sa ( ). (3 A 3, 3 B, 5 D, 6 B and subsections)

1. Muqádtu ba (si, ni) Husí sa Mabúlu karúng hápun?
2. Waq (níya, siyá) himúqa ang íyang trabáhu.
3. Uy, (ikáw, ka) ba si Mis Wílbi?
4. Muqinúm ba gyud (si, ni) Nuy Tibúq ug kukakúla?
5. Si Místir Abáya (ang, sa) mukáqun sa ságing.
6. Kuháqun na (kamú, nínyu) ang putús?

7. Ságdi lang kay (námuq, kamí) ang muhumán sa ímung trabáhu.
8. Maqú (kiní, niqíni) ang gipangítaq sa ákung amígu.
9. Kanúsqa kaháq (silá, níla) muqánhi sa baay?
10. Bátaq pa (siyá, níya) kaqáyu.
11. Níndut ba (sa, ang) siníng ('movie') gitánqaw nínyu gahápun?
12. Ákung gipalít (ang, sa) dyip (si, ni) Nuy Prid.
13. Dínhi (námuq, kamí) palitá ang aríyus.
14. (Kádtu, Niqádtu) ang níndut sa tanáng gibalígyaq.
15. Dádqun (nátuq, kitá) silá dídtu karúng gabíqi.
16. Hapít unyáq (kamú, nínyu) sa baay.
17. Kanúsqa man (silá, níla) musakáy sa dyip?
18. Mangádtu ta sa (silá, íla)ng Nída úgmaq..
19. Kalayúq (ang, sa) íyang lúngsud.
20. Mupalít (akú, nákuq) ug káluq sa tindáhan.

IV C. (To be preceded by PP-N) Change the regular genitives to preposed genitives and the preposed genitives to regular genitives. (6 B, 6 B 1, 6 B 2).

1. Dádqun lang námuq si Lítu sa Amiriká.
2. Ákuq lang ibílin ning amígu nákuq sa tindáhan.
3. Adtúqun gyud kunú níla si Místir Abáya.
4. Tanqáwun pa níya ug makalakáw ba siyá.
5. Ámuq ra ba siyáng imbitahún sa písta ('fiesta').
6. Ákuq na lang súgtun si Huwán.
7. Palitún ba nínyu ang gibalígyaq?
8. Íla bang gilútuq ang kaság?
9. Báyran lagí ka námuq sa giqútang ('debt') ni Husí.
10. Ínyu diqáyng huwatún ang dyip?
11. Úsbun ('change') námuq ang púrma ('form') sa baay.
12. Maqáyu pag himúqun ('make') lang níla ang kurtína ('curtain').
13. Giqiháp diqáy nímu ang sinsíyu?
14. Ang kinhasún nínyu hikalímtan.
15. Íyang nalímtan ang káluq sa dyip.
16. Huwatún námung muqabút siyá.
17. Ílang gikúhaq ang mga síya ('chairs') sa kwártu.
18. Lutúqun na ba kaháq nákuq ang súdqan?

19. Íya gyung balíkun ang íyang nalímtan. 'He will surely go back for what he forgot.'

20. Abángan námuq ang tindáhan ug barátu ra.

IV D. Gámqa nga negative ang musunúd nga mga túdling púlung. (2 B, 3 C 3, 6 B 3)

1. Gihumán námuq ang ámung trabáhu.
2. Kánqa ang súdqan nga gibílin nímu. 'Eat the food that you left.'
3. Dádqun níla ang mga kaság sa Kárbun.
4. Kalímti na lang ang nahitabúq gabíqi. 'Just forget what happened last night.'
5. Giqimbitár mi ni Pírla sa ílang lúngsud.
6. May bisíta ta karúng búntag.
7. Muqádtu silá si Nuy Tibúq ug si Pírla sa Pulambatú sunúd túqig ('next year').
8. Ímu bang gipalít ang mga aríyus nga gibalígyaq?
9. Mahímuq bang mangutána?
10. Dághan bag dyip átbang sa tindáhan?
11. Ibílin lang nákuq silá dínhi.
12. Ámuq na lang ibalígyaq ang bir.
13. Muqinúm ka bag kukakúla?
14. Gikúhaq ni Husí ang mga síya ('chairs') gíkan sa kwártu.
15. Manáqug ming tanán sa Banáwaq.

V A. Ibúngat ang mga musunúd nga mga púlung sa hústung panínugug. (234 statement)

1. Únu utsínta. (6 b 37)
2. Tagáqi lang kug únu singkwínta. (6 b 39)
3. Uu sigí. (6 b 40)
4. Únu singkwínta. (6 b 40)
5. Suklíqi uh. (5 b 41)
6. Waq man kuy sinsíyu pára síngku. (6 b 42)
7. Ambí nang síngku. (6 b 44)
8. Díqay únu singkwínta. (6 b 46)
9. Básin pa. (3 a 44)
10. Mangutána ta. (3 a 8)

11. Ayáw na lang. (1.14)
12. Manakáy na ta. (2 a 17)

V B. (423 question)

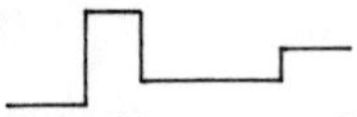

1. Tagpíla man ni? (6 a 3)
2. Unsáqun man nákuq pagpatáy? (6 a 32)
3. Ása man ku musakáyg dyip páras Mabúlu? (6 b 49)
4. Giqúnsa man nímu pagqabút ánang idára? (5.14)
5. Pilá man nang kaság?
6. Ngánung únu utsínta man?
7. Únsa man nang ímung balígyaq?
8. Háqin man ang ákung síngku?
9. Únsa kaháy ákung hikalímtan sa tindáhan? (6 a 18)

V C. (423 statement)

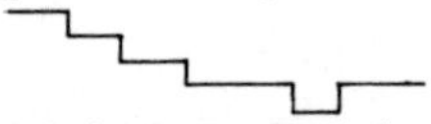

1. Kiní si Nuy Tibúq. (5.8)
2. Náqa say usá sa ubús. (3 b 21)
3. Ádtu naq sa Mabúlu. (6 b 51)
4. Maqúy muqádtus Mabúlu. (6 b 55)
5. Kiní si Místir Gamílu. (1.10)
6. Íngna nga dyis ray ákung (6 a 12)
7. Úna báynti ray ákung ihátag.

V D. (324 question)

1. Diq ba mahímug dyis na lang? (6 a 8)
2. Diq ba gyud diqáy mahímung dyis? (6 a 10)
3. Ákung pangutánqun siyá ha? (6 a 13)
4. Diq ka kaháq samúkans mga bátaq? (3 c 11)
5. Lábqas ba kanáq? (6 a 30)
6. Salámat Nuy ha? (6 b 52)
7. Ádtu ba nis Mabúlu? (6 b 53)
8. Aa, waq kay sinsíyu? (6 b 43)

VI A. Pagbása

1. Retell the story.
2. Have one informant ask you questions.
3. Do the exercise on the verbs below (VI B).

Si Nída Namalít ug Kaság

Nída: Anáaq náqay nagbalígyag kaság. Tanqáwun nákuq.

Pírla: Únsa na man puy ímung palitún? Aa, kaság diqáy.

Nída: Dalíq Iyáq, arí ági. Pirlá, pilá may átung palitún? Hústu pa kaháq ug átung lutúqun páras paniqúdtu?

Pírla: Hústu pa tingáli. Isáq pa. Pangitáqun pa nákuq ang bag.

(Taqudtaqúd, humáns pagpalít)

Pírla: Ihapún* saq nákuq ug hústu ba ning mga kaság. Uy! Kúlag usá. ('There is one missing.')

Nída: Uy, Iyáq. Ísaq pa kay ákung adtúqun. Túqa ra. Pangutánqun pud nákuq siyá ug íya na ba kung gisuklíqan.

Pírla: Ay na lang. Natagáqan na ka níyas súkliq. Ságdi na lang tung usá ka kaság. Ang maqáyu pústun mu naq pagqáyu arún díliq makalakáw. Dádqun ku ning báskit diháq?

Nída: Sigí kay kiníy ákung buhátug úna. Yaaaay, agúuuuy. Pátyun ta gyud ka. (I'll kill you!')

Pírla: Uy! Ngánu? Ngánu? Naqúnsa ka?

Nída: Karún lutúqun tiká dáyun. Pátyun ta gyud ka úsaq.

Pírla: Aa, ag kaság diqáy! ('Oh! It's just the crabs!')

VI B. Pagbánsay

Si Nída Namalít ug Kaság

Ibutáng sa lunáq ang hústung púrma sa bírbung gilikupán sa ( ).

Nída: Anáaq náqay nagbalígyag kaság. (Tánqaw) nákuq.

Pírla: Únsa na man puy ímung (palít)? Aa, kaság diqáy.

Nída: Dalíq Iyáq, arí ági. Pirlá, pilá may átung (palít)? Íguq pa kaháq ug átung (lútuq) páras paniqúdtu?

Pírla: Hústu pa tingáli. Isáq pa. (Pangítaq) pa nákuq ang bag.

(Taqudtaqúd, humáns pagpalít)

Pírla: (Iháp) saq nákuq ug hústu ba ning mga kaság. Uy! Kúlag usá. ('There is one missing.')

---

* Íphun is also possible. (It has the same meaning as ihapún.)

Nída: Uy, Iyáq! Ísaq pa kay ákung adtúqun. Túqa ra (pangutána) pud nákuq siyá ug íya na ba kung gisuklíqan.

Pírla: Ay na lang. Natagáqan na ka níyas súkliq. Ságdi na lang tung usá ka kaság. Ang maqáyu (putús) mu naq pagqáyu arún díliq makalakáw. (Dalá) ku ning báskit diháq?

Nída: Sigí kay kiníy ákung (búhat)g úna. Yaaaay, agúuuuy. Pátyun ta gyud ka. ('I'll kill you!')

Pírla: Uy! Ngánu? Ngánu? Naqúnsa ka?

Nída: Karún (lútuq) tiká dáyun. (Patáy) ta gyud ka úsaq.

Pírla: Aa, ag kaság diqáy! ('Oh! It's just the crabs!')

VII. Sultiqánay

Si Mis Wílbi Namalít

A: Únsa may átuq Day?

B: Nangítaq kug kuqán—kiníng ihátag sa usá ka amíga.

A: Díqay mga aríyus. Gústu ka ba áni?

B: Uy anáaq kanindut! Tagpíla man ni?

A: Kuqán lang naq Day . . . tris písus ang par.

B: Mahímuq bag dus?

A: Aa—Díliq ra ba Day. Waq na tay ganánsya ánaq. Tányag lag dus singkwínta ug ákung pangutánqun ang Ínsik.

B: Ay na lang kay dus ray ákung ibáyad. Ádtu na lang ku.

Tubagág <u>hústu</u> u <u>díliq</u>:

1. Nangítaq si Mis Wílbig kaság.
2. Nakakitáq si Mis Wílbig aríyus nga nagustuqán níya.
3. Ang prísyu sa aríyus barátu ra. Dus písus ang par.
4. Waq siyá makapalít dáyun.
5. Mihángyuq si Mis Wílbi ug dus, pirú miqingún ang nagbalígyaq nga waláq siláy ganánsya niqánaq.
6. Giputús ang aríyus kay napalít ni Mis Wílbi.

A: Aa Mis! Mis! Bálik!

B: Uy anáaq! Gitawág man ku níla! Únsa kaháy ákung nalímtan dídtus tindáhan?

A: Aa Mis—miqingún ang Ínsik nga makapalít kag dus kun duháy ímung palitún.

B: Aa, tanqáwun saq nátuq. Aa, ang gikinahánglan nákuq usá ra ka par.

A: Maqáy ning pagkapalíta. Níndut ni kaqáyu.

B: Pústa na lang nang usá. Díqay dus.

A: Uu. Na sigí. Níqa puy mga káluq. Gústu ka?

B: Ay na lang. Nagdalíq man ku. Salámat na lang.

A: Balikbálik ha? Ayáwg tagám ha?

Tubagág <u>hústu</u> u <u>díliq</u>:

7. Hunaqhúnaq ni Mis Wílbing dúnay íyang hikalímtan dídtus tindáhan.
8. Giqíngnan si Mis Wílbi nga barátu na tung aríyus ug mupalít siyág duhá ka par.
9. Duháy íyang gipalít kay barátu man.
10. Nagkinahánglan si Mis Wílbig duhá ka par.
11. Namalígyaq sad silág káluq pirú waq si Mis Wílbi mupalít.
12. Si Mis Wílbi waláq mupalít ug káluq kay ang Ínsik díliq makasinsíyu sa íyang síngku.

LESSON 7. REVIEW

Ripásu

Sugilánun:

Písta Sa Árgaw

Nída: Maqáyu.

Lína: Dayún, únsa may átuq?

Nída: Day, níqa ba si Línda?

Lína: Uu. Túqa siyá sa íyang kwártu. Língkud úsaq ha, kay ákuq siyáng táwgun.

Línda: Uy, Nidá, ikáw man diqáy. Únsa na?[1]

Nída: Díqay túrtang[2] ákung gidáa nímu, uh. Waq man gud ka makaqubán námuq.

Línda: Uy kalamíq niqíni. Salámat, ha? Diqín man ni nínyu?

Nída: Sa Árgaw.

Línda: Sa Árgaw? Dídtu diqáy mu?

Nída: Ay úqu. Sus, kaníndut dídtu, uy. Giqimbitár man gud mi níla ni Dúdung sa písta[3] gahápun dídtu. Giqánhi[4] ka námuq apán dídtu ka man kunú sa Úpun, maqú nga waq na lang mi maghuwát nímu.

Línda: Daqúy, may pag[5] waq ku muqádtu sa Úpun daq. Únsa may ínyung gisákyan?

Nída: Pagpadúung námuq ngádtu, dyip ang ámung gisákyan kay nagqábang man mi sa dyip níla ni Dyuu.[6]

Línda: Sayún ra diqáy ang ínyung biyáhi[7] kay kaqugalíngun man ang sakyanán. Kaníndut úntag nakaqubán ku nu? Waq pa ra ba ku makaqádtu sa Árgaw.

Nída: Uy waq pa diqáy? Bísag túqa si Tiyáq Márta nímu magpuyúq, waq pa gyud ka mubisíta ngádtu?

Línda: Waq pa gyud táwun.[8] Unyáq kang kínsa mang baay ang ínyung giqádtu?

Nída: Sus, dághan kaqáyu ang ámung giqádtu uy, diq na maqiháp. Ang ubán gániq nalímtan na nákuq kun kínsa tung ílang ngaan.

Línda: Waq mu muqádtu sa ka Pípi?

Nída: Waq gyud. Gipangítaq námuq ang ílang baláy apán gikápuy na lang mig[9] lakawlákaw[10] waq gyud gihápun námuq hikítqi.[11]

---

* See page 268 for list of new words. The raised numerals in this text correspond to the numbers on that list.

Línda: Aw diqáy? Saq pa ra gud. Nagsígi[12] na man lang hinúqun tag istúrya.[13] Liná, dádqi ra gud mi diríg kukakúla. Pagdáa usáb ug pínggan árun súdlan niqíning túrta.

Lína: Níqa na ang kuk, uh.

Línda: Inúm úsaq Nidá, uh. Ipáris[14] ni nátuq sa túrta.

Nída: Salámat. Kuk ray ákuq. Diq na lang ku mukáqun niqánang túrta. Dághan kaqáyu kug nakáqun ánaq dídtus Árgaw.

Línda: Kuqán hinúqun[15] Liná, pagkúhag bískwit.[16] Dádqa ngarí.

Nída: Aa, ayáw na lang. Hústu na lang ring kuk.

Línda: Lamíq ning turtáha daq. Kínsay gahímuq niqíni?

Nída: Gihátag naq námuq ni Mísis Kintanár. Kamí gyung tanán gitagáqan. Dághan kaqáyu tung ílang túrta, uy. Unyáq, ang ákung báhin[17] maqúy ákung gidalá ngánhi nímu.

Línda: Sus kabuqútan[18] gyud nímu uy.

Nída: Nangutána diqáy tu si Místir Almirántig ngánu kunú nga waq ka man muqubán.

Línda: Aw, dídtu sab diqáy mu sa íla?

Nída: Úqu. Unyáq ákuq na lang siyáng gisultíhan kun ngánung waq ka makaqádtu.

Línda: Nangáqun ba mu dídtu sa íla?

Nída: Aw úqu. Lamíq kaqáyu ang ílang súdqan uy. Siyá kunúy naglútuq sa ubán niqádtu.

Línda: Aa, úqu, kay kahibáwu man naq siyá manglútuq.

Nída: Unyáq, pagkahumán námuq dídtu sa íla nu, íya ming gihatúd[19] ngádtu sa simbahán.

Línda: Nanánqaw ba mu sa báyli?

Nída: Diq lang kay tánqaw ra, namáyli pa gyud[20] mi.

Línda: Diqáy? Kaqalígri[21] diqáy nínyu nu? Dídtu diqáy mu matúug?

Nída: Waq uy. Pagkahumán sa báyli, misakáy dáyun mi sa dyip arún mubálik dáyun ngánhi sa Sibú. Naghángyuq gániq tung ámung kaqúban nga sa búntag na lang mi mamaqúliq,[22] apán waq man mi musugút, kay gústu na man gyud ming mupaqúliq.

Línda: Unyáq, únsa na man mung urása miqabút ngánhi?

Nída: Sus, alás síngku na tingáli tu, kay ang dyip nga ámung gisákyan, kanúnay lang nga muhúnung. Íguq lang[23] ming nakadúlhug ug gamáy gíkan sa Árgaw mihúnung na usáb kay nadáqut ang ligíd.[24] Nanganáqug na lang ming tanán. Maqáyu kay dúnay miqáging traak, namálhin na lang mi.

Línda: Gibiyáqan[25] na lang nínyu ang dyip?

Nída: Aw úqu. Unsáqun man námuq tung dyípa nga díliq na man mudágan. Dúna hinúqun miy duhá ka kaqúban nga nagpabílin[26] dídtu.

Línda: Pilá man diqáy mu ka buqúk nga nangádtu?

Nída: Dúsi man tingáli mi.

Línda: Aq, usá ka dusína man gyud diqáy mu.

Nída: Bítaw,[27] makapunúq[28] gud dáyun mig lamísa kun mangáqun na mi. Uy, díliq na lang ku magdúgay ha, kay dúna pa kuy palitúnun.

Línda: Únsa gud nang ímung palitúnun?

Nída: Papalitún man gud ku ni Tíyaq ug aríyus nga kinhasún, íyang ihátag sa amígang Amirikána. Dúna man tuy tindáhan dínhis mga aláhas nga kinhasún sa ínyung dúqul, nu?

Línda: Uu duqúl ra. Subáya lang ning daan, unyáq likúq sa walá diháq sa primírung iskína. Ang ikaduhá nga baláy gíkan sa beauty parlor maqú naq ang ílang Mísis Maglásang. Dághan kaqáyu naq silág balígyang níndut nga aláhas. Silá man gániq ang mamúhat sa ubán.[29]

Nída: Na, muqádtu na lang ku, ha? Magkítaq na lang ta úgmaq sa upisína.

Línda: Sigí. Salámat sa túrta, ha?

Nída: Way sapayán. Ádtu na ku. Bábay.

Línda: Bábay. Balikbálik.

Notes

1.	únsa na	'how are things?'
2.	túrta	[kind of cake]
3.	písta	'fiesta'
4.	giqánhi ka námuq	'we came by for you'
5.	Daqúy, may pag . . .	'Oh heck. It would have been better . . .'
6.	níla ni Dyuu	'Joe and his family'
7.	biyáhi	'trip'
8.	táwun	'poor me'
9.	gikápuy na lang mi	'we got tired'
10.	lakawlákaw	'walking around'
11.	hikítqi	'found'
12.	nagsígi	'all we are doing is'
13.	istúrya	'chatting'
14.	ipáris	'have along with'
15.	hinúqun	'instead'
16.	bískwit	'cookies'
17.	báhin	'share'
18.	kabuqútan	'how good of'

19. gihatúd 'took (in a vehicle)'
20. diq lang kay —— ra . . . pa gyud 'not only —— but also . . .'
21. kaqalígri 'how gay!'
22. mamaqúliq 'returned'
23. íguq lang 'just as we had'
24. nadáqut ang ligíd 'something went wrong with the wheel'
25. gibiyáqan 'abandoned'
26. nagpabílin 'stayed behind'
27. bítaw 'yes, that's so'
28. makapunúq 'we could fill up'
29. sa ubán 'some of them'

Pattern Practices and Exercises

I. Deictics and interrogatives (1 A 2, 2 A and subsections) (This exercise may follow Pattern Practice PP-B, Lesson 2.) Ibutáng ang hústung púlung sa lúnang gipaqángay sa matág túdling púlung. Tanqáwa ang laráwan.

1. (C-D) __________ na tingáli ta __________ sa baláy ni Dúktur Pirnándis.
2. (D-A) May dyip ba __________ng muqági pára Lahúg?
3. (D-A) __________ man ta musakáy ug dyip pára Banáwaq?
4. (C-A) __________ mi __________ kay ákung gidalá si Huwán.
5. (B-CD) Dayún. __________ lang mu __________ sa pantáwan.
6. (A-CD) Uy, __________ pa man kamú gíkan?
7. (D-A) __________ man diqáy si Mísis Abilyána? __________ba?
8. (B-A) __________ man si Huwán?
9. (A-B) __________ siya sa sílung.
10. (A-CD) Dayún lang mu __________ sa táqas.
11. (C-B) __________ ba si Místir Abáya?
12. (B-CD) Saká lang mu. __________ si Místir Abáya sa suud.
13. (B-A) __________ lang ta __________ sa pantáwan manihápun.
14. (B-A) __________ na ba ang duktúr nga ákung gitawág?
15. (C-D) __________ lang ta sa pantáwan ági. 'Let's go in by way of the back porch.'
16. (D-B) __________ na ba si Dúktur Pirnándis?
17. (B-CD) Waláq pa, __________ pa sa Lahúg.

A
C

18. (C-D) Maqú diqáy niy ílang baláy? __________ man ku sa miqáging ádlaw.
19. (CD-A) __________ na ba ang ímung anák __________ sa sulúd?
20. (C-D) __________ na si Líta sa baláy.
21. (B-CD) __________ pa man mu padulúng? __________ pa ba mu sa Kárbun?
22. (D-B) __________ man gud mi sa ílang baláy ni Lúling.
23. (A-CD) __________ si Lúling diq pa dúgay, pirú waq na.
24. (A-B; B-A) "__________ ba sa pantáwan si Huwán?" "__________ tingáli sa sílung."
25. (B-A) Dádqi ku __________ ug kukakúla.

II. Kamí or kitá. (1 B)

1. Kuqán man gud Dung, __________ mang duhá ang musakáy. 'We two are going to get on, driver.'
2. Taná manaká __________ sa táqas.
3. Ay sus! Hápun na man diqáy kaqáyu. Ádtu na lang __________ Mam! Magquná lang __________ nínyu.
4. Mamalít úntaq __________ nínyug aláhas nga kinhasún. Pilá man ang inyung aríyus?
5. Manakáy u manlákaw ba lang __________? 'Shall we ride or just walk?'
6. __________y magsakáy. Kamú na lay lakáw.
7. Íngna lang si Mis Wílbi nga muqánhaq __________ dínhaq. (spoken on the telephone)
8. Kun díliq ka muqubán __________ na lang duhá.
9. Padulúng na ba __________ sa Karbún Dung?
10. Salámat na lang. Humán na __________ maniqúdtu.
11. Dádqun ka (nátuq, námuq) sa Amiriká Dung.
12. (Ámuq, Átuq) lang ibílin siÚsting dínhi nínyu.
13. Níqa na gyud __________ sa baláy sa ímung amígu.
14. Díliq na ba lang __________ nímu ipaqilaqíla sa ímung asáwa?
15. Diq na ka kinahánglang mubáyad—tutál ('anyway') (ámuq, átuq) man kang amígu.

III. Gamíta ang laráwan ug isulát sa lunáq nga gipaqángay sa matág túdling púlung sa ubús, ang hústung púlung nga makahátag sa hústung demonstrative: kirí, kiní, kanáq, kadtú. (1 A 1)

1. (D-C) Maqú __________ ang baláy ni Saníng.
2. (B-A) Aa, dádqi __________ng sunúyg makáqun. 'Bring this rooster here some food.'
3. (B-A) __________ng ákung bag sa kwártu, dádqa ngarí. 'Bring that bag here into the room.'

4. C-D: Tanqáwa __________ng sunúy. Dakúq kaqáyu, nu?

5. C-D: __________ ng baláya ang ákung balhínan. 'This house is the one I will move to.'

6. B-A: __________ng díqa sa pantáwan ang ákung dádqun.

7. B-A: Kínsa man __________ng duhá ka táwu sa sílung?

8. D-C: __________ng náqa sa táqas maqú ang ákung amíga, si Saníng.

9. CD-B: Imúk, ibalígyaq mu ba __________ng sunúy mu sa pantáwan?

IV. Tubagá ang musunúd nga mga pangutána sa mga túdling púlung nga mugámit sa díliq, waláq, ug ayáw. (2 B)

1. Mahál bang ábang sa íyang baláy?
2. Dúna bay mga Amirikánu dínhi?
3. Dịdtu ba mu ági sa Piláys pagpaqingún nínyu ngánhi?
4. Níqa ba magpuyúq si Mis Abáya?
5. Dráybir man ang ímung anák, únsa nu?
6. Midágan ba ang bátaq ni Místir Gamílu?
7. Muqánhi akú dínhi káda búlan, ha?
8. Káda búntag ka ba musakáy sa dyip?
9. Dághan bang musakáy pára Banáwaq?
10. Gitúgnaw ka ba Dyuu?
11. Dúna bay dálan paqingún sa ka Duktúr Pirnándis?
12. Musugút ka bang ánhi mi mupuyúq dínhi?
13. Ihatúd ku ikáw sa iskína, ha? 'Shall I take you to the corner?'
14. Ákung táwgun ang duktúr, ha? 'Shall I call the doctor?'
15. May dyip ba si Místir Gamílu?

V. Gamíta dínhi niqíning mga túdling púlung ang -a (kun mahímuq). (2 C)

Pananglítan: Kiníng líbru ang ákung palitún pára ni Lítu.
Tubág: Kiníng librúha ang ákung palitún pára ni Lítu.

1. Dínhi dapít siyá namatáy.
2. Únsang kwártu ang ímung gústu?
3. Diqíng lugár silá muqádtu?
4. Dínhi íning tindáhan ku ni palitá.
5. Únsang úras si Pírla milakáw?
6. Kanáng baláy maqúy níndut sa tanán. 'That house is the most beautiful of all.'
7. Maqú kadtúng daan nga giqagíqan sa dyip.
8. Kádtung tigúwang maqúy gabalígyag kaság.

9. Dínhi íning iskína mi manáqug.
10. Kanáng bátaq apú ni Nuy Tibúq.

VI. Hubára sa Sinibwanú ang musunúd nga mga túdling púlung. (3 A 1)

1. I have visitors coming.
2. There are many jeeps on the corner.
3. Do you have crabs for sale?
4. Are there many rooms in your house?
5. Is there a toilet here?
6. Someone went to your town last week. (Literally: There was one who went to your town last week.)
7. Does John have a beautiful house?
8. There were men in the street yesterday.
9. You know I have books in the house.
10. She has four grandchildren.
11. I know they have hats for sale.
12. The store over there has jewelry.
13. There are no more crabs for sale.
14. I know she did not have a husband.
15. Are there rooms for rent in Perla's house?
16. A man came here looking for you. (Literally: There was a man here looking for you.)
17. Did you have many friends in America?
18. She doesn't have any children in the house.
19. Do you have sisters living in Mabolo?
20. Were there many people in Carbon this morning?

VII. (This exercise may be preceded by PP-I, Lesson 5.) Gámqa nga exclamatory ang musunúd nga mga declarative nga túdling púlung. (5 A)

1. Lamíq kaqáyu ang súdqan nga gilútuq ni Pírla.
2. Míngaw gyud ang ámung lugár ug tímpung bakasyún. (tímpung bakasyún 'during vacation')
3. Níndut tanqáwun ang mga aríyus nga gipalít ni Mis Wílbi.
4. Lábqas pa ang mga kaság nga balígyaq dínhis Sibu.
5. Mahál diqáy ang mga balígyaq dínhis Sibú.
6. Gamáy ra diqáy ang baay níla sa lúngsud.
7. Layúq ang ámung baay sa sinihán.
8. Dalíq ra siyáng mibálik gíkan sa simbahán.

9. Dághan ka gyug apú.
10. Mahál ka diqáyng mubalígyaq.

VIII A. (This exercise may be preceded by PP-J, Lesson 5.) Pilíqa ang túkmang púlung nga náqa diháq sa ( ). (4 B and subsections; 6 A 3 and subsections)

1. (Muqabút, Miqabút) mi sa Sibú karúng gabíqi.
2. Waq níya (palitá, palitún, gipalít) ang aríyus nga gibalígyaq námuq.
3. Waq nákuq (malútuq, nalútuq) ang ságing.
4. (Gipangítaq, Pangitáqun) námuq silá sa syudád sunúd simána.
5. Ug (makasakáy, nakasakáy) mig dyip (miqági, muqági) mi sa ínyu.
6. Maqáyu kay (mubálik, mibálik) ka sa baay gabíqi. (gabíqi 'last night')
7. Padúung silá sa Karbún kay ádtu man silá (namalígyaq, mamalígyaq).
8. Waq ku kahibáwung (makaqági, nakaqági) ba ta dínhi.
9. Gústu kung (muhátag, mihátag) ni Mis Wílbig líbru.
10. Mahímuq ka bang (mubálik, mibálik) dínhi sa Pilipínas?
11. Waq na siyá (makalútuq, nakalútuq) kay gabíqi na kaqáyu.
12. Ug may lugár pa kunú (mibálik, mubálik) silá dídtu sa ínyu.
13. Maqáyu gániq kay (nakalíngkud, makalíngkud) mu sa sinihán.
14. (Palitún, Palitá) gyud diqáy ni Huwán ang dyip ni Nuy Tibúq.
15. (Gibúhat, Buhátun) ba nímu karún ang trabáhu nákuq?
16. Ábi nákug (I thought) (maputús, naputús) na níya ang ákung gipamalít ganíha.
17. (Musugút, Misugút) ba kaháq si Pírlag abángan nákuq ang íyang baláy?
18. (Makapangutána, Nakapangutána) ba tag diqín padúung ning dána? 'May we ask . . . ?'
19. Íngna siyág mahímuq bang (makaqánhaq, nakaqánhaq) mi dínhaq.
20. Waq níya (gikúhaq, kuháqa) ang aláhas dídtu sa lamísa.
21. Gústu ku (muhátag, mihátag) níyag kwárta.
22. Mahímuq bang (bálhina, balhínun) nínyu ang ínyung tindáhan?
23. Arí ta dirí (maglíngkud, naglíngkud) sa sála.
24. Tingálig (musugút, misugút) siyág ímung hangyúqun.
25. Mahímuq bang (makabisíta, nakabisíta) sa ínyu?

VIII B. Pilíqa ang hústung púrma sa mga bírbu (nag-/mag-, mi-/mu-, naka-/maka-). (4 A; 5 C and subsections)

1. Kanúsqa ka (miqabút, nagqabút) dínhi?
2. (Nagsakáy, Nakasakáy) ka ba dáyun sa pagpadúung nímu dínhi?

3. Díliq na (maputús, pústun) ang líbru kay waláq nay papíl. Ug dúnay papíl mahímung pústun.
4. Díliq kitá (naglútuq, maglútuq) ug súpas karún. (súpas: a kind of cake)
5. (Milakáw, Naglakáw) ka ba lang sa pagqánhi nímu ('when you came')?
6. Gústu kung (magqinúm, muqinúm).
7. Gústu kung (mulakáw, maglakáw) ug sayú ngádtu sa Karbún.
8. (Nakahátag, Naghátag) na ba mus sulát ni Mis Wílbi?
9. (Maghúnung, Muhúnung) ba dínhing mga dyip nga páras Mabúlu?
10. (Makaqánhi, Magqánhi) ka ba úgmaq sa hápun?
11. (Nakabisíta, Nagbisíta) si Pídru sa ámuq makaqusá ra. (makaqusá ra 'just once')
12. Dúgay kung (nakahulát, naghulát) nímu dínhi.
13. (Naglakáw, Milakáw) ba kamúng duhá padulúng dínhi?
14. Tingálig díliq ka na (makabálik, magbálik) dínhi.
15. (Miqánhi, Nagqánhi) ku arún (mutábang, magtábang) kanímu.

PP-Y. Díliq vs. waláq: Direct Passive (6A)

Step I. (Change of verbs)

'She will not cook the bananas.'

Díliq níya lutúqun ang ságing.	(waláq)
Waláq níya lutúqa ang ságing.	(palitá)
Waláq níya palitá ang ságing.	(díliq)
Díliq níya palitún ang ságing.	(dádqun)
Díliq níya dádqun ang ságing.	(waláq)
Waláq níya dádqa ang ságing.	(pústa)
Waláq níya pústa ang ságing.	(díliq)
Díliq níya pústun ang ságing.	(kánqun)
Díliq níya kánqun ang ságing.	(waláq)
Waláq níya kánqa ang ságing.	(ípha)
Waláq níya ípha ang ságing.	(díliq)
Díliq níya íphun ang ságing.	(pilíqun)
Díliq níya pilíqun ang ságing.	(waláq)
Waláq níya pilíqa ang ságing.	(pangitáqa)
Waláq níya pangitáqa ang ságing.	(díliq)
Díliq níya pangitáqun ang ságing.	(hangyúqun)
Díliq níya hangyúqun ang ságing.	(waláq)

Waláq níya hangyúqa ang ságing.	(tanqáwa)
Waláq níya tanqáwa ang ságing.	(díliq)
Díliq níya tanqáwun ang ságing.	

Step II. (Díliq and waláq with meanings given)

'They asked the old man.'

Gipangutána níla ang tigúlang.	(they didn't)
Waláq níla pangutánqa ang tigúlang.	(they won't)
Díliq níla pangutánqun ang tigúlang.	(they will)
Pangutánqun níla ang tigúlang.	(they didn't)
Waláq níla pangutánqa ang tigúlang.	(they won't)
Díliq níla pangutánqun ang tigúlang.	(pangitáqun)
Díliq níla pangitáqun ang tigúlang.	(they didn't)
Waláq níla pangitáqa ang tigúlang.	(they will)
Pangitáqun níla ang tigúlang.	(they won't)
Díliq níla pangitáqun ang tigúlang.	(dádqun)
Díliq níla dádqun ang tigúlang.	(they will)
Dádqun níla ang tigúlang.	(they didn't)
Waláq níla dádqa ang tigúlang.	(táwga)
Waláq níla táwga ang tigúlang.	(they won't)
Díliq níla táwgun ang tigúlang.	(they will)
Táwgun níla ang tigúlang.	(íngnun)
Íngnun níla ang tigúlang.	(they didn't)
Waláq níla íngna ang tigúlang.	(they won't)
Díliq níla íngnun ang tígulang.	(they will)
Íngnun níla ang tigúlang.	

Step III. Díliq vs. waláq with preposed genitives (meanings given).

'We just called the boy.'

Ámuq na lang gitawág ang bátaq.	(didn't)
Waláq na lang námuq táwga ang bátaq.	(won't)
Diq na lang námuq táwgun ang bátaq.	(will)
Ámuq na lang táwgun ang bátaq.	(gipangítaq)
Ámuq na lang gipangítaq ang bátaq.	(didn't)
Waláq na lang námuq pangitáqa ang bátaq.	(won't)
Diq na lang námuq pangitáqun ang bátaq.	(súndun)

Diq na lang námuq súndun ang bátaq.	(didn't)
Waláq na lang námuq súnda ang bátaq.	(will)
Súndun na lang námuq ang bátaq.	(dádqun)
Dádqun na lang námuq ang bátaq.	(won't)
Diq na lang námuq dádqun ang bátaq.	(didn't)
Waláq na lang námuq dádqa ang bátaq.	(pangutánqa)
Waláq na lang námuq pangutánqa ang bátaq.	(won't)
Diq na lang námuq pangutánqun ang bátaq.	(will)
Pangutánqun na lang námuq ang bátaq.	(huwatún)
Huwatún na lang námuq ang bátaq.	(didn't)
Waláq na lang námuq huwatá ang bátaq.	(won't)
Díliq na lang námuq huwatún ang bátaq.	(we will)
Huwatún na lang námuq ang bátaq.	

Step IV. <u>Díliq</u> vs. <u>waláq</u> (including potentials)

'We just bought the crabs.'

Ámuq na lang gipalít ang kaság.	(didn't)
Waláq na lang námuq palitá ang kaság.	(won't)
Diq na lang námuq palitún ang kaság.	(didn't)
Waláq na lang námuq palitá ang kaság.	(didn't have the chance)
Waláq na lang námuq mapalít ang kaság.	(can't)
Diq na lang námuq mapalít ang kaság.	(íphun)
Diq na lang námuq íphun ang kaság.	(didn't)
Waláq na lang námuq ípha ang kaság.	(didn't have the chance)
Waláq na lang námuq maqiháp ang kaság.	(will)
Ámuq na lang íphun ang kaság.	(lutúqun)
Ámuq na lang lutúqun ang kaság.	(won't)
Diq na lang námuq lutúqun ang kaság.	(didn't)
Waláq na lang námuq lutúqa ang kaság.	(didn't have the chance)
Waláq na lang námuq malútuq ang kaság.	(can't)
Diq na lang námuq malútuq ang kaság.	(pústun)
Diq na lang námuq pústun ang kásag.	(didn't)
Waláq na lang námuq pústa ang kaság.	(didn't have the chance)
Waláq na lang námuq maputús ang kaság.	(can't)
Diq na lang námuq maputús ang kaság.	(will)
Ámuq na lang pústun ang kaság.	

PP-S Transformation of active to passive (6A)

Step I. (Real, direct passive only) (no shift in emphasis)

a. 'He got some bananas.'
b. 'He got the bananas.'

1. a. Nagkúhaq siyág ságing.
   b. Gikúhaq níya ang ságing.

2. a. Nagkúhaq siyág kwárta.
   b. Gikúhaq níya ang kwárta.

3. a. Mitánqaw siyág ísdaq.
   b. Gitánqaw níya ang ísdaq.

4. a. Gadalá siyág gátas.
   b. Gidalá níya ang gátas.

5. a. Nagpalít siyág líbru.
   b. Gipalít níya ang líbru.

6. a. Naglútuq siyág ísdaq.
   b. Gilútuq níya ang ísdaq.

7. a. Nagkúhaq siyág sinínaq.
   b. Gikúhaq níya ang sinínaq.

8. a. Mikáqun siyág prútas.
   b. Gikaqún níya ang prútas.

9. a. Nagtawág siyág tartanílya.
   b. Gitawág níya ang tartanílya.

10. a. Nagtawág siyág dúktur.
    b. Gitawág níya ang dúktur.

11. a. Nagtánqaw siyág aríyus.
    b. Gitánqaw níya ang aríyus.

12. a. Gakúhaq siyág paan.
    b. Gikúhaq níya ang paan.

13. a. Nagdalá siyág manúk.
    b. Gidalá níya ang manúk.

14. a. Gakaqún siyág kánqun.
    b. Gikaqún níya ang kánqun.

15. a. Gahátag siyág gása.
    b. Gihátag níya ang gása.

16. a. Nagpalít siyág gása.
    b. Gipalít níya ang gása.

17. a. Nagqiháp siyág kwárta.
    b. Giqiháp níya ang kwárta.

18. a. Nagqinúm siyág túbig.
    b. Giqinúm níya ang túbig.

19. a. Nagbalígyaq siyág bag.
    b. Gibalígyaq níya ang bag.

20. a. Naghatúd siyág sinínaq.
    b. Gihatúd níya ang sinínaq.

Step II. (Real, direct passive only) (shift of emphasis)

a. 'He cooked some bananas.'
b. 'Bananas are what he cooked.'

1. a. Naglútuq siyág ságing.
   b. Ságing ang íyang gilútuq.

2. a. Nagbúhat siyág lamísa.
   b. Lamísa ang íyang gibúhat.

3. a. Nagqinúm siyág bir.
   b. Bir ang íyang giqinúm.

4. a. Nagkúhaq siyág paan.
   b. Paan ang íyang gikúhaq.

5. a. Nagpalít siyág bag.
   b. Bag ang íyang gipalít.

6. a. Nagtánqaw siyág sini.
   b. Siní ang íyang gitánqaw.

7. a. Nagkúhaq siyág pípsi.
   b. Pípsi ang íyang gikúhaq.

8. a. Nagbúhat siyág baláy.
   b. Baláy ang íyang gibúhat.

9. a. Nakadalá siyág gása.
   b. Gása ang íyang nadalá.

10. a. Naglútuq siyág ítlug.
    b. Ítlug ang íyang gilútuq.

11. a. Nagqinúm siyág gátas.
    b. Gátas ang íyang giqinúm.

12. a. Nagpalít siyág bárku.
    b. Bárku ang íyang gipalít.

Step III. Real and unreal, direct passive only (shift of emphasis)

a. 'He'll see the show.'
b. 'The show is what he'll see.'

1. a. Mutánqaw siyás siní.
   b. Siní ang íyang tanqáwun.

2. a. Nagtánqaw siyág siní.
   b. Siní ang íyang gitánqaw.

3. a. Mudalá siyág líbru.
   b. Líbru ang íyang dádqun.

4. a. Nagdalá siyág líbru.
   b. Líbru ang íyang gidalá.

5. a. Mupalít siyág ísdaq.
   b. Ísdaq ang íyang palitún.

6. a. Nagpalít siyág ísdaq.
   b. Ísdaq ang íyang gipalít.

7. a. Mukáqun siyág ságing.
   b. Ságing ang íyang kánqun.

8. a. Gakaqún siyág ságing.
   b. Ságing ang íyang {gikáqun / gikaqún}.

9. a. Nagkaqún siyág ságing.
   b. Ságing ang íyang {gikáqun / gikaqún}.

10. a. Mukúhaq siyág pitáka.
    b. Pitáka ang íyang kuháqun.

11. a. Nagkúhaq siyág pitáka.
    b. Pitáka ang íyang gikúhaq.

12. a. Musulúd siyás kwártu.
    b. Kwártu ang íyang súdlun.

13. a. Mutawág siyág táksi.
    b. Táksi ang íyang táwgun.

14. a. Nagtawág siyág táksi.
    b. Táksi ang íyang gitawág.

15. a. Mulútuq siyág ísdaq.
    b. Ísdaq ang íyang lutúqun.

16. a. Naglútuq siyág ísdaq.
    b. Ísdaq ang íyang gilútuq.

VIII C. Ibutáng sa lunáq ang hústung púrma sa bírbu. Pagpíliq kun active u direct passive ba. (4 A, 6 A 1)

Pananglítan: (Dalá) na ba nímu ang bir ngádtu?
Tubág: Gidalá na ba nímu ang bir ngádtu?

1. Díliq na lámang (palít) ni Pírla ang kaság kay mahál kaqáyu. 'Perla won't buy the crabs because they're very expensive.'
2. Kínsa man ang (tawág) kanákuq? 'Who's calling me?'
3. (Pangítaq)ba kag kinhasún nga aláhas? 'Are you looking for jewelry made of sea shells?'
4. Mamatáy bítaw kanáq kun ímu nang (lútuq). 'It will die when you cook it. Don't worry!'
5. Díliq ba masukúq ang Ínsik kun (dalá) ku kiníng tanán? 'Won't the Chinaman get mad if I take all of these with me?'
6. (Kítaq) ba diqáy nímung ákung káluq? 'Have you really seen my hat?'
7. Ása man diqáy ka (huwát) kang Huwán? 'Where will you wait for John, then?'

8. Muqádtu ku sa Lahúg kay ákung (bisíta) si Índay. 'I'm going to Lahug because I'm going to visit Inday.'

9. (Bálik) ba kaháq kitá dáyun ngádtu sa Banáwaq? 'Shall we go right back to Banawa?'

10. Waq man diqáy (kúhaq) ni Lítu ang kukakúla dirí. 'Lito didn't take the Coca-Cola away from here, after all.'

11. Díliq na lang ku (ádtu) sa Banáwaq. 'I won't bother going to Banawa.'

12. (Bálik) ka pa ba ngánhi úgmaq sa hápun? 'Will you come back again tomorrow afternoon?'

13. (Kúhaq) sa bátaq ang kaság nga ákung (palít) dídtus Karbún. 'The child took the crabs which I had bought in Carbon.'

14. Díliq pa (kítaq) nátuq ang ílang baláy kay layúq pa man kaqáyu.

15. Díliq ka lang ba (pangutána) sa Ínsik kun tagpíla ang dusína sa káluq?

16. Waláq na lang nákuq (káqun) ang kaság kay waq ka pa man makakaqún.

17. Pagdalá ngánhig dághang kinhasún kay ákung (hímuq) nga aríyus.

18. Gústung (pangutána) si Lítu báhin sa aríyus kay íya mang (palít).

19. Níndut kaqáyung (tánqaw) kiníng aríyus diháq nímu.

20. Kínsa may ínyung (pangítaq)? Si Huwán ba?

IX. Ihátag ang hústung púrma sa pronouns nga anáqa sa suud sa parentheses. (1 B, 5 D, 6 B and subsections)

1. Dádqun na ba (siyá) ang rigálu mu kaníya?

2. Kanáq ba ang (kamú)ng baláy Day?

3. Ádtu únaq (kitá) sa ámuq Mis.

4. Kiní ang giqingún (siyá)ng íyang amígu.

5. Háqin mang tung (ikáw)ng gidalá?

6. Dághan ba (kamú)g ságing sa (kamú)?

7. Ákuq na lang (kiní)ng dádqun, ha?

8. Ma, níqay (kitá)ng bisíta.

9. Ásа mang dapíta ang (kamú)ng kanaqúgan? 'Where are you getting off?'

10. Díliq ba mulikúq ning (ikáw)ng dyip sa Pidíl Rusáryu?

11. Túqa (siyá) ang ákung líbru. 'He has my book.'

12. Taná ádtu (kitá) sa (kamí)ng baláy. Mangáqun ta.

13. Unsáqun man (silá) pagpatáy ánang kaság?

14. Dúnay mangasáwa (siyá). 'There is someone who will marry her.'

15. Diqín man (kamú) palitá kanáng kaság?

16. Háqin na man ang putús (kamí)? (putús 'package')

17. Túqa ku magpuyúq sa (silá) ni Místir Abáya.

18. May nagqimbitár (kamí) ug paniqúdtu.
19. Subáya lang (kamú) kanáng Pidíl Rusáryu.
20. Díliq lang (silá) tanqáwun ang kwártu.

XA. (This exercise may be preceded by PP-E, Lesson 3.) Idúgang ang mga púlung gústu, kinahánglan, dáyun, mahímuq, ug ayáw sa musunúd nga mga túdling púlung ug gámqa ang gikinahánglang pagqusáb. (3 C 3 a)

Pananglítan: Muqádtu na lagí akú. (gústu)
Tubág: Gústu na lagí akúng muqádtu.

1. Manáqug úntaq mi dínhi. (gústu)
2. Muqádtu ba mi sa ínyung baláy karún? (mahímuq)
3. Humanún nímu karún. (kinahánglan)
4. Dínhi ka lang, Pirlá, ha? (kinahánglan)
5. Dung, dádqun ka námuq sa Amiriká. (díliq)
6. Muqádtu na lang úntaq ku kay hápun na man. (gústu)
7. Muqinúm ka ba ug bir? (gústu)
8. Ákuq na ba ning lutúqun? (mahímuq)
9. Ihátag ku na ba ning sulát níya? (mahímuq)
10. Ánhi úntaq ku matúlug sa ínyu karún. (gústu)
11. Dádqun ku na lang ni. (díliq)
12. Ákuq na lang ning lutúqung kaság. (gústu)
13. Makalakáw na ba ku? (mahímuq)
14. Ibálhin nátuq kiní arún díliq mahúgaw. (kinahánglan)
15. Muhulát lang ku nímu. (díliq)
16. Mupalít akúg sapátus úgmaq. (gústu)
17. Táwga na lang siyá karún. (ayáw)
18. Ikáw gayúd ang muqádtu. (kinahánglan)
19. Makasulúd ba akú? (mahímuq)
20. Mubáyad na lang ku. (gústu)

XB. Gámqag negative ang musunúd nga mga túdling púlung. (2 B, 3 C 3 a)

1. Mahímu bag dyis na lang ang dusína sa aríyus?
2. Gitawág man ku nímu. Dúna ba kuy hikalímtan?
3. Buháta naq run dáyun.
4. Kádtung dyip nga túqas tumúy, maqú ba tung padulúng sa Mabúlu?
5. Palitá na lang naq, Day.
6. Búhiq ba nang kaság mu Yaq?
7. Lutúqa na nang kaság. (Change na to saq)

8. May ikasinsíyu ka bas dyis písus?
9. Mahímu bang tanqáwun ku ang mga aríyus?
10. Tanqáwa ra gud nang kaság Day.
11. Mitánqaw dáyun siyá sa kaság.
12. Gústu ku úntang makaganánsyag dyútay.
13. Dung, pasákya ra si Huwán sa ímung dyip ug ihatúd siyás Mabúlu.
14. Miqánhi man si Mis Wílbi kagahápun.
15. Balígyaq ba nang kaság Nang?

XC. Ipunúq ang agent ug recipient sa musunúd nga mga túdling púlung. (6A)

	Recipient	Agent
Panangl ítan: Gidalá _____ _____ dínhi. Tubág: Gidalá nákuq si Mis Wílbi dínhi.	Mis Wílbi	I
1. _____ _____ng gibálhin sa ámuq.	them	I
2. Kuháqun _____ úntaq _____ sa ínyu.	you (sing.)	we (excl.)
3. Dádqun _____ _____ sa ámuq.	Lítu	I
4. Mubisíta ra ba kunú _____ _____ úgmaq.	you (sing.)	he
5. Mangutána úntaq _____ _____: Mahímu ba?	you (sing.)	I
6. Taná, manánqaw _____g _____.	siní	we (incl.)
7. Pátyun ba dyud _____ _____?	him	you (sing.)
8. Gústu _____ mutánqaw _____ karún.	you (sing.)	he
9. Gústu _____ muqábag _____ sa ínyung baay.	kwártu	they
10. Mamisíta _____ _____ únyaq.	you (pl.)	we (excl.)
11. Gitawág man _____ _____.	them	I
12. Nangítaq _____ _____ ganína.	you (sing.)	they
13. Mupalít usáq _____g _____.	ságing	we (incl.)
14. Uy, gipangítaq _____ ra ba _____.	him	I
15. Pangutánqun ra gud _____ _____.	Mísis Abilyána	we (incl.)
16. Díliq _____ samúkun _____.	Índay	we (incl.)
17. Sigí, kánqun _____ _____.	ságing	we (incl.)
18. _____ nang giqiháp _____.	kwártu	we (excl.)
19. Giputús na _____ _____.	kaság	we (excl.)
20. Dádqun _____ _____ ngádtus dúktur.	bátaq	I

Additional exercise: Reverse the columns marked agent and recipient if possible and fill in the blanks.

Sagquluhúnun

First Part	Únang Báhin
driver	dráybir
the one	maqú
boat	bárku
going to	pára sa
Ormoc (city in Leyte)	Úrmuk
1. Driver, is this the boat for Ormoc?	1. Draybír, maqú ba kiníng bárku ... páras Úrmuk?
is now (as contrasted with earlier)	na
mark, sign	márka
[linker between márka and Úrmuk]	nga
2. Ah, this is it now because there is a sign (saying) Ormoc.	2. Aa, maqú na ni kay náqa may ... márkang Úrmuk.
it is so	túqud
3. Oh yes, that's right (pointing).	3. Túqud uh.
let's go	taná
get on	manaká

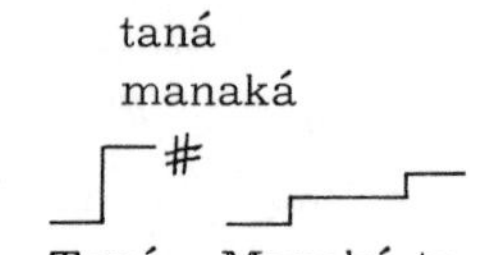

4. Let's go. Let's get on.	4. Taná. Manaká ta.
heavens! (expression of surprise)	anáaq
it seems	mu ra
[linker between mu ra and the rest of the sentence]	ug
completely	pulús
already	na
occupied	giqukupahán
cot	tihíras

5. Heavens, it looks as though the cots here are all taken already.

*5. Anáaq, mu ra mag pulús na giqukupahán ang mga tihíras dínhi.

reserved — girisírba
[linker between girisírba and tihíras] — nga
for — pára
[dative particle] — kang

6. Boy, do you have a cot reserved for Miss Wilby?

*6. Dung, may girisírba ka bang tihíras pára kang Mis Wílbi?

[dative particle] — ni

7. Yes, there is one reserved for Miss Wilby.

*7. Uu. Náqay usáng girisírba pára ni Mis Wílbi.

upstairs — táqas

8. It is upstairs.

8. Túqas táqas.

cool — búgnaw
and — ug
fresh — hayáhay

9. It's good there because it's cool and fresh.

9. Maqáyu dídtu kay búgnawg hayáhay.

10. Come on, let's go up.

10. Taná. Manaká ta.

carry — dalá (short for mudalá)
bag — bag

11. Let me carry your bag, Miss. (Lit. I shall be the one to carry this bag of yours, Miss.)

11. Akúy dalá íning bag nímu Mis.

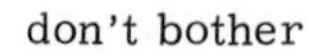

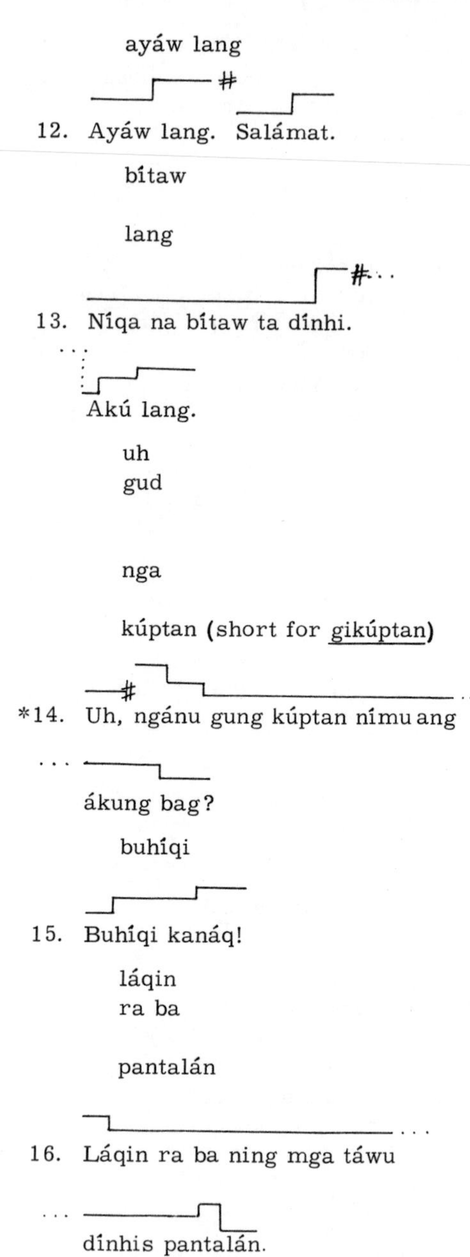

don't bother	ayáw lang
12. Don't bother, thanks.	12. Ayáw lang. Salámat.
[particle giving reason; reassuring]	bítaw
just, only	lang
13. We are already here anyway. I'll do it myself. (Lit. I'll just be the one to do it.)	13. Níqa na bítaw ta dínhi. ... Akú lang.
[exclamation of surprise]	uh
[question particle after interrogatives showing strong surprise]	gud
[linker between ngánu and kúptan]	nga
hold	kúptan (short for gikúptan)
14. Hey, what do you think you're doing holding my bag? (Lit. Hey, why are you holding my bag?)	*14. Uh, ngánu gung kúptan nímu ang ... ákung bag?
to be let go	buhíqi
15. Let go of that!	15. Buhíqi kanáq!
of a bad type	láqin
[particle with statement giving advice]	ra ba
pier	pantalán
16. The people here at the waterfront are not of a nice sort.	16. Láqin ra ba ning mga táwu ... dínhis pantalán.
should watch out	magbántay
17. You should be careful here.	*17. Magbántay ka dínhi.
18. Here we are now at our cots.	*18. Níqa na kitás átung tihíras.
when [someone] arrives	inigqabút

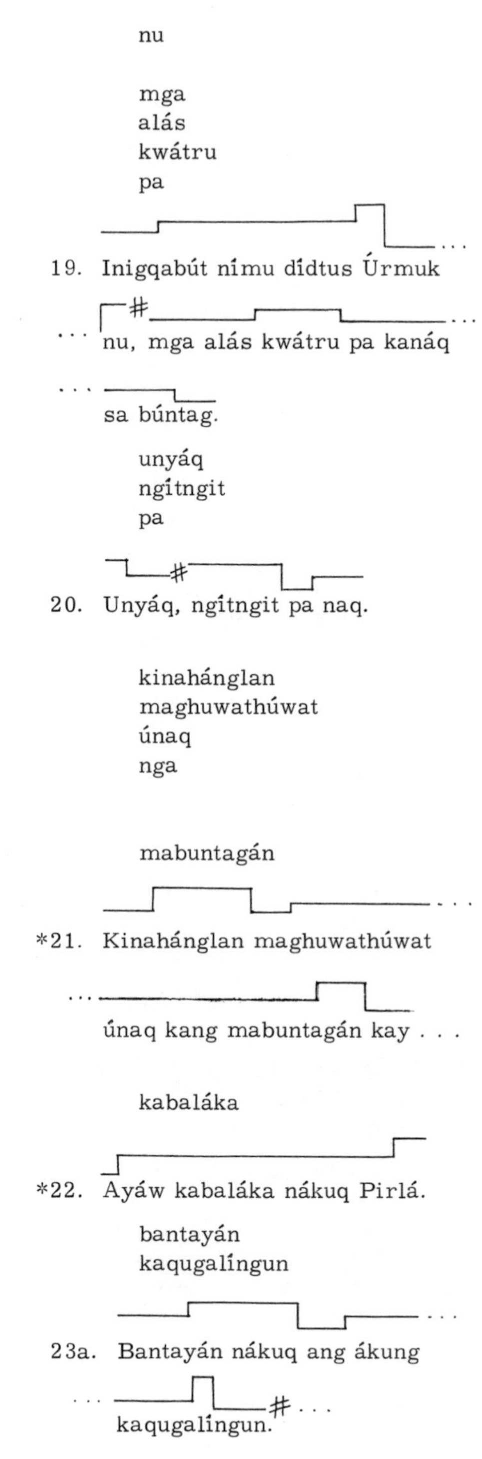

you know? do you understand?	nu
about	mga
o'clock	alás
four	kwátru
still	pa
19. You know, when you arrive there in Ormoc, it (lit. that) will be about four o'clock in the morning.	19. Inigqabút nímu dídtus Úrmuk . . . nu, mga alás kwátru pa kanáq . . . sa búntag.
furthermore	unyáq
dark	ngítngit
still	pa
20. Furthermore, it (lit. that) will still be dark.	20. Unyáq, ngítngit pa naq.
it is necessary	kinahánglan
wait for a bit	maghuwathúwat
first	únaq
[linker between maghuwathúwat and the rest of the sentence]	nga
be overtaken by morning	mabuntagán
21. You'll have to wait until morning first because . . . (Lit. It is necessary for you to wait to be overtaken by morning because . . .)	*21. Kinahánglan maghuwathúwat . . . únaq kang mabuntagán kay . . .
worry	kabaláka
22. Don't worry about me, Perla.	*22. Ayáw kabaláka nákuq Pirlá.
to be taken care of	bantayán
self	kaqugalíngun
23a. I will take care of myself.	23a. Bantayán nákuq ang ákung . . . kaqugalíngun.
and	ug
go down, get off	manáqug
while	sámtang

yet, still	pa
bright	háyag
23b. And I will certainly not get off before it is light (lit. while it is still not light).	23b. Ug díliq gyud akú manáqug sámtang díliq pa háyag.
come here	daliq
[particle making a polite command]	ra gud
24. Boy, come here.	*24. Dung, daliq ra gud.
reserved for	girisirbahán
place	lugár
25. This is Miss Wilby, the American I reserved a place for here on the boat.	*25. Maqú kinís Mis Wílbi ang Amirikánang ákung girisirbahág lugár dínhis bárku.

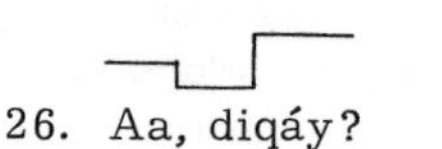

26. Oh, really?	26. Aa, diqáy?
to be taken care of	bantayí
later	unyáq
[particle asking for agreement]	ha

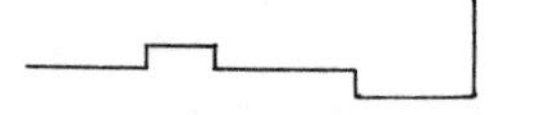

27. Take care of her, will you? (Lit. Take care of her later, will you?)	27. Bantayí unyáq siyá ha?
be attended to	tágdun
well	pagqáyu
don't	ay (short for <u>ayáw</u>)
[particle linking <u>ayáw</u> and the imperative]	ug
28. Yes, I will attend to her well, don't you worry.	28. Uu, ákuq siyáng tágdun pagqáyu. Ayg kabaláka.
tip	tip

[particle for pointing at something]	uh
29. Here's your tip. Here.	29. Níqay ímung tip uh.
30. Thank you very much.	30. Dághang salámat.
31. Don't mention it.	31. Way sapayán.
probably	tingáli
[linker between maqáyu and the rest of the sentence]	nga
32. I should probably be going now. (Lit. Maybe it is good that I just go now.)	32. Maqáyu tingáling ádtu na lang ... ku.
forget	paghikalimút
to write	pagsuwát
33. Also don't forget to write me, will you?	33. Unyáq, ayáw paghikalimút ... pagsuwát kanákuq ha?
of course	aw uu
should write	magsuwát
immediately	dáyun
34. Of course, I will make it a point to write you immediately.	34. Aw uu, magsuwát gyud ku nímu ... dáyun.

Mga Pangutána

Únang Báhin

1. Náqa na bang bárku páras Úrmuk?
2. Manaká na ba ta?
3. Dúna na ba muy tihíras nga girisírba?
4. Búgnaw tingális táqas nu?
5. Mabuntagán kaháq kus bárku?

6. Láqin ba ning mga táwu dînhis pantalán?
7. Ngîtngit pa ba inigqabút kus Úrmuk?
8. Maqú ba kiníng átung tihîras?
9. Ngánung magbántay man ku dînhi?
10. Mahîmuq bang akúy dalá îning bag nîmu Mis?
11. Dîliq tingáli maqáyung manáqug ku sámtang dîliq pa háyag nu?
12. Ikáw ba ang Amirikánang girisirbahág lugár dînhis bárku?
13. Tágdun mu kaháq siyá pagqáyu?
14. Magsuwát ba kaháq siyá nákuq nu?
15. Ngîtngit pa ba inigqabút sa bárku sa Úrmuk?
16. Háqin man ang girisîrbang tihîras pára kang Mis Wîlbi?
17. Hayáhay ba dîdtu sa táqas?
18. Ngánung kúptan man nîmu ning ákung bag?
19. Kinahánglan ba gyung magbántay sa pantalán?
20. Ása man ku maghuwathúwat ug sakyanán ('transportation')?

Mga Pangutána (Matching)

Únang Báhin

1. Kiní na ba ang bárku páras Úrmuk?
2. Unyáq, inigqabút nîmu dîdtu, magsuwát ka dáyun ha?
3. Dúna ka na bay girisîrbang tihîras?
4. Mahîmuq bang akúy dalás îmung bag Mis?
5. Búntag na kaháq kung muqabút dîdtus Úrmuk?
6. Kiní ba ang Amirkánang girisirbahág tihîras?
7. Ása man ang maqáyu, sa táqas u sa ubús?
8. Kamú bang duháy musakáy?
9. Nîndut ba kaháq ang Úrmuk?

(a) Ayáw na lang Dung. Salámat.
(b) Úqu. Siyá.
(c) Búntag na kaqáyu. Mga alás útsu gyud.
(d) Aw uu. Diq gyud naq nákuq kalîmtan.
(e) Dúna na.
(f) Uy, nîndut gyud kaqáyu. Makagústu ka gyud.
(g) Dîliq, siyá ra.
(h) Maqáyus táqas kay búgnaw.
(i) Aa, úqu. Dúnay márkang páras Úrmuk.

Sagquluhúnun

Second Part	Ikaduháng Báhin
thing to be attended to	bantayí
[particle preceding manner of action]	ug
book	líbru
1. Take good care of our bookstore, will you? (Lit. Attend to our bookstore well, will you?)	1. Bantayíg maqáyu ang átung tindáhan sa mga líbru ha?
then	nyaq
take care of yourself	pagqayuqáyu
2. And take care of yourself here in Cebu.	2. Nyaq, pagqayuqáyu dínhis Sibú.
next	sunúd
month	búwan
see each other	magkítaq
3. We won't see each other till next month. (Lit. It will just be next month when we meet.)	3. Sunúd na lang búwan kitá magkítaq.
(A lady enters into conversation with Miss Wilby.)	(Gipakigsultíhan si Mis Wílbi sa usá ka babáyi.)

4. Oh, so you are an American?	4. Uy, Amirkána ka diqáy?
yes	úqu
missionary	misyunáryu
5. Yes, I'm a missionary here in Cebu.	5. Úqu, misyunáryu ku dínhis Sibú.
my!	uy
surprised	natingála
[linker between natingála ku and the rest of the sentence]	nga
speak Visayan	mubinisayáq
6. My, I am very much surprised	*6. Uy, natingála kaqáyu kung

that you speak Visayan well.	. . . maqáyu kang mubinisayáq.
(Miss Wilby is sold her ticket.)	(Gibaligyáqan si Mis Wílbig tíkit.)
ticket	tíkit
four-fifty	kwátru singkwínta
7. Ticket, Ma'am; four-fifty.	7. Tíkit Day, kwátru singkwínta.
8. Four-fifty?	8. Kwátru singkwínta?
9. How cheap!	9. Kabarátu!
five-fifty	síngku singkwínta
[particle correcting a misstatement]	diqáy
10. Oh no! It's actually five-fifty.	10. Aa, síngku singkwínta diqáy.
[particle expressing surprise]	uh
is it really	maqú ba gyud
fare	pasáhi
from	gíkan
11. Oh! Is that really the fare from here to Ormoc?	11. Uh, maqú ba gyud nang pasáhi . . . gíkan dínhi ngádtus Úrmuk?
is said	giqingún
on	sa
12. What does it say on the ticket? (Lit. What is it that is said on the ticket?)	12. Únsa may giqingún dihás tíkit?
give it to me	bi

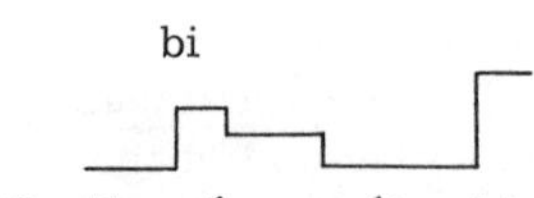

13. Let's look at it.	13. Tanqáwun nátuq bi.
14. Here it is.	14. Díqa uh.
according to	mátud sa

four-fifty	kwátru singkwínta
this and no more	ra
[particle: 'contrary to what you say']	lagí
15. According to this ticket here, it's only four-fifty.	15. Uh, mátud sa tíkit dirí, kwátru ... singkwínta ra man lagí.
is	maqú
no more than	ra
to be given	ihátag
16. That's all I'm giving you.	16. Maqú ra nay ákung ihátag nímu.
was mistaken	nasayúp
[particle used upon saying something one has just remembered]	diqáy
17. Ah, I was mistaken then.	17. Aa, nasayúp diqáy ku.
(Miss Wilby sees a boy selling things.)	(Nakakitáq si Mis Wílbig bátang namalígyaq.)
being sold	gibalígyaq
18. Boy, what is that you're selling?	18. Dung, únsa man nang ímung ... gibalígyaq?
coconut-milk caramel	kalamáy
19. This? This is coconut-milk caramel.	19. Kiní? Kalamáy ni.
20. What's that?	20. Únsa man naq?
coconut milk	túnuq
to which is added	gipúnqan
brown sugar	kalámay
boiled to let the liquid evaporate	giqítus
21. Well, kalamay is coconut milk with brown sugar added	*21. Aa, kiníng kalamáy—túnuq ning

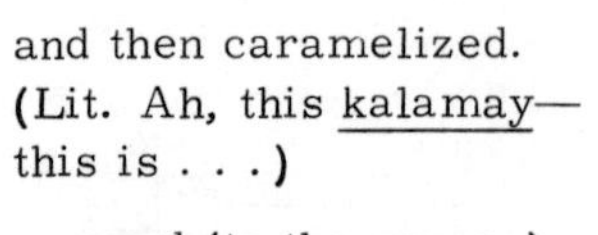

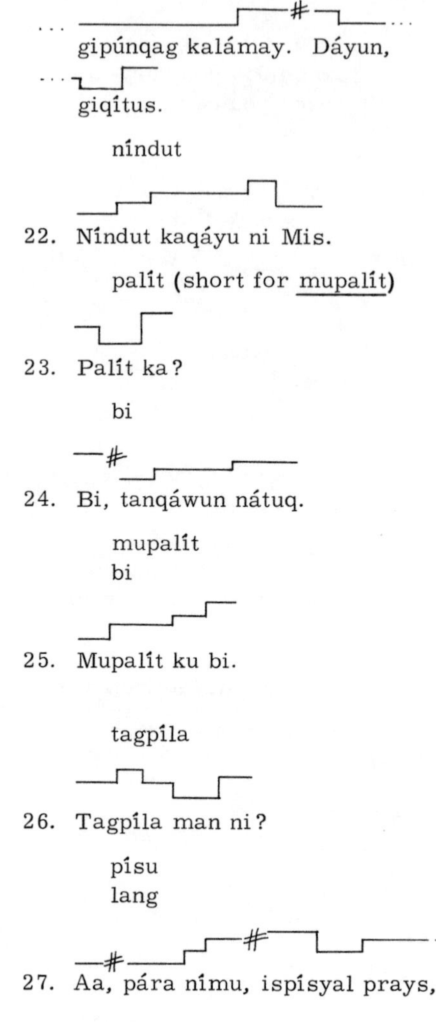

and then caramelized. (Lit. Ah, this kalamay—this is . . .)	gipúnqag kalámay. Dáyun, giqítus.
good (to the senses)	níndut
22. It's very good, Miss.	22. Níndut kaqáyu ni Mis.
buy	palít (short for mupalít)
23. Will you buy (some)?	23. Palít ka?
[particle: 'let me see']	bi
24. Here, let's look at it.	24. Bi, tanqáwun nátuq.
will buy [particle: 'let me see it']	mupalít bi
25. I'll take some. (Lit. I'll buy; give it to me.)	25. Mupalít ku bi.
how much apiece?	tagpíla
26. How much are these (apiece)?	26. Tagpíla man ni?
one peso just	písu lang
27. Umm, it's a special price for you. Only one peso.	27. Aa, pára nímu, ispísyal prays, 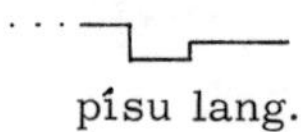 písu lang.
28. Oh, one peso?	28. Aa, písu?
how expensive! fifty not more than O. K.?	kamahál singkwínta ra ha
29. How expensive! Make it fifty! (Lit. No more than fifty, O. K.?)	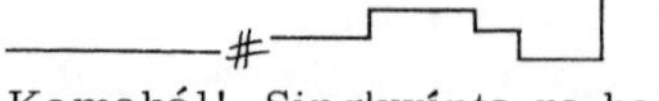 29. Kamahál! Singkwínta ra ha?
all right	sigí

30. Well, all right.	30. Aa, sigí.
oh (particle of surprise)	uh
nevertheless (particle insisting that a statement is true)	lagí
woman	babáyi
no more than	ra
[particle with statement giving information]	man
was paid	gibáyad
31. Oh! Why did that woman who bought some pay only thirty-five? (Lit. That woman who bought, why was it that thirty-five was all she paid?)	*31. Uh,ngánu man lagí tung babáying ... nagpalít nga trayntaysíngku ra ... man ang íyang gibáyad?

Mga Pangutána

Ikaduháng Báhin

1. Háqin man dápit ang ínyung tindáhas mga líbru Pirlá?
2. Anúsqa man ta magkítaq pagqusáb?
3. Diq ba Amirkána ka man?
4. Ngánung natingála ka man?
5. Ikáw mang misyunáryu dínhis Sibú nu?
6. Pilá man ang pasáhi gíkan dínhi ngádtus Úrmuk?
7. Únsa may náqas tíkit?
8. Waq ka kaháq masayúp?
9. Palít kag kalamáy Day?
10. Mahímuq bang tanqáwun ku úsaq?
11. Unyáq mupalít ka?
12. Mahímuq bag singkwínta lay ákung ibáyad Duq?
13. Ngánung tráynta ra man lagí tung sa babáyi Dung?
14. Waq man lagíy giqingúng síngku singkwínta diháq sa tíkit?
15. Magkítaq ba ta sa sunúd búwan?
16. Dúna ka na bay tíkit Day?

17. Maqáyu ka na bang mubinisayáq?
18. Mahímuq bang tanqáwun ku úsaq ang tíkit?
19. Ngánung síngku singkwínta man?
20. Únsa nang gibalígyaq mu Dung?
21. Dághan ka pa bag kalamáy Dung?
22. Maqáyu ba ning kalamáy Pirlá?
23. Mupalít ka íning kalamáy Mis?
24. Ispisyál prays man kaháq, pilá man?
25. Pilá, trayntaysíngku?

Mga Pangutána (Matching)

Ikaduháng Báhin

1. Unyáq anúsqa man ta magkítaq?
2. Ngánung natingála ka man?
3. May tíkit ka na Day?
4. Pilá may pasáhi gíkan dínhi ngádtus Úrmuk?
5. Diq ba kwátru singkwínta ra may díqas tíkit?
6. Únsa nang balígyaq nímu Dung?
7. Mahímuq bang tanqáwun ku únaq?
8. Tagpíla man ni Dung?
9. Kumústang átung tindáhan sa líbru?

(a) Aw, natingála ku kay maqáyu ka na mang mubinisayáq.
(b) Waaq. Ása man nákuq palitá?
(c) Sunúd na lang búwan ku muqánhi. Magkítaq nyaq ta.
(d) Kalamáy ni Mis.
(e) Síngku singkwínta Mis páras Úrmuk.
(f) Singkwínta ang usá Mis.
(g) Maqáyu man apán dyútay na lang ang átung líbrung gibalígyaq.
(h) Aa, úqu. Pirú síngku singkwínta na man run.
(i) Uu, mahímuq. Mupalít ka man kaháq.

Sagquluhúnun

Third Part	Ikatulúng Báhin
come back	bálik
[particle making command less harsh]	ra
here	ngarí

1. Boy! Boy! Come back here.	1. Dung! Dung! Bálik ra ngarí.
[question particle after interrogative showing impatience]	gud
amount made to pay	gipabáyad
me	kanákuq
2. Why is it that you made me pay fifty, . . .	2. Ngánu gung singkwínta man ang . . .
	. . . ímung gipabáyad kanákuq,
when (linker between two sentences)	nga
no more than	ra
[particle giving reason]	man
3. . . . when that woman paid only thirty-five?	3. Nga kádtung babáyi . . .
	. . . trayntaysíngku ra man.
because	man gud
4. Because you're an American.	4. Amirkána ka man gud.
can pay	kabayád
without a doubt (despite what you say)	gyud núqun (short for <u>gayúd hinúqun</u>)
also, anyway	pud
5. Anyway, you can certainly afford it.	*5. Kabayád ka gyud núqun pud.
[linker between <u>maqáyu</u> and the rest of the sentence]	nga
person made to pay	pabáyrun
more	mas
big	dakúq
than	sa
usual	kasagáran
price	prísyu
6. But it's not good to make me pay more than the	6. Pirú díliq naq maqáyung . . .
	. . . pabáyrun ku nímug mas dakús . . .

usual price.	kasagárang prísyu.
pity	malúquy
7. Ah, have pity on us, Miss. (Lit. you just be the one to pity us.)	7. Aa, ikáw lay malúquy námuq Mis.
poor	púbri
because	man gud
8. Because we are very poor.	8. Púbri man gud kaqáyu mi.
in order	arún
can live	mabúhiq
mother	inahán
candy, sweets	dúlsi
9. In order for us to make a living, my mother cooks this candy.	9. Arún mabúhiq kamí, ákung inahán mulútuq niqíning dúlsi.
and	ug
is sold	ibalígyaq
can eat	makakaqún
10. And we sell it in order to eat.	*10. Ug ámung ibalígyaq arún kamí makakaqún.
something to eat	makáqun
sometimes	usáhay
whole	tibuqúk
day	ádlaw
even	bísan
[particle indicating best of limited choices]	na lang
if	ug
bananas	ságing
11. And sometimes we don't have anything to eat all day long, not even bananas.	*11. Ug waq miy makáqun usáhay sa tibuqúk ádlaw bísan na lag ságing.

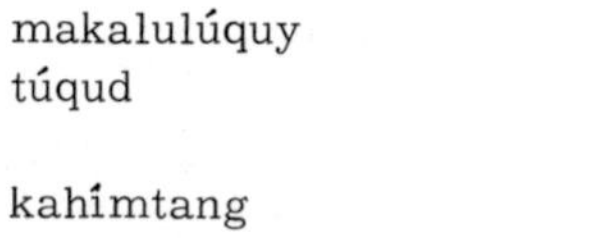

pitiful — makalulúquy
really (agreeing with foregoing) — túqud
situation — kahímtang

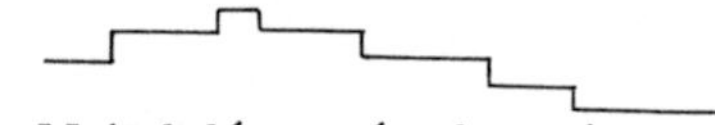

12. Your situation is really pitiful.

12. Makalulúquy túqud ang ínyung ... kahímtang.

13. Now I'll buy some candy from you.

13. Karún, mupalít ku nímug dúlsi.

then — unyáq

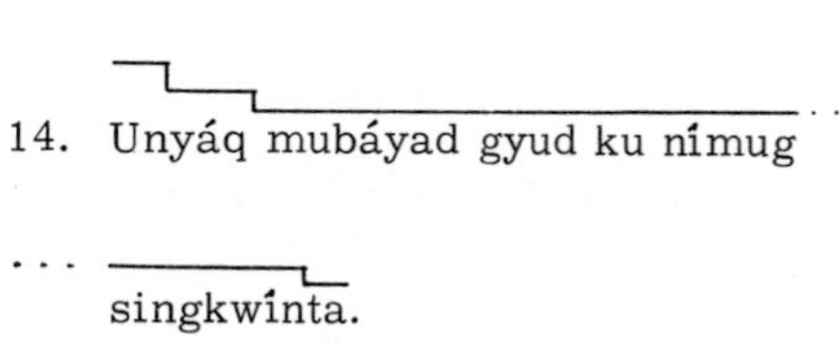

14. And I'll gladly pay you fifty. (Lit. I'll pay you fifty without a doubt.)

14. Unyáq mubáyad gyud ku nímug ... singkwínta.

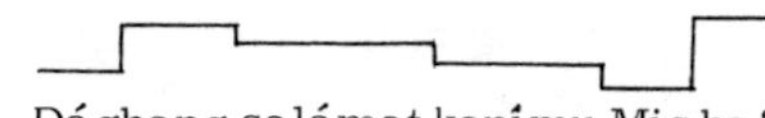

15. Many thanks to you, Miss.

15. Dághang salámat kanímu Mis ha?

yes — úqu
but — pirú
to be remembered — hinumdumí
be sure to (particle with imperatives) — bayáq
that (linker between hinumdumí and the rest of the sentence) — nga
cheat — manlímbung

16. Yes, but be sure to remember that it's not good for you to cheat people.

16. Úqu, pirú hinumdumí bayáq nga ... díliq maqáyung manlímbungkas ... mga táwu.

it is necessary — kinahánglan
sell things — mamalígyaq
in the right way — sa minatarúng

17. You must sell in an honest way.

*17. Kinahánglan mamalígyaq kas ... minatarúng.

to be remembered — hinumdumán

18. I will be sure to remember that, Miss.

18. Ákuq gyud nang hinumdumán ... Mis.

(The next morning) — (Pagkabúntag)

arrived — naqabút

19. Miss Wilby! Miss Wilby! We've (already) arrived. We're here now.

19. Mis Wílbi! # Mis Wílbi! # Naqabút ... na ta. Níqa na ta.

arrived — abút (short for naqabút)

20. Why, we're here already! (Lit. Oh, so we have already arrived.)

20. Abút na man diqáy ta.

never mind — sigí lang
not yet — díliq pa
go down, get off a vehicle or ship — manáqug

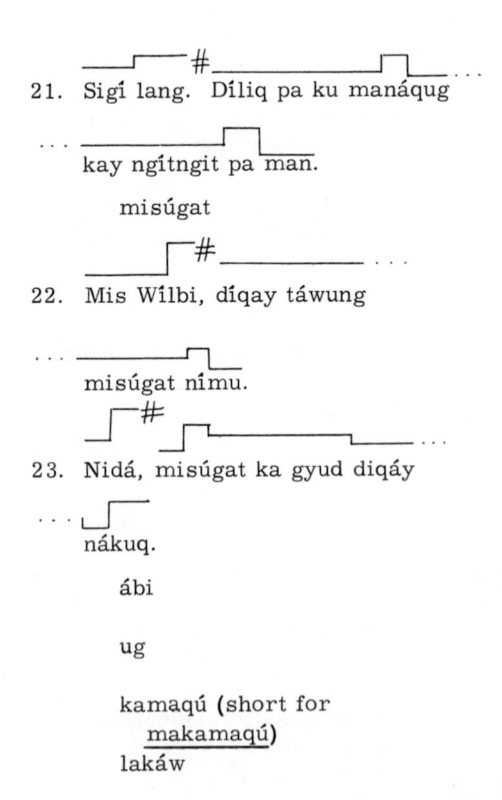

21. Never mind. I won't get off yet because it's still dark.

21. Sigí lang. # Díliq pa ku manáqug ... kay ngítngit pa man.

met — misúgat

22. Miss Wilby, there's someone here to meet you. (Lit. here is a person who met you.)

22. Mis Wílbi, # díqay táwung ... misúgat nímu.

23. Nida, so you've really come to meet me.

23. Nidá, # misúgat ka gyud diqáy ... nákuq.

thought, assumed, took for granted — ábi
[linker for ábi and the rest of the sentence] — ug
know — kamaqú (short for makamaqú)
way, direction — lakáw

24. I thought you didn't know your way.	24. Ábi nákug diq ka kamaqús ímung lakáw.
therefore	maqú nga
came for	giqánhi
make it a point to . . .	gyud
in order	arún
to get	pagkúhaq
25. So I came to get you. (Lit. So I made it a point to come for you in order to get you.)	25. Maqú nga giqánhi ta gyud ka arún pagkúhaq nímu.
come here	dalíq
let's go	taná
26. Come, let's go. We'd better get going now. (Lit. we will just go already.)	26. Dalíq. Taná. Muqádtu na lang ta.
how?	kumústa
trip	biyáhi
27. How was your trip?	27. Kumústang ímung biyáhi?
28. Oh, I had a good trip here.	28. Aa, maqáyung ákung biyáhi ngánhi.
29. H'm. So this is Ormoc.	29. Aa, maqú diqáy ning Úrmuk.
two-wheeled horse-drawn rig	tartanílya
come here	dalíq
30. Rig! Come here.	30. Tartanílya, dalíq.
31. Let me carry your bag, Miss. (Lit. I will be the one to carry your bag, Miss.)	31. Akúy dalás ímung bag Mis.
never mind	ayáw lang
we	kamí
only	ra

32. Never mind. We'll carry it ourselves. (Lit. we'll be the ones alone to take this.)
32. Ayáw lang. Kamí ray daa áni.

will get for — kuháqan
taxi — táksi

33. Shall I get you a taxi?
33. Kuháqan ta kag táksi?

never mind, don't bother — sigí lang
will ride — manakáy

34. Never mind, we won't take a taxi.
34. Sigí lang, diq mi manakáyg táksi.

merely — ra
thing to be ridden — sákyan
is that not so? — nu

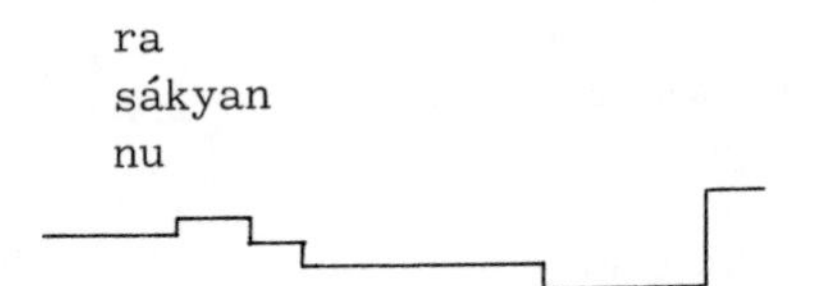

35. Let's just take a rig, shall we? (Lit. It is only a rig we will ride, isn't it?)
35. Tartanílya ray átung sákyan nu?

to — sa
one twenty-three — siyíntu báynti tris
Real Street — Riyál Strit

36. We [are going] to 123 Real Street, boy.
36. Sa siyíntu báynti tris Riyál ... Strit kamí Dung.

37. You two?
37. Kamúng duhá?

well (particle bringing something to a close) — na
let's go — taná

38. Yes. Well, let's go.
38. Uu. Na, taná.

Mga Pangutána

Ikatulúng Báhin

1. Ngánung gipabáyad man ku nímug singkwínta, Dung?
2. Diq ka ba malúquy námuq Mis? Púbri kaqáyu mi.

3. Kínsa man diqáy mulútuq niqíning dúlsi, Dung?
4. Unyáq may makáqun pa mu?
5. Tibuqúk ádlaw ka bang mamalígyaq?
6. Diqín mu man diqáy palitá ang bugás? (bugás, 'rice')
7. Diq ba gud túqud makalulúquy ang ílang kahímtang?
8. Unyáq dághan pa nang dúlsi nímu diháq Dung?
9. Mukúyug ba ni siyá nímu Mis Wílbi?
10. Maqáyu ba ang ímung biyáhi?
11. Muqádtu na ba ta?
12. Mahímuq bang kuháqan ta kag táksi?
13. Kamúng duhá ang muqádtus Riyál Strit?
14. Pilá tuy gipabáyad nímu kanákuq Dung?
15. Trayntaysíngku ra man lagí kádtung sa babáyi Dung?
16. Díliq ka ba gud kabayád sa trayntaysíngku?
17. Ngánung pabáyrun man ku nímug dakúq sa kasagárang prísyu?
18. Makakaqún na ba ang gamáy mung bátaq?
19. Ang ímung inahán bay naglútuq niqíning dúlsi?
20. Ngánung giqánhi pa man ku nímu Nidá?
21. Ngánung manlímbung ka man Dung?

Mga Pangutána (Matching)

Ikatulúng Báhin

1. Ngánung singkwínta may ipabáyad nímu nákuq Dung?
2. Pilá may kasagárang prísyu nímu Dung?
3. Diq ka ba diqáy malúquy Mis? Púbri kaqáyu mi.
4. Kínsa may naglútuq íning dúlsi, Dung?
5. Maqú na ba ni ang Úrmuk?
6. Díliq pa ba ka manáqug Mis?
7. Ngánung misúgat ka pa man gyud Nidá?
8. Magtawág ba kug táksi?
9. Gústu ka bang muqubán Dung?

(a) Ása man? Sa Úrmuk?

(b) Ábi nákuq gud ug diq kang kamaqú sa ímung lakáw.

(c) Ayáw na lang. Tartanílya lay ámuq.

(d) Mu man gud nay hústung prísyu.

(e) Trayntaysíngku Mis.

(f) Kínsa may malúquy nga manlímbung ka man.

(g) Ang ákung inahán Mis.

(h) Uu, maqú na ni. Díliq ba níndut?

(i) Díliq lang úsaq kay ngítngit pa man.

Commentary to Basic Sentences

8 a 5 tihíras — Cots for the passengers are placed on the decks of the larger interisland vessels.

8 a 6, pára kang, 8 a 7 pára ni — There is no difference in meaning between pára ni, pára kang, and párang. Cf. chart, 1 B, p. 14.

8 a 14 ngánu — Ngánu is a prepositive. It is always linked with nga, but attraction of postpositives to ngánu is optional: 3 C 3 a.

8 a 17 magbántay — An example of the hortative mag-: 5 C 2 b, p. 179.

8 a 18 átuq — Átuq is used because both are interested parties.

8 a 21 maghuwathúwat — The mag- here shows that the action is durative (5 C 2 a, p. 179). (Muhuwathúwat could also be used, with no difference in meaning: 4 B 2, p. 143.)

8 a 22 ayáw kabaláka — Ayáw is not linked with ug here: cf. 8 D, p. 312. Note that ay (short for ayáw) in 8 a 28 IS linked with ug.

nákuq — Short form of the dative kanákuq.

8 a 24 dalíq ra gud — A nice way of saying 'Come here.'

8 a 25 s — Short form of si.

8 b 6 mubinisayáq — Cebuano is usually called Binisayáq ('Visayan') by Cebuano speakers. However, this name is also given to other languages spoken in the central Philippines (Ilonggo, Waraywaray, Aklanon, Kinaray-a, and others); to avoid ambiguity, therefore, we call the language of these lessons Cebuano.

8 b 21 dáyun — Note that dáyun is used as a prepositive, not linked with nga. (Dáyun also occurs at the end of some sentences.)

8 b 31 tung babáying nagpalít — This is the grammatical topic of the sentence. A TOPIC is a form that comes first in the sentence and has the function of announcing the referent of the assertion. 'As for that lady who bought (some), why did she pay no more than thirty-five cents?'

8 c 5 kabayád — The full form of this prefix ka- is maka-.

8 c 10 makakaqún — With certain bases (each must be learned separately), the naka-/maka- prefixes cause the stress to move to the end. (Cf. also kabayád 'can pay,' in 8 c 5 above, vs. mubáyad 'will pay.')

8 c 11 waq miy makáqun — The y after the i of mi is difficult for English speakers to hear.

8 c 17 kinahánglan — The linking of the prepositive kinahánglan is optional. Kinahánglan here is not linked (though it could have been, with no change in meaning: Kinahánglang mamalígyaq kas minatarúng).

Grammatical Section

8 A. Local passives

In Lesson 6 we took up direct passives: in this lesson, we study LOCAL PASSIVES. The following chart shows their forms:

Local Passive Forms

	Real	Unreal	Subjunctive
Nonpotential	gi- . . . -an	-an	-i
Potential	na- . . . -an	{ma- . . . -an / ka- . . . -an}	{ma-. . .-i / ka- . . .-i}

As the chart shows, all of the forms except two (nonpotential unreal and nonpotential subjunctive) are made by simultaneously adding a prefix and a suffix to the base.

Anáaq mu ra mag púlus na giqukupahán ang mga tihíras dínhi. (8 a 5) 'Heavens, it looks as though the cots here are all taken already.' [base: ukupár]
Uh, ngánu gung kúptan nímung ákung bag? (8 a 14) 'Hey! What do you think you're doing holding my bag?' [base: kupút]
Bantayí únyaq siyá, ha? (8 a 27) 'Take care of her later, will you?' [base: bántay]
Kinahánglan maghuwathúwat únaq kang mabuntagán kay . . . (8 a 21) 'It is necessary for you to wait until morning . . . because . . . ' [base: búntag]

8 A 1. Local passives with place meaning

In one kind of local passive sentence, the local passive form is used in the predicate when the subject names the location where the action of the passive verb takes place. (As usual, the subject is a nominative or a form preceded by ang, y, or si.) As in other passive sentences, the agent is a genitive or a form preceded by sa.

Giqagíqan ku ang Riyál Strit padulúng ngánhi. 'I came here by way of Real Street.' (Lit. 'Real Street was gone over by me coming here.')
Gikuháqan níyag dyútay ang ákung kalamáy. 'He took a little bit of my kalamay.' (Lit. 'My kalamay was taken away from a little bit by him.')

In another type of sentence, the local passive is used in the subject when the predicate refers to the location of the action of the verb:

Ákung kalamáy ang íyang gikuháqan. 'He took some of my kalamay.' (Lit. 'My kalamay was what was taken from by him.')

Kínsay ímung gipalitág kalamáy Day? 'Who did you buy kalamay from, Miss?' (Lit. 'Who was the one who was bought some kalamay from by you?')

When a verb modifies a noun, the local passive form is used if the noun refers to the location where the action of the verb takes place:

Nangítaq ku sa bátang ákung gipalitág kalamáy. 'I am looking for the boy I bought some kalamay from' (lit. the boy who was bought some kalamay from by me).
Nakasakáy kus dyíp nga gisákyan ni Manáng. 'I happened to get on the jeep which Big Sister was riding (lit. which was being ridden by Big Sister).'

8 A 2. Local passives with personal behalf meaning

Other local passive sentences mean 'be [done] for or to someone.' In this type of sentence, the local passive is used in the predicate when the subject names the person on whose behalf the action is done:

Gipalitán ku ni Mámag kalamáy. 'Mama bought me some kalamay.' (Lit. 'I was bought some kalamay by Mama.')
Suwatán nákuq pírmi si Pápa. 'I will always write to Dad.' (Lit. 'Father will always be written to by me.')

The local passive is used in the subject when the predicate names the person on whose behalf the action is done:

Si Níday ákung gikuháqag táksi. 'I got a taxi for Nida.' (Lit. 'Nida is the one I got a taxi for.')

When a verb modifies a noun, the local passive form is used if the noun refers to the person on whose behalf the action is done:

Maqú kiní si Mis Wílbi, ang Amirikánang ákung girisirbahág lugár dínhis bárku. (8 a 25) 'This is Miss Wilby, the American I reserved a place for, here on the boat (lit. the American, a place was reserved for).'

Note that the same local passive verb may occur in either the personal behalf meaning or in the place meaning: context allows us to determine which of the two meanings is present. Thus the first sentence of this section is ambiguous:

Gipalitán ku ni Mámag kalamáy. 'Mama bought some kalamay for me.' or 'Mother bought kalamay from me (lit. I was bought from by Mother, some kalamay).'

8 A 3. Local passives with direct meaning

Direct passive sentences (6 A, above, p. 227) have subjects that specify the recipient of the action:

Gipalít ni Mis Wílbi ang aríyus. 'The earrings were bought by Miss Wilby.'

Certain local passive sentences also have subjects which specify the recipient. The verb in these sentences are those which have no direct passive forms:

Gihinumdumán ni Mis Wílbi ang aríyus. 'The earrings were remembered by Miss Wilby.' [There is no direct passive of the verb hinúmdum 'remember,' and the local passive is used in the meaning 'the subject is the recipient of the action.']

Anaáq mu ra mag púlus na giqukupahán ang mga tihíras dínhi. (8 a 5) 'Heavens, it looks as though the cots here are all taken already!'

Ngánu gung kúptan nímu ang ákung bag? (8 a 14) 'What do you think you're doing holding my bag?' (Lit. 'Why is my bag being held by you?')

Ákuq gyud nang hinumdumán Mis. (8 c 18) 'I will be sure to remember that, Miss.' (Lit. 'That will certainly be remembered by me.')

Bantayán nákuq ang ákung kaqugalíngun. (8 a 23) 'I will take care of myself.' (Lit. 'Myself will be watched by me.')

When verbs like these appear as the subject, the predicate is the recipient of the action:

Maqú kiní ang kanúnay nákung hinumdumán. 'This is what I will always remember (lit. what will always be remembered by me).'

When they modify a noun, the noun is the recipient of the action:

Háqin na man ang bag nga gikúptan sa táwu? 'Where is the bag which the man took hold of?' (Lit. 'Where is the bag now which was taken hold of by the man?')

8 A 4. Local passives in the meaning 'affected by'

Some local passive sentences say that the subject is indirectly affected by the action of the verb. The verb action (appearing in the predicate) happened at, on, near, in, or to the subject; or, if the verb is the subject, the action indirectly affected the predicate; or, if the verb modifies a noun, the action indirectly affected the noun modified:

Tingálig magabhiqán ta. (4 b 41) 'We'll probably be overtaken by night.' (Lit. 'We will have night (gabíqi) happen to us.')

Local passive verbs in such sentences are of three types: (1) local passive verbs with a noun base* (verbs whose bases occur also as nouns, e.g. magabhiqán 'affected by nightfall' from a base gabíqi 'night'); (2) local passive verbs with a verb base (verbs whose bases occur only as verbs, e.g. nabúthan 'have something explode on one' from a base butú 'explode'); and (3) local passive verbs with an adjective base (verbs whose bases also occur as adjectives, e.g. gimahalán 'consider something expensive' from a base mahál 'expensive').

8 A 4 a. Local passives in the meaning 'affected by' formed from noun bases and verb bases.

When a local passive verb form made from a noun base (N) occurs as the predicate, the sentence means that the subject was affected by the occurrence of the noun base N:

Kinahánglan maghuwathúwat únaq kang mabuntagán kay . . . (8 a 21) 'You have to wait until morning, because . . . ' (Lit. 'You have to wait that you will be affected by the occurrence of morning, because . . . ') (búntag 'morning')

Giqulanán ku sa ákung pagqánhi 'I was caught in the rain (lit. I was affected by rain) coming here.' (ulán 'rain')

---

* The BASE is the form to which the affixes are added: see 4 A, p. 142.

In the same type of sentence, local passives of verbs with a verb base mean 'the action of the verb happened to the subject':

> Nabúthan siyág dinamíta. 'He had dynamite explode on him.' (Lit. 'He had exploding of dynamite happen to him.') (butú 'explode')

8 A 4 b. Local passives formed from adjective bases

Local passive verbs with an adjective base, in the same type of sentence, mean that the subject considers the goal to have the quality of the adjective:

> Gimahalán si Huwán sa plíti ngádtu sa Úrmuk. 'John considered the fare to Ormoc expensive.'
> Nindután ba kaháq si Máma sa ákung gipalít kaníya? 'Do you think Mama will think that what I bought for her is beautiful?'
> Gipubríhan da siyá kanátuq dínhi sa Pilipínas. 'He considered us poor here in the Philippines.'
> Diq gyud siyá lísdan sa Binisayáq. 'He won't find Visayan difficult at all.'

8 A 5. Local passive of hátag 'give'

The regularly formed local passives of hátag 'give' are quite formal in tone. In natural colloquial speech, a special set of local passive forms are used, as follows:

	Real	Unreal	Subjunctive
Nonpotential	gitagáqan	tagáqan	tagáqi
Potential	natagáqan	{matagáqan / katagáqan}	{matagáqi / katagáqi}

> Tagáqi lang kug únu singkwínta. (6 b 39) 'Just give me one-fifty.'
> Gitagáqan ku níyag kalamáy. 'She gave me some kalamay.'
> Diq ka katagáqag dúlsi kay diq man ka buqútan. 'You cannot be given any candy because you aren't good.'

Exercises 8.I A, 8.I C, 9.I A, 9.I C, 12.I A (2). (See also the list of exercises after 8 B 3.)

8 B. Local passives with a place meaning contrasted with direct passives

The following pairs of examples demonstrate the contrast between local passive sentences and direct passive sentences. (The local passive is given first in each pair.)

a. Gikuháqan níya ang ákung kalamáy. 'He took some of my kalamay (lit. took something from my kalamay).'
a (1). Gikúhaq níya ang ákung kalamáy. 'He took my kalamay.'
b. Ang bátaq maqúy íyang palitán sa kalamáy. 'He'll buy kalamay from the boy'—that is, 'The boy is the one he will buy the kalamay from.'
b (1). Ang kalamáy maqúy íyang palitún sa bátaq. 'He'll buy kalamay from the boy'—that is, 'The kalamay is what he'll buy from the boy.'
c. Sulatán níya ang lamísa sa istúrya. 'He will write the story at the table.'
c (1). Sulatún níya ang istúrya sa lamísa. 'He'll write the story at the table.'
d. Iskína ang hulatán ni Mis Wílbi sa dyíp. 'The corner is where Miss Wilby will wait for the jeep.'

d (1). Dyíp ang hulatún ni Mis Wílbi sa iskína. 'A jeep is what Miss Wilby waits for at the corner.'

e. Pústan níya ang papíl sa mga kaság. 'He'll use the paper to wrap the crabs.'

e (1). Pústun níya ang mga kaság sa papíl. 'He'll wrap the crabs in the paper.'

f. Lutúqan níya ang láta sa ísdaq. 'He'll use the can to cook the fish in (and the pot, he will use for the rice).'

f (1). Lutúqun níya ang ísdaq sa láta. 'She'll cook the fish in the can (and the rice, she will cook in the pot).'

g. Lamísa ang íyang íphan sa kwárta. 'The table is where he counts the money.'

g (1). Kwárta ang íyang íphun sa lamísa. 'It is money that he counts at the table.'

h. Makuháqan ku ra ang kalamáy unyáq. 'I can always take some of the kalamay later.'

h (1). Makúhaq ku ra ang kalamáy unyáq. 'I can always take the kalamay later.'

i. Kasulatán ba nákuq nang papíl ug istúrya? 'Can I use that paper to write the story on?'

i (1). Masulát ba nákuq ang istúrya sa papíl? 'Can I write the story on the paper?'

j. Kabalhínan níya ang tihíras sa íyang bag. 'She can move her bag to the cot.'

j (1). Mabálhin níya ang íyang bag sa tihíras. 'She can move her bag to the cot.'

k. Kapalitán ku ang tindáhan sa ságing. 'I can buy the bananas in the store (but not anywhere else).'

k (1). Mapalít ku ang ságing sa tindáhan. 'I can buy the bananas in the store (but I can't buy the sugar in the store).'

8 B 2. Local passives in the personal behalf meaning vs. direct passives

a. Kuháqan ta kag táksi? (8 c 33) 'Shall I get you a taxi?'

a (1). Kuháqun nákuq ang táksi pára kanímu. 'I'll get the taxi* for you.'

b. Palitán ku ni Máma ug kalamáy.

b (1). Palitún ni Máma ang kalamáy pára nákuq. 'Mama will buy the kalamay for me.'

c. Gisulatán ni Mis Wílbi si Dúdung ug istúrya. 'Miss Wilby wrote a story for Dodong.'

c (1). Gisulát ni Mis Wílbi ang istúrya pára ni Dúdung. 'Mis Wilby wrote the story for Dodong.'

d. Gipústan níya ug aríyus si Mis Wílbi. 'He wrapped some earrings for Miss Wilby.'

d (1). Giputús níya ang aríyus pára kang Mis Wílbi. 'He wrapped the earrings for Miss Wilby.'

---

* The subject usually is definite in meaning—that is, it refers to a specific, previously mentioned person or thing, often corresponding to English nouns modified by 'the.' The goal may be definite or indefinite depending on whether marked by sa or ug (see 5 D 2, p. 181). Thus in some pairs of examples a definite noun in one corresponds to an indefinite noun in the other.

e. Gibuhátan níya si Mis Wílbi ug bag. 'He made a bag for Miss Wilby.'
e (1). Gibúhat níya ang bag párang Mis Wílbi. 'He made the bag for Miss Wilby.'
f. Lutúqan ku ikáw ug ísdaq. 'I'll cook you some fish.'
f (1). Lutúqun ku ang ísdaq pára nímu. 'I'll cook the fish for you.'
g. Gikuháqan ku siyá ug prútas. 'I got some fruit for her.'
g (1). Gikúhaq ku ang prútas pára níya. 'I got the fruit for her.'
h. Kapalitán ku siyá ug sinínaq. 'I can buy her a dress.'
h (1). Mapalít ku ang sinínaq pára níya. 'I can buy the dress for her.'
i. Kapangitáqan ku siyá ug papíl. 'I can look for a piece of paper for her.'
i (1). Mapangítaq ku ang papíl pára níya. 'I can look for the piece of paper for her.'
j. Katagáqan ku ang bátaq ug gása. 'I can give the boy a gift.'
j (1). Mahátag ku ang gása sa bátaq. 'I can give the gift to the boy.'
k. Kaqíphan ku siyá ug kwárta. 'I can count some money out for her.'
k (1). Maqiháp ku ang kwárta pára níya. 'I can count the money out for her.'
l. Nadádqan ku siyá ug gása. 'I happened to bring her a gift.'
l (1). Nadáa ku ang gása pára níya. 'I have brought the gift for her.'

8 B 3. Which passive to choose with verbs that take both local and direct passive affixes

In sentences consisting of two parts, one of which is a noun or noun phrase and the other a verb or verb phrase, if the noun (or noun phrase) is emphasized, it is made the predicate and the verb (or verb phrase) becomes the subject (3 B 2, p. 94). If the noun emphasized is the place of the action, or the person on whose behalf the action is done, the local passive verb is used; if the noun emphasized is the recipient of the action, the direct passive is used:

a. Si Lítuy ákung palitán sa dúlsi. 'Lito is the one I am buying the candy for [or from] (not Perla).'
a (1). Dúlsiy ákung palitún kang Lítu. 'Candy is what I am buying for Lito (not ice cream).'
b. Únsa may ímung kánqan? 'What are you going to eat off of [or eat part of]?'
b (1). Únsa may ímung kánqun? 'What are you going to eat?'

In sentences consisting of a noun part and a verb part with no special emphasis on the noun, the verb is the predicate. The local passive is used if the subject is the place at which, or person on whose behalf, the action of the verb is done; the direct passive is used if the subject is the recipient of the action.

Remember that a subject construction has the meaning 'thing about which (or person about whom) the predicate is said' (3 B, p. 93). Another way of stating the distinction between the uses of the local and direct passives is this: If the context is such that the predicate is being said about the place of the action or the person on whose behalf the action is performed, the local passive verb is used. If the context is such that the predicate is being said about the recipient of the action, the direct passive is used.

c. Gilutúqan ku ang látas ságing. 'I cooked the bananas in the can.' [This could be said, for example, in talking about a series of things used for various purposes: I soaked the fish in the bowl; I boiled the meat in the pot; I cooked the bananas in the can.]

c (1). Gilútuq ku ang ságing sa láta. 'I cooked the bananas in the can.' [Said when talking about the bananas, for example in answer to the question 'Have you cooked the bananas?']

d. Gipalitán ku si Lítu sa dúlsi. 'I bought the candy for Lito.' [Said, for example, when considering several people: I didn't buy the candy for you, but I bought the candy for Lito.]

d (1). Gipalít ku ang dúlsi párang Lítu. 'I bought the candy for Lito.' [Said, for example, on considering various things bought: The cookies, I bought for you; the candy, I bought for Lito.]

e. Gidádqan ku si Lítu niqíning dúlsi. 'I brought this candy for Lito.' [Said, for example, when talking about people: I brought Lito this candy; I brought Jaime these toys.]

e (1). Gidalá ku kiníng dulsíha kang Lítu. 'This candy I brought for Lito. [That candy I brought for Jaime.]'

8 B 4. Verbs having the same meaning in the direct and local passive

Some verbs meaning 'say, ask, tell,' and the like mean the same thing in both local and direct passive sentences. Verbs of this type we have had so far are ingún 'say' and pangutána 'ask.'

Íngnun [or Íngnan] ku siyá nga diq gyud naq mahímuq. 'I'll tell him that it is impossible.'

Kínsay ákung mapangutána [or mapangutánqan or kapangutánqan]? 'Whom can I ask?'

Verbs meaning 'open' and 'close' also mean the same thing in local and direct passive sentences:

Ablíhun [or Ablíhan] ku ang bintánaq. 'I will open the window.'

Exercises 8.I B, 9.I B; Pattern practices PP-Q, PP-T, PP-Z.

8 C 1. Agents

In local passive sentences, as with other passives, the agent (the one who does the action) is a genitive form (6 B 2, p. 233):

Bantayán nákuq ang ákung kaqugalíngun. (8 a 23) 'I will take care of myself.'

With the local passive, as with other passives, the preposed genitive is interchangeable with the regular genitive:

Ngánung ímu man siyáng gilimbúngan? 'Why did you cheat her?'

Ákuq gyud nang hinumdumán. (8 c 18) 'I'll be sure to remember that.'

8 C 2. Goals

Local passive sentences, like active sentences and other passive sentences, occur with goals (forms preceded by ug or sa or the dative forms of the pronouns).

Girisirbahán ku si Mis Wílbi ug tihíras sa bárku. 'I reserved Miss Wilby a cot on the boat.'

Karún palitán tikág dúlsi. 'Now I will buy some candy for you.'

8 D. Linking with ug

Some prepositives are linked to the words or phrases they modify with ug.* (See 3 C 3 a, p. 97, for a definition and discussion of prepositives.) So far, we have had the following prepositives linked with ug: maqú ra 'seem,' ábi 'take for granted,' and ayáw 'don't.' Ayáw is sometimes linked to the word or phrase it modifies; ábi and maqú ra are always linked to the word or phrase they modify.

Ábi nakug diq ka kamaqús ímung lakáw. (8 c 24) 'I didn't think you knew your way.'

Ayáw is always linked, by ug, to a verb with no affix:

Ayáwg lakáw. 'Don't go away.'

If the verb has a prefix pag-, ayáw is not linked to the verb:

Ayáw paglakáw. 'Don't go away.'

If the verb has an affix other than pag-, ayáw is optionally linked to it by ug:

Ayáw lagí siyá íngnang níqa ku. or Ayáw lagí siyág íngnang níqa ku. 'Don't tell him I am here, I said.' [Íngna has a suffix -a; therefore, ayáw is optionally linked to it with ug.]
Ayáw ug kabaláka. or Ayáw kabaláka. 'Don't worry.' [Kabaláka has a prefix ka-; therefore, ayáw is optionally linked to it with ug.]

(On the linking of ayáw, see also 3 E 1, p. 99.)

Pattern Practices and Exercises

I A. Supply the affixes to the words in parentheses (local passives only). (8 A and 6 A 3 and subsections)

Pananglítan: Waq ku (súkliq) sa babáying ákung (palít).
Tubág: Waq ku suklíqi sa babáying ákung gipalitán.

1. Ang Amirkána (risírba) nag tihíras sa buy.' 'The boy has already reserved a cot for the American.'
2. (Kupút) ta ning bag mu Mis. 'Let me (lit. Let us) hold your bag, Miss.'
3. Waláq (bántay) sa buy ang ubáng tihíras. 'The boy did not watch the other cots.'
4. (Abút) siyág kwárta ganínang búntag. 'She got some money this morning.'
5. Maqú kiníng barkúha ang íyang (sakáy) padúung ngánhi. 'This is the boat that he took coming here.'
6. Waláq níya (báyad) ang kalamay. 'He didn't pay for the kalamay.'
7. (Balígyaq) siyá sa bátaq ug kalamay sa íyang pagpadúung ngánhi. 'The boy sold her some kalamay on her way here.'

---

* The majority of prepositives we have had up to now are linked to the words or phrases they modify by nga.

8. Kanáng baláya ang átung (bisíta) úgmaq. 'We'll visit that house tomorrow.'

9. (Hatúd) kamí ni Pírla ug kalamáy nga íyang gipalít sa bárku. 'Perla brought us some kalamay which she had bought on the boat.'

10. Waláq pa níya (língkud) ang tihíras. 'He hasn't sat on the cot yet.'

11. (Dágan) níya ang bágqung pantalán inigqabút sa Úrmuk. 'He'll run over the new pier when he arrives at Ormoc.'

12. Waq pa (sakáy) ang bárku gíkan sa Súgbu. 'No one has boarded the boat from Cebu yet.'

13. (Sáqad) na námuq silá nga ánhi manihápun. 'We already promised them that we'd eat supper here.'

14. Kanáng básu maqúy (sulúd) nímug lítsi, díliq kiríng díqa kanákuq. 'You should put milk in that glass there, not this one here.'

15. Waq pa (sulúd) ang básu níyag túbig. 'She hasn't put water in the glass yet.'

16. Ámung (bisíta) ang mga masakitún sa uspitál unyáng hápun. (masakitún 'sick people')

17. Waq siyá (ubán) ni Pírla sa Úrmuk.

18. Sa pagqabút námuq (lútuq) na diqáy kamí ni Lúling ug súdqan.

19. (Súkliq) pa tingáli ta níyag báynti kay kúlang pa man ning súkliq. (kúlang 'not enough')

20. Kanáng baláya ang (bálhin) níla sa sunúd Sabadú.

21. Táwga ra gud ang bátaq nga átung (palít) ug kalamáy. 'Call the boy we bought the kalamay from.'

22. Waq námuq (bisíta) si Iyúq Ámbuq sa Pulambatú.

23. Waq níya (hibalú) nga misúgat diqáy si Nída.

24. Ásа bang dapíta ang átung (dúlhug) inigkahumán dínhi?

25. Waq ba diqáy nímu (dalá) ug kalamáy si Nída?

PP-Q Direct vs. local (no transformations) (8 A)

Step I. (Real direct vs. real local, in direct meaning)

'We looked at the book.'

Ámung gitánqaw ang líbru.	(dalá)
Ámung gidalá ang líbru.	(hátag)
Ámung gihátag ang líbru.	(palít)
Ámung gipalít ang líbru.	(pangítaq)
Ámung gipangítaq ang líbru.	(si Lítu)
Ámung gipangítaq si Lítu.	(báyad)
Ámung gibáyran si Lítu.	(bisíta)

Ámung gibisitáhan si Lítu.	(báyad)
Ámung gibáyran si Lítu.	(ang bag)
Ámung gibáyran ang bag.	(iháp)
Ámung giqiháp ang bag.	(kupút)
Ámung gikúptan ang bag.	(bántay)
Ámung gibantayán ang bag.	(kúhaq)
Ámung gikúhaq ang bag.	(ang babáyi)
Ámung gikúhaq ang babáyi.	(huwát)
Ámung gihuwát ang babáyi.	(bisíta)
Ámung gibisitáhan ang babáyi.	(hinúmdum)
Ámung gihinumdumán ang babáyi.	(hángyuq)
Ámung gihángyuq ang babáyi.	(báyad)
Ámung gibáyran ang babáyi.	

Step II. (Unreal direct vs. unreal local, direct meaning)

'I will call Pedro.'

Táwgun ku si Pídru.	(dalá)
Dádqun ku si Pídru.	(hinúmdum)
Hinumdumán ku si Pídru.	(bántay)
Bantayán ku si Pídru.	(si Tátay)
Bantayán ku si Tátay.	(imbitár)
Imbitahún ku si Tátay.	(huwát)
Huwatún ku si Tátay.	(ang traak)
Huwatún ku ang traak.	(sakáy)
Sákyan ku ang traak.	(búhat)
Buhátun ku ang traak.	(ukupár)
Ukupahán ku ang traak.	(dalá)
Dádqun ku ang traak.	(si Lína)
Dádqun ku si Lína.	(pangutána)
Pangutánqun / Pangutánqan } ku si Lína.	(tubág)
Tubagún ku si Lína.	(pangítaq)
Pangitáqun ku si Lína.	(Nánay)
Pangitáqun ku si Nánay.	(kalímut)
Kalímtan ku si Nánay.	(ang babáyi)
Kalímtan ku ang babáyi.	(bisíta)

Bisitáhun / Bisitáhan } ku ang babáyi.	(báyad)
Báyran ku ang babáyi.	

Step III. (Direct vs. local, real and unreal, direct meaning)

'I looked at the bus.'

Gitánqaw nákuq ang traak.	(I'll ride)
Sákyan nákuq ang traak.	(I'll watch for)
Bantayán nákuq ang traak.	(si Nánay)
Bantayán nákuq si Nánay.	(I'll remember)
Hinumdumán nákuq si Nánay.	(I asked)
Gipangutạna nákuq si Nánay.	(I'll forget)
Kalímtan nákuq si Nánay.	(ang siními naq)
Kalímtan nákuq ang siníinaq.	(I'll wash)
Lábhan nákuq ang siníinaq.	(I'll pay for)
Báyran nákuq ang siníinaq.	(si Líta)
Báyran nákuq si Líta.	(I'll wait for)
Huwatún nákuq si Líta.	(I visited)
Gibisitáhan / Gibisíta } nákuq si Líta.	(I waited for)
Gihuwát nákuq si Líta.	(I accompanied)
Giqubanán nákuq si Líta.	(I'll look for)
Pangitáqun nákuq si Líta.	(I'll remember)
Hinumdumán nákuq si Líta.	(I'll call)
Táwgun nákuq si Líta.	(I called)
Gitawág nákuq si Líta.	(I looked at)
Gitánqaw nákuq si Líta.	(ang tihíras)
Gitánqaw nákuq ang tihíras.	(I reserved)
Girisírba nákuq ang tihíras.	(I occupied)
Giqukupahán nákuq ang tihíras.	(I paid for)
Gibáyran nákuq ang tihíras.	(I'll wash)
Lábhan nákuq ang tihíras.	

Step IV. (Direct vs. local, all meanings)

'Perla was looking for Big Brother.'

Gipangítaq ni Pírla si Mánuy.	(dalá)
Gidalá ni Pírla si Mánuy.	(palít ug gása)

Gipalitág gása ni Pírla si Mánuy. (risírba ug tihíras)

Girisirbahág tihíras ni Pírla si Mánuy. (báyad)

Gibáyran ni Pírla si Mánuy. (bántay ug maqáyu)

Gibantayág maqáyu ni Pírla si Mánuy. (hátag ug plíti)

Gitagáqag plíti ni Pírla si Mánuy. (tánqaw)

Gitánqaw ni Pírla si Mánuy. (hátag ug gása)

Gitagáqag gása ni Pírla si Mánuy. (dalá ug makáqun)

Gidádqag makáqun ni Pírla si Mánuy. (bisíta)

Gibisitáhan } ni Pírla si Mánuy. (súkliq)
Gibisíta }

Gisuklíqan ni Pírla si Mánuy. (suwát)

Gisuwatán ni Pírla si Mánuy. (kúhaq)

Gikúhaq ni Pírla si Mánuy. (límbung)

Gilimbúngan ni Pírla si Mánuy. (balígyaq ug kalamáy)

Gibaligyáqag kalamáy ni Pírla si Mánuy.

Step V. (Direct vs. local, with preposed forms of the agent)

'We took Miss Wilby along.'

Ámung gidalá si Mis Wílbi. (watched)

Ámung gibantayán si Mis Wílbi. (cheated)

Ámung gilimbúngan si Mis Wílbi. (ang tigúwang)

Ámung gilimbúngan ang tigúwang. (will buy for)

Ámung palitán ang tigúwang. (helped)

Ámung gitabángan ang tigúwang. (will make change for)

Ámung suklíqan ang tigúwang. (promised)

Ámung gisaqáran ang tigúwang. (will cook for)

Ámung lutúqan ang tigúwang. (ang bátaq)

Ámung lutúqan ang bátaq. (will call)

Ámung táwgun ang bátaq. (waited for)

Ámung gihuwát ang bátaq. (will bring)

Ámung dádqun ang bátaq. (asked)

Ámung gipangutána ang bátaq. (will remember)

Ámung hinumdumán ang bátaq. (remembered)

Ámung gihinumdumán ang bátaq.

Step VI. (Direct vs. local, with various types of agents)

'We looked at Lina.'

Gitánqaw námuq si Lína.	(you)
Gitánqaw nímu si Lína.	(he)
Gitánqaw níya si Lína.	(suwatán)
Gisuwatán níya si Lína.	(I)
Gisuwatán ku si Lína.	(ni Mis Wílbi)
Gisuwatán ni Mis Wílbi si Lína.	(imbitár)
Giqimbitár ni Mis Wílbi si Lína.	(he)
Giqimbitár níya si Lína.	(we)
Giqimbitár námuq si Lína.	(you)
Giqimbitár nímu si Lína.	(siyá)
Giqimbitár nímu siyá.	(ni Pírla)
Giqimbitár siyá ni Pírla.	

Step VII. (Direct vs. local, with preposed agents and various subjects)

'They paid Miss Wilby.'

Ílang gibáyran si Mis Wílbi.	(him)
Íla siyáng gibáyran.	(ang táwu)
Ílang gibáyran ang táwu.	(me)
Íla kung gibáyran.	(hangyúqun)
Íla kung hangyúqun.	(ang tindíra)
Ílang hangyúqun ang tindíra.	(her)
Íla siyáng hangyúqun.	(Máma)
Ílang hangyúqun si Máma.	(kádtung bayhána)
Ílang hangyúqun kádtung bayhána.	(kiní)
Íla kiníng hangyúqun.	

Step VIII. (Direct vs. local, with agents and subjects of all types)

'Miss Wilby paid me.'

Gibáyran ku ni Mis Wílbi.	(Tátay, Pídru)
Gibáyran ni Tátay si Pídru.	(he, them)
Gibáyran níya silá.	(he, Mísis Milíndris)
Gibáyran níya si Mísis Milíndris.	(I, Pírla)
Gibáyran ku si Pírla.	(them, Pírla)
Gibáyran níla si Pírla.	(Máma, ang tindíra)
Gibáyran ni Máma ang tindíra.	(Místir Mílir, ang tindíra)
Gibáyran ni Místir Mílir ang tindíra.	(Pírla, ang babáyi)
Gibáyran ni Pírla ang babáyi.	(Lína, the doctor)

Gibáyran ni Lína ang dúktur. (I, kutsíru)

Gibáyran {ku / nákuq} ang kutsíru. (they, driver)

Gibáyran níla ang dráybir. (she, the boy)

Gibáyran níya ang bátaq. (he, Místir Abáya)

Gibáyran níya si Místir Abáya. (Místir Abáya, ang tigúlang)

Gibáyran ni Místir Abáya ang tigúlang.

Step IX. (Direct vs. local, with agents and subjects of all types)

'Mother can buy candy from you.'

Kapalitán kag dúlsing Nánay. (mother, from him)

Kapalitán siyág dúlsing Nánay. (Pídru, from me)

Kapalitán kug dúlsing Pídru. (he, from me)

Kapalitán ku níyag dúlsi. (he, from her)

Kapalitán siyá níyag dúlsi. (Pídru, from him)

Kapalitán siyág dúlsing Pídru. (Pídru, from Mánuy)

Kapalitág dúlsi ni Pídru si Mánuy. (Máma, from the lady)

Kapalitág dúlsi ni Máma ang babáyi. (she, from the lady)

Kapalitán níyag dúlsi ang babáyi.

IB. Ibutáng ang hústung púrma sa bírbu ginámit ang local passives ug direct passives. (8 B, 6 A)

Pananglítan: Waláq níya (lútuq) ang súdqan.
Tubág: Waláq níya lutúqa ang súdqan.

1. Ngánu gung waq man tu nímu (palít)? 'Why on earth didn't you buy that?'

2. Waq pa nákuq (palít) ug dúlsi si Lítu. 'I haven't bought any candy for Lito yet.'

3. (Palít) ku si Nída ug kalamáy inigqabút nákuq sa bárku. 'I'll buy Nida some kalamay as soon as I get to the boat.'

4. (Dalá) na ku ni Pírla sa Úrmuk kaqusá. 'Perla has already taken me to Ormoc once.'

5. Únyaq igbálik nímu sa Súgbu (dalá) bayáq gyud mig gása ha? 'When you come back from Cebu, be sure to bring us gifts, will you?'

6. Ayáw lang kabaláka kay (dalá) ka lagí námuq ug gása. 'Don't you worry. We certainly will bring you gifts.'

7. (Dalá) níya ang líbru kay diq man nákuq kinahanglánun. 'He took the book because I won't be needing it.'

8. Ang bir waláq pa (kúhaq) sa ámuq. 'Nobody has gotten the beer from our house yet.'

9. Ákuq unyáq tung (kúhaq) ug gamáy. 'I'll take a little bit of that later on.'

10. Maqú ni ímung (kúhaq) iniglakáw nímu. 'Take this one when you go out.'

11. (Bálhin) na ba ni Mis Wílbi ang íyang bag sa tihíras? 'Has Miss Wilby moved her bag to the cot yet?'

12. Kiníng kwartúha ang átung (bálhin) sa sunúd búlan. 'This is the room we'll move into next month.'

13. (Ubán) ku si Pírla sa bárku. 'I went to the boat with Perla.'

14. Waq (ubán) ni Pírla si Mis Wílbi sa Úrmuk. 'Perla didn't go to Ormoc with Miss Wilby.'

15. (Risírba) sa buy ang tihíras pára sa Amirkána.

16. (Risírba) ra akúg lugár sa bárku.

17. Únsay (pangítaq) mu diháq sa pridyidír?

18. Ayáw na lang mig (pangítaq) ug dyip kay manglákaw na lang mi.

19. (Pangítaq) ku silág dyip apán waláq diqáy silá musakáy.

20. (Pangítaq) tiká. Diqín ka man?

21. (Súbay) lang ning dálan Piláys.

22. Kiníng dalána ang (súbay) nátuq kun muqádtu tas Kapitúl.

23. Waláq ba tu nímu (iháp) ng líbru?

24. Ákuq na lang kang (iháp) kútub sa napúuq.

25. (Iháp) na siyá apán waláq gihápun mudágan.

IC. Ibutáng sa línya ang hústung púrma sa bírbu nga anáqa sa parentheses ginámit ang active ug passive. (8 A, 8 B, 6 A, 5 C)

Pananglítan: Ákung (bántay) ug maqáyu si Mis Wílbi.
Tubág: Ákung bantayán ug maqáyu si Mis Wílbi. or Ákung gibantayán. . . .

1. (Dalá) siyá ug kalamáy párang Nída. 'He brought some kalamay for Nída.'

2. (Dalá) na ba níya ang mga gása sa Pulambatú? 'Has he taken the gifts to Redstone?'

3. (Dágan) hinúqun ang túntu. 'The fool ran away instead.'

4. Kínsa tung túqa dídtung (dágan)? 'Who is that running there?'

5. Ayáw nig (dágan)ng simíntu kay basáq pa. 'Don't run on this cement because it's still wet.'

6. Waláq na silá dínhi. (Bálhin) na silá. 'They're not here any more. They've moved away.'

7. Maqú nang baláya ang ílang (bálhin) úgmaq. 'That's the house they are moving to tomorrow.'

8. Háqin guy ímung (bálhin) Pírla ganína? Kiní bang líbru? 'Which book did you move a while ago, Perla? This one?'

9. (Hatúd)pa kang Mis Wílbi si Pírla. 'Perla still has to take Miss Wilby home.'

10. (Hatúd) ku ni Lúling ug súdqan ganína. 'Loling brought me some food a while ago.'

11. Waláq silá (hatúd) ug gása ni Mis Wílbi. 'Miss Wilby didn't bring them any gifts.'

12. Isáq pa kay (tawág) kug dyip pára nímu. 'Excuse me. I'll call a jeep for you.'

13. Ákuq pang (tawág) ang dráybir. Hulatá lang ku. 'I'll have to call the driver first. Just wait for me.'

14. Kínsa man tung (tawág)? 'Who's that calling?'

15. Waq níya (tawág) ang buy nga (bántay) sa tihíras. 'He didn't call the boy who was taking care of the cots.'

16. (Bántay) nákuq si Pírlag maqáyu hángtud nga maqabút siyá.

17. Kiníng kwartúha waq pa (ábang).

18. (Ábang) ni nílang baláya sa waq pa silá mulárga sa Úrmuk.

19. Kádtung únang (ábang) dínhi (báyad) ug kwarínta písus ang búlan.

20. (Báyad) mig dyis písus matág búlan sa túbig. Búsaq, díliq mahángyuq ang ábang.

21. Waláq nákuq (báyad) ang girisírba nátung tihíras.

22. (Ági) ba tu dínhing bárku páras Úrmuk? 'Does the boat for Ormoc pass by here?'

23. (Ági) lang ang Súgbu sa bárku gahápun.

24. (Lútuq) ka na bag súdqan Lulíng pára dádqun sa bárku?

25. (Lútuq) ku unyáq tung kárni nga dalá mu sa Pulambatú. (kárne,'meat')

II. Ang vs. sa or ug, si vs. ni, siyá vs. níya. Gíkan sa mga púlung sa parentheses pilíqa ang hústung púlung. (I B 1, I D, 5 D, 6 B, 6 C, 8 C)

Pananglítan: Pagqabút ni Mis Wílbi sa Úrmuk waq (siyá, níya) manáqug sámtang waq pa muqabút (ang, sa) íyang amíga.

Tubág: Pagqabút ni Mis Wílbi pa Úrmuk wag siyá manáqug sámtang waq pa muqabút ang íyang amíga.

1. Waq gyud (siyá, níya) palití (ang, sa) bátang nagbalígyag kalamáy kay (siyá, níya) nga malimbúngan.

2. Nagdalá (si, ni) Pilár (ug, ang) paan arún makáqun (níya, siyá).

3. Díliq (siyá, níya) maglútuq (ug, ang) lamíng súdqan pára (ni, si) Místir Abáya.

4. Waláq pa (siyá, níya) makaqánhi (sa, ang) átuq.

5. Mubálhin (si, ni) Mis Wílbi (sa, ang) sunúd búlan sa ka Mísis Abilyána. (Siyá, Níya) rang usá.

6. Huwatún nátuq (si, ni) Ínting (ang, sa) iskína kay waláq (siyá, níya) y kaqúban.
7. Waláq pa (siyá, níya) muqábang (sa, ang) baláy (ni, si) Mísis Abilyána.
8. (Si, Ni) Mis Wílbi ang pasákya niqíning dyip padulúng (ang, sa) Banáwaq. 'Let Miss Wilby be the one to take this jeep to Banawa.'
9. (Siyá, Níya) na lay mahibalú (ni, si) Mis Wílbi (sa, ang) bárku. 'She might as well be the one to take care of Miss Wilby on the boat.'
10. Waláq mubalígyaq (ang, sa) bátaq (siyá, níya) ug kalamáy kay dínhaq man (si, ni) Nída.
11. Mubálik run tu (si, ni) Ínting kay níqa man (ang, sa) asáwa (siyá, níya).
12. Nagputús na (siyá, níya) (sa, ang) kalamáy pára (ni, si) Mis Wílbi.
13. Giqimbitár mi (ni, si) Nída (sa, ang) ádlaw (níya, siyá) (ádlaw 'birthday').
14. Misugút ku (sa, ang) hángyuq (ni, si) Ínting nga mangítaq (ang, sa) baláy nga abángan (níya, siyá).
15. Ubanán ku (si, ni) Pírla (sa, ang) Pulambatú arún (siyá, níya) díliq masukúq.
16. Paglútuq nag súdqan Lulíng kay níqa na tu run (si, ni) Tásyu ug ang amígu (níya, siyá).
17. Nasámuk ba (siyá, níya) sa mga bátaq (ni, si) Mísis Abilyána nga níqa (sa, ang) sílung?
18. Mikanáqug na (ni, si) Mis Wílbi (sa, ang) bárku kay gústu na (níya, siyá) ng makítaq ang Úrmuk.
19. Nadungúg (níya, siyá) (sa, ang) áwit (ni, si) Lúling.
20. Midúlhug na (ang, sa) dyip nga gisákyan (ni, si) Pírla ug mipadulúng na sa baláy (níya, siyá).

III A. Ibungát ang mga musunúd nga mga túdling púlung sa hústung paníngug. (423 question)

1. Únsa man nang ímung gibalígyaq? (8 b 18)
2. Únsa man naq? (8 b 20)
3. Tagpíla man ni? (8 b 26)
4. Ngánu man lagí tung babáying nagpalít nga trayntaysíngku ra man ang íyang gibáyad? (8 b 31)
5. Ngánu gung kúptan nímu ang ákung bag? (8 a 14)
6. Ngánung gipabáyad man ku nímug singkwínta?
7. Pilá man ni?
8. Ása man ning dyípa Dung? (3 c 24)
9. Unsáqun man nákuq pagpatáy? (6 a 32)

III B. All questions also occur with a falling intonation: high pitch on the first syllable and falling throughout the sentence to the end. This intonation is symbolized 432—E.g.:

Ngánu gung kúptan nímu ang ákung bag. (8 a 14)

Pronounce the questions of III A above with a falling intonation.

III C. Ibungát ang mga musunúd nga mga túdling púlung sa hústung paníngug. (423 statement)

1. Daliq ra gud. (8 a 24)
2. Maqáyu tingáling ádtu na lang ku. (8 a 32)
3. Kínsi písus ang dusína. (6 a 6)
4. Kiní si Nuy Tibúq. (5.8)
5. Dúlhug ngádtug gamáy. (3 a 22)
6. Maqú ra nay ákung ihátag nímu. (8 b 16)
7. Kinahánglan mamalígyaq kas minatarúng. (8 c 17)

III D. (234 statement)

1. Manaká ta. (8 a 4)
2. Buhíqi kanáq. (8 a 15)
3. Níqa na kitás átung tihíras. (8 a 18)
4. Ayáw kabaláka nákuq Pirlá. (8 a 22)
5. Sunúd na lang búwan kitá magkítaq. (8 b 3)
6. Tíkit Day. (8 b 7)
7. Aa, síngku singkwínta diqáy. (8 b 10)
8. Níndut kaqáyu ni. (8 b 22)
9. Mupalít ku bi. (8 b 25)
10. Aa, sigí. (8 b 30)
11. Ikáw lay malúquy námuq Mis. (8 c 7)
12. Akúy dalás ímung bag Mis. (8 c 31)
13. Sa syíntu báynti tris Riyál Strit kamí Dung. (8 c 36)

III E. (324 question)

1. Kwátru singkwínta? (8 b 8)
2. Tanqáwun nátuq bi? (8 b 13)

3. Palît ka? (8 b 23)
4. Singkwînta ra ha? (8 b 29)
5. Misúgat ka gyud diqáy nákuq? (8 c 23)
6. Kamúng duhá? (8 c 37)

IV A. Pagbása. Retell the story. Answer questions on the story put to you by your informant. Do the exercise on the underlined verbs.

Miqádtus Pírla sa Pîstas Pulambatú.

Pírla : Plurá, ádtu tas Pulambatú. Gisulatán kung Nuy Tibúq gahápun ug nagqingún siyá nga maqáyu untáq ug ikáw ákung iqubán ('take along') ngádtu. Taná!

Plúra: Túqud nu. Nahinumdumán pa gyud diqáy tas tigúwang. Katúltul pa tingáli gihápun ta. (túltul 'know how to get to [a place]')

Pírla : Gisúgat man tas úna, sugátun pud tingáli gihápun ta run.

Plúra: Ádtu na ta kay giqukupahán na run ang mga lingkuránan. Ikanáqug saq tung átung dadqunún kay ihátag pa nákuq ring ságing ngádtu ni Ínsi Isíd.

Pírla : Taná. Ayáwg kalîmti tung kwártang náqas lamîsa kay mu tuy átung ibáyads plîti ('pay the fare with').

(Sa dîdtu nas istasyunáns traak)

Pírla : Ngánung ímu mang gikúptan nang ákung bag? Ibutáng naq! Ngánung waq man nîmu tágdang bag Plurá?

Plúra: Ákuq bîtaw nang gibantayán. Nagtánqaw pa man gud ku áring gibalîgyang kaság.

Pírla : Pagqáyu bayáq ('be very careful!'). May mag usá pay gilimbúngan niqánang mga nagbalîgyag kaság.* Sigí, sakáy na ta.

(Dîdtus Pulambatú)

Plúra: Uy, nalîmut man diqáy ku! Ákuq na ba tung gibáyran ag kalamáyng átung gikaqúns traak?

Pírla : Balú nîmu ('I don't know if you did'). Ábi kug gihatágan† nîmu ang tigúwang sa kwártang gisúkliq sa átung plîti. Ságdi na lang. Níqa na tas baláyng Nuy Tibúq.

---

* The sentence May . . . kaság means literally: 'It would be all right [not to be careful] if that seller of crabs had cheated no more than one person [but actually he has cheated many].'

† Or gitagáqan.

IV B. Pagbánsay sa Pagbása

(Ádtu)s Pírla sa Pístas Pulambatú

Pírla : Plurá, ádtu tas Pulambatú. (Sulát) kung Nuy Tibúq gahápun ug nagqingún siyá nga maqáyu untáq ug ikáw ákung iqubán ('take along') ngádtu. Taná!

Plúra: Túqud nu. (Hinúmdum) pa gyud diqáy tas tigúwang. Katúltul pa tingáli gihápun ta. (túltul 'know how to get to')

Pírla : (Súgat) man tas úna, sugátun pud tingáli gihápun ta run.

Plúra: Ádtu na ta kay (ukupár) na run ang mga lingkuránan. Ikanáqug saq tung átung dadqunún kay ihátag pa nákuq ring ságing ngádtu ni Ínsi Isíd.

Pírla : Taná. Ayáwg (kalímut) tung kwártang náqas lamísa kay mu tuy átung ibayads plíti ('pay the fare with').

(Sa dídtu nas istasyunáns traak)

Pírla : Ngánung ímu mang (kupút) nang ákung bag? (Butáng) naq! Ngánung waq man nímu (tagád)ng bag Plurá?

Plúra: Ákuq bítaw nang (bántay). Nagtánqaw pa man gud ku áring (balígyaq)ng kaság.

Pírla : Pagqáyu bayáq ('be very careful!'). May mag usá ray (límbung) niqánang mga nagbalígyag kaság. Sigí, sakáy na ta.

(Dídtus Pulambatú)

Plúra: Uy, nalímut man diqáy ku! Ákuq na ba tung (báyad) ag kalamáyng átung (káqun)s traak?

Pírla : Balú nímu ('I don't know if you did'). Ábi kug (hátag) nímu ang tigúwang sa kwártang (súkliq) sa átung plíti. Ságdi na lang. Níqa na tas baláyng Nuy Tibúq.

V. Sultiqánay

Si Mísis Únru ug si Mis Wílbi Nangádtus
Ilígan Sakáy sa Bárku

A: Náqa nay átung bárku páras Ilígan. Taná Istír. Manaká na ta.

B: Uy anáaq. Murág pulús giqukupahán ang tanáng tihíras dínhi.

A: Ayáw lag kabaláka Istír. Dúna na may ákung girisírba ganínang búntag.

B: Dung, dalíq ra gud. Háqin mang mga tihíras girisírba pára námuq?

A: Ságdi na lang Dung. Díqa ra. Arí dirí Istír, manglíngkud ta.

B: Uy kápuy. Kapalít na kag tíkit Iliná?

A: Waláq pa. Muqánhi ra bítaw nang nagbalígyag tíkit.

1. Nangádtu silá si Mis Wílbis Úrmuk.
2. Nanaká ang duhá.

3. Pagsaká nílang Mis Wílbig Mísis Únru dághang tihíras nga waq pa kaqukupahí.

4. Dúna siláy girisírbang tihíras.

5. Gibalígyaq dínhas bárkung tíkit.

(Sunúd ádlaw)

A: Dalíq ngarí Iliná. Nakítaq nang Mindanáw.

B: Háqin gud—waq ku kakitáq.

A: Díliq diháq. Díqa ra.

B: Tinúqud nu—túqa ra.

A: Kádtung túqa dídtu—mga lubí tu.

B: Uu. Náqa na ang syudád—ug náqay pantalán uh.

A: Hápit na diqáy ta muqabút.

B: Inigqabút nátuq magbántay gyud ta sa átung mga butáng—kay láqin ra ba kunú nang mga táwu dídtus pantalán.

A: Hústu naq. Kuqán ra ba—waq ra bay musúgat nátuq.

6. Sunúd ádlaw makítaq nang Mindanáw.

7. Pirú diq pa makítang pantalán.

8. Díliq bantayán ang butáng inigqábut nílas pantalán.

9. Kay náqay musúgat kaníla.

A: Tána Istír. Ánhi ra dínhi ta makasakáyg traak páras Inítaw.

B: Uu. Níqay traak. Muhatúd tingáli nas Inítaw.

A: Sakáy ta.

B: Mahál gyud núqun ning plíti dínhi. Tíqaw mu bay dus singkwíntang gipabáyad nátuq.

A: Ngánung dus singkwínta gud? Nga niqádtung usáng ádlaw únu singkwínta ra man lagíy giplíti nákuq.

B: Bítaw nu. Básta Amirkánu pabáyrun ka gyug mahál.

10. Waláy muhatúd nílas Inítaw.

11. Gipabáyad silág labáws kasagárang plíti.

12. Tris singkwínta ang ílang giplíti pagqádtu sa Inítaw.

LESSON 9. A VISIT TO PULAMBATO

Sagquluhúnun

Miss Wilby goes to Redstone to visit her friends the Olivars.

Miqádtu si Mis Wílbi sa Pulambatú arún mubisíta sa pamílya sa mga Ulibár.

First Part

Únang Báhin

Flora (girl's name) — Plúra (shortened form, Plur)
proper — ángay
Pulambato (barrio in northern Cebu: translated 'Redstone') — Pulambatú

1. Flor, Flora, what should I take to Redstone?

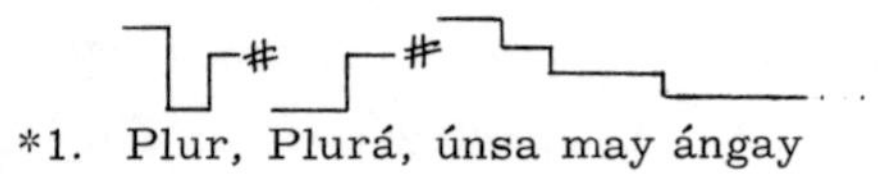

*1. Plur, Plurá, únsa may ángay

... ———————————— ...

nákung dádqun ngádtus

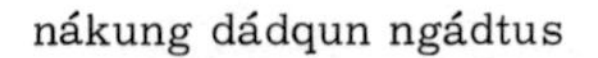

Pulambatú?

uh (fumbling for a word) — kuqán
[hesitation word] — kanáq nga
soap — sabún
towel — tuqálya
mosquito net — muskitíru

2. Well—soap, towel, and mosquito net.

2. Kuqán, kanáng, sabún, tuqálya

... ug muskitíru

that (well known, you know what I mean) — kanáq
toilet paper — papíl pára ilú

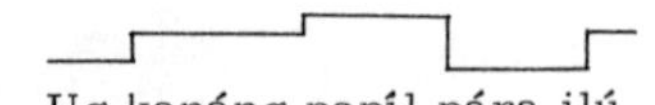

3. And toilet paper. (Lit. And that toilet paper.)

3. Ug kanáng papíl pára ilú.

for sure — gyud
[particle indicating that the speaker remembered something] — diqáy

4. That I will take along for sure.	4. Kanáq gyud diqáy ákung dádqun ngádtu.
what else?	únsa pa
other	ubán
5. What else should I take?	5. Únsa pa may ubán nákung dádqun?
should bring	magdalá
gifts	gása
6. Should I bring gifts?	6. Magdalá ba kug mga gása?
of course	aw
it is necessary	kinahángan
7. Oh yes. You certainly should.	*7. Aw, kinahángan gyud.
8. But aren't you afraid to go to Redstone?	8. Pirú diq ka ba mahádluk muqádtus Pulambatú?
[particle of admonition]	ra ba
[particle: 'they say']	kunú
9. They say the people there are very poor.	9. Mga púbri ra ba kunú kaqáyu nang mga táwu dîdtu.
[contrary to interlocutor's statement]	man
10. I'm not afraid.	*10. Diq man ku mahádluk.
anyway	tutál
11. Anyway, that's just what my job here in the Philippines is.	11. Tutál, maqú man gyud nang ákung trabáhu dînhis Pilipínas.

helping	pagtábang
[particle preceding goal]	sa
12. Helping the people.	12. Ang pagtábang sa mga táwu.
[particle with agent after passive verbs]	sa
eyes	matá
13. And I absolutely must see their situation with my own eyes . . .	13. Ug kinahángan gyung makítaq sa ákung mga matá ang ílang kahímtang,
if	ug
want	buqút
14. . . . if I want to help them.	*14. Ug buqút kung mutábang kaníla.
what do you say? (lit. how about it?)	únsa ba
accompany	kuyúgan
the worthwhile thing to do	lang
rather, instead	hinúqun
15. What do you say? Hadn't I better go (lit. Shall I just rather go) with you to Redstone?	*15. Únsa ba, kuyúgan ku ba lang hinúqun ka ngádtus Pulambatú?
16. Don't bother.	16. Ayáw na lang.
waste time	paghaguqhagúq
[particle preceding infinitive]	ug
accompany	kúyug
17. Don't waste time going to Redstone with me.	17. Ayáw paghaguqhagúg kúyug nákus Pulambatú.
anyway	tutál
know	kahibáwu (short for nakahibáwu)

18. Anyway, I already know how to get there.	18. Tutál, kahibáwu na man kung ... muqádtu.
have gone	nakaqádtu
before (lit. that time in the past)	niqádtu
[linker preceding kaqusá]	ug
once	kaqusá
19. We've already been there before (lit. that one time).	*19. Nakaqádtu na man ta niqádtug ... kaqusá.
come on	taná
bus station	istasyunán
of	sa
truck; bus	traak
20. Come on. Let's go to the bus station now.	20. Taná, ádtu na tas istasyunán ... sa traak.
will leave	mulárga
right now	karún dáyun
21. Is this (bus) leaving right now?	21. Mulárga ba ni karún dáyun
will leave	mulárga
right away	dáyun
22. Yes, it's leaving right away, Miss.	22. Uu, mulárga dáyun ni Day.
will leave	mulárga
[particle giving new information]	man
[particle said upon receiving new information]	diqáy
right away	dáyun
23. Oh my! So it's leaving right away.	23. Ay sus, mulárga man diqáy ... dáyun.

no more	wánqa (= waq na)
time	úras
to buy	pagpalít
[particle preceding goal]	sa
things to be bought	palitúnun

24. I have no more time to buy things (that are to be bought).

*24. Wánqa kuy úras pagpalít sa ... ákung mga palitúnun.

go ahead	sigí
wait	hulatún
I [will direct an action to] you	tikáw

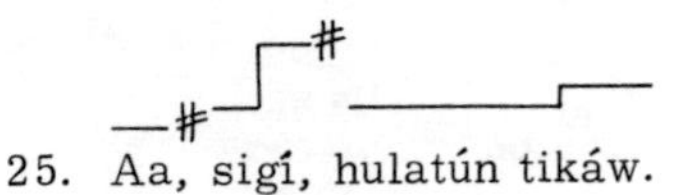

25. Go ahead. I'll wait for you.

25. Aa, sigí, hulatún tikáw.

come on	taná
shall buy	mamalít

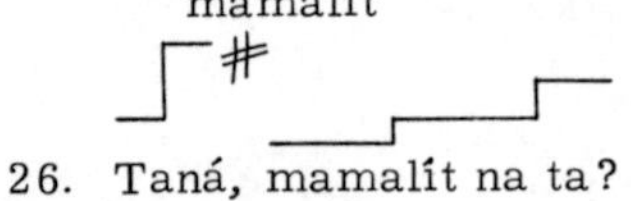

26. Come on, shall we go buy (our things) now?

26. Taná, mamalít na ta?

(A bit later) (Pagkataqudtaqúd)

well (particle before broaching a new subject)	na
all right	sigí
better	mas maqáyu
[particle following comparison]	pa

27. All right, Flora, you'd probably better get back to the store (lit. it's better you just go back there to the store).

27. Na sigí Plurá, mas maqáyu ... pang mubálik ka na lang ... ngádtus tindáhan.

good-by	sigí
I agree (though I would rather it were otherwise)	hinúqun

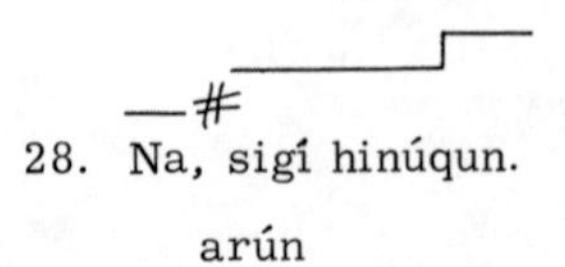

28. O. K., I'd better go then.

28. Na, sigí hinúqun.

so that	arún

can be watched — mabantayán

29. So that I can attend to the books. (Lit. So that the books will be watched for sure.)

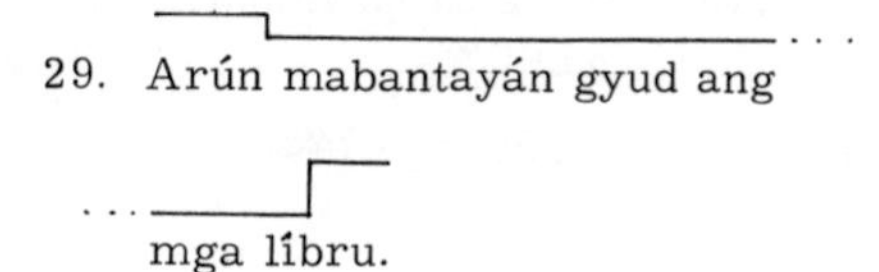

29. Arún mabantayán gyud ang mga líbru.

Mga Pangutána

Únang Báhin

1. Ángay bang magdalág sabún, tuqálya ug muskitírus Pulambatú?
2. Waq ka ba mahádluk?
3. Únsa pa may ubán kung dádqun?
4. Dádqun ba diqáy kanáng papíl pára ilú?
5. Kinahánglan ba ang pagtábang sa mga táwus Pilipínas?
6. Muqádtu ka gyud sa Pulambatú?
7. Diq ka mahádluk?
8. Magdalá kag mga gása?
9. Púbri ba gyud ang kahímtang sa mga táwu ngádtu?
10. Únsa may trabáhu dínhi?
11. Buqút ka gyung muqádtu?
12. Nakaqádtu ka bas Pulambatú?
13. Kuyúgan ta ba ka ngádtus Pulambatú?
14. Mubálik ka ngádtus tindáhan?
15. Mulárga ba ni dáyun?
16. Únsang adláwa ka mubálik Mis?
17. Maqáyu ba ang ílang kahímtang karún sa Pulambatú?
18. Ngánu ba gyung gahaguqhagúq ka pa mag ánhi?
19. Sugátun ta ba ka dínhi sa istasyunán inigbálik mu?
20. Únsang urása ta mamalít sa ímung dadqunún sa Pulambatú?

Mga Pangutána (Matching)

Únang Báhin

1. Únsa may angayán kung dádqun sa Pulambatú?

(a) Uu. Sakáy na lang dirí.

2. Diq ka ba mahádluk muqádtu?
3. Kahibáwu ka ba sa ímung lakáw ngádtu?
4. Púbri ba ang mga táwu dínhaq?
5. Mamalít tag líbrus tindáhan?
6. Mulárga ba ni dáyun Dung?
7. Ádtu ka ba musakáy sa istasyunán sa traak?
8. Nakaqádtu na ba kas Pulambatú?
9. Kínsay gústu nímung tabángan?
10. Únsa man ang trabáhu dínhi? (Únsa 'how is?')

(b) Díliq. Ánhi lang ku dínhi musakáy.
(c) Ang mga táwu dídtus Pulambatú.
(d) Waq pa ra ba ku kaqádtu.
(e) Maqáyu.
(f) Diq man. Únsa guy kahadlúkan?
(g) Púbri kunú ang mga táwu dínhaq.
(h) Uu. Kahibáwu ku. Kaqádtu na man ku dídtug kásqa.
(i) Diq na lang ta mamalít kay waq na tingáliy úras.
(j) Pagdalág muskitíru ug ayáwg kalimút pagdalág rigálu.

Sagquluhúnun

Second Part	Ikaduháng Báhin
(A talkative woman gets on the bus.)	(Misakáy ang usá ka tabiqáng babáyi.)
expensive	mahál
without a doubt (despite what you think)	gyud núqun (short for gayúd hinúqun)
fare	plíti
1. The (lit. This) fare here certainly is expensive.	1. Mahál gyud núqun ning plíti ... dínhi.
will pay	mubáyad
no matter how much	biság pilá
as long as	básta
can go home	makapaqúliq
2. But I will (just) pay any amount as long as I can get home (there).	2. Pirú mubáyad lang ku biság ... pilá básta makapaqúliq ku ... dídtu.
it's better than	silabí

[particle linking silabí and the rest of the sentence] — ug
walk — magbáklay
[do] when it should not be necessary — pa
go back home — pagpaqúliq

3. It's better than walking home.
*3. Silabíg magbáklay pa kus ... ákung pagpaqúliq sa baláy.

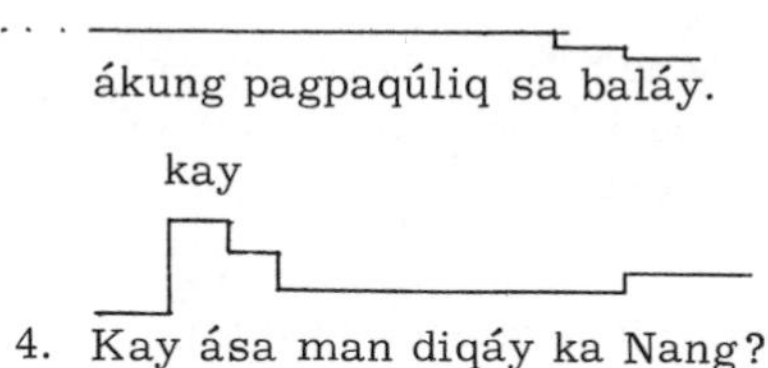

because — kay

4. Why (lit. Because)? Where are you going, Ma'am?
4. Kay ása man diqáy ka Nang?

far — layúq
destination — adtúqan

5. Is the place you're going to a long way?
5. Layúq bang ímung adtúqan?

no — díliq
about to go back home — umuqúliq
just, merely — lang
Carmen (name of town) — Kármin

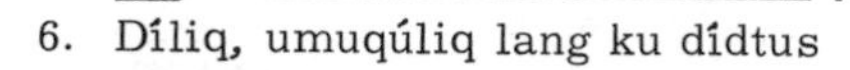

6. No, I'm going home to (lit. just back to) Carmen.
6. Díliq, umuqúliq lang ku dídtus ... Kármin.

[fumbling word] — kuqán
believe it or not — lagí
[particle of hesitation] — kanáng

7. Well, you know, my children are there. (Lit. Er, believe it or not—umm, there are children.)
7. Kuqán lagí, kanáng, sus, túqay ... mga bátaq,

rumble — nagkutúy
their — íla
stomach — tiyán

8. Their stomachs are already rumbling.
8. Nagkutúy na tung ílang tiyán.

waiting and waiting [expression of pity]	naghuwathúwat intáwun
9. They (lit. Those) are waiting for what I am bringing (lit. will have brought) them, poor things.	9. Naghuwathúwat intáwun tus . . . ákung madalá.
watch	nagbántay
10. Why? Isn't there anybody there now to take care of them?	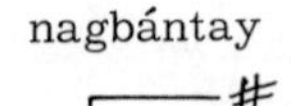 10. Ngánu man, waq díqay ruy 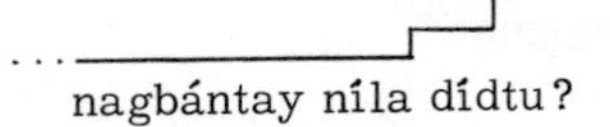 . . . nagbántay níla dídtu?
[expression of pity]	intáwun
11. No, poor things.	11. Waq intáwun.
[particle said upon giving new information]	man
[particle said upon receiving new information]	diqáy
12. Oh, here we are in Carmen now.	12. Aa, níqa na man diqáy tas . . . Kármin.
here's where I get off for now	ánhi ra ku úsaq
13. This is as far as I'll be going for now, O.K.?	*13. Ánhi ra ku úsaq, ha?
oh (particle preceding an exclamation at new information obtained)	uh
here is where [someone] gets off	ánhi lang
14. Oh, here's where you get off?	*14. Uh, ánhi lang diqáy ka?
good-by (lit. well, all right)	na sigí
[title of address for woman older than speaker]	Nang

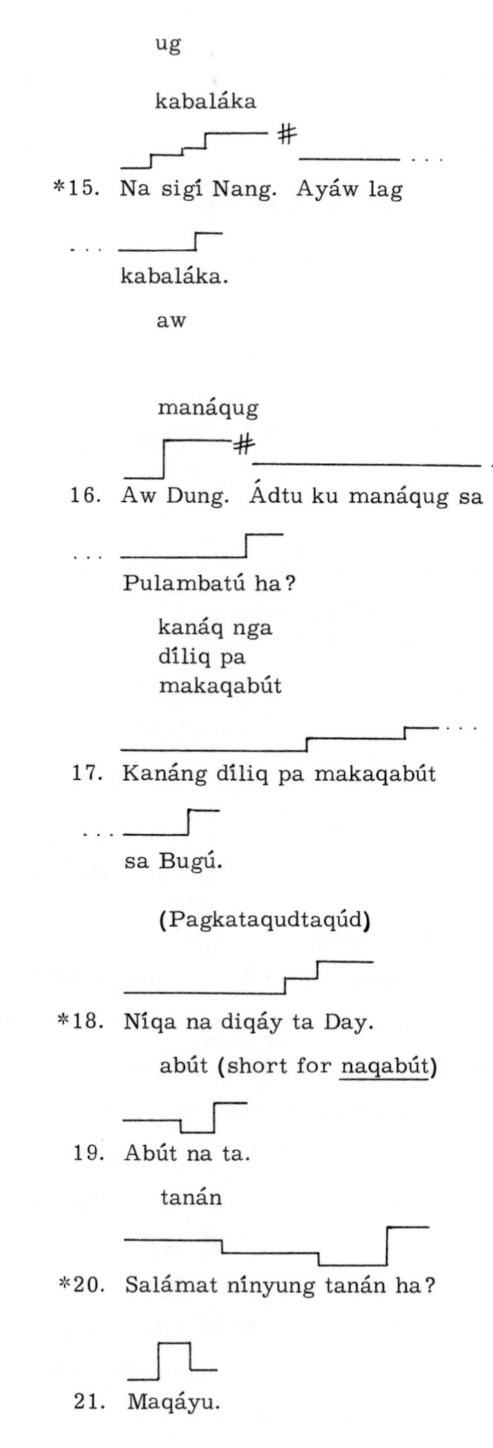

[particle linking ayáw and kabaláka]	ug
worry	kabaláka
15. Good-by, Ma'am. Just don't worry.	*15. Na sigí Nang. Ayáw lag ... kabaláka.
oh (particle said upon remembering to ask or say something)	aw
get off	manáqug
16. Oh, conductor. I'm getting off (lit. I'll get off) at Redstone, O.K.?	16. Aw Dung. Ádtu ku manáqug sa ... Pulambatú ha?
when	kanáq nga
not yet	díliq pa
reach	makaqabút
17. Before we get to Bogo. (Lit. When it has not yet reached Bogo.)	17. Kanáng díliq pa makaqabút ... sa Bugú.
(A little later)	(Pagkataqudtaqúd)
18. We're here now, Miss.	*18. Níqa na diqáy ta Day.
arrived	abút (short for naqabút)
19. We've (already) arrived.	19. Abút na ta.
all	tanán
20. Thank you, folks. (Lit. Thank you, O.K.?)	*20. Salámat nínyung tanán ha?
21. Hello! (Lit. Good.)	21. Maqáyu.
22. Come in.	22. Dayún.

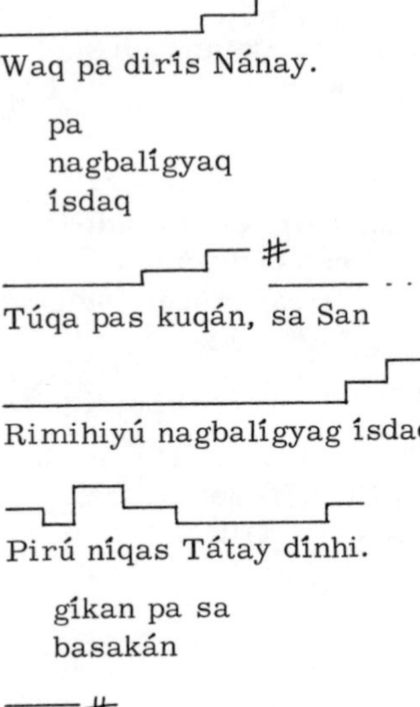

23. Is Mrs. Olivar in?

23. Náqa si Mísis Ulibár?

not yet — waq pa

24. Mom is not here yet.

24. Waq pa dirís Nánay.

still — pa
selling — nagbalígyaq
fish — ísdaq

25. She is still at—you know—at San Remigio, selling fish.

25. Túqa pas kuqán, sa San ... Rimihiyú nagbalígyag ísdaq.

26. But Dad is here.

26. Pirú níqas Tátay dínhi.

just back from — gíkan pa sa
rice fields — basakán

27. He's there, just back from the rice fields.

27. Náqa, gíkan pas basakán.

Mga Pangutána

Ikaduháng Báhin

1. Ngánung mahál mang plíti dínhi?
2. Maglakáw ka ba lang padulúng sa ínyu?
3. Díliq ba layúq ang ímung adtúqan Nang?
4. Ása ka man mupaqúliq Nang?
5. Kínsa man diqáy nagbántay sa baláy karún?
6. Naghuwathúwat ba siyá kanákuq?
7. Ánhi ka ra dínhi Nang?
8. Magbáklay ka ba lang ngádtu?
9. Makaqabút kaháq tas Bugú Dung?
10. Ádtu ka ba manáqug sa Pulambatú?
11. Ngánung miqádtu man siyás San Rimihiyú Day?
12. Si Tátay mu, náqa ba?
13. Gíkan na ba siyás basakán?

14. Anúsqa man muqabút si Nánay nímu Day?
15. Ngánu, waq pa ba tay makáqun?
16. Niqabút na ba si Mísis Ulibár?
17. Nagqúnsa man si Tátay nímu sa basakán Dung?
18. May madalá ba ku páras mga bátaq Plurá?
19. Unsáqun ku man karún pagpaqúling waláq na man diqáy kuy kasákyan?
20. May nagbántay ba sa ímung mga bátaq karún Nang?

Mga Pangutána (Matching)

Ikaduháng Báhin

1. Ang plíti dínhi diq ba mahál?
2. Unyáq maglakáw ka na lang Nang?
3. Kínsa man diqáy nagbántays ímung mga bátaq run Nang?
4. Nagqúnsa ang mga bátaq?
5. Háqins Tátay mu Day?
6. Si Nánay nímu Day, níqa ba?
7. Layúq ba nang ímung adtúqan Day?
8. Háqin man tung Pulambatú?
9. Ánhi ka ba lang manáqug Nang?

(a) Si Tátay, díqa dirís táqas.
(b) Ang Pulambatú? Kanáng sa diq pa muqabút sa Bugú.
(c) Sus, mahál kaqáyu.
(d) Maglakáw na lang gyud ug diq makasakáy.
(e) Naghuwathúwat tu run nákuq.
(f) Waq intáwun. Silá ra intáwung mga bátay túqas baay.
(g) Waláq ra ba Nang. Túqas Nánay sa San Rimihiyú namalígyaq.
(h) Ánhi na lang ku Dung. Salámat ha?
(i) Díliq. Diháq ras Pulambatú.

Sagquluhúnun

Third Part	Ikatulúng Báhin
1. Good afternoon.	1. Maqáyung hápun.
oh (interjection upon receiving surprising information)	uh
arrived	ningqabút
2. My! You're already here!	*2. Uh, ningqabút na diqáy ka?

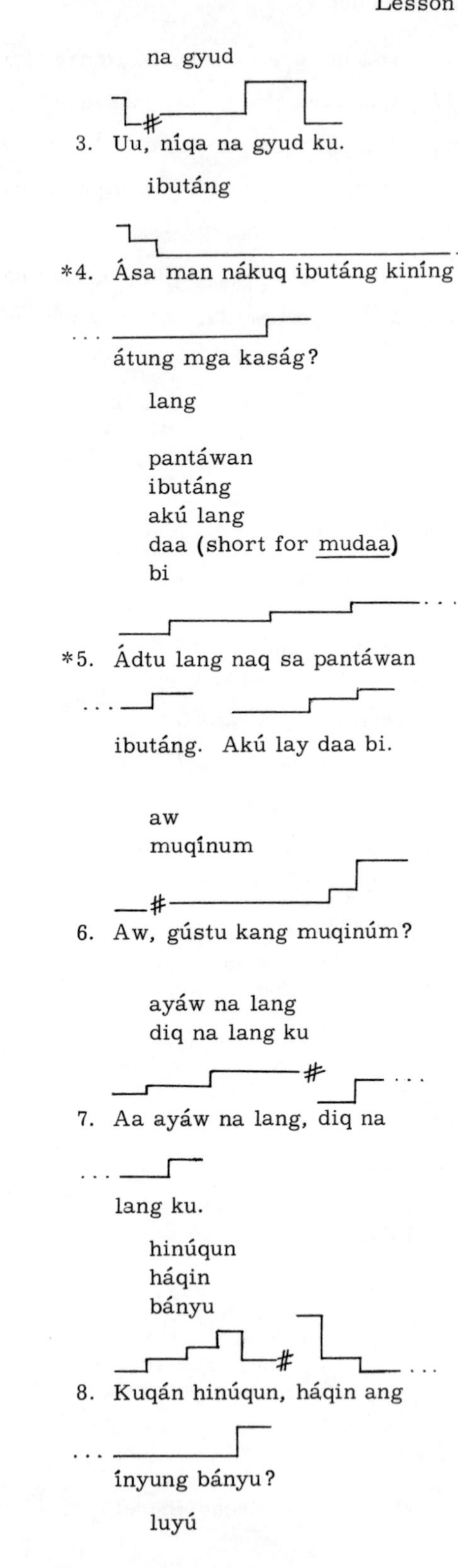

at last	na gyud
3. Yes, I'm here at last.	3. Uu, níqa na gyud ku.
put	ibutáng
4. Where shall I put these crabs I brought? (Lit. Where shall I put these crabs of ours?)	*4. Ásà man nákuq ibutáng kiníng ... átung mga kaság?
[deprecating particle with imperative]	lang
back porch	pantáwan
put	ibutáng
let me be the one to [do]	akú lang
take	daa (short for mudaa)
give it to me	bi
5. Just put them on the back porch. Here, let me take them (lit. I will just be the one to take them; give them to me).	*5. Ádtu lang naq sa pantáwan ... ibutáng. Akú lay daa bi.
by the way	aw
drink	muqínum
6. Oh, would you like (something) to drink?	6. Aw, gústu kang muqinúm?
never mind, no thanks	ayáw na lang
I don't care for any	diq na lang ku
7. No thanks; I don't care for any(thing).	7. Aa ayáw na lang, diq na ... lang ku.
however	hinúqun
where	háqin
bathroom	bányu
8. But, umm . . . where is your bathroom?	8. Kuqán hinúqun, háqin ang ... ínyung bányu?
back	luyú

	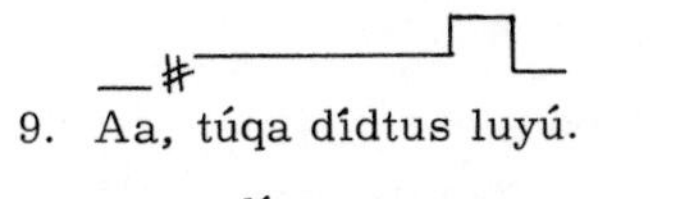
9. There at the back.	9. Aa, túqa dídtus luyú.
want to bathe	malíguq
	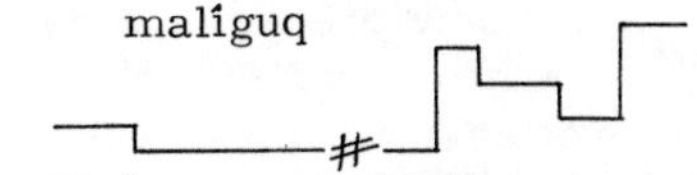
10. Why? Are you going to take a bath?	10. Ngánu man? Malíguq ka ba?
have water fetched for I [will (do) to] you [particle preceding goal] water	pakáwsan tiká ug túbig
11. I will have water fetched for you.	11. Pakáwsan tikág túbig.
never mind urinate [particle contradicting interlocutor]	ayáw lang mangíhiq man
12. Oh no, I just want to urinate.	12. Ayáw lang. Mangíhiq man lang ku.
(The children peek at the visitor.)	(Gisulingsúling sa mga bátaq ang bisíta.)
go away	lakáw
13. Now, you just get out of here.	13. Na, lakáw na lang mu.
stop [do]ing! look	ayáw na tanqáwa
14. You all stop looking at me now because I'm going to urinate.	14. Ayáw na lang ku nínyug tanqáwa kay mangíhiq ku.
(After urinating)	(Humág pangíhiq)
let's go visit	talá mubisíta
15. Let's go and visit our	15. Talá, mubisíta na tas mga

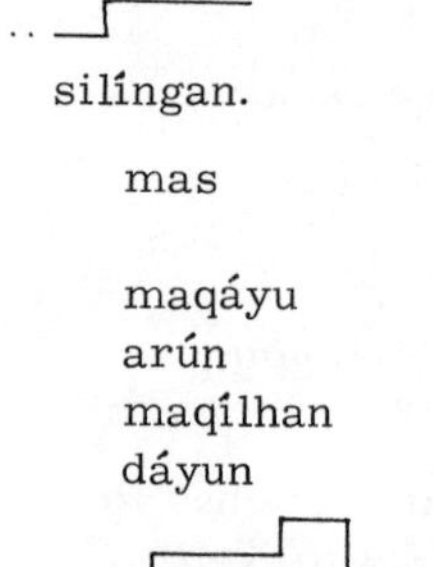

neighbors now.	silíngan.
[particle preceding comparative adjective]	mas
better	maqáyu
so that	arún
will be known	maqílhan
right away	dáyun
16. Fine. I want to meet them right away. (Lit. It's better so that I may know them right away.)	16. Mas maqáyu arún maqílhan ku silá dáyun.
17. Who is that woman carrying a child (in her arms)?	17. Kínsa man tung babáying nagdalág bátaq?

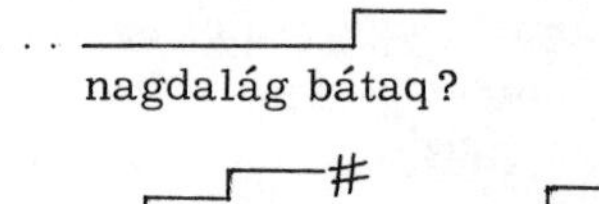

18. That is—what's-her-name—Mrs. Melendres.	18. Kuqán naq, si Mísis Milíndris.
daughter	anák
of	sa
barrio lieutenant (political head of the barrio)	tinyínti dil báryu
19. She is the daughter of the barrio lieutenant here.	19. Siyá ang anák sa tinyínti dil báryu dínhi.
thirteen	trísi
[linker for numerals]	ka
piece, segment [of a larger whole] (counter)	buqúk
20. She has thirteen children (lit. thirteen pieces of children).	20. May anák siyáng trísi ka buqúk.
how many!	kadághan
[particle exclaiming about a fact found out for the first time]	gud

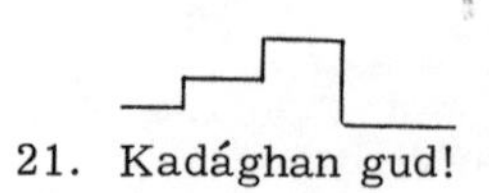

21. What a lot!	21. Kadághan gud!

(Miss Wilby talks to Mrs. Melendres.)	(Nagsúlti silá si Mis Wílbi ug si Mísis Milíndris.)
how?	unsáqun
feed	pagpakáqun
22. How do you feed thirteen children?	22. Unsáqun man nínyu pagpakáqun sa trísi ka buqúk bátaq?
hard	lisúd
really (emphasizer)	gyud
more than you realize	núqun
23. It's really very hard (harder than you think).	23. Lisúd gyud núqun.
my!	sus
how hard! (exclamatory adjective)	pagkalisúd
really	gyud
life	kinabúhiq
24. My! How hard our life is!	*24. Sus! Pagkalisúd gyud sa ámung kinabúhiq.
[particle preceding abstract form]	sa
fetch (water)	pagkalús
water	túbig
have to [do], cannot escape [do]ing	kinahángan gyud
[particle preceding goal]	ug
25. Just to fetch water, you have to walk one whole kilometer (lit. you can't escape walking one kilometer).	25. Sa pagkalús lag túbig kinahángan gyung mulakáwg usá ka kilumítru.
place from which one fetches water	kalusán
26. The place you fetch water	26. Usá ka kilumítru ang ínyung

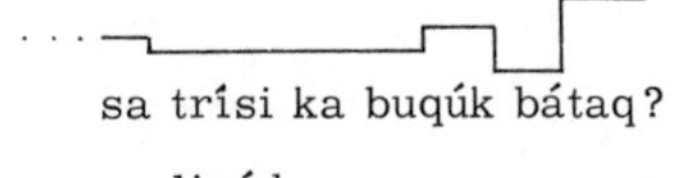

from is one kilometer away?	kaluság túbig?
fetching	magkáwus
27. Who fetches the water here?	*27. Kínsa may magkáwus ug túbig ngánhi?
since	sukád
got cut off	maputúl
hand	kamút
of	sa
husband	bána
28. I do. Since my husband's hand got cut off.	*28. Akú sukád maputúl ang kamút sa ákung bána.
now (as contrasted with earlier)	na
[expression of pity]	intáwun
do by oneself	nangunáy
fetching	pagkáwus
for	pára sa
whole	tibuqúk
family	pamílya
29. Now, I fetch water for the whole family by myself, poor me.	29. Akú na intáwun ang mangunáy pagkáwus páras tibuqúk pamílya.
how big!	kadakúq
job	trabáhu
isn't it?	nu
30. What a big job it is, isn't it?	30. Kadakúng trabáhu nu?
it is	maqú
[particle agreeing with interlocutor's exclamation]	bítaw
31. It certainly is!	31. Maqú bítaw.

[particle with a statement which confirms something]	bítaw
grow fat	mutámbuk

32. Look at me. You see I haven't gotten fat!

32. Tanqáwa, waq bítaw ku mutámbuk.

Mga Pangutána

Ikatulúng Báhin

1. Ása ku man ibutáng kiníng isdáqa?
2. Diq ba mahímu dihás pantáwan?
3. Gústu ka bang muqinúm?
4. Háqin mang ínyung bányu?
5. Ása man ka lakáw?
6. Mubisíta ba ta karún sa átung mga silíngan?
7. Diq ba maqáyu mang makaqilá dáyun akú níla?
8. Kínsa man kanáng babáying nagdalág bátaq?
9. Pilá na man ka buqúk ang íyang anák karún?
10. Magkalús ka na bag túbig?
11. Díliq ba lisúd ang ínyung kinabúhiq dínhi?
12. Ngánung malíguq ka pa man?
13. Ása man ku mangíhiq?
14. Ngánung mulakáw pa man mug usá ka kilumítru?
15. Waq ba muy makúhang táwu nga magkáwus pára kanínyu?
16. Ngánung naputúl man ang kamút sa ímung bána?
17. Layúq ba dínhi ang ínyung kalusánag túbig?
18. Dághan ba mug silíngan Mísis Milíndris?
19. Únsang urásang ningqabút ang traak sa Pulambatú?
20. May maqinúm ba mu dínhing búgnaw?

Mga Pangutána (Matching)

Ikatulúng Báhin

1. Mubisíta ba ta karún sa átung mga silíngan?
2. Kínsa may mukáwus ug túbig sa ínyu?
3. Anúsqa man ta manglákaw?
4. Kanáq bang babáying nagdalág bátaq ang anák sa tinyínti dil báryu?
5. Ása ku man ibutáng kiníng dalá kung ísdaq?
6. Pilá na man ka buqúk ang ímung anák Mísis Milíndris?
7. Layúq ba ang kalusánag túbig?
8. Diqín ka man ánang isdáqa Plurá?
9. Pilá ka pamílya ang átung bisitáhun karún Mis?

(a) Sus, dághan na kaqáyu. Trísi naq silá ka buqúk.

(b) Úqu arún maqílhan ku silá dáyun.

(c) Akú intáwun sukád maputúl ang kamút sa ákung bána.

(d) Upát lang usáq kay tingálig maqábtan tag ulán.

(e) Uu kanáq siyá. Ang íyang ngálan si Mísis Milíndris.

(f) Layúq. Usá gyud ka kilumítru.

(g) Ádtu lang naq ibutáng dídtu sa pantáwan.

(h) Karún dáyun.

(i) Dídtu sa istasyunán sa traak. Diháq may namalígyaq.

Commentary to Basic Sentences

9 a 1	ángay	A prepositive linked with nga.
9 a 7	kinahángan	A form of kinahánglan, common in Cebu City.
9 a 10		Note that the speaker uses diq. 'To be afraid to do something' is expressed by the unreal: mahádluk 'is (am, etc.) afraid to . . . '; or, in the negative, diq mahádluk 'is (am, etc.) not afraid to . . . ' 'To be afraid of something' is expressed by the real: nahádluk 'is afraid (of) . . . ' or, in the negative, waq mahádluk 'is not afraid (of) . . . ' "Nahádluk ka ba?" "Waq." '"Are you afraid?" "No."'
9 a 14	buqút	A prepositive like gústu, etc., linked with nga.
9 a 15		Note the use of the agent ku with a subject ka when the two are separated by several words: cf. 9A below.
9 a 19	ug kaqusá	When kaqusá (kásqa) 'once' does not begin the sentence, it is linked by ug to what precedes.
9 a 24	wánqa	Waq na is often pronounced wánqa in colloquial speech.
9 b 3	silabí	A prepositive which is linked with ug.

9 b 13 ha? — When one takes leave in Cebuano, he asks permission to go; that is why ha 'O. K. ?' is often used. The answer is sigí or halá 'go ahead.'

úsaq — This is a courteous word used upon asking permission to leave. (The implication is one won't be gone long.)

9 b 14 — The expression ánhi ra (or ánhi lang) is interchangeable with the dínhi lang (dínhi ra) and ngánhi lang (ngánhi ra) that have appeared in previous lessons. These all mean the same thing.

9 b 15 — Miss Wilby tells the lady not to worry because she wants to show that she is concerned with her problems. She implies that she is willing to help her out any time.

9 b 18 diqáy — The connotation of diqáy here is that neither the conductor nor Miss Wilby had noticed, until then, that they had arrived at Pulambato.

9 b 20 — Miss Wilby is saying good-by to everyone on the bus because the trip has been lively, and she has been talking with many of the other passengers.

9 c 2 ningqabút — Ningqabút 'arrived' is an alternative form for miqabút or niqabút with the same meaning. Some verbs (we will have to learn each case separately) occur with a prefix ning- as well as ni- and mi- in the same meaning.

9 c 4 — One usually brings something special to eat when coming for a long visit; this is why Miss Wilby is bringing crabs to the Olivars.

9 c 5 pantáwan — The pantáwan is a back stoop (usually uncovered) where the water containers are kept.

9 c 24 pagkalisúd — This is the same in meaning as the exclamatory kalisúd 'how difficult!': see 5 A, above, p. 174. (We will discuss the prefix pagka- in Lesson 12.

9 c 27 magkáwus — Káwus (= kalús) is one of the few bases which does not occur with the prefix mu- in the meaning 'habitual action.' (See 5 C 1 (3), p. 177.) 'Usually fetch water' is magkáwus.

9 c 28 maputúl — This is a subjunctive form. After sukád 'since,' humán 'after,' and other words with similar meaning, the subjunctive passive occurs in place of the real (just as after waláq 'no'). (Words which are followed by a subjunctive are discussed in detail in Lesson 13.)

Grammatical Section

9 A Use of ta, kitá, etc., for first person singular

If the agent is 'I' and the recipient is 'you' (either singular or plural), the form ta is used for 'I' and ka or ikáw (mu or kamú) is used for 'you'; or, instead, tiká or tikáw—combinations of the first and second persons—replace the separate forms: 'I . . . (to) you.'

Kuháqan ta kag táksi? (8 c 33) 'Shall I get you a taxi?
Maqú nga giqánhi ta gyud ka arún pagkúhaq nímu. (8 c 25) 'So I came here to get you.'
Pakáwsan tikág túbig. (9 c 11) 'I'll have water fetched for you.'

Ta . . . ka (ikáw, mu, kamú) or tiká or tikáw are also used with nouns, when the first person (genitive) is the possessor of the noun and second person is the subject:

Amígu ta man ka. 'You are my friend.'

Compare also the use of the first person inclusive plural when the speaker and the hearer are both interested parties (comment 8 a 18, above, p. 304):

Níqa na kitá sa átung tihíras. (8 a 18) 'Here we are at our cots.' (Actually Miss Wilby was the only person for whom a cot had been reserved.)

Exercise 9.II A.

9 B. Abstract forms

All Cebuano verbs have an ABSTRACT FORM, made by adding to the base an ABSTRACT PREFIX. The abstract prefixes are pag-, pagka-, and inig- (short form ig-). The abstract forms are used in the constructions described below.

9 B 1 a. Abstract forms as clauses

An abstract form followed (optionally) by a genitive agent and/or a goal (the agent precedes if there is both an agent and a goal) is a clause meaning 'when . . .':

Pagqabút nínyu sa iskína Hwan Lúna, likúq sa tuqú. 'When you arrive at the corner of Juan Luna, turn to the right.' [Pagqabút 'upon arriving' is an abstract form; nínyu 'you' is a genitive and is the agent of pagqabút; sa iskína Huwan Luna 'the corner of Juan Luna' is a goal.]
Pagbálik níla sa Úrmuk, waq na diháq si Pápa níla. 'When they got back to Ormoc, their father was not there any longer.'

9 B 1 a (1). Inig-/ig- abstract forms

The abstract form with inig-/ig- (plus agent and/or goal) occurs only as a clause and only when the time reference is to unreal (future or habitual) action.

Inigqabút nímu dídtus Úrmuk nu, mga alás kwátru pa kanáq sa búntag. (8 a 19) 'You know, when you get to Ormoc, it will only be about four o'clock in the morning.'
Igbálik nímu, pagdalá bayág mga rigálu, ha? (5.61) 'When you come back, be sure to bring presents, will you?'

Exercise 9.II B.

9 B 1 a (2). Sa with abstracts followed by an agent and/or a goal.

Abstract forms with pag- or pagka- occurring as clauses may be preceded by sa, with no difference in meaning. Sa may thus be inserted before the pag- abstracts in the example of 9 B 1 a above. Another example is the following:

Sa pagkáwus lag túbig kinahánglan gyung mulakáwg usá ka kilumítru. (9 c 25) 'Just to fetch water you have to walk a whole kilometer.'

9 B 1 b. Abstract forms in the infinitive construction

An abstract form with pag- or pagka- followed optionally by a goal may occur following a verb. An abstract in such a construction is an INFINITIVE and functions as the complement of the verb. The infinitive is often translated by English 'to [do]': 'I want to go,' 'it began to rain,' and so forth. The abstract form with pag- or pagka- in the infinitive construction may be preceded by sa, with no difference in meaning.

Nagsúgud (sa) pagqulán. 'It began to rain.'
Waq mu maglisúd (sa) pagqánhi ngánhi? (2 b 17) 'Didn't you have a hard time getting here?'
Unyáq ayáw paghikalimút (sa) pagsuwát kanákuq ha? (8 a 33) 'Also, you won't forget to write me, will you?'
Unsáqun man nákuq (sa) pagpatáy? (6 a 32) 'How can I kill it?'

9 B 1 c. Abstract forms in the imperative construction

Abstract forms with pag- or pagka- followed optionally by a goal also occur in the imperative construction. An IMPERATIVE verb gives a command: 'do!' 'go!' 'eat!' etc. The agent of an imperative is 'you,' either singular or plural; if singular, it is usually omitted:

Uy, Lulíng, pagdalá diríg bír. (2 b 26) 'Loling, bring some beer here.'
Nyaq, pagqayuqáyu dínhis Sibú. (8 b 2) 'Also, have a good time here in Cebu.'

If the agent is 'you' (plural) and the imperative is an abstract, the agent is kamú or mu:

Pagqayuqáyu kamú dínhi ha? 'You all have a good time, hear?'

9 B 1 d. Abstract forms with pag- used as nouns

Abstract forms with pag- occur also in any construction in which a noun occurs. The meaning is 'action of [the verb],' often expressed in English by an -ing participle or an infinitive:

Ang ímung pagdáag mga rigálu makalípay sa mga táwu. 'Your bringing of presents will make the people happy.'
Maqúy lisúd kaqáyu ang pagpatáy sa kaság. 'What was difficult was to kill the crabs.'
Lamíq kaqáyu ang pagmatág sayú. 'It is very nice to wake up early.'

9 B 2. The genitive with abstracts in clauses or with abstracts occurring as nouns

The genitive in the agent usage occurs with abstracts in clauses (9 B 1 a) and with abstracts used as nouns (9 B 1 d):

Inigqabút nímu dídtus Úrmuk nu, mga alás kwátru pa kanáq sa búntag. (8 a 19) 'When you arrive at Ormoc, it will only be around four in the morning.'
Maqúy ákung gikabalákqan ang pagdúgayg abút ni Pápa. 'What I'm worried about is that it's taking Dad so long to get here.' (Lit. 'What I am worried about is the taking long of Daddy to get here.')

9 C. Expressions of manner

Expressions telling how—that is, in what manner—something is done (well, slowly, carefully, etc.) are said in several ways in Cebuano. Three of these are:

1. Adjective of manner preceding the verb and linked to it with nga;
2. Adjective of manner following the verb and linked to it with ug;
3. Verb followed by infinitive of manner.

9 C 1. Adjective plus nga plus unreal verb

A sentence consisting of an adjective plus nga plus an unreal verb plus a subject is used only in unreal tense meaning. If the verb is active, the sentence means '[subject] does (did, will do) the action in an [adjective] manner'; if the verb is passive, the sentence means '[subject] has (etc.) the action happen to him in an [adjective] manner.' (For the use of the unreal see 4 B 2 b, above, p. 143.)

Maqáyu kang mubinisayáq. (8 b 6) 'You speak Visayan well.' [Maqáyu 'well' is an adjective linked by nga (in its alternant form ng) to the active verb mubinisayáq 'speak Visayan.' Ka 'you' is the subject.]
Nīndut ka man lagi diqáyng mulútuq. 'Why, you're a wonderful cook (lit. you cook deliciously)!'
Bátaq pa siyá kaqáyung tanqáwun. 'He still looks very young.'

9 C 2. Verb plus ug plus adjective

A sentence consisting of a verb (real or unreal) plus ug plus an adjective plus a subject is used in any tense meaning. If the verb is active, the sentence means '[subject] does (did, will do) the action in an [adjective] manner'; if the verb is passive, the sentence means '[subject] has (etc.) the action happen to him in an [adjective] manner.'

Milakáw siyág hīnay. 'He walked away slowly.' [Milakáw 'walked away,' an active verb, is linked with ug to hīnay 'slowly,' an adjective. Siyá 'he' is the subject.]
Bantayīg maqáyu ang átung tindáhan ha. 'Take good care of our store, will you?' (Lit. 'Watch our store well, will you?')

9 C 3. Verb plus infinitive

A sentence consisting of a verb plus an infinitive (9 B 1 b) plus a subject is used in any tense meaning. If the verb is active, the sentence means '[subject] does (did, will do) the action in an [adjective] manner'; if the verb is passive, the sentence means '[subject] has (etc.) the action happen to him in an [adjective] manner.' The kind of infinitives used in this construction are those from verbs meaning '[do] in a certain manner': 'do slowly, 'do carefully,' etc.

Milakáw siyá paghīnay. 'He walked away slowly.' [Hīnay is an adjective meaning 'slow' and also a verb meaning 'do slowly.']
Bantayī pagqáyu ang átung tindáhan. 'Take good care of our store.' (Lit. 'Watch our store well.') [Áyu is a verb meaning 'do well.']
Ákuq siyáng tágdun pagqáyu. (8 a 28) 'I shall watch her carefully.'

Expressions of manner are further treated below, 14 A.

Exercise 9.III.

9 D. Exclamations of manner

A sentence consisting of ka- plus adjective plus linker plus verb plus genitive means 'how [adjective-ly] [the genitive] habitually [does]!'* The genitive is the person or thing about whom the exclamation is made.

Kamaqáyu nímung mubinisayáq. 'How well you speak Visayan.' [Nímu 'you,' the one about whom the exclamation is made, is a genitive. The exclamatory adjective kamaqáyu 'how well!' is linked to the verb with ng. The verb mubinsayáq 'speak Visayan' is unreal.]
Kanindut gyud diqáy nímung mulútuq. 'How well you cook!'
Kabátaq nímung tanqáwun. 'How young you look!'

Exercise 9.III.

Pattern Practices and Exercises

IA. Pilíqa ang hústung púrma sa bírbu nga anáqa sa parentheses. Pilíqa kun real, unreal, u subjunctive ba sa local passive. (8 A and subsections; 6 A 3 and subsections)

Pananglítan:

a: (Kúhaq) níya ang kalamáy ni Mis Wílbi. 'She took part of Miss Wilby's kalamay.'

Tubág: Gikuháqan níya ang kalamáy ni Mis Wílbi.

b: (Dalá) siyá ug prútas sa kwártu. 'Bring her some fruit into the room.'

Tubág: Dádqi siyá ug prútas sa kwártu.

1. Iskínay (hulát) ni Dyuu sa íyang amígu. 'It was at the corner that Joe waited for his friend.'
2. Kiní lang dyípay (sakáy) nínyu. 'Just take this jeep.'
3. (Ágí) níla ang baay ni Huwán pagqádtu níla sa Dyuns Abinyú. 'They passed by John's house on their way to Jones Avenue.'
4. "Dádqa ring gása, Liná." "Diq ku kay (pangítaq) unyáq ku ánaq sa ímung inahán." '"Take this gift, Lina." "No, I won't, because your mother might ask me for it."'
5. Mu ning barkúha ang ílang (sakáy) padúung ngánhi. 'This is the boat they'll take coming back.'
6. Diq kunú ni (paqábang) nga kwartúha. 'This room is not for rent.'
7. Pulambatú ang (ádtu) nílang Mis Wílbi ug Pírla. 'Pulambato was where Miss Wilby and Perla went.'

---

* This is the exclamatory adjective (above, 5 A, p. 174) followed by nga plus an unreal verb as described in 9 C 1.

8. Kanáng tindáhan ímung (pangutána) kun háqin magpuyúq si Iyúq Tibúq. 'You can ask in that store where Tibo lives.'
9. (Hímuq) ku ni Dúdung ug lamísa. 'Dodong will make a table for me.'
10. (Báyad) na níya ang aláhas nga kinhasún. 'He has already paid for the seashell earrings.'
11. (Báyad) bayáq ang tindíra, Dung; tingálig makalimút ka unyáq.
12. (Hatúd) níla sa Mis Wílbi ug gása sa íyang baay.
13. Waq (sámuk) si Mis Wílbi sa dághang bátaq.
14. (Sáqad) ku níyang dádqun sa siní.
15. (Puyúq) ra ba ning baláya úgmaq sa Amirkána nga bágqung naqabút gíkan sa Amiriká.
16. (Ubán) ku run sa siní, Liná.
17. Kiníng lamisáha íyang (iháp)g kwárta gahápun.
18. Bátaq ang ákung (palít)g dúlsi niqánang tindahána ganíha.
19. (Bálik) si Mísis Mílir sa íyang sakít.
20. Díqay síngku písus. (Súkliq) ku bi.

IB. (Practice PP-Q of Lesson 8 before this exercise.) Ibutáng ang hústung púrma sa bírbu ginámit ang local passives ug direct passives. (8 A, 6 A)

Pananglítan:

a: Gústu kung (palít) ang aríyus nga gibalígyaq sa babáyi. 'I would like to buy the earrings the woman is selling.'

Tubág: Gústu kung palitún ang aríyus nga gibalígyaq sa babáyi.

b: (Palít) ku únyaq si Mis Wílbi gása. 'I'll buy Miss Wilby a present later.'

Tubág: Palitán ku únyaq si Mis Wílbi gása.

1. (Sakáy) níla ang píkqap pagqádtu níla sa Talísay. 'They took an unscheduled bus to Talisay.'
2. Mirlí, (bántay) bayáq nang átung mga butáng. 'Merlie, watch our things.'
3. Ayáwg kabaláka kay ákung (bántay)g maqáyu ang tindáhan. 'Don't worry, for I'll watch the store carefully.'
4. Mahímuq nga ímung (káqun)g dyútay nang kalamáy nga ákung gidáa. 'It's all right if you eat a little of that kalamay I brought.'
5. Liná, (dalá) si Mísis Pirnándis ug túbig sa íyang kwártu. 'Lina, bring a glass of water to Mrs. Fernandez in her room.'
6. (Súbay) lang ning dalána kay makítqan ra nínyu ang ínyung (pangítaq)ng baay. (Tánqaw)g sígi ang dapít sa tuqú. 'Follow this road and you'll find the house you're looking for. Keep looking to the right.'

7. (Láqay) si Mírli pagpinaqábut sa íyang amígu. 'Merlie got sick of waiting for her friend.'

8. Ay, kanáng haluqháluq (sakút) naq nílag áyskrim. 'Well, that halo-halo was mixed with ice cream.'

9. Átuq ning (pangutána)ng dyípa kun muqádtu ba ni sa Talísay. 'We'll ask this jeep driver (lit. this jeep) whether he goes to Talisay.'

10. (Ubán) ba kaháq nátuq ni siyá sa Talísay? 'Shall we go with her to Talisay?'

11. Ása mang lugára sa Talísay ang átung (ádtu)?

12. Diq ku. Waláy angáy ning lugárang (kalíguq).

13. (Píliq) nátuq nang dyip nga mudirítsus Sibú.

14. Únsa man diqáy ang átung (sakáy) padúung sa Banáwaq?

15. Ayáw kug (límbung) Dung.

16. (Súlti) gyud si Dúdung sa tinúqud. 'Tell Dodong the truth.'

17. Lamísa ang íyang (sulát) sa istúrya. 'It was on the desk that she was writing the story.'

18. Mahímuq bang (káqun) ku ning ságing? 'May I eat some of these bananas?'

19. (Kúyug) si Níniq sa íyang gitrabahúqan. 'Go with Nene to the place where she works.'

20. Anáaq mu rag púlus nang (ukupár)ang mga lugár dínhi.

IC. Ibutáng sa línya ang hústung púrma sa bírbu nga anáqa sa parentheses ginámit ang active ug passive. Gamíta ang local u direct sa passive. (8 A, 6 A)

1. (Palít) níya si Mis Wílbi ug kalamáy. 'She bought some kalamay for Miss Wilby.'

2. (Putús) na nang aríyus, Day, kay ákung (palít). 'Wrap up those earrings, Miss. I'll take them.'

3. (Kúhaq) ra gud si Mísis Abáya ug ságing sa kusína Litú. 'Please get a banana from the kitchen for Mrs. Abaya, Lito.'

4. (Tánqaw) kug siní rung gabíqi. 'I'll go to the show this evening.'

5. (Pangutána) ta ang tigúlang kun háqin run (balígyaq)g kalamáy ang bátang átung (palít) gahápun. 'Let's ask the old man where the boy we bought kalamay from yesterday is selling now.'

6. (Súkliq) na nang babáyi, Liná, kay (dalíq) tingáli naq siyá. 'Give the woman her change, Lena, because she's probably in a hurry.'

7. (Pangítaq) ang ákung pitáka kay kun makítqan, (hátag) ta kag kwárta. 'Look for my wallet. If you find it, I'll give you some money.'

8. Díliq ku Dung (ági) sa taytáyan. 'I don't want to cross the bridge.'

9. Ngánu mang waq ka (ánhi) sa písta. 'Why didn't you come for the fiesta?'

10. (Dágan) si Lítu nga (dalá) sa íyang líbru. 'Lito ran away taking his book with him.'
11. (Diritsu) ba nis Gutsán? 'Does this (jeep) go straight to the Go Chan?'
12. Uu, (pangítaq) ku si Mírli. 'Yes, I'll look for Merlie.'
13. (Ingún) si Dyuu nga diq siyá (ubán). 'Joe said that he wouldn't come along.'
14. (Buhíq) ang kaság arún diq ka paqákun. 'Let the crab loose so that you won't be bitten.'
15. (Ítus) ni Nuy Tibúq ang tunúq nga may kalámay. 'Tibo caramelized the coconut milk that had brown sugar in it.'
16. Maqáyu man lagí kang (binisayáq) Mis Wílbi.
17. (Lárga) si Pírla úgmaq padúung sa Pulambatú.
18. (Káwus) si Buy ug túbig arún mu makakaligúq.
19. Akú lay (báyad) sa plíti nátuq Mísis Kapangpángan. 'Let me pay the fare, Mrs. Kapangpangan.'

ID. Ang vs. sa or ug, si vs. ni, siyá vs. níya, etc. Gíkan sa mga púlung sa parentheses pilíqa ang hústung púlung. (1 B 1, 3 A 3, 3 B, 5 A 1, 5 D and subsections, 6 B and subsections, 6 C, 8 C and subsections, 9 B 2)

1. Kanáng sabún, tuqálya ug muskitíru dádqun (siyá, níya) dídtu (sa, ang) Pulambatú.
2. Kinahánglan sultíhan ta (siyá, níya) nga (sa, ang) íyang amíga niqabút gíkan (sa, ug) Amiriká.
3. Adtúqun (níya, siyá) (si, ni) Pírla (sa, ang) tindáhan sa mga líbru. 'He will go see Perla at the bookstore.'
4. Misakáy (ang, ug) usá ka tabiqáng babáyi.
5. Muqádtu silá (sa, ang) baay (ni, si) Mírli.
6. Giqimbitár siyá (si, ni) Pírla (sa, ang) ristáwran.
7. Sigurúqa (ug, ang) dalá (ang, sa) líbru ngádtu sa upisína.
8. Dádqa ngarí (ang, ug) kukakúla nga pára (sa, ang) bisíta (ni, si) Dína.
9. Kuháqun (níya, siyá) (ang, ug) kalamáy (si, ni) Huwán.
10. Bárku ang gisákyan (níya, siyá) pagqádtu (níya, siyá) sa Úrmuk.
11. Gipangutána (siyá, níya) (sa, ang) tindíra kun ibalígyaq bag barátu (ang, sa) aríyus.
12. Mubálhin (siyá, níya) (ug, ang) láqing baay nga paqabángan.
13. Táwga lang (níya, siyá) (ang, sa) tilipunú.
14. Gisamúkan (siyá, níya) (sa, ug) mga bátaq (ni, si) Mísis Kapangpángan.
15. Pilíqi (siyá, níya) Dung (ug, ang) maqáyung sinínaq.
16. Muqulíq na (níya, siyá) úgmaq (sa, ang) Sibú.

17. Gilaqáyan (níya, siyá) ug hulát (ang, sa) amígu níya. 'He got tired of waiting for his friends.'
18. Nalímtan (níya, siyá) ug dalá (ang, sa) tuqálya (ni, si) Mis Wílbi.
19. Naquwanán (níya, siyá).
20. Mipasílung (siyá, níya) (sa, ang) baláy (si, ni) Pírla.

PP-O Use of the agent and the subject (6 D, direct and local passive)

Step I. (Changing the agent)

'I bought some kalamay for her.'

Gipalitán ku siyág kalamáy.	(námuq)
Gipalitán námuq siyág kalamáy.	(nímu)
Gipalitán nímu siyág kalamáy.	(níya)
Gipalitán níya siyág kalamáy.	(nákuq)
Gipalitán nákuq siyág kalamáy.	(nátuq)
Gipalitán nátuq siyág kalamáy.	(níla)
Gipalitán níla siyág kalamáy.	(nímu)
Gipalitán nímu siyág kalamáy.	(ku)
Gipalitán ku siyág kalamáy.	(námuq)
Gipalitán námuq siyág kalamáy.	(nátuq)
Gipalitán nátuq siyág kalamáy.	

Step II. (Changing the agent in negative sentences)

'I won't give her any kalamay.'

Díliq siyá nákuq tagáqag kalamáy.	(nátuq)
Díliq siyá nátuq tagáqag kalamáy.	(námuq)
Díliq siyá námuq tagáqag kalamáy.	(nímu)
Díliq siyá nímu tagáqag kalamáy.	(námuq)
Díliq siyá námuq tagáqag kalamáy.	

Step III. (Changing the agent in negative sentences)

'I didn't watch her.'

Waláq siyá nákuq bantayí.	(nínyu)
Waláq siyá nínyu bantayí.	(námuq)
Waláq siyá námuq bantayí.	(nátuq)
Waláq siyá nátuq bantayí.	(nímu)
Waláq siyá nímu bantayí.	(nátuq)
Waláq siyá nátuq bantayí.	(nínyu)

Waláq siyá nínyu bantayí. (námuq)

Waláq siyá námuq bantayí.

Step IV. (Changing the subject)

'They bought something for her.'

Gipalitán siyá níla. (mi)

Gipalitán mi níla. (ni)

Gipalitán ni níla. (mu)

Gipalitán mu níla. (naq)

Gipalitán naq níla. (silá)

Gipalitán silá níla. (kanáq)

Gipalitán kanáq níla. (ta)

Gipalitán ta níla. (ri)

Gipalitán ri níla. (akú)

Gipalitán akú níla. (ri)

Gipalitán ri níla.

Step V. (Changing the verb)

'I watched him.'

Gibantayán ku siyá. (palitán)

Palitán ku siyá. (gihágkan)

Gihágkan ku siyá. (sultíhan)

Sultíhan ku siyá. (giqíngnan)

Giqíngnan ku siyá. (dádqan)

Dádqan ku siyá.

Step VI. (Changing the subject using both long and short forms)

'You're holding my bag.'

Kúptan man nímu ang ákung bag. (tanqáwun)

Tanqáwun man nímu ang ákung bag. (siyá)

Tanqáwun man nímu siyá. (si Lína)

Tanqáwun man nímu si Lína. (hatágan)

Hatágan man nímu si Lína. (palitán)

Palitán man nímu si Lína. (siyá)

Palitán man nímu siyá. (silá)

Palitán man nímu silá. (kamí)

Palitán man nímu kamí. (si Dína)

Palitán man nímu si Dína.	(siyá)
Palitán man nímu siyá.	(baligyáqan)
Baligyáqan man nímu siyá.	(ang táwu)
Baligyáqan man nímu ang táwu.	(si Mis Wílbi)
Baligyáqan man nímu si Mis Wílbi.	(kuháqun)
Kuháqun man nímu si Mis Wílbi.	(ang lamísa)
Kuháqun man nímu ang lamísa.	(kúptan)
Kúptan man nímu ang lamísa.	

Step VII. (Position of long and short forms of the genitive agent)

'I'll buy some bread for her.'

Palitán ku siyág paan.	(nímu)
Palitán siyá nímug paan.	(ta)
Palitán ta siyág paan.	(níla)
Palitán siyá nílag paan.	(mu)
Palitán mu siyág paan.	(nínyu)
Palitán siyá nínyug paan.	(námuq)
Palitán siyá námug paan.	(ta)
Palitán ta siyág paan.	

Step VIII. (Position of pronoun and noun subjects and pronoun and noun agents)

'I didn't give him a present.'

Waláq ku siyá tagáqig gása.	(si Mis Wílbi)
Waláq ku tagáqig gása si Mis Wílbi.	(silá)
Waláq ku silá tagáqig gása.	(si Pírla)
Waláq ku tagáqig gása si Pírla.	(námuq)
Waláq námuq tagáqig gása si Pírla.	(siyá)
Waláq námuq siyá tagáqig gása.	(si Bíbi)
Waláq námuq tagáqig gása si Bíbi.	(níla)
Waláq níla tagáqig gása si Bíbi.	(kamí)
Waláq níla kamí tagáqig gása.	(si Ústing)
Waláq níla tagáqig gása si Ústing.	(siyá)
Waláq nilá siyá tagáqig gása.	(si Manáng)
Waláq níla tagáqig gása si Manáng.	(naq siyá)
Waláq níla naq siyá tagáqig gása.	(kádtu si Mis Alpapára)

Waláq níla tagáqig gása kádtu si Mis Alpapára. (kiní)

Waláq níla kiní tagáqig gása. (si Lína)

Waláq níla tagáqig gása si Lína. (mi)

Waláq mi níla tagáqig gása. (si Mánung)

Waláq níla tagáqig gása si Mánung. (mu)

Waláq mu níla tagáqig gása. (si Mánuy)

Waláq níla tagáqig gása si Mánuy. (ta)

Waláq ta níla tagáqig gása. (si Tátay)

Waláq níla tagáqig gása si Tátay. (ku)

Waláq ku níla tagáqig gása. (si Nánay)

Waláq níla tagáqig gása si Nánay. (nínyu)

Waláq nínyu tagáqig gása si Nánay. (si Dalíng)

Waláq nínyu tagáqig gása si Dalíng. (níla)

Waláq níla tagáqig gása si Dalíng. (ang bátaq)

Waláq níla tagáqig gása ang bátaq. (nátuq)

Waláq nátuq tagáqig gása ang bátaq. (ni Índay)

Waláq tagáqig gása ni Índay ang bátaq. (ang mádri)

Waláq tagáqig gása ni Índay ang mádri. (níya)

Waláq níya tagáqig gása ang mádri. (ni Piríng)

Waláq tagáqig gása ni Piríng ang mádri. (si Sílsu)

Waláq tagáqig gása ni Piríng si Sílsu. (síya)

Waláq siyá tagáqig gása ni Piríng. (ang anák)

Waláq tagáqig gása ni Piríng ang anák. (námuq)

Waláq námuq tagáqig gása ang anák.

Step IX. (Preposed form of agent)

'I watched over the child.'

Ákung gibantayán ang bátaq. (ímu)

Ímung gibantayán ang bátaq. (ínyu)

Ínyung gibantayán ang bátaq. (íla)

Ílang gibantayán ang bátaq. (ámuq)

Ámung gibantayán ang bátaq. (ákuq)

Ákung gibantayán ang bátaq. (ámuq)

Ámung gibantayán ang bátaq. (átuq)

Átung gibantayán ang bátaq.

Step X. (Word order)

'Are we going to look at the baby?'

Átuq bang tanqáwun ang bátaq?	(nátuq)
Tanqáwun ba nátuq ang bátaq?	(ámuq)
Ámuq bang tanqáwun ang bátaq?	(námuq)
Tanqáwun ba námuq ang bátaq?	(íla)
Íla bang tanqáwun ang bátaq?	(níla)
Tanqáwun ba níla ang bátaq?	(ínyu)
Ínyu bang tanqáwun ang bátaq?	(nínyu)
Tanqáwun ba nínyu ang bátaq?	(ákuq)
Ákuq bang tanqáwun ang bátaq?	(nákuq)
Tanqáwun ba nákuq ang bátaq?	(íya)
Íya bang tanqáwun ang bátaq?	(níya)
Tanqáwun ba níya ang bátaq?	(ku)
Tanqáwun ku ba ang bátaq?	(ímu)
Ímu bang tanqáwun ang bátaq?	(mu)
Tanqáwun mu ba ang bátaq?	(íla)
Íla bang tanqáwun ang bátaq?	(nímu)
Tanqáwun ba nímu ang bátaq?	

Step XI. (Word order)

'Did you watch Perla?'

Ímu bang gibantayán si Pírla?	(siyá)
Ímu ba siyáng gibantayán?	(si Adúr)
Ímu bang gibantayán si Adúr?	(ku)
Ímu ba kung gibantayán?	(ang bátaq)
Ímu bang gibantayán ang bátaq?	(silá)
Ímu ba siláng gibantayán?	(ang babáyi)
Ímu bang gibantayán ang babáyi?	(kiní)
Ímu ba kiníng gibantayán?	(si Lísa)
Ímu bang gibantayán si Lísa?	(kanáq)
Ímu ba kanáng gibantayán?	(ang ákung amígu)
Ímu bang gibantayán ang ákung amígu?	(tu)
Ímu ba tung gibantayán?	(si Mísis Mindúsa)
Ímu bang gibantayán si Mísis Mindúsa?	(mi)
Ímu ba ming gibantayán?	

Step XII. (Word order)

'I might as well call Perla.'

Ákuq na lang táwgun si Pírla.	(siyá)
Ákuq na lang siyáng táwgun.	(si Mis Wílbi)
Ákuq na lang táwgun si Mis Wílbi.	(silá)
Ákuq na lang siláng táwgun.	(nákuq)
Táwgun na lang silá nákuq.	(níya)
Táwgun na lang silá níya.	(íya)
Íya na lang siláng táwgun.	(si Mis Wílbi)
Íya na lang táwgun si Mis Wílbi.	(níla)
Táwgun na lang níla si Mis Wílbi.	(námuq)
Táwgun na lang námuq si Mis Wílbi.	(ámuq)
Ámuq na lang táwgun si Mis Wílbi.	(siyá)
Ámuq na lang siyáng táwgun.	(nákuq)
Táwgun na lang siyá nákuq.	(ímu)
Ímu na lang siyáng táwgun.	(si Dína)
Ímu na lang táwgun si Dína.	(níya)
Táwgun na lang níya si Dína.	(ta)
Táwgun na lang ta níya.	(íla)
Íla na lang tang táwgun.	

Step XIII. (Word order)

'They might as well call Perla.'

Íla na lang táwgun si Pírla.	(siyá)
Íla na lang siyáng táwgun.	(námuq)
Táwgun na lang siyá námuq.	(ni Pídru)
Táwgun na lang siyá ni Pídru.	(nímu)
Táwgun na lang siyá nímu.	(si Pípi)
Táwgun na lang nímu si Pípi.	(ni Pírla)
Táwgun na lang ni Pírla si Pípi.	(siyá)
Táwgun na lang siyá ni Pírla.	(nákuq)
Táwgun na lang siyá nákuq.	(ákuq)
Ákuq na lang siyáng táwgun.	(si Pírla)
Ákuq na lang táwgun si Pírla.	(ni Pídru)
Táwgun na lang ni Pídru si Pírla.	(ímu)
Ímu na lang táwgun si Pírla.	(ni Maríng)

Táwgun na lang ni Maríng si Pírla. (siyá)
Táwgun na lang siyá ni Maríng. (íla)
Íla na lang siyáng táwgun. (ni Manáng)
Táwgun na lang siyá ni Manáng. (ákuq)
Ákuq na lang siyáng táwgun. (ni Mánuy)
Táwgun na lang siyá ni Mánuy. (íla)
Íla na lang siyáng táwgun. (ni Manáng)
Táwgun na lang siyá ni Manáng. (ang babáyi)
Táwgun na lang ni Manáng ang babáyi. (kamí)
Táwgun na lang kamí ni Manáng. (ang bátaq)
Táwgun na lang ni Manáng ang bátaq. (ámuq)
Ámuq na lang táwgun ang bátaq.

Step XIV. (Word order)

'Did you watch Perla?'
Ímu bang gibantayán si Pírla? (siyá)
Ímu ba siyáng gibantayán? (nímu)
Gibantayán ba siyá nímu? (íla)
Íla ba siyáng gibantayán? (níla)
Gibantayán ba níla siyá? (níya)
Gibantayán ba níya siyá? (ákuq)
Ákuq ba siyáng gibantayán? (nákuq)
Gibantayán ba nákuq siyá? (íya)
Íya ba siyáng gibantayán? (ni Pídru)
Gibantayán ba siyá ni Pídru? (mu)
Gibantayán mu ba siyá? (ínyu)
Ínyu ba siyáng gibantayán? (nínyu)
Gibantayán ba nínyu siyá? (ku)
Gibantayán ku ba siyá? (átuq)
Átuq ba siyáng gibantayán?

Step XV. (Word order)

'Did you cut the banana tree down?'
Ímu bang giputúl ang ságing? (íla)
Íla bang giputúl ang ságing? (níla)
Giputúl ba níla ang ságing? (átuq)

Átuq bang giputúl ang ságing?	(nátuq)
Giputúl ba nátuq ang ságing?	(ku)
Giputúl ku ba ang ságing?	(nímu)
Giputúl ba nímu ang ságing?	(mu)
Giputúl mu ba ang ságing?	(nátuq)
Giputúl ba nátuq ang ságing?	(ta)
Giputúl ta ba ang ságing?	(námuq)
Giputúl ba námuq ang ságing?	(ni Huwán)
Giputúl ba ang ságing ni Huwán?	(níya)
Giputúl ba níya ang ságing?	(íya)
Íya bang giputúl ang ságing?	(mu)
Giputúl mu ba ang ságing?	(ákuq)
Ákuq bang giputúl ang ságing?	(nákuq)
Giputúl ba nákuq ang ságing?	(mu)
Giputúl mu ba ang ságing?	(nímu)
Giputúl ba nímu ang ságing?	(ímu)
Ímu bang giputúl ang ságing?	(nínyu)
Giputúl ba nínyu ang ságing?	

IIA. Use of kitá (ta) for 'I.' Ibutáng ang hústung púrma sa agent ug sa recipient. (9A)

		Recipient	Agent
1.	Gikuháqan ____ ____ ug dúlsi.	me	Lítu
2.	Nakítqan ____ ____ gabíqi sa bárku.	you (sing.)	I
3.	Inigqabút nákuq gíkan sa Úrmuk dádqun ____ ____ sa ámuq.	you (sing.)	I
4.	Ánhi ____ ____ huwatá dínhi.	us (incl.)	he
5.	Gihimúqan ____ ____ ug sílya.	Ínting	I
6.	Anhíqun ____ ____ úgmaq ha? (anhíqun 'person one comes to fetch')	you (sing.)	I
7.	Gipangutána ____ ____ báhin sa Pulambatú.	me	Mis Wílbi
8.	Tagáqan ____ ____ unyág síngku.	you (sing.)	I
9.	Ánhi nyaq kay tagáqan ____ ____ gása.	you (sing.)	I

		Recipient	Agent
10.	Mahál ____ gyud ____ Pirlá.	you (sing.)	I
11.	Adtúqun ____ ____ sa ínyu? (adtúqun 'person one goes to fetch')	you (sing.)	I
12.	Uu. Adtúqun ____ ____ sa ámuq.	me	you
13.	Pangitáqan ____ lang ____g dyip páras Banáwaq.	you (sing.)	I
14.	Waláq ____ subáya ____ padulúng sa Kapitúl.	dálan	I
15.	Palitán ____ ____ug dúlsi unyáq.	you (pl.)	I
16.	Gitawág ____ ____?	me	you (sing.)
17.	Kalímtan na lang ____ ____.	me	you (sing.)
18.	Lutúqan ____ ____g maqáyung súdqan.	me	Pírla
19.	Bisitáhan ____ ba ____ úgmaq?	you (sing.)	I
20.	Inigqabút námuq sa bárku palitán ____ ____g kalamáy.	you (sing.)	we
21.	Táwgun ____ ____ sa ínyu sa mga alás útsu.	you (sing.)	I
22.	Giqíngnan ____ ____ nga níqa si Mis Wílbi sa Úrmuk.	me	she
23.	Waláq ____________ báyri sa kalamáy.	her	I
24.	Gisuwatán ____ ____. Waq ba nímu madáwat?	you (sing.)	I
25.	Waláq ____ hátdi ____ ug kalamáy.	me	Pírla

II B. Ibálhin ang musunúd nga abstract ngádtu sa púrmang inig- kun mahímuq. (9 B)

Pananglítan:

a: Pagqábut nímu dídtu sa Úrmuk nu, mga alás kwátru pa kanáq sa búntag.

Tubág: Inigqabút nímu dídtu sa Úrmuk nu, mga alás kwátru pa kanáq sa búntag.

b: Pagqabút nákuq sa baláy milakáw na si Tátay.

Tubág: Díliq maqilísan ang pagqabút sa inigqabút.

1. Si Lítu ang muqubán pagpalít nákug dúlsi.
2. Unyáq na ku mulakáw pagqabút níya.

3. Manágan dáyun ta pagsulúd níla dínhi.
4. Pagsúgud nákug iháp, dágan lang dáyun.
5. Unyáq na lang ku muhátag sa plíti paghúnung íning dyip.
6. Táwga si Pírla pagkanáqug níya sa dyip.
7. Ayáw siyág tubagá pagpangutána níya nímu.
8. Pagqabút nákuq sa baláy waq na diháq si Pipíng. Milakáw.
9. Tagáqi nyaq mig kuk pagqánhaq námuq dínhaq.
10. Pagbálhin níya sa bágqung baláy dídtu na pud si Máma níya.
11. Átung palitán ug dúlsi si Lítu pagpadulúng nátuq sa baláy.
12. Dádqan ka námug ságing pagqádtu námuq sa Pulambatú.
13. Paglíngkud níya sa sílya, nahúlug siyá dáyun.
14. Hibaluqán gyud mi nínyu pagqági námuq dínhi.
15. Húnung dáyun mu pagqiháp nákug dus.

III. (Expression of Manner) Hubára ang musunúd sa Binisayáq. (9C, 9D)

1. You speak Visayan well.
2. This jeep runs slowly. (slowly: hínay)
3. He cooks well.
4. John runs fast. (fast: kusúg)
5. He ran quickly.
6. How slowly you walk!
7. How well she cooks!
8. She takes good care of her children.

Pagbása

IV A. Retell the story and answer questions.

Túnyu: Gisulatán ku ni Nída. Nahinúmdum pa gyud diqáy intáwun siyá.

Ártur: Aa kádtung misúgat nátus bárku? Nahinúmdum túqud ku. Apán waq dyud ka malímut, niqádtung* gilimbúngan siyá ádtung bátang nagbalígyag kalamáy.

Túnyu: Bísag ikáw nalimbúngan ka na gyud.

Ártur: Aw úqu, kásqa ra núqun. Kádtung* waq ku tagáqi sa ákung súkliq. Kádtu* pung waq ku tagáqi sa ákung girisírbang tihíras†.

---

* Kádtu and niqádtu linked with nga are used to mean 'that past time when —— happened.'

† Ákung girisírbang tihíras 'the cots which had been reserved by me.'

Túnyu: Taná. Ádtu na tas bárku. Tingálig giqukupahán na ang átung tihíras.

Ártur: Díliq diqáy úsaq ka mukáqun sa diq pa ta muqádtu?

Túnyu: Diq na lang. Sigí, manáqug na ta kay náqa nang dyip. Akúy mudalá ning ímung bag arún díliq mawálaq ('get lost').

(Taqudtaqúd)

Pilá may átung ibáyad Dung?

Draybir: Únu singkwínta lang. Naqukupahán man ang lugár sa ínyung gikárga.

Ártur: Ngánung únu singkwínta gud? Sa úna ang ámung gibáyad sa pagsúgat námung Pírla, písu ra. Dídtu pa mi manáqug sa Banáwaq.

IV B. Add the proper affixes to the verbs in parentheses.

Túnyu: (Sulát) ku ni Nída. Nahinúmdum pa gyud diqáy intáwun siyá.

Ártur: Aa kádtung (súgat) nátus bárku? Nahinúmdum túqud ku. Apán waq gyud ka malímut niqádtung (límbung) siyá ádtung bátang (balígyaq)g kalamáy.

Túnyu: Bísag ikáw (límbung) ka na gyud.

Ártur: Aw úqu, kásqa ra núqun. Kádtung waq ku (hátag) sa ákung súkliq. Kádtu pung waq ku (hátag) sa ákung (risírba)ng tihíras.

Túnyu: Taná. Ádtu na tas bárku. Tingálig (ukupár) na ang átung tihíras.

Ártur: Díliq diqáy úsaq ka (káqun) sa diq pa ta (ádtu)?

Túnyu: Diq na lang. Sigí, manáqug na ta kay náqa nang dyip. Akúy (dalá) ning ímung bag arún díliq mawálaq.

(Taqudtaqúd)

Pilá may átung ibáyad Dung?

Dráybir: Únu singkwínta lang. (Ukupár) man ang tanáng lugár sa ínyung gikárga.

Ártur: Ngánung únu singkwínta gud? Sa úna ang ámung (báyad) sa pagsúgat námung Pírla, písu ra. Dídtu pa mi manáqug sa Banáwaq.

V A. Ibungát ang mga musunúd nga mga túdling púlung sa hústung paníngug. 234 statement)

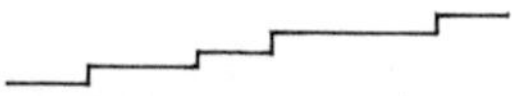

1. Diq man ku mahádluk. (9 a 10)
2. Ayáw na lang. (9 a 16)
3. Ayáw paghaguqhagúg kúyug nákus Pulambatú. (9 a 17)
4. Nakaqádtu na man ta niqádtug kaqusá. (9 a 19)

5. Waq na kuy úras pagpalít sa ákung mga palitúnun. (9 a 24)
6. Mamalít na ta. (9 a 26)
7. Na sigí Plurá. (9 a 27)
8. Umuqúliq lang ku dídtus Kármin. (9 b 6)
9. Na sigí Nang. (9 b 15)
10. Níqa na diqáy ta Day. (9 b 18)
11. Waq pa dirís Nánay. (9 b 24)
12. Ádtu lang naq sa pantáwan ibutáng. (9 c 5)
13. Aa ayáw na lang. (9 c 7)
14. Pakáwsan tikág túbig. (9 c 11)
15. Lakáw na lang mu. (9 c 13)

V B. (423 question)

1. Únsa may ángay nákung dádqun sa ... Pulambatú? (9 a 1)
2. Únsa pa may ubán nákung dádqun? (9 a 5)
3. Ása man nákuq ibutáng kiníng átung mga kaság? (9 c 4)
4. Tagpíla man ni? (6 a 3)
5. Pilá may bayranán ánaq sa káda búwan? (3 b 25)
6. Kínsa man tung babáying nagdalág bátaq? (9 c 17)
7. Kínsa may magkawús ug túbig ngánhi? (9 c 27)
8. Ása man ku musakáyg dyip páras Mabúlu? (6 b 49)
9. Háqin ang ínyung bányu? (9 c 8)
10. Ása man diqáy ka Nang? (9 b 4)

V C. (324 question)

1. Magdalá ba kug mga gása? (9 a 6)
2. Diq ba ka mahádluk muqádtus Pulambatú? (9 a 8)
3. Níqa ba si Místir Abáya? (1.4)
4. Layúq ba ang ímung adtúqan? (9 b 5)
5. Ánhi lang diqáy ka? (9 b 14)
6. Abút na ta? (9 b 19)

7. Salámat nínyung tanán ha? (9 b 20)
8. Náqa si Mísis Ulibár? (9 b 23)
9. Ningqabút na diqáy ka? (9 c 2)
10. Kadakúng trabáhu nu? (9 c 30)
11. Diq ba gyud diqáy mahímung dyis? (6 a 10)
12. Kínsay ímung ngálan Dung? (2 b 19)

VI. Sultiqánay

Nangádtu Silás Pírla ug Mis Wílbi sa Talísay

A: Pirlá, muqádtu man tingáli tas Talísay; ádtu na ta.

B: Ísaq pa kay maglútuq pa kug pagkáqun.

A: Ay na lang naq. Dághan bítawng pagkáqung mapalít dídtu.

B: Waq na tay láqing dádqun?

A: Pagdalág sabún ug tuqálya.

B: Ug kuqán pud diqáy. Kwárta kay ibáyad sa pagkáqun.

1. Giqimbitár si Pírla ni Mis Wílbi sa Talísay.
2. Dúna pay lutúqun si Mis Wílbi.
3. Waláy gibalígyang pagkáqun sa Talísay.
4. Nagqingún si Pírla nga magdalá pud silág papíl pára ilú.
5. Díliq na níla dádqun ang sabún.
6. Mamalít silá ug pagkáqun kay dághan mang gibalígyaq.

(Sa dídtu na silá sa Talísay)

New words: sirádu 'closed'; luyú 'back (rear part of something)'

B: Ásaq man ta paqingún?

A: Kuqán—dúnay bányu dínhi Pirlá?

B: Ngánu man, malíguq ka na?

A: Díliq. Malíguq man tas dágat. Mangíhiq lang ku.

B: Aa taná. Mangíhiq pud ku.

A: Uy sirádu man diqáy ang bányu.

B: Aa ádtus luyú.

A: Pagquná.

B: Diq ku uy. Dághang mga bátang nagsulingsúling.

A: Sa dágat na lang hinúqun.

B: Náqay balaybálay uh. Ádtu lang ta dídtu.

7. Nangítaq si Mis Wílbi bányu kay malíguq.
8. Pagqabút nílas bányu nakapangíhiq na gyud silá.
9. Dídtu silás luyú mangíhiq kay sirádu man ang bányu.

A: Mahímuq bang ánhi mi dínhi língkud Nang?

C: Uu sigí. Waq may naglíngkud dínhi.

A: Kiníng mga bátaq, ímu ba ning tanán?

C: Aa díliq. Kádtu rang usá—nga dalága.

A: Kínsa man nang ubán?

C: Mga bátaq naq ni Mísis Milíndris, asáwa sa tinyínti dil báryu.

A: Dághan silág anák?

C: Sus kadághan. Napúuq ka buqúk. Naglisúd gud siyá pagpakáqun kay naputúl ang kamút sa íyang bána.

10. Giqukupahán na ang tanáng lugár sa balaybálay.
11. Si Mísis Milíndris dághag anák—napúuq ka buqúk.
12. Anák síya sa tinyínti dil báryu.
13. Napútlan intáwug kamút si Mísis Milíndris.

LESSON 10. OCCUPATIONS IN THE BARRIO

Sagquluhúnun

First Part	Únang Báhin
let's go around (from place to place)	manúruy ta (base súruy plus prefix paN-)
beach	baybáyun
do first	magqúna
1. Miss Wilby, come on. Let's go places. Let's go to the beach first.	1. Mis Wilbí. Taná. Manúruy ta. Ádtu ta sa baybáyun magqúna.
2. O.K. Let's go.	2. Sigí. Ádtu na ta.
is the one	maqú
[subject marker]	ang
dative marker (meaning 'belonging to')	kang
[title or term of address for males older than speaker]	Nuy
masculine name (short for Tiburcio)	Tibúq
3. That house there—it (lit. that one) is (Noy) Tibo's.	*3. Kanáng náqang baay diháq, maqú naq ang kang Nuy Tibúq.
most	labí
[linker between labí and tigúwang]	nga
old (of people)	tigúwang
village	balángay
4. He is the oldest man here in the village.	4. Siyá ang labíng tigúwang táwu dínhis balángay.

him (just referred to and not present)	naq siyá
because	kay
fisherman	mangingísdaq
because	man
merely	lang

5. He is very poor because he is only a fisherman.

*5. Púbri kaqáyu naq siyá kay ... mangingísdaq man lang.

besides	gawás pa
now	na
as well	sad
in order to	pára
go fishing	mangísdaq

6. Besides, he's (also) too old now to go fishing.

*6. Gawás pa, # tigúlang na sad ... kaqáyu siyá pára mangísdaq.

what?	unsingálan (dialectal form)
[question particle following interrogatives]	man
bamboo slat about one inch wide	lipák
bamboo	kawáyan
[linker between kawáyan and gipamaqátan]	nga
tied together (plural)	gipamaqátan (báqat plus paN-)

7. What are those bamboo slats tied together?

*7. Unsingálan man nang mga lipák ... sa kawáyan nga gipamaqátan?

for	pára sa
type of fish trap	búngsud

8. Ah, those? Those are bamboo slats for fish traps.

*8. Aa kanáq? # Mga kawáyan naq ... pára sa búngsud.

those (previously mentioned)	kanáq
of	sa

way	paqági
of	sa
fishing	pangísdaq
in our place	sa ámuq

9\. A búngsud is one of the means of fishing here. (Lit. That búngsud—that is one of the means of fishing here in our place.)

9\. Kanáng búngsud—usá naq ... sa paqági sa pangísdaq dínhi ... sa ámuq.

use to surround, place around the perimeter of	ilíbut
[particle preceding goal]	sa
one	usá
[linker between usá and párti]	ka
part	párti
of	sa
sea	dágat

10\. They use those bamboo slats to enclose (lit. surround) a part of the sea.

10\. Kanáng mga kawáyan, íla ... nang ilíbut sa usá ka párti ... sa dágat.

also	sad
doorway	pultahán

11\. And there's also a doorway.

11\. Ug dúna say pultahán.

thing into which [something] is put	butangán

12\. They put a doorway into (it).

12\. Butangán nílag pultahán.

fish	ísdaq
[linker between ísdaq and masúud]	nga
happen to enter	masúud
corral	kurál
[linker between kurál and gihímuq]	nga

was built	gihímuq
have a hard time	maglisúd
now	na
to go out	paguwáq (guwáq + pag-)
13. The fish that get inside that corral (that was made) have a hard time getting out again.	*13. Ang mga ísdaq nga masúud ánang kurál nga gihímuq, maglisúd na paguwáq.
obstruction (vertical or horizontal)	alí
[linker between alí and the following clause]	nga
[subject marker]	ang
fish	ísdaq
can no longer	díliq na
14. Because the door has also an obstruction so that the fish can no longer . . .	14. Kay ang pultahán dúna man say alí nga ang mga ísdaq díliq na . . .
can	mahímuq
[linker between mahímuq and muguwáq]	nga
get out	muguwáq
15. They can't get out.	15. Díliq mahímung muguwáq.
16. Oh, really?	16. Aa diqáy?
parents	ginikánan
brothers and sisters	igsúqun
earn (lit. are earning) their livelihood	nanginabúhiq
in	sa
17. My parents and my brothers and sisters make their	*17. Ang ákung mga ginikánan ug mga igsúqun, nanginabúhiq

living by fishing.	sa pangísdaq.

[subject marker]	ang
my	ákuq
likewise	bítaw
[linker between ákuq and bána]	nga
husband	bána
fisherman	mangingísdaq
[particle with statement giving information]	man
also	sad

18. My husband was (also) a fisherman, too.	18. Ang ákuq bítawng bána mangingísdaq man sad.

but	apán
got cut off	naputúl
affected by an explosion	nabúthan
because	man
[particle preceding goal]	ug
dynamite	dinamíta

19. But one of his hands was cut off in a dynamite explosion. (Lit. But one of his hands was cut off because he was affected by dynamite.)	*19. Apán naputúl ang íyang usá ... # ka kamút kay nabúthan mag dinamíta.

small	dyútay
[linker between dyútay and lunáq]	nga
piece of land	lunáq
of	sa
land	yútaq

20. We also have a small piece of land in San Remigio.	20. Dúna sad miy dyútayng lunáq sa yútaq sa San Rimihiyú.

is the one	muqú (dialectal for maqú)
[subject marker]	y
working	nagtrabáhu

21. And my husband (is the one who) works there.	21. Ug ang ákung bána muqúy nagtrabáhu dídtu.
male	laláki
also	sad
are working	gatrabáhu
cornfield	kamaqisán
22. My sons are also there, working in the cornfield.	22. Ang ákuq sang mga anák nga laláki, # túqa sad gatrabáhu sa kamaqisán.
instead	hinúqun
23. Let's go there instead.	23. Ádtu hinúqun ta dídtu.
24. Let's take a look at the corn.	24. Tanqáwun nátuq ang mga maqís.
25. This is our cornfield.	25. Maqú kiní ang ámung kamaqisán.
this	kaní (= kiní)
ours	ámuq
still	gihápun
26. These here and those there are ours too (lit. are still ours).	26. Kaníng níqa ug kádtung túqa, # ámuq gihápun.
next	sunúd
week	simána
will harvest corn	manánggiq (sánggiq plus paN-)
now	na
27. Next week we'll be harvesting corn (lit. will be harvesting corn now).	27. Sunúd simána, # manánggiq na mi sa maqís.

so that	arún
again, also	usáb
thing that can be planted on	katámnan
right away	dáyun

28. So that we can plant again on it right away.

28. Arún usáb katámnan námuq ... dáyun.

how many?	pilá
[question particle after interrogative]	man
[linker between pilá and sánggiq]	ka
harvest of corn	sánggiq

29. How many harvests can you get in a year?

29. Pilá man ka sánggiq ang ... ínyung mahímuq sa usá ka ... túqig?

is the same	magsáma

30. Oh, it varies. (Lit. It's not the same.)

30. Aa, díliq magsáma.

sometimes	usáhay
three times	katulú
four times	kaqupát

31. Sometimes three times, sometimes four.

*31. Usáhay katulú, usáhay ... kaqupát.

helper	katábang
in	sa
harvesting	panánggiq
neighbor	silíngan

32. Our helpers here in the harvest are our neighbors,

32. Ang ámung mga katábang dínhi ... sa panánggiq maqú ang ámung

(and) my children.	mga silíngan, ákung mga anák.
people from other places	tagaláqing lugár
[linker between tagaláqing lugár and the rest of the sentence]	nga
come (plural)	mangánhi
merely in order to	arún lang
[particle preceding infinitive]	sa
help	pagtábang
[particle preceding goal]	sa
harvesting	panánggiq

33. And there are also people from other places who come here just to help in the harvest.	33. Ug dúna say tagaláqing lugár ... nga mangánhi arún lang sa ... pagtábang sa panánggiq.

Mga Pangutána

Únang Báhin

1. Díliq ba ta manúruy Mis Wílbi?
2. Diq ba si Nuy Tibúq man nang tiguwánga?
3. Mangingísdaq man naq si Nuy Tibúq nu?
4. Ngánung gipamaqátan man nang mga lipák sa kawáyan?
5. Dúna ba diqáy mu dínhiy búngsud?
6. Ang ímung ginikánan, nanginabúhiq ba usáb sa pangísdaq?
7. Ang ímung bána, únsa may trabáhu?
8. Giqúnsa man sa ímung bána ang dinamíta?
9. May kamaqisán ba sab mu sa San Rimihiyú?
10. Ang ímung mga anák gatrabáhu ba sab sa ínyung kamaqisán?
11. Pilá ka simána úsaq masánggiq ang maqís?
12. Anúsqa man mu manánggiq?
13. Dúna na ba muy katábang sa panánggiq?
14. Katámnan na ba nig maqís sunúd simána?
15. Kanáng ínyung mga silíngan, díliq ba mutábang sa panánggiq?

16. Magsáma ba ang báhin sa mga katábang sa panánggiq?
17. Dághan ba mug masánggiq sa ikatulú nínyung tanúm?
18. Dúna ba say tagaláqing lugár nga mangánhi dínhi kun manánggiq na?
19. Butangán ba sab nílag pultahán kanáng ílang búngsud?
20. Díliq ba muguwáq nang mga ísdaq sa kurál?

Mga Pangutána (Matching)

Únang Báhin

1. Ása man ta manúruy Mis Wílbi?
2. Háqin mang dapíta ang baay ni Nuy Tibúq?
3. Únsa may trabáhu sa ímung anák?
4. Únsa man nang búngsud?
5. Kanáng kawáyan nga gipamaqátan, unsáqun man naq níla?
6. Ang ísdang musulúd, díliq na ba makaguwáq?
7. Ang mga mangingísdaq, háqin man magpuyúq?
8. Ang ímung bána, mangingísdaq ba sad?
9. May mutábang ba sad sa panánggiq nga díliq tagadínhi?

(a) Uu, apán naputúl ang usá níyang kamút kay nabúthan man sa dinamíta.
(b) Kanáng mga kawáyan, íla nang ilíbut sa usá ka párti sa dágat.
(c) Dúnay dághan nga muqánhi lang dínhi sa panahún sa panánggiq.
(d) Díliq na kay may alí man ang pultahán sa búngsud.
(e) Kanáng náqang baay diháq sa baybáyun, maqú nang kang Nuy Tibúq.
(f) Kanáng mga baay diháq sa baybáyun, maqú nay gipúyqan sa mga mangingísdaq.
(g) Kanáng búngsud, maqúy usá ka paqági sa pangísdaq.
(h) Ay, pangísdaq lang intáwun.
(i) Ádtu ta manúruy sa baybáyun ug únyaq, muqádtu ta sa kamaqisán.

Sagquluhúnun

Second Part	Ikaduháng Báhin
rice field	humayán
1. There are rice fields here as well.	1. Dúna usáb dínhiy humayán.

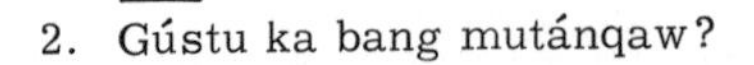

2. Would you like to look at (them)?	2. Gústu ka bang mutánqaw?

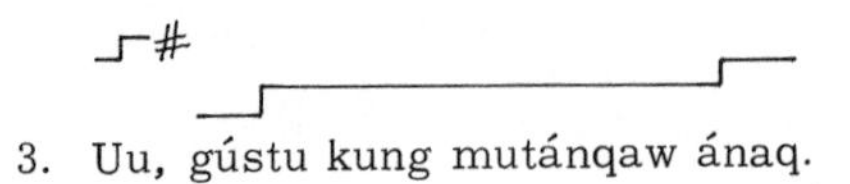

3. Yes, I'd love to look at that.	3. Uu, gústu kung mutánqaw ánaq.
[exclamation of surprise]	anáaq

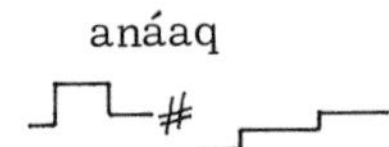

4. My! How beautiful!	4. Anáaq, kaníndut!
ready for [do]ing, ready to be [done]	hústu
yet, by now	na
[linker between hústu and aníhun]	nga
to be harvested	aníhun
rice (ground or unground)	humáy
5. Is this rice ready to be harvested yet?	*5. Hústu na bang aníhun ning ... humáya?
not yet	díliq pa
approximately	mga
still	pa
[linker between duhá and búwan]	ka
month	búwan
before	úsaq
can be harvested	maqáni
6. Oh, not yet. It will take around two more months before it can be harvested.	6. Aa, díliq pa. Mga duhá pa ... ka búwan naq úsaq maqáni.
(at the time) when	kanáng
yellow-brown	pulá
becomes yellow-brown	mupulá
grain-bearing head of grasses	uháy
now	na
[subject marker]	y
proper	hústu
[linker between hústu and tímpu]	nga
season	tímpu
[particle preceding infinitive]	sa

harvesting	pagqáni
7. When the heads turn yellow, that's the right time for harvesting the rice. (Lit. When those heads of theirs are becoming yellow now, that's the right time now for harvesting rice.)	*7. Kanáng mupulá na nang ílang . . . uháy, maqú na nay hústung . . . tímpu sa pagqáni sa humáy.
not either	díliq sad
good	maqáyu
[linker between maqáyu and the rest of the sentence]	nga
delay	dugáyun
8. (Because) it's not good for you to delay harvesting (them) either.	8. Kay díliq man sad maqáyu . . . nga ímung dugáyun pagqáni.
will become bad	madáqut
because	man
9. Because the rice will be spoiled.	9. Kay madáqut man ang humáy.
especially	labí na
if	ug
falls on the side	matúmba
whatchamacallit will happen to it	makuqán
already	na
10. Especially if it [the rice] has fallen—it will, you know . . .	*10. Labí nag matúmba na naq. . . . Makuqán na . . .
will get immersed	mahúmul
in	sa
water	túbig
will become bloated	mubúrut
[particle with information given]	man
they (referred to immediately before)	naq silá

11. It will get immersed in the water. It (lit. Those them) will get bloated.	11. Mahúmul sa túbig, mubúrut man naq silá.
owner	tagqíya
12. The owner of that rice field doesn't live here. He's in Cebu (City).	12. Ang tagqíya ánang humayána waláq dínhi magpuyúq. Túqa sa Súgbu.
thing caused to be run by tenants	gipasápqan (root, saqúp)
merely	lang
13. He just has it run by tenants here.	*13. Gipasápqan lang naq níya dínhi.
tenants	saqúp
take	mukúhaq
only	lang
share	báhin
[linker between báhin and kwarínta pursíntu]	nga
40 per cent	kwarínta pursíntu
of	sa
all	tanán
[linker between tanán and áni]	nga
harvest	áni
14. And his tenants here in Redstone just get a 40-per-cent share of the entire harvest.	14. Ug ang íyang saqúp dínhi sa Pulambatú, mukúhaq lag báhin nga kwarínta pursíntu sa tanáng áni.
from there	gíkan diháq
[subject marker]	ang

money to pay a salary	isúhul
[particle preceding goal]	sa
[linker between táwu and mitábang]	nga
helped	mitábang
15. And from that they take out what they pay to the people who helped harvest.	15. Ug gíkan diháq, ánhaq níla kuháqa ang isúhul sa mga táwu nga mitábang sa pagqáni.
how many?	pilá
[interrogative particle]	man
[linker between pilá and áni]	ka
harvest	áni
can be obtained	mahímuq
in	sa
16. How many harvests do you get a year?	16. Pilá man ka áni mahímuq sa usá ka túqig?
17. Of rice?	17. Sa humáy?
18. Yes.	18. Uu.
oh (pause before starting to speak)	aa
two times	kaduhá
no more than	ra
for sure	gyud
19. Oh, never more than two (times).	*19. Aa, kaduhá ra gyud.
sometimes	usáhay
even	gániq
once	kásqa
no more than	ra

20. Sometimes, we even have only one.	20. Usáhay gániq, kásqa ra.
goes along with	magnunút
because	man gud
weather	panahún
21. It (lit. That) depends upon (lit. goes along with) the weather.	21. Magnunút man gud naq sa panahún.
even	gániq
if	kun
rain	ulán
not once, not at all	diq gyud
even	gániq
can plant	makatanúm
22. There are even years when there is no rain—they can't even plant once.	22. Dúna say túqig gániq, kun waláy ulán, diq gániq gyud silá makatanúm.
necessary	kinahánglan
come back	mubálik
23. You must come back here.	23. Kinahánglan mubálik ka dínhi.
[linker between sunúd and pagbálik]	nga
return	pagbálik
thing made to coincide	iqatúl
[linker between iqatúl and the rest of the phrase]	nga
that time when	kanáng
they are harvesting	mangáni
already	na
24. And when you come here next time, come at harvest	24. Ug sa sunúd nímung pagbálik, ...

time (lit. make it coincide with when they are harvesting the rice).	iqatúl nga kanáng mangáni na sa humáy.
nice	níndut
[linker between níndut and tanqáwun]	nga
to be looked at	tanqáwun
when	kun
25. Because it's very beautiful to look at when they are harvesting the rice.	25. Kay níndut kaqáyung tanqáwun kun mangáni na sa humáy.

Mga Pangutána

Ikaduháng Báhin

1. Gústu ka bang mutánqaw sa ámung humayán?
2. Pilá ka búwan úsaq maqáni ang humáy?
3. Madáqut ba nang humáy kun díliq maqáni dáyun?
4. Kanáng humayána, kang kínsa man naq?
5. Únsa may paqági sa pagbáhin sa áni dínhi sa ínyu?
6. Ang báhin sa mga katábang, ása man kuháqa?
7. Únsa may ínyung isúhul sa mutábang pagtanúm—kwárta ba?
8. Dúgay bang aníhun nang humáy?
9. Dághan ba sang táwu nga mutábang sa pangáni?
10. Níqa ba sab dínhi magpuyúq ang tagqíya ánang humayána?
11. Díliq ba maqúnsa kanáng humáy kun mahúmul naq silá sa túbig? (maqúnsa 'something will happen to')
12. Ang aníhun nínyung humáy ása man nínyu ibutáng?
13. Piláy maqáni nínyu ánang lunáqa nínyu sa yútaq?
14. Ngánung díliq man nínyu aníhun ang humáy kun díliq pa mupulá ang ílang uháy?
15. Dúna ba sab muy mga saqúp Misís?
16. Ínyu bang gipasápqan ang yútaq nínyu sa San Rimihiyú?
17. Dághan ba mug báhin sa káda pangáni?
18. Anúsqa man ka mubálik Mis Wílbi?

19. Anúsqa man ang sunúd nínyung pangáni Misís?

20. Níndut bang tanqáwun nang mangáni sa humáy?

Mga Pangutána (Matching)

Ikaduháng Báhin

1. Dúna ba sab muy humayán?
2. Aníhun na ba nínyu nang humáya?
3. Pilá pa ka búwan úsaq naq aníha?
4. Unsáqun man nínyu pagkahibalú nga hústu nang aníhun ang humáy?
5. Ngánung karún pa man ka mubálik?
6. Kanáng humayána, kínsa may tagqíya?
7. Díliq ba madáqut ang humáy kun mahúmul sa túbig?
8. Pilá man ka pursíntu ang mabáhin sa saqúp?
9. Kapilá man mu muqáni sa humáy sulúd sa usá ka túqig?

(a) Kay ákuq mang iqatúl ang ákung pagbálik sa pagqáni sa humáy.

(b) Gamáy ra. Kwarínta pursíntu ra.

(c) Aa, kanáq? Ang tagqíya ánaq, túqa sa Súgbu magpuyúq.

(d) Díliq pa kay waláq pa man naq sa tímpu.

(e) Dúna. Gústu ka bang mutánqaw?

(f) Madáqut kay kun mahúmul na ang humáy sa túbig, mubúrut man.

(g) Aa, díliq magsáma kay magnunút man gud naq sa panahún.

(h) Mga duhá pa ka búwan.

(i) Mupulá man nang ílang uháy kun hústu nang aníhun.

Commentary to Basic Sentences

10 a 3	ang kang Nuy Tibúq	The meaning 'belong to' is expressed by the dative form of names, titles, and pronouns; with common nouns, sa 'of' is placed first (see 2 E 1, above, p. 46). (Kang is the particle that makes names and titles dative.)
10 a 5	mangingísdaq	The root of mangingísdaq is ísdaq 'fish.'
10 a 6	tigúlang	For the meaning 'too [adjective] to [do this or that]' Cebuano uses 'very [adjective] to [do this or that]' e.g. here 'too old to fish' is tigúlang kaqáyu pára mangísdaq, i.e. 'very old to fish.'

10 a 7	unsingálan	This is a dialectal form of únsa 'what.'
10 a 8	búngsud	A kind of fence made by tying bamboo slats together, resembling a snow fence. Put in shallow water, it is placed in such a way that when the tide is in, the fish can get behind it, but when the tide is out, they cannot return to the other side and are trapped.
10 a 13	masúud	Short for mahasúud (= mahasulúd) 'happen to enter.'
10 a 17	nanginabúhiq	Formed from a base panginabúhiq 'earn a living' (kinabúhiq 'life' plus paN-).
10 a 19	nabúthan mag dinamíta	For this use of the local passive see 8 A 4, p. 307.
10 a 31	katulú, kaqupát	The prefix ka- (short for maka-) is used with numbers to mean '[that number of] times.'
10 b 5	áni	The general word for harvesting any crop (except corn) that is not picked.
10 b 7	mupulá	Note that pulá 'red' includes various shades of yellow and brown.
10 b 10	matúmba	Katúmba 'fall down' refers to something that was standing upright.
10 b 13	gipasápqan	The root is saqúp 'till the soil for someone else' (cf. 12 C 5).
10 b 19	kaduhá	See comment to sentence 10 a 31.

Grammatical Section

10 A. The instrumental passive

The following chart shows the form of the INSTRUMENTAL PASSIVE.

	Real	Unreal	Subjunctive
Nonpotential	gi-	i-	i-
Potential	{na- / gika-}	{ma- / ika-}	{ma- / ika-}

Maqú ra nay ákung ihátag nímu. (8 b 16) 'That is all I am giving you.'
Únsay íyang gihátag nímu? 'What did he give you?'
Ikahátag [or mahátag] ba ning mga butánga? 'Can these things be given away?'
Gikahátag [or nahátag] na níya ang tanáng gása. 'He has already given all the presents away.'

Not all verbs have an instrumental passive form. Of those that do, not all have it in every one of its meanings.

A sentence whose verb is in the instrumental passive form is an INSTRUMENTAL PASSIVE SENTENCE. Such sentences have two different types of meaning. In one type, the use of the instrumental passive verb form implies one of the following relationships of the subject to the verb predicate:

INSTRUMENTALITY. The subject is the instrument used to perform the action of the verb.

CONVEYANCE. The subject is directly acted upon in the course of being conveyed or transferred from its point of origin to its goal.

BENEFACTION. The subject is the person for whose benefit the action is performed.

In the second type of meaning (TEMPORAL), the instrumental verb form means 'It is time to [do the action of the verb].'

10 A 1. Instrumental passive sentences expressing instrumentality

The following sentences are examples of instrumental sentences with the subject as the instrument used to perform the action of the verb. (The subjects are underlined once, the predicates twice.)

Ipalít ku kiníng kwártag kalamáy. 'I will buy kalamay with this money.'
Kiníng ákung tiqíl díliq na ikalakáwg layúq. 'These feet of mine can't walk far (lit. can't be used to walk far) any longer.'
Hústu ba ning ákung kwárta iplíti ngádtu sa Urmuk? 'Is this money of mine enough to pay the fare to Ormoc?'

If the instrumental passive verb is the subject of the sentence, the predicate may be the instrument used to perform the action of the verb:

Maqú kiníy ákung ipalít ug kalamáy. 'This is what I will buy kalamay with.'

If the instrumental passive verb modifies a noun, the noun may be the instrument used to perform the action of the verb. (The noun and the verb which modifies it are underlined):

Waláq akúy kwártang iplíti ngádtu sa Úrmuk. 'I have no money to pay the fare to Ormoc.'

10 A 2. Instrumental passive sentence expressing conveyance

To express conveyance, the instrumental passive form occurs with verbs meaning 'give, pay, put, throw, sell,' and the like—that is, verbs having direct objects that are conveyed from one point to another. (This construction usually occurs with verbs that have no direct passive forms, though not always: see below, 12 C 4, 14 F.) The subject is the thing acted upon directly, or conveyed.

Ibutáng ang kwárta sa lamísa. 'Put the money on the table.' (More literally, 'The money is to be put on the table.')
Ilábay nang papíl. 'Throw that paper away.' ('That paper is to be thrown away.')
Ug ámung ibalígyaq ang kalamáy arún kamí makakaqún. (8 c 10) 'And we sell the kalamay in order to eat.'

If the instrumental passive verb is the subject, the predicate may be the thing acted upon directly or conveyed:

Maqú ra nay ákung ihátag kanímu. (8 b 16) 'That is all I am giving you.'
Dung, únsa man ang ímung gibalígyaq? (cf. 8 b 18) 'Boy, what are you selling?'

If the instrumental passive verb modifies a noun, the noun may be the thing acted upon directly or conveyed (the noun and modifying verb are underlined):

> Maqú ba kiní ang papíl nga ímung ilábay? 'Is this the paper that you are going to throw away?'

This meaning is also common with verbs meaning 'say,' 'tell,' and the like (see also 14 F 4 below). The subject (to a verb predicate) or the predicate (to a verb subject) is 'the thing said or told':

> Únsa may giqingún dihás tikít? (8 b 12) 'What is said on the ticket?'
> Únsa kaháy ákung itubág kaníya? 'What shall I answer him?'

Verbs having the prefix pa- also use the instrumental passive in this meaning (see also 12 C 4 below):

> Gústu nákung ipaqilaqíla ang ákung asáwa nímu. (cf. 2 b 14) 'I would like to introduce my wife to you.'

10 A 3. The instrumental passive to express benefaction

In this usage of the instrumental passive form, nearly all verbs are used in the imperative, while very few are used in forms other than the imperative. (This is a polite imperative, and we translate it with 'please.') The subject is the person for whose benefit the action of the verb is performed. (The instrumental forms in the examples below are underlined twice, the subjects once.)

> Day, ikúhaq ra kug bir. 'Day, please bring me some beer.' (More literally, 'I am to be brought beer for.')
> Ilútuq ra siyá áring ságing. 'Please cook these bananas for him.' (Lit. 'He is to have these bananas cooked for him.')
> Itawág ra akúg táksi. 'Please call a taxi for me.'

10 A 4. Instrumental passive in the temporal meaning

In the temporal meaning, the instrumental passive means 'time to [do the action],' and occurs with almost all verbs.

> Díliq pa run hústung ibáyad sa plíti. 'It (lit. Now) is not time to pay the fare yet.'
> Alás syíti tingáli ang igíkan sa bárku. 'The boat probably leaves at seven o'clock.'

The instrumental passive in the temporal meaning is used only in the unreal.

PP-P, PP-R, and PP-AA. See also the pattern practices listed at the end of 10 C. Exercises X.I A; XII.I A 3; also the exercises listed at the end of 10 C.

10 B. Comparison between the local and instrumental passives for verbs with a meaning of conveyance

In conveyance constructions, where an object is conveyed or transferred and the verb means 'give, throw, sell, pay, say,' or the like, either an instrumental passive or a local passive form is used, as follows: The instrumental passive is used when the subject is the thing conveyed (pay the MONEY to the driver; sell the BOOK to him; etc.). The local passive is used when the subject is the origin or the destination (person or place) of the thing conveyed (pay the DRIVER the money; sell HIM the book; etc.).

In each of the following pairs of examples demonstrating this contrast, the instrumental passive sentence is given first and the local passive sentence second. The subjects are underlined once and the passive verb forms twice.

1. (a) Ibalígyaq ku ning mga kinhasún kang Dyuu. 'I will sell these sea shells to Joe.'
   (b) Baligyáqan kug kinhasún si Dyuu. 'I will sell Joe some sea shells.
2. (a) Waláq ku pa man iqúliq ang kwárta kaníya. 'But I still haven't returned the money to him.'
   (b) Waláq ku pa man siya ulíqig kwárta. 'I still haven't given him any money.'
3. (a) Gibáyad ku ang ákung sinsíyu sa dráybir. 'I paid my change to the driver.'
   (b) Gibáyran ku ang dráybir sa ákung sinsíyu. 'I paid the driver my change.'
   (c) Gibáyran ku ang ákung útang. 'I paid my debt off.'
4. (a) Ihátag ku ning líbru kangÚsting. 'I will give this book to Osting.'
   (b) Hatágan kug líbru si Ústing. 'I will give Osting a book.'
5. (a) Gisúlti na ba nímu níya ang báhin sa abangán? 'Have you already told him about the rental?'
   (b) Gisultíhan na ba nímu siyá báhin sa abangán? 'Have you already told him about the rental?'
6. (a) Ilábay ku ning paan sa irúq. 'I will throw this piece of bread to the dog.'
   (b) Labáyan kug paan ang irúq. 'I will throw a piece of bread to the dog.'
7. (a) Ihatúd ku ning súdqan sa ka Pípi. 'I will deliver this food to Pepe's.
   (b) Hátdan kug súdqan si Pípi. 'I will deliver Pepe some food.'
8. (a) Gibílin níya ang bag kang Pírla. 'She left the bag with Perla.'
   (b) Gibínlan níyag bag si Pírla. 'She left Perla a bag.'
9. (a) Isáqad ku níya ang lamíng pagkáqun kun mubisíta siyá nákuq. 'I promise the delicious food to her if she visits me.'
   (b) Saqáran ku siyág lamíng pagkáqun kung mubisíta siyá nákuq. 'I will promise her delicious food if she visits me.'
10. (a) Isúkliq ku ning báynti ni Pídru. 'I will give this twenty-centavo piece as change to Pedro.'
    (b) Suklíqan kug báynti si Pídru. 'I will give Pedro a twenty-centavo piece as change.'
    (c) Suklíqan ku ning báynti ni Pídru. 'I will change this twenty-peso bill of Pedro's.'
11. (a) Nahátag na níya ang plítis dráybir. 'He has already given the fare to the driver.'
    (b) Nahatágan na níyag plíti ang dráybir. 'He has already given the driver his fare.'
12. (a) Gitínda sa tindíra ang mga kaság sa Karbún. 'The vendor sold the crabs at Carbon.'

(b) Gitindáhan sa tindíra ang Karbún ug kaság. 'The vendor sold crabs in Carbon.'

13. (a) Gibutáng níya ang túbig sa básu. 'He put the water in the glass.'
(b) Gibutangán níyag túbig ang básu. 'He put water into the glass.'

(For further examples of instrumental passives of verbs meaning 'say,' see 14 F 4 below.)

10 C. Verbs meaning both 'put' and 'go'

The following verbs (among others to be learned later) mean 'go up,' 'go back,' 'go down,' or 'go in' in the direct and local passives and 'put up,' 'put back,' 'put down,' or 'put in' in the local and instrumental passives: saká 'go or put up (etc.),' bálik 'go or put back (etc.),' kanáqug 'go or put down (etc.),' sulúd 'go or put in (etc.).' In the direct passive they mean either (1) 'place gone up (etc.) to' or (2) 'thing which one has gone up, back (etc.) to get.' (Cf. the discussions in Lesson 16, Part 2.) In the local passive they mean either (1) place gone up (etc.) on, place gone up (etc.) over' or (2) 'place where something is put up (etc.),' 'person for whom something is put up (etc.).' In the instrumental passive these verbs mean 'thing put up (etc.).' In the following sets of examples demonstrating this contrast, the direct passive sentence is given first, the local passive sentence next, and the instrumental passive sentence last:

saká

1 (a) Sákqun ku ang ságing. 'I will climb the banana tree.' (Lit. 'I will go up to the [top of] the banana tree.')
(b) Ngánung sákqan nínyu kanáng hágdan nga gabúk man naq? 'Why are you all climbing that ladder (lit. 'Why is that ladder being climbed on by you), when it is rotten?'
(c) Ngánung siyá may ímung gisákqag túbig pagqúna nga akú man úntay únang nipalít? 'Why was he delivered water first (lit. taken water up for), when I was the first one to buy?'
(d) Isaká na lang ang sílya sa táqas kay gabíqi na. 'Bring the chairs upstairs because it's getting late.'

bálik

2 (a) Balíkun ku ang líbrung ákung nalímtan sa íla. 'I will go back for the book I left (lit. forgot) at their place.' (Lit. The book . . . will be gone back for by me.')
(b) Ayáw patúnqug diháq. Balíkan nyaq ka sa ímung hilánat. 'Don't expose yourself to the draft. Your fever might return.' (Lit. 'You might be the place your fever returns to.')
(c) Ibálik ku ang líbru kanímu. 'I will return the book to you.'

kanáqug

3 (a) Kanaqúgun pa nákuq tung grípu kay waq ku kasírhi. 'I still should go downstairs to that faucet, because I haven't turned it off.' (Cf. example C.)
(b) Kanaqúgi ra gud akúg tulú ka buqúk sílya dirí. 'Please bring three chairs to me down here.' (Lit. 'I am to be brought down for, three chairs.')
(c) Mu nang dapíta ang gikanaqúgan sa babáyi. 'That's the place where the woman got off.'

(d) Ikanáqug ra ang putús ku, Dung. 'Please take my package off, Boy.'

sulúd

4 (a) Súdlun níya ang lángub. 'He will enter the cave.' (Lit. 'The cave is to be gone into by him.')
(b) Súdlan níya ang básug túbig. 'He will put water into the glass.' (Lit. 'The glass is the place water is to be put into by him.')
(c) Isulúd ang túbig sa básu. 'Put the water into the glass.'

With verbs meaning 'ride,' there is no direct passive; the local passive means 'thing ridden.'

sakáy

5 (a) Nahitabúq nga ang dyip ámung nasákyan mu say gisákyan ni Gámbi. 'It so happened that the jeep we were riding on was also the one Gambe was riding on.'
(b) Isakáy ku gyud siyá sa primírung biyáhi sa Nága. 'I'll put him on the very first bus to Naga.'

(This subject is discussed again in Lesson 14.)

PP-V, PP-W, PP-X. Exercise X.I A, I B; XII.I B; XIII.I B; XIV.I A.

Pattern Practices and Exercises

PP-R Local vs. instrumental (no transformation) (10 A)

Step I. (Instrumental in the direct meaning [conveyance])

'I'll put the boy on the truck.'

Ákung isakáy ang bátaq sa traak.	(sulúd)
Ákung isulúd ang bátaq sa traak.	(kanáqug)
Ákung ikanáqug ang bátaq sa traak.	(ang dúlsi)
Ákung ikanáqug ang dúlsi sa traak.	(butáng)
Ákung ibutáng ang dúlsi sa traak.	(lábay)
Ákung ilábay ang dúlsi sa traak.	(tínda)
Ákung itínda ang dúlsi sa traak.	(balígyaq)
Ákung ibalígyaq ang dúlsi sa traak.	(sa bátaq)
Ákung ibalígyaq ang dúlsi sa bátaq.	(hátag)
Ákung ihátag ang dúlsi sa bátaq.	(hatúd)
Ákung ihatúd ang dúlsi sa bátaq.	(bálik)
Ákung ibálik ang dúlsi sa bátaq.	(ang báynti)
Ákung ibálik ang báynti sa bátaq.	(súkliq)
Ákung isúkliq ang báynti sa bátaq.	(punúq)

Ákung ipunúq ang báynti sa bátaq. (báyad)

Ákung ibáyad ang báynti sa bátaq. (kiní)

Ákung ibáyad kiní sa bátaq. (táwu)

Ákung ibáyad kiní sa táwu. (súlti)

Ákung isúlti kiní sa táwu. (sulát)

Ákung isulát kiní sa táwu. (tubág)

Ákung itubág kiní sa táwu.

Step II. (Instrumental vs. the direct vs. the local)

'I'll tell Pedro the truth.'

Sultíhan ku si Pídru sa tinúqud. (ang tinúqud)

Isúlti ku ang tinúqud. (tubág)

Itubág ku ang tinúqud. (si Pídru)

Tubagún ku si Pídru. (suwát)

Suwatán ku si Pídru. (ang tinúqud)

Isuwát ku ang tinúqud. (si Tátay)

Suwatán ku si Tátay. (hátag)

Tagáqan ku si Tátay. (ang gása)

Ihátag ku ang gása. (bálik)

Ibálik ku ang gása. (si Tátay)

Balíkan ku si Tátay. (lábay)

Labáyan ku si Tátay. (ang ságing)

Ilábay ku ang ságing. (lútuq)

Lutúqun ku ang ságing. (hatúd)

Ihatúd ku ang ságing. (si Pápa)

Hátdan ku si Pápa. (ang traak)

Hátdan ku ang traak. (ang suwát)

Ihatúd ku ang suwát. (bása)

Basáhun ku ang suwát. (tubág)

Tubagún ku ang suwát. (ang tinúqud)

Itubág ku ang tinúqud. (súlti)

Isúlti ku ang tinúqud. (si Pápa)

Sultíhan ku si Pápa. (huwát)

Huwatún ku si Pápa. (pangutána)

Pangutánqun
Pangutánqan } ku si Pápa. (ang tinúqud)

Ipangutána ku ang tinúqud.	(hinúmdum)
Hinumdumán ku ang tinúqud.	(si Mánuy)
Hinumdumán ku si Mánuy.	(dalá)
Dádqun ku si Mánuy.	(báyad)
Báyran ku si Mánuy.	(ang kwárta)
Ibáyad ku ang kwárta.	(bálik)
Ibálik ku ang kwárta.	(bántay)
Bantayán ku ang kwárta.	(butáng)
Ibutáng ku ang kwárta.	(dalá)
Dádqun ku ang kwárta.	(hátag)
Ihátag ku ang kwárta.	(pangítaq)
Pangitáqun ku ang kwárta.	(kalímut)
Kalímtan ku ang kwárta.	(traak)
Kalímtan ku ang traak.	(tánqaw)
Tanqáwun ku ang traak.	(hinúmdum)
Hinumdumán ku ang traak.	(huwát)
Huwatún ku ang traak.	(sakáy)
Sákyan ku ang traak.	(bátaq)
Isakáy ku ang bátaq.	(imbitár)
Imbitahún ku ang bátaq.	(saká)
Isaká ku ang bátaq.	(ang baay)
Sákqun ku ang baay.	(ukupár)
Ukupahán ku ang baay.	(pangítaq)
Pangitáqun ku ang baay.	(hinúmdum)
Hinumdumán ku ang baay.	(si Pápa)
Hinumdumán ku si Pápa.	(hátag)
Hatágan ku si Pápa.	(ang gása)
Ihátag ku ang gása.	(báyad)
Báyran ku ang gása.	(lábay)
Ilábay ku ang gása.	(huwát)
Huwatún ku ang gása.	(kanáqug)
Ikanáqug ku ang gása.	(bántay)
Bantayán ku ang gása.	

Step III. (Instrumental vs. local vs. direct)

'I gave (it to) Daddy.'

Gitagáqan ku si Pápa.	(will write to)
Suwatán ku si Pápa.	(ang tinúqud)
Isuwát ku ang tinúqud.	(I wrote)
Gisuwát ku ang tinúqud.	(will tell the truth)
Isúlti ku ang tinúqud.	(I told)
Gisúlti ku ang tinúqud.	(will answer)
Itubág ku ang tinúqud.	(ang pangutána)
Tubagún ku ang pangutána.	(answered)
Gitubág ku ang pangutána.	(tinúqud)
Gitubág ku ang tinúqud.	(will ask)
Ipangutána ku ang tinúqud.	(will remember)
Hinumdumán ku ang tinúqud.	(am waiting for)
Gihuwát ku ang tinúqud.	(si Mánuy)
Gihuwát ku si Mánuy.	(will buy for)
Palitán ku si Mánuy.	(ang kwárta)
Ipalít ku ang kwárta.	(bought with)
Gipalít ku ang kwárta.	(will return)
Ibálik ku ang kwárta.	(si Lítu)
Balíkan ku si Lítu.	(will wait for)
Huwatún ku si Lítu.	

Step IV. (Instrumental vs. local vs. direct)

'I will look for Ósting.'

Pangitáqun ku si Ústing.	(ang tihíras)
Pangitáqun ku ang tihíras.	(balígyaq)
Ibalígyaq ku ang tihíras.	(risírba)
Irisírba ku ang tihíras.	(ang kwárta)
Irisírba ku ang kwárta.	(palít ug gása)
Ipalít kug gása ang kwárta.	(si Pápa)
Palitán kug gása si Pápa.	(búhat ug húngut)
Buhátan kug húngut si Pápa.	(balígyaq ug kalamáy)
Baligyáqan kug kalamáy si Pápa.	(ang kalamáy)
Ibalígyaq ku ang kalamáy.	(lábay)
Ilábay ku ang kalamáy.	(kúhaq)

Kuháqun ku ang kalamáy.	(si Mánuy)
Kuháqun ku si Mánuy.	(suwát)
Suwatán ku si Mánuy.	(ang lápis)
Isuwát ku ang lápis.	(palít)
Palitún ku ang lápis.	(bálik)
Ibálik ku ang lápis.	(ang papíl)
Ibálik ku ang papíl.	(sulát)
Sulatán ku ang papíl.	(putús)
Iputús ku ang papíl.	(kalamáy)
Pústun ku ang kalamáy.	

Step V. (Instrumental vs. local vs. direct)

'I'll use the pencil to write.'

Isulát ku ang lápis.	(paper)
Sulatán ku ang papíl.	(will watch: bántay)
Bantayán ku ang papíl.	(will throw away)
Ilábay ku ang papíl.	(will buy)
Palitún ku ang papíl.	(bought)
Gipalít ku ang papíl.	(ang bag)
Gipalít ku ang bag.	(will bring)
Dádqun ku ang bag.	(I gave away)
Gihátag ku ang bag.	(I will give away)
Ihátag ku ang bag.	(will remember)
Hinumdumán ku ang bag.	(ang bátaq)
Hinumdumán ku ang bátaq.	(waited for)
Gihuwát ku ang bátaq.	(will ask)
Pangutánqun ku ang bátaq.	

Step VI. (Instrumental with various agents)

'I will write with the pencil.'

Isulát ku ang lápis.	(you)
Isulát nímu ang lápis.	(he)
Isulát níya ang lápis.	(Miss Wilby)
Isulát ni Mis Wílbi ang lápis.	(hátag)
Ihátag ni Mis Wílbi ang lápis.	(I)
Ihátag ku ang lápis.	(ságing)

Ihátag ku ang ságing.	(them)
Ihátag níla ang ságing.	(ni Pírla)
Ihátag ni Pírla ang ságing.	(lábay)
Ilábay ni Pírla ang ságing.	(we)
Ilábay námuq ang ságing.	

Step VII. (Instrumental and local with various subjects and preposed agents)

'I will give the pencil away.'

Ákung ihátag ang lápis.	(that)
Ákuq kanáng ihátag.	(ságing)
Ákung ihátag ang ságing.	(this here)
Ákuq ring ihátag.	(ang líbru)
Ákung ihátag ang líbru.	(that there)
Ákuq tung ihátag.	(tagáqan)
Ákuq tung tagáqan.	(siyá)
Ákuq siyáng tagáqan.	(si Pírla)
Ákung tagáqan si Pírla.	(silá)
Ákuq siláng tagáqan.	

Step VIII. (Exercise in a variety of subjects and agents)

'I will give the book to Perla.'

Ihátag ku ang líbru kang Pírla.	(she–the boy)
Ihátag níya ang líbru sa bátaq.	(them–driver)
Ihátag níla ang líbru sa dráybir.	(Mr. Abáya–the old man)
Ihátag ni Místir Abáya ang líbru sa tigúlang.	(Lína–the doctor)
Ihátag ni Lína ang líbru sa dúktur.	(I–Pírla)
Ihátag ku ang líbru kang Pírla.	(them–Lína)
Ihátag níla ang líbru kang Lína.	(Tátay–Lítu)
Ihátag ni Tátay ang líbru kang Lítu.	(Místir Mílir–Mísis Abáya)
Ihátag ni Místir Mílir ang líbru kang Mísis Abáya.	(Lítu–Lína)
Ihátag ni Lítu ang líbru kang Lína.	(Máma–Mánuy)
Ihátag ni Máma ang líbru kang Mánuy.	(lady–old man)
Ihátag sa babáyi ang líbru sa tigúlang.	

Step IX. (Exercise in a variety of subjects and agents, including preposed forms of the agent.)

'I will throw the can away.'

Ákuq na lang ilábay ang láta.	(you–the book)
Ímu na lang ilábay ang líbru.	(he–the candy)
Íya na lang ilábay ang dúlsi.	(they–the paper)
Íla na lang ilábay ang papíl.	(I–kalamáy)
Ákuq na lang ilábay ang kalamáy.	(I–kaság)
Ákuq na lang ilábay ang kaság.	(she–that)
Íya na lang nang ilábay.	(she–the book)
Íya na lang ilábay ang líbru.	(she–this)
Íya na lang ning ilábay.	(she–the can)
Íya na lang ilábay ang láta.	(he–básu)
Íya na lang ilábay ang básu.	(Pírla–bag)
Ilábay na lang ni Pírla ang bag.	(Lítu–kutsílyu)
Ilábay na lang ni Lítu ang kutsílyu.	(Lítu–this)
Ilábay na lang kiní ni Lítu.	(basúra)
Ilábay na lang ni Lítu ang basúra.	(that)
Ilábay na lang kanáq ni Lítu.	

IA. Ibutáng ang hústung púrma sa bírbu nga anáqa sa parentheses ginámit ang real, unreal, u subjunctive sa instrumental. (10 A)

1. Maqú ba ning líbrung íyang (hatúd) gabíqi? 'Is this the book he delivered last night?'
2. (Sakáy) ku na lang ning mga gása sa traak. 'I will just put these gifts on the bus.'
3. (Sulúd) na ba nímu ang tuqálya sa bag? 'Have you put the towel in the bag yet?'
4. Isáq pa kay dúna kuy (hatúd) sa ka Mísis Milíndris. 'Excuse me (because) I still have something to deliver to Mrs. Melendres.'
5. (Báyad)ku ning kwartáha sa sabún ug káwuq. 'I'll pay this money for the soap and the hat.'
6. Ákuq lang (palít) ug líbru kiníng kwárta ug diq ka muqabút, ha? 'I'll just use this money to buy a book with if you don't get there, may I?'
7. (Súklíq) na hinúqun nákuq ang sinsílyu dirí. 'I have already used up my loose change.' (Lit. 'I have already given out my change here as loose change.')

8. (Balígyaq) ta ba ning kaság Plur? 'Shall we sell these crabs, Flor?'

9. Waq nay (lútuq) ng mantíkaq. 'There's no more lard to cook with.'

10. (Balígyaq) lang ning kalamáy ug tagdyis arún mahálin dáyun. 'Just sell this kalamáy at ten centavos apiece so that it can be sold out immediately.' (mahálin 'can be sold out')

11. Ámbi nang lápis kay ákung (súwat). 'Give me that pencil because I want to write with it.'

12. Waq níya (kanáqug) ang íyang mga dalá. 'He did not take his things off (the vehicle).'

13. Háqin na man tung (butáng) nákuq dínhi sa lamísa? 'Where are those things I put here on the table?'

14. Dúna ka bay (pangutána) nákuq unyáq? 'Will you have something to ask me later?'

15. Waq gyud naq nákuq (sáqad) níya. 'I certainly did not promise him that.'

16. (Ubán) ku si Plúra sa Pulambatú inigqádtu nákuq. 'I will let Flora go to Pulambato with me when I go there.'

17. (Sulúd) na ba nímu ang súkliq sa bag? 'Have you already put the change in the bag?'

18. Kiníng kutsílyu ang (putúl), díliq nang martílyu. 'Use this knife for cutting, not that hammer.' (martílyu 'hammer')

19. Maqú ba ning tubíga ang ímung (kalíguq)? 'Is this the water you are going to bathe with?'

20. Ang íyang mga anák (tábang) na sa mga buluhatún kay dágkuq na man.

21. Maqú ba ning librúha ang (hatúd) níya gabíqi?

22. Waláq pa níya (saká) ang túbig nga íyang gikáwus.

23. (Hátag) na hinúqun nákuq ang mga gása nga (dalá) ku.

24. Átuq na bang (balígyaq) kiníng ísdaq karún?

25. Díqay ákung kwárta apán (ábang) ku man ni sa baláy.

26. (Huwát) ta ba kag traak sa istasyunán?

27. Waq ku níya (hángyuq) sa ákung nánay nga díliq pa ku muqulíq sa San Rimihiyú.

28. Waláq (likúq) sa dráybir ang dyip sa iskína.

29. Dúna ba kuy (tábang) nímu Plurá?

30. Ngánung waq man mi nímu (tawág) ug sakyanán?

IB. (Local vs. Instrumental vs. Direct) Ibutáng ang hústung púrma sa bírbu nga anáqa sa parentheses ginámit ang local, instrumental, ug direct passives. (6 A 1, 8 A, 10 A and subsections)

1. (Káqun) ku ganíha ang paan nga dalá níla. 'I ate the bread they brought a while ago.'

2. (Káqun) níyag gamáy ang ísdaq nga gidalá sa bisíta. 'He ate a little bit of the fish the visitor brought.'

3. Kanáng platúha waq námuq (káqun). 'We did not eat from that plate.'

4. Isáq pa kay (tawág) ku pa si Nánay. 'Excuse me, (for) I still have to call Mother.'

5. Ngánung níqa ka man nga waláq ka man nákuq (tawág)? 'Why are you here when I did not call you?'

6. Waláq nákuq (sáqad) níya nga muqádtu ku sa íla. 'I didn't promise him that I would go to their place.'

7. (Sáqad) ba sab ka ni Mísis Ulibár nga paqadtúqun sa Pulambatú? 'Did Mrs. Olivar also promise to have you come to Pulambato?'

8. Únsay (dalá) nímu Plurá pagqádtu nímu sa ka Mísis Ulibár? 'What did you bring, Flora, when you went to Mrs. Olivar's?'

9. (Dalá) mu nákug kaság. Búhiq pa kiní. 'I've brought you some crabs. They're still alive.'

10. (Balígyaq) ku níla ang mga dalá kung kaság. 'I sold them the crabs that I brought.'

11. Kínsay ímung (balígyaq) niqádtung líbru? 'Who did you sell that book to?'

12. Waláq lang námuq (pangítaq) ang baláy níla. 'We didn't bother looking for their house.'

13. Ngánung kamí man únyaq ang (pangítaq) nínyu sa súkliq? 'Why should you ask us for the change?'

14. (Pangítaq) ta lang kag baláy dínhi sa Pulambatú. 'I'll just look for a house for you here in Pulambato.'

15. Kiníng kwárta nímu maqúy (báyad) ku sa ákung plíti. 'I'm going to pay my fare with this money of yours.'

16. Singkwínta ray ákung (báyad) pára sa kaság. 'Fifty centavos is all I'm going to pay for the crabs.'

17. (Báyad) na ba nímu ang dráybir sa traak? 'Have you paid the bus driver yet?'

18. (Sulúd) ku únyaq dínhaq sa kahún ang dalá kung sabún. 'Later on I'll put the soap I brought there in that box.'

19. Waláq na kuy kwárta. (Ábang) ku na sa baláy. 'I have no more money. I've used it all up for the house rent.'

20. (Ábang) únyaq naq námung baláya inigkahumán ánaq.

21. Waq man ni námuq (ábang). Gipapuyúq man lang mi. 'We don't rent this [house]. We were just given permission to stay here.'

22. (Pangutána) ta únyaq ka kun ngánung waláq dínhi si Tátay mu.

23. Kanáng baláya ang ámung (pangutána) gahápun kun níqa ba tinúqud si Mísis Milíndris.

24. Kínsa man tung (bisíta) mu sa úna?

25. Waq na gyud ku (bisíta) níla.
26. Ánhi lang dínhi nákuq (butáng) kiníng mga dalá kung gása.
27. Únsa may (butáng) nátuq íring kaság Dung?
28. Ngánung waq pa man nímu naq (butáng) sa lamísa?
29. Kiríng lápis lang ang (suwát) nákuq.
30. Kínsa may (suwát) nímu diháq nga waq pa man ka mahumán?

PP-P Use of agent and subject (6 D) (Direct, local, and instrumental passive)

Step I. (Changing the agent)

'I bought the man's kalamay.'

Gipalít ku ang kalamáy sa táwu.	(námuq)
Gipalít námuq ang kalamáy sa táwu.	(nímu)
Gipalít nímu ang kalamáy sa táwu.	(níya)
Gipalít níya ang kalamáy sa táwu.	(nákuq)
Gipalít nákuq ang kalamáy sa táwu.	(nátuq)
Gipalít nátuq ang kalamáy sa táwu.	(níla)
Gipalít níla ang kalamáy sa táwu.	(nímu)
Gipalít nímu ang kalamáy sa táwu.	(ku)
Gipalít ku ang kalamáy sa táwu.	(námuq)
Gipalít námuq ang kalamáy sa táwu.	(nátuq)
Gipalít nátuq ang kalamáy sa táwu.	

Step II. (Changing the agent)

'I won't buy her kalamay.'

Díliq siyá nákuq ipalít ug kalamáy.	(nátuq)
Díliq siyá nátuq ipalít ug kalamáy.	(námuq)
Díliq siyá námuq ipalít ug kalamáy.	(nímu)
Díliq siyá nímu ipalít ug kalamáy.	(níla)
Díliq siyá níla ipalít ug kalamáy.	

Step III. (Changing the agent)

'I didn't take her home.'

Waláq siyá nákuq ihatúd sa baláy.	(nínyu)
Waláq siyá nínyu ihatúd sa baláy.	(námuq)

Waláq siyá námuq ihatúd sa baláy.	(nátuq)
Waláq siyá nátuq ihatúd sa baláy.	(nímu)
Waláq siyá nímu ihatúd sa baláy.	(níla)
Waláq siyá níla ihatúd sa baláy.	(nínyu)
Waláq siyá nínyu ihatúd sa baláy.	(níya)
Waláq siyá níya ihatúd sa baláy.	(nímu)
Waláq siyá nímu ihatúd sa baláy.	

Step IV. (Changing the subjects)

'They will buy some kalamay for her.'

Ipalít siyá nílag kalamáy.	(mi)
Ipalít mi nílag kalamáy.	(ni)
Ipalít ni nílag kalamáy.	(mu)
Ipalít mu nílag kalamáy.	(naq)
Ipalít naq nílag kalamáy.	(silá)
Ipalít silá nílag kalamáy.	(kanáq)
Ipalít kanáq nílag kalamáy.	(ta)
Ipalít ta nílag kalamáy.	(ri)
Ipalít ri nílag kalamáy.	(akú)
Ipalít akú nílag kalamáy.	

Step V. (Changing the verb)

'I'll just throw the crabs away.'

Ilábay ku na lang ang kaság.	(ibutáng)
Ibutáng ku na lang ang kaság.	(ihátag)
Ihátag ku na lang ang kaság.	(ibutáng)
Ibutáng ku na lang ang kaság.	(irisírba)
Irisírba ku na lang ang kaság.	(gibalígyaq)
Gibalígyaq ku na lang ang kaság.	

Step VI. (Changing agent and verb)

'You gave my bag away.'

Anáaq gihátag man nímu ang ákung bag.	(kúptan)
Anáaq kúptan man nímu ang ákung bag.	(níya)
Anáaq kúptan man níya ang ákung bag.	(gibalígyaq)
Anáaq gibalígyaq man níya ang ákung bag.	(ang patáyng kaság)
Anáaq gibalígyaq man níya ang patáyng kaság.	(gidalá)

Anáaq gidalá man níya ang patáyng kaság.

Step VII. (Changing agent with short and long forms of pronouns)

'I'll get some bread for her.'

Ikúhaq ku siyág paan.	(nímu)
Ikúhaq siya nímug paan.	(ta)
Ikúhaq ta siyág paan.	(níla)
Ikúhaq siyá nílag paan.	(mu)
Ikúhaq mu siyág paan.	(nínyu)
Ikúhaq siyá nínyug paan.	(námuq)
Ikúhaq siyá námug paan.	(níya)
Ikúhaq siyá níyag paan.	

Step VIII. (Replacing pronoun agents and subjects by noun agents and subjects)

'I didn't sell the earrings.'

Waláq ku ibalígyaq ang aríyus.	(kanáq)
Waláq ku kanáq ibalígyaq.	(námuq)
Waláq námuq kanáq ibalígyaq.	(níla)
Waláq níla kanáq ibalígyaq.	(ang kwíntas)
Waláq níla ibalígyaq ang kwíntas.	(níya)
Waláq níya ibalígyaq ang kwíntas.	(nínyu)
Waláq nínyu ibalígyaq ang kwíntas.	(ni Lína)
Waláq ibalígyaq ni Lína ang kwíntas.	(kiní)
Waláq kiní ibalígyaq ni Lína.	(ku)
Waláq ku kiní ibalígyaq.	(níya)
Waláq níya kiní ibalígyaq.	(níla)
Waláq níla kiní ibalígyaq.	(ang lamísa)
Waláq níla ibalígyaq ang lamísa.	(ku)
Waláq ku ibalígyaq ang lamísa.	(níya)
Waláq níya ibalígyaq ang lamísa.	(ni Piríng)
Waláq ibalígyaq ni Piríng ang lamísa.	(ang bag)
Waláq ibalígyaq ni Piríng ang bag.	(nátuq)
Waláq nátuq ibalígyaq ang bag.	(níla)
Waláq níla ibalígyaq ang bag.	(ri)
Waláq ri níla ibalígyaq.	(ang líbru)
Waláq níla ibalígyaq ang líbru.	(ni)

Waláq ni níla ibalígyaq.	(ang dúlsi)
Waláq níla ibalígyaq ang dúlsi.	(naq)
Waláq naq níla ibalígyaq.	(ni Huwán)
Waláq naq ibalígyaq ni Huwán.	(níya)
Waláq naq níya ibalígyaq.	(ku)
Waláq ku naq ibalígyaq.	(ni Pírla)
Waláq naq ibalígyaq ni Pírla.	(mu)
Waláq mu naq ibalígyaq.	(ni Huwán)
Waláq naq ibalígyaq ni Huwán.	(ta)
Waláq ta naq ibalígyaq.	(ni Mánuy)
Waláq naq ibalígyaq ni Mánuy.	(ku)
Waláq ku naq ibalígyaq.	(ang líbru)
Waláq ku ibalígyaq ang líbru.	(ni Pírla)
Waláq ibalígyaq ang líbru ni Pírla.	(níya)
Waláq níya ibalígyaq ang líbru.	(naq)
Waláq naq níya ibalígyaq.	(ang gása)
Waláq níya ibalígyaq ang gása.	(ni Pírla)
Waláq ibalígyaq ang gása ni Pírla.	

Step IX. (Preposed genitive agents)

'I cut the banana tree with a knife.'

Ákung giputúl ang ságing sa kutsílyu.	(ímu)
Ímung giputúl ang ságing sa kutsílyu.	(ínyu)
Ínyung giputúl ang ságing sa kutsílyu.	(íla)
Ílang giputúl ang ságing sa kutsílyu.	(ámuq)
Ámung giputúl ang ságing sa kutsílyu.	(átuq)
Átung giputúl ang ságing sa kutsílyu.	(ákuq)
Ákung giputúl ang ságing sa kutsílyu.	(ámuq)
Ámung giputúl ang ságing sa kutsílyu.	(átuq)
Átung giputúl ang ságing sa kutsílyu.	

Step X. (Preposed genitive agents vs. other types of agents)

'Did we drink the milk in the glass?'

Átuq bang giqinúm ang gátas sa básu?	(nátuq)
Giqinúm ba nátuq ang gátas sa básu?	(ámuq)
Ámuq bang giqinúm ang gátas sa básu?	(námuq)

Giqinúm ba námuq ang gátas sa básu?	(íla)
Íla bang giqinúm ang gátas sa básu?	(níla)
Giqinúm ba níla ang gátas sa básu?	(ínyu)
Ínyu bang giqinúm ang gátas sa básu?	(nínyu)
Giqinúm ba nínyu ang gátas sa básu?	(ákuq)
Ákuq bang giqinúm ang gátas sa básu?	(nákuq)
Giqinúm ba nákuq ang gátas sa básu?	(íya)
Íya bang giqinúm ang gátas sa básu?	(níya)
Giqinúm ba níya ang gátas sa básu?	(ku)
Giqinúm ku ba ang gátas sa básu?	(ímu)
Ímu bang giqinúm ang gátas sa básu?	(mu)
Giqinúm mu ba ang gátas sa básu?	(nímu)
Giqinúm ba nímu ang gátas sa básu?	

Step XI. (Changing the subject)

'Because I'll throw the rock.'

Ákuq man gung ilábay ang bátu.	(naq)
Ákuq man gud nang ilábay.	(ang sinínaq)
Ákuq man gung ilábay ang sinínaq.	(ni)
Ákuq man gud ning ilábay.	(ang ísdaq)
Ákuq man gung ilábay ang ísdaq.	(ri)
Ákuq man gud ring ilábay.	(tu)
Ákuq man gud tung ilábay.	(karí)
Ákuq man gud karíng ilábay.	(ang pitáka)
Ákuq man gung ilábay ang pitáka.	(kaní)
Ákuq man gud kaníng ilábay.	(naq)
Ákuq man gud nang ilábay.	(ang lamísa)
Ákuq man gung ilábay ang lamísa.	(ni)
Ákuq man gud ning ilábay.	(tu)
Ákuq man gud tung ilábay.	

Step XII. (Changing agent, using all types)

'He will just sell the bag.'

Ibalígyaq na lang níya ang bag.	(ákuq)
Ákuq na lang ibalígyaq ang bag.	(námuq)
Ibalígyaq na lang námuq ang bag.	(ni Pírla)

Ibalígyaq na lang ang bag ni Pírla.	(níla)
Ibalígyaq na lang níla ang bag.	(ku)
Ibalígyaq ku na lang ang bag.	(íla)
Íla na lang ibalígyaq ang bag.	(níya)
Ibalígyaq na lang níya ang bag.	(átuq)
Átuq na lang ibalígyaq ang bag.	(ta)
Ibalígyaq ta na lang ang bag.	(ni Lína)
Ibalígyaq na lang ang bag ni Lína.	(ku)
Ibalígyaq ku na lang ang bag.	(ámuq)
Ámuq na lang ibalígyaq ang bag.	(námuq)
Ibalígyaq na lang námuq ang bag.	(íya)
Íya na lang ibalígyaq ang bag.	(ni Mis Wílbi)
Ibalígyaq na lang ang bag ni Mis Wílbi.	(nátuq)
Ibalígyaq na lang nátuq ang bag.	(ta)
Ibalígyaq ta na lang ang bag.	(sa babáyi)
Ibalígyaq na lang ang bag sa babáyi.	(níla)
Ibalígyaq na lang níla ang bag.	(ákuq)
Ákuq na lang ibalígyaq ang bag.	(mu)
Ibalígyaq mu na lang ang bag.	

Step XIII. (Changing agent and subject using all types)

'I'll just put the money on the table.'

Ákuq na lang ibutáng ang kwártas lamísa.	(íya)
Íya na lang ibutáng ang kwártas lamísa.	(námuq)
Ibutáng na lang námuq ang kwártas lamísa.	(ang pitáka)
Ibutáng na lang námuq ang pitákas lamísa.	(kanáq)
Ibutáng na lang námuq kanáq sa lamísa.	(ákuq)
Ákuq na lang kanáng ibutáng sa lamísa.	(ang prútas)
Ákuq na lang ibutáng ang prútas sa lamísa.	(námuq)
Ibutáng na lang námuq ang prútas sa lamísa.	(ri)
Ibutáng na lang námuq ris lamísa.	(ni Pírla)
Ibutáng na lang ri ni Pírlas lamísa.	(ang bag)
Ibutáng na lang ni Pírla ang bag sa lamísa.	(níya)
Ibutáng na lang níya ang bag sa lamísa.	(íya)
Íya na lang ibutáng ang bag sa lamísa.	(ku)
Ibutáng ku na lang ang bag sa lamísa.	(átuq)

Átuq na lang ibutáng ang bag sa lamísa.	(naq)
Átuq na lang nang ibutáng sa lamísa.	(ta)
Ibutáng ta na lang naq sa lamísa.	(ang líbru)
Ibutáng ta na lang ang líbrus lamísa.	(ni Lína)
Ibutáng na lang ni Lína ang líbrus lamísa.	(íya)
Íya na lang ibutáng ang líbrus lamísa.	(ámuq)
Ámuq na lang ibutáng ang líbrus lamísa.	(naq)
Ámuq na lang nang ibutáng sa lamísa.	(ni)
Ámuq na lang ning ibutáng sa lamísa.	(níya)
Ibutáng na lang ni níyas lamísa.	(naq)
Ibutáng na lang naq níyas lamísa.	(ni Maríng)
Ibutáng na lang naq ni Maríng sa lamísa.	(ri)
Ibutáng na lang ri ni Maríng sa lamísa.	(átuq)
Átuq na lang ring ibutáng sa lamísa.	(íla)
Íla na lang ring ibutáng sa lamísa.	(níla)
Ibutáng na lang ri nílas lamísa.	

II A 1. Ibúngat ang mga musunúd nga mga túdling púlung sa hústung paníngug. (342 Statement: early rise)

1. Kay díliq man sad maqáyu nga ímung dugáyun pagqáni. (10 b 8)
2. Kay níndut kaqáyung tanqáwun kun mangáni na sa humáy. (10 b 25)
3. Ang ákung mga ginikánan ug mga igsúqun nanginabúhiq sa pangísdaq. (10 a 17)
4. Ang ákuq bítawng bána mangingísdaq man sad. (10 a 18)
5. Sunúd simána manánggiq na mi sa maqís. (10 a 27)
6. Usáhay katulú. (10 a 31)

II A 2. (342 Statement: rise at end)

1. Túqas Banáwaq. (3 a 4)
2. Kay madáqut man ang humáy. (10 b 9)
3. Pangutánqa nang dyip. (3 a 32)

4. Tris písus ang par. (6 a 4)
5. Tutál, kahibáwu na man kung muqádtu. (9 a 18)
6. Lisúd gyud núqun. (9 c 23)
7. Arún usáb katámnan námuq dáyun. (10 a 28)

II B. (234 Statement)

1. Ádtu ta sa baybáyun magqúna. (10 a 1)
2. Maqáyu man. (1.8)
3. Ádtu na ta. (10 a 2)
4. Kumústa. (1.7)
5. Mga kawáyan naq pára sa búngsud. (10 a 8)
6. Ádtu hinúqun ta dídtu. (10 a 23)
7. Waq man kaqáyu mi maglisúd. (2 b 18)
8. Tanqáwun nátuq ang mga maqís. (10 a 24)
9. Díliq magsáma. (10 a 30)
10. Salámat na lang Duktúr. (2 b 29)
11. Gústu kung mutánqaw ánaq. (10 b 3)
12. Náqay márkang Banáwaq. (3 a 36)
13. Díliq pa. (10 b 6)
14. Sayún ra naq. (5.15)
15. Mga duhá pa ka búwan naq úsaq maqáni. (10 b 6)
16. Gamáy ra kaqáyung mga dápit dídtung dúnay ságing. (5.31)
17. Magnunút man gud naq sa panahún. (10 b 21)
18. Tagáqi lang kug únu singkwínta. (6 b 39)
19. Níqa na tas átung tihíras. (8 a 18)
20. Ayáw kabaláka nákuq Pirlá. (8 a 22)

II C. (423 Statement)

1. Maqú naq ang kang Nuy Tibúq. (10 a 3)
2. Usá naq sa paqági sa pangísdaq dínhi sa ámuq. (10 a 9)
3. Íla nang ilíbut sa usá ka párti sa dágat. (10 a 10)
4. Ug dúna say pultahán. (10 a 11)
5. Ákuq lang ibílin ning ákung amígu dínhi. (1.16)

6. Butangán nílag pultahán. (10 a 12)
7. Díliq mahímung muguwáq. (10 a 15)
8. Dúna sad miy dyútayng lunáq sa yútaq sa San Rimihiyú. (10 a 20)
9. Maw ni siyá ang nangítag kwártu. (3 b 13)
10. Maqú kiní ang ámung kamaqisán. (10 a 25)
11. Ánhi ta dínhi maghuwát ug dyip. (3 c 22)
12. Dúna usáb dínhiy humayán. (10 b 1)
13. Ádtu naq sa Mabúlu. (6 b 51)
14. Maqú na nay hústung tímpu sa pagqáni sa humáy. (10 b 7)
15. Maqáyu tingáling ádtu na lang ku. (8 a 32)
16. Tigúlang na sad kaqáyu siyá pára mangísdaq. (10 a 6)
17. Naputúl ang íyang usá ka kamút kay nabúthan mag dinamíta. (10 a 19)
18. Maqú diqáy ning Úrmuk. (8 c 29)
19. Ug dúna say tagaláqing lugár nga mangánhi arún lang sa pagtábang sa panánggiq. (10 a 33)
20. Níqa na man diqáy tas Kármin. (9 b 12)

III. Pagbása

Sulúd Sa Siní (Movie)

Ártur: Taná, ádtu na tas siní. Nahatágan ka bag ibáyad? 'Have you been given money to pay with?'

Túni: Díqa, apán waq ra ba nákuq kasultíhi si Mámang mutánqaw kug siní. Únsa may itubág nákuq nyaq? 'What should I answer later on?'

Ártur: Sayún ra naq. Sa? ('How about it?') Sigí, kay díqay prádang gahuwát. Maqúy átung sákyan. (práda 'rig')

Túni: Taa, sakáy na ta. Pilá may ibáyads práda? Gahuwát man kaháq ni nátuq.

Ártur: Báyrig dúbli. Hústu ra naq, kay dakúq ra ug písus ihátag. 'Pay him double. That's enough, because one peso is too much.'

Túni: Pangutánqa ang kutsíru ug únsay náqa run sa Liin.

(Mihukúm siyá nga díliq níya dádqun ang kahúng íyang nadalá.)

Túni: Isáq. Ibálik ning prádag kadyút. Ákung ikanáqug ring ákung kahún. Ákuq ning ibílins tindáhan. Diq lang nákuq dádqun.

(Sa dídtu nas siní)

Ártur: Diqín man nímu ibutáng ag kahúng ímung gibílin? (ag = ang)

Túni: Aa, dídtu nákuq isulúd sa kwártu sa luyú sa tindáhan.

Ártur: Língkud ta ári. Pangutánqa nang táwug giqukupahán na ba nang lugára diháq. Ug waláq pa, sultíhi ug mahímuq bang mubálhin siyág língkud ádtung usá.

Túni: Diq ku, ikáw lang. Sultíhi na siyá.

(Ang táwung gisultíhan waláq musugút ug únyaq sa pipilá ka gútluq)

Ártur: Uy! Ikáw man diqáy ni. Ingún nákug kínsa. ('Oh, it's you! I thought it was someone else!')

Túni: Uy, si Nuy Tibúq man diqáy. Kumústa Nuy? Ngítngit man gud. Waq lang nátuq kahatágig maqáyung pagtagád.

III. Pagbánsay

Sulúd Sa Siní (Movie)

Ártur: Taná, ádtu na tas siní. (Hátag) ka bag (báyad)? 'Have you been given money to pay with?'

Túni: Díqa, apán waq ra ba nákuq (súlti) si Mámang mutánqaw kug siní. Únsa may (tubág) nákuq nyaq? 'What should I answer later on?'

Ártur: Sayún ra naq. Sa? ('How about it?') Sigí, kay díqay prádang gahuwát. Maqúy átung (sakáy). (práda 'rig')

Túni: Taa, sakáy na ta. Pilá may (báyad)s práda? Gahuwát man kaháq ni nátuq.

Ártur: (Báyad)g dúbli. Hústu ra naq kay dakúq rag písus (hátag). 'Pay him double. That's enough, because one peso is too much.'

Túni: (Pangutána) ang kutsíru ug únsay náqa run sa Liin.

(Mihukúm siyá nga díliq níya dádqun ang kahúng íyang nadalá.)

Túni: Isáq. (Bálik) ring prádag kadyút. Ákung (kanáqug) ning ákung kahún. Ákuq ning (bílin)s tindáhan. Diq lang nákuq (dalá).

(Sa dídtu nas siní)

Ártur: Diqín man nímu (butáng) ag kahúng ímung (bílin)? (ag = ang)

Túni: Aa, dídtu nákuq (sulúd) sa kwártu sa luyú sa tindáhan.

Ártur: Língkud ta ári. (Pangutána) nang táwug (ukupár) na ba nang lugára diháq. Ug waláq pa, (súlti) ug mahímuq bang mubálhin siyág língkud ádtung usá.

Túni: Diq ku, ikáw lang. (Súlti) na siyá.

(Ang táwung gisultíhan waláq musugút ug únyaq sa pipilá ka gútluq)

Ártur: Uy! Ikáw man diqáy ni. Ingún nákug kínsa. ('Oh, it's you! I thought it was someone else!')

Túni: Uy, si Nuy Tibúq man diqáy. Kumústa Nuy? Ngítngit man gud. Waq lang nátuq (hátag) maqáyung pagtagád.

IV. Sultiqánay

Sulúd sa Siní

Ártur: Túní, mulakáw man kaháq ta runs siní, taná!

Túni: Kínsa may átung kúyug?

Ártur: Kitá ra, arún waláy dághang sámuk.

Túni: Sigí gud. Maay pud arún makapaqúliq ta dáyun.

Ártur: Magdalá tag kuuk kay átung ímnun.

Túni: Díliq lang kay waláq na tay úras. Nagdalíq ta.

Ártur: Sakáy tag tartanílya. Dalíq.

Túni: Kuqán, táksi lang. Nagdalíq ra ba ta.

Ártur: Uu. Díqa nay usá. Táwga.

1. Milakáw silás Talísay.
2. Siláng duhá may kúyug.
3. Gústu siláng makapaqúliq dáyun.
4. Waláq silá magdalág kuuk.
5. Nagsakáy silág tartanílya.
6. Waláq silá makasakáys táksi.

Ártur: Huwán Lúna mi Bay.

Túni: Ása man diqáy ta? Ádtu dídtus Huwán Lúna?

Ártur: Ádtu úntaq tas Liin.

Túni: Níqa na ta.

Ártur: Pilá may átung plíti? Únsa may náqas kuntadúr? (kuntadúr 'meter')

Túni: Únu báynti.

Ártur: Ikáw lang say hátag ha?

Túni: Uy, waq ra ba ku kadalág ibáyad.

Ártur: Hásta pud ku. Díqa núquy písus.

Túni: Singkwíntay síngku ra ring ákuq. Íguq diqáy.

Ártur: Díliq na ta katánqawg siní.

Túni: Ádtu na lang tas Magalyánis.

7. Singkwíntay ílang plíti sa táksi.
8. Nakatánqaw silás siní.
9. Waláq siláy daláng plíti.
10. Dídtu na lang silás Magalyánis.

(Sa pilá ka gútluq)

Ártur: Díqa man diqáy dyis. Taa. Dayún lang tag tánqaws siní.

Túni: Sigí, hústu pa run.

Ártur: Sakáy na pud ta.

Túni: Diq lang, maglakáw lang ta. Níqa na bítaw ta.

Ártur: Tutál níqa na man gyud ta. Taa. Sulúd na ta. Uy, láqin man lagíy salída?

Túni: Ii, diq na lang gyud ku.

11. Dínhaq diqáy dyis písus ni Ártur.
12. Midayún silág tánqaw sa siní.
13. Waláq na lang silá musakáy ug táksi.
14. Layúq ra silás sinihán.

Sagquluhúnun

First Part	Únang Báhin
Miss Wilby and Mrs. Olivar continue their stroll in Pulambato.	Nagsígig suruysúruy silá si Mis Wílbi ug si Mísis Ulibár sa Pulambatú.
make sure	sigurúqa
for sure	gyud
[linker between sigurúqa and the rest of the sentence]	nga
can come back	makabálik
time	panahún
harvesting	pangáni
1. Make sure you can come back here during harvest time.	1. Sigurúqa gyud nga makabálik ... ka ngánhi sa panahún sa ... pangáni.
will make	magbúhat
rice crunch	pilípig
2. I'll make some rice crunch.	2. Magbúhat nyaq kug pilípig.
what?	singáan (dialectal form for únsa)
that (just mentioned)	naq
3. What is rice crunch?	3. Singáan man nang pilípig?
ah (pause before speaking)	aa
that (well known)	kanáq
whatchamacallit	kuqán
4. Ah, (that) pilípig—that's whatchamacallit.	4. Aa, kanáng pilípig, kuqán naq.
you know? do you understand?	ba

rice	humáy
ripe	hinúg
is the one	muqú (= maqú)
thing to be taken	kuháqun
5. That, er, rice, you know, which isn't very ripe yet—that's what you take.	5. Kanáq bang humáy ba, díliq pa kaqáyu hinúg, muqú nay ímung kuháqun.
then	únyaq
to be roasted in a pan	sangágun
6. Then you roast it (lit. that).	6. Únyaq, ímu nang sangágun.
after	inigkahumán
[particle preceding infinitive]	ug
roast in a pan	sángag
to be pounded	lúbkun (base, <u>lubúk</u>)
7. After you have roasted (it) you pound (it).	*7. Inigkahumán nímug sángag, ímung lúbkun.
thing to have brown sugar put in it	kamayán
8. Then it (lit. that) has brown sugar put on it?	8. Aa, únyaq kamayán naq?
9. No. (Lit. No longer.)	9. Díliq na.
[particle preceding infinitive]	ug
pound in a mortar	lubúk
when [something] has been taken away	inigkúhaq
[particle preceding goal]	sa
husks	tahúp
delicious	lamíq
already	na
[linker between <u>lamíq</u> and <u>kánqun</u>]	nga
to be eaten	kánqun

10. After you have pounded it (lit. that), when you have removed the husks, it's very good to eat (lit. that is good already).

*10. Inigkahumán nímu ánag lubúk, inigkúhaq nímus tahúp, lamíq na kaqáyu nang kánqun.

my!	sus
how delicious!	nindúta

11. My, how delicious!

11. Sus, nindúta!

but	pirú
little	dyútay
very	ra
[particle: 'have']	ug

12. But we have only very few corn and rice fields here.

12. Pirú dyútay ra kaqáyu mi dínhig kamaqisán ug kahumayán.

usual	kasagáran
of	sa
land	yútaq
in	sa
place planted	gitámnan
[particle preceding goal]	ug
sugar cane	tubú

13. Usually the land here in Pulambato (lit. The usual type of land here in Pulambato) is planted to sugar cane.

13. Ang kasagáran dínhis yútaq sa Pulambatú, gitámnag tubú.

with	sa
sugar cane	tubú
once	kaqusá
no more than	ra
for sure	gyud
can harvest	makaqáni

14. Then with sugar cane, we can harvest only once a year.

14. Únyaq sa tubú, kaqusá ra gyud mi makaqáni sa usá ka túqig.

long time	dúgay
[linker between dúgay and the rest of the sentence]	nga
can be gathered	makúhaq
15. Because it takes a long time to harvest the sugar cane. (Lit. Because that is a long time, that the sugar cane can be gathered.)	15. Kay dúgay man kaqáyu nang ... makúhang tubú.
in	sa
preparing	pagqándam
field in which something is planted	baqúl
persons made to help	patabángun
[particle preceding infinitive]	sa
16. In preparing the field, I have my sons help (in the preparation).	16. Sa pagqándam sa baqúl, ang ... ákung mga anák, ákung ... patabángun sa pagqándam.
earn	mukítaq
one-fifty	únu singkwínta
per day	ang ádlaw
17. (Because) they earn one-fifty a day.	17. Kay mukítaq man silág únu ... singkwínta ang ádlaw.
other	ubán
also	sab
[linker between ubán and kuqán]	nga
neighborhood	kasilinganán
18. The other whatchamacallit—families who are very poor here in our neighborhood . . .	18. Ang ubán sang mga kuqán, ... mga pamílya nga púbri kaqáyu ... dínhi sa ámung kasilinganán,

in which (linker between <u>pamílya</u> and the rest of the sentence)	nga
not	waq
even	gániq
[existential particle]	y
[measurement of distance between fingertips of arms outstretched]	dupá
[linker between <u>dupá</u> and <u>yútaq</u>]	nga
land	yútaq
there	ánhaq ra
also	sad
earn their living	manginabúhiq

19. . . . who do not even have a yard of land here, (they) also earn their living that way (lit. there) . . .

19. Nga waq gániq dínhiy usá ka dupá nga yútaq, ánhaq ra sad manginabúhiq,

[particle preceding infinitive]	sa
help	pagtábang
[particle preceding goal of infinitive]	sa
planting	pananúm
[particle preceding goal]	sa

20. . . . by helping plant the sugar cane.

20. Sa pagtábang sa pananúm sa tubú.

in	sa
harvesting	pangáni
of	sa
sugar cane	tubú
there	náqa
[particle expressing humility]	táwun

21. We earn our living by harvesting sugar cane. (Lit. In harvesting the sugar cane, it's there that we earn our living, poor us.)

21. Sa pangáni sa tubú—náqa táwun mi manginabúhiq diháq.

come on	dalíq
let's go over	arí ta
the center	tungaqtúngaq
artesian well	púsu
previously	kaniqádtu

22. Come on. Let's go to the center, (because) that's where our artesian well used to be (lit. here is where our artesian well was before).

*22. Dalíq. Arí ta sa tungaqtúngaq kay díqa dirí ang ámung púsu kaniqádtu.

particular well	pusúha
thing made	gibúhat
in	sa
time	panahún
still	pa
of (particle preceding names)	ni

23. This artesian well—it (lit. this) was constructed during President Magsaysay's time (lit. in the time still of President Magsaysay).

23. Kiníng pusúha, gibúhat ni sa panahún pa ni Prisidínti Magsáysay.

long time ago now	dúgay na
that (past time)	tu
anyway (particle explaining that something is unimportant)	uy
seven	pitú
already	na
[linker between pitú and túqig]	ka
year	túqig
more than	kapín

24. But anyway that was a long time ago. It's more than seven years now.

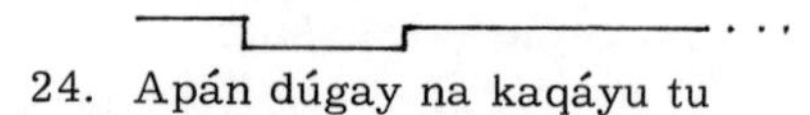

24. Apán dúgay na kaqáyu tu uy. Pitú na ka túqig kapín.

work	búhat
[linker between búhat and dinaliqdalíq]	nga

done hastily	dinaliqdalíq
quickly	dalíq
very	ra
also	sad
[linker between dalíq and nagubáq]	nga
broken down	nagubáq

25. Then because the work was done hurriedly, it wasn't long (either) before it broke down.

*25. Unyáq kay búhat nga dinaliqdalíq, dalíq ra sad kaqáyung nagubáq.

[particle of pity]	táwun

26. And now, poor us, we fetch water from the hacienda.

26. Ug karún táwun, ádtu táwun mi magkúhag túbig sa asyínda.

very	pwírti
[linker between pwírti and layúqa]	nga
how far!	layúqa
[particle expressing sympathy]	táwun

27. We're awfully far away. (Lit. How very far away we are, poor us.)

27. Pwírting layúqa táwun námuq.

suffer	magqántus
[particle preceding infinitive]	ug
walk	lakáw

28. We have to walk all that way. (Lit. We suffer walking.)

28. Magqántus mig lakáw.

Mga Pangutána

Únang Báhin

1. Anúsqa man mu mangáni?
2. Nakakitáq ka na bag nagbúhat ug pilípig?
3. Únsa may buhátung pilípig?
4. Kanáng pilípig dúna ba nay kalámay?
5. Ngánung lúbkun man nínyu nang pilípig?
6. Únsa pa may ínyung tanúm gawás sa maqís ug humáy?
7. Lisúd bang itanúm nang tubú?
8. Dúgay bang andámun ang yútaq nga támnan sa tubú?
9. Dághan bang pamílya dínhi sa Pulambatú nga may tanúm nga tubú?
10. Ang ínyung túbig dínhi diqín man nínyu kuháqa?
11. Pilá na ka túqig ning pusúha?
12. Dúgay na bang nagubáq ning pusúha?
13. Únsa may ímung sangágun Misís?
14. Ngánung díliq man kamayán kanáng pilípig?
15. Kínsa may tagqíya ánang mga kahumayán?
16. Dúna ba muy yútang gitámnag tubú?
17. Ngánung kaqusá ra man mu makaqánig tubú sulúd sa usá ka túqig?
18. Patabángun ba sab nímu ang ímung mga anák sa pagpananúm ug tubú?
19. Karún nga gubáq na ning ínyung púsu túqa na mu magkúhag túbig sa asyínda?
20. Dúgay na bang gibúhat ning pusúha?

Mga Pangutána (Matching)

Únang Báhin

1. Lisúd bang buhátun kanáng pilípig?
2. Humág tahúp butangán ba nag kalámay? (tahúp 'winnow')
3. Hinúg bang humáy ang ímung sangágun?
4. Anúsqa ka man mubálik kay magbúhat únyaq kug pilípig?

(a) Gamáy ra gyud kay ang kasagáran sa mga yútaq gitámnan mag tubú.

(b) Díliq man. Dalíq ra man gániq kaqáyu.

(c) Sunúd búlan pa ku makabálik kay ádtu pa man kus Úrmuk.

(d) Uu, kay mukítaq man silág únu singkwínta ang ádlaw.

5. Kanáng kamaqisána ínyu ba naq?
6. Ngánung gamáy ra man ning ínyung kamaqisán ug kahumayán dínhi?
7. Kiníng ínyung púsu, ngánung nagubáq man ni dáyun?
8. Mutábang ba sab ang ímung mga anák sa pagqáni sa tubú?
9. Ngánung dághan man ang tubú nga gitanúm kay sa maqís?

(e) Díliq. Kanáng díliq pa hinúg maqúy sangágun kay maqú man gyud nay buhátung pilípig.

(f) Kanáng náqang kamaqisána, ámuq naq ug kádtu pung humayán.

(g) Díliq na kay waq na man kinahanglána ang kalámay.

(h) Dághan gyud kay dakúq mag makítang kwárta ang tubú tungúd sa kalámay.

(i) Nagubáq naq dáyun kay dinaliqdalíq mang pagkabúhat.

Sagquluhúnun

Second Part

what?

1. What's that the children are playing?

[exclamation dismissing something as unimportant]
Lord!
is called
[particle preceding goal]
[name of game]

2. Oh, that? That's what we call sátung here.

that (well known)
[linker between kanáq and nakítqan]
see
is there (pointing)
short
stick
[linker between káhuy and gihapakhápak]

Ikaduháng Báhin

unsingáan (dialectal for únsa)

1. Unsingáan man nang gidúlaq sa mga bátaq?

ay
sus
gitawág
ug
sátung

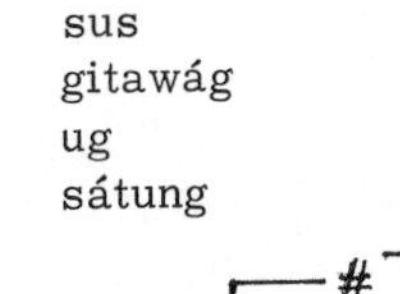

*2. Ay, sus kanáq? Maqú nay

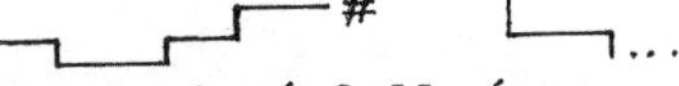

gitawág námuq dínhig sátung.

kanáq
nga
nakítqan
náqay
mubúq
káhuy
nga

thing being batted continuously	gihapakhápak

3\. Satung . . . You see—that very short stick there that they keep on batting at . . .

*3. Kanáng sátung, kanáng nakîtqan mu, nang náqay mubúq kaqáyung káhuy nga ịlang gihapakhápak . . .

4\. Oh yes, that short one.

4\. Uu, kanáng mubúq.

be placed across	ipátung
over	sa
hole	lungág
[linker between lungág and gamáy]	nga
small	gamáy
is thrown	ilábay
far place	layúq

5\. They place that across a small hole, then they flip it far away.

*5. Íla nang ipátung sa lungág nga gamáy, unyáq ilábay ngádtu sa layúq.

long	taqás
stick	káhuy
also	sab
thing to be used	gamítun
[particle preceding infinitive]	sa
to throw	paglábay

6\. And that longer stick there, that's what they use in throwing away (the small stick).

6\. Ug kanáng náqang taqás nga káhuy sab, maqúy gamítun

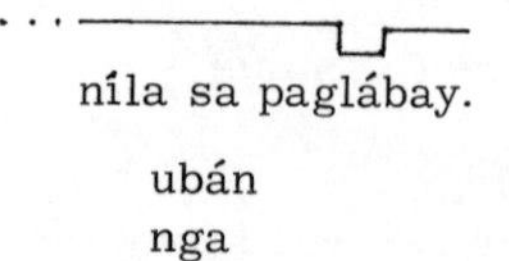

níla sa paglábay.

other	ubán
[linker between ubán and gadúwaq]	nga

are playing	gadúwaq
strive	maningúhaq
[linker between maningúhaq and what follows]	nga
can catch	makasáwuq

7. And those other players try to catch that short stick.

*7. Ug kádtung ubáng gadúwaq, ... maningúhaq nga makasáwuq ... niqánang mubúng káhuy.

is the one	mu (= maqú)

8. Ah, so that's it.

8. Aa, mu diqáy naq.

upon catching	inigkasáwuq
already	na
points	púntus

9. If they catch it, they get a point. (Lit. When they catch that, they have points now.)

9. Inigkasáwuq níla ánaq, dúna ... na siláy púntus.

besides	gawás pa
that particular one (past time)	ang kádtu
did the throwing	naglábay
now	na
also	sad
watch	mubántay

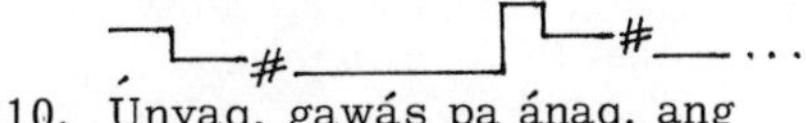

10. And furthermore, the one (lit. that one) who threw the small stick becomes the one (lit. is now the one) who has to watch (to catch it).

*10. Únyaq, gawás pa ánaq, ang ... kádtung naglábay ánang mubúng ... káhuy, mu na say mubántay.

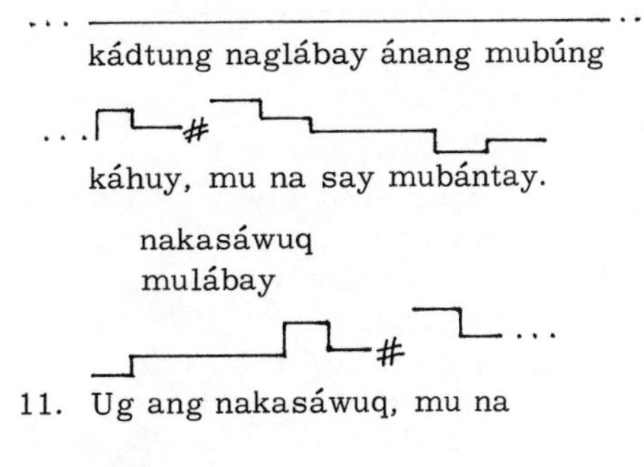

managed to catch	nakasáwuq
will do the throwing	mulábay

11. And the one who catches the small stick becomes the one who throws it away in turn (lit. is now the one also who throws it away).

11. Ug ang nakasáwuq, mu na ... say mulábay.

succeeds in getting	makakuháq
least	kinagámyan
12. The one who gets the least number of points . . .	12. Ang makakuhás kinagámyang . . . púntus—
thing over which an agreement was made	gikasabútan
[linker between gikasabútan and what follows]	nga
how many?	pilá
[linker between pilá and púntus]	ka
for example	kínta
before	úsaq
stop (plural)	mangúndang
13. Because they agree on how many points to play (lit. they have an agreement as to how many points, say, before they quit).	13. Kay dúna man siláy gikasabútan . . . nga pilá ka púntus kínta . . . úsaq silá mangúndang.
something used as	sílbi
[linker between sílbi and kastígu]	nga
punishment, penalty	kastígu
14. There is also something which serves as penalty.	14. Dúna say sílbing kastígu.
that (before mentioned)	kanáq
15. That short stick—(they) throw (it) far away.	15. Kanáng káhuyng mubúq, . . . ilábay naq sa layúq.
approximately	mga
three times	katúu
is repeatedly thrown	ilabaylábay
child	bátaq
[linker between bátaq and nakadaqúg]	nga
won	nakadaqúg

16. The child that wins (lit. won) throws it (lit. that) around three times.

16. Mga katúu naq ilabaylábay ... sa bátang nakadaqúg.

that one	kádtu
lost	napíldi
starts from	manukád (root sukád)
[linker between ádtu and gilabáyan]	nga
place to which a thing is thrown	gilabáyan
[particle preceding goal]	sa

17. Then the loser (lit. Then that one who lost) starts from the place where the stick was thrown to.

*17. Únyaq kádtung napíldi, ... manukád ádtung gilabáyan ... sa káhuy.

that one (past time)	kádtu
[linker between kádtu and katapúsan]	nga
last one	katapúsan
[linker between katapúsan and lábay]	nga
act of throwing	lábay
that (place where)	kádtu
place something hit the ground	gitugdúnan

18. That last throw, where it hit the ground . . .

*18. Kádtung katapúsang lábay, ... kádtung gitugdúnan . . .

afterward	humán
runs	mudágan
back	bálik
here	ngarí
hole	lungág
[linker between lungág and gibutangán]	nga
place where something was put	gibutangán
[particle preceding goal]	sa

19. Afterward, starting from there, he runs back (here) to the hole where they had (first) placed the stick. (Lit. Afterward, he starts from there—he runs back to the hole where they put the stick over.)	19. Humán, ádtu siyá manukád dídtu, mudágan bálik ngarí sa lungág nga ílang gibutángán sa káhuy.
for example	pananglítan
if	ug
forceful	kusúg
[linker between kusúg and mulábay]	nga
throws	mulábay
quite far	layuqlayúq
also	sad
[particle: 'has']	ug
place to be run to	dagánan
20. If the child throws the stick very hard, he (the other one) has quite a long distance to run, too.	20. Pananglítag ang bátaq kusúg kaqáyung mulábay, layuqlayúq sad siyág dagánan.
not allow air to enter the mouth or nose	muqutúng
he (previously mentioned)	naq siyá
21. Also, he holds his breath.	*21. Únyaq, muqutúng naq siyá.
continually	sígi
[linker between sigí and sínggit]	nga
shouts	sínggit
22. He keeps on shouting satoong.	22. Síging sínggit, sátuung . . .
until	hángtud
place reached	maqabút
how shall we call it?	lugár
[linker between íla and biis]	nga
base	biis

23. Until he gets to . . . shall we say . . . their base . . .	*23. Hángtud maqabút níya ang ... íla lugár nga biis,
home base	baláy
24. Their home base.	24. Ílang baláy.
25. Ah, so that's it.	25. Aa, maqú diqáy naq.
that particular one	ang kádtu
thing being played	gidúlaq
26. That child there, what is he playing?	26. Ang kádtung bátaq ngádtu, ... únsa may íyang gidúlaq?
27. Mm, that one over there?	27. Aa, kádtung túqa dídtu?
play tákyan	nagtákyan
that one	naq
28. He's playing tákyan.	*28. Nagtákyan naq.
game	dúwaq
[linker between dúwaq and lisúd]	nga
difficult	lisúd
29. That's a very difficult game.	29. Maqú nay dúwang lisúd kaqáyu.
necessary	kinahángan (dialectal for kinahánglan)
without a doubt	gyud
practice	magbánsay
without a doubt	gyud
well	pagqáyu
30. You really have to practice it well. (Lit. That is really necessary to practice it well.)	*30. Kinahángan gyud nang ... magbánsay ka gyud pagqáyu.
that (previously mentioned)	kanáq

[name of a game or name of the object with which the game is played]	tákyan
[linker between kanáq and tsápa]	nga
washer (metal ring)	tsápa
[particle assuring hearer that what has been stated is really so]	bítaw
31. That tákyan—that's a whatchamacallit—just a (lit. that) washer.	*31. Kanáng tákyan—kuqán kanáq—kanáng tsápa bítaw.
32. Washer?	32. Tsápa?
that (well known)	kanáq
[linker between kanáq and sa kuqán]	nga
belong to a whatchamacallit	sa kuqán
belonging to	sa
roof	atúp
[linker between atúp and siin]	nga
galvanized iron	siin
33. That thing from a whatchamacallit—that thing put on a tin roof . . .	33. Kanáng sa kuqán—kanáng sa atúp nga siin . . .
that one	kanáq
[linker between kanáq and náqa]	nga
[particle: 'is there' (pointing)]	náqay
round	língin
34. That round thing there.	*34. Kanáng náqay língin.
35. Yes. Right.	35. Uu. Hústu.
thing used for making	gibúhat
that	ánaq

36. That's what it's (the takyan) made of. (Lit. That's what was used to make that.)	36. Maqú nay gibúhat ánaq.
thing over or under which something was placed as a cushion	gihanigán
[particle preceding goal]	ug
leather	pánit
37. It is cushioned (underneath) with a piece of leather.	37. Gihanigán ug pánit.
place on which something is put	gibutangán
[particle preceding goal]	ug
feathers	balhíbu
38. Then chicken feathers are put on it.	38. Unyáq, gibutangág balhíbu ... sa manúk.
thing made to stand	gipatíndug
those (just mentioned)	kanáq
small (plural)	gágmay
[linker between balhíbu and dapít sa líqug]	nga
near	dapít sa
neck	líqug
39. Those small feathers near the neck (of the chicken) are set upright on it.	*39. Gipatíndug kanáng mga ... gágmayng balhíbung dapít ... sa líqug.
thing caused to stand	gipatíndug
as (a)	sílbi
[linker between sílbi and kuqán]	nga
whatchamacallit	kuqán
for it	níya
so that	pára
will fall to the side	matúmba

40. They are set upright as a whatchamacallit for it—so that the takyan doesn't fall on its side (i.e. so that it will fall vertically).

40. Gipatíndug sílbing kuqán níya pára díliq matúmba ang tákyan.

then — unyáq
thing kicked — patíran

41. Then you kick it. (Lit. Then that is kicked.)

41. Unyáq, # patíran naq.

[particle giving assurance] — bítaw

42. There—you see that child.

42. Nakakitáq ka bítaw ánang bátaq.

[particle expressing that it is actually that way] — uy

43. That's very difficult, you know.

*43. Lisúd kaqáyu naq uy.

44. Do you know (how to do) that?

44. Maqantígu ka ánaq?

Mga Pangutána

Ikaduháng Báhin

1. Unsingáan mang duláqa kanáng gidúlaq sa mga bátaq?
2. Maqantígu ka ba mudúlag sátung?
3. Gamítun ba níla sa ílang dúlaq kanáng gamáyng lungág?
4. Ása man níla ilábay nang káhuy?
5. Kun makasáwuq ang bátaq, síya na ba puy mulábay?
6. Pilá man diqáy ka púntus ang ihátag sa makasáwuq?
7. Kádtung túqa dídtu, unsingáan man nang ílang giduwáqan?
8. Únsa may ílang gihaníg ánang tsápa?

9. Diqín mang partíha sa manúk naq níla kuháqang balhíbu?
10. Ang mga gágmayng balhíbu sa manúk, maqú nay ílang gibutáng ánang ílang tákyan nu?
11. Kanáq bang batáqa ang nakakuháq sa kinadaghanáng púntus?
12. Únsa tuy átung gikasabútan Dyuu?
13. Kínsa man karúy napíldi niqánang duháng gadúlaq?
14. Ása man ta manukád?
15. Kanáng gidúlaq sa duhá ka bátaq, maqú man nay tákyan nu?
16. Maqantígu ka bang mutákyan?
17. Kanúsqa tung katapúsan mung pagqádtu sa San Rimihiyú?

Mga Pangutána (Matching)

Ikaduháng Báhin

1. Maqantígu ka bang mudúlag sátung?
2. Únsa mang duláqa kanáng gidúlaq sa duhá ka bátaq?
3. Pilá ka púntus ang ihátag sa makasáwuq?
4. Ngánung muqutúng man nang bátaq kun mudágan na?
5. Maqantígu ka bang mutákyan, Dyuu?
6. Únsa man nang buhátun nílag tákyan?
7. Kinahángan ba gyud tang magbánsay kun mudúlaq tag tákyan?
8. Diqín man níla kuháqa kanáng balhíbu nga ílang gigámit?
9. Maqantígu ka bang mubúhat ug tákyan, Dyuu?

(a) Muqutúng gyud naq siyá kay kastígu man naq sa íyang pagkapíldi.

(b) Kinahángan gyud. Kay kun díliq ka magbánsay mapíldi ka man.

(c) Maqantígu man. Maqáyu kaqáyu kung mubúhat ánang tákyan.

(d) Tsápa sa atúp nga siin, pánit, ug balhíbu sa manúk. Mu nay ílang buhátug tákyan.

(e) Magnunút lang sa gikasabútan sa magdúlaq.

(f) Díliq. Únsa mang duláqa nang sátung?

(g) Uu. Bánsay kaqáyu ku ánang tákyan. (bánsay 'skilled')

(h) Aa, kanáng náqa? Maqú nay gitawág ug sátung.

(i) Aa, kanáng mga balhibúqa? Mga balhíbu naq sa manúk nga náqa dapít sa líqug.

Sagquluhúnun

Third Part	Ikatulúng Báhin
coming	nagpaqingún
1. Ah, here's an old man coming this way.	1. Aa, níqay tigúwang nagpaqingún ngánhi.
is carrying	nagdáa
rooster	sunúy
2. He's carrying a rooster.	2. Nagdáag sunúy.
ah (dismissing something as ordinary)	aa
he (referred to previously)	kanáq siyá
[masculine nickname]	Ántuy (= Huwán)
3. Oh, him. That's Antoy. (Lit. Ah, that one. He is Noy Antoy.)	3. Aa, kanáq siyá—. Si Nuy Ántuy naq.
famous in fighting	banggiqítan
4. That cock (lit. chicken) of his, that's the best fighter here in our place.	*4. Kanáng íyang manúk—maqú nay banggiqítan dínhi sa ámung lugár.
which one?	háqi
fierce fighter	ísug
5. Which one? This cock of mine? This one is a very fierce fighter.	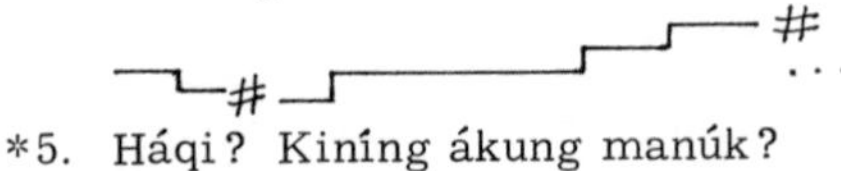 *5. Háqi? Kiníng ákung manúk? Ísug kaqáyu ni.
ten times	kanapúluq
already	na

6. I've won ten times (here at our place) with this one. | *6. Kanapúluq na ku makadaqúg ... niqíni dínhi sa ámuq.

whatchamacallit — kuqán
because — man gud
Texas (breed of rooster) — Tíksas

7. Because this is a whatchamacallit—because this is a 'Texas.' | *7. Kuqán man gud ni. Tíksas man ... gud ni.

genuine — pyur
without a doubt — gyud
condition or state of being a 'Texas' — pagkatíksas

8. He's a genuine 'Texas.' (Lit. This 'Texas-ness' of his is genuine.) | 8. Pyur gyud ning pagkatíksas ... níya.

particular chicken — manúka

9. This chicken is a very good fighter. | 9. Banggiqítan kaqáyu ning ... manúka.

have won — kadaqúg

10. Where did you win? | 10. Diqín man ka kadaqúg?

[particle dismissing what follows as unimportant] — ay
when it is Sunday — madumínggu

11. Ah, in that whatchamacallit—on Sunday (lit. when it's Sunday) . . . | 11. Ay sa kuqán—kanáng ... madumínggu—

illegal cockfight — tigbakáy

12. There at the tigbakáy. | *12. Ánhaq sa tigbakáy.

no more than	ra
because	man
for sure	gyud
when	ug
on Sundays	madumínggu

13. For what we have here on Sundays is merely a tigbakay. — 13. Kay tigbakáy ra man gyud ... ning ámuq dínhig madumínggu.

far from	layúq sa
very	ra
because	man
cockpit (where cockfights are held)	bulangán

14. Because we are very far from the cockpit. — 14. Layúq ra man kaqáyu mis ... bulangán.

15. We can't get to the cockpit at San Remigio. — 15. Díliq man mi makaqádtu sa ... bulangán sa San Rimihiyú.

difference	kalaqínan
between	sa
illegal cockfight	tigbakáy
and	ug
legal cockfight	búlang

16. What is the difference between tigbakay and bulang? — 16. Únsa may kalaqínan sa ... tigbakáy ug búlang?

[particle indicating that what follows is easy or unimportant]	ay
that (referred to previously)	kanáq
just the same	paríha ra
[particle with information about which hearer may wonder]	gud
[linker between paríha and búlang]	ug

cockfight	búlang
still	gihápun
17. Well, a (lit. that) tigbakay—it's just the same as a bulang.	17. Ay kanáng tigbakáy—paríha ra gud nag búlang gihápun.
because	tungúd kay
because	man
permission	pagtúgut
therefore	maqú nang
is called	gitawág
[particle preceding goal]	ug
18. But they don't have permission to hold it, so it's called a tigbakay. (Lit. But because there is no permission for it, therefore that is called a tigbakay.)	18. Tungúd kay waq man nay pagtúgut, maqú nang gitawág nag tigbakáy.
mutual killing	patyánay
because	man gud
[particle with information on something hearer may wonder about]	gud
19. That's when the chickens kill each other, you know. (Lit. Because that—that is killing of the chickens.)	19. Kay kanáq patyánay man gud naq sa mga manúk gud.
20. Oh, really?	20. Aa, diqáy?
[particle with statement giving information]	man
to be lifted up	alsáhun
dead	patáy
already	na
for sure	gyud
opponent	kúntra
21. Because the cock is not picked up unless the	*21. Díliq man alsáhun ang manúk

opponent is really dead.	kun dîliq patáy na gyud ang kúntra.
[linker between <u>únsa</u> and <u>rasáha</u>]	nga
particular breed	rasáha
22. What is the breed of that cock? (Lit. What breed is that of the cock, Noy?)	22. Únsa mang rasáha naq sa sunúy Nuy?
23. Ah, this one? This is 'Texas.'	23. Aa, kiní? Tíksas ni.
[particle expressing that it actually is that way]	uy

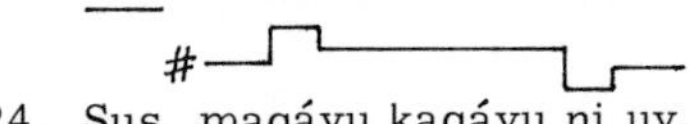

24. My! It's a good one, you know.	24. Sus, maqáyu kaqáyu ni uy.
want	gústu
for sure	gyud
[linker between <u>gústu</u> and <u>mutánqaw</u>]	nga
cockfight without knives	sábung

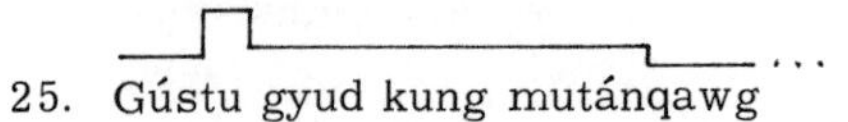

25. I really would like to see a sparring match.	25. Gústu gyud kung mutánqawg sábung.
come on	taná
let's go over here	arî ta
another	pa
other	láqin

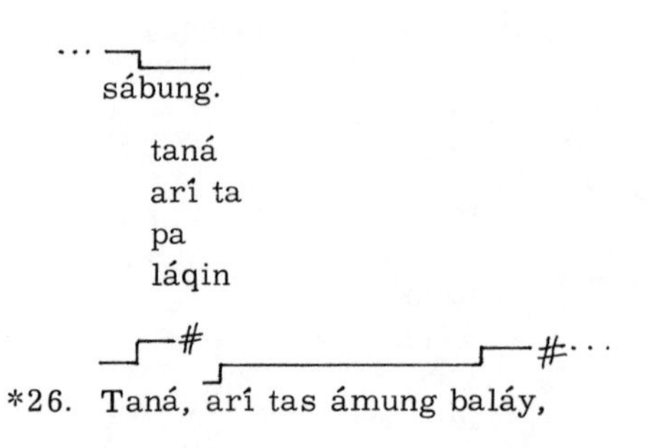

26. Come on, let's go over to my house; I have some other cocks over there (lit. because there are some other chickens of mine over here).	*26. Taná, arî tas ámung baláy, kay dîqa pa may ákung láqing manúk.

thing to be pitted (without knives)	isábung
27. Let's pit this one (against one of them).	27. Isábung nátuq ni.

Mga Pangutána

Ikatulúng Báhin

1. Kanáng manúk nga gidalá ánang tigúwang, pára ba naq sa búlang?
2. Magdáa ba gyud naq siyág sunúy káda lakáw níya?
3. Ása man nímu dádqa nang ímung manúk Nuy?
4. Ibúlang ba nímu nang manúka sa Dumínggu Nuy?
5. Muqádtu ba ta run sa tigbakáy Dyuu?
6. Ása man ang tigbakáy karún Nuy?
7. Duqúl ra ba dínhi ang bulangán Nuy?
8. Paríha ba nang búlang ug kanáng gitawág ug tigbakáy Dyuu?
9. Mamúlang ka ba karúng Dumínggu Nuy?
10. Banggiqítan ba sab ning ímung manúk Nuy, paríha sa kang Dyuu nga tíksas?
11. Ímu bang isábung nang ímung tíksas Nuy?
12. Diqín mang lugára níya mapalít nang íyang manúk?
13. Alsáhun ku na ba nang átung manúk Nuy Antúy?
14. Waq ba kaháy pagtúgut sa búlang dínhi sa ínyung lugár Nuy?
15. Níndut bang tanqáwun nang mga manúk nga magpatyánay Nuy?
16. Dúna ka bay balígyang manúk nga tíksas Nuy Antúy?
17. Nakakitáq ka na bag sábung Dyuu?
18. Dúna ka pa bay láqing manúk Nuy?
19. Gústu ka bang mutánqawg sábung ubán kanákuq?
20. Pilá na ka manúk ang napatáy íning ímung tíksas Nuy?

Mga Pangutána (Matching)

Ikatulúng Báhin

1. Kínsa man nang tigúwang nga nagpaqingún ngánhi Dyuu?	(a) Dúna. Duqúl sa ámung baláy dúnay gasábung.

2. Únsang rasáha sa sunúy nang ímung gidáa Nuy?
3. Ása man naq níya dádqang sunúy Nuy Antúy?
4. Kapilá ka na makadaqúg ánang ímung tíksas Nuy Tibúq?
5. Únsa mang adláwa ang búlang Nuy?
6. Duqúl dínhis ínyu ang bulangán Nuy?
7. Ngánung díliq man alsáhun ang manúk kun díliq patáy na gyud ang kúntra.
8. Waláq bay sábung karún dínhi Nuy?
9. Ngánu? Gústu ka bang mutánqaw ug sábung?

(b) Kuqán, kanáng madumínggu ra apán díliq dínhi sa ámuq. Ádtu ra sa San Rimihiyú.

(c) Gústu úntaq Nuy. Isábung ta hinúqun nang ímung tíksas Nuy?

(d) Layúq uy. Mga dyis kilumítrus gíkan dínhi.

(e) Ádtu tingáli naq níya dádqa sa tigbakáy. May tigbakáy man gud run.

(f) Maqú man gyud naq ang kasabútan sa tigbakáy. Patyánay man gyud.

(g) Aa kiní? Tíksas ni siyá. Pyur tíksas gyud ni.

(h) Háqi? Kiní? Kanapúluq na ku makadaqúg niqíni. Ísug kaqáyu ni.

(i) Háqin? Kanáng nagdáag manúk? Si Nuy Ántuy naq.

Commentary to Basic Sentences

11 a 7	sángag	'To heat in a pan with or without cooking oil.'
11 a 10	lubúk	'To pound with a pestle.'
11 a 22		Mrs. Olivar uses arí, dirí, and díqa because she is motioning to Miss Wilby to go to her further side.
11 a 25	dinaliqdalíq	An adjective meaning 'done hastily.'
11 b 2	sátung	The name of a game; it is taken from the penalty (described in the course of the sentences).
11 b 3	nakítqan	The meaning here is the same as for nakítaq.
11 b 3	náqay	This meaning of náqay is the same as náqa except that there is definite pointing. Túqay is used similarly for things far away.
11 b 5	ilábay	'Thing to be knocked away.' This is not the usual meaning for ilábay. The root lábay means 'to throw'; 'thing to be knocked away' is ipalábtik.
11 b 7	makasáwuq	'Can catch.' Salúq means 'to catch, with the hands, something falling or thrown.'

11 b 10	ang kádtu	Note that the subject marker is used with kádtu when the meaning is 'that particular one (out of a choice of several).'
11 b 17	manukád	'Start from.' The base of this word is panukád from the root sukád 'from [a time].'
11 b 18	túgdun	'To land on the ground.'
11 b 21	utúng	'Not to inhale.'
11 b 23	lugár	This particle means the same thing as kínta: 'let's call it [so-and-so]' or 'let's settle on [so-and-so] as . . . '
11 b 28	tákyan	Tákyan is a game, named for the object it is played with—something that looks like a shuttlecock but is hit with the foot rather than a racket. The tákyan is bounced on the inner edge of the foot (the part beneath the ankle anywhere between the toes and the heel).
11 b 30	kinahángan	Dialectal form of kinahánglan. This is the form commonly used in Cebu City.
11 b 31	tsápa	A flat metal ring. In the Philippines they commonly use washers on metal roofs as part of the means for attaching the roofing to the frame.
11 b 34	náqay	The same usage as in 11 b 3; however, here the thing being pointed to is not actually there. (Cf. a similar usage in substandard English 'that there washer.' This usage is standard colloquial Cebuano, however.)
11 b 39		The bunched feathers are tied to one end of a leather thong. The other end is passed through the washer, to which are affixed round pieces of leather, slit to allow passage of the thong.
11 b 43	uy	Mrs. Olivar says uy because she feels that Miss Wilby thinks it is easy.
11 c 4	banggiqítan	The basic meaning of this word is 'notorious'—i.e. 'famous for something bad.'
11 c 5	háqi	Colloquial for háqin.
11 c 6	makadaqúg	The unreal is used here because the sentence is introduced by kanapúluq. (Cf. 13 F.)
11 c 7	Tíksas	This is a breed of cock, with a special type of beak which is considered especially good for fighting. The breed is said to originate in Texas.
11 c 12		Cockfighting is divided into the following types:
	táriq	Any cockfight with gaffs (knives on legs) and with betting.
	tigbakáy	Illegal cockfight with gaffs; originally without betting but now more commonly with bets.
	búlang	Legal cockfight in the cockpit, with betting and with gaffs.
	sábung	Cockfight with no gaffs (usually a warm-up).

patáyan	Cockfight with no gaffs, fought till one cock runs away.
karambúla	Cockfight with gaffs (often one on each leg) and with bets, involving many cocks in a free-for-all.
pintakási	Cockfight meet, with victors being matched against each other.

11 c 21 Actually the speaker is slightly inaccurate. If one of the cocks runs away, the adversary is put near him; if he shies away a second time, the adversary is declared winner.

11 c 26 Arí, díqa are used because Antoy's house is on the side near him and away from Miss Wilby.

Grammatical Section

11 A. The derivative verb prefix paN-*

A DERIVATIVE VERB PREFIX is a prefix which is attached at the beginning of a root to form a verb base. To this new verb base the active or passive affixes are added.

The following charts summarize the active and passive affixes added to bases having a paN- prefix. Note that the shape of the active volitional and durative affixes when added to bases with a paN- prefix is different from their shape when added to other bases. (See the chart of 4 A, p. 142, to compare these to the other active affixes.)

Active

	Real	Unreal	Abstract
Volitional or Durative †	naN-	maN-	pagpaN-
Potential	nakapaN-	makapaN-	pagkapaN-

Passive

	Real	Unreal	Subjunctive
Direct	gipaN-	paN- -un	paN- -a
Potential	napaN-	mapaN-	mapaN-
Local	gipaN- -an	paN- -an	paN- -i
Potential	napaN- -an	{mapaN- -an / kapaN- -an}	{mapaN- -i / kapaN- -i}
Instrumental	gipaN-	ipaN-	ipaN-
Potential	{gikapaN- / napaN-}	{ikapaN- / mapaN-}	{ikapaN- / mapaN-}

* For the meaning of N, cf. 4 E.

† There are also forms nagpaN-/magpaN-, but these are for fancy language only. We will study them later.

The verb forms in the examples below are underlined:

[active]

Ug dúnay mangasáwa nímu musugút kaháq ka? (5 b 45) 'If there is some-one who wants to marry you, will you by any chance accept?'
Nangapú na gániq tingáli ang ímung mga apú. (5 a 24) 'Even your grand-children probably already have grandchildren.'

[direct passive]

Ákung pangutánqun siyá, ha? (6 a 13) 'I'll ask him, shall I?'

[local passive]

Gipanghatágan silág mga gása. 'They were given gifts.'

[instrumental passive]

Díqay kaság nga gipamalígyaq. (6 a 27) 'There are crabs for sale here.'

All roots may occur with the paN- prefix. Bases containing paN- are of several types. We discuss the three most important here:

(1) bases consisting of a verb root plus paN-, where the verb root also occurs alone without paN- but with verb affixes;
(2) bases consisting of a noun root plus paN-;
(3) bases containing paN- which never (or rarely) occur without it.

11 A 1. PaN- with verb roots

In bases consisting of a verb root plus paN-, the paN- prefix shows that the action is done by several agents or affects several recipients. In the following examples mangádtu '[several people] go' and mangáqun '[several people] eat' or 'eat [several things]' are formed by adding paN- and the verb affixes to the verb roots ádtu and káqun respectively:

a. Aa, mangádtu mus Banáwaq? (3 a 17) 'Oh, are you going to Banawa?'
b. Mangáqun na ta. 'Let's eat.'

Verb forms without paN- are used when the agents or the recipients are either singular or plural: that is to say, they are ambiguous with respect to the number of agents or recipients involved. Verbs with paN-, on the other hand, as described in this section, specifically indicate that the agent or the recipient is plural. Thus the above examples can also be said without the paN- affix:

a(1). Aa, muqádtu mus Banáwaq? 'Oh, are you going to Banawa?
b(1). Mukáqun na ta. 'Let's eat.'

PP-CC exercises this plural-denoting use of paN-.

11 A 2. PaN- forming verbs from nouns

PaN- forms verbs from certain nouns. This is a common type of formation. Some of the nouns we have had which occur with paN- to form a verb are anák 'child' (panganák 'give birth'), apú 'grandchild' (pangapú 'have grandchildren'), asáwa 'wife' (pangasáwa 'take a wife'), bána 'husband' (pamána 'get married [of a woman]').

Nangapú na gániq tingáli ang ímung mga apú. (5 a 24) 'Even your grand-children probably already have grandchildren.'

11 A 3. Verbs that occur only with paN-

Some bases occur either never or only rarely without paN-. For example, pangutána 'ask' does not occur without it:*

Pangutánqa nang dyip, uh. (3 a 32) 'Ask that jeep [driver] there.'

11 B. The derivative verb prefix ka-

Another common derivative verb prefix is ka-. The following chart shows its forms. Note that there are no potentials or direct passives and very few instrumental passives to verbs containing the prefix ka-.

	Active	
Real	Unreal	Abstract
na-†	ma-†	pagka-
	Local Passive	
Real	Unreal	Subjunctive
{gika- -an / na- -an}	ka- -an	ka- -i

The ka- is dropped from the base and replaced by na-/ma-.

Kun matúug mi ngánhi, kamú ngádtu sa Amiriká magmatá. (5 b 37) 'When we are asleep here, you in America are awake.

Uy, natingála kaqáyu kung maqáyu kang mubinisayáq. (8 b 6) 'My, I am very surprised that you speak Visayan well.'

Natingádqan [or gikatingádqan] níla ang Amirkánang maqáyung mubinisayáq. 'They were amazed at the American who spoke Visayan well.'

The meanings of the ka- prefix are similar to those of the potential (above, 5 C 3, p. 179).

11 B 1. Ka- meaning 'accidentally happen to [something]'

Aa, nasayúp diqáy ku. (8 b 17) 'Oh, I was mistaken, wasn't I?' [Nasayúp 'be mistaken' happened to ku 'me.']

Diq ka mahádluk muqádtus Pulambatú? (9 a 8) 'Aren't you afraid to go to Pulambatú?' [Mahádluk 'be afraid' will not happen to ka 'you.']

The prefix ka- is always used with verbs meaning 'to fall,' since falling is always accidental.

Natúmba ang dakúq kaqáyung káhuy. 'The huge tree fell down.'

---

* The fact that the volitional and durative active forms are nangutána/mangutána: (cf. chart, 11 A) is proof that the form does indeed have the paN- prefix.

† Na- and ma- are used for both the volitional and the durative forms. In fancy language nag- and mag- also occur to bases with ka- (nagka-/magka-, discussed in Lesson 18, Part Two).

11 B 2. Ka- meaning 'can'

Arún mabúhiq kamí, ang ákung inahán mulútuq niqíning dúlsi. (8 c 9) 'So that we can live, my mother cooks this candy.'

11 B 3. Ka- meaning 'become'

An adjective base prefixed with ka- means 'become [adjective]':

Waq gyud ku matigúwang. (5 a 17) 'I have never grown old.' [tigúwang 'old (of persons)']
Nadakúq ang matá sa bátaq pagkakitáq níya sa gásang gidáa ni Máma níya. 'The child's eyes grew large when he saw the present his mother brought him.'

11 B 4. Ka- with no meaning

The ka- prefix with a small number of common verbs has no meaning: it simply appears whenever the roots to which it is attached are used as verbs. Verbs of this type we have had so far are: kanáqug 'go down, bring down,' kalîguq 'bathe,' and katúlug 'sleep.'

Dîliq pa ku manáqug kay ngîtngit pa man. (8 c 21) 'I won't get off yet because it's still dark.'
Kun matúug mi ngánhi, kamú ngádtus Amiriká magmatá. (5 b 37) 'When we are asleep here, you in America are awake.'

11 B 5. PaN- derivatives of verbs with ka-

All bases containing ka- may have paN- added to them, resulting in a prefix panga- (paN- + ka). This is the paN- of 11 A 1 and the meaning is plurality, of the agent or of the recipient of the action.

Ug magmatá mi ngánhi mangatúug sab mu dîdtu. (5 b 38) 'When we are awake here, you are asleep there.'
Pagpangatúmba sa mga káhuy, nanágan ang mga táwu. 'When the trees fell down, the people ran.'

11 B 6. The abstract form of bases with ka-

All ka- bases occur with the prefixes pag- and inig- (or its alternant ig-). When the abstract prefix pag- is attached to ka- bases, the prefixes combine to form the shape pagka- (cf. chart, p. 438). Similarly, the prefix inig- (or its alternant ig-) combines with ka- into the shape inigka- (igka-).

Inigkahumán, mubálik dáyun sa Sibú. (5 b 58) 'After that (is finished), I will return immediately to Cebu.'

Exercises XI.IV and XV.VII.

11 C. Imperative verb forms

The imperative form is used to express a command. Imperative forms, like other verb forms, are either active or passive; they have special shapes, described in the following subsections.

11 C 1. Active imperative

The active imperative has two alternative shapes, with no difference in meaning: (1) base alone, or (2) base prefixed by pag-.

Dalá [or pagdalá] diríg bir. 'Bring some beer here.'

The active imperative with pag- is most common with the negative ayáw.

An active imperative without a subject implies 'you [singular]' as agent. If the agent is 'you [plural],' the subject is kamú or mu. The goal is preceded by ug or sa as with other active verbs. In the following example the subject is underlined once, the imperative twice, and the goal three times:

Pagdalá mu diríg bir. 'You all bring some beer here.'

11 C 2. Passive imperative

A passive imperative form, like other passive verb forms, is either direct, local, or instrumental. The agent is genitive, as with other passives. The only agent that occurs with passive imperatives is nínyu 'you [plural].' A passive imperative without a genitive agent implies 'you [singular].' The following chart gives the passive imperative affixes:

Passive	Imperative affixes
Direct passive	-a or pag- -a*
Local passive	-i or pag- -i*
Instrumental passive	i- or pagqi-*

11 C 2 a. Direct passive imperative

With the direct passive imperative, as with other direct passives, the subject is the recipient of the action (cf. 6 A). The subjects in the examples below are underlined once, the imperatives, twice.

Ayáw na lang ku nínyug tanqáwa. (9 c 14) 'Don't look at me.'
Ayáw intáwun akú pagpátya. 'Don't kill me, please.'

11 C 2 b. Local passive imperative

With the local passive imperative, as with other local passives, the subject is the place of the action, the beneficiary of the action, or the recipient of the action (cf. 8 A 1, 8 A 2, 8 A 3).

Bantayí únyaq siyá ha? (8 a 27) 'Take good care of her, will you?'
Tagáqi lang kug únu singkwínta. (6 b 39) 'Just give me one-fifty.'

11 C 2 c. Instrumental passive imperative

With the instrumental passive imperative, as with other instrumental passives, the subject is either the instrument of the action, the beneficiary of the action, or the thing conveyed by the action (cf. 10 A 1, 10 A 2, and 10 A 3).

Ikúhaq kug bir Day. 'Bring me some beer.'
Ayáwg ihátag kanáng ímung gása. 'Don't give that present of yours away.'
Ibutáng ang kwárta sa lamísa. 'Put the money on the table.'

11 C 3. Imperative forms of bases with paN- or ka-

---

* Passive affixes containing pag- are not frequently used. They occur only with the negative, ayáw.

11 C 3 a. Active

The active imperative of bases containing the prefixes paN- or ka- have two shapes: (1) base alone (i.e. having no affix other than paN- or ka-) or (2) base plus a pag- prefix (i.e. having a prefix pagpaN- or pagka-).

[with paN-]

Pangítaq lang mug pára sa Kapitúl. (2 a 10) 'Just look for one [a jeep] going to the Capitol.'
Ayáw na pagpangutána. 'Stop asking questions.'

[with ka-]

Katúug na diháq. 'Go to sleep now.'
Ayáw pagkanáqug. 'Don't get off.'

11 C 3 b. Passive

The passive imperative forms of bases containing paN- or ka- have the same affixes as those described in 11 C 2 above.

Pangutánqa nang dyip uh. (3 a 32) 'Ask that jeep [driver] there.'

11 D. Obligatory use of the potentials

Some verb bases do not occur with the volitional or durative active prefixes but only with the potential active prefixes (naka-/maka-), and in the passive they occur only with the potential affixes. Verbs of this type we have had so far are kítaq 'see' and dungúg 'hear.'

Nakakitáq siyág dakúng káhuy. 'He saw a huge tree.'
Únsa man nang ákung nadungúg? (5 b 36) 'What is that I heard?'
Kinahánglan gyung makítaq sa ákung mga matá ang ílang kahímtang. (9 a 13) 'I absolutely must see their situation with my own eyes.'

Exercise XI.IV.

Pattern Practices and Exercises

PP-T Direct vs. local (transformations of active to passive) (8 A)

Step I. (Real, direct only. Transformation to passive)

a. 'He got some bananas.'
b. 'He got the bananas.'

1. a. Nagkúhaq siyág ságing.
   b. Gikúhaq níya ang ságing.

2. a. Nagkúhaq siyág kwárta.
   b. Gikúhaq níya ang kwárta.

3. a. Mitánqaw siyág ísdaq.
   b. Gitánqaw níya ang ísdaq.

4. a. Gadalá siyág gátas.
   b. Gidalá níya ang gátas.

5. a. Nagpalít siyág líbru.
   b. Gipalít níya ang líbru.

6. a. Naglútuq siyág ísdaq.
   b. Gilútuq níya ang ísdaq.

7. a. Nagkúhaq siyág sinínaq.
   b. Gikúhaq níya ang sinínaq.

8. a. Mikáqun siyág prútas.
   b. Gikaqún níya ang prútas.

9. a. Nagtawág siyág tartanílya.
   b. Gitawág níya ang tartanílya.

10. a. Nagtawág siyág dúktur.
    b. Gitawág níya ang dúktur.

11. a. Nagtánqaw siyág aríyus.
    b. Gitánqaw níya ang aríyus.

12. a. Gakúhaq siyág paan.
    b. Gikúhaq níya ang paan.

13. a. Nagdalá siyág manúk.
    b. Gidalá níya ang manúk.

14. a. Gakaqún siyág kánqun.
    b. {Gikaqún / Gikáqun} níya ang kánqun.

15. a. Gahátag siyág gása.
    b. Gihátag níya ang gása.

Step II. (Real only, direct only. Transform active to passive, with change of emphasis.)

a. 'He cooked some bananas.'
b. 'It was bananas he cooked.'

1. a. Naglútuq siyág ságing.
   b. Ságing ang íyang gilútuq.

2. a. Nagbúhat siyág lamísa.
   b. Lamísa ang íyang gibúhat.

3. a. Nagqinúm siyág bir.
   b. Bir ang íyang giqinúm.

4. a. Nagkúhaq siyág paan.
   b. Paan ang íyang gikúhaq.

5. a. Nakakitáq siyág aláhas.
   b. Aláhas ang íyang nakítaq.

6. a. Nagpalít siyág bag.
   b. Bag ang íyang gipalít.

7. a. Nagtánqaw siyág siní.
   b. Siní ang íyang gitánqaw.

8. a. Nagkúhaq siyág pípsi.
   b. Pípsi ang íyang gikúhaq.

9. a. Nagbúhat siyág baláy.
   b. Baláy ang íyang gibúhat.

10. a. Naglútuq siyág ítlug.
    b. Ítlug ang íyang gilútuq.

11. a. Nagqinúm siyág gátas.
    b. Gátas ang íyang giqinúm.

12. a. Nagpalít siyág bárku.
    b. Bárku ang íyang gipalít.

Step III. (Real and unreal, direct only. Shift of emphasis)

a. 'He is going to see a show.'
b. 'It is a show he is going to see.'

1. a. Mutánqaw siyág siní.
   b. Siní ang íyang tanqáwun.

2. a. Nagtánqaw siyág siní.
   b. Siní ang íyang gitánqaw.

3. a. Mudalá siyág líbru.
   b. Líbru ang íyang dádqun.

4. a. Nagdalá siyág líbru.
   b. Líbru ang íyang gidalá.

5. a. Mupalít siyág ísdaq.
   b. Ísdaq ang íyang palitún.

6. a. Nagpalít siyág ísdaq.
   b. Ísdaq ang íyang gipalít.

7. a. Mukáqun siyág ságing.
   b. Ságing ang íyang kánqun.

8. a. Gakaqún siyág ságing.
   b. Ságing ang íyang gikáqun.

9. a. Nagkaqún siyág ságing.
   b. Ságing ang íyang gikáqun.

10. a. Mukúhaq siyág pitáka.
    b. Pitáka ang íyang kuháqun.

11. a. Nagkúhaq siyág pitáka.
    b. Pitáka ang íyang gikúhaq.

12. a. Musulúd siyá sa kwártu.
    b. Kwártu ang íyang súdlun.

13. a. Mutawág siyág táksi.
    b. Táksi ang íyang táwgun.

14. a. Nagtawág siyág táksi.
    b. Táksi ang íyang gitawág.

15. a. Mulútuq siyág ísdaq.
    b. Ísdaq ang íyang lutúqun.

16. a. Naglútuq siyág ísdaq.
    b. Ísdaq ang íyang gilútuq.

Step IV. (Real and unreal and potential, direct only. Shift of emphasis)

'He can see the movie.'

1. a. Makatánqaw siyág siní.
   b. Siní ang íyang matánqaw.

2. a. Nakatánqaw siyág siní.
   b. Siní ang íyang natánqaw.

3. a. Nagtánqaw siyág siní.
   b. Siní ang íyang gitánqaw.

4. a. Makadalá siyág líbru.
   b. Líbru ang íyang madalá.

5. a. Gadalá siyág líbru.
   b. Líbru ang íyang gidalá.

6. a. Nagdalá siyág líbru.
   b. Líbru ang íyang nadalá.

7. a. Nakadalá siyág líbru.
   b. Líbru ang íyang nadalá.

8. a. Mupalít siyág ísdaq.
   b. Ísdaq ang íyang palitún.

9. a. Nakapalít siyág ísdaq.
   b. Ísdaq ang íyang napalít.

10. a. Nagpalít siyág ísdaq.
    b. Ísdaq ang íyang gipalít.

11. a. Gapalít siyág ísdaq.
    b. Ísdaq ang íyang gipalít.

12. a. Makapalít siyág ísdaq.
    b. Ísdaq ang íyang mapalít.

13. a. Mipalít siyág ísdaq.
    b. Ísdaq ang íyang gipalít.

14. a. Makakaqún siyág ságing.
    b. Ságing íyang makáqun.

15. a. Mikáqun siyág ságing.
    b. Ságing íyang gikaqún.

Step V. (Real and unreal, direct and local, in direct meaning. Shift of emphasis)

a. 'He'll look at Perla.'
b. 'Perla is the one he is going to look at.'

1. a. Mutánqaw siyáng Pírla.
   b. Si Pírla ang íyang tanqáwun.

2. a. Mitánqaw siyáng Pírla.
   b. Si Pírla ang íyang gitánqaw.

3. a. Nagtawág siyá sa dúktur.
   b. Dúktur ang íyang gitawág.

4. a. Miqábli siyá sa pultahán.
   b. Pultahán ang íyang giqablíhan.

5. a. Nagbántay siyás tindáhan.
   b. Tindáhan ang íyang gibantayán.

6. a. Muháwuk siyá sa bátaq.
   b. Bátaq ang íyang {háwkan / hágkan}.

7. a. Miháwuk siyá sa bátaq.
   b. Bátaq ang íyang {giháwkan / gihágkan}.

8. a. Mubántay siyá sa anák.
   b. Anák ang íyang bantayán.

9. a. Nagbántay siyá sa anák.
   b. Anák ang íyang gibantayán.

10. a. Mutánqaw siyág siní.
    b. Siní ang íyang tanqáwun.

11. a. Mitánqaw siyá sa aláhas.
    b. Aláhas ang íyang gitánqaw.

12. a. Musulúd siyá sa tindáhan.
    b. Tindáhan ang íyang súdlun.

13. a. Nagbalígyaq siyág ságing.
    b. Ságing ang íyang gibalígyaq.

14. a. Mubántay siyás tindáhan.
    b. Tindáhan ang íyang bantayán.

15. a. Nagbántay siyás tindáhan.
    b. Tindáhan ang íyang gibantayán.

16. a. Naghulát siyá ni Maríng.
    b. Si Maríng ang íyang gihulát.

17. a. Maglútuq siyág ísdaq.
    b. Ísdaq ang íyang lutúqun.

18. a. Mulabá siyág sinínaq.
    b. Sinínaq ang íyang lábhan.

19. a. Naglabá siyág sinínaq.
    b. Sinínaq ang íyang gilábhan.

20. a. Nagbúhat siyág baláy.
    b. Baláy ang íyang gibúhat.

Step VI. (Same as Step V)

a. 'She can watch the store.'
b. 'The store is what she can watch.'

1. a. Makabántay siyá sa tindáhan.
   b. Tindáhan ang íyang {kabantayán / mabantayán}.

2. a. Nakabántay siyás tindáhan.
   b. Tindáhan ang íyang nabantayán.

3. a. Nagkúhaq siyág ságing.
   b. Ságing ang íyang gikúhaq.

4. a. Mukúhaq siyág ságing.
   b. Ságing ang íyang kuháqun.

5. a. Nakaqábli siyás pitáka.
   b. Pitáka ang íyang naqablíhan.

6. a. Makaqábli siyás pitáka.
   b. Pitáka ang íyang {maqablíhan / kaqablíhan}.

7. a. Makabúhat siyág baláy.
   b. Baláy ang íyang mabúhat.

8. a. Galabá siyás sinínaq.
   b. Sinínaq ang íyang gilábhan.

9. a. Magqinúm siyág gátas.
   b. Gátas ang íyang ímnun.

10. a. Makakuháq siyág paan.
    b. Paan ang íyang makúhaq.

11. a. Miqinúm siyág gátas.
    b. Gátas ang íyang giqinúm.

12. a. Milabá siyás sinínaq.
    b. Sinínaq ang íyang gilábhan.

13. a. Nakabúhat siyág baláy.
    b. Baláy ang íyang nabúhat.

14. a. Milútuq siyág ságing.
    b. Ságing ang íyang gilútuq.

15. a. Makalútuq siyág ságing.
    b. Ságing ang íyang malútuq.

16. a. Maglútuq siyág paan.
    b. Paan ang íyang lutúqun.

17. a. Mitánqaw siyáng Pírla.
    b. Si Pírla ang íyang gitánqaw.

18. a. Nakatánqaw siyáng Pírla.
    b. Si Pírla ang íyang natánqaw.

19. a. Makahalúk siyás anák.
    b. Anák ang íyang mahágkan.

20. a. Makatawág siyás kutsíru.
    b. Kutsíru ang íyang matawág.

Step VII. (Local and direct in all meanings; change of emphasis)

a. 'He's drinking from the glass.'
b. 'It's the glass he is drinking from.'

1. a. Gaqinúm siyás básu.
   b. Básu ang íyang giqímnan.

2. a. Nagqinúm siyás básu.
   b. Básu ang íyang giqímnan.

3. a. Makaqinúm siyás básu.
   b. Básu ang íyang {maqímnan / kaqímnan}.

4. a. Miqinúm siyás básu.
   b. Básu ang íyang giqímnan.

5. a. Maglabá siyág sinínaq.
   b. Sinínaq ang íyang lábhan.

6. a. Makapuyúq siyás baláy.
   b. Baláy ang íyang {mapúyqan / kapúyqan}.

7. a. Mikúhaq siyág paan.
   b. Paan ang íyang gikúhaq.

8. a. Nakaqinúm siyás básu.
   b. Básu ang íyang naqímnan.

9. a. Nagkúhaq siyág paan.
   b. Paan ang íyang gikúhaq.

10. a. Makakúhaq siyág kwárta sa pitáka.
    b. Pitáka ang íyang {makuháqag / kakuháqag} kwárta.

11. a. Makalútuq siyás kusína.
    b. Kusína ang íyang {malutúqan / kalutúqan}.

12. a. Nagbúhat siyág baláy.
    b. Baláy ang íyang gibúhat.

13. a. Makaqádtu siyás siní.
    b. Siní ang íyang {maqadtúqan / kaqadtúqan}.

14. a. Mukúhaq siyág kwárta sa pitáka.
    b. Pitáka ang íyang kuháqag kwárta.

15. a. Muqádtu siyás siní.
    b. Siní ang íyang adtúqan.

16. a. Gaqinúm siyág lítsi sa básu.
    b. Básung íyang giqímnag lítsi.

17. a. Nakaqinúm siyág gátas.
    b. Gátas ang íyang naqinúm.

18. a. Muqinúm siyág gátas sa básu.
    b. Básung íyang ímnag gátas.

19. a. Makaqinúm siyág gátas.
    b. Gátas ang íyang maqinúm.

20. a. Makaqádtu siyás uspitál.
    b. Uspitál ang íyang {maqadtúqan / kaqadtúqan}.

I. (May be preceeded by PP-R and PP-T.) Ibutáng ang hústung púrma sa bírbu nga anáqa sa parentheses. Gamita ang active ug passive. (4 A, 12 A)

1. Díqay tindáhan sa mga aláhas. (Suud) ku. 'Here's a jewelry store. I'll go inside.'
2. (Suud) na ánang tindáhan sa aláhas si Mis Wílbi. 'Miss Wilby has already gone inside that jewelry store.'
3. (Suud) ra gud ang mga líbru sa tindáhan. 'Please put the books inside the store.'
4. Ug (palít) kug usá ka dusína, pilá man? 'If I buy a dozen, how much (will it cost)?'
5. Tibuqúk dusína ba ang ímung (palít) ganíha? 'Did you buy a whole dozen a while ago?'
6. Kínsay ímung (palít) niqánang aríyus? 'Who did you buy those earrings from?'
7. (Hátag) mig prísyung ispisyál pára nímu. 'We can give you a special price.'
8. (Hátag) ka na námuq sa ultimúng prísyu. 'We have already given you the lowest price.'
9. Waláq pa ku nímu (hátag) sa báyad uy! 'You have not given me the payment yet.'
10. Uy anáaq, (tawág) man ku níla. 'Oh my! They're calling me!'
11. (Tawág) ra ku ánang dráybir Dung. 'Please call that driver for me, Boy.'
12. Ang Ínsik bay (tawág) nákuq Day? 'Is it the Chinaman who is calling me, Miss?'
13. Kínsa tung (tawág) ganíha? 'Who was it that called a while ago?'

14. Huwat lang kay (tánqaw) pa níya kun dúna ba siyáy ikasinsíyu sa ímung báynti. 'Wait a second. He's going to see if he can change your twenty.'
15. Waláq pa níya (tánqaw) ang súkliq sa íyang báynti písus. 'She hasn't looked at the change for her twenty pesos yet.'
16. (Tánqaw) ang mga bátaq ni Mis Wílbi. 'Miss Wilby looked at the children.'
17. Ayáw ku nínyug (tánqaw). 'Don't look at me.'
18. Ása man ku (sakáy)g dyip páras Mabúlu?
19. Maqú ning dyípa ang(sakáy) ku gahápun padulúng sa Lahúg.
20. Pulús na (ukupár) ang mga tihíras.
21. Kiníng tihirása waláq pa ba (ukupár)?
22. Kínsa may (ukupár) únyaq áning tihíras? Si Mis Wílbi ba?
23. Ása man nákuq (butáng) ning mga kaság? Sa pantáwan ba?
24. (butáng) na ni Plúra ang dalá níyang muskitíru sa suud.
25. Kínsay (butáng) áring sabún sa bányu?

PP-CC Change Singular to Plural (11 A)

Step I. (No imperatives)

'He is eating.'

1.	a.	Nagkaqún siyá.	(silá)
	b.	Nangáqun silá.	
2.	a.	Muqinúm akú.	(kitá)
	b.	Manginúm kitá.	
3.	a.	Mukáqun siyá.	(silá)
	b.	Mangáqun silá.	
4.	a.	Matúlug akú.	(kamí)
	b.	Mangatúlug kamí.	
5.	a.	Manáqug siyá.	(silá)
	b.	Manganáqug silá.	
6.	a.	Mulakáw akú.	(kitá)
	b.	Manglákaw kitá.	
7.	a.	Musakáy siyá.	(silá)
	b.	Manakáy silá.	
8.	a.	Musaká akú.	(kamí)
	b.	Manaká kamí.	
9.	a.	Muhúnung siyá.	(silá)
	b.	Manghúnung silá.	

10. a. Mubálik akú. (kitá)
    b. Mamálik kitá.

11. a. Nagpalít siyág líbru. (ang mga táwu)
    b. Namalít ang mga táwug líbru.

12. a. Gibalígyaq níya ang básu. (ang mga kaság)
    b. Gipamalígyaq níya ang mga kaság.

13. a. Gilábay níya ang láta. (ang mga láta)
    b. Gipanglábay níya ang mga láta.

14. a. Gilútuq níya ang ságing. (ang mga ságing)
    b. Gipanglútuq níya ang mga ságing.

15. a. Giputús níya ang kaság. (ang mga kaság)
    b. Gipamutús níya ang mga kaság.

Step II. (Imperatives)

'Just get on.'

1. a. Sakáy na lang. (mu)
   b. Panakáy na lang mu.

2. a. Kanáqug na diháq. (mu)
   b. Panganáqug na mu diháq.

3. a. Katúlug na. (mu)
   b. Pangatúlug na mu.

4. a. Káqun na Pidrú. (mu)
   b. Pangáqun na mu Pidrú.

5. a. Kuháqa náq. (nínyu)
   b. Panguháqa naq nínyu.

6. a. Kúyug dirí. (kamú)
   b. Pangúyug kamú dirí.

7. a. Itúsa na lang ang sabáw. (nínyu ang mga sabáw)
   b. Pangitúsa na lang nínyu ang mga sabáw.

8. a. Pútla na ang káhuy. (nínyu ang mga káhuy)
   b. Pamútla na nínyu ang mga káhuy.

9. a. Sakáy na lang dídtu. (mu)
   b. Panakáy na lang mu dídtu.

10. a. Tagáqi na lang siyá. (silá)
    b. Panagáqi na lang silá.

11. a. Púnqa ang básug túbig. (ang mga básu)
    b. Pamúnqa ang mga básug túbig.

12. a. Lutúqa na lang ang kaság. (nínyu ang mga kaság)
    b. Panglutúqa na lang nínyu ang mga kaság.

13. a. Úsba ang pagkabutáng sa líbru. (mga líbru)
    b. Pangúsba ang pagkabutáng sa mga líbru.

14. a. Samúka ang táwu nga nagbáyli. (nínyu ang mga táwu)
    b. Panamúka nínyu ang mga táwung nagbáyli.

15. a. Pústa ang líbru ni Pírla. (mga líbru)
    b. Pamústa ang mga líbru ni Pírla.

16. a. Pátya ang bábuy ni Ústing. (mga bábuy)
    b. Památya ang mga bábuy ni Ústing.

Step III. (Mixture of nonimperative and imperative)

'I'm going to the dance now.'

1. a. Muqádtu na ku sa báyli. (kamí)
   b. Mangádtu na kamí sa báyli.

2. a. Palitá na lang ang kaság. (ang mga kaság)
   b. Pamalitá na lang ang mga kaság.

3. a. Mubálik na lang siyá sa baláy. (silá)
   b. Mamálik na lang silá sa baláy.

4. a. Balhína ang lamísa sa kusína. (mga lamísa)
   b. Pamalhína ang mga lamísa sa kusína.

5. a. Magbúhat kug muskitíru. (mga muskitíru)
   b. Mamúhat kug mga muskitíru.

6. a. Sulúd na sa kwártu. (kamú)
   b. Panulúd na kamú sa kwártu.

7. a. Muhátag kug kwárta. (silá)
   b. Manghátag silág kwárta.

8. a. Hangyúqa ang bátaq. (nínyu ang mga bátaq)
   b. Panghangyúqa nínyu ang mga bátaq.

9. a. Mutánqaw siyág sini. (silá)
   b. Manánqaw silág sini.

10. a. Pútla na ang káhuy. (nínyu ang mga káhuy)
    b. Pamútla na nínyu ang mga káhuy.

II. Ibutáng ang hústung púrma sa bírbu nga anáqa sa parentheses. (11 A and subsections, 11 B and subsections)

Pananglítan: Sus! Waq pa gániq akú (pangapú).

Tubág: Sus! Waq pa gániq akú mangapú.

1. Pagqabút námuq sa baláy (pangáqun) na ang mga bátaq. 'When we reached home, the children had already eaten.'

2. Dínhi lang saq mu kay (panghatúd) ku pa ring mga kaság sa ílang Mísis Ulibár. 'Just stay here for a while because I still have to deliver these crabs to Mrs. Olivar's.'
3. (Kabúhiq) mi sa gamáy námung basakán. 'We live on the proceeds of our small rice field.'
4. Maqáyung (panglútuq) si Mísis Milíndris. 'Mrs. Melendres cooks well.'
5. Diqín man nímu (pamutáng) ang mga dalá mung gása? 'Where did you put the gifts you brought?' (Use the subjunctive for this sentence.)
6. Ikáw Day. Diq pa ba ka (kanáqug) nga Pulambatú na man ni? 'You, Miss. Aren't you getting off yet? This is Pulambato now.'
7. Díliq ba nátuq (panghátag) kiníng mga líbru? 'Aren't we going to give these books away?'
8. Sa sunúd búlan pa mi (pamálhin) sa Banáwaq. 'We aren't going to move to Banawa till next month.'
9. Sámtang waláq pa tay baláy, (pangábang) lang saq ta. 'As long as we don't have a house, let's just rent one for now.'
10. Túqa si Nánay nilakáw arún (panínda) ug kalamáy. 'Mother went out to sell kalamay.'
11. Dínhi sa San Rimihiyú (kamatáy) tung tigúwang Amirkánu. 'That old American died here in San Remigio.' (Use the unreal.)
12. Náqa ba siyá sa bányu (kalíguq)? (Use the unreal for this sentence.)
13. Diq pa gániq ku (pangasáwa) (pangimbitár) ka na. 'I'm not even getting married yet, but you're already inviting people.'
14. May (pangítaq) ba nákuq dínhi sa ínyu? 'Was there someone who was looking for me here at your place?'
15. Ádtu pa ku sa gawás (pamalít) ug sabún nga ákung dádqun sa Pulambatú.
16. Túqa silá sa tihíras (panglíngkud). Adtúqa lang. 'There they are sitting on the cots. Just go see them there.'
17. Si Nánay ang (pamutús) ánang mga dadqunún nímu.
18. Karúng hápun (pangádtu) ta sa ílang Mísis Milíndris.
19. Kínsa may (pangúhaq) sa mga gása dirí?
20. Úgmaq kay Dumínggu man (pamisíta) ta nílang Pírla ug Mis Wílbi.
21. (Kahibalú) ba si Tátay nímung níqa mi?
22. Dínhi lang ka kay (panulúd) pa mi dirí sa kwártu. (dínhi lang ka 'you stay here')
23. Unyáq lang mu sakáy ug (pangabút) ang mga bátaq.
24. Túqa na silá sa Úrmuk (pamuyúq) karún. (Use the unreal.)
25. Ngánung (kahádluk) man silá nákuq nga díliq man ku mangúnsa?

III. Ibutáng ang hústung púrma sa imperative sa parentheses. (11 C and subsections)

Pananglítan: (Tánqaw) ra nang nagbalígyag mga káwuq.

Tubág: Tanqáwa ra nang nagbalígyag mga káwuq.

b. Halá mga bátaq. (pangatúlug) na mu.

Tubág: Halá mga bátaq. Pangatúlug na mu.

1. (Kúhaq) ra ku ánang tuqálya Day. 'Get me that towel, Miss.'
2. Únyaq sa hápun, (panghatúd) nínyu ning mga gása sa ka Mísis Ulibár. 'Later this afternoon, deliver these gifts to Mrs. Olivar's.'
3. Huy Plurá, (dalá) ning sabún ug tuqálya sa bányu. 'Hey, Flora, take this soap and towel to the bathroom.'
4. Inigkahumán diháq sa ímung búhat (káwus) nyaq kug túbig. 'After your work there is finished, get me some water.'
5. (Sakáy) na ring mga dalá kung gása sa traak Dung. 'Put these gifts I brought on the bus now, Boy.'
6. (Tánqaw) nu ngádtu sa istasyunán ug náqa na bang traak. 'Go to the station and see if the bus is there now.'
7. Ayáwg (butáng) nang túbig dínhi. (Sulúd) lang naq sa bányu. 'Don't put that water here. Just put it in the bathroom.'
8. Dung, (hatúd) ku sa Banáwaq run. 'Boy, take me to Banawa now.'
9. (Pangítaq) ku ug baláy nga paqabángan. 'Find me a house for rent.'
10. Ayáw nag (búhat) kay díliq naq maqáyu. 'Don't do that because it's not nice.'
11. Kiríng dalá kung kaság (bálhin) dídtu sa kusína kay arún lutúqun ni Lúling. 'Take these crabs I brought into the kitchen so that Loling can cook them.'
12. Day, (huwát) ku dínhi kay adtúqun ku pa si Tátay nímu sa basakán. 'Miss, wait for me here because I am going to get your father in the rice field.'
13. Duq, (húnung) na lang ku dínhi kay maqú na man ning baláy námuq. 'Boy, just drop me off here because this is our house now.'
14. Lulíng, (lútuq) nyaq ring súdqan dirí sa lamísa. 'Later on, Loling, cook the food that's here on the table.'
15. (Putús) na ring sabún Day kay mulakáw na ku. 'Wrap this soap up, Miss, because I'm going out now.'
16. Díqay písu uh. (Súkliq) rig báynti.
17. (Pangutána) akú níya kun miqabút na ba si Mísis Milíndris.
18. (Hátag) ra nang bátag dúlsi arún diq na muhílak. (Use the colloquial form.)
19. Pirlá, (ubán) si Mis Wílbi sa bárku karúng gabíqi.

20. (Iháp) nu ning kaság ug nakaqabút ba ug napúuq.
21. Ayáw na lang ug kaguqúl. (Kalímut) na lang tung tanán. 'Don't fret anymore. Just forget the whole thing.'
22. Dung, (palít) ra kug kalamáy ánang bátang nagtínda.
23. (risírba) mig tihíras Duq kay manglákaw pa mi.
24. Ayáwg (búhiq) ning mga kaság kay manágan nyaq ni.
25. (kupút) ra saq ning bag ku Pirlá.

IV. Gamíta ang hústung púrma sa bírbu nga anáqa sa <u>parentheses</u> ginámit ang <u>potentials</u>. (11 D)

Pananglítan:

a. Únsa tung ákung (dungúg) nga waq pa mu (kítaq) ug baláy? (kítaq 'find, see)

Tubág: Únsa tung ákung <u>nadungúg</u> nga waq pa mu <u>makakitáq</u> ug baláy.

1. (Dungúg)ming mulárga ka rung gabíqi sa Úrmuk Mis Wílbi. 'We heard that you were leaving for Ormoc this evening, Miss Wilby.'
2. Waq pa gyud ku (kítaq)g basakán Plurá. 'I haven't seen a rice field yet, Flora.'
3. Únsa may (kítaq) nínyung níndut sa Pulambatú Day? 'What did you see that was nice in Pulambato, Miss?'
4. (dungúg) ba ku nínyu diháq? 'Can you hear me there?'
5. Waq nákuq (kítaq) kanáng tawhána dídtu sa ílang Mísis Ulibár. 'I didn't see that man at Mrs. Olivar's.'
6. Waláq pa ba mu (dungúg) ug Amirkánang kamaqúng mubinisayáq? 'Haven't you ever heard of an American who can speak Visayan?'
7. (Kitáq) na gyud námuq ang baláy nílang Nída. Níndut diqáy. 'At last we saw Nida's house. It was beautiful.'
8. Kiníng awíta (song), waláq pa ba nímu (dungúg)? 'Haven't you heard this song yet?'
9. Ug (kítaq) lang nínyu ang Úrmuk, sigúrung makagústu gyud mung muqádtu. 'If you only could see Ormoc, you would surely want to go there.'
10. Waq pa gyud ku (kítaq) ánang amíga mung si Mísis Milíndris. 'I haven't seen your friend, Mrs. Melendres yet.'

V A. Ibúngat ang mga musunúd nga mga túdling púlung sa hústung paníngug. (<u>324</u> Question)

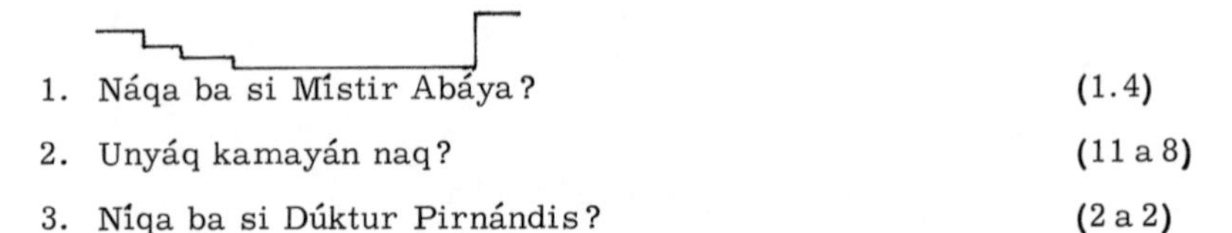

1. Náqa ba si Místir Abáya? (1.4)
2. Unyáq kamayán naq? (11 a 8)
3. Níqa ba si Dúktur Pirnándis? (2 a 2)

4. Kádtung túqa dídtu? (11 b 27)
5. Kínsa ning nagtawág? (2 a 4)
6. Padúung ba naq sa Banáwaq? (2 a 11)
7. Maqantígu ka ánaq? (11 b 44)
8. Lítu diqáy ímung ngálan? (2 b 24)
9. Diq ka kaháq únyaq samúkans mga bátaq? (3 c 11)
10. Dúna muy mga lubí sa ínyung dápit? (5 a 27)
11. Diq ba mahímug dyis na lang? (6 a 8)

V B. (234 Statement)

1. Díliq na. (11 a 9)
2. Níqa na kitás átung tihíras. (8 a 10)
3. Ayáw na lang. (1.14)
4. Pitú na ka túqig kapín. (11 a 24)
5. Manakáy na ta. (2 a 17)
6. Dúna say sílbing kastígu. (11 b 14)
7. Nagtákyan naq. (11 b 28)
8. Waq na ra bay bir Nyur. (2 b 27)
9. Nakakitáq ka bítaw ánang bátaq. (11 b 42)
10. Sayún ra naq. (5 a 15)

V C. (423 Statement)

1. Ákuq lang ibílin ning ákung amígu dínhi. (1.16)
2. Aa, maqú diqáy nis Mis Wílbi. (3 b 10)
3. Kaqusá ra gyud mi makaqáni sa usá ka túqig. (11 a 14)
4. Náqa táwun mi manginabúhiq diháq. (11 a 21)
5. Mu ni si Índay. (3 c 4)
6. Maqú nay gitawág námuq dínhig sátung. (11 b 2)
7. Mu nang waq gyud ku matigúwang. (5 a 17)
8. Dúna na siláy púntus. (11 b 9)
9. Hángtud maqabút níya ang íla lugár nga biis. (11 b 23)
10. Maqáyu tingáling ádtu na lang ku. (8 a 32)
11. Maqú nay dúwang lisúd kaqáyu. (11 b 29)
12. Maqú nay gibúhat ánaq. (11 b 36)

13. Maqú nay banggiqítan dínhi sa ámung lugár. (11 c 4)
14. Maqú nang gitawág nag tigbakáy. (11 c 18)

V D. (423 Question)

1. Únsa may átuq? (1.3)
2. Singáan man nang pilípig? (11 a 3)
3. Ánhi lang ta manihápun? (2 b 31)
4. Unsingáan man nang gidúlaq sa mga bátaq? (11 b 1)
5. Ása man tung baay ni Mísis Abilyána? (3 a 1)
6. Únsa may íyang gidúlaq? (11 b 26)
7. Ása man ta musakáy ug muqádtu tas Banáwaq? (3 a 16)
8. Únsa mang rasáha naq sa sunúy Nuy? (11 c 22)
9. Pilá may bayranán ánaq sa káda búwan? (3 b 25)
10. Ása man ning dyípa Dung? (3 c 24)
11. Únsa pa may ubán nákung dádqun? (9 a 5)

V E. (431 Statement)

1. Magbúhat nyaq kug pilípig. (11 a 2)
2. Túqas Banáwaq. (3 a 4)
3. Kay dúgay man kaqáyu nang makúhang tubú. (11 a 15)
4. Pangutánqa nang dyip. (3 a 32)
5. Kay mukítaq man silág únu singkwínta ang ádlaw. (11 a 17)
6. Pwírting layúqa táwun námuq. (11 a 27)
7. Mga katúu naq ilabaylábay sa bátang nakadaqúg. (11 b 16)
8. Tutál kahibáwu na man kung muqádtu. (9 a 18)
9. Kanapúluq na ku makadaqúg niqíni dínhi sa ámuq. (11 c 6)
10. Kay tigbakáy ra man gyud ning ámuq dínhig madumínggu. (11 c 13)
11. Gústu gyud kung mutánqawg sábung. (11 c 25)

V F. Ibúngat ang mga túdling púlung sa itáqas (Exercise V E) ginámit ang 231 Statement nga túnu.

1. Magbúhat nyaq kug pilípig. (11 a 2)

V G. The following sentences consist of a 243 contour followed by a pause and a 423 contour. The pause occurs where the comma is written. This contour, symbolized 243#423, is used for statements.

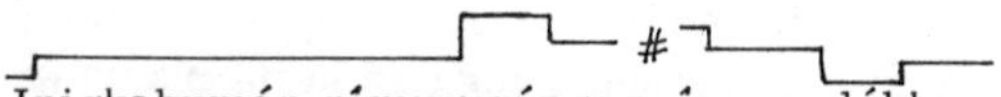

1.	Inigkahumán nímug sángag, ímung lúbkun.	(11 a 7)
2.	Unyáq sa tubú, kaqusá ra gyud mi makaqáni sa usá ka túqig.	(11 a 14)
3.	Sa pangáni sa tubú, náqa táwun mi manginabúhiq diháq.	(11 a 21)
4.	Kay búhat nga dinaliqdalíq, dalíq ra sad kaqáyung nagubáq.	(11 a 25)
5.	Ug kanáng náqang taqás nga káhuy sab, maqúy gamítun níla sa paglábay.	(11 b 6)
6.	Inigkasáwuq níla ánaq, dúna na siláy púntus.	(11 b 9)
7.	Ang kadtúng naglábay ánang mubúng káhuy, mu na say mubántay.	(11 b 10)
8.	Ug ang makasáwuq, mu na say mulábay.	(11 b 11)
9.	Kanáng káhuyng mubúq, ilábay naq sa layúq.	(11 b 15)
10.	Kadtúng napíldi, manukád ádtung gilabáyan sa káhuy.	(11 b 17)
11.	Ádtu siyá manukád dídtu, mudágan bálik ngarí sa lungág nga ílang gibutangán sa káhuy.	(11 b 19)
12.	Pananglítag ang bátaq kusúg kaqáyung mulabáy, layuqlayúq sad siyág dagánan.	(11 b 20)
13.	Kanáng íyang manúk, maqú nay banggiqítan dínhi sa ámung lugár.	(11 c 4)
14.	Ay kanáng tigbakáy, paríhà ra gud nag búlang gihápun.	(11 c 17)
15.	Tungúd kay waláq may pagtúgut, maqú nang gitawág nag tigbakáy.	(11 c 18)

VI A. Pagbása

Gása sa mga Bátaq

Asáy: Únsa may gipamalít nímu? Bágqu pa man kang namalít ádtung miqáging simána.

Lína: Aa, ákuq man gung ipanghátag sa átung mga higála dídtus Pulambatú.

Asáy: Pamústa lang nang mga gása kay mawálaq nyaq naq.

Lína: Kahádluk na man nímu! ('How scared you are!') Ngánung mahádluk ka mag mawálaq naq nga kitá ra man? Waq na mans Lítu.

Asáy: Panádqun ta ni dirís sulúd kay ipamutáng nátus aparadúr. (aparadúr 'cabinet')

Lína: Panguháqa saq tung mga sulúd sa aparadúr.

Asáy: Pamalhínun nákuq ring mga tuqálya ug usá ka muskitíru. Liná, ikupút saq ku áring muskitíru kay ákung pamalhínun ring mga tuqálya.

Lína: Malímut ka nyaq nga mamaqúliq bayáq ta dáyun kay dághan pa akúg buhátun. Mamutús pa kus ubáng mga gása ug mangutána pa kung Mísis Mílir anúsqa ipanghátag ang mga gása. Humán niqánaq mamálik pa ta dídtus Pulambatú kay kitáqun nátus Nuy Tibúq. 'We'll go to see Tibo.'

Asáy: Ngánu mang mamálik ta ngádtu?

Lína: Ii, mangasáwa na man gud nang íyang apú ug mangádtu únyaq ta kay nangimbitár siyá nátuq. Siyá ra ba gyuy nangunáy pagpangingún sa mga higála nga gipangimbitár.

Asáy: Mamatáy na pud ta ínis kakápuy. Sigí, ámbi na nang muskitíru ug átung ipanganáqug ring mga líbru.

(Unyáq)

Asáy: Uy! Díqa ra man lagí ag ímung bag nga nawálaq!

Lína: Sus salámat! Diq na gyud ku mabaláka sa ákung singkwínta písus. Náqa na kuy ipamáyad sa palitún kung mga gása.

VI B. Pagbánsay. (Ibutáng ang hústung púrma sa mga púlung nga anáqa sa parentheses.)

Gása sa mga Bátaq

Asáy: Únsa may (pamalít) nímu? Bágqu pa man kang (pamalít) ádtung miqáging simána.

Lína: Aa, ákuq man gung (panghátag) sa átung mga higála dídtus Pulambatú.

Asáy: (pamutús) lang nang mga gása kay mawálaq nyaq naq.

Lína: Kahádluk na man nímu! ('How scared you are!') Ngánung (kahádluk) ka mag (kawálaq) naq nga kitá ra man? Waq na mans Lítu.

Asáy: (panalá) ta ni dirís sulúd kay (pamutáng) nátus aparadúr.

Lína: (pangúhaq) saq tung mga sulúd sa aparadúr.

Asáy: (pamálhin) nákuq ring mga tuqálya ug usá ka muskitíru. Liná, ikupút saq ku áring muskitíru kay ákung (pamálhin) ring mga tuqálya.

Lína: (kalímut) ka nyaq nga (pamaqúliq) bayáq ta dáyun kay dághan pa akúg buhátun. (pamutús) pa kus ubáng mga gása ug (pangutána) pa kung Mísis Mílir anúsqa (panghátag) ang mga gása. Humán niqánaq (pamálik) pa ta dídtus Pulambatú kay kitáqun nátus Nuy Tibúq. 'We'll go to see Tibo.'

Asáy: Ngánu man tang (pamálik) ngádtu?

Lína: Ii, (pangasáwa) na man gud nang íyang apú ug (pangádtu) únyaq ta kay (pangimbitár) siyá nátuq. Siyá ra ba gyuy (pangunáy) pagpangingún sa mga higála nga (pangimbitár).

Asáy: (Kamatáy) na pud ta ínis kakápuy. Sigí, ámbi na nang muskitíru ug átung (panganáqug) ring mga líbru.

(Únyaq)

Asáy: Uy! Díqa ra man lagí ag ímung bag nga (kawálaq)!

Lína: Sus, salámat! Diq na gyud ku (kabaláka) sa ákung singkwínta písus. Náqa na kuy (pamáyad) sa palitún kung mga gása.

VII. Sultiqánay

A: Nidá, díqay ákung gása pára nímu.

B: Aa diqáy. Diqín man naq nímu palitá?

A: Dídtus Magalyánis. Gahápun nákuq mapalít. Ayáwg tanqáwa saq run.

B: Sultíhi lang saq ku rug únsay suud Pirlá.

A: Aa diq ku! Uh, ayáwg sulingsulínga!

B: Aa halá gud. Túqa puy ákung ihátag nímu. Ayáw pug tanqáwa. Dídtu nákuq mapalít sa Huwán Lúna.

A: Náqa bay tindáhan diháq sa Huwán Lúna?

B: Uu, náqa. Ag Usyánik diqáy.

1. Waláq si Nida palití ug gása.
2. Dídtu sa Magalyánis mapalít ang gása.
3. Gisultíhan si Nída ug únsay gásang gipalít álang kaníya.
4. Sulingsulíngun ni Nída arún mahibálqag únsay suud.
5. Gipalitán pud si Pírla ug gása ni Nída.

A: Únsa man tung igása nímu nákuq Nidá? Sultíhi lang ku.

B: Díliq maqáyung mahibalú ka. Hulát lag dyútayng panahún.

(Ni Pírla pa sa íyang kaqugalíngun.)

A: Ákung tagúqan ring ákung igása níya arún díliq níya makítaq. Íya pa lang tanqáwun nyaq.

(Ug ni Nída pa sa íyang pagsúltis íyang kaqugalíngun.)

B: Ákuq lang ibutáng sa lamísa, bir ug íya ba gyung tanqawtanqáwun.

(Nakítqan ni Pírla ang gibutángs lamísa.)

A: Íya pa gyung gibutangbútang sa lamísa.

6. Si Pírla na puy nangutánag únsay gásang ihátag kaníya.
7. Gipahulát siyág dyútayng panahún.
8. Waláq tagúqi ni Pírla ang íyang gása párang Nída.
9. Ang gásang Pírla gibutáng langs lamísa.

(Sa pagkapásku* na gyud)

A: Maqáyung Pásku Nidá!

B: Ug maqáyu pung Bágqung Túqig.

A: Átung pananqáwun ang átung mga gása.

B: Uu sigí, dúngan tag ábli.

A: Hulatá saq kug kadyút kay ákung kuháqun ang ákung gása nímu.

B: Díliq ta magtanqawáy.

(Pagkahumán)

A: Uy!

B: Uy! Anáaq!

A ug B: Paríhas man tag gipanghátag.

10. Waláq níla pananqáwa ang ílang mga gása.
11. Nagquná si Pírlag ábli sa íyang gása.
12. Gikúhaq pa úsaq ang gása ni Pírla pára kang Nída.
13. Paríhas diqáy ang ílang mga gása.

---

* Pásku 'Christmas.'

LESSON 12. IN THE BOOKSTORE

Sagquluhúnun

First Part	Únang Báhin
[hissing sound to draw attention]	sst—sst
[term of address for males same age as or younger than speaker]	Dung
1. Hey! Rig, Boy!	*1. Sst—sst tartanílya Dung.
[term of address for females same age as or younger than speaker]	Day
2. Where are you going, Miss?	2. Âsa man ka Day?
3. To Borromeo Street.	3. Sa Burumíyu.
[particle contradicting]	man
just	ra
because	man
near	duqúl
4. No, I can't, Miss; I'm just working in this neighborhood. (Lit. Ah, not me, Miss, because I'm just going near here.)	4. Aa, dîliq man ku Day. Ánhi ra ... man kus duqúl.
come on!	sígi
just (particle with command implying it is a little thing to do)	lang
5. Oh, come on!	5. Sîgi lang.
heck (expression of disgust about something speaker did not want to have happen)	da
it is raining	nagquwán

now (as contrasted with before)	na
[expression about an event one did not want to have happen]	hinúqun
6. Heck, it's starting to rain now.	*6. Da, nagquwán na hinúqun.
rig	tartanílya
over here	ngarí
[particle drawing attention of hearer]	uh
7. Rig! Over here!	7. Tartanílya, ngarí uh.
8. Yes.	8. Uu.
let ride	pasákya
9. Let me get in.	*9. Pasákya ku nínyu.
10. Where are you going, Miss?	10. Ása man ka Day?
take	ihatúd
[particle asking for agreement]	ha
11. Take me to Borromeo, will you?	11. Ihatúd ku sa Burumíyu ha?
ah (pause for polite refusal)	aa
get off	kanáqug
just	lang
market place	tiyánggi
12. Please get off, Miss, because I'm going to the market place.	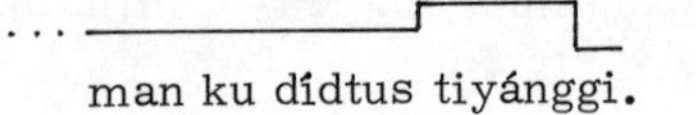 12. Aa, kanáqug lang Day kay ádtu ... man ku dídtus tiyánggi.
oh (coaxing)	uh
just	lang
13. Oh, just take me over there to Borromeo St.	13. Uh, ihatúd lang ku dídtus ... Burumíyu.

it's raining	nagquwán
because	man gud
new	bágqu
[particle with a reason which is an admonition]	ra ba
dress	sinínaq

14. Because it's raining and my dress is new. — 14. Nagquwán man gud. Bágqu ra ba ning ákung sinínaq.

still	pa
because	man
downtown	sa ubús

15. (Ah), I can't because I still have to go downtown — 15. Aa, diq mahímuq kay ádtu pa man ku dídtus ubús.

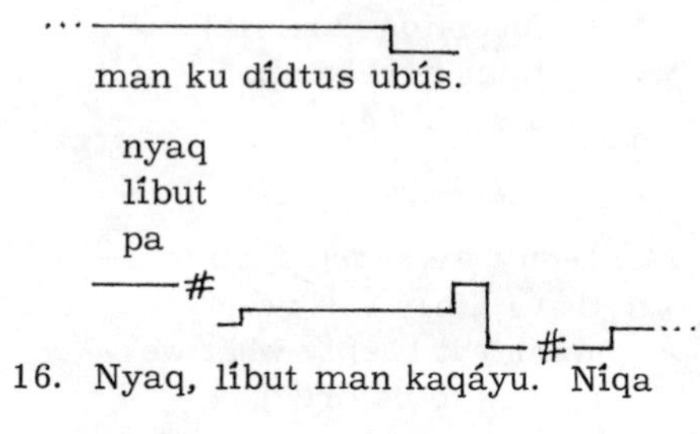

furthermore	nyaq
roundabout	líbut
still	pa

16. Furthermore, it's a very roundabout way. I still have somebody here to take. — 16. Nyaq, líbut man kaqáyu. Níqa pa may ákung ihatúd.

come on!	sígi na

17. Come on, Boy! — 17. Sígi na Dung.

will make double	dublíhun
fare	plíti

18. I'll pay you double. (Lit. I'll double my fare to you.) — *18. Dublíhun nákuq ákung plíti nímu.

all right	halá
go on	sígi

19. All right, get in. — 19. Halá, sígi.

here	ngánhi
just	lang

20. Here's where I get off. (Lit. Just here.)	20. Ngánhi lang.
[particle drawing attention of hearer]	uh
twenty cents	báynti
	—#
21. Here's twenty cents.	21. Uh, díqay báynti.
22. Thirty cents, Miss.	22. Tráynta Day.
oh! (expression of surprise)	uh
[question particle indicating surprise]	gud
	—#
23. Why, how come it's thirty?	23. Uh! Ngánung tráynta gud?
[question particle]	ba
thing agreed upon	gikasabútan
a while ago	ganíha
24. Didn't we agree a while ago that I'd pay you twenty? (Lit. Wasn't it twenty what we agreed to before?)	24. Diq ba báyntiy átung ... gikasabútan ganíha?
ah (pause after acceding to a mistake)	aa
right	hústu
isn't that so	túqud nu
	—# #
25. Ah, that's right, isn't it— twenty cents, wasn't it?	25. Aa, hústu túqud nu? Baynti ... túqud nu?
I thought	nákuq
[word linking nákuq and the sentence which follows it]	ug
26. I thought you would pay thirty.	*26. Nákug mubáyad kag tráynta.

Mga Pangutána

Únang Báhin

1. Ása tung ímu Day, sa Burumíyu?
2. Nagquwán ba?
3. Ihatúd ba ku nímu Dung?
4. Únsa na Dung, ihatúd ku nímu u díliq?
5. Kun dublíhun nákuq ang ákung plíti Dung, ihatúd ku nímu?
6. Bágqu kag sinínaq Day nu?
7. Ngánu gung líbut? Duqúl ra kaqáyu naq.
8. Ngánung báynti ra man ni Day?
9. Náqa na bay tartanílya?
10. Duqúl ba dínhing tiyánggi?
11. Ása ka man mukanáqug Nang?
12. Dídtu na bas tiyánggi si Nánay?
13. Diqín sa Burumíyu ang ímung adtúqan Nang?
14. Waq pa ba muhúnung ang uwán?
15. Ngánung waq man nínyu pasákya tung babáyi?
16. Kay pilá man diqáy?
17. Mubáyad kag tráynta Nang?
18. Pilá may átung gikasabútan, diq ba tráynta?
19. Bágqu pa ning uwána nu? (bágqu pa 'was just now')
20. Ganíha ka pa bang naghulát ug tartanílya Day?

Mga Pangutána (Matching)

Únang Báhin

1. Nagtawág ka na bag tartanílya?
2. Nagquwán pa ba?
3. Túqa na bas tiyánggi si Nánay nímu Day?
4. Ádtu ka man manáqug sa Burumíyu Day nu?
5. Ngánung báynti ra man lagi ni Day?
6. Únsa, pasakáy ka, díliq?

a. Uu Dung, sa Burumíyu.
b. Uu. Díliq pa gyud tu dúgayng milakáw.
c. Kay pilá man diqáy? Diq ba báynti ra may átung gikasabútan?
d. Waláq na; mihúnung na.
e. Díqa na; ákuq lang usáng gipahuwát.

7. Pilá may plíti íning ákung mga dalá Dung?

8. Ása ka man pahatúd Nang?

9. Pilá may gústu nímung ibáyad Nang?

f. Báyri lang kug singkwínta sintábus Nang; dalá na ang ímung plíti. ('That includes your fare.')

g. Duqúl ra kaqáyu Dung; diháq lang sa Burumíyu.

h. Kwarínta sintábus; dyis sintábus sa ákung plíti; tráynta sintábus sa ákung mga dalá.

i. Díliq lang, Nang. Layúq man gud kaqáyu.

Sagquluhúnun

Second Part	Ikaduháng Báhin
oh! (particle of surprise on seeing someone)	uh
27. Oh, good morning, Miss.	27. Uh, maqáyung búntag Mis.
er	aa
want to go out	mulakáw
would like	taq
28. Er, I'd like to go out.	*28. Aa, mulakáw taq ku.
ask permission	manánghid
would like	taq
[particle preceding clause, linking manánghid and the rest of the sentence]	nga
take care of	mubántay
head	úlu
29. I'd like to ask permission not to look after the store today because I have a severe headache.	*29. Manánghid taq kung diq ku mubántays tindáhan karúng adláwa kay labád kaqáyu ákung úlu.

30. All right.	30. Na halá.
tomorrow	úgmaq
if	ug
able to come back	makabálik
person to be told	sultíhi
[particle asking for agreement]	ha
so that	arún
can, uh, you know (fumbling for the right word)	makakuqán
31. But if you are not able to come back here tomorrow, tell me, will you? So I can whatchamacallit somebody else to help.	*31. Pirú úgmaq ug diq ka ... makabálik, sultíhi ku ha, arún ... makakuqán kug láqing ... mutábang.
yes	uu
person to be told	sultíhan
I—you	tiká
if	ug
32. Yes, I'll tell you if I can't come here tomorrow.	32. Uu, sultíhan tiká ug diq ku ... makaqánhi úgmaq.
33. Yes.	33. Uu.
34. All right, I'm going now, O.K.?	34. Na, ádtu na ku ha?
35. Go on.	35. Halá.
(A young man comes in.)	(Ningsúud ang usá ka batánqun.)
36. Good (morning).	36. Maqáyu.
come in	dayún
just	lang
[term of address for males same age as or younger than speaker]	Duq

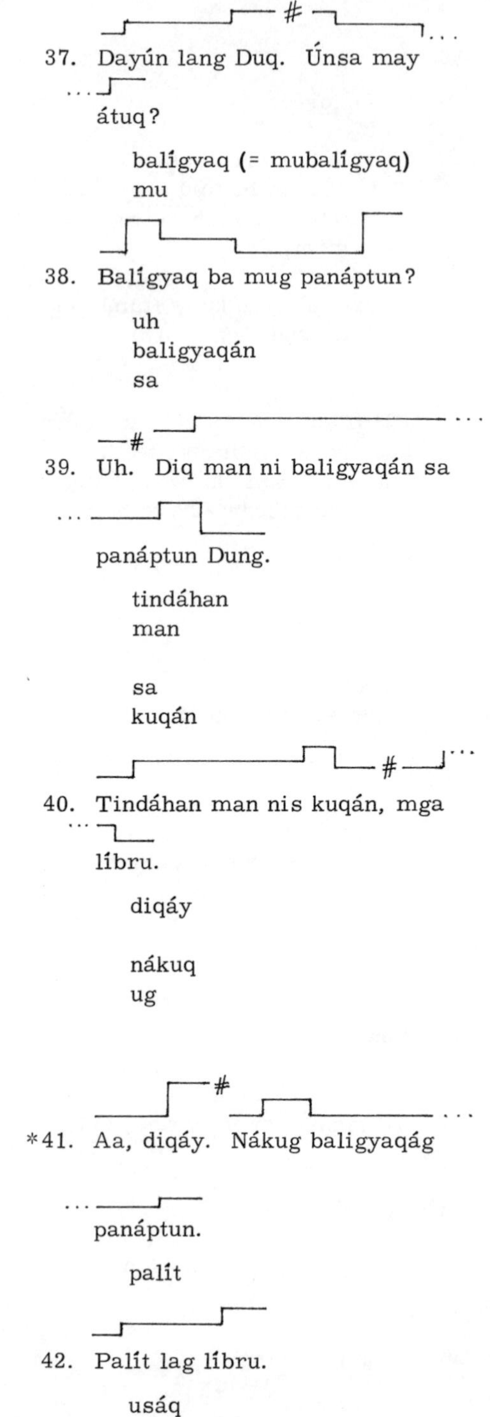

37. Just come in, Boy. What can I do for you (Lit. what is ours)?
    — 37. Dayún lang Duq. Únsa may átuq?

    sell — baligyaq (= mubaligyaq)
    you (plural) — mu

38. Do you sell cloth?
    — 38. Balígyaq ba mug panáptun?

    oh (expression of surprise) — uh
    place where they sell — baligyaqán
    [particle preceding goal] — sa

39. Oh, this isn't a textile store, Boy!
    — 39. Uh. Diq man ni baligyaqán sa panáptun Dung.

    store — tindáhan
    [particle used in giving information] — man
    for — sa
    whatchamacallit — kuqán

40. This is a whatchamacallit, a bookstore (lit. a store of books).
    — 40. Tindáhan man nis kuqán, mga líbru.

    [particle used on acquisition of new information] — diqáy
    I thought — nákuq
    [particle introducing clause after nákuq, linking nákuq and what follows] — ug

41. Oh, really? I thought this was a textile store.
    — *41. Aa, diqáy. Nákug baligyaqág panáptun.

    buy (imperative) — palít

42. Just buy a book.
    — 42. Palít lag líbru.

    for now — usáq
    take shelter — pasílung
    it is raining — ulán (= nagqulán)
    still — pa

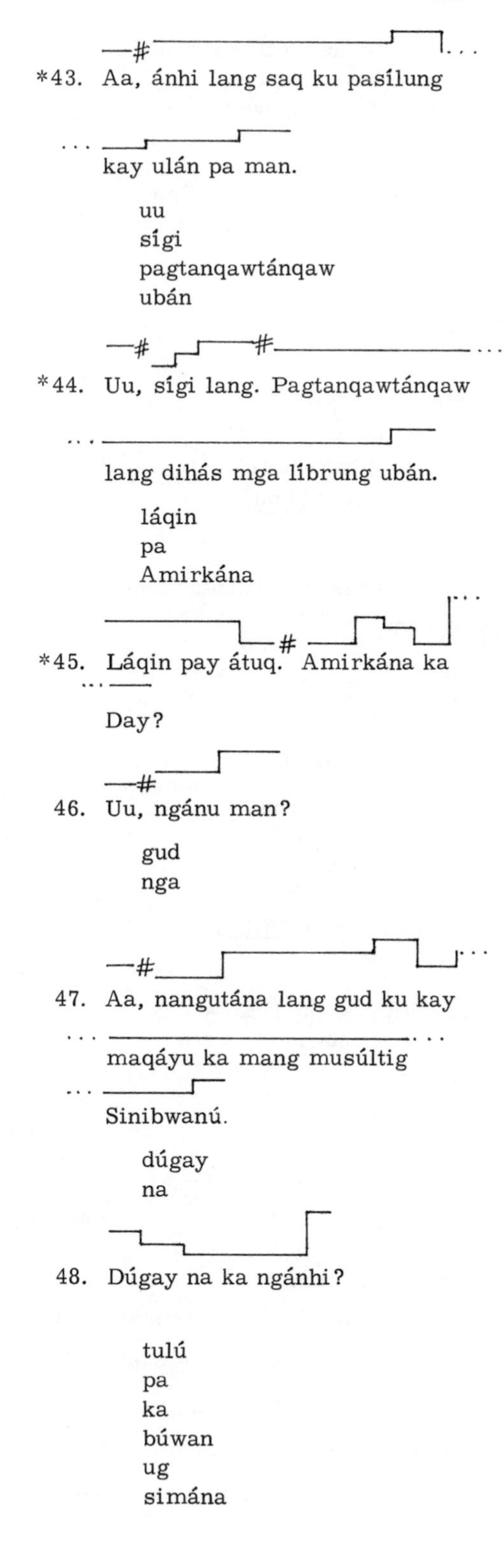

43. Well, I'll just take shelter here for the time being, for it's still raining.

*43. Aa, ánhi lang saq ku pasílung kay ulán pa man.

yes — uu
go ahead — sígi
look around — pagtanqawtánqaw
other — ubán

44. Yes, just go ahead. Look around there at the other books.

*44. Uu, sígi lang. Pagtanqawtánqaw lang dihás mga líbrung ubán.

different — láqin
still — pa
(female) American — Amirkána

45. By the way (lit. Ours is different), are you an American, Miss?

*45. Láqin pay átuq. Amirkána ka Day?

46. Yes, why?

46. Uu, ngánu man?

[particle with an explanation] — gud
[linker between maqáyu and musúlti] — nga

47. Oh, I'm just asking, because you speak Cebuano well.

47. Aa, nangutána lang gud ku kay maqáyu ka mang musúltig Sinibwanú.

long time — dúgay
already — na

48. Have you been here for a long time now?

48. Dúgay na ka ngánhi?

three — tulú
only [so much] up to now — pa
[linker for numbers] — ka
month — búwan
and — ug
week — simána

[linker following time expression]	nga
am studying	nagtuqún
49. I've been studying Cebuano for only three months and a week.	*49. Tulú pa ka búwag usá ka simána kung nagtuqún sa Sinibwanú.
50. Oh, really!	50. Aa, diqáy!
because	man gud
[linker between maqáyu and mutúdluq]	nga
51. Because the woman teaches me Cebuano well.	51. Maqáyu man gung mutúdluq ang babáyi nákuq sa Sinibwanú.
52. Oh, really!	52. Aa, diqáy!
that is why	maqú nang
quite well	maqarangqaráng
already	na
[linker between maqarangqaráng and musúlti]	nga
53. That's why I can speak all right now.	53. Maqú nang maqarangqaráng na kung musúlti.

Mga Pangutána

Ikaduháng Báhin

1. Únsa mang adláwa ta manlákaw?
2. Nakapanánghid ka na bang mulakáw ka?
3. Kínsa man diqáy ang ímung paqanhíqun úgmaq?
4. Unyáq kanúsqa ka man mubálik?
5. Nagbalígyaq ba mug panáptun dínhi?

6. Únsang tindahána ang gipalitán mu niqíning mga panaptúna?
7. Nakaqilá ka ba niqánang táwung nagpasílung sa tindáhan níla ni Mis Wílbi?
8. Mis Wílbi, dúgay ka na ba dínhis Sibú?
9. Únsay ímung gitanqawtánqaw dínhaq Dung?
10. Ngánung waq man ku nímu dáyun sultíhi?
11. Únsa tuy ímung gipangutána Dung?
12. Kínsa may nagtúdluq kanímu pagsúltis Sinibwanú?
13. Dúna ka na bay napalít nga líbru Day?
14. Kumústang ínyung pagpaníndag mga líbru?
15. Únsa mang mga librúha ang ínyung gipamalígyaq dínhi?
16. Únsang adláwa tu kang nanánghid?
17. Makabalík ka ba sulúd sa tulú ka ádlaw?
18. Háqin man dapít ang baligyaqánag panáptun?
19. Díliq ba lang ta mupasílung?
20. Ngánung waq ka man mangutána?

Mga Pangutána (Matching)

Ikaduháng Báhin

1. Manánghid untáq kung mulakáw ku.
2. Makaqánhi ka sunúd ádlaw?
3. Mutúdluq ka bag Sinibwanú?
4. Maqáyu ba kus Sinibwanú?
5. Nangutána ka ngánhi?
6. Maqáyu na kang musúltig Sinibwanú nu?
7. Mahímuq bang mupasílung ku dínhi?
8. Únsa may gipalít mu?
9. Kabalík ka úgmaq?
10. Baligyaqán ba nig panáptun?

a. Uu sigí lang, gaquwán pa man.
b. Waaq. Nahádluk man kung mangutána.
c. Maqarangqaráng na kang musúltig Sinibwanú.
d. Díliq pa kay kuqán man, náqay ákung bisíta.
e. Uu, ug patúdluq ka nákuq.
f. Ngánu man, únsa may ímung lákwun? (lákwun 'reason for going')
g. Uu. Tulú na ka búwan ku ngánhi, maqú nga makasúlti na kug Sinibwanú.
h. Díliq. Ádtu kus tiyánggi úgmaq tibuqúk ádlaw.
i. Dayún lang Sir. Níqay dághan.
j. Waaq na lang ku mamalít. Mahál man ang mga balígyaq.

Sagquluhúnun

Third Part	Ikatulúng Báhin
by the way (lit. ours is yet another)	láqin pay átuq
need	magkinahánglan
helper	katábang
in	sa
54. By the way, don't you need a helper in your store?	54. Láqin pay átuq, waq ba ka magkinahánglag katábang sa ímung tindáhan?
already	na
55. I have a helper already.	55. Dúna na man kuy katábang.
only, but, however	gániq
able to come	makaqánhi
now	karún
aches	nagsakít
because	man gud
56. Only she couldn't be here today because she has a headache (lit. for her head is painful).	56. Gániq, waq siyá makaqánhi karún kay nagsakít man gud ang íyang úlu.
I thought	nákuq
[particle linking nákuq with what follows]	ug
need	nagkinahánglan
57. Oh, I thought you needed (one).	*57. Aa, nákug nagkinahánglan ka.
ah (expressing regret at being unable to fulfill the request)	ay
no more	waláq na
just right	hústu ra
one	usá
[linker for numbers]	ka
piece	buqúk

58. I'm sorry, I don't any more. That one is just enough.	*58. Ay, waláq na Hústu ra nang usá ka buqúk.
small	gamáy
very	ra
because	man gud
also	usáb
59. Besides this is a very small store. (Lit. Also because this my store is very small.)	59. Gamáy ra man gud usáb ning ákung tindáhan.
furthermore	unyáq
very	ra
[particle 'have']	ug
profit	ganánsya
not yet	díliq pa
[linker between díliq and kakuqán]	nga
can whatchamacallit	kakuqán
[particle preceding goal]	ug
helper (one who will help)	tumatabáng
60. Also, the profit is very small. I can't whatchamacallit another helper here in the store yet.	*60. Unyáq, gamáy rag ganánsya. Diq pa kung kakuqán karúg láqing tumatabáng dínhis tindáhan.
oh! (exclamation of surprise)	uy
no more	waláq na
[particle upon giving new information]	man
[particle upon receiving new information]	diqáy
61. Oh! It's not raining any more (Lit. There is no more rain.) I might as well be going.	61. Uy! Waq na man diqáy ulán. Ádtu na lang ku.
[particle asking for agreement]	ha

might as well let me have it	ákuq na lang
souvenir	handumánan
62. May I take this book? Just let me have it as a souvenir, O.K.? (Lit. I'll take this one book, O.K.? Let me just have this as a souvenir, O.K.?)	62. Ákung dádqun ning usá ka buqúk líbru ha? Ákuq na lang ning handumánan ha?
sorry!	ay
still	pa
63. Sorry, Boy! This store of mine is still very small.	63. Ay Dung. Gamáy pa kaqáyu ning ákung tindáhan.
not yet	díliq pa
can give (several things)	makapanghátag
64. We can't give (things) away yet. (Lit. We cannot give away yet now.)	64. Diq pa mi makapanghátag karún.
small	gamáy
very	ra
[particle: 'have']	ug
profit	ganánsya
just make it next time	sunúd na lang
I hope	básin pa
[linker between básin and what follows]	ug
become bigger	mudakuqdakúq
65. The profit is very small. Just make it next time. I hope (then) this store will be a little bit bigger.	65. Gamáy ra kaqáyug ganánsya. Sunúd na lang. Básin pag mudakuqdakúq ning tindáhan.
all right (particle introducing a new subject)	na
never mind	way sapayán
just	lang
good-bye	ádtu na ku

66. All right. It doesn't matter. Good-bye.

66. Na, waq lay sapayán. Ádtu na ku.

Mga Pangutána

Ikatulúng Báhin

1. Anúsqa man diqáy ka mubálik?
2. Sakít ba gyud kaqáyu ang ímung úlu?
3. Anúsqa man diqáy mubálik ang ímung katábang sa tindáhan Mis?
4. Waláq ka na ba magkinahánglag katábang sa ímung tindáhan?
5. Maqáyung búntag. Ikáw ba ang nagkinahánglag láqing tumatabáng sa tindáhan?
6. Mulakáw ka na bang gaqulán pa man?
7. Únsa may ákung dádqun?
8. Háqing librúha ang ímung palitún Dung?
9. Gamáy ra ba gug ganánsya kining mamalígyag líbru?
10. Waláq ba diqáy kay líbrung ipanghátag?
11. Makaqánhi ka ba únyang hápun?
12. Pilá ka buqúk líbru ang ímung palitún Dung?
13. Hústu na ba ang duhá ka buqúk nga katábang?
14. Gágmay pa ba ang ímung mga anák?
15. Anúsqa ka man diqáy mubálik sa Úrmuk?
16. Ngánung waq ka man usáb makaqánhi niqádtung usáng ádlaw?
17. Ngánung karúng gikinahánglan ka kaqáyu, nagsakít pa urúy ang ímung úlu?
18. Pilá man ka buqúk ang gikinahánglan mung katábang Mis?
19. Nagqulán pa ba?
20. Makahátag ka ba kanákug usá ka líbru Mis?

Mga Pangutána (Matching)

Ikatulúng Báhin

1. Ikáw bay nagkinahánglag katábang sa tindáhan?
2. Pilá ra man diqáy ímung gikinahánglan?

a. Palitún ku na lang. Díliq ka pa man kaháq makapanghátag.

b. Úqu, píru dúna na akúy katábang karún.

3. Palitún mu ba kanáng librúha?
4. Únsa may sakít sa ímung katábang?
5. Nagqulán pa ba?
6. Dakúq bag ganánsya kiníng maníndag líbru?
7. Dúgay na bang nasakít ang ímung katábang?
8. Dúna ka na bay katábang dínhis tindáhan?
9. Ádtu ka na ba?

c. Usá ra ka buqúk kay gamáy ra man gud kiníng ákung tindáhan.
d. Úqu, dúna ka bay ipadalá?
e. Usá pa lang ka ádlaw.
f. Dúna na, píru waláq makaqánhi karún kay gisakitán sa íyang úlu.
g. Sa úna dakúq. Píru karún gamáy na lang.
h. Ay, gamáy ra kaqáyu. Gisakitán lang sa úlu.
i. Waq na. Muqádtu na diqáy ku.

Commentary to Basic Sentences

12 a 1	sst	A common way to attract the attention of equals or inferiors. (It would not be polite to call superiors this way.)
12 a 6	na	This use of na is explained below, 12 G 1 a, p. 484.
12 a 9	nínyu	Miss Wilby addresses the passengers as she gets in.
12 a 18		The ang is omitted before the subject—a common colloquial usage when the verb is passive and the subject is a recipient of the action if the subject does not precede the predicate.
12 a 26	nákuq	This form, short for gipakaqingún nákuq or kaqingún nákuq, is used at the beginning of a sentence and is linked with ug; it means 'I thought.'
12 b 28	taq	Short for úntaq. Úntaq after a verb gives a meaning similar to 'would like' as contrasted with 'want.'
12 b 29		Note the absence of ang before the subject when the subject is a noun and the predicate is an adjective. This is common usage if the subject does not precede the predicate (cf. comment to 12 a 18 above).
12 b 31	mutábang	A verb preceded by ang or g or sa means 'one who [does the action of the verb].'
12 b 41	nákuq	Cf. comment to 12 a 26.
12 b 43	pasílung	Short for magpasílung, a usage explained below (12 C 2).
12 b 44	ubán	The young man has already started looking at some books.
12 b 45	láqin pa	The pa is explained below (12 G 2 e).
12 b 49	tulú pa	The pa is used to mean 'only . . . now'; whereas na would mean 'already . . . now' (12 G 2 d).

12 c 57 nákuq — Nákuq is explained in the comment to 12 a 26.

12 c 58 waláq — Note waláq in answer to nagkinahánglan? (a real verb).

12 c 60 diq kung — The ng after diq is explained below (12 D).

Grammatical Section

12 A. Summary of passive verb forms

You have now studied all of the passive types: direct, local, and instrumental. In addition to the forms discussed in the preceding lessons, other forms—'fancy' forms*—occur from time to time. These forms are discussed in the subsections below, and are included also in the following review chart:

	Real	Unreal	Subjunctive
Direct			
Direct nonpotential	gi-	-un	-a
Habitual-durative	gina-†	paga- -un†	paga- -a†
Potential	na-	ma-	ma-
Local			
Nonpotential	gi- -an	-an	-i
Habitual-durative	gina- -an†	paga- -an†	paga- -i†
Potential	na- -an	{ma- -an / ka- -an}	ma- -i
Instrumental			
Nonpotential	gi-	i-	i-
Habitual-durative	gina-†	iga-†	iga-†
Potential	{na- / gika-}	{ma- / ika-}	{ma- / ika-}

12 A 1. Habitual-durative passive verb forms

The habitual-durative passive forms are used in fancy language when a passive verb is required and the context calls for a form with a habitual or durative meaning—the meanings discussed and illustrated with active verb forms in 5 C 2 (1), and 5 C 2 a. Note that in ordinary speech the habitual and durative meanings are expressed by the ordinary forms of the passive.

---

* "Fancy" forms are those used in writing and formal speeches, and on other occasions requiring high-flown language.

† Fancy forms.

[direct passive]

Kanúnay níyang pagatanqáwun ang pultahán kay nagpaqábut man siyá sa íyang inahán. 'He keeps looking at the door because he's waiting for his mother.'

Dúgay na níyang ginapaqábut ang íyang anák. 'He's been waiting for his child for a long time.'

[local passive]

Nagsúhul siyá ug napúluq ka mga táwu arún níla pagabantayán ang bulánwan. 'He hired ten people to watch the gold.'

Ang nahitabúq nahímung ginasultíhan sa mga táwu sa lúngsud. 'The event became a subject of conversation for the people in the town.'

[instrumental passive: confined to a few set expressions]

Maqú ba nay ímung igabálus sa ákung kaqáyu? 'Is that the way you repay my kindness?'

12 B. Forms with the base únsa 'what?'

Únsa 'what?' occurs as a verb base with nag-/mag-/maka-, naN-/maN-, na-/ma-, gi-/-un/-a, and gi-/i-.

12 B 1. Nag-/mag-/maka- plus únsa

When one of these prefixes is attached to the base únsa, a q is inserted be- them. Únsa with nag-/mag- means 'do what?':

Nagqúnsa ka ba sa Banáwaq? 'What were you doing in Banawa?'

Magqúnsa ka karúng Dumínggu? 'What will you be doing this Sunday?'

Maka- with únsa means 'can do harm':

Diq naq makaqúnsa. 'That can do no harm.'

12 B 2. Únsa with naN-/maN-

With naN-/maN-, únsa means 'do harm':

Ayáw kahádluk, díliq bítaw naq mangúnsang amúq. 'Don't be afraid, that monkey won't do anything to you.'

Nangúnsa na man sab si Lítu dídtu? 'Now, what (harm) did Lito do there?'

12 B 3. Na-/ma- with únsa

Na-/ma- with únsa means 'what happened to [the subject]?' The subject is the portion underlined once:

Naqúnsa ka gud Litú? Nabúqang ka man kaháq. 'What's the matter with you, Lito? Have you gone crazy?'

Ibutáng lang naq diháq. Diq bítaw naq maqúnsa. 'Just put that there. Nothing will happen to it.'

12 B 4. Gi-/-un/-a with únsa

A construction made up of a subject plus únsa affixed with gi-, -un, or -a specifies that the subject (underlined once) is the thing to which something was done:

Ngánung nasukúq ka man? Waq ta bítaw ka unsáqa. 'Why are you mad? I didn't do anything to you.'

Giqúnsa man nímu ang bátaq? 'What did you do to the child?'

Unsáqun ku man ning mga batáqa? Nagsígi man nig sulingsúling nákuq.

'What shall I do with these children? They keep peeping at me.'
(For special uses of unsáqun and giqúnsa, cf. 12B6 below.)

12B5. Gi-/i- with únsa

A construction made up of a subject plus únsa affixed with gi- or i- asks how the subject is used:

Giqúnsa man naq nímung kutsílyus tanúm? 'What did you do to the plant with that knife?'

Iqúnsa man ni nímung tútpik sa paghímug kik? 'How will you use these toothpicks in making a cake?'

12B6. Special types of sentences with unsáqun and giqúnsa meaning 'how?'

Giqúnsa 'how?' (real) and unsáqun 'how?' (unreal) occur in sentences consisting of a predicate without a subject. The predicate is giqúnsa or unsáqun plus a genitive agent plus an abstract form (form with a pag- prefix) plus a goal of the abstract. The meaning of such a sentence is 'how does [the agent] do [the abstract] to [the goal]?' In the following sentences the agent is underlined once, the abstract twice, and the goal three times:

a. Giqúnsa man nímu pagqabút niqánang idára? (5a14) 'How did you reach that age?'
b. Unsáqun man nínyu pagpakáqun sa trísi ka buqúk mga bátaq? (9c22) 'How do you feed thirteen children?'

The meanings expressed by this type of sentence can also be expressed by sentences consisting of a predicate and a subject, where the predicate consists of giqúnsa or unsáqun 'how?' plus a genitive agent plus an abstract, and the subject is the recipient of the action of the abstract. The subject is underlined once and the predicate twice:

a(1). Giqúnsa man nímu pagqabút kanáng idára? 'How did you reach that age?'
b(1). Unsáqun man nínyu pagpakáqun ang trísi ka buqúk bátaq? 'How do you feed thirteen children?'

PP-BB, exercise XII.II.

12C. The derivational verb prefix pa-

The prefix pa- may be added to any root which is a verb. The meaning of pa- is 'cause someone to do the action of the verb.' Káwus means 'fetch water,' pakáwus 'have someone fetch water.'

Pakáwsan tikág túbig. (9c11) 'I will have someone get you some water.'

Báyad means 'pay,' pabáyad 'have someone pay.'

Ngánu gung síngkwínta man ang ímung gipabáyad kanákuq? (8c2) 'Why did you make me pay fifty cents?'

Pirú díliq naq maqáyung pabáyrun ku nímug mas dakús kasagárang prísyu. (8c6) 'But it's not fair to make me pay more than the usual price.'

12C1. Active forms of bases containing pa-

The active forms of the bases containing pa- have two meanings (depending on the context): (1) the agent does the action to himself or has it done to him; (2) the agent has (lets, makes) someone do the action. The affixes mi-/mu- are infrequent with bases containing pa-.

Meaning (1):

a. Magpatahúm kitá. 'Let's make ourselves beautiful.' [tahúm 'beautiful']

Meaning (2):

b. Díliq gayúd siyá magpakítaq. 'She won't let anyone see her.' [kítaq 'see']

c. Magpalútuq ku nímu sa ákung ságing. 'I'll have you cook my bananas.'

12 C 2. Dropping of mag- before bases containing pa-

Bases with pa- and no other affix occur interchangeably with bases having magpa-: that is, a base with pa- has unreal meanings and is used in the same contexts in which the same base with magpa- could occur.

a (1). Patahúm kitá. 'Let's make ourselves beautiful.'

b (1). Díliq gayúd siyá pakítaq. 'She won't let anyone see her.'

c (1). Palútuq ku nímu sa ákung ságing. 'I'll have you cook my bananas.'

Other examples of pa- in meaning (1):

d. Diq siya pabuyág. 'He won't shut up (lit. let someone quiet him down).'

e. Pabílin lang akú sa baláy. 'I'll just stay home.' [bílin 'be left behind']

Other examples of pa- in meaning (2):

f. Palabá ka ba sa ímung sinínaq? 'Do you want to have your shirt washed?'

g. Diq gyud siyá pakáqun sa íyang kik. 'He won't let anyone eat his cake.'

12 C 3. Direct passive forms of bases with pa-

The direct passive form of a verb containing pa- means that the word the verb refers to (the subject if the verb is the predicate, or the predicate if the verb is the subject) was caused to do the action of the verb. The word the verb refers to is underlined once and the verb twice in the following sentences:

Pasákya ku nínyu. (12 a 9) 'Let me get on.' (Lit. 'I am to be caused to get on.') [sakáy 'get on (a vehicle)']

Ambí Iyáq, papalitá kug tungás dusína. (6 b 36) Here, let me buy (lit. I am to be caused to buy) half a dozen.' [palít 'buy']

Pirú díliq naq maqáyung pabáyrun ku nímug mas dakús kasagárang prísyu. (8 c 6) 'But it's not good to make me pay more than the usual price (lit. that I am to be caused to pay).'

12 C 4. Instrumental passive forms of bases with pa-

The instrumental passive form of a verb containing pa- means that the word the verb refers to was caused to be the recipient of the action of the verb. The word the verb refers to is underlined once and the verb twice:

Ngánu gung singkwínta man ang ímung gipabáyad kanákuq? (8 C 2) 'Why did you make me pay fifty cents?' (Lit. 'Why was fifty caused by you to be paid?')

Ipapalít na lang naq nákuq Iyáq. 'Let me buy that.' (Lit. 'Let that be caused to be bought.')

Únsay ímung ipakáqun sa ínyung mga bátaq? 'What do you feed your children?' (Lit. 'What do you cause to be eaten by your children?')

12 C 5. Local passive forms of bases with pa-

In a sentence having a local passive verb form containing pa-, the word the verb refers to (the subject, if the verb is the predicate; the predicate, if the verb is the subject) is the beneficiary of the action or is the place where the action occurs. The word the verb refers to is underlined once, the verb twice:

Pakáwsan tikág túbig. (9 C 11) 'I'll have someone get you some water.' (Lit. 'You will be caused to be gotten for, some water.' [kawus 'fetch water'])

Díliq ka papalitán ni máma nímug dúlsi. 'Your mother won't let anyone buy candy for you.' (Lit. 'You won't be caused to be bought for, some candy.' [palít 'buy'])

Díliq nákuq papalitán kanímu ang tindáhan ni Imúk, kay mahál diháq. 'I won't allow you to buy at Imoc's store, because (things) are expensive there.' (Lit. 'Imoc's store will not be caused to be bought at.')

12 C 6. Examples of the active and three passives of a base with pa-

A context is suggested for each of the following to demonstrate the emphasis of the parts in each sentence.

[active]

Magpapalít si Máma kang Lítu ug kalamáy sa tindáhan ni Imúk. 'Mama will have Lito buy some kalamay at Imoc's store [and then she will give it to the children].'

[direct passive]

Papalitún ni Máma si Lítu ug kalamáy sa tindáhan ni Imúk. 'Mother will have Lito buy some kalamay at Imoc's store [while she will have Loling do something else].'

[instrumental passive]

Ipapalít ni Máma kang Lítu ang kalamáy sa tindáhan ni Imúk. 'Mama will have Lito buy the kalamay at Imoc's store [but the vegetables, she will have him buy somewhere else].'

[local passive]

Papalitán ni Máma ug kalamáy kang Lítu ang tindáhan ni Imúk. 'Mama will have Lito buy kalamay at Imoc's store [and then at another store, she will have him buy something else].'

PP-DD, exercises XII.III A, III B; XIII.I D; XV.III A.

12 D. Linking of díliq and waláq

The negatives díliq (diq) and waláq (waq) are optionally linked by nga to verbs with a prefix ka- (short for naka-/maka-).

Diq pa kung kasúhul run ug láqing tumatabáng. (See 12 c 60) or Diq pa ku kasúhul run ug láqing tumatabáng. 'I can't hire another helper yet.'

12 E. Complements

A COMPLEMENT is an expression that follows a word or phrase and modifies it. Complements are either infinitives or sentences (the latter often consisting of a verb, though not in an infinitive form).

12 E 1. Infinitive complement following verbs

An INFINITIVE COMPLEMENT has the infinitive shape—that is, one of the following three alternatives: (1) abstract form (pag- plus verb base); (2) abstract form preceded by sa; or (3) ug plus verb base. (Review 9 B 1 b.) The following examples contain an infinitive complement following a verb (the infinitive is underlined):

Waq mu maglîsud pagqánhi [or sa pagqánhi, or ug ánhi] nganhi? (2 b 17) 'Didn't you have a hard time coming here?'

Unsáqun man nákuq pagpatáy [or sa pagpatáy]? (6 a 32) 'How can I kill it?'

Giqánhi ta gyud ka arún pagkúhaq [or sa pagkúhaq] nímu. (8 c 25) 'I came to get you.'

Ayáw paghikalimút pagsulát [or sa pagsulát or ug sulát] kanákuq. (8 a 33) 'Don't forget to write me.'

All three shapes of the infinitive have the same meaning and in most cases are used interchangeably, with the exception that sa plus the abstract is a sign of fancy language. (There are some contexts in which an infinitive with ug is rarely used: three of these are after arún 'in order to' and after giqúnsa and unsáqun 'how?').

12 E 2. Infinitive complement following a noun

In the following example the noun úras 'time' has an infinitive complement pagpalít 'to buy.'

Waq na kuy úras pagpalít [or sa pagpalít, or ug palít] sa ákung mga palitúnun. (9 a 24) 'I have no more time to make my purchases.'

12 E 3. Sentence complements

Some words have complements that consist not of an infinitive but of a sentence. Sentence complements are preceded by nga (or its short form ng). In the following example, the verb kahibáwu 'know' is followed by the complement nga plus muqádtu 'go' (a sentence consisting of a verb):

Tutál kahibáwu na man kung muqádtu. (9 a 18) 'Anyway, I already know how to go.'

Words you are familiar with that may take sentence complements are verbs meaning 'know how to' and 'be afraid.'

Pirú diq ka ba mahádluk muqádtu sa Pulambatú? (9 a 8) 'But aren't you afraid to go to Pulambato?' *

Often, the translation 'to [do]' serves for both types of complements—infinitive and sentence complements. There is no way of knowing from the English meaning what type of complement to use; it is necessary to learn which Cebuano words take which.

12 E 4. Sentence complement following maqáyu 'it is good'

Maqáyu in the meaning 'it is good' takes nga plus a sentence complement.

---

* In this example there is no linker nga after mahadluk. Remember that when the linker nga comes after words ending in consonants other than n or q, it is either pronounced nga or is silent. If the word order in the example is changed so that the linker comes after a vowel, the linker reappears in the shape ng:

Pirú diq ba mahádluk kang muqádtu sa Pulambatú? 'But aren't you afraid to go to Pulambatu?'

Maqáyu pang mubálik ka na lang ngádtu sa tindáhan. (9 a 27) 'It would be better for you just to go back to the store.'

12 E 5. Sentence complement following verbs meaning 'say,' 'think,' and the like

Verbs meaning 'say,' 'think,' and the like may take nga (ng) plus a sentence complement. In such contexts nga often corresponds to English 'that.'

Niqingún siyá nga díliq na lang siyá muqánhi. 'He said that he might as well not come.'

Manánghid taq kung diq ku mubántay sa tindáhan karúng adláwa. (12 b 29) 'I would like to ask permission not to look after the store today.'

Exercise XII.IV.

12 F. Exclamatory sentences with pagka- and -a

Sentences containing ka- plus an adjective meaning 'how [adjective] (something is)!' are EXCLAMATORY SENTENCES (cf. 5 A). For example:

Kalisúd gayúd sa ámung kinabúhiq! 'How difficult our life is!'

Forms consisting of pagka- or -a plus an adjective root are used in exclamatory sentences interchangeably with ka- plus adjective root.* (There is no difference in meaning among the exclamatory affixes ka-, pagka-, and -a.)

Pagkalisúd gayúd sa ámung kinabúhiq! 'How difficult our life is!'
Lisúra gayúd sa ámung kinabúhiq! 'How difficult our life is!'

12 G. Postpositive particles

Words we have been calling postpositive particles (3 C 2), like the small colloquial words in every language, are important to the meaning of the Cebuano sentences and very difficult to find equivalents for in English. In many contexts, the Cebuano sentence expresses with these particles a certain meaning, which is not expressed at all in the corresponding English sentences.

The following sections discuss the meanings of the particles na and pa.

12 G 1. Na

Na modifies a predicate, and the basic meaning it gives to the predicate is that the action of the predicate has been started or completed at a certain point in time, or that the predicate has come into existence as of a certain point in time. English 'now' or 'by now' (as, for example, in, 'Now can you see me?' or 'How many children have you got by now?') is the closest equivalent; in fact, for whatever English context the meaning 'now' or 'by now' is appropriate, the corresponding Cebuano sentence without fail contains na, even though the English sentence does not necessarily contain 'now' or 'by now.'

The following subsections illustrate na in this basic meaning and related meanings.

---

* Adjectives which consist of a root plus other affixes do not take the suffix -a. For example, malipáyun 'happy' consists of a root lípay plus affixes ma- and -un; thus there are forms kamalipáyun 'how happy!' and pagkamalipáyun 'how happy!' but the affix -a is not added to malipáyun.

12 G 1 a. Na meaning 'by now'

Naqabút na ta. 'We're here now.'

Údtu na man diqáy kaqáyu. (1 a 24) 'It's very late (lit. I notice it's very late now).'

Anáaq, mu ra mag púlus na giqukupahán ang mga tihíras dínhi. (8 a 5) 'Heavens, it looks as though the cots here have all been taken by now.'

Nangapú na gániq tingáli ang ímung mga apú. (5 a 24) 'Even your grandchildren probably have grandchildren by now.'

In questions na corresponds to English 'yet.'

Náqa na ba si Pápa nímu? 'Is your father there yet?'—i.e. 'Is your father there by now?'

12 G 1 b. Na with negatives díliq and wálaq

The phrases díliq (diq) na and waláq (waq) na mean 'no longer, not any more.'

Waq na kuy úras pagpalít sa ákung mga palitúnun. (9 a 24) 'I haven't got time any longer to buy my things.'

Diq na ku mubálik dídtu. 'I won't go back there any longer.' [Said with either of the following connotations: 'I was going to go there, but now I won't'; or 'I usually go back there, but from now on I won't.']

Adúnay dághan. Diq na gániq ku makaqiháp. (5 a 23) 'There are many of them. I can't even count them any longer.'

12 G 1 c. Na with unreal verbs, imperative verbs, nouns, or pronouns

Unreal verb plus na means '[verb] will happen now (when something else had been happening up to now).'

Taná. Muquwán na daq. (4 b 51) 'Let's go. It's going to rain now.'

Unreal verbs meaning 'let's [verb]' plus na mean 'let's [verb] now (when we had been doing something else up to now).'

Manakáy na ta. (2 a 17) 'Let's get on now.'

Mangítaq na tag dyip. 'Let's look for a jeep now.' [They have finished doing the other things they had to do.]

With imperative verbs, na adds the connotation: 'stop what you are doing now and do what I'm telling you.'

Halá mga bátaq, katúug na mu. 'O.K., children, (stop what you are doing and) go to sleep now.'

Ayáw na ku nínyug tanqáwa. (9 c 14) 'Stop looking at me.'

Noun or pronoun plus na means '[noun or pronoun] is the one now (when it was something else before).'

Aa, maqú na ni kay náqa may márkang Úrmuk. (8 a 2) 'Ah, this is it now, because there's a sign "Ormoc".'

Akú na intáwun ang mangunáy pagkáwus ug túbig. 'Now I'm the one who has to fetch all the water [since my husband can't do it any longer].'

12 G d. Na lang

The combination na lang is often used to modify a predicate and give it the connotation '[the predicate] might as well be,' '[the predicate] is the best thing under the circumstances, though something else is probably more desirable.'

Na, ikáw na lay sakáy Pirlá. Maghuwát na lang kug láqin. (3 c 33, 34) 'You (might as well) get on, Perla. I'll just wait for another one.'

Kay wánqa may láqing dyip, manlákaw na lang ta. 'Since there are no jeeps at this hour, let's just walk.'
Ádtu na lang ku. (1.25) 'I should be going now.' [The implication is that I would rather not go, but I am forced to.]
Sunúd na lang. (12c65) 'Just make it next time.'
Waq ka bay sinsíyu gawás ánang pisíta? Na halá. Ambí na lang nang pisíta bi. 'You have nothing other than that twenty-cent piece? All right. Just give me the twenty-cent piece then.'

12G2. Pa

12G2a. Pa meaning 'still,' 'yet'

Únyaq ngítngit pa naq. (8a20) 'Furthermore, it will still be dark.'
Túqa pa si Máma sa kuqán, San Rimihiyú. (Cf. 9b25) 'Mama is still in San Remigio.'

Díliq (diq) or waláq (waq) plus pa corresponds sometimes to 'not yet,' sometimes to 'before'—lit. 'while . . . not . . . yet.'
Waq pa dirí si Nánay. (9b24) 'Mother is not here yet.'
Waq pa gyud intáwuy mihángyuq nákuq. (5b48) 'There is nobody who has asked me yet.'
Sigí lang. Díliq pa ku manáqug kay ngítngit pa man. (8c21) 'Never mind. I won't get off yet, because it's still dark.'
Díliq gyud akú manáqug sámtang díliq pa háyag. 'I won't get off before it is light (lit. while it is not yet light).'
Sa waláq pa akú dínhi, díliq pa akú makabinisayáq. 'Before I came here (lit. While I was not here yet), I could not speak Visayan.'

12G2b. Pa in comparisons

Adjective plus pa means 'more [adjective]' or '[adjective]-er.'
Taqás pa siyá nákuq. 'He is taller than I am.'
Na sigí Plurá, maqáyu pang mubálik ka na lang ngádtu sa tindáhan. (9a27) 'O.K., Flora, it's better for you to go back to the store (than that you stay here any longer).'
Támbuk pay dyis. 'A dime is fatter [than he is]'—i.e. He is very thin.

12G2c. Pa meaning 'just now, just a moment ago'

Karún ka pa muqabút? Karún pa gyud. (2b11, 12) 'Have you just arrived?—Just now?'
Anáqa, gíkan pas basakán. (9b27) 'There he is, just back from the rice fields.'

12G2d. Pa with numbers or quantities

A number plus pa means 'only [number] up to now.'
Tulú pa ka búwan kung nagtuqún sa Sinibuwanú. (12b49) 'I've been studying Cebuano for only three months now.'
Inigqabút nímu dídtu sa Úrmuk, mga alás kwátru pa kanáq sa búntag. (8a19) 'When you arrive at Ormoc, it will be only about four o'clock in the morning.'

12G 2e. Pa meaning '. . . else (in addition)'

Some predicates with pa have the meaning '[predicate] else (in addition).'

Kinsa pay muqánhi? Si Huwán pa? 'Who else is coming? John? (Lit. John in addition?)'

Níqay ímung áyskrim. Únsa pa? 'Here's your ice cream. What else (do you want)?'

Láqin pay átuq . . . (12b 45) 'By the way . . .' (lit. 'ours—i.e. our conversation—is a different one in addition.')

If the predicate is a verb, the use of pa gives the meaning 'still have [verb]ing to do in addition to what has been done already.' (Cf. 12G 2a above.)

Muqádtu pa ra ba tas Gútsan. (4 a 3) 'We still have to go to the Go Chan (building).'

12Gf. Expressions with pa

The expressions ísaq pa, taym pa, úsaq pa, and kadyút pa ra gud are used in asking people to wait a second, or to interrupt a conversation.

Saq pa diqáy. Kanúsqa ka man mubálhin dínhi? (3 c 16) 'By the way [interrupting the speaker], when are you going to move here?'

Taym pa ra gud, kúwang man ang ímung gisúkliq. 'Just a second, you haven't given me enough change.'

Exercises XII.V, X.III.IF, XIV.ID, XV.X.

12G 3. Negatives of predicates containing na, pa

In negative predicates, na is replaced by pa and pa is replaced by na:

Níqa na ba siyá?—Waq pa siyá dínhi. 'Is he here yet (by now)?—He's not here yet.'

Milakáw na tu siyá.—Waq pa tu siyá mulakáw. 'He has gone out (by now).—He hasn't gone out yet.'

Níqa pa siyá dínhi.—Waq na siyá dínhi. 'He is still here.—He isn't here any longer.'

Nagqulán pa ba?—Waq na ba magqulán? 'Is it still raining?—Isn't it raining any more?

Exercises XII.VI A and XII.VI B.

Pattern Practices and Exercises

I A. Butangí ang lunáq sa hústung púrma sa bírbung náqa sa sulúd sa parentheses. 'Real,' 'unreal,' ug 'subjunctive' sa (1) direct passives
(2) local passives
(3) instrumental passives.

(1) Direct passives (Gamíta ang 'direct passive' sa musunúd nga mga tudling púlung.)

1. Gústu úntaq kung (tawág) mu lang kug Pírla.
'I would like it if you'd just call me Perla.'

2. Uy, waq man nákuq (dalá) ang ímung líbru.
'Oh! I didn't bring your book.'

3. (Dalá) úntaq nákuq kádtung ímung líbru apán nalímut ku.
'I should have brought your book, but I forgot.'

4. Ayáw ku nínyug (tánqaw) kay malíguq ku.
'Don't look at me because I'm going to take a bath.'

5. (Ingún) ku na siyá sa ímung túgun.
'I already gave him your message.'

6. Kay ngánu, (palít) úntaq tu nímu?
'Why? Would you have bought it?'

7. Ákuq bang líbru ang ímung (dalá) únyaq ngádtu sa ínyu?

8. Ábi ku bag akú ang (tawág) níla. (Ábi ku 'I took for granted')
'I thought they were calling me.'

9. Ngánung (dúbli) man nímu ímung báyad sa dyip?
Waq ka ba kasakáy nga dyis ray báyad?
'Why did you pay double . . . ?'

10. (Kinahánglan) ku ra ba kádtu, maqúng ákung gidáa ngánhi.

(2) Local passives (8 A)

1. Duq, (báyad) ka na ba nákuq sa kalamáy?
'Boy, have I paid you for the kalamay yet?'

2. Uy, (hátag) ka na nákug písu.
(Use the colloquial form gitagáqan, tagáqan, or tagáqi.)
'Oh, I already gave you a peso.'

3. Waq pa man gániq ku nímu (súkliq).
'You haven't even given me the change yet.'

4. Diq na úntaq ku nímu (límbung).
'You shouldn't cheat me any more.'

5. Kun waq pa ku mahinúmdum (dúbli) úntaq ka nákug báyad.
'Had I not remembered, I would have paid you double.'

6. Maqáyu gániq kay waq ka nákuq (hátag) pagqusáb.
(Use the colloquial form.)
'Good that I didn't give it to you twice.'

7. Sultíhi si Máma nímu arún (tábang) ka níya.
'Tell your mother so that she may help you.'

8. (Palít) pa kug láqin Mam.
'Buy another one from me, Ma'am.'

9. Kínsa may ímung (palít) niqánang dulsíha Mis?
'Whom are you going to buy that candy for, Miss?'

10. Kanáng bayhána ay, (balígyaq) man gud ku níya.

(3) Instrumental passives (10 A)

1. Dung, (líbut) ra ning tartanílya sa tiyanggihán.
'Boy, have the rig go around to the marketplace.'

2. Ákung bawíqun tung súbrang kwártang ákung (báyad) sa tindíru. (báwiq 'take back')
'I'll take back the extra money I paid the salesman.'

3. Waq pa ra ba gyud níya (hátag) ang ákung napalít.
   'He still hasn't given me what I bought.'

4. Kiní bang dus písus ang ímung (palít) niqádtung sinínaq?
   'Is this the two pesos you are going to use to buy that dress?'

5. Pilá may ákung (plíti) Dung?
   'How much is my fare, Boy?'

6. (Kanáqug) ra ku niqánang bukág (basket) Dung.
   'Get that basket down for me, Boy.'

7. Ang batánqun nga misulúd sa tindáhan ni Mis Wílbi waláq masáyud nga líbru ra ang (balígyaq) dídtu.
   'The young man that went inside Miss Wilby's store didn't know that she only had books for sale there.'

8. Maqú nay íyang (súlti) nákuq kay nasukúq siyá. (nasukúq 'angry')
   'That's what she said to me. She was mad.'

9. Mis Wílbi, maqú kádtu ang íyang (pangutána).
   'Miss Wilby, that was what he asked.'

10. (Bántay) ra kug tartanílya Dung.

IB. (May be preceded by PP-R.) Local vs. instrumental vs. direct. (5 A, 8 A, 10 A) Butangí ang lunáq sa hústung púrma sa bírbung náqa sa sulúd sa parentheses.

1. Pirlá, únsa may átung (sakáy) ngádtu sa Mabúlu?
   'Perla, how are we going to Mabolo?'

2. Dyis na lang gyud ang ákung kwárta nga (plíti) sa tartanílya.
   'The only money I have to pay the rig fare with is ten centavos.'

3. Díliq ba naq magsábaq nang irúq kun ímung (sakáy) sa traak?
   'Won't that dog make noise if you put him on the bus?'

4. (Plíti) ku diháq ha, kay waq na gyud kuy kwárta.
   'Pay my fare, will you please, because I haven't any money.'

5. Ímu bang (dalá) ang ímung líbru ngádtu sa tindáhan?
   'Did you bring your book to the store?'

6. (Dalá) ka nákuq ug támbal (medicine) únyaq kay (labád) ka man kaháq sa ímung úlu.
   'I'll bring you some medicine, since you say you have a headache.'

7. (Dalá) ra gud ku niqíning bukág (basket) kay magpalít pa kug kíndi nga ákung (dalá) sa mga bátaq.
   'Take this basket for me, please, because I still have to buy candy to bring to the children.'

8. Layúq pa ba ang ímung (kanáqug) Mis?
   'Is the place you're getting off at still far away, Miss?'

9. Palíhug Dung, (kanáqug) ra gud ku sa ákung bukág kay búgqat ra kaqáyu.
   'Take this basket off please, Boy, because it's very heavy.'

10. Ánhaq ra mis tyanggihán kay adúna miy (palít).
 'We'll get off at the market because we have to buy something.'

11. Díqay dyis uh. (Palít) ni dídtug ságing. Ayáw (palít) nang gágmay kaqáyu, ha?
 'Here's ten centavos. Buy bananas with it. Don't buy the very small ones, will you?'

12. Kang kínsang kwárta ang ímung (palít) niqíning líbru nga ímung (palít) sa ka Pírla?
 'Whose money did you use to buy this book that you bought at Perla's?'

13. Ayáw na ang kutsíru (hátag) ug plíti kay (hátag) ku na siyág báynti sintábus. (Use colloquial forms.)
 'Don't give the rig driver any more fare because I already have given him twenty centavos.'

14. (Hátag) ba kiní nímu nákung líbru?
 'Will you give this book to me?'

15. Kínsa may ímung (báyad) sa ábang nátuq sa baláy?
 'Who did you pay our house rent to?'

16. Kun waq pa nímu (báyad) ang átung útang sa tindáhan pagdalá na lang dáqan ug kwártang ímung (báyad).
 'If you haven't paid off our debt at the store yet, take some money with you (in advance) to pay it with.' (dáqan 'beforehand')

17. Muqádtu kus tindáhan kay (tánqaw) nákuq kun túqa na ba dídtu si Pírla.
 'I'm going to the store to see if Perla is there yet.'

18. Únsa kaháq nang (tánqaw) níla dídtu sa átbang, nu?
 'What could they be looking at across the way?'

19. Mamálik ta ngádtus átung (tánqaw) ug siní, básin pag túqa dídtu ang ímung pitáka. (pitáka 'purse')
 'Let's go back to where we sat (watched from) in the show. Your purse might be there.'

20. Waq na kuy úras (tánqaw) ug siní karún kay dághan kug buhatúnun.
 'I don't have time to see the show now, because I've got lots to do.'

IC. Butangí ang lunáq sa hústung active u passive nga púrma sa bírbung náqa sa sulúd sa parentheses. (4 A, 6 A, 8 A, 8 B, 10 A, 11 C and subsections)

1. (Ádtu) si Mis Wílbi sa Pulambatú úgmaq arún mubisíta sa mga táwu dídtu.
 'Miss Wilby will go to Redstone tomorrow to visit the people there.'

2. Ug mubálik ku dínhi (dalá) ba kug gása?
 'If I come back here, shall I bring gifts?'

3. (Dalá)g dághang gása páras mga bátaq.
 'Bring a lot of presents for the children.'

4. (Dalá) bayáq kug gása inigbálik nímu ha?
 'Be sure to bring me a present when you come back, O.K.?'

5. Siyá ang (hátag) nákuq niqíning líbru ganína.
   'She was the one who gave me the book a while ago.'

6. (Hátag) ku na ba lang kaníya kiníng támbal páras labád sa úlu arún mamaqáyu dáyun siyá?
   'Shall I give her this medicine for her headache? Then she'll get over it right away.'

7. Ling, (hátag) rag túbig si Mis Wílbi kay giquháw kunú siyá. (giquháw 'thirsty')
   'Loling, give Mis Wilby some water, because she's thirsty.'

8. (Hatúd) usáq ku sa istasyunán sa traak, Plurá, sa diq ka pa mupaqúliq.
   'Take me to the bus station first, Flora, before you go home.'

9. (Hatúd) ra ku diríg kukakúla.
   'Bring me some Coca-Cola, please.'

10. Siyá ang gústung (hatúd) nákuq dínhi sa baay gahápun.
    'He was the one who wanted to take me home yesterday.'

11. (Bántay) bayág maqáyu ang mga líbru ha?
    'Watch the books carefully, will you?'

12. Kínsay (bántay) sa tindáhan gahápun?
    'Who looked after the store yesterday?'

13. Uy, saq pa diqáy kay may (palít) pa ku.
    'Oh, wait, I still have to buy something else.'

14. Maqáyu gániq kay waq ku (palít) sa ímung kaság. Patáy na man diqáy tu.
    'It's good that I didn't buy your crabs. They were already dead.'

15. Ása man ta (sakáy) kun muqádtu tas Burumíyu?
    'Where do we get on if we go to Borromeo?'

16. Nakaqilá ka ba niqádtung táwung (sakáy) sa tartanílya?
    'Did you know that man who got on the rig?'

17. Únsa may ímung (sakáy) pagpadúung nímu dínhi?
    'What did you come here on?

18. Ngánung waq man ka (súlti) dáyun nákuq nga gilábdan kas úlu?
    'Why didn't you tell me at once that you had a headache?'

19. Lakáw. (Súlti) si Nánay mu nga miqabút na si Mis Wílbi.
    'Go tell your Mama that Miss Wilby is here now.'

20. Kínsay (súlti) kanímu nga adúnay balígyang panáptun dínhi?
    'Who told you that there was cloth for sale here?'

ID. Butangí ang lunáq sa hústung púrma sa imperative sa bírbung náqa sa sulúd sa parentheses. (11 C and subsections)

Pananglítan: (Pangítaq) lang mug láqing dyip páras Kapitúl.
Tubag: Pangítaq lang mug láqing dyip páras Kapitúl.

1. (Kanáqug) na Mis kay Pulambatú na man ni.
   'Get off Miss, because this is Redstone now.'

2. Mísis Ulibár, (hátag) ra gud nang mga bátaq íning ákung gása.
'Mrs. Olivar, please give those children my gifts.'

3. (Hatúd) usáb niqánaq kádtung ímung mga higála.
'Take some of that to your friends, too.'

4. Uy, mga bátaq, (kanáqug) na mu kay manglákaw na mi ni Mis Wílbi.
'O.K., children, get off, because Miss Wilby and I are going now.'

5. Mga bátaq, ayáw saq mug (lakáw) kay magkúyug lang ta.
'Children, don't go away yet because we should go in a group.'

6. (Súlti) nínyu ang ínyung Nánay nga muqádtu ku sa ínyu.
'Tell your Mama that I am going to your place.'

7. (Ánhi) mu dínhi úgmaq, ha?
'Come here tomorrow, will you?'

8. Píru (panánghid) mu sa ínyung Nánay arún díliq silá mangítaq nínyu.
'But ask permission from your mothers so that they will not look for you.'

9. Kay gabíqi na man, (katúlug) saq mu sa ínyu.
'Go home and go to bed please, because it's night now.'

10. Sus ning mga anáka. Ayáw mug (ubán) kay kadalíq ra mi.
'Heavens, children! You can't come with us. We'll be right back.'

11. (Palít) gániq nig kukakúla Ting, arún díliq muqubán nákuq.
'Buy Coca-Cola for this (child), Ting, so that he won't want to go along with me.'

12. Dung, (pangutána) kunú ang ímung nánay kun nakaqándam na ba sa panihápun.
'Boy, ask your mother whether supper is ready.'

13. (Tábang) hinúqun nínyu siyá arún sayú tang makapanihápun.
'You help her instead so that we can eat supper early.'

14. Maríya, (tábang) ra ning ímung mga kaqúban kun únsay buhatún.
'Mary, help your friends in whatever there is to be done.'

15. Uy, Maryú, Litú, (tuqún) sab mug únsay buluhatún dínhis baay.
'Oh, Mario, Lito, better find out what's to be done here in the house.'

16. (Kanáqug) lang mu Mis kay díliq man ku muhatúd ngádtu sa Kárbún.
'Just get off, Miss, because I don't take passengers to Carbon.'

17. (Tánqaw) ra gud nínyu ang mga dalá ni Ínting kun dúna bay mga panáptun.
'Look at the things Inting brought and see if there's any cloth.'

18. Day, (balígyaq) ning kalamáy arún dúna kitáy ikapalít ug makáqun.
'Sell this kalamay, child, so that we can have something to buy food with.'

19. (Súlti) ku dáyun úgmaq kun makaqánhi ka ba sa tindáhan.
'Tell me first thing tomorrow whether you can come to the store.'

20. Sigí, (saká) na mu kay ngítngit na.
'Come on. Come in now because it's dark now.'

PP-BB Giqúnsa vs. Unsáqun (12B)

Step I. (With nímu as agent)

'How did you get it?'

Giqúnsa man nímu pagqabút ádtu?	(how will you)
Unsáqun man nímu pagqabút ádtu?	(paglútuq)
Unsáqun man nímu paglútuq ádtu?	(how did you)
Giqúnsa man nímu paglútuq ádtu?	(paghatúd)
Giqúnsa man nímu paghatúd ádtu?	(how will you)
Unsáqun man nímu paghatúd ádtu?	(pagdalá)
Unsáqun man nímu pagdalá ádtu?	(how did you)
Giqúnsa man nímu pagdalá ádtu?	

Step II. (With various agents)

'How can I go there?'

Unsáqun ku man pagqádtu dídtu?	(how did you)
Giqúnsa mu man pagqádtu dídtu?	(how did they)
Giqúnsa man níla pagqádtu dídtu?	(cook)
Giqúnsa man níla paglútuq dídtu?	(how will he)
Unsáqun man níya paglútuq dídtu?	(how are we to)
Unsáqun ta man paglútuq dídtu?	(sleep)
Unsáqun ta man pagkatúlug dídtu?	(how did you)
Giqúnsa mu man pagkutúlug dídtu?	

II. Ibutáng ang hústung púrma sa únsa nga gipaqángay. (12B and subsections)

Pananglítan: Tábiq Nuy (excuse me, Sir) ________ ku man pagqádtu sa Banáwaq?

Tubág: Tábiq Nuy, unsáqun ku man pagqádtu sa Banáwaq?

1. ________ ku man pagtábang sa mga púbri?
2. Pangutánqa siyá kun ________ níya pagkúhag túbig.
   'Ask him how he got the water.'
3. ________ man nímu pagtuqún sa Sinibwanú nga maqáyu ka na mang musúlti?
4. Ngánung muqádtu ka man sa Úrmuk, ________ ka man dídtu?
   'What will you do there?'
5. ________ ka gud dídtu sa Pulambatú nga dúgay ka man kaqáyu dídtu?
   'What happened to you that you stayed there so long?'
6. ________ ba kaháq kiníng batáqa nga naghilák man?
7. ________ nímu ang ságing nga ákung gidalá gíkan sa Úrmuk? Gihurút ba nímug káqun?

8. ________ ka man? Ngánung díliq ka man mutrabáhu dínhis tindáhan karún?

9. ________ kaháq si Lítu dídtus Kárbun nga waq man tu siyáy daláng kwárta?

10. ________ man ta dídtu sa ínyu karúng gabíqi?

11. Nuy, ________ man nímu pagqabút niqánang ímung idára?

12. Pangutánqun nákuq si Nánay kun ________ paglútuq niqíning kaság.
'I'll ask Mom how to cook these crabs.'

13. ________ na man lang kug díliq na ku makalakáw?
'What shall I do when I can't walk any more?'

14. ________ kaháq si Pírla nga waq man muqánhi?
'What could have happened to Perla . . . ?'

15. Mihílak man lang naq siyá dáyun bísag waq naq siyá námuq ________.

16. ________ man nátuq pagqádtus Banáwaq nga waq pa may dyip?

17. ________ man naq nímung líbru, Dung, nga diq man ka makabasá ('can't read')?

18. Dídtu diqáy ka sa ka Mísis Abilyána? ________ ka man dídtu?

19. ________ man nákuq pagkahibáwu kun háqin ka magpuyúq?

20. Ayáwg kahádluk sa mga táwu dídtu, díliq bítaw naq silá ________.

PP-DD Direct, local and instrumental of causatives (12C)

Step I. (Direct to instrumental)

a. 'Have Perla cook some bananas.'
b. 'Bananas is what you should have Perla cook.'

1. a. Palutúqag ságing si Pírla. (ságing)
b. Ságing ang ipalútuq ni Pírla.

2. a. Pakuháqag túbig si Lítu. (túbig)
b. Túbig ang ipakúhang Lítu.

3. a. Paqímnag lítsi si Pírla. (lítsi)
b. Lítsi ang ipaqinúm ni Pírla.

4. a. Pakánqag paan si Pírla. (paan)
b. Paan ang ipakáqun ni Pírla.

5. a. Pahátdag súdqan si Lúling. (súdqan)
b. Súdqan ang ipahatúd ni Lúling.

6. a. Patanqáwag siní si Manáng. (siní)
b. Siní ang ipatánqaw ni Manáng.

7. a. Papalitág dúlsi si Buy. (dúlsi)
b. Dúlsi ang ipapalít ni Buy.

8. a. Pahimúqag lamísa si Mánuy. (lamísa)
b. Lamísa ang ipahímung Mánuy.

9. a. Papilíqag sinínaq si Pírla. (sinínaq)
   b. Sinínaq ang ipapíling Pírla.

10. a. Padádqag bir si Ínting. (bir)
    b. Bir ang ipadaláng Ínting.

Step II. (Direct to instrumental [three elements])

a. 'He'll have Perla cook some bananas.'
b. 'Bananas are what he'll have Perla cook.'

1. a. Palutúqun níyag ságing si Pírla. (ságing)
   b. Ságing ang ipalútuq níya ni Pírla.

2. a. Padádqun nákug gása si Pírla. (gása)
   b. Gása ang ipadalá nákuq ni Pírla.

3. a. Papalitún nílag kukakúla si Ínting. (kukakúla)
   b. Kukakúla ang ipapalít níla ni Ínting.

4. a. Patanqáwun níyag siní ang mutsátsa. (siní)
   b. Siní ang ipatánqaw níya sa mutsátsa.

5. a. Pakuháqun námug túbig si Pírla. (túbig)
   b. Túbig ang ipakúhaq námuq ni Pírla.

6. a. Patáwgun níyag dyip ang buy. (dyip)
   b. Dyip ang ipatawág níya sa buy.

7. a. Papangitáqun nílag traak si Pírla. (traak)
   b. Traak ang ipapangítaq níla ni Pírla.

8. a. Pahimúqun nákug dúlsi si Manáng. (dúlsi)
   b. Dúlsi ang ipahímu nákuq ni Manáng.

9. a. Pabaligyáqun nátug kaság si Manáng. (kaság)
   b. Kaság ang ipabalígyaq nátuq ni Manáng.

10. a. Paqímnun námug bir ang bisíta. (bir)
    b. Bir ang ipaqinúm námuq sa bisíta.

Step III. (Instrumental and direct passives)

a. 'He'll have Big Sister cook some rice.'
b. 'Big Sister is the one he'll have cook the rice.'

1. a. Palutúqun níya si Manáng ug kánqun. (Manáng)
   b. Si Manáng ang palutúqun níyag kánqun.

2. a. Palutúqun níya si Manáng ug kánqun. (kánqun)
   b. Kánqun ang ipalútuq níyang Manáng.

3. a. Palimpyuhún nákuq si Índay ug básu. (Índay)
   b. Si Índay ang palimpyuhún nákug básu.

4. a. Paplitíhun níya ang babáying támbuk ug dúbli. (babáying támbuk)
   b. Babáying támbuk ang paplitíhun níyag dúbli.

5. a. Paplitíhun níya ang babáying támbuk ug dúbli. (dúbli)
   b. Dúbli ang ipapliti níyas babáying támbuk.

6. a. Pakuháqun níya si Pírlag ságing. (ságing)
   b. Ságing ang ipakúhaq níyang Pírla.

7. a. Patanqáwun níya ang mutsátsag sini. (sini)
   b. Sini ang ipatánqaw níyas mutsátsa.

8. a. Paqíphun níla ang babáyig napúluq. (napúluq)
   b. Napúluq ang ipaqiháp nílas babáyi.

9. a. Paqíphun níla ang babáyig napúluq. (babáyi)
   b. Babáyi ang paqíphun nílag napúluq.

10. a. Padádqun ku si Tátay ug paan. (tátay)
    b. Si Tátay ang padádqun kug paan.

11. a. Padádqun ku si Tátay ug paan. (paan)
    b. Paan ang ipadalá kung Tátay.

12. a. Papangitáqun níyag trabáhu si Mánuy. (Mánuy)
    b. Si Mánuy ang papangitáqun níyag trabáhu.

13. a. Papangitáqun níyag trabáhu si Mánuy. (trabáhu)
    b. Trabáhu ang ipapangítaq níyang Mánuy.

14. a. Paqimbitarún ku si Máma kang Dyiin. (Máma)
    b. Si Máma ang paqimbitarún ku kang Dyiin.

15. a. Paqimbitarún ku si Máma kang Dyiin. (Dyiin)
    b. Si Dyiin ang ipaqimbitár ku kang Máma.

16. a. Palibríhun ta si Kíkuy kang Ánghil. (Ánghil)
    b. Si Ánghil ang ipalíbri ta kang Kíkuy.

17. a. Palibríhun ta si Kíkuy kang Ánghil. (Kíkuy)
    b. Si Kíkuy ang palibríhun ta kang Ánghil.

Step IV. (Instrumental and direct)

a. 'They had him fix the food.'
b. 'The food is what they had him fix.'

1. a. Pahikáyun síyag pagkáqun. (pagkáqun)
   b. Pagkáqun ang ipahíkay níya.

2. a. Ipahíkay níya ang pagkáqun. (siyá)
   b. Siyá ang pahikáyun sa pagkáqun.

3. a. Papústun níya ang tindíras íyang pinalít. (íyang pinalít)
   b. Íyang pinalít ang ipaputús níya sa tindíra.

4. a. Ipaputús níya ang íyang pinalít sa tindíra. (ang tindíra)
   b. Ang tindíra ang papústun níyas íyang pinalít.

5. a. Pakuháqun níya si Plúrag sabún. (sabún)
   b. Sabún ang ipakúhaq níyang Plúra.

6. a. Ipakúhaq níya ang sabún ni Plúra. (Plúra)
   b. Si Plúra ang pakuháqun níyag sabún.

7. a. Ipapamînaw níya ang áwit ni Nîda. (Nîda)
   b. Si Nîda ang papamináwun níyag áwit.

8. a. Papamináwun nîya si Nîdag áwit. (áwit)
   b. Âwit ang ipapamînaw níyang Nîda.

9. a. Ipaqîtsa ku ang láta ni Ânghil. (Ânghil)
   b. Si Ânghil ang paqitsáhun kus láta.

10. a. Paqitsáhun ku si Ânghil sa láta. (láta)
    b. Láta ang ipaqîtsa ku kang Ânghil.

11. a. Paqisturyáhun námuq siyá báhing Núwa. (báhing Núwa)
    b. Báhing Núwa ang ipaqistúrya námuq níya.

12. a. Paqisturyáhun námuq siyá báhing Núwa. (siyá)
    b. Siyá ang paqisturyáhun námuq báhing Núwa.

13. a. Ipadúlaq níya ang sîndul pándul sa mga bátaq. (mga bátaq)
    b. Mga bátaq ang paduláqun níyag sîndul pándul.

14. a. Paduláqun níya ang mga bátag sîndul pándul. (sîndul pándul)
    b. Sîndul pándul ang ipadúlaq níyas mga bátaq.

15. a. Ipadakúp níya ang abát kang Kîkuy. (Kîkuy)
    b. Si Kîkuy ang padákpun níyas abát.

16. a. Padákpun níya si Kîkuy ug abát. (abát)
    b. Abát ang ipadakúp níyang Kîkuy.

17. a. Ipatînda námuq ang bukháyuq ni Nánay. (Nánay)
    b. Si Nánay ang patindáhun námug bukháyuq.

18. a. Patindáhun námuq si Nánayg bukháyuq. (bukháyuq)
    b. Bukháyuq ang ipatînda námuq ni Nánay.

19. a. Ipasaká níya ang lubî ni Lîtu. (Lîtu)
    b. Si Lîtu ang pasákqun níyag lubî.

20. a. Pasákqun níyas Lîtug lubî. (lubî)
    b. Lubî ang ipasaká níyang Lîtu.

Step V. (Instrumental and direct: advanced)

a. 'He'll have Big Brother eat some hot soup.'
b. 'Hot soup is what he'll have Big Brother eat.'

1. a. Pahigúpun níya si Mánuy ug înit sabáw. (înit sabáw)
   b. Înit sabáw ang ipahígup níya ni Mánuy.

2. a. Ipasúlti nîya ang Binisayáq kang Mis Wîlbi. (Mis Wîlbi)
   b. Si Mis Wîlbi ang pasultîhun níyag Binisayáq.

3. a. Paqímnun ni Nída ang íyang bisíta ug túbig. (túbig)
   b. Túbig ang ipaqinúm ni Nídas íyang bisíta.

4. a. Pakánqun níyag paan ang dráybir. (paan)
   b. Paan ang ipakáqun níya sa dráybir.

5. a. Ipahímuq níya ang lamísa sa mutsátsa. (mutsátsa)
   b. Mutsátsa ang pahimúqun níyag lamísa.

6. a. Patáwgun nílag dyip si Lítu. (dyip)
   b. Dyip ang ipatawág nílang Lítu.

7. a. Ipapalít níya ang sabún ni Manáng. (Manáng)
   b. Si Manáng ang papalitún níyag sabún.

8. a. Pasugátun ku si Nídang Lína. (Nída)
   b. Si Nída ang pasugátun kung Lína.

9. a. Ipahígup níya ang ínit sabáw ni Mánuy. (Mánuy)
   b. Si Mánuy ang pahigúpun níyag ínit sabáw.

10. a. Pasultíhun níyag Binisayáq si Mis Wílbi. (Binisayáq)
    b. Binisayáq ang ipasúlti níyang Mis Wílbi.

11. a. Ipaqinúm ni Nída ang túbig sa íyang bisíta. (íyang bisíta)
    b. Ang íyang bisíta ang paqímnun ni Nídag túbig.

12. a. Ipatawág níla ang dyip ni Lítu. (Lítu)
    b. Si Lítu ang patáwgun nílag dyip.

13. a. Pahimúqun níya ang mutsátsug lamísa. (lamísa)
    b. Lamísa ang ipahímu níyas mutsátsu.

14. a. Ipakáqun níya ang paan sa dráybir. (dráybir)
    b. Dráybir ang pakánqun níyag paan.

15. a. Papalitún níya si Manáng ug sabún. (sabún)
    b. Sabún ang ipapalít níyang Manáng.

16. a. Pasugátun ku si Nídang Lína. (Lína)
    b. Si Lína ang ipasúgat kung Nída.

Step VI. (Direct, local, and instrumental)

a. 'Lina will be allowed to rent the room for thirty pesos.'
b. 'Lina is the one who will be allowed to rent the room for thirty pesos.'

1. a. Paqabángug tráynta si Línas kwártu. (Lína)
   b. Si Lína ang paqabángug tráyntas kwártu.

2. a. Paqabángug tráynta si Línas kwártu. (tráynta)
   b. Tráynta ang ipaqábang ni Línas kwártu.

3. a. Paqabángug tráynta si Línas kwártu. (kwártu)
   b. Kwártu ang paqabángag tráynta ni Lína.

4. a. Parisirbahún siyá ug tihíras párang Ínting. (siyá)
   b. Siyá ang parisirbahúg tihíras párang Ínting.

5\. a. Parisirbahún siyág tihíras párang Ínting. (tihíras)
   b. Tihíras ang iparisírba níya párang Ínting.

6\. a. Parisirbahún siyág tihíras párang Ínting. (Ínting)
   b. Si Ínting ang parisirbahán níyag tihíras.

7\. a. Pabáyrun si Plúrag kwaríntas kaság. (Plúra)
   b. Si Plúra ang pabáyrug kwaríntas kaság.

8\. a. Pabáyrun si Plúrag kwaríntas kaság. (kwarínta)
   b. Kwarínta ang ipabáyad ni Plúras kaság.

9\. a. Pabáyrun si Plúrag kwaríntas kaság. (kaság)
   b. Kaság ang pabáyran ni Plúrag kwarínta.

10\. a. Patudlúqun si Dyuug Binisayáng Mis Wílbi. (Dyuu)
    b. Si Dyuu ang patudlúqun ni Mis Wílbig. Binisayáq.

11\. a. Patudlúqun si Dyuug Binisayáng Mis Wílbi. (Binisayáq)
    b. Binisayáq ang ipatúdluq ni Dyuung Mis Wílbi.

12\. a. Patudlúqun si Dyuug Binisayáng Mis Wílbi. (Mis Wílbi)
    b. Si Mis Wílbi ang patudlúqan ni Dyuug Binisayáq.

13\. a. Pasuwatún nákuq si Ánghil ni Máma. (Máma)
    b. Si Máma ang pasuwatán nákuq ni Ánghil.

14\. a. Pasuwatán nákuq si Máma ni Ánghil. (Ánghil)
    b. Si Ánghil ang pasuwatún nákuq ni Máma.

15\. a. Palabáyun ku si Mams batú. (Mam)
    b. Si Mam ang palabáyun kus batú.

16\. a. Palabáyun ku si Mam sa irísir. (irísir)
    b. Irísir ang ipalábay nákung Mam.

17\. a. Ipalábay ku ang batú ngádtung Kíkuy. (Kíkuy)
    b. Si Kíkuy ang palabáyan nákus batú.

18\. a. Patagúqun níya ang mutsátsag bir. (bir)
    b. Bir ang ipatáguq níyas mutsátsa.

19\. a. Ipatáguq níya ang bir sa mutsátsa. (mutsátsa)
    b. Mutsátsa ang patagúqun níyas bir.

20\. a. Patagúqun ang mutsátsag bir sa kahún. (kahún)
    b. Kahún ang patagúqag bir sa mutsátsa.

21\. a. Ipakítaq ta ang gása níla. (silá)
    b. Silá ang {pakitáqun / pakítqun} tas gása.

22\. a. Pakítqun ta silás gása. (gása)
    b. Gása ang ipakítaq ta níla.

23\. a. Pasákqun námug lubí si Nuy Tibúq. (Nuy Tibúq)
    b. Si Nuy Tibúq ang pasákqun námug lubí.

24. a. Pasákqun námug lubí si Nuy Tibúq. (lubí)
    b. Lubí ang {ipasaká / pasákqan} námung Nuy Tibúq.

25. a. Ipahatúd ang súdqan níya sa lamísa. (siyá)
    b. Siyá ang pahátdug súdqan sa lamísa.

26. a. Pahátdun siyág súdqan sa lamísa. (súdqan)
    b. Súdqan ang ipahatúd níya sa lamísa.

27. a. Pahátdun síyag súdqan sa lamísa. (lamísa)
    b. Lamísa ang pahátdan níyag súdqan.

28. a. Pahulatún si Plúra ug traak sa istasyunán. (traak)
    b. Traak ang ipahulát ni Plúras istasyunán.

29. a. Ipahulát ang traak ni Plúra sa istasyunán. (Plúra)
    b. Si Plúra ang pahulatúg traak sa istasyunán.

30. a. Pahulatún si Plúra ug traak sa istasyunán. (istasyunán)
    b. Istasyunán ang pahulatán ni Plúrag traak.

31. a. Pasuwatún nákuq si Ânghil sa lamísa. (lamísa)
    b. Lamísa ang pasuwatán nákung Ânghil.

32. a. Pahatágun si Plúra ug gása sa mga bátaq. (mga bátaq)
    b. Mga bátaq ang pahatágan ni Plúrag gása.

33. a. Pahatágun si Plúra ug gása sa mga bátaq. (gása)
    b. Gása ang ipahátag ni Plúras mga bátaq.

34. a. Pahatágan ang mangá bátag gása ni Plúra. (Plúra)
    b. Si Plúra ang pahatágug gása sa mga bátaq.

35. a. Pabaligyáqun si Ínting ug kukakúla. (kukakúla)
    b. Kukakúla ang ipabalígyaq ni Ínting.

36. a. Pabaligyáqun si Ínting ug kukakúla. (Ínting)
    b. Si Ínting ang pabaligyáqug kukakúla.

37. a. Pabaligyáqun si Mis Wílbig paan. (paan)
    b. Paan ang ipabalígyang Mis Wílbi.

38. a. Ang tindíra pahatágan nákug kwárta. (akú)
    b. Akú ang pahatágug kwártas tindíra.

39. a. Pahatágun akúg kwárta sa tindíra. (kwárta)
    b. Kwárta ang ipahátag nákus tindíra.

40. a. Pahatágun akúg kwárta sa tindíra. (tindíra)
    b. Tindíra ang pahatágan nákug kwárta.

III A. Ibutáng ang hústung púrma sa pa- sa lunáq nga gipaqángay. (12 C)

Pananglítan: Ngánung waq man nímu (patánqaw) ang mutsátsa sa siní?
Tubág: Ngánung waq man nímu patanqáwa ang mutsátsa sa siní?

1. (Pahátag) ni Mis Wílbi kiníng líbru kang Pírla.
   'Miss Wilby will have someone give this book to Perla.'

2. Únsay ímung (papalít) ni Pírla sa Karbún ganíha?
   'What did you have Perla buy at Carbon a while ago?'

3. Dung, (pasakáy) úsaq ku sa ímung dyip.
'Boy, let me ride in your jeep for a while.'

4. Ákuq na lang siyáng (pasakáy) sa traak padúung sa Banáwaq.
'I'll just have him take the bus going to Banawa.'

5. Íya ba kaháq kung (pasúlti) kang Mis Wílbi báhin sa nahitabúq? (báhin sa nahitabúq 'about what happened')
'Will she let me tell Miss Wilby about what happened?'

6. (Paplíti) pa ba diqáy ning gamáyng bátaq?
'You mean to say this small boy is going to have to pay fare too?'

7. Ug mahímuq (paqánhi) úntaq nákuq silá karúng gabíqi.
'If possible I would like to have them come over this evening.'

8. (Pahatúd) ni Máma nákuq kiníng íyang gása ngádtu kang Mísis Abilyána.
'Mother had me take her gift to Mrs. Abellana's.'

9. Tingáli (paqubán) ku níya sa Amiriká.
'Perhaps he will have me go with him to America.'

10. (Pabálik) siyá sa íyang trabáhu kay waq na nákuq siyá kinahangléna dínhi.
'Have him go back to his work, because I don't need him here any more.'

11. Gústu ku níyang (pasílhig) sa tibuqúk baláy.
'She wanted to have me sweep the whole house.'

12. (Pahátag) na lang ni Pírla ang gásang Huwán.
'Just have Perla give John's present away.'

13. Maqáyu pag (papalít) nímu siyá sa ímung kinahanglánun.
'It would be better if you would have him buy what you need.'

14. (Papanánghid) si Mis Wílbi sa ímung amahán arún túgtan ka sa báyli.
'Have Miss Wilby ask your father.'

15. (Patánqaw) námuq ang ímung gisulát.

16. Ngánu gung ímu pa kung (pahulát)? Ngánung waq ku nímu (paqádtu) dáyun?

17. (Pasakáy) ba kaháq ku sa ílang dyip?

18. Gústu níya ning (papalít) arún ihátag nímu.

19. (Palakáw) na silá arún makaqabút sa traak nga padúung sa Nága.

20. Íla úntaq kung (paqubán) sa Pulambatú pirú waq ku musugút.

III B. Gamíta ang musunúd nga mga púlung sa pagbúhat ug mga túdling púlung. (12C)

ipapalít	paqabángan
pakítaq	padádqun
pabáyad	patáwga
pahatúd	ipatawág

pahunúngun	ipaputús
ipahúnung	pabuhátun
palutúqa	ipabálik
pahulatún	pahimúqa
magpahímuq	pakanaqúga
magpahibalú	pakáwsan
ipasúkliq	ipakúhaq
pakánqa	

IV. (Infinitive or finite complements of verbs) Ibutáng ang hústung púrma sa bírbu nga náqa sa parentheses. Ipunúq ang nga u ug kun kinahanglánun. (12E and subsections)

Pananglítan: a. Miqingún siyá (ánhi) dínhi.
Tubág: Miqingún siyáng muqánhi dínhi.

b. Nahikalímtan ni Dyuu (dalá) ang líbru.
Tubág: Nahikalímtan ni Dyuu pagdalá ang líbru.

1. Miqingún silá (palít) silá ug sílhig.
   'They said they would buy a broom.'
2. Ayúhun níya (sílhig) ang mga iskína.
   'He will do a good job sweeping in the corners.'
3. Tinúqud bang nahumán nímu (trápu) ang mga síya? (síya 'chair')
   'Is it true that you've wiped off all the chairs?'
4. Kahibáwu ka na ba (límpyu) sa kwártu?
   'Do you already know how to clean the room?'
5. Gústu si Pírla (ádtu) sa Pulambatú.
   'Perla would like to go to Redstone.'
6. Muqubán ka kang Mis Wílbi (bisíta) kang Iyúq Tibúq.
   'You will go along with Miss Wilby to visit Uncle Tibo.'
7. Gustuqán ba siyá (ádtu) sa lúngsud sunúd simána?
   'Would she like to go to town next week?'
8. Kahibáwu ka ba (tánqaw) mig siní karúng hápun?
   'Do you know that we're going to the show this afternoon?'
9. Nahumán na ba níla (lútuq) ang paniqúdtu?
   'Have they cooked dinner yet?'
10. Gústu ka ba (hígup) ug sabáw?
    'Would you like to eat some soup?'
11. Uy, nalímut man ku (bisíta) nímu.
    'Oh! I forgot that I was going to visit you.'
12. Kinahánglan (bálik) mu dínhi sa ámuq úgmaq sa búntag.
    'You must come back here to our place tomorrow morning.'

13. Miqingún silá (sakáy) ug dyip padúung sa Mabúlu.
'They said they'd take a jeep to Mabolo.'

14. Nahumán na ba nímu (lútuq) ang pagkáqun?
'Have you finished cooking the food yet?'

15. Diq ba siyá mahádluk (ádtu) sa Pulambatú?
'Isn't she afraid to go to Redstone?'

V. Hubára ang musunúd ngádtu sa mga túdling púlung nga mugámit sa pa ug na. (12G and subsections)

1. Stop looking at me.
2. Here we are.
3. I'd better be going now.
4. It's better for me to go home.
5. Nobody has asked me yet.
6. Come on now. Let me get on.
7. Even though he is old, he still drinks a hungut of tuba every day.
8. He was already in Cebu before the war. (war 'gíra')
9. Come on. Let's get on!
10. Mother is just back from San Remigio.
11. Have you sold all the hats yet?
12. Jolo is part of the Philippines. (Ang Hulú sákup sa Pilipínas.) Tawitawi is still part of the Philippines. But Borneo—that is not the Philippines.
13. This one goes to Ormoc and so does that one. But that one there does not.
14. I have never seen a rice field.
15. Let's look for a jeep. I can't walk any more.
16. Go to sleep now in there!
17. He is even bigger than I am. (than I am 'kay kanákuq')
18. Excuse me. Did you just get here?
19. Don't get off [the boat] before it's light.
20. In 1956 I was in France, but by 1957 I was in the Philippines.
21. I haven't eaten kinilaw yet. (kinílaw 'raw food eaten with vinegar')
22. Excuse me (interrupting speaker). Isn't this Banawa yet?
23. Yes. This is it now because there is Dr. Fernandez' house.
24. Before I came to Cebu, I didn't know him.
25. Do you have anything else to buy?
26. It's better for you to get on now while it's still light.

27. There isn't any more beer, Sir.
28. My! It's late. There are probably no more jeeps. Let's just take this taxi.
29. Stop your talking! Go to sleep now!
30. 'Turn that off (págnga).' 'The radio?' 'Yes, what else?'
31. I have been here for just four days.
32. Have you been here a long time already?
33. Here's another jeep. Let's ask him if he's going now.

VI A. Mga pagbánsay sa mga túdling púlung ginámit ang na ug pa.

(1) Gámqang negative ang musunúd nga mga túdling púlung ginámit ang na ug pa. (12G 3, 2B)

Mga pananglítan: a. Nagkinahánglan pa ba kag tumatabáng dínhi?
Tubág: Waq na ba ka magkinahánglag tumatabáng dínhi?

b. Mibálhin na ba diqáy silá pagpuyúq sa íla ka Pírla?
Tubág: Waq pa ba diqáy silá mubálhin pagpuyúq sa íla ka Pírla?

1. Ma, muqádtu na kunús Burumíyu si Mis Wílbi.
2. Túqa pa si Mis Wílbi sa kusína.
3. Nanáqug na siyá kay musakáy sa tartanílya.
4. Nakasakáy na ba si Mis Wílbi Day?
5. Naghulát pa siyág tartanílya páras Burumíyu.
6. Dung, muqági ka pa bas tyánggi?
7. Karúng panahúna, lisúd na kaqáyu pagpangítag tartanílya.
8. Nagpahuwát pa si Pírla kang Mis Wílbi.
9. Muqádtu na ku kay náqa nay tartanílya.
10. Day, muqádtu na ku kay muhapít pa kus tindáhan.
11. Uy, nakasakáy na man diqáy si Pírla.
12. Manlákaw na ta Day kay údtu na man.
13. Nagsakít pa man diqáy ning ákung úlu.
14. Ínyu na ba ning tindáhan Day?
15. Dúna ka pa bay palitúng líbru Day?

(2) Buhátang affirmative ang musunúd nga mga túdling púlung ginámit ang na ug pa.

Pananglítan: a. Diq pa ku mulakáw.
Tubág: Mulakáw na ku.

b. Waq na man diqáy magqulán.
Tubág: Nagqulán pa man diqáy.

1. Diq na ku muqubán nímu ngádtus tindáhan.
2. Diq pa ku mulakáw run kay waq pa may tartanílya.
3. Nagqingún ang dráybir nga diq na siyá makahuwát nímu.
4. Waq pa siyá makasakáyg tartanílya kay waq pa may miqági.
5. Ikáw ba tung nagsúlti nákuq nga diq ka pa makaqádtug Lahúg?
6. Day, waq na ba mu dínhiy líbru?
7. Dung, díliq na ba mi makasakáy sa ímung tartanílya?
8. Anáaq, diq pa man diqáy ku makalakáw kay waq pa man ku níya kahatágig sinsílyu.
9. Uy, waq pa man diqáy kung kabayád sa kutsíru.
10. Waq na ba dínhi tung líbrung ákung gitanqawtánqaw ganíha?
11. Diq ka na ba magkinahánglan sa ákung tábang karún Mis?
12. Waq pa ba kay nabaligyáqag líbru karún Day?
13. Diq pa mu musakáy Day? Diq na man ku makahulát nínyu.
14. Pirlá, waq na ba gyud kay láqing tartanílyang nakítqan?
15. Diq na ku mupalít ug líbru dínhi uy.

VI B. Tubagá sa negative ang musunúd nga mga pangutána ginámit ang na ug pa.

Pananglítan: a. Nagqulán pa ba?
Tubág: Waq na magqulán.

b. Nakaqádtu ka na bas Burumíyu?
Tubág: Waq pa kung kaqádtus Burumíyu.

1. Náqa na ba ang tartanílyang ákung gitawág Day?
2. Nakasakáy na ba si Mis Wílbi?
3. Nabáyran na ba nímu ang kutsíru?
4. May sinsíyu ka pa ba Dung?
5. Makasakáy pa ba ku diháq Dung?
6. Dághan pa ba rung táwu sa tindáhan?
7. Dídtu na ba kas Burumíyu paghúnung sa ulán?
8. Nakapalít ka pa bag líbrus tindáhan nga gabíqi na man?
9. Ádtu ka na ba Day nga gaqulán pa man?
10. Túqa na ba kaháq si Mis Wílbi sa tindáhan?
11. May katábang na ba kaháq silá karún sa tindáhan?
12. Báyran pa ba naq nímung líbru?
13. Gisuklíqan ka na ba sa tindíra?
14. Gibáyran na ba nímu ang kutsíru?
15. Gihulát ka pa ba ni Mis Wílbi?

VII A. (May be preceded by PP-I.) Exclamatory sentences. Úsba ang musunúd nga mga túdling púlung nga declarative ngádtu sa exclamatory. (5 A, 12 F)

Pananglítan: Lisúd gyud núqun kiníng ákung kinabúhiq.

Tubág:
- Pagkalisúd gyud núqun níng ákung kinabúhiq! or
- Kalisúd gyud núqun níng ákung kinabúhiq! or
- Lisúra gyud núqun íning ákung kinabúhiq!

1. Dúgay kang miqabút.
2. Labád ang ákung úlu.
3. Sakít ang ákung tiyán ganína.
4. Dalíng nahumán ang ákung trabáhu.
5. Dághan kiníng ímung líbrung balígyaq.
6. Níndut kiníng balígyaq nínyung panáptun.
7. Maqáyu kang musinibwanú.
8. Sayúp ang ímung gibúhat.
9. Sámuk kiníng dapíta.
10. Arangqaráng ka na karúng musúltig Sinibwanú.
11. Sayún ra diqáy nang buhátun.
12. Layúq diqáy ang Pulambatú.
13. Gamáy ra ang ámung ganánsya sa tindáhan.
14. Dakúq ang baláy ni Mísis Abilyána.
15. Dághan kanáng kaság nga ímung gipalít.

VII B. Pilíqa ang hústung púrma nga anáqa sa sulúd sa parentheses.

Pananglítan: Giqúnsa man (nímu, ikáw) (kádtu, niqádtu)ng bátaq?
Tubág: Giqúnsa man nímu kadtúng bátaq?

1. Kun gústu (ka, nímu)ng muqubán, panánghid usáq (si, ni) Máma.
2. Dádqi ra (nákuq, ku)g bir dirí Dung.
3. Inigkahumán (ikáw, nímu) (niqánaq, kanáq), pahibáwqa (ku, nákuq).
4. Ánhi lang (nákuq, ku) ibutáng (ang, sa) mga kaság sa pantáwan.
5. Gústu (ni, si) Mis Wílbing muqinúm ug túbig.
6. Mangíhiq kunú (siyá, níya) sa bányu.
7. Ayáw ku (kamú, nínyu)g tanqáwa.
8. Díliq (ka, nímu) diqáy malíguq?
9. Tagáqan ra ba kunú tag dúlsi (si, ni) Lítu.
10. Biság nagkalisudlisúd ku dirí waq lang gyud (ku, nákuq) (nínyu, kamú) tabángi.
11. Mubisíta ra ba kunú (silá, níya) (nátuq, kamí) úgmaq.

12. Inigpaqúliq (ikáw, nímu) dádqa (ang, sa) líbrung ákung giqingún (nímu, ka).
13. Ayáw bayáq (siyá, níya)g sultíhi ha?
14. Gústu kung maqílhan (silá, kaníla) dáyun.
15. Waq ra ba ku (niqádtu, kádtu) makakitáq.
16. Waq (námuq, kamí) níya tudlúqi kun unsáqun pagbúhat niqánaq.
17. Tanqáwun (nákuq, akú) kun natúlug na ba siyá.
18. Kamí na lang si Lítu (ang, sa) muqádtus Kárbun.
19. Uy! Ikáw diqáy (ni, si) Místir Abáya?
20. Pangutánqa (ang, sa) bátaq kun háqin (sa, ang) íyang maqístra. (maqístra 'teacher')

VIII A. Ibúngat ang mga musunúd nga mga túdling púlung sa hústung paníngug. (423 Question)

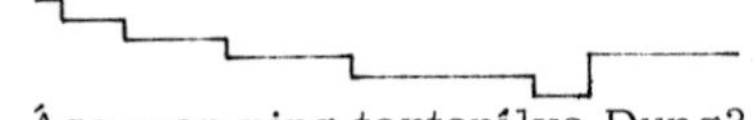

1. Ása man ning tartanílya Dung?
2. Ngánung diq man mahímuq?
3. Ása man siyá nákuq ihatúd?
4. Ngánung ádtu pa man kas ubús?
5. Piláy ímung ibáyad?
6. Kínsa pa may ímung ihatúd?
7. Ása man ka mulakáw?
8. Ngánung maqáyu man kang musúltig Sinibwanú?
9. Únsa may gitánqaw mu diháq?
10. Pilá may plíti?

VIII B. (234 Statement)

1. Tartanílya Dung. (12a 1)
2. Sa Burumíyu. (12a 3)
3. Nagquwán man gud. (12a 14)
4. Ngánhi lang. (12a 20)
5. Maqáyung búntag Mis. (12b 27)
6. Mulakáw taq ku. (12b 28)
7. Na halá. (12b 30)
8. Palít lag líbru. (12b 42)

9. Dúna na man kuy katábang. (12 c 55)
10. Gamáy ra man gud usáb ning ákung tindáhan. (12 c 59)
11. Gamáy ra kaqáyug ganánsya. (12 c 65)
12. Sunúd na lang. (12 c 65)
13. Básin pag madakuqdakúq ning tindáhan. (12 c 65)
14. Ikúhaq kug bir. (1.13)

VIII C. (324 Question)

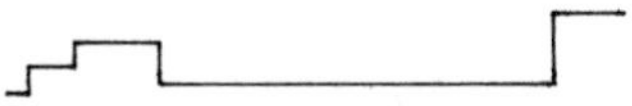

1. Ihatúd ku sa Burumíyu ha? (12 a 11)
2. Diq ba báyntiy átung gikasabútan ganíha? (12 a 24)
3. Dúgay na ka ngánhi? (12 b 48)
4. Ákuq na lang ning handumánan ha? (12 c 62)
5. Singkwínta ra ha? (8 b 29)
6. Língkud saq mu ha? (3 b 9)
7. Kínsay ímung ngálan Dung? (2 b 19)

VIII D. (234 # 231)

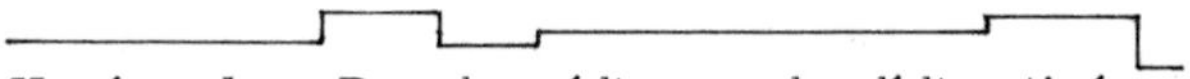

1. Kanáqug lang Day, kay ádtu man ku dídtus tiyánggi. (12 a 12)
2. Ang ákuq bítawng bána, mangingísdaq man sad. (10 a 18)
3. Ang kasagáran dínhis yútaq sa Pulambatú, gitámnag tubú. (11 a 13)
4. Sunúd simána, manánggiq na mi sa maqís. (10 a 27)
5. Diq mahímuq, kay ádtu pa man ku dídtus ubús. (12 a 15)
6. Ang ámung mga katábang dínhi sa panánggiq, maqú ang ámung mga silíngan. (10 a 32)
7. Ug ang íyang saqúp dínhi sa Pulambatú, mukúhaq lag báhin nga kwarínta pursyíntu sa tanáng áni. (10 b 14)

VIII E. (234 # 234)

1. Ánhi lang ku pasílung, kay ulán pa man. (12 b 43)
2. Arí ta sa tungaqtúngaq, kay díqa dirí ang ámung púsu kaniqádtu. (11 a 22)
3. Kun waláy ulán, diq gániq silá makatanúm. (10 b 22)
4. Nangutána lang gud ku, kay maqáyu ka mang musúltig. Sinibwanú. (12 b 47)

5. Sultíhan tiká, ug diq ku makaqánhi úgmaq. (12b32)
6. Inigbálik nátuq, maglísud tag sakáy. (4a18)
7. Mas maqáyu, arún maqílhan ku silá dáyun. (9c16)
8. Kanáng mga irúqa, mga laqág naq. (4a25)
9. Sakáy na ta, kay dirítsu man nis Sibú. (4b48)

IX A. Pagbása

Nasakít nga Maqáyug Láwas

Lúling: Uy! Naqúnsa man si Lítu? Pasákqas táqas ug pahigdáqa.

Saníng: Sigí, dalíq. Ipatawág si Dúktur Pirnándis.

Lúling: Kuqán, Saníng, únsa may gipakáqun nímu kang Lítu?

Saníng: Waláq ku magpakáqun ni Lítu uy. Alás says pa gániq. Nagqúnsa man siyá ganíha?

Lúling: Balú. (I don't know.) Siyá ra man tung usá dídtus táqas. (tu 'at that time')

Saníng: Waláy balubálu. Ikáw bayáy gipatánqaw sa bátaq. Maqúnsa gániq nyaq siyá, bántay ka lang gyuds dúktur. 'If anything happens to him, you watch out for what the doctor will do!'

Lúling: Magqúnsa man ku nga dághan man kug búhat.

Saníng: Miqabút nang dúktur. Pasúdla. Ipatánqaw si Lítu.

Lúling: Unsáqun kaháq ta run íni sa dúktur?

(Taqudtaqúd)

Saníng: Nan, únsa may súltis dúktur?

Lúling: Aa. Way kásu.* Waláq maqúnsa si Lítu.

Saníng: Lagí, makapahádluk man lang. Únsa may nakapakatúlug níya?

Lúling: Ang pagkawaláy tulúg.

IX B. Pagbánsay

Nasakít nga Maqáyug Láwas

Lúling: Uy! (Únsa) man si Lítu? (Pasaká)s táqas ug (pahígdaq).

Saníng: Sigí, dalíq. (Patawág) si Dúktur Pirnándis.

Lúling: Kuqán, Saníng, únsa may (pakáqun) nímu ni Lítu?

Saníng: Waláq ku (pakáqun) ni Lítu uy. Alás says pa gániq. (Únsa) man siyá ganíha?

Lúling: Balú. (I don't know.) Siyá ra man tung usá dídtus táqas. (tu 'at that time')

---

* Way kásu 'nothing wrong.'

Saníng: Waláy balubálu. Ikáw bayáy (patánqaw)sa bátaq. (Únsa) gániq nyaq siyá, bántay ka lang gyuds dúktur.

Lúling: (Únsa) man ku nga dághan man kug búhat.

Saníng: Miqabút nang dúktur. (Pasulúd). (Patánqaw) si Lítu.

Lúling: (Únsa) kaháq ta run íni sa dúktur?

(Taqudtaqúd)

Saníng: Nan. (Únsa) may súltis dúktur?

Lúling: Aa. Way kásu. Waláq (únsa) si Lítu.

Saníng: Lagí, (pahádluk) man lang. Únsa may (pakatúlug) níya?

Lúling: Ang pagkawaláy tulúg.

X. Sultiqánay: Si Mis Wílbi ug si Pírla Nagpaqábut ug Traak.

A: Sus, bugqáta ning mga librúha uy!

B: Bítaw nu, dágkuq man gud kaqáyu.

A: Anáaq! Hápit na man muqulán.

B: Daq, mabasáq na hinúqun ni. Layúq pa ra ba tung átung tindáhan.

A: Layúq ra ba tag baláy. Sigúru gyud ning mabasáq.

B: Pirlá, pagtawág ug tartanílyas iskína. Maqáyu kay waq pa muqulán.

A: Básig náqay tartanílyang gahulát.

1. Nagdalá silás Mis Wílbig líbru.
2. Hápit na muquwán pirú duqúl na lang ang tindáhan.
3. Layúq pang tindáhan pirú dághang baláys dúqul.
4. Mahádluk siláng maqulanán kay bágqu ra ba silág sinínaq.
5. Miqulán na ug midágan si Pírla pagpangítag tartanílya.

B: Lisúd tingáling itawág tartanílya kay ulán ra ba. Aa. Túqa. Ssst. Dung, dalíq ra.

C: Díliq ku Day kay paqúliq na ku.

B: Sigí Dung kay kuqán kiníng—túqay ákung mga líbru, mabasáq nyaq tug muqulán.

C: Ásà man?

B: Sa Burumíyu lang Dung.

C: Ádtu man kus Práybit.

B: Sigí na lang Dung. Hápit na hinúqun muqulán.

C: Singkwínta sa Burumíyu Day ha?

B: Uy kamahál gud. Kwarínta lang.

C: Nyaq ikáw ra?

B: Duhá mi. Hústu, sígi singkwínta. Bálik ra dídtus iskína kay túqa may ákung amígang gahuwát dídtu.

C: Hiq. Kl-kl-kl-

B: Únyaq dádqa mis Burumíyu tupád sa Rusítas Basár.

6. Naglisúd si Pírla pagtawág tartanílya, kay dyútay ra básta magqulán.
7. Nakakitáq na gyud siyág paráda, pirú paqúliq na man hinúqun.
8. Paríhug padúlngan si Pírlag ang tartanílya.
9. Kwarínta ra úntay ibáyad ni Pírla, pirú misugút na lang siyág singkwínta.
10. Gipabálik níya ang paráda sa gihuwatán ni Mis Wílbi.
11. Ang ílang tindáhan náqa sa duqúl sa Rusítas Basár.

C: Singkwínta ug ikáw ug ang líbru ra. Náqa pa man diqáy kaqúban mu.

B: Únyaq pilá na man pud.

C: Láqin na pud naq.

B: Halá sigí gud. Ákung pakyáwun nang ímung tartanílya. Básta ihatúd lang mis Burumíyu. Hápit na ra ba gyud muqulán.

C: Aa sigí. Sakáy na lang. Gústu kung makapaqulíq dáyun.

B: Likúq sa walá kay túqa dídtung ákung kaqúban.

C: Hiip ulán na.

12. Waláq mahímug singkwínta ang plíti.
13. Gipákyaw ni Pírla ang tartanílya.
14. Dídtu silás Mis Wílbi ihatúd sa Burumíyu.
15. Waláq mulíkuq ang tartanílya, midiritsu lang.
16. Nagqulán na paggíkan níla.

LESSON 13. AT SCHOOL

Sagquluhúnun

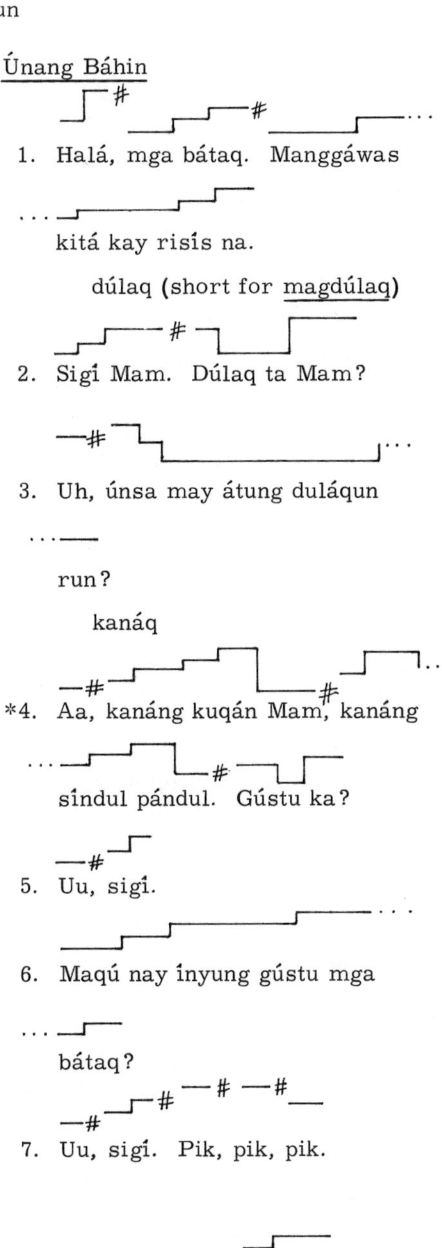

First Part	Únang Báhin
1. All right, children, let's go out, (because) it's recess now.	1. Halá, mga bátaq. Manggáwas kitá kay risís na.
let's play	dúlaq (short for magdúlaq)
2. Come on, Ma'am. Let's play (a game).	2. Sigí Mam. Dúlaq ta Mam?
3. Oh, what shall we play now?	3. Uh, únsa may átung duláqun run?
that (well known)	kanáq
4. Ah, whatchamacallit, Ma'am, hide and seek (lit. that whatchamacallit. That hide and seek). Do you want to?	*4. Aa, kanáng kuqán Mam, kanáng síndul pándul. Gústu ka?
5. Yes, all right.	5. Uu, sigí.
6. Is that what you want, children?	6. Maqú nay ínyung gústu mga bátaq?
7. All right. Let's see who's It. (Lit. Yes, all right. Pik, pik, pik.)	7. Uu, sigí. Pik, pik, pik.
8. Me and Lito first (Ma'am).	8. Kamí úsaq si Lítu Mam.

9. One, two, three.	9. Únu, dus, tris.
lost (a game)	píldi (short for napíldi)
10. Ah, Lito lost.	10. Aa, píldis Lítu.
11. Because his was paper (Ma'am).	11. Papíl man iyáha Mam.
12. Mine was scissors.	12. Ákuq gúnting.
13. You lost, Lito. Now the teacher and me.	13. Ikáw may píldi Litú. Kamí na sad si Mam.
14. All right. One, two, three.	14. Na sigí. Únu, dus, tris.
15. Oh. Scissors is defeated by stone.	15. Uh, pílding gúnting sa batú.
16. Ah, so I lost.	16. Aa, píldi diqáy ku.
17. Ah, the teacher lost. You're It, Ma'am, you're It (lit. you are the witch).	17. Aa, píldi si Mam. Ikáy abát Mam, ikáy abát.
18. All right, I'm It (lit. I am the fool).	18. Na sigí. Akúy búqang.
19. Who's going to throw the can?	19. Kínsa may mulábays láta?
20. Me (Ma'am), me.	20. Akú Mam, akú.
21. All right.	21. Na sigí.
22. Toss (it).	22. Ítsa.

let's hide — táguq (short for <u>magtáguq</u>)

23. Yes, run! Let's hide right away.

23. Uu dágan. Táguq dáyun ta.

24. Come on! Run!

24. Sigí na, dágan.

25. Yes.

25. Uu.

26. Coming, ready or not! (Lit. All right, I'm here now, O. K.?)

26. Na, níqa na ku ha?

was caught — sákpan (= <u>hisákpan</u>)

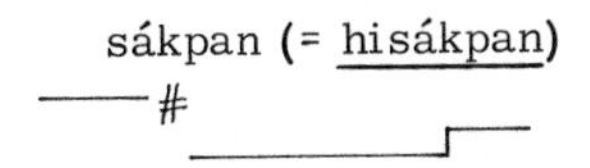

27. One-two-three on you! (Lit. Ha! I caught you.)

*27. Bung, sákpan ku ikáw.

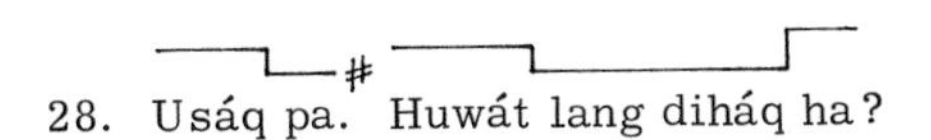

28. Wait a minute. Just wait there, will you?

28. Usáq pa. Huwát lang diháq ha?

29. I'll look for someone else (lit. another one).

29. Mangítaq pa kug ubán.

30. Oh, I've caught someone.

30. Uh, hmm, sákpan nákuq.

31. All free.

31. Líbring tanán.

32. Well, you're still It (lit. the witch), Ma'am.

32. Na, ikáw gihápuy abát Mam.

33. You're still It.

33. Ikáw gihápun.

34. (Yes,) O. K., you all hide again.

34. Uu sigí, panáguq na sab mu.

35. (Yes,) O. K.

35. Uu sigí.

36. Well, I really have to look

36. Na, mangítaq na gyud ku áni

for them.

37. Where can they (lit. these) be hiding?

38. Oh, there they are.

39. One-two-three on Kikoy. (Lit. Ha, Kikoy, I got you.)

40. Ah, you really got me (lit. we were really caught).

41. All right, you're the whatchamacallit now, Kikoy, O.K.?

42. (Yes,) O.K. You all hide again.

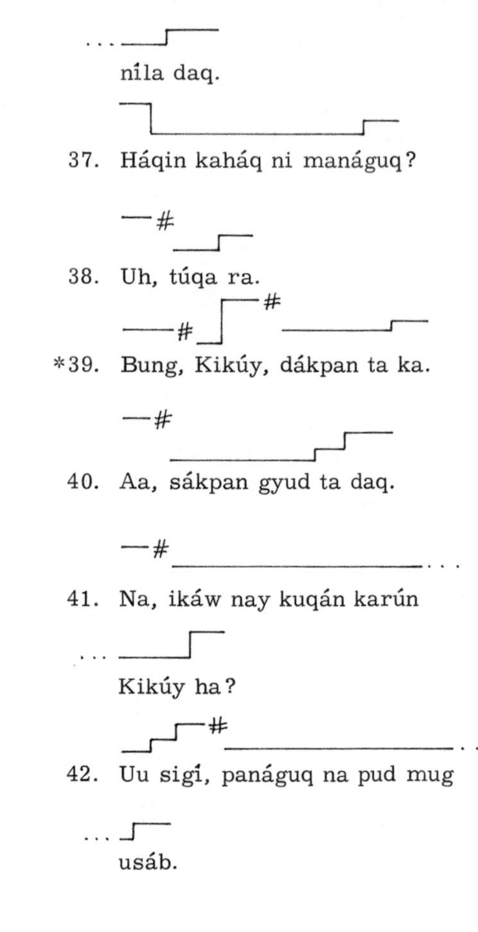

nîla daq.
37. Háqin kaháq ni manáguq?
38. Uh, túqa ra.
*39. Bung, Kikúy, dákpan ta ka.
40. Aa, sákpan gyud ta daq.
41. Na, ikáw nay kuqán karún
Kikúy ha?
42. Uu sigî, panáguq na pud mug
usáb.

Mga Pangutána

Únang Báhin

1. Mga bátaq, únsay gústu nínyung dúlaq?
2. Háqin may pîldi, papîl ug gúnting?
3. Kînsa may abát?
4. Pilá may nasákpan?
5. Nakatáguq na bang tanán?
6. Si Kîkuy bay búqang?
7. Kînsa pay pangitáqun?
8. Únsa pay înyung gihuwát? Táguq na mu.
9. Nakîtqan na ba ang tanán Mam?
10. Diqîn ka man táguq Kikúy?
11. Makahibáwu ka ba sa dúlaq nga sîndul pándul sa láta Mam?

12. Mam díliq pa ba ta magrisís?
13. Gústu ba mu sa dúlang síndul pándul?
14. Kínsay píldi nínyu ni Kíkuy Litú?
15. Kínsa may píldi námuq? Ákuq batú; íya gúnting.
16. Si Kíkuy na ba lay waq hidákpi?
17. Únsa pa may ínyung gihuwát?
18. Pilá nay nasákpan nímu Mam?
19. Kay nalíbri mang tanán, akú ba giházpun ruy abát?
20. Manáguq na ba mi Mam?

Mga Pangutána (Matching)

Únang Báhin

1. Únsay gústu nínyung dúlaq?
2. Ikáy píldi Litú? Ikáy abát?
3. Kínsay nakalíbring Lítu?
4. Sa átuq pa, búqang díqay gihápun ku?
5. Kínsa man diqáy mulábay sa láta?
6. Kínsa pay waq hidákpi Mam?
7. Kínsa may napíldi nínyung Lítu?
8. Diqín man mu manáguq?
9. Kinahánglan bang pangitáqun ang tanán?

(a) Si Lítu Mam, kay papíl ang íya, únyaq ang ákuq gúnting.
(b) Akú lay lábay. Sigí, táguq na mu.
(c) Si Kíkuy na lang. Ang ubán hidákpan na.
(d) Uu, kay nalíbri man ni Lítu si Píya; ug kamí pud, nakalíbri man mi; waq man mi nímu hidákpi.
(e) Si Kíkuy, Mam, siyáy nakalíbring Lítu.
(f) Kanáng kuqán Mam, síndul pándul.
(g) Díliq uy! Papíl may ákuq ganíha. Ímu batú.
(h) Aw uu. Pangitáqun gyud ang tanán únaq manáguq pagqusáb.
(i) Dídtus átung kwártu, Mam. Níndut kaqáyung tagúqan dídtu.

Sagquluhúnun

Second Part	Ikaduháng Báhin
43. All right. That's enough	43. Na, hústu na tas átung dúwaq

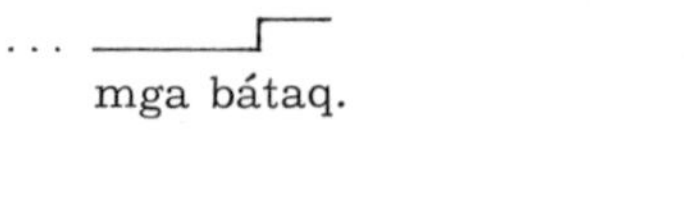

now, children (lit. we are enough now of our playing). ... mga bátaq.

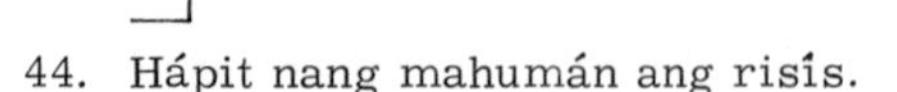

44. Recess is almost over now. — 44. Hápit nang mahumán ang risís.

45. Get in line over here now. — 45. Línya na mu dirí.

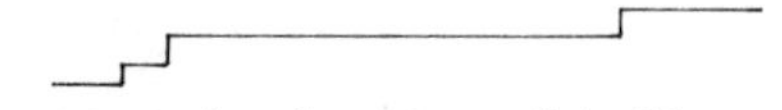

46. May I get a drink first, Ma'am? (Lit. I'll get a drink of water first.) — 46. Muqinúm úsaq kug túbig Mam.

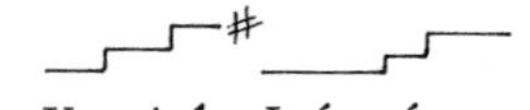

47. All right, get a drink first. — 47. Uu sigí. Inúm úsaq.

[particle used in pointing out something or accusing] — ay

mucus in the nose — sípqun

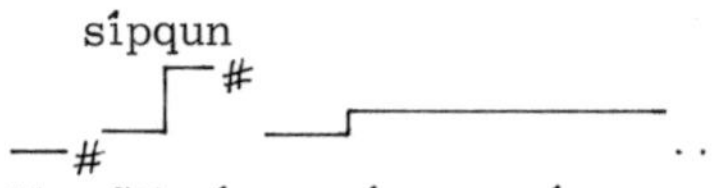

48. Hey, Sebya, your nose is running. Wipe it. (Lit. Your mucus. Wipe it.) — 48. Uy, Sibyá, ang ímung sípqun ... ay. Pahíra.

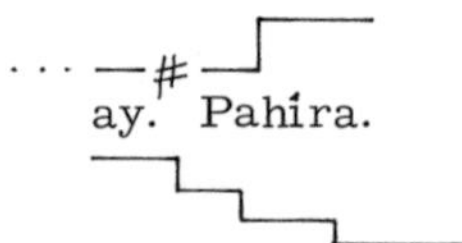

49. Who else has to go to the bathroom (lit. wants to urinate)? — 49. Kínsa pay gústung mangíhiq?

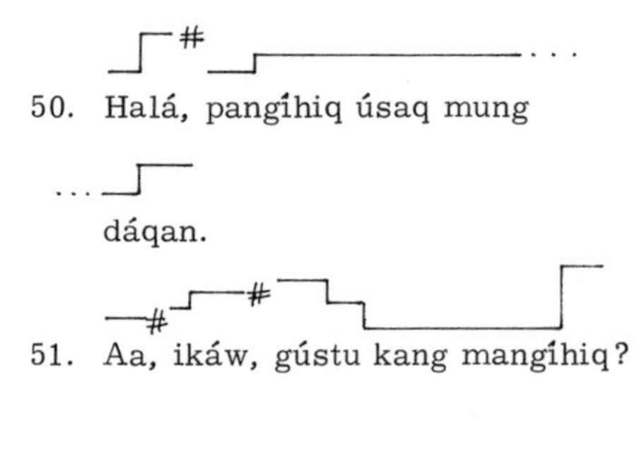

50. All right. Go to the bathroom (lit. urinate) first. — 50. Halá, pangíhiq úsaq mung ... dáqan.

51. Ah, you. Do you have to go to the bathroom? (Lit. Do you want to urinate?) — 51. Aa, ikáw, gústu kang mangíhiq?

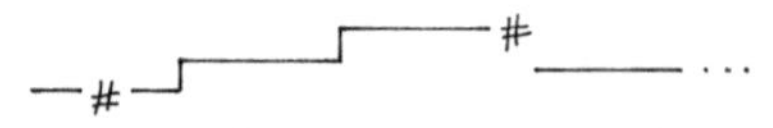

52. Oh, I've already gone, Ma'am. I've finished. (Lit. Oh, it's finished already.) — 52. Uh, humán na Mam. Humán ... na ku.

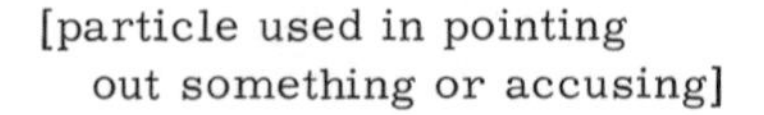

[particle used in pointing out something or accusing] — ay

53. Pedro, there. He hasn't yet.	53. Si Pídru ay. Waláq pa.
54. Oh, Pedro, go on.	54. Uh, lakáw Pidrú.
55. Who has not gotten a drink yet?	55. Kínsay waq pa kaqinúm?
56. Get a drink first.	56. Inúm mung dáqan.
57. Is everybody done now?	57. Humán nang tanán?
58. All right. Go in this way. (Lit. All right. You all enter here now.)	58. Uh sigí. Suud na mu dirí.
59. Sit down now, sit down.	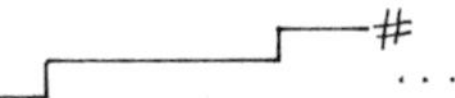 59. Panglíngkud na mu. ... Panglíngkud.
that one (in the past)	tu
60. Who was it that was in charge of erasing the blackboard?	*60. Kínsa tuy tigpápas sa ... blákburd?
61. Angel, Ma'am.	61. Si Ánghil Mam.
62. It's his turn to clean the blackboard now.	62. Iyáha nang túrnu pagqirís ... sa blákburd.
63. Oh, it's your (turn) now, Angel?	63. Aa, ímu run Anghíl?
64. (Oh,) over here.	64. Uh dirí.

65. Erase all that there.	65. Papása naq diháng tanán.
66. Then after you finish, clean the eraser.	66. Únyaq inigkahumán, limpyúhi ang irísir.
67. Afterward, I'll tell you a story.	67. Inigkahumán, magqistúrya ku nínyu.
68. What story, Ma'am?	68. Únsang isturyáha Mam?
69. This is a story from the Bible.	69. Usá kiní ka sugilánun gíkan sa Biblíya.
70. Oh, how beautiful!	70. Aa kaníndut!
71. What story?	71. Únsang isturyáha?
that (well known)	kanáq
72. Whatchamacallit . . . about Noah and his ark.	72. Kanáng kuqán, báhin ni Nuwág íyang Árka.
isn't it?	sa?
73. It's a nice one, isn't it?	*73. Níndut Mam sa?
74. Yes. Do you know what an ark is?	74. Uu. Kahibáwu kag únsay árka?
75. (Ah,) I know (Ma'am).	75. Aa, kahibáwu ku Mam.
76. Who knows?	76. Kínsay kahibáwu?

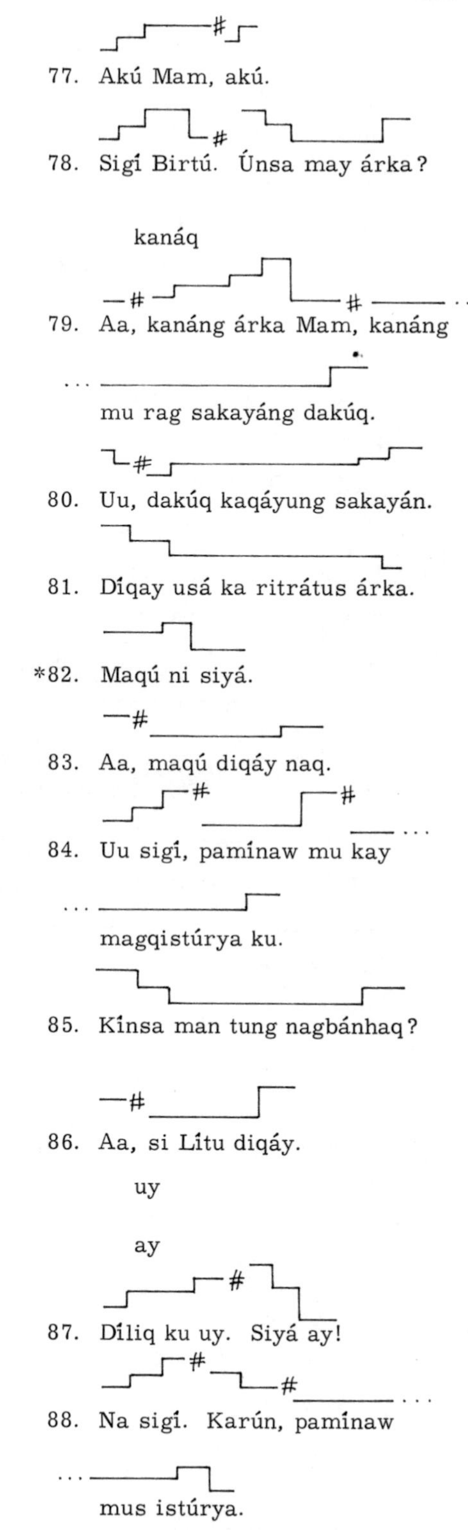

77. Me (Ma'am). Me.	77. Akú Mam, akú.
78. All right, Berto. What is an ark?	78. Sigí Birtú. Únsa may árka?
that (previously mentioned)	kanáq
79. Ah . . . arks (Ma'am)—they're those things that are like big boats.	79. Aa, kanáng árka Mam, kanáng . . . mu rag sakayáng dakúq.
80. Yes, a very big boat.	80. Uu, dakúq kaqáyung sakayán.
81. Here's a picture of an ark.	81. Díqay usá ka ritrátus árka.
82. This is it.	*82. Maqú ni siyá.
83. Ah, so that's it.	83. Aa, maqú diqáy naq.
84. All right, you listen; (because) I'm going to tell a story.	84. Uu sigí, pamínaw mu kay . . . magqistúrya ku.
85. Who is it that's making noise?	85. Kínsa man tung nagbánhaq?
86. Ah, so it's Lito.	86. Aa, si Lítu diqáy.
[particle emphatically contradicting interlocutor]	uy
[pointer]	ay
87. It's not me. It's him!	87. Díliq ku uy. Siyá ay!
88. All right. Now listen to the story.	88. Na sigí. Karún, pamínaw . . . mus istúrya.

Mga Pangutána

Ikaduháng Báhin

1. Humán nang átung risís Mam?
2. Sibyá, diq ka ba makamaqúng mupáhid niqánang ímung sípqun?
3. Kínsay gústung mangíhiq?
4. Nakaqinúm na ba mung tanág túbig?
5. Ngánung waq ka pa man mulíngkud Pidrú?
6. Kínsang túrnu karúns pagpápas sa blákburd?
7. Únsay ímung iqistúrya Mam?
8. Kínsa kanínyuy nakakitág ritrátus árka?
9. Kanáng árka Mam, paríhu ba nag sakayán?
10. Papásun ku ba kiníng tanán nga níqas blákburd Mam?
11. Níndut bang tanqáwun kanáng árka Mam?
12. Ikáw tung nagbánhaq Litú nu?
13. Anghíl, ímu na bang túrnus pagqirís sa blákburd?
14. Mam, kínsa man nas Núwa?
15. Mamínaw na ba mu mga bátaq?
16. Níndut ba nang isturyáha Mam?
17. Únsa man nang árka Mam, sakayán ba naq?
18. Humán ka na bag pápas sa blákburd Anghíl?
19. Mam, ása man nákuq ibutáng kiríng irísir?
20. Magqistúrya ka na ba Mam?

Mga Pangutána (Matching)

Ikaduháng Báhin

1. Litú, ngánung waq pa man nímu papása ang blákburd?
2. Pidrú, únsa pa may ímung gihuwát nga waláq ka pa man mulínya?
3. Háqin nang ritrátus árka?
4. Kínsay waláq pa makapangíhiq?
5. Kirí diríng iskináha, papásun pa ba ri?
6. Ímu bang túrnu pagpápas Anghíl?

(a) Túqang Síbya Mam. Gitagúqan.

(b) Díliq man ákung túrnu karún Mam. Kang Ánghil man.

(c) Mangíhiq pa man gud úntaq ku Mam.

(d) Aw uu. Ayúhag pápas kanáng tanán.

(e) Siyá ay. Waláq pa naq siyá mangíhiq.

(f) Akú Mam. Nakakitáq na ku Mam.

7. May nakakitáq na ba kanínyug ritrátus árka?
8. Paríha mag sakayán kanáng árka Mam nu?
9. Kínsay waláq pa makaqinúm ug túbig?

(g) Úqu Mam. Ákuq karúng túrnu.
(h) Akú Mam. Waláq pa ku kaqinúm Mam.
(i) Uu. Paríhag sakayán pirú dakúq kaqáyu.

Commentary to Basic Sentences

13.4	síndul pándul	The game of Kick the Can: the can is kicked, and while the player who is It replaces the can, the others hide.
13.27	bung	This is an exclamation used in games when the one who is It catches someone.
13.39	dákpan ta	Short for hidákpan, which in this case means the same as sákpan. Remember the plural ta is used for ku if there is a subject ka or kamú.
13.60	tu	'That one in the past.' Literally, the sentence says: 'Who was that one (I designated) to erase the blackboard?'
13.60	tigpápas	'The one who erases the blackboard.' Tig- has a meaning similar to English -er 'one who [does].'
13.73	sa	This word, like nu, is used at the end of sentences to mean 'isn't it?'
13.82	ni siyá	The speaker's use of ni indicates that the children are near the picture. Note that siyá is used after ni to refer to a thing. Siyá follows a demonstrative and refers to a thing when the thing is being explained. Thus ni siyá means 'this thing.'

Grammatical Section

13A. Obligatory use of the passive

There are certain constructions where passive forms must always be used, and active forms never.

13A1. Passives used when agents follow ang, y, nga, sa

A phrase meaning 'agent does an action' is expressed by a passive verb and a genitive agent after ang, y, nga, or sa. In the following examples the genitive agent is underlined once and the passive verb twice:

Maqú kiní ang ákung gisúlti níya.
'This is what I told him.'

(The corresponding active construction misúlti aku does not occur after ang.)

Únsay gústu nímung tanqáwun?
'What would you like to see?'

(Active construction gústu kang mutánqaw does not occur after y.)

Únsa man tung gibalígyaq nímu?
'What is that you are selling?'

(Active construction mibalígyaq ka does not occur after a linking nga.)

Waq ku kasabút sa ímung gisúlti.
'I didn't understand what you said.'

(Active construction misúlti ka does not occur after a goal marking sa.)

Unsa may átung duláqun run?
'What shall we play now?' (13a 3)

(Active construction magdúlaq kitá does not occur after y.)

13 A 2. Passives used when recipient of the action precedes the verb

A passive form must be used when the verb is preceded by the recipient of the action, the place where the action occurs, or the instrument producing the action. (This rule also applies in most of the examples in 13 A 1 above and reinforces the choice of the passive there.) The recipient of the action is underlined once and the verb twice in the following examples:

Waq man siyáy táwung nakítaq. 'He saw no one (lit. there was no one he saw).' (táwu man, the thing seen, precedes the verb; thus the verb is passive.)

Which passive is used depends upon what meaning relation there is between the verb and the noun preceding. In the two examples below the direct passive is used because the noun preceding is the recipient of the action and the verbs are of the type which take the direct passive.

Kiníng ságing díliq pa makáqun kay hiláw pa. 'These bananas cannot be eaten yet because they're still green.'
Si Huwáy napíliq. 'John is the one who was chosen.'

13 A 3. Passives in existential sentences

In existential sentences which have an existent (the portion of the sentence following the particle y: 3 A 1) that contains a verb, if there is a subject with the agent meaning, the passive form is obligatory. In the following sentence the subject is underlined once and the passive verb twice:

a. Ug dúna kay makítaq, sultíhi akú. 'If you see [someone], tell me.' (Lit. 'If you have [someone] seen, tell me.') [The subject ka 'you' is the agent—the one who does the seeing—and since the sentence is existential, the verb is passive.]

In existential sentences which have an existent containing a verb plus nga plus recipient, the passive is obligatory. The verb is underlined twice and the recipient three times in the following sentence:

b. Ug dúna kay makítang táwu, sultíhi akú. 'If you see a man, tell me.'

(Lit. 'If you have a man seen, tell me.')

c. Waláy trabáhung nahumán na. 'There is no work that has been finished.'

Exercises for this section are listed under 13 D 5.

13 A 3 a. Meaning of a passive verb in an existential sentence

In existential sentences, a passive verb means '[do] to [the recipient].' (See examples b and c of 13 A 3, where the recipient is underlined three times.) If no recipient is expressed, the passive verb means '[do] to someone, something, anyone, anything, no one, or nothing.'

Ug dúna kay makítaq, sultíhi akú. 'If you see (anyone), tell me.'
Ug náqay gibutáng sa ímung báqbaq, kuháqa dáyun. 'If you have something in your mouth (lit. If there is (something) put in your mouth), take it out right away.'
Náqa bay ímung nadalá? 'Did you bring (anything)?' (Lit. 'Is there anything brought by you?')
Waq ra ba kuy ikahátag kanímu. 'I have nothing to give you.' (Lit. 'I have nothing to be given to you.')
Waláq na kuy ikasúlti. 'I have nothing more to say.' (Lit. 'I have nothing to be said any longer.')

Do Step I of PP-EE. (Do the other steps after you have studied 13 B and its subsections.)

13 B. Obligatory use of the active

13 B 1. Agent preceding verb

Use of an active form is obligatory if the agent—the one who does the action—precedes the verb (unless the agent is a genitive form). The agent is underlined once and the verb twice:

Ikáw lay magpíliq. 'You be the one to choose.' [Ikáw, the agent, precedes the action; therefore the active form magpíliq is used.]
Ngánung diq man nímu ibalígyaq nang dyip nga díliq mudágan? 'Why don't you sell that jeep, since it won't run?' [The active mudágan is obligatory, because the agent dyip precedes the verb.]

Exercises for this section are listed under 13 D 5.

13 B 2. Meaning of an active verb in an existential sentence

In existential sentences, an active verb means '[agent] does [do].' The agent is underlined once and the active verb twice:

Ug dúnay táwung muqánhi, sultíhi akú. 'If a man comes, tell me.' (Lit. 'If there is a man who comes, tell me.')

If no agent is expressed, the active verb means 'somebody, something, anyone, anything, no one, or nothing [does].'

Ug dúnay muqánhi, sultíhi akú. 'If (somebody) comes, tell me.'
Ug maqalás útsug waq gihápuy mupalít, paqúliq na lang. 'If eight o'clock comes around and still no one buys (it) (lit. still there is no one who buys), just go on home.'

Náqay nahigúgma nákuq. Kínsa kaháq? 'Somebody loves me (lit. There is [someone] who loves me). I wonder who?'
Waláy nakakitáq níya. 'Nobody saw him.' (Lit. 'There was no one who saw him.')

Pattern Practice PP-EE. (Other exercises for 13 A 3 a and 13 B 2 are listed under 13 C.)

This construction is the only Cebuano equivalent of the English indefinite pronouns (someone, somebody, something, anybody, anything, anyone, no one, nobody, nothing). If the recipient of the verb action is indefinite, you use an existential predicate containing a passive form (described in 13 A 3 a). If the agent of the action is indefinite, you use an existential predicate containing an active form (described in 13 B 2).

13 C. Bísan kínsa

Bísan kínsa means 'Anyone.'

Ayáwg isúlti kang bísan kínsa. 'Don't tell anyone.'
Bísan kínsa makahímuq pagpatáy niádtung Bákir. 'Anyone at all was allowed to kill Baker (the outlaw).'

Exercises XIII.III, XIV.II B, and XV.XV covers this section, as well as 13 A 3 a and 13 B 2 above.

13 D. Meanings of active and passive verb forms: review

In Lesson 6, pp. 228ff., you studied differences in meaning between the active and the passive verb forms. It will be useful at this time to observe the differences in greater detail, in order to choose the form that expresses your meaning accurately in constructions where either is possible.

13 D 1. Meanings of active and passive imperative forms

The active imperative is a simple command to someone to do something, so that the emphasis is on the action itself:

a. Likúq sa tuqú. 'Turn right.'
b. Píliq lang mu diháq. (4 b 35) 'You choose.'
c. Sunúd lang nákuq. (4 a 23) 'Just follow me.'

The passive imperative, by contrast, is used when attention is focused on the thing to be affected by the command—that is, a command for something to happen to something else:

Súnda akú. 'Follow me.' [The attention is focused on who should be followed—not on what somebody should do. This command might be given in response to a question 'Who do we follow?' or 'What should we do to you?']

13 D 2. Other active meanings

In sentences having an active form other than imperative, the predicate tells what someone or something does (or did, or will or can do)—that is, the predicate answers the question 'What does (etc.) [someone] do?' Examples:

a. Díqay tindáhan sa aláhas. Musúud tingáli ku. 'Here's a jewelry store. I think I'll go in.' [The active is used because the sentence might answer the question 'What will you do?']
b. Muqábang nu siyá sa usá sa mga kwártu. 'She says she wants to rent one of the rooms.' [The active is used because the sentence could answer the question 'What does she want to do?']
c. Ánhaq muhúnung ang mga dyip. (3 a 25) 'That's where the jeeps stop.' [The active is used because the sentence might answer the question 'What do the jeeps do there?']

The potential active verb form is used in predicates when the predicate tells what someone or something can do:

d. Átung tanqáwun ug makasakáy ba tas píkqap. (4 a 8) 'Let's see if we can get on an irregular trip.'

The unreal verb predicate with a hortatory meaning ['let's . . .': 4 B 2 a] calls for an active form:

e. Mangutána ta. (3 a 8) 'Let's ask.'
f. Manakáy ta. 'Let's get on.'

The unreal verb meaning 'should [do]' (5 C 2 (2)) must also be active:

g. Magbántay ka dinhi. (8 a 17) 'You should watch out here.'

13 D 3 a. Other passive meanings

A passive verb form is used in predicates that tell what happens to somebody or something. To put it another way, if the predicate answers the question 'Does [the action] happen to [someone, something]?' a passive verb form is used. For example:

Díliq ku abángan kanáng kwártu kay duqúl sa kusína. Ug dúnay kwártung mas layúq sa kusína, ákung abángan. 'I won't rent that room because it's near the kitchen. If there's a room farther from the kitchen, I'll rent it.' [The predicate tells what will happen to the room; attention is focused on what room I want to rent, rather than on what I want to do. The sentence might answer a question about the room, as 'How about this room? Do you want it?']

A passive form is used for an unreal verb if it is to have a hortatory meaning ('let's . . .) with attention focused on the recipient of the action. For example:

Náqay dyip. Átuq ning pangutánqun. (4 a 9) 'There's a jeep. Let's ask there (lit. this one).' [Attention is focused on the jeep and what should be done to it, rather than what we should do. It could answer a question about the jeep, as: 'How about this jeep? Shall we ask if it goes to Talisay?']

A potential passive verb form is required in predicates that tell what can be done to something:

Diq na naq mahángyuq? (3 b 29) 'Can't we bargain for that?' [The question is whether that is something one can bargain over—not whether or not we are able to bargain.]

13 D 3 b. Passive verbs with specific recipients

A passive form must be used when the recipient of the action is specific—when it is a name, a word preceded by a demonstrative, or a noun modified by a genitive possessor—and when it is this specific recipient that is emphasized. (The verb is underlined twice and the recipient once in the examples below.)

Ngánu gung kúptan nímung ákung bag? (8 a 14) 'What do you think you're doing holding my bag?'
Ákung gidalá si Mis Wílbi. (3 b 6) 'I brought Miss Wilby.'
Ákuq lang ibílin ning ákung amígu dínhi. (1 a 16) 'I'll just leave my friend here.'

13 D 4. Verbs that tend to be used in the passive

Certain verbs tend to be used in the passive even in situations which would usually call for an active verb. An example of this type of verb is tánqaw 'look, see.'

a. Muqádtu kus tindáhan kay tanqáwun nákuq kun túqa na ba dídtu si Pírla. 'I am going to the store to see (lit. because I want to see) if Perla is there yet.' [Since attention is focused on what I am going to do in the store, we would expect an active verb, as in the example just below; but since the verb is tánqaw, the passive is used rather than the active.]*

Contrast this with the following parallel example, where the normal active form appears:

b. Muqádtu kus tindáhan kay mupalít pa ku ug panáptun. 'I am going to the store because I still have to buy cloth.'

13 D 5. Active and passive verbs as subjects

If a predicate names the agent of a verb that appears as the subject, the subject verb form is active:

Akúy mangutána? (3 a 10) 'Shall I ask?' (Lit. 'I'll be the one to ask?') [The predicate akú 'I' is the agent of the action in the subject, mangutána 'ask'; therefore, the verb is active.]
Ang nakasáwuq mu na say mulábay. (11 b 11) 'The one who caught (the ball) becomes the one who throws it in turn.' [The predicate ang nakasáwuq 'the one who caught it' is the agent of the verb in the subject, mulábay 'will throw it'; therefore, the verb is active.]

(The rule of 13 B 1—stating that if the agent precedes the verb, the verb is active—also applies to sentences of this type.)

If the subject of a sentence is a verb and the predicate does not have the agent meaning, the verb is passive:

Únsa may átung duláqun run? (13 a 3) 'What shall we play now?' [Because the predicate únsa 'what?' is not the agent of the action of the verb in the subject duláqun 'play' (it is the recipient), a passive verb form is used.]

---

* The active form of tánqaw is indeed used, but usually only in constructions which require an active or in the meaning 'watch a performance.'

For 13 D and its subsections, do Exercises XIII.II A, XIII.II B, XIII.IV A, XIV. II A, XV.II. (These exercises also apply to 13 A 1, 13 A 2, 13 A 3, and 13 B 1.)

13 E. Kitá, kamí, kamú, silá si/ni X

Kitá, kamí, kamú, or silá followed by si or ni X (where X is a name) mean 'we and X,' 'X and I (that is, we),' 'X and you,' and 'X and they' respectively. There is no difference in meaning between si and ni in this usage.

Kamí ni Dyuu ang maqádtu. 'Joe and I will go.'
Kamí úsaq si Litu Mam. (13 a 8) 'Lito and me first, Ma'am.'
Diqín ba díqay kamú si Ústing? 'Where were you and Osting?'

Silá si/ni X has the special meaning 'X and his companions':

Níqa man diqáy siláng Mísis Abáya. 'Ah, here is Mrs. Abaya and her companions.'

(In this sentence ng appears rather than ni: cf. chart, 1 B 1, p. 14.)

13 F. Use of the subjunctive passive and unreal active after certain words

Up to now you have used the subjunctive and the unreal active after waláq. These same forms are used, optionally, with qualifying expressions of time or place, if they precede the verb form. The qualifier is underlined once and the verb form twice:

Dídtu silá maglíngkud sa sála. 'They were sitting (there) in the living room.'
Humán níya táwga ang doktór, misulúd na pud siyá sa kwártu. 'After he called the doctor, he went back into the room.'
Sa sunúd na lang ádlaw níya lutúqa ang ísdaq. 'He will just cook the fish the next day.'
Kanúsqa man níya hibáwqi? 'When did he find out about it?'

Exercise XIII.IV B.

13 G. Particles lang and diqáy

13 G 1. Lang (short for lámang)

Lang together with a predicate means 'only [predicate], out of several possibilities.' Lang appears in the position of the postpositives (see 3 C 2 and 3 C 3ff.).

13 G 1 a. Lang with predicates meaning '[the predicate] is the only thing remaining'

A number followed by lang means 'only [number]'—that is, 'not an implied or expressed larger number.'

Pára nímu prísyung ispisyál—písu lang. (8 b 27) 'For you, a special price—just a peso.'

Lang in this meaning often combines with na (forming na lang) to modify numbers which are less than a previously stated number: 'now (it is) only [so much].'

Tagpíla ang aríyus?—Dus písus ang par.--Únu singkwínta na lang. 'How much are the earrings?'—'Two pesos a pair.'—'Make it one-fifty.' (Lit. 'Now just one-fifty.')

Na lang also modifies nouns or pronouns to mean 'only [noun or pronoun] now (as contrasted with more earlier).'

Namatáy ang amahán ni Huwán. Maqú nga si Huwán na lang ang nahibilín. 'John's father died. So John was the only one left.' (Lit.'Now only John was the one left.')

13 G 1 b. Lang modifying predicates in sentences with verb subjects

In sentences with a verb subject lang modifies a predicate (in the postpositive position—3 C 2, 3 C 3ff.) to give the meaning 'let [predicate] do [the verb]'—literally '[the predicate] will just be the one to [do].' The subject is underlined once and the predicate twice:

Akú lay dalá ining bag nímu. 'Let me carry your bag.' (Lit. 'I will just be the one to carry your bag.')
Ikáw lay magpíliq. (3 b 22) 'You be the one to choose.'

Lang modifies predicates in sentences without a subject in the meaning, 'let [predicate] do it, let [predicate] be the one.'

Níqa na bítaw ta dínhi. Akú lang. (8 a 13) 'We're almost there now anyway. I'll carry it myself.' (Lit. 'I'll just be the one.')

13 G 1 c. Lang following commands or exhortations

A command or exhortation with lang after it means '[do]!' or 'let's [do]!' with the implication that it's a small thing to do.

Pangítaq lang mug pára sa Kapitúl. (2 a 10) 'Just look for one for the Capitol.'
Ánhi lang ta manihápun. (2 b 31) 'Let's just eat supper here.'
Subáya lang naq nínyu, kanáng dálan Piláyis. (3 a 21) 'Just follow Pelaez Street.'

The phrases ayáw lang and ságdi lang mean 'never mind.'

13 G 1 d. Lang with verbs meaning 'have to [do the less desirable alternative]':

A phrase consisting of verb plus lang means that the verb is the thing to be done, though it would be preferable to do otherwise.

Ikáw na lay sakáy Pirlá. Maghuwát lang kug láqin. 'You get on, Perla. I'll just wait for another.' [The speaker would like to get on the same jeep as Perla, but since there is room for only one person, she will wait for the next one.]
Magquná lang ku nimu. 'I'll go ahead of you.' [I would prefer to go together with you, but it is impossible.]

In this meaning lang is the same as na lang (discussed in 12 G 1 d), and in the above sentences na lang could be substituted for lang without changing the meaning.

13 G 1 e. Lang meaning 'merely'

A verb or noun plus lang means 'merely, no better than [noun or verb].' In this usage lang is synonymous with ra (14 G 2 f in Lesson 14).

Tíqaw mu bay mutsátsu lang, únyaq mangasáwa sa anák sa prisidínti. 'Imagine, a mere servant, yet he wants to marry the president's daughter!'

Ang urkístra nagyáqyaq lang. 'The orchestra is no good.' (Lit. 'The orchestra is no better than sloppy.')

13 G 1 f. Expressions with lang

[Mu lang]

Mu lang is an exclamation of emphatic agreement or an emphatic affirmative.

Iníta árun aq.—Mu lang. 'Boy! Is it hot today!'—'It sure is.'

Gústu kag surbíti?—Gústu mu lang. 'Do you want some ice cream?'—'I sure do!'

[Pa lang]

Pa lang plus a predicate means 'lest [predicate] happen,' '(or else) [the predicate] might happen.'

Diq ku musaká sa káhuy uy. Mahúlug pa lang nyaq ku. 'I won't climb the tree! I might fall.'

13 G 2. Diqáy

13 G 2 a. Diqáy modifies the predicate of a statement in which the speaker responds to having received some new information. The meaning is something like 'I have just discovered that [predicate] is the case.'

Uh! Údtu na man diqáy kaqáyu. (1 a 24) 'Oh my! It has gotten to be very late.' (Lit. 'I see that it is very late now.') [The speaker has just discovered that it is late, and diqáy modifying the statement indicates that the information is new.]

Uy, dúna man diqáy tay mga bisíta Ma! 'Oh, we have visitors, Ma' (Lit. 'I see we have visitors!') [The speaker has just found out.]

Diq diqáy mahímuq Mis. (6 a 14) 'It can't be done, Miss.' (Lit. 'I have found out that it cannot be done.')

The same meaning is present in questions with no interrogatives—something like, 'Oh, so [the predicate] is the case, is it?'

Kamú bang duhá diqáy muqábang sa uság kwártu? (3 c 7) 'So you two will rent the other room?'

13 G 2 b. Diqáy with interrogatives

Diqáy with interrogatives has one of two meanings. It may indicate that the question is not being asked for the first time: 'What, then, is the case (if it isn't what I thought)?'

Únsa man diqáyng dyip ámung sákyan padúung sa Banáwaq? (2 a 9) 'What jeep DO we get then to go to Banawa (if it isn't this one)?'

Nyaq ása man diqáy ta manakáyg dyip páras Kárbun? 'Where DO we get on, then, to go to Carbon?'

Or, if the question is being asked for the first time, diqáy has the effect of showing a stronger interest than ordinary.

Kay ása man diqáy ka Nang? (9 b 4) 'Why? Where are you going, Ma'am?'

13 G 2 c. Diqáy plus predicate meaning '[predicate] should also be taken into consideration'

Diqáy modifies the predicate of statements or questions calling attention to something of which the speaker or the hearer is not aware. To such a statement, diqáy gives a meaning something like, 'Oh, yes, [the predicate] is also the case, isn't it.' The questions mean, 'How about [the predicate]?' or '[predicate] is the case, isn't it?'

Akú diqáy? Waq man ku nímu tagáqig bukháyuq. 'How about me? You forgot to give me any bukhayo.'
Diq man kung kaqádtu. Waq man kuy ikasapátus.—Ang ímung putíq diqáy? 'I can't go because I haven't any shoes to wear.'—'How about your white ones?'
Makahímuq pa kag ádtu. Inighumág kasál diqáy, muqádtus báylig pásyun syuu. 'You can still go. After the wedding is over (lit. How about after the wedding is over?) you can go to the dance and the fashion show.'
Únyaq náqay ímung ilúng dalá?—Aw uu, kanáq diqáy. Sus hápit nákuq kalímti. 'Do you have toilet paper?'—'Oh yes, of course (lit. that of course), I almost forgot it!'

In expressions used to interrupt a conversation or change the topic (e.g. isáq pa diqáy or taym pa diqáy), diqáy has this same meaning: 'Oh yes, something else should also be taken into consideration.'

Isáq pa diqáy. Amirkána ka Day nu? (5 a 25) 'Excuse me (lit. I'm reminding you I want to say something). You're an American, aren't you?'

13 G 2 d. Diqáy to correct oneself

Diqáy is used in statements to correct one's spoken error:

Ámbi ra gud nang ímung búlpin—aw díliq diqáy ang búlpin. Ang papil diqáy. 'Let me have your ballpoint pen. Er—I don't mean your ballpoint pen. I mean your paper.'

Pattern Practices and Exercises

IA. (Review) PP-R in Lesson 10—p. 388. (Local vs. instrumental vs. direct passive) Ihátag ang túkmang púrmas bírbung anáqa sa parentheses. (6 A 1, 8 A, 10 A)

1. (Inúm) ba ning túbig dínhi?
   'Can you drink this water here?'
2. Mahímung (inúm) nínyu nang túbig diháq.
   'You may drink that water there.'

3. (Inúm) na gyud núqun níya ang túbig.
'He actually had already drunk the water.'

4. Níndut kaqáyung (tánqaw) ang mga bátang nagdúwaq.
'It's very nice to see the children playing.'

5. Ngánung (tánqaw) man nímu siyá?
'Why did you look at her?'

6. (Límpyu) nang trapú dínhis lamísa Day.
'Use that rag for cleaning the table here.'

7. Húgaw man gihápun ning ímung (límpyu).
'That place you cleaned is still dirty.'

8. (Límpyu) gyug maqáyu ning átung baláy Plurá ha?
'Do a good job cleaning our house, Flora, will you?'

9. Ása man kaháq siyág kwártang (palít) niqánaq?
'Where can she possibly get the money to buy that?'

10. (Palít) na úntaq nákuq siyág líbru kun gipahángyuq pa ku níla.
'I could have bought a book for her if they had let me bargain.'

11. Dághan pa kaqáyu kug (palít)ng mga butáng nga (dalá) nákuq sa Banáwaq.
'I still have many things to buy to take to Banawa.'

12. Tingáli kun dakúq na ning ákung tindáhan (hátag) na mu nákug mga gása.

13. (Hátag) ku na ba nímu ang ímung líbru, waq pa?

14. Ikáw lay íyang (hátag) sa prímyu. (Use the colloquial form.)

15. Waq ba nákuq (hátag) ang suwát kanímu?

16. Únsa kaháy (páhid) níya dínhi ganíha?

17. Musínaw ba kaháq nig (páhid)?

18. (Páhid) ku na lang ni dínhi kay abugún pa man. (abugún 'dusty')

19. Ánhi na lang nátuq (hulát) ang mga sakyanán. (Use the subjunctive. See 13F, p. 527.)

20. Ása man nátuq siyá (hulát)? (Use the subjunctive. See 13F.)

IB. Ibutáng sa lunáq ang túkmang púrmas bírbung (passive or active) anáqas suud sa parentheses. (4A, 6A, 8A, 8B, 10A, 11C and subsections)

1. (Ánhi) kunú siyás sunúd búlan.
'They say he will come here next month.'

2. Pirlá, (ádtu) na diqáy kus Úrmuk.
'Perla, I have already been to Ormoc.'

3. (Pangíhiq) ka na ba Pidrú?
'Are you done urinating, Pedro?'

4. Si Lítu ray (líbri) apán (dakúp) gyud nákuq ang ubán.
'Only Lito has come in free, but I'll be sure to catch the rest.'

5. (Báklay) na lang ku gíkan ngánhi ngádtus Banáwaq kay waq na kuy (plíti) sa traak.

'I will just walk from here to Banawa because I don't have anything to pay the bus fare with.'

6. Siyáy (balígyaq) nákuq niqíning líbru.
'He was the one who sold me this book.'

7. Ang íyang kaqáyu díliq (báyad) ug salapíq. (salapíq 'money')
'His kindness cannot be repaid with money.'

8. Únyaq na ku (báyad) kanímus ákung útang.
'I will pay my debt to you later.'

9. Waq pa intáwun miy (báyad) niqánaq karún Day.
'We don't have any money to pay for that now, Miss.'

10. Arún diq siyá masukúq (inúm) na lang kus támbal nga íyang (palít).
'I'll just take the medicine he bought, so he won't get mad.'

11. Búgnaw kaqáyung (inúm) ang túbig sa atábay. (atábay 'well')
'The water in the well is too cold to drink.'

12. (Inúm) na ba mung tanán?
'Are you all done drinking?'

13. Waq na gyud kuy láqing (táguq) daq!
'I have no other place to hide.'

14. (Kalús) ku naq siyág túbig káda ádlaw kay maqú kanáy ámung gikasabútan.
'I fetch water for him every day because that's what we have agreed to.'

15. Túqa pa si Místir Mílir (kalús) ug túbig sa atábay. (atábay 'well')

16. (Istúrya) ku nínyu básta mamínaw mug maqáyu nákuq.

17. Waq pa ba nákuq (istúrya) kanínyu ang mahitungúd kang Núwa ug ang íyang Árka? (mahitungúd 'concerning')

18. (Hígup) na gyud ta áning ínit nga sabáw. Lamíqang (lútuq) si Mísis Mílir.
'Now we can eat this hot soup. Mrs. Miller cooks delicious (food).'

19. Si Pídru, Mam, waq pa (irís) sa blákburd.

20. Waq pa gyud (irís) ang blákburd ni Lítu.

I C. Ibutáng ang hústung púrmas mga bírbung (imperative) anáqas suud sa parentheses. (11 C)

1. Halá mga bátaq, (sulúd) na mus átung kwártu.
'All right, children, come into the room now.'

2. (Dúwaq) lang mu diháq kay níqa pay ákung buhátun.
'Just play there, because I still have something to do.'

3. Kun gústu kang mupahúlay (rest) úsag trabáhu (panánghid) lang ngádtu níya.
'If you want to take a break from your work, just ask permission from him.'

4. Plurá, (húgas) ra gud ring mga pínggan dirí.
'Flora, wash these dishes here for me, please.'

5. (Límpyu) ra gud diháq Plurá.
'Clean up there, please, Flora.'

6. Mis Wilbí, (bántay) bayáq ang ímung kaqugalíngun.
   'Miss Wilby, be sure to take care of yourself.'

7. Ayáwg (inúm) niqánaq kay tingálig mahílu ka. (hilú 'poison')
   'Don't drink that. You might get poisoned.'

8. (Katúng) na mu ngádtu kay gabíqi na.
   'Go to sleep there; (because) it's late now.'

9. Halá mga bátaq, (hígdaq) na mu arún mu makapahúlay.
   'All right, children, go to bed now so that you can rest.'

10. Mga bátaq (línya) na mu kay hápit na matápus ang átung risís.
    'Children, line up now; (because) recess is about over.'

11. (Tagád) naq silág maqáyu ha?
    'Take good care of them, will you?'

12. Pirlá, (hulát) ra gud kug kadiyút.
    'Perla, please wait for me for a while.'

13. Dung, (risírba) nang usá ka tihíras ni Mis Wílbi ha?
    'Boy, reserve that cot for Miss Wilby, will you?'

14. Nidá, (súgat) gyud úgmaq si Mis Wílbi sa piir.
    'Nida, make sure to meet Miss Wilby at the pier tomorrow.'

15. (Punúq) ra gud ning ákung kalamáy Dung.
    'Give me some more kalamay.'

ID. (Review PP-DD, in Lesson 12, if desired.) Pilíqa ang hústung púrmas bírbung anáqa sa sulúd sa parentheses (ipa- vs. pa- -un). (12 C)

1. (Pasilhígun, Ipasílhig) ni Mísis Mílir kanáng mga ságbut diháq nímu. (ságbut 'rubbish')

2. Si Lítu maqúy (paqirisún, ipaqirís) nátuq sa blákburd karún.

3. Siyáy (palabáyun, ipalábay) nátuq sa búla ha?

4. Muqádtu mis ílang Dyiin kay ámuq siyáng (ipaqinúm, paqímnun) niqíning támbal.

5. Ngánung (pabakláyun, ipabáklay) man nímu naq siyá nga gikapúy man kaháq naq? (gikapúy 'is tired')

6. Ang maqáyu áni (ipatábang, patabángun) nátuq siyá.
   'The best thing to do is have him help out.'

7. Mga bátaq, (ipagawás, pagáwsun) mu nákuq pirú kinahánglan díliq mu muqádtus kalsáda. (kalsáda 'street')

8. (Pagáwsun, Ipagawás) naq únyaq ngádtus sála Day, ha?

9. Ikáw kunúy (palutúqun, ipalútuq) niqíning sabáws manúk Dyiin.

10. Ngánhi únyaq Day kay (pabaligyáqun, ipabalígyaq) ta kag mga líbrus ákung tindáhan.

11. (Pasákyun, Ipasakáy) ka na lang níya arún mas madalíq.

12. Nidá, (pabaligyáqun, ipabalígyaq) ku ni nímu sa átung tindáhan úgmaq, ha?

13. (Pasúdlun, Ipasulúd) ta na úntaq mu pirú dúgay pa man matápus ang átung risís.

14. Únyaq ug gústu ka na (paqanhíqun, ipaqánhi) ta lang ka ni Pírla.

15. Nagqingún si Pírla nga (pahulatún, ipahulát) gyud nátuq ang gilútuq níyang ságing.

16. (Ipadalíq, Padaliqún) kunú nang túbig pagdalá ngádtu Day.

17. Silá ray átung (pakalusún, ipakalús) ug túbig kay ikáw maqúy ákung (palimpyúhun, ipalímpyu) dínhis táqas.

18. Ikáw lay ámung (ipatábang, patabángun) sa tindáhan kay mu ra kag kasalígan. (kasalígan 'reliable')

19. (Paqisturyáhun, Ipaqistúrya) nátuq ni Mam ang mahitungúd ni Núwa ug ang íyang Árka.

20. Kun gústu mu, (ipatánqaw, patanqáwun) nátuq si Mísis Mílir ug usá ka dúktur.

IE. Pilíqa ang hústung púlung. (1 B, 1 D, 3 A 3, 3 B, 5 A, 5 D, 6 B, 6 C, 8 C, 9 B 2, and their subsections)

1. Ihátag nákuq (si, ni) Dyiin ang sabáws manúk.

2. Únsay gitawág nímu (ni, si) Plúra Mísis Mílir?

3. Day, íngna (sa, ang) ímung maqístra nga (sa, ang) íyang mga bátaq atúqa na sa kalsáda.

4. Mahál kaqáyu (sa, ang) giplíti námuq (si, ni) Nída sa tartanílya.

5. Pagpanggáwas (sa, ang) mga bátaq, (si, ni) Lítu gyud maqúy miqúnag dágan.

6. Gipalitán ku (sa, ang) mga bátaq (ug, ang) mga líbru dídtus Burumíyu.

7. Súnda lang (si, ni) Dyiin ug únsay íyang isúlti kanímu.

8. Gipaqirís (si, ni) Mam kang Ústing ang blákburd.

9. Manghátag únyaq ku (ug, ang) mga gása kun (sa, ang) ákung ganánsya mudakúq na.

10. Sigí, panánghid na lang (ni, si) Mis Wílbi nga magquná na lang tag lakáw.

11. Ngánung waq na man lang (ikáw, nímu) pahugási (si, ni) Plúra (sa, ang) átung mga plátu?

12. Akú na lang ug (ni, si) Síbya maqúy mulímpyu (sa, ang) irísir Mam.

13. Tágda (silá, níla) ug maqáyu ha, Mísis Abilyána?

14. Nakítqan (siyá, níya) (ang, ug) babáyi nga nagdalá (ang, ug) báskit paqingún (ang, sa) Karbún.

15. Paqímna (ang, ug) támbal (ni, si) Kíkuy arún maqáyu naq (siyá, níya) dáyun.

IF. Hubára ning musunúd nga mga túdling púlung ngádtus Binisayáq nga mugámit ug na ug pa. (12 G and subsections)

1. Noah's ark is bigger than a ship.
2. It isn't Angel's turn to erase the blackboard yet. (Say: 'Angel's turn . . . hasn't arrived yet.')
3. Ma'am, we've finished our game now.
4. I haven't seen a picture of an ark (yet).
5. Have you seen one (already), Pedro?
6. Maybe I'd better let you drink some water before we start our classes.
7. Ma'am, can I go home now?
8. Has Jane recovered from her headache yet?
9. The rain hasn't stopped yet.
10. Has Lina brought you a glass of water yet?
11. I still have to write her a letter.
12. Don't bother visiting me if your maids are off.
13. Have you heard the story of Noah and his ark?
14. It will still be dark when you get there.
15. Is there no other game we can play?
16. There's no other boat going to Ormoc but this one.
17. I've gone to many places already, but I like Pulambato best.
18. They haven't defeated us yet.
19. I haven't told you the story of Noah yet, have I?
20. You may go home now, children.
21. We walked to Borromeo because we couldn't get a ride here.
22. We're still waiting for them here.
23. I'm sorry there's no ice cream left.
24. Let's eat now.
25. Why don't we just get (a jeep) here, even though there are many people waiting?
26. Have you all gone to the bathroom yet?
27. We've all gone (already), Ma'am.
28. Angel is even taller than Lina.
29. I just came from Pulambato, Lina.
30. Why haven't you let them in yet?

I G. Hubára ning musunúd nga mga túdling púlung ngádtus Binisayáq ginámit ang lang, na lang, ug diqáy. (12 G 1, 13 G and subsections)

1. The fare now is only four pesos.
2. Oh, it's five-fifty. I thought it is four-fifty.
3. Excuse me, are you an American?
4. You be the one to carry the bag.
5. Just follow Pelaez Street.
6. Oh! It's (already) late (afternoon).
7. Where do we get a jeep for Carbon then?
8. By the way, will you stay long in Cebu?
9. So you two will play hide and seek?
10. You might as well do the buying.
11. Who will cook the crabs then (if you don't)?
12. Crabs are only twenty (centavos) apiece now.
13. You might as well take another jeep. (Lit. Just take another jeep.)
14. Oh my, the crabs are already done (cooked).
15. What did he buy then (if he didn't buy that)?
16. We should be going now.
17. Can't it be sold for ten (pesos) then?
18. We'll just see each other next month.
19. So this is Ormoc.
20. Ah, so there are no jeeps any longer. We might as well walk.
21. I couldn't sell it for ten (pesos), so I settled for five pesos (lit. just sold it for five).
22. How about me? You didn't give me any.

II A. Pilíqa ang hústung tubág. (13 D)

1. Dúnay dághan. Diq na gániq (ku makaqiháp, nákuq maqíphan).
2. Ug dúnay ságing sa ámuq (nagdáa lang silá ánaq, gidáa lang naq) gíkan sa ubáng mga lúngsud.
3. Waq pa dyuy mihángyuq nákuq, píru kanúnay kung (gipaqábut, nagpaqábut).
4. Maqáyu nang (maqílhan ku silá, makaqilá ku níla).
5. Pagbálik ngánhi sa panahún sa pangáni. (Magbúhat nyaq kug pilípig, Buhátun nyaq nákuq ang pilípig.)
6. Kanáng pilípig, kuqán naq. (Sangágun naq nímu, Musángag ka ánaq.)
7. Kiníng pusúha (nagbúhat silá áni, gibúhat ni níla), sa panahún pang Prisidínti Magsáysay.

8. Nakitqan mu ba nang náqay mubúq kaqáyung káhuy? (Mulábay silá ánaq, Íla nang ilábay) ngádtu sa layúq.

9. Humán ádtu siyá manukád dídtu (mudágan siyá bálik ngarí sa, dagánun níya bálik ngarí ang) lungág nga ílang gibutangán sa káhuy.

10. Únyaq (muqutúng naq siyá, utúngun ánaq níya).

11. (Nagpatíndug silá niqánang, Gipatíndug níla kanáng) mga gágmayng balhíbu dapít sa líqug.

12. (Nakakitáq ka bítaw ánang, Nakítaq bítaw nímu kanáng) bátaq. Lisúd kaqáyu naq uy.

13. Nangutána lang gud ku kay maqáyu (man nímung isúlti ang, ka mang musúltig) Sinibuwanú.

14. Manánghid taq kung diq ku (bantayán ang, mubántay sa) tindáhan. 'I would like to ask permission to be excused from taking care of the store.'

II B. Ibutáng ang hústung púrma sa bírbu (passives or actives) ug sa pronoun nga anáqa sa suud sa parentheses. (13 A, 13 B, 13 D)

Pananglítan:

a. Únsa man tuy (tánqaw) (ikáw) karúng gabíqi?

Tubág: Únsa man tuy tanqáwun nímu karúng gabíqi?

b. Kun dúnay (suud) ngánhi, sultíhi ku.

Tubág: Kun dúnay musúud ngánhi, sultíhi ku.

c. (Akú) na lay (dalá) íning bag nímu Mis.

Tubág: Akú na lay mudalá íning bag nímu Mis. (or Akú na lay dalá . . .)

1. Únsay (patánqaw) (ikáw) sa mga bátaq gahápun Mam?

2. Únsa may ínyung gústung (istúrya) (akú) karún?

3. Ang átung (dúlaq) run Mam síndul pándul.

4. Díliq pa (mu, nínyu) (dúlaq) run mga bátaq kay nagquwán pa.

5. Waq pa muy (tánqaw) dínhi karún kay waq pa mi makapamalít.

6. Ug dúnay (tawág) (akú) dínhi, (ingún) lang nga may giqádtu pa ku.

7. Ngánung siyá may (ikáw)ng (padágan) nga hinayán (slow) man kaqáyu naq siyá? 'Why did you have him run . . . ?'

8. Díliq ka ba kamaqúng (dágan)?

9. Sírhi (close) na lang ang tindáhan ug waq nay (palít) sa ímung tínda.

10. (Bánhaq) ganiq mu, diq gyud (ku, nákuq) (istúrya) (kamú, nínyu) run.

11. Dúna man siyáy (súlti) (ikáw) ganíha. Únsa man tu?

12. Ikáw lang tingáliy (pasúlti) (siyá) kang Mis Kintána mahitungúd sa nahitabúq. 'He'll probably make you tell Miss Quintana about what happened.'

13. (Panánghid) tang Mam nga manggáwas únaq ta.

14. Uy Day, (panánghid) ka úsaq kunú (siyá) úsaq ka mulakáw.

15. (Si, Ni) Pídru lay (irís) sa blákburd.

PP-EE. Transforming statements into negative existential sentences. (13 A 2, 13 C)

Step I. (Using passives only. Use the word order noun nga verb, even though verb nga noun is equally correct.)

'He saw the man.'
'He didn't see anyone.'

1. a. Nakítaq níya ang táwu.
   b. Waq siyáy táwung nakítaq.

2. a. Gisúlti níya ang tinúqud.
   b. Waq siyáy tinúqud nga gisúlti.

3. a. Giqabángan níya ang kwártu.
   b. Waq siyáy kwártung giqabángan.

4. a. Gilábhan níya ang sinínaq.
   b. Waq siyáy sinínang gilábhan.

5. a. Gikúhaq níya ang bag.
   b. Waq siyáy bag nga gikúhaq.

6. a. Gidalá níya ang báskit.
   b. Waq siyáy báskit nga gidalá.

7. a. Giqádtu níya ang dúktur.
   b. Waq siyáy dúktur nga giqádtu.

8. a. Gibálik níya ang kwárta.
   b. Waq siyáy kwártang gibálik.

9. a. Kánqun níya ang ságing.
   b. Waq siyáy ságing nga kánqun.

10. a. Dádqun níya ang líbru.
    b. Waq siyáy líbrung dádqun.

11. a. Gikúptan níya ang bátaq.
    b. Waq siyáy bátang gikúptan.

12. a. Gigámit níya ang kutsílyu.
    b. Waq siyáy kutsílyung gigámit.

13. a. Nalútuq níya ang ítlug.
    b. Waq siyáy ítlug nga nalútuq.

14. a. Ihátag níya ang gása.
    b. Waq siyáy gásang ihátag.

15. a. Ímnan níya ang básu.
    b. Waq siyáy básung ímnan.

16. a. Tanqáwun níya ang ritrátu.
    b. Waq siyáy ritrátung tanqáwun.

17. a. Gisakáy níya ang bábuy.
    b. Waq siyáy bábuy nga gisakáy.

18. a. Giqiháp níya ang lápis.
    b. Waq siyáy lápis nga giqiháp.

19. a. Baligyáqan níya ang ínsik.
    b. Waq siyáy ínsik nga baligyáqan.

20. a. Gihátag níya ang láta.
    b. Waq siyáy látang gihátag.

Step II. (Using actives. Use the word order noun nga verb, except if the noun ends in a consonant other than n or q: in that case use the word order verb nga noun.)

'He was cooking fish.'
'He didn't cook any fish.'

1. a. Naglútuq siyág ísdaq.
   b. Waq siyáy ísdang gilútuq.

2. a. Nagkúhaq siyág papíl.
   b. Waq siyáy gikúhang papíl.

3. a. Magbalígyaq siyág aríyus.
   b. Waq siyáy ibalígyang aríyus.

4. a. Nagqiháp siyág kwárta.
   b. Waq siyáy kwártang giqiháp.

5. a. Gaputús siyág gása.
   b. Waq siyáy gásang giputús.

6. a. Mutánqaw siyág siní.
   b. Waq siyáy siníng tanqáwun.

7. a. Musulúd siyás kwártu.
   b. Waq siyáy kwártung súdlan.

8. a. Nagkaqún siyág ságing.
   b. Waq siyáy gikaqúng ságing.

9. a. Mubisíta siyás táwu.
   b. Waq siyáy táwung bisitáhun.

10. a. Nagsúlti siyás tinúqud.
    b. Waq siyáy gisúlting tinúqud.

11. a. Nakakitáq siyág aríyus.
    b. Waq siyáy nakítang aríyus.

12. a. Gatawág siyág tartanílya.
    b. Waq siyáy tartanílyang gitawág.

13. a. Makabalígyaq siyág pitáka.
    b. Waq siyáy pitákang mabalígyaq.

14. a. Muqádtu siyás uspitál.
    b. Waq siyáy adtúqung uspitál.

15. a. Nagqábang siyág kwártu.
    b. Waq siyáy kwártung giqabángan.

16. a. Makatawág siyás tindíra.
    b. Waq siyáy tindírang matawág.

17. a. Gakupút siyás bátaq.
    b. Waq siyáy bátang gikúptan.

18. a. Nagputúl siyág káhuy.
    b. Waq siyáy káhuyng giputúl.

19. a. Gabántay siyág irúq.
    b. Waq siyáy irúng gibantayán.

20. a. Misakáy siyás tartanílya.
    b. Waq siyáy tartanílyang gisákyan.

Step III. (Actives and passives mixed. Use the word order noun nga verb unless the noun ends in a consonant other than n or q, in which case use verb nga noun.)

'He was watching a show.'
'He wasn't watching any show.'

1. a. Nagtánqaw siyág siní.
   b. Waq siyáy siníng gitánqaw.

2. a. Gilábay níya ang láta.
   b. Waq siyáy látang gilábay.

3. a. Giqubanán níya ang táwu.
   b. Waq siyáy táwung giqubanán.

4. a. Nakakitáq siyág aríyus.
   b. Waq siyáy nakítang aríyus.

5. a. Gilingkúran níya ang sílya.
   b. Waq siyáy sílyang gilingkúran.

6. a. Gakaqún siyág prútas.
   b. Waq siyáy gikaqúng prútas.

7. a. Nagsakáy siyág tartanílya.
   b. Waq siyáy tartanílyang gisákyan.

8. a. Nabalígyaq níya ang gatas.
   b. Waq siyáy nabalígyang gátas.

9. a. Giqagiqán níya ang balay.
   b. Waq siyáy giqagiqáng baláy.

10. a. Nakaqinúm siyág pípsi.
    b. Waq siyáy pípsing naqinúm.

11. a. Nagpalít siyág pitáka.
    b. Waq siyáy pitákang gipalít.

12. a. Nadáwat níya ang líbru.
    b. Waq siyáy líbrung nadáwat.

13. a. Gisákyan níya ang dyip.
    b. Waq siyáy gisákyang dyip.

14. a. Gipalít níya ang ísdaq.
    b. Waq siyáy ísdang gipalít.

15. a. Mihátag siyág gása.
    b. Waq siyáy gásang gihátag.

16. a. Gibáyad níya ang kwárta.
    b. Waq siyáy kwártang gibáyad.

17. a. Báyran níya ang babáyi.
    b. Waq siyáy babáying báyran.

18. a. Nagdalá siyág gása.
    b. Waq siyáy gásang gidalá.

19. a. Gilábay níya ang batú.
    b. Waq siyáy batúng gilábay.

20. a. Nagkúhaq siyág pínggan.
    b. Waq siyáy pínggang gikúhaq.

Step IV. (Changing the agents; mixed actives and passives)

'I called the rig.'
'I didn't call any rig.'

1. a. Gitawúg ku ang tartanílya.
   b. Waq kuy tartanílyang gitawág.

2. a. Nagkaqún silág prútas.
   b. Waq siláy gikaqúng prútas.

3. a. Naglútuq si Pírlag ísdaq.
   b. Waq si Pírlay gilútung ísdaq.

4. a. Nagsúlti siyás tinúqud.
   b. Waq siyáy gisúlting tinúqud.

5. a. Gisúkliq níla ang kwárta.
   b. Waq siláy kwártang gisúkliq.

6. a. Nakahátag si Lítug gása.
   b. Waq si Lítuy gásang {nahátag / gikahátag}.

7. a. Nakaqábang si Nítag líbru.
   b. Waq si Nítay líbrung naqabángan.

8. a. Gilábay ku ang láta.
   b. Waq kuy látang gilábay.

9. a. Giputúl námuq ang káhuy.
   b. Waq miy káhuyng giputúl.

10. a. Nakakuháq kug ságing.
    b. Waq kuy nakúhang ságing.

11. a. Gibaligyáqan níya ang ínsik.
    b. Waq siyáy gibaligyáqang ínsik.

12. a. Makaqádtu silás siní.
    b. Waq siláy siníng {maqadtúqan / kaqadtúqan}.

13. a. Maghátag si Lítag gása.
    b. Waq si Lítay gásang ihátag.

14. a. Hátdan níla ang tigúlang.
    b. Waq siláy tigúlang hátdan.

15. a. Dádqun námuq ang lamísa.
    b. Waq miy lamísang dádqun.

16. a. Muqukupár kus kwártu.
    b. Waq kuy kwártung ukupahán.

17. a. Nagqábang mig baláy.
    b. Waq miy baláyng giqabángan.

18. a. Mibálik silás bárku.
    b. Waq siláy bárkung gibalíkan.

19. a. Gigámit ku ang líbru.
    b. Waq kuy líbrung gigámit.

20. a. Gibáyran níla ang tindíra.
    b. Waq siláy tindírang gibáyran.

21. a. Tanqáwun ku ang búlak.
    b. Waq kuy tanqáwung búlak.

22. a. Nagsúlti si Dínas tinúqud.
    b. Waq si Dínay gisúlting tinúqud.

23. a. Ímnan námuq ang básu.
    b. Waq miy básung ímnan.

24. a. Gipútlan nákuq ang sinínaq.
    b. Waq kuy sinínang gipútlan.

25. a. Ibáyad ku ang kwárta.
    b. Waq kuy kwártang ibáyad.

III. Hubára sa Binisayáq kiníng musunúd nga mga túdling púlung nga existential. (13 A 3 a, 13 B 2)

Pananglítan:

a. I didn't see anything.

Tubág: Waláq kuy nakítaq.

b. Did anybody see Kikoy?

Tubág: Dúna bay nakakitáng Kíkuy?

1. Did somebody throw me a ball?
2. Somebody came over to visit Jane.
3. Somebody's knocking at the door. (knock: túktuk)
4. If somebody comes, tell him I'm out.

5. Someone helped me find my way to Pulambato. (find my way: pagdúmdum)
6. Somebody is calling the teacher.
7. Someone's calling you.
8. Did anybody come?
9. Nobody helped me sweep the floor.
10. Nobody's listening to your story.
11. Somebody listened to my story carefully.
12. I didn't hear anybody call me at all.
13. Is somebody watching the children in the yard?
14. Somebody told me you need help.
15. Has anyone seen Angel?
16. Did someone call?
17. Anything at all will do.
18. Somebody might call you.
19. There's somebody in Pulambato who needs your help.
20. If anyone wants to drink, let him come over.

IV A. Ibutáng ang hústung púrma sa bírbung anáqa sa parentheses ug pilíqa ang hústing púrma sa pronouns, particles, ug demonstratives nga anáqa gihápun sa suud sa parentheses. (13 A, 13 D)

Pananglítan:

Unsáqun ku ning librúha, (hátag) (si, ni) Mis Wílbi?

Tubág: Unsáqun ku ning librúha, ihátag ni Mis Wílbi?

1. Gústu ba nímung (hátag) nákuq (si, ni) Ústing ning ákung líbru Mam?
2. Ustíng, gústu mu bang (hátag) ni Lítu kanímu (kanáng, niqánang) íyang líbru?
3. Kínsay gústung (hátag) (si, ni) Ústing (ang, sa) íyang báskit?
4. Ustíng, níqay líbru nákuq uh. (kúhaq).
5. Mam, akúy (dalá) (kanáng, niqánang) líbru ngádtu ni Ústing.
6. Aa, ayáw na lang Niná kay (bílin) ku na lang (naq, ánaq) diháq.
7. (Kúhaq) na (naq, ánaq) (mu, nínyu)ng mga líbru diháq ni Nína.
8. Ngánung (kúhaq) man naq (kamí, námuq) nga waq pa man naq (námuq, kamí) (kinahánglan)?
9. Ngánung diq man (kamú, nínyu) gústung (kúhaq) (ang, sa) líbrung náqa diháng Nína.
10. (Panggáwas) lang únaq (kamí, ta) ug magdúwaq Mam.
11. Karíng lamisáha maqúy (ínyung, ikáw) (butáng) (ang, sa) líbru.

12. (Sa, Ang) gústung (gawás) run maqúy (irís) (sa, ang) blákburd.
13. Akú lay (irís) (kanáng, niqánang) blákburd.
14. Litú, díqay irísir uh. (Irís) na nang blákburd.
15. Úsaq ta (gawás) mangutána úsaq kug magqúnsa ta ngádtus gawás.
16. (Dúwaq) lang (nátuq, kitá)g síndul pándul.
17. (Panggáwas) únyaq tag mahumán na (si, ni) Lítug irís sa blákburd.
18. (Irís) na (akú, nákuq) (ang, sa) blákburd Mam. Mahímuq nang (panggáwas) kitá?
19. (Lakáw)(námuq, ta) ngádtus gawás.
20. Na halá. (Butáng) na (nang, niqánang) ínyung mga dalá diháq sa lamísa.
21. Mam, gústu (kamí, námuq)ng (dúwaq) ug síndul pándul.
22. (Dúwaq) lang (nínyu, mu)g únsay ínyung gústu diháq.
23. Kínsay (lábay) ug úna sa láta? 'Who will throw the can first?'
24. Ganína, si Kíkuy muqúy (lábay) sa láta. Karún (akú, ákuq) na say (lábay) sa láta.
25. Túqa na ang láta ay! Halá (táguq) na Niná.

IV B. Ibutáng ang púlung nga náqa sa parentheses sa sinúgdan sa musunud nga mga túdling púlung ug himúqa ang gikinahánglang pagqusáb. (13 F)

Pananglítan:

Naglíngkud silás sála.	(dídtu)

Tubág: Dídtu silá maglíngkud sa sála.

1.	Nagdúlaq silág síndul pándul.	(dínhi)
2.	Nakadúlaq gyud silág usáb.	(kanúsqa)
3.	Gibutáng ni Ánghil ang irísir.	(dídtu)
4.	Nakagústu ra silás ílang dúlaq.	(únyaq)
5.	Midúlaq pug apíl si Mis Sántus.	(úgmaq)
6.	Nasákpan níyas Ústing.	(diháq)
7.	Midágan man gud silá si Nínig si Kíkuy.	(kanúsqa)
8.	Gidakúp si Kíkuy.	(diháq)
9.	Gibutáng níla ang ílang dalá.	(dínhi)
10.	Nakahibáwu ra siyá sa dúlaq.	(inigkataqudtaqúd)
11.	Nakaqinúm si Pídrug túbig.	(dínhaq)
12.	Nagqistúrya na lang si Mis Wílbi.	(sa sunúd ádlaw)
13.	Nakakitáq kug ritrátus árka.	(diháq)
14.	Gihuwát ba silá ni Mis Wílbi?	(kanúsqa)

15. Nanginúm ug túbig ang mga bátaq. (inigkahumán)
16. Nagdúlaq pa silás gawás. (únyaq)
17. Nagqistúrya ku nínyu. (kásqa ra)
18. Nakaqistúrya ka? (kanúsqa na man pud)
19. Naghuwát si Lítu níla. (dínhi)
20. Nagdúlaq silág usáb. (kanúsqa)
21. Nagtíndug si Mis Wílbi duqúl sa blákburd. (diháq)
22. Gibutáng ni Nína ang líbru. (dínhi)
23. Hikítqan ni Mam ang mga ilagáq. (ilagáq 'mouse') (diqín man)
24. Nagdalá si Lítug líbru. (sa Byírnis)
25. Nagdúlaq siláng tanán. (karún dáyun)

V A. Ibúngat ang mga musunúd nga mga túdling púlung sa hústung paníngug. (423 Question)

1. Únsa may átung duláqun run? (13 a 3)
2. Únsa may átuq? (1.3)
3. Kínsa may mulábays láta? (13 a 19)
4. Ása man ta musakáy ug muqádtus Banáwaq? (3 a 16)
5. Kínsa pay gústung mangíhiq? (13 b 49)
6. Pilá na man diqáy idád nímu Iyúq? (5 a 10)
7. Únsa may árka? (13 b 78)
8. Kínsa may magkáwus ug túbig ngánhi? (9 c 27)
9. Kínsa man tung nagbánhaq? (13 b 85)

V B. (234 Statement)

1. Sigí Mam. (13 a 2)
2. Kamí úsaq si Lítu. (13 a 8)
3. Pílding gúnting sa batú. (13 a 15)
4. Dúna na man kuy katábang. (12 c 55)
5. Síngku singkwínta diqáy. (8 b 10)
6. Mangítaq pa kug ubán. (13 a 29)
7. Hústu na tas átung dúwaq mga bátaq. (13 b 43)
8. Hápit nang mahumán ang risís. (13 b 44)
9. Línya na mu dirí. (13 b 45)

V C. (324 Question)

1. Naqa ba si Místir Abáya? (1.4)
2. Dúlaq ta Mam? (13 a 2)
3. Padúung ba naq sa Banáwaq? (2 a 11)
4. Gústu ka? (13 a 4)
5. Mahímuq bang mangutána? (3 a 14)
6. Níqa na ku ha? (13 a 26)
7. Huwát lang diháq ha? (13 a 28)
8. Ádtu nyaq sa baay ha? (5 b 50)
9. Gústu kang mangíhiq? (13 b 51)
10. Ayáw paghikalimút pagsuwát kanákuq ha? (8 a 33)

V D. (423 Statement)

1. Kiní si Místir Gamílu. (1.10)
2. Kamí na sad si Mam. (13 a 13)
3. Píldi diqáy ku. (13 a 16)
4. Maqáyu tingáling ádtu na lang ku. (8 a 32)
5. Maqú diqáy ning Úrmuk. (8 c 29)
6. Níqa na man diqáy tas Kármin. (9 b 12)

V E. (423 # 312)

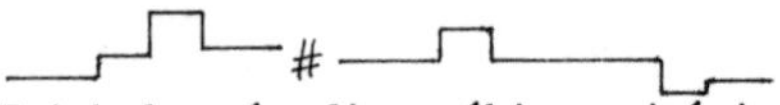

1. Inigkahumán, limpyúhi ang irísir. (13 b 66)
2. Ug gíkan diháq, ánhaq níla kuháqa ang isúhul sa mga táwu nga mutábang sa pagqáni. (10 b 15)
3. Ug ang ákung bána, maqúy nagtrabáhu dídtu. (10 a 21)
4. Ang ákuq sang mga anák nga laláki, túqa sad gatrabáhu sa kamaqisán. (10 a 22)
5. Kanáng mga kawáyan, ila nang ilíbut sa usá ka párti sa dágat. (10 a 10)
6. Ang mga ísdaq nga masúud ánang kurál nga gihímuq, maglisúd na pagúwaq. (10 a 13)

VI A. Pagbása

Túrtang Ispisyál

Pírla: Humán na gyud kug lútug túrta. Hay kapúya! Láqay kaqáyu ning maghíkayg mapísta. (maghíkay 'prepare a banquet')

Lína : Uy, humán na kag lútug túrta? Dalíq ra man diqáy.

Pírla: Únsay dalíq? Limá bayáq ka úras nákung lutuqlútuq. Díliq lalím uy! ('It's no joke.')

Lína : Waláq may mitábang nímu nu?

Pírla: Dínhi tus Lítu apán milakáw na. Nagpaqábut tu nímu. Akúq lang úsang gipatábangs paglútuq nákug túrta.

Lína : Bi, átuq kunúng tilawán. ('Let me taste it.') Uy, ásgad ('salty') man. Únsa, asín ('salt') bay ímung gitímpla ('seasoned with')?

Pírla: Ngánung asín gud? Kang Lítu na ning ági. ('That's Lito's doing.') Sus, dághan ra ba ning ámung gilútuq.

Lína : Tanqáwag ásgad ba nang tanán. Básig dyútay ra.

Pírla: Tilawán ('Let's taste') gyud nátuq ning tanán.

Lína : Ánhaq gyud. ('You'd better'—i.e. 'It's got to be that way.')

Pírla: Kiní, aa, maqáyu. Kiríng díqa, maay pud. Aa, ásgad ri.

(Sa pipilá ka gútluq)

Lína : Nan, dághan?

Pírla: Díliq. Pilá lang ka buqúk. Bálig usá ka háqun. ('About one batch.')

Lína : Dyútay man lang diqáy.

Pírla: Kirí na lang pilá ka buqúk. Daq lagí. ('Just as I thought.') Díqa rag síngsing. Si Lítu íniy nagbutáng.

VI B. Pagbánsay

Butangí ang mga lunáq sa mga púlung na, lang, man ug diqáy.

Pírla: Humán _____ gyud kug lútug túrta. Hay kapúya! Láqay kaqáyu ning maghíkayg mapísta. (maghíkay 'prepare a banquet')

Lína : Uy, humán _____ kag lútug túrta? Dalíq ra man _____.

Pírla: Únsay dalíq? Limá bayáq ka úras nákung lutuqlútuq. Díliq lalím uy! ('It's no joke.')

Lína : Waláq may mitábang nímu, nu?

Pírla: Dínhi tus Lítu apán milakáw _____. Nagpaqábut tu nímu. Ákuq _____ úsang gipatábangs paglútuq nákug túrta.

Lína : Bi, átuq kunúng tilawán. ('Let me taste it.') Uy, ásgad ('salty') man. Únsa, asín ('salt') bay ímung gitímpla ('seasoned with')?

Pírla: Ngánung asín gud? Kang Lítu _____ ning ági. ('That's Lito's doing.') Sus, dághan ra ba ning ámung gilútuq.

Lína : Tanqáwag ásgad ba nang tanán. Básig dyútay ra.

Pírla: Tilawán ('Let's taste') gyud nátuq ning tanán.

Lína : Ánhaq gyud. ('You'd better'—i.e. 'It's got to be that way.')

Pírla: Kiní, aa, maqáyu. Kiríng díqa, maay pud. Aa, ásgad ri.

(Sa pipilá ka gútluq)

Lína : Nan, dághan?

Pírla: Díliq. Pilá _____ ka buqúk. Bálig usá ka háqun. ('About one batch.')

Lína : Dyútay man lang _____.

Pírla: Kirí na _____ pilá ka buqúk. Daq lagi. ('Just as I thought.') Díqa rag síngsing. Si Lítu íniy nagbútang.

VII. Sultiqánay

Pagdúlaq Sa Risís

B: Risís na man, magdúlaq tag láqin. Diq na lang tung síndul pándul.

A: Aa kádtung ímung giqingún? Hústu, abatqábat. (abatqábat 'tag')

B: Uu sigí dáyun. Halá pik na mu mga bátaq.

A: Dalíq Mam. Dúlaq ta Mam.

B: Sigí lang. Díliq ku kay sakít ning ákung tiqíl. Kamú lang diháq. Diq ku.

A: Na. Akú na lay abát. Sigí. Lárga na mu.

1. Ang mga bátaq magdúlag síndul pándul.
2. Waláq pay klási siláng nagdúlaq.
3. Apíl pud si Mam ug dúlaq. (apíl 'take part')
4. Si Mam maqúy abát.
5. Si Mam gisakitág tiqíl maqúng waláq siyá muqapíl ug dúlaq.

B: Hústu na mga bátaq kay taym na. Paglínya na mu dirí. Ikáw Litú. Ngánung galuksulúksu ka pa man dínhaq. Apíl na sa línya.

A: Mangíhiq pa man ku Mam.

B: Ngánung waq man ka mangíhiq ganíha ubán níla?

A: Mahímuq ba Mam—kaqihiqún na ku kaqáyu.

B: Kínsa pay láqing mangíhiq? Sigí. Kúyug na mu ni Lítu. Apán sunúd magdúngan dyud mu ha!

6. Gipadúlaq silág sigí sa ílang maqístra.
7. Buqútan kaqáyu ang tanán. Waláq sila maglihuklihúk.
8. Mangíhiq úntaq si Lítu.
9. Waláq siyá papangihíqa sa maqístra. Waq man gud siyá mangíhiq sa hústung panahún.
10. Si Lítu ray gipapangíhiq.

LESSON 14. SICK IN BED

Sagquluhúnun

First Part | Únang Báhin

(Mrs. Miller is at home. She has a headache.)

*(Si Mísis Mílir túqa sa ílang baay. Gilábdag uu.)

[particle following commands to make them softer] — ra gud

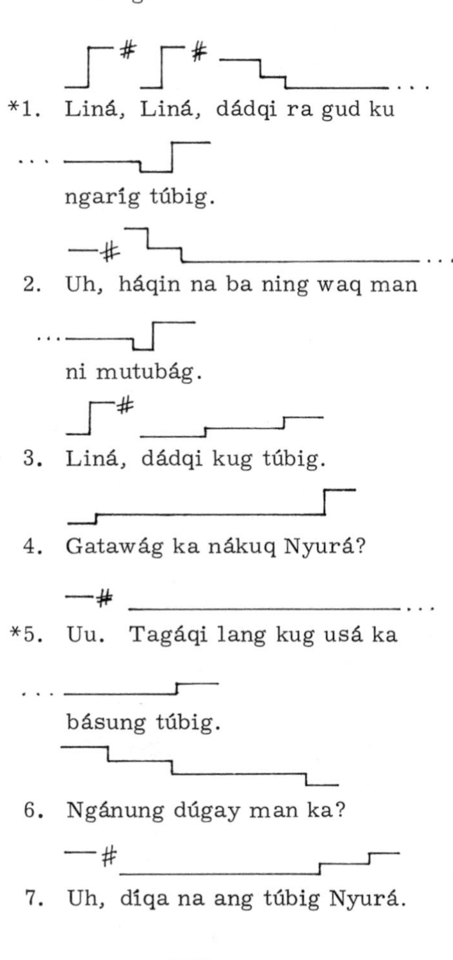

1. Lena! Lena! Please bring me some water.

*1. Liná, Liná, dádqi ra gud ku ngaríg túbig.

2. Oh, where can she be now? She didn't answer. (Lit. Where is this? This didn't answer.)

2. Uh, háqin na ba ning waq man ni mutubág.

3. Lena! Bring me some water.

3. Liná, dádqi kug túbig.

4. Were you calling me, Ma'am?

4. Gatawág ka nákuq Nyurá?

5. Yes. Just give me a glass of water.

*5. Uu. Tagáqi lang kug usá ka básung túbig.

6. Why did it take you so long?

6. Ngánung dúgay man ka?

7. Here. Here's the water now, Ma'am.

7. Uh, díqa na ang túbig Nyurá.

8. Oh, thank you.

8. Uh, salámat.

(Mrs. Miller gets up to inspect the maid's work.)

(Mibákun si Mísis Mílir pagtánqaw sa ági sa mutsátsa.)

9. Let me inspect her work— how it turned out. (Lit. I'll look at this way of sweeping of hers, what happened to this now.)

9. Tanqáwun nákuq ning íyang ... panílhig ug naqúnsa na ni.

10. My! Here's a corner she didn't sweep well.

*10. Sus, díqay iskína, waq ayúhag ... sílhig.

come	dalíq
[particle to make command more polite]	ra gud

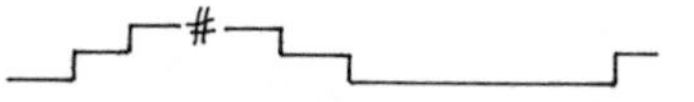

11. Hey, Lena! Come over here please.

11. Uy Linā, dalíq ra gud ngarí.

12. Yes, Ma'am.

12. Uu, Nyurá.

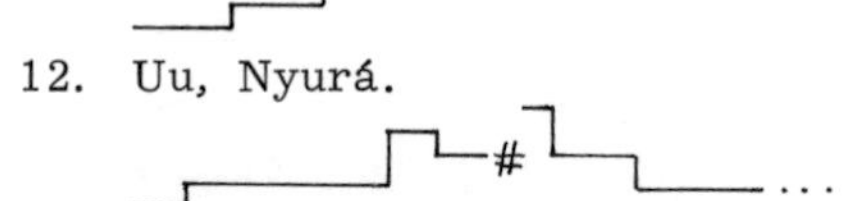

13. This corner—you should have given it a good sweeping.

13. Kiníng iskináha, ímu úntaq ... ning silhígag maqáyu.

things to be done well	pangayúhun

14. Also, do a good job wiping there. (Lit. Also, that over there, you will do a good job wiping.)

*14. Unyáq, kadtú dídtu, ímung ... pangayúhug trápu.

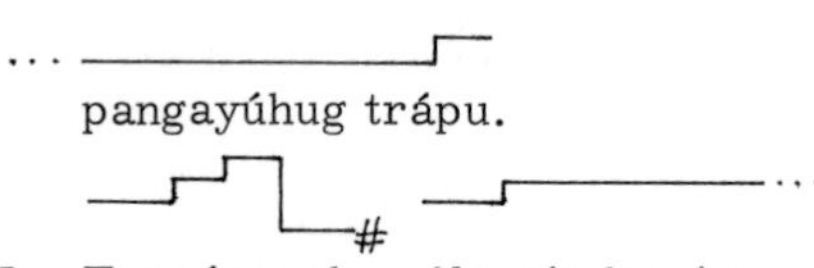

15. Look here! It's very dusty in the corner.

15. Tanqáwa uh. Abugún kaqáyu ... sa suqúk.

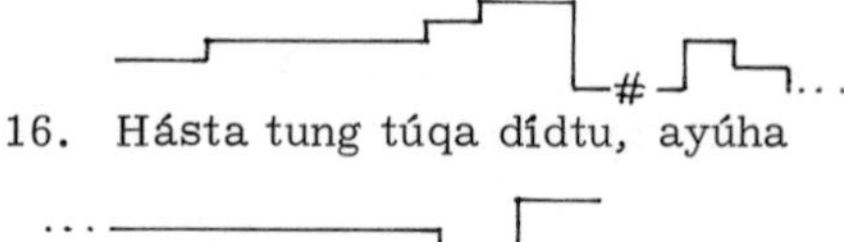

16. Also (lit. Including the one that is over there), do a good job cleaning over there as well.

16. Hásta tung túqa dídtu, ayúha ... pa tu ngádtug límpyu.

17. Then when you finish cleaning,

17. Únyaq inigkahumán nímug

wash the dishes.	... límpyu, panghúgas unyáq sa ...
	... mga pínggan.
18. Go on. Hurry up.	18. Sigí. Daliqá.
(Mr. Miller comes home from work.)	(Naqabút si Místir Mílir gíkan sa trabáhu.)
19. How are you, Jane?	19. Kumústa ka Dyiin?
20. Is your head all right now?	20. Maqáyu na bang ímung úlu?
21. Does it still ache? (Lit. Is it not painful any more?)	21. Waláq na ba magsakít?
22. Not too much any more, but I still have a little fever (lit. my fever is still there a little).	22. Waláq na man kaqáyu, pirú ... ang ákung hilánat, náqa pay ... gamáy.
(Their neighbor visits them.)	(Gibisitáqan silá sa ílang silíngan.)
23. Hello. Good afternoon.	23. Maqáyu. Maqáyung hápun.
24. Hello. (Lit. Yes.) Come in.	24. Uu. Dayún.
this	ni
25. It (lit. This) is the Abayas.	*25. Silá man diqáy ning Mísis ... Abáya.
26. Come in, Mrs. Abaya. Come in.	26. Dayún Mísis Abáya. Dayún.

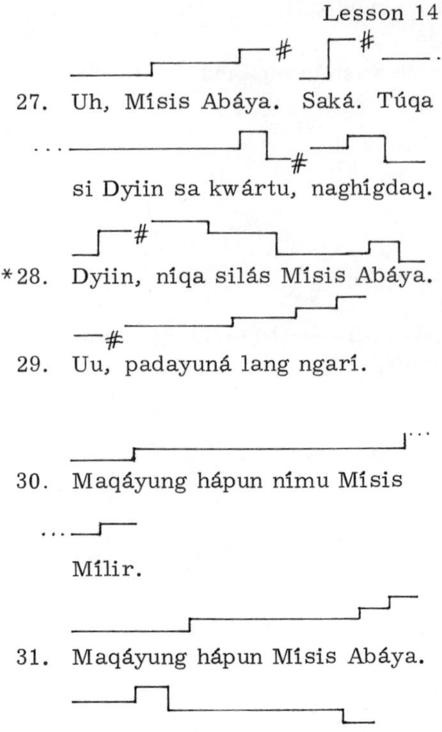

27. Oh, come upstairs, Mrs. Abaya. Jane is in (her) room, in bed.

27. Uh, Mísis Abáya. Saká. Túqa si Dyiin sa kwártu, naghígdaq.

28. Jane, the Abayas are here.

*28. Dyiin, níqa silás Mísis Abáya.

29. Yes, just have them come up here.

29. Uu, padayuná lang ngarí.

30. Good afternoon to you, Mrs. Miller.

30. Maqáyung hápun nímu Mísis Mílir.

31. Good afternoon, Mrs. Abaya.

31. Maqáyung hápun Mísis Abáya.

32. I'm glad (lit. It's good because) you've come.

32. Maqáyu kay nakaqánhi mu.

Mga Pangutána

Únang Báhin

1. Liná, háqin ka gud?
2. Nakapanílhig ka na ba?
3. Giqúnsa man nímu kiní paglímpyu?
4. Kiní. Ngánung waláq man ni nímu ayúha paglímpyu?
5. Nakapanghúgas ka nas mga pínggan?
6. Kumústa. Taqás ba gihápun ang ímung hilánat?
7. Ngánung waq ka man mutubág dáyun?
8. Búgnawng túbig bay ímung gústu Nyurá?
9. Usá ra ka básu Nyurá?
10. Diqín ka gung dúgay ka mang nakadúqul?
11. Gitrapúhan na ba nímu ang gibutangán sa átung mga líbru?
12. Hásta ba kiníng mga iskína Nyurá?
13. Kínsa karúng nagtawág?
14. Akú bay ímung gitawág Nyurá?

15. Maqáyu na ba si Mísis Mílir?
16. Ngánung mibákun ka pa man Misís?
17. Ang ákung kwártu gisilhígan mu na ba?
18. Manghúgas na ba ku sa pínggan Misís?
19. May hilánat ka pa ba Dyiin?
20. Uy Mísis Abáya, ngánu gung waq man ka mudayún?

Mga Pangutána (Matching)

Únang Báhin

1. Únsay trabáhu mu Liná?
2. Ikáw bay nagtawág kanákuq Nyurá?
3. Usá ra ka bású Nyurá?
4. Ang gibutangán sa mga líbru, gitrapúhan mu ba?
5. May hilánat ba gihápun si Mísis Mílir?
6. Ngánung waq ka man manílhig dirí?
7. Maqáyu. Makadayún ba?
8. Kumústa. Nagsakít ba gihápun ang ímung úlu?
9. Diqín ka gung dúgay ka man kaqáyung midúqul?

(a) Gihumán ku man gud úsaq paghúgas ang mga pínggan Nyurá.
(b) Waláq na. Pirú níqa giхápuy hilánat gamáy.
(c) Úqu Nyurá. Humán na.
(d) Uy! Si Mísis Abáya! Dayún.
(e) Adúna pay gamáy.
(f) Usá ra. Kanáng búgnaw.
(g) Uu. Tagáqi kug usá ka básung túbig.
(h) Nanghúgas ug mga pínggan Nyurá.
(i) Gisilhígan ku na naq ganíhang búntag Nyurá, pirú náqa na pud tingáliy dághang abúg.

Sagquluhúnun

Second Part

33. Here, I brought you some soup. (Lit. Here, I made it a point to bring you soup.)

34. This is chicken soup.

drink, sip (a hot food or beverage)

Ikaduháng Báhin

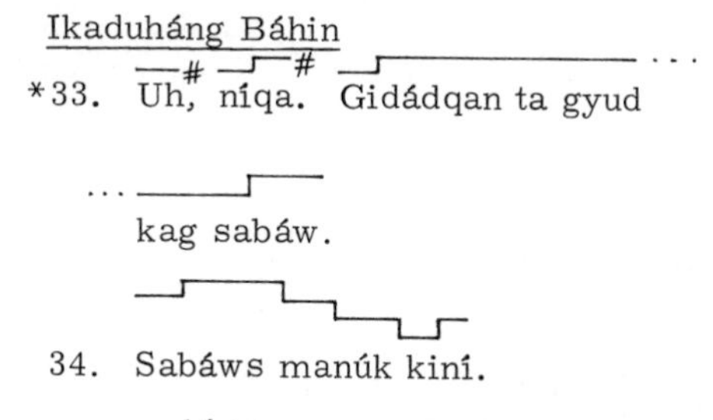

*33. Uh, níqa. Gidádqan ta gyud kag sabáw.

34. Sabáws manúk kiní.

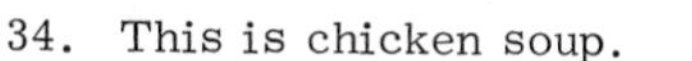

hígup

35. It's good for you to drink this while it's still hot.

*35. Maqáyu ning higúpun nímu ...

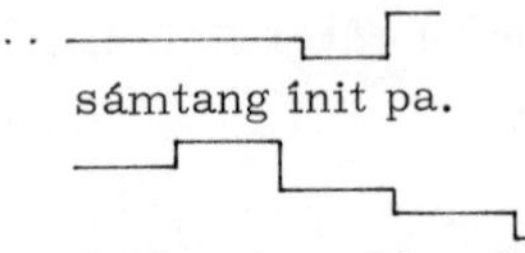

... sámtang ínit pa.

36. Thank you very, very much.

36. Salámat gyud kaqáyu.

how good! how well behaved! — kabuqútan

[particle exclaiming over something unexpected but not necessarily surprising] — bayáq

[expression of surprise in exclamatory sentences] — uy

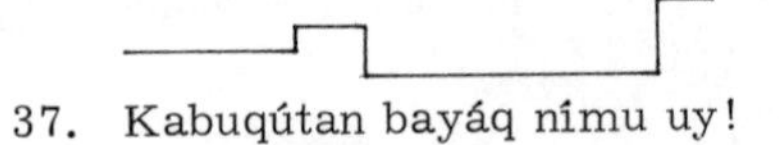

37. How very good of you!

37. Kabuqútan bayáq nímu uy!

go to trouble bringing things — naghatudhátud

in addition (more than necessary) — pa

38. You shouldn't have bothered bringing soup here. (Lit. You make it a point to keep bringing soup here as well.)

38. Naghatudhátud ka pa gyud ... ngánhig sabáw.

nonsense! come now! (dismissing something as unimportant) — adá

39. Nonsense, it's no trouble. (Lit. Nonsense, you're bothering about it now.)

39. Adá, # tagád ka na man.

tasty — lamíq

[particle giving advice about something the speaker has tried] — ra ba

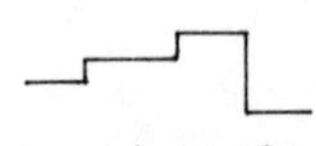

40. It certainly is good.

*40. Lamíq ra ba.

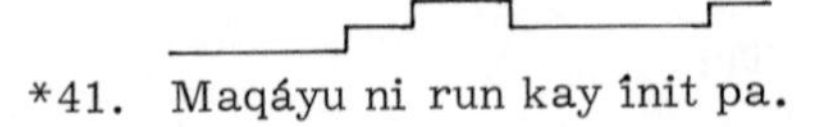

41. This is good now, because it's still hot.

*41. Maqáyu ni run kay ínit pa.

if perhaps — básin

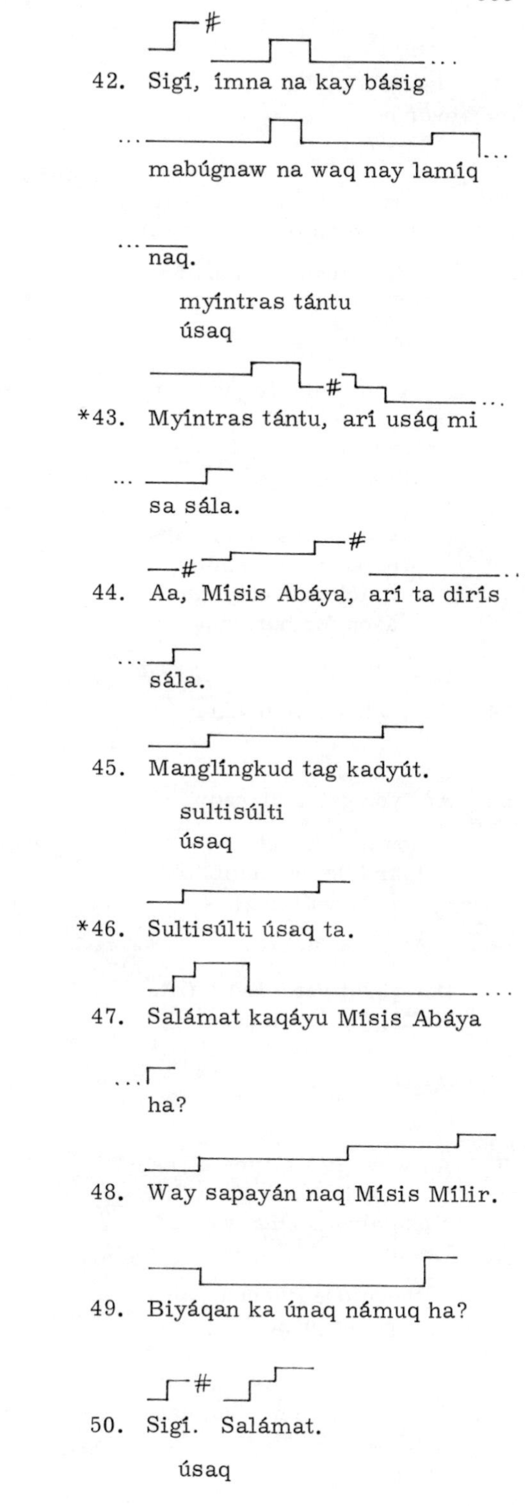

42. Go ahead, drink it now, because if it gets cold, it will lose its flavor (lit. that won't have any flavor any more).

42. Sigí, ímna na kay básig mabúgnaw na waq nay lamíq naq.

in the meantime — myíntras tántu
for a while — úsaq

43. In the meantime, we'll go over here to the living room for a while.

*43. Myíntras tántu, arí usáq mi sa sála.

44. Ah, Mrs. Abaya, let's go to the living room.

44. Aa, Mísis Abáya, arí ta dirís sála.

45. Let's sit down for a while.

45. Manglíngkud tag kadyút.

converse, chit-chat — sultisúlti
for a while — úsaq

46. Let's chat for a while.

*46. Sultisúlti úsaq ta.

47. Thank you very much, Mrs. Abaya.

47. Salámat kaqáyu Mísis Abáya ha?

48. Don't mention it (lit. That's no trouble), Mrs. Miller.

48. Way sapayán naq Mísis Mílir.

49. We'll leave you for a while, may we?

49. Biyáqan ka únaq námuq ha?

50. Go ahead. And thank you.

50. Sigí. Salámat.

meanwhile — úsaq

51. Meanwhile, I'll just stay over here.	*51. Arí lang úsaq ku dirí.
52. I'll stay in bed. (Lit. I'll still keep on lying around.)	52. Maghigdaqhígdaq pa ku.
[man's name, short for <u>Pídru</u> and others]	Dru
	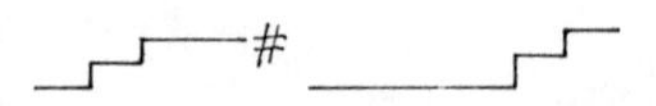
53. Let's go to the living room, Dro.	*53. Talá Dru. Ádtu tas sála.
(A little later)	(Pagkataqudtaqúd)
hey (expression of surprise at something which suddenly came up)	uy
reason for hurrying	daliqán
	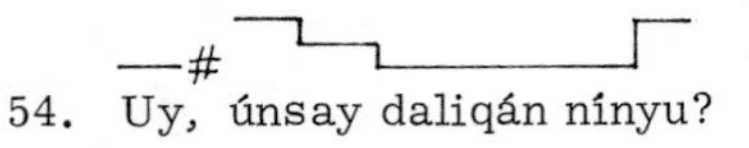
54. Hey, what's your hurry?	54. Uy, únsay daliqán nínyu?
	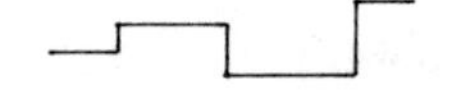
55. Are you going already?	55. Mangádtu na mu?
don't . . . yet	ayáw úsaq
[particle emphatically contradicting]	uy
56. Don't (go) yet. Let's (lit. We'll) eat lunch here.	56. Ayáw úsaq uy. Ánhi ta ... maniqúdtu.
57. Anyway, it's eleven already. It's nearly lunch time (lit. close already that we eat lunch).	57. Tutál, alás únsi na man. Duqúl nang maniqúdtu.
therefore (inescapable consequence)	diq

58. So, why don't we just eat lunch here?	*58. Diq, ánhi lang gyud ta ... maniqúdtu.

59. We'll (just) be going now, because I still have to cook (lit. I still have to cook our food there).

59. Muqádtu na lang kamí kay ... maglútuq pa man ku dídtus ... ámung pagkáqun.

60. Really?

60. Aw diqáy?

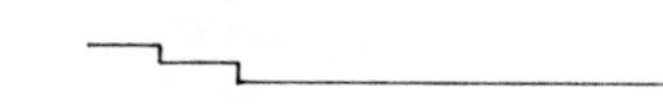

61. Why? Isn't there anyone (lit. anyone who stayed behind) at your place?

61. Waláq diqáy nahabilín sa ínyu?

62. The children.

62. Mga bátaq.

63. I let the maid go to the show. (Lit. I let the maid see the show.)

63. Gipatánqaw nákuq ang ... mutsátsag siní.

64. Oh, that's right, isn't it? Actually there's no one who can fix your lunch.

64. Aa, # túqud nu. # Waq túquy ... makahíkays ínyung paniqúdtu.

65. All right then. But come back later, will you?

65. Na sigí. # Píru balikbálik ... únyaq ha?

66. Yes, because it's just close by.

66. Úqu. # Duqúl ra man.

[reply to a person who agrees to a point after some debate]

aw lagí

67. Of course. It (lit. That) is good to keep coming over for visits.

67. Aw lagí. # Maqáyu nang ... magaduqawdúqaw.

anyway, even so

hinúqun

68. Anyway Jane won't be sick much longer. (Lit. Because, anyway, this Jane, it won't be long any more.)

68. Kay kiní si Dyiin, díliq na hinúqun madúgay.

will get well — maqáyu
again — na pud
slight cold — sipqunsípqun

69. She'll get well again, (for) it's only a slight cold.

69. Maqáyu na pud ni, kay sipqunsípqun man lang.

70. I hope that you won't get worse.

70. Hináqut pa úntaq nga díliq ka mugrábi.

[hesitation word] — kiníng
nasty (lit. rather difficult) — lisudlisúd
being sick all the time — magdaqutdáqut

71. Because you know—it's nasty to be sick all the time.

*71. Kay kiní gung lisudlisúd man ning magdaqutdáqut.

72. I hope I won't.

72. Hináqut úntaq.

73. Well, we'll just be going now.

73. Na halá. Ádtu na lang mi ha?

74. Yes, good-bye. (Lit. Yes. All right.) Come again.

74. Uu, na sigí. Balikbálik.

Mga Pangutána

Ikaduháng Báhin

1. Ngánung nagdalá ka pa man gyug sabáw?
2. Sa únsa man ning sabáwa Mísis Abáya?
3. Únsa may gústu nímung ímnun Mísis Abáya?
4. Ínit pa ba nang sabáwa?

5. Mangádtu na ba tas baláy ni Mísis Mílir?
6. Uy, muqádtu na ba gud ka?
7. Kínsa man diqáy ang naglútuq niqíning sabáw?
8. Gipatánqaw na ba nímu kanás dúktur?
9. Kínsa may ngálan sa ímung mutsátsa?
10. Magdúgay ka bas Pulambatú?
11. Maqáyu na bas Dyiin?
12. Dúgay ka na bang gadaqút?
13. Diq ka ba magpahatúd? 'Won't you have someone take you?'
14. Lamíq ba kaqáyu ang sabáws manúk?
15. Ngánu man gyung gadalíq man mu?
16. Duqúl ra ba ang ínyung baláy Mísis Abáya?
17. Uy, únsa na man diqáyng urása?
18. Nigrábi ba ang sakít ni Mísis Mílir?
19. Nakahíkay na ba mug paniqúdtu?
20. Anúsqa ka man mubálik pagdúqaw?

Mga Pangutána (Matching)

Ikaduháng Báhin

1. Lamíq bang sabáws manúk Dyiin?
2. Nakalútuq ka na ba Liná?
3. May nahabilín pa bang ilímnun? (ilímnun 'drinks')
4. Waq ba guy láqing makahíkay sa ínyung paniqúdtu?
5. Mubálik ka pa ba paghígdaq Dyiin?
6. Grábi ba ang íyang sakít?
7. Dághan ka bag manúk sa ínyung baláy Mísis Abáya?
8. Únsay gústu mung ímnun Dyiin?
9. Gitánqaw na ba naq siyás dúktur?

(a) Náqay singkwínta ka buqúk.

(b) Túbig lay ákuq.

(c) Waq. Bísag grábi kaqáyung íyang sakít.

(d) Úqu, díqa pay dághan.

(e) Uu, kay sakít pa man ning ákung úlu.

(f) Uy, lamíq kaqáyu.

(g) Waláq gyud. Kay pulús mga bátaq ang nahabilín.

(h) Uu, Nyurá. Humán na kug lútuq.

(i) Aa, díliq hinúqun grábi.

Commentary to Basic Sentences

[Stage direction]	gilábdag uu	Short for gilábdan ug ulu 'affected by a headache' (local passive of the type described in 8 A 4).
14 a 1	ra gud	This particle after an imperative makes the command polite; cf. 14 a 3, where the particle is omitted because the speaker is annoyed.
14 a 5	lang	The particle lang implies that it is a small thing: 'I have nothing else to ask except [imperative].'
14 a 5	básung túbig	Notice that 'a glass of water' is usá ka básu nga túbig (in this case nga, and not sa, corresponds to English 'of'). Cf. discussion below, 14 D, p. 563.
14 a 10	waq ayúhag sílhig	'Did not do a good job sweeping.' See 14 A 1.
14 a 14	pangayúhun	This is the root áyu 'do well' with paN- prefix: [do] to several recipients.'
14 a 25	siláng Mísis Abáya	'Mrs. Abaya and her companions.' Cf. 13 E.
14 a 28	silás Mísis Abáya	'Mrs. Abaya and her companions.' Cf. 13 E.
14 b 33	uh níqa	It is polite to say níqa after uh at the beginning of sentences when attracting attention to something offered.
14 b 35	higúpun	In Cebuano one does not say káqun 'eat' or inúm 'drink' when referring to the partaking of hot liquids (soup, tea, coffee, etc.); instead, one uses hígup, the nearest translation of which is 'sip.'
14 b 40 and 14 b 41		Said by Mrs. Miller.
14 b 43		Said by Mrs. Miller's husband.
14 b 46	sultisúlti	Short for magsultisúlti.
14 b 51		Said by Mrs. Miller.
14 b 53	Dru	Mrs. Abaya is addressing her companion, named Dru (short for Pídru).
14 b 58	diq	This diq means 'therefore' (not to be confused with diq 'not') and is usually followed by a pause.
14 b 71	kiní gung	Kiníng, marking a pause for thought at the beginning of a sentence, plus gud, a particle indicating that the speaker wants to explain something which might puzzle the hearer.

Grammatical Section

14A. Other ways of expressing manner

Review 9C, where you learned that an adjective followed by nga plus an unreal verb means '[do] in an [adjective] manner,' implying that it is the usual manner. In the following examples the adjective is underlined once and the verb twice:

Maqáyu kang mubinisayáq. 'You speak Visayan well.'
Níndut si Ústing mulútug kasag. 'Osting cooks crabs well.'

14A1. Manner expressed by a verb followed by an infinitive

A verb meaning 'do in a certain way' followed by an infinitive means '[do the infinitive] in a [verb] way.' This construction differs from that of 9C in that it may be used for expressing how a particular action is done, as well as how that action is generally done (the construction described in 9C expresses only the latter meaning). The verb is underlined twice and the infinitive once in the following examples:

a. Mikalít siyá paglúksu pagkakitáq níya sa sawá diháq sa íyang duqúl. 'He suddenly jumped, upon seeing the snake near him.'
b. Mihínay si Ínting ug língiq. 'Inting looked back slowly.'

The verb corresponding to maqáyu 'good' is áyu 'do well.'

c. Sus, díqay iskína, waq ayúhag sílhig. (14a10) 'My! Here's a corner she did not sweep well.'
d. Hásta tung túqa dídtu, ayúha pa tu ngádtug límpyu. (14a16) 'Also that one over there. Do a good job of cleaning over there as well.'

14A2. Manner expressed by an infinitive preceded by a verb

An infinitive meaning '[do in a certain way]' preceded by a verb means '[do the verb] in an [infinitive] way'—the same as the construction described in 14A1 above except that the verb and the infinitive are reversed. The verb is underlined twice and the infinitive once in the following examples:

a(1). Milúksu siyá pagkalít, pagkakitáq níya sa sawá diháq sa íyang duqúl. 'He suddenly jumped, upon seeing the snake near him.'
b(1). Milíngiq si Ínting ug hínay. 'Inting looked back slowly.'
c(1). Sus, díqay iskína, waq silhígig maqáyu. 'My! Here's a corner she did not sweep well.'
d(1). Hásta tung túqa dídtu, limpyúhi pa tu ngádtug maqáyu. 'Also that one over there. Do a good job of cleaning over there as well.'

The infinitive form corresponding to maqáyu 'good' is either pagqáyu or ug maqáyu, used interchangeably. See examples c(1) and d(1) above and the following two examples:

c(2). Hásta tung túqa dídtu, limpyúhi pa tu ngádtu pagqáyu. 'Also that one over there. Do a good job of cleaning over there as well.'
e. Kiníng iskináha, ímu úntaq ning silhígag maqáyu. (14a13) This corner —you should have swept it well.'

Pattern Practice PP-FF; Exercises XIV.III and XV.XIV.

14 B. Naga-/maga-/ga-

Naga-/maga- has a durative meaning, as described in 5 C 2(1).

a. Nagaqulán ba run? Waq magaqulán. 'Is it raining now?' 'No, it isn't raining.'

In normal conversational speech naga- is usually shorted to ga-.

a(2). Gaquwán ba run? 'Is it raining now?
b. Gatawág ka nákuq Nyurá? (14 a 4) 'Were you calling me, Ma'am?'

As stated in 5 C 2(1), the durative meaning is also expressed by nag-/mag-.*

14 C. Doubled verb roots

Any verb root may be doubled: for example, káqun 'eat,' kaqunkáqun.† A doubled verb root means either (a) '[do the action of the root] for a while without purpose' or (b) '[do] repeatedly,' depending on the context:

Meaning (a):

Arí lang úsaq ku dirí. Maghigdaqhígdaq pa ku. (14 b 51-52) 'I'll just stay here. I'll lie around for a while.'
Maglíngkud tag kadiyút. Sultisúlti saq ta. (14 b 45-46) 'Let's sit down for a while and chit-chat.'

Meaning (b):

Aw lagí. Maqáyu nang magduqawdúqaw. (14 b 67) 'Of course. It's good to keep coming over for visits.'
Balikbálik. 'Come back.' (Lit. 'Keep coming back.')

14 C 1. Special meanings

With some verb roots, doubling results in a special meaning. For example, doubled hatúd 'bring' gives hatudhátud 'bother bringing':

Naghatudhátud ka pa gyud ngánhig sabáw. (14 b 38) 'You shouldn't have bothered bringing soup here.'

---

* Wherever naga- is used nag- may be substituted for it, and wherever maga- is used mag- may be substituted for it; thus, example a of this section may also be said:

Nagqulán ba run? Waq magqulán. 'Is it raining now?' 'No, it isn't raining.'

The reverse, however, is not true: there are some meanings of nag-/mag- for which naga-/maga- may not be substituted.

† In doubled forms, if there is a prefix ending with N (paN-, maN-, or naN-), the changes represented by N occur only in the first of the doubled words. E.g. paN- added to the doubled root sultisúlti 'speak' gives panultisúlti 'manner of speaking':

Ang panultisúlti níya mu rag dághang táwu. 'The way he speaks, it sounds as though there were a lot of people (talking).'

14 C 2. A substitute for doubling

Bases of more than two syllables do not double; instead, they receive a prefix ulu- (if they begin with a vowel) or, if they begin with a consonant, they receive a prefix consisting of their initial consonant plus -ulu-. (This process is symbolized as (C)ulu-, with (C) indicating a sometimes-present consonant.) For example, pahúlay 'rest,' instead of doubling (it has three syllables), takes the prefix (C)ulu-: pulupahúlay 'rest awhile.' Further examples are:

panánghid	'ask permission to leave'	pulupanánghid	'keep asking permission to leave'
pangutána	'ask a question'	pulupangutána	'keep asking questions'
balíbad	'refuse something offered'	bulubalíbad	'keep refusing'

For speakers who drop the l (see the introduction to the glossary for a discussion of dropping of l), the prefix (C)ulu- has the shape (C)u-. Thus pulupahúlay 'rest awhile' is pronounced pupahúway by speakers who drop l.

Some common roots of two syllables take the prefix (C)ulu- or Cu- as an interchangeable alternative to doubling. One such root is sulti 'speak':

Magsulusúlti ta. 'Let's chat awhile.' or
Magsultisúlti ta. 'Let's chat awhile.'

14 D. Measurements and amounts

A measurement or amount of a [noun] is expressed by either of two formulas:

(a) measurement nga noun
(b) noun nga measurement

Example, usá ka básung túbig 'a glass of water.'

In the following examples, the measurement is underlined once and the noun twice:

Tagáqi lang kug usá ka básung túbig. (14 a 5) 'Just give me a glass of water.

Mupalít kug kaság nga bálig písus. 'I want to buy a peso's worth of crabs.'

Muqinúm kug usá ka húngut tubáq káda ádlaw. (5 a 16) 'I drink a coconut shell full of toddy every day.' [The nga linking the measurement and the noun is dropped in this case, as is normal when nga follows a word which ends in a consonant.]

14 E. The accidental passive -an/-i

Most verbs occur with an ACCIDENTAL PASSIVE verb form. The ACCIDENTAL PASSIVE is a verb form with an affix -an (used for the real and unreal meanings) and -i (used in constructions requiring the subjunctive). In the following sentences the accidental passive verb forms are underlined:

a. Kítqan ku siyá sa simbahán. 'I saw (or might see) him in church.'
b. Waláq ku níla sákpi. 'They did not catch me.'

The accidental passive has the meanings of either the direct or the local passive (depending on the context) (see 6 Aff. and 8 Aff.). The accidental passive differs from the local and direct passive in that it means the action of the verb is accidental (was done involuntarily or happened accidentally to the recipient). Thus the accidental passive means either (1) the subject (or predicate if the verb is the subject) was the person or thing accidentally affected by the action (i.e. the direct passive meaning) or (2) the subject (or predicate if the verb is the subject) is the person or thing for whom the action was accidentally done, or the place at which the action was accidentally done (i.e. the local passive meaning). Thus in examples a and b above the accidental passives have a direct passive meaning. In the following examples the accidental passive has the local meaning:

c. Biyaqán ku sa dyip padúung sa Banáwaq, maqúng atrasáwu kung miqabút dínhi. 'I missed (lit. accidentally was left by) the jeep going to Banawa, so I arrived late.'
d. Tagaqán ku ang bátaq ug pagkáqun nga díliq úntaq níya kánqun. 'I accidentally gave the child some food which he should not have eaten.'

14 E 1. Simultaneous prefixing of hi- or hing- to accidental passives

All accidental passive forms may optionally add a prefix hi- or hing- forming an affix hi- -an or hing- -an (with real or unreal meanings) and hi- -i or hing- -i for the subjunctive. There is no difference in meaning between the accidental passive with hi- and the accidental passive with hing- (whether hi- or hing- is used varies from speaker to speaker). There is also no difference in meaning between the accidental passive with hi- or hing- and the accidental passive without hi- or hing-. Thus the examples of 14 E above can also be said accidental passive with verbs having a prefix hi- or hing- with no change or meaning:

a(1). Hikítqan (or hingkítqan) ku siyá sa simbahán. 'I saw (or might see) him in church.'
b(1). Waláq ku níla hisákpi (or hingsákpi). 'They did not catch me.'
c(1). Hibiyaqán (or hing biyaqán ku sa dyip padúung sa Banáwaq, maqúng atrasáwu kung miqabút dínhi. 'I missed (lit. was accidentally left by) the jeep going to Banawa, so I arrived late.'
d(1). Hitagaqán (or hingtagaqán) ku ang bátaq ug pagkáqun nga díliq úntaq níya kánqun. 'I accidentally gave the child some food which he should not have eaten.'

Pattern practice PP-GG.

14 F. Verbs with direct passives and instrumental passives in similar meanings

Certain verbs have both a direct and an instrumental passive, both of them meaning that the subject is the recipient of the action. The types listed in 14 F 1 and 14 F 2 below were presented earlier (10 C and 12 C) and are included here for review; those given in 14 F 3 and 14 F 4 are discussed here for the first time.

14 F 1. The instrumental and direct passives or verbs with a meaning 'go' or 'come'

Some bases mean 'go' in the direct and local passive and 'put' in the local and instrumental passive. (Review the discussion of this verb type in 10 C.) The direct passive of such verbs has the meaning 'the subject (or the predicate, if the verb is the subject) is the place gone to.' For example, for sulúd 'go into' the direct passive means 'the subject is the place the agent went into.' The verb is underlined twice and the subject once in the following examples:

Súdlun ku ang kwártu. 'I will go into the room.' (Lit. 'The room is what I will go into.')

The instrumental passive of such verbs means 'the subject (or the predicate) is the person or thing put.'

Isulúd ku ang irúq sa kwártu. 'I will put the dog inside the room.'

There are many other verbs of this type. One such verb is saká 'go up':

[direct passive]

Sákqun ku nang taqás nga káhuy. 'I am going to climb that tall tree.'

[instrumental passive]

Isaká ra gud dídtus táqas kanáng túbig Ting. 'Take that water up into the house, Ting.'

14 F 2. The instrumental and direct passives of verbs containing a prefix pa-

The direct passive of a verb with a prefix pa- means 'the subject (or the predicate, if the verb is the subject) is the person or thing caused to do the verb.' The instrumental passive of a verb with a prefix pa- means 'the subject (or the predicate) is the recipient of the action of the verb.' (See 12 C 3 and 4.)

[direct passive]

Papalitún nákuq si Lúling sa ságing. 'I'll have Loling buy the bananas.' (Idang, I will have to do something else.)

[instrumental passive]

Ipapalít nákuq ang ságing kang Lúling. 'I'll have Loling buy the bananas.' (The mangoes, I'll buy myself.)

14 F 3. Verbs meaning '[do] together' or '[do] one to another'

Verbs of this type are those meaning 'go (come, ride) together' or 'be put together.' For such verbs the direct passive means 'those named in the subject (or the predicate, if the verb is the subject) are the things or persons who were put together or made to go together.' The verb is underlined twice and the word the verb refers to once:

Sagúla ang kámay ug lubí, dáyun inítа. 'Mix the sugar and coconut. Then heat them.'
Kuyúgun ku silá sa simbahán kay waq man siláy ubán. 'I'll have them go to church together because they have no one else to go with.'

The instrumental passive means 'the subject (or the predicate) is the thing or person that is put or made to go with something else.'

Mu ning kámayng iságul sa lubí. Díliq tung putíq. 'This is the sugar to mix into the coconut. Not that white (sugar).'
Ikáw lay ákung ikúyug kay waq man dínhi si Dyuu. 'I'll just take you (lit. You will just be the one I will have go along), because Joe isn't here.'

14F4. Verbs meaning 'say,' 'call,' and the like

For verbs of this type the direct passive means 'the subject (or the predicate, if the verb is the subject) is the person spoken to.' The instrumental passive means 'the subject (or predicate) is the thing that is said.'*

Únsa may giqingún dihás tíkit? (8b12) 'What does it say on the ticket?' [instrumental passive]
Giqingún ku níya nga diq siyá makaqádtu. 'He told me he could not go.' [direct passive]
Únsa kaháy ákung itubág níya? 'What can I answer him?'
Diq ku na lang siyá tubagún. 'I won't bother answering him.'
Abír kun únsay ílang itawág nákuq. 'Let's see what they call me.'
Isáq pa. Ákung táwgun ang dúktur. 'Just a second. I'll call the doctor.'
Bísag únsay ákung isúguq níya, diq gyud siyá mutúqu. 'No matter what I tell him to do, he won't obey.'
Si Ústing na lay sugúqa. 'Just tell Osting to do it.' (Lit. 'Osting is the one you should tell to do it.')

14G. More postpositive particles: man, ra

14G1a. Man in questions with interrogatives

In questions with interrogatives (question words) man modifies the interrogative. In this usage it has no English equivalent. Man is used in a neutral question (a question with no special nuance of surprise or the like) which contains an interrogative.

Ása ka man paqingún? 'Where are you going?'
Kínsa may mupápas sa blákburd? 'Who will erase the blackboard?'

14G1b. Man in statements meaning 'because'

Man modifies the predicates of statements which give a reason. It can be translated as 'because,' though it is much more frequent than 'because' and hence often corresponds to nothing, or to a slight pause, in corresponding English sentences.

Muqádtu na lang kamí kay maglútuq pa man ku dídtus ámung pagkáqun. (14b59) 'We'll just be going now, (because) I still have to cook.'
Pirú balikbálik únyaq ha?—Úqu. Duqúl ra man. (14b65–66) 'But come back later, will you?'—'Yes. Anyway (lit. Because) it's not far.'
Maqáyu na pud ni kay sipqunsípqun man lang. (14b69) 'She'll get well again—(because) she only has a slight cold.'

14G1c. Man in statements which give information

Man modifies the predicates of statements which give a fact not known to the hearer. There is no English equivalent for this usage.

---

* Some verbs have both a direct and a local passive in the meaning 'the subject is the person spoken to' (among them ingún 'say' and pangutána 'ask'). (See 8B4.)

Waláq na ba magsakít?—Waláq na man kaqáyu pirú ang ákung hilánat, náqa pay gamáy. (14 a 21-22) 'Does it still ache?'—'Not too much any more, but I still have a little fever.'

Nyaq líbut man kaqáyu. Níqa pa may ákung ihatúd. (12 a 16) 'Furthermore, it is very much out of the way. I still have other passengers (lit. people to deliver).' [Both man's have this meaning]

Díliq man alsáhun ang manúk kun díliq patáy na gyud ang kúntra. (11 c 21) 'The rooster is not picked up until his opponent is completely dead.'

14 G 1 d. Man contradicting a previous statement

Man modifies the predicate of a statement which contradicts something the hearer has assumed. (Again man has no English equivalent.)

Diq ba diqáy dyis ang plíti?—Diq na man kay mahál na man ang gasulína. 'Isn't the fare ten (centavos)?—'No, it isn't any longer (because) gas is expensive now.' [The second man means 'because']

Samúkan ka tingáli sa mga bátaq—Díliq man. Gústu kug mga bátaq. 'You'll consider the children a nuisance.'—'No, I won't. I like children.'

14 G 1 e. Diqáy vs. man diqáy

Man modifying the predicate of a statement which gives information (14 G 1 c, above) combines with the diqáy that indicates the information received is new (13 G 2 a p. 529). The combination man diqáy modifies statements containing newly received information that the speaker is now giving out for the first time.

a. Uh! Údtu na man diqáy kaqáyu. (1 a 24) 'My! It's very late.'

In the context of example a, the speaker has found it is late by looking at his watch and now gives that information to his hearer. Without man, the context would be one in which the hearer already knew it was late: the speaker says, 'Oh, so it's late, is it?'

b. Maqáyu man diqáy kang mubinisayáq. 'You speak Bisayan well.'

In example b the speaker uses man diqáy because he has heard the hearer speak Cebuano, discovered it was well done, and now passes this new information on to the hearer. Without man, the implied context is that the hearer has remarked that he himself speaks good Cebuano and the speaker now repeats that statement: 'Oh, so you speak good Cebuano.'

Exercise XIV.IV B (1) deals with the difference between man, man diqáy, and diqáy. (Other exercises for man are listed at the end of 14 G 2 h.)

14 G 2. Ra*

Ra modifies predicates. Its basic meaning is 'only, precisely [the predicate]' that is, '[the predicate] and nothing else: 'no more, no less.'

---

* In old-fashioned or fancy speech da replaces ra, with no difference except in style:

Gúgmang pútliq maqú day pasálig. (from the song Mátud Níla) '(My) only guarantee (to you) is (my) pure love.'

14 G 2 a. With predicates consisting of numbers, nouns, or pronouns

With numbers ra implies 'not more than.' It can be translated by 'only,' though it is much more commonly used than 'only.'

Piláy ímung gústu? — Duhá ra. 'How many do you want?' — '(Only) two.'
Tagpíla man ang kaság Iyáq? — Tagbáynti ra. 'How much are the crabs apiece?' — '(Only) twenty (centavos).'

Compare the use of lang (13 G 1 a, p. 527), where the implication is that a higher number was quoted previously.

A noun or pronoun plus ra means '[noun or pronoun] is the only one who . . .':

Kamú bang duhá? Díliq. Siyá ra. 'Both of you?' 'No, just him. (He's the only one who will stay here.)'
Si Huwán ray muqádtu. 'John is the only one who is going.'
Waláy láqin. Siya ra. 'There's no one else. He is the only one.'

14 G 2 b. Ra with deictics

If a predicate consists of a single deictic, the deictic is obligatorily followed by ra:

Díqa ra ku. 'Here I am.'
Túqa ra uh. 'There (he) is.'

If the predicate contains two deictics the use of ra is optional (ra follows the first deictic):

Níqa siyá dínhi. or Níqa ra siyá dínhi. 'Here he is.'

Deictics in an existential sentence are not followed by ra:

Níqay ákung amígu. 'I have a friend here.'

14 G 2 c. Ra with adjectives

An adjective followed by ra means 'very [adjective]' or 'too [adjective]':

Mahál ra kiníng kinhasún. 'These shellfish are too (or very) expensive.'

Some adjectives are automatically followed by ra whenever they are predicates, with no meaning of 'very' or 'too.' Two examples are duqúl 'nearby' and paríha 'same':

Tutál duqúl ra man ang ínyu. 'Anyway, your place is nearby.'
Paríha ra pára nákuq. 'It's all the same to me.'

14 G 2 d. Ra modifying imperatives

Ra modifies imperatives to make the command a request.

Tanqáwa ra nang nagbalígyaq dihág mga káluq. (6 b 50) 'Do you see that (man) there selling hats?' (Lit. 'Look at that (man) selling hats there.')

Without ra or any other particle, the imperative is a demand. Compare the following:

Ámbi ra nang lápis. 'May I have that pencil?'

Compare the sentence without ra:

Ámbi nang lápis! 'Give me that pencil!'

The phrase ra gud after an imperative makes the request even nicer:

Ámbi ra gud nang lápis. 'May I see that pencil a second please?'
Uy Liná, dalíq ra gud ngarí. (14 a 11) 'Lena! Come here a minute, please.'

14 G 2 e. Ra with other verbs

Ra modifies verbs that are not imperative to give the meaning '[verb] is certain to happen.'

Lutúqa. Mamatáy ra bítaw naq. (6 a 34) 'Cook it. It will die for sure.'
Báslan ra nákuq ang ímung kaqáyu. 'I'll repay your kindness for sure.'
Magkítaq ra kitá, bastús. 'We'll meet again (for sure), you rat.'

14 G 2 f. Ra with nouns

Ra modifies noun predicates to give the meaning 'no better than [noun].' In this usage ra has the same meaning as lang (13 G 1 e, p. 529).

Usá ra siyá ka mutsátsu únyaq mangasáwa sa anák sa prisidínti. 'He is no more than a servant, yet he wants to marry the president's daughter.'

14 G 2 g. Ra ba in predicates giving advice

Ra ba modifies the predicate of a statement which gives advice of various kinds: perhaps a warning, or a piece of advice recommending a course of action.

Magbántay ka dínhi. Láqin ra ba ning mga táwu dínhis pantalán. (8 a 16, 17) 'Watch out here (because) the people here at the wharf are not of a nice type.'
Itúgqan ra ba tikáng Máma. 'Watch it. I'll tell Mama on you!'
Da nagqulán na hinúqun. Bágqu ra ba ning ákung sinínaq. (9 a 6) 'Heck! It has already started to rain, and here I have a new dress on.' [The speaker is warning herself that there are going to be unpleasant consequences because she is going to get caught in the rain.]
Lamíq ra ba. (14 b 40) 'It is good.' [Mrs. Miller has just been given some soup and she is advising her hearers that it is delicious—implied 'take some.']

14 G 2 h. Ra ba modifying an apology

Ra ba also modifies the predicate of a statement of apology:

Wánqa ra ba tay bir Nyur. 'I'm sorry, Sir, we have no more beer.'
Muhatúd ba ni sa Karbun? — Díliq ra ba Day. Ádtu ni sa Kalámba. 'Will this (jeep) take me to Carbon?' —'Sorry, no, Miss. This (jeep) goes to Calamba Street.'

Exercises XIV.IV A and B.

Pattern Practices and Exercises

IA. (PP-R may be practiced before Exercise IA.) Ibutáng ang túkmang púrma sa bírbu (local vs. instrumental vs. direct) nga náqas sulúd sa parentheses. (6A, 8A, 10A)

1. Liná (dalá) ra gud ku ngarig usá ka básung túbig.
   'Lina, please bring me a glass of water.'
2. Túbig ba kanáng ímung (dalá)?
   'Is that water you are carrying?'
3. (Dalá) rag bálik kiníng básu.
   'Please take this glass back with you.'
4. (Tánqaw) nákuq ning íyang panílhig kun naqúnsa na.
   'I'm going to see what kind of job she did sweeping.'
5. Waq nákuq (tánqaw) ang íyang panílhig kun giqúnsa níya.
   'I haven't looked to see how she swept.'
6. (Tánqaw) ni Mísis Mílir ang ági sa mutsátsag maqáyu bang pagkalímpyu.
   'Mrs. Miller inspected the maid's work to see if it was well done.'
7. Waq naq (áyu) ug sílhig Nyurá kay nagdalíq man ku.
   '(I) didn't sweep it well Ma'am, because I was in a hurry.'
8. Sus, waq níya (áyu)g sílhig ning iskína.
   'Goodness, she didn't do a good job sweeping this corner.'
9. (Áyu) ku nag sílhig kanáng iskináha uy.
   'I did do a good job sweeping that corner.'
10. Kiníng iskináha ímu úntaq ning (sílhig)g maqáyu.
    'You should have done a good job sweeping this corner.'
11. (Sílhig) ku na kanáng iskináha Nyurá.
    'I've already swept that corner, Ma'am.'
12. Kanáng silhíga nga náqa diháq ang (sílhig) niqíning iskináha.
    'Use that broom there for this corner.'
13. (Límpyu)g maqáyu tung túqa dídtu.
14. (Límpyu) ku na kádtug maqáyu. Úsbun ba nákuq?
15. (Límpyu) ra ku niqádtung túqa dídtu.

IB. Ibutáng ang túkmang púrma sa bírbung náqas sulúd sa parentheses (active vs. passive). (4A, 4B; 5C, 6A, 8A, 10A and subsections)

1. (Hatudhátud) ka pa man gyud ngánhig sabáw.
   'You shouldn't have bothered bringing the soup.'
2. (Hatúd) pa man gyud ku nímu ngánhig sabáw.
   'I'll bring you some soup again sometime.'
3. Sigí, (inúm) na kay básin mabúgnaw mawáaq na nay lamíq.
   'Go ahead, drink it now; [for] if it gets cold, it will lose its flavor.'

4. (Inúm) na bítaw ku. Lamíq man gániq.
   'I already drank some. It's good (though I didn't expect it would be).'

5. (Bíyaq) ka únaq námuq ha?
   'We'll leave you for a moment, may we?'

6. (Bíyaq) ka man lang dáyun námuq.
   'You just left right away (without saying goodbye).'

7. Uy, únsay (dalíq) nínyu?
   'Hey! What's your hurry?'

8. Ngánung (dalíq) man mu?
   'Why are you in such a hurry?'

9. (Ádtu) na lang mi kay údtu na.
   'We have to go now, it's late.'

10. (Pangádtu) na mu?
    'Are you going now?'

11. Ánhi lang ta (paniqúdtu).
    'Let's just eat lunch here.'

12. (Paniqúdtu) na ba mu úsaq mung mangánhi?
    'Did you eat lunch before you came here?'

13. (Lútuq) ra gud si Pípi sa íyang panihápun.
    'Please cook Pepe's dinner.'

14. Muqádtu na lang mi kay (lútuq) pa ra ba ku sa ámung pagkáqun.
    'We have to go now. I still have to cook dinner.'

15. (Tánqaw) ug siní ang ámung mutsátsa maqúng mga bátaq ray nahibilín sa ámuq.

16. Waq túquy (híkay) sa ínyung paniqúdtu.
    'Oh yes. There's nobody to fix your dinner.'

17. Maqáyu lag (híkay) run ang ámung paniqúdtu sa mga bátaq.
    'It would be all right if the children could fix dinner.'

18. Uh, háqin na ba ning waq man ni (tubág)?

19. Ngánu kaháng waq man ku (tubág) ni Lína?

20. Únsay ímung (tubág) ánaq? Gitawág man kang irúq!

I C. Ibutáng ang hústung púrma sa púlung nga náqas sulúd sa parentheses. (3 A 3, 3 B, 5 A 1, 5 D, 6 B, 6 C, 6 D, 8 D, 9 B 2 and subsections)

1. Uy. Nalímtan ku man pagdalá (ang, sa) gása nímu!

2. Aa, píldi (ni, si) Lítu kay papíl man (ang, sa) iyáha.

3. Kay (ikáw, ímu) may píldi Litú, (kamí, nínyu) na sab si Mam.

4. Uu, píldi (ang, sa) gúnting (ang, sa) batú.

5. Ikáw ba (ang, sa) mulábay (ang, sa) láta?

6. Na, hústu na ta (sa, ang) (átuq, nátuq)ng dúwaq mga bátaq.

7. Muqinúm usáq (ku, nákuq) (ang, ug) túbig Mam.
8. Aa, gústu (nímu, ka) (nga, ug) mangíhiq?
9. Uy Sibyá, pahíri (sa, ang) (ímu, nímu)ng sípqun.
10. Kínsa (tu, ádtu)ng tigpápas (sa, ang) blákburd?
11. Iyáha nang túrnu pagqirís (sa, ang) blákburd.
12. Papása naq diháq (nga, ug) tanán.
13. Únyaq inigkahumán limpyúhi (sa, ang) irísir.
14. Karún pamínaw (nínyu, kamú) (sa, ang) istúrya.
15. Kínsa man (niqádtu, kádtu)ng nagbánhaq?

I D. Hubára ning musunúd nga mga túdling púlung ngádtus Binisayáq nga mugámit ug na, pa, diqáy, lang, ug na lang. (12 G, 13 G)

1. I'll just have to ask Father.
2. Five pesos a dozen. But I'll give you a special price, just three pesos.
3. Just have Lina clean the room.
4. There are very few jeeps here. Let's (just) go to Juan Luna and wait there.
5. Never mind, we'll just come back tomorrow.
6. They don't have any more of the small size. We might as well buy the big one.
7. Oh, it's noon already. I'll have to go now.
8. So, this is the house you two will live in.
(you two will live in: púyqan nínyung duhá)
9. What do you want to eat then (if you don't want to eat this)?
10. Just a minute, aren't you Mr. Abaya's grandson?
11. Uncle Tibo's children are already grown up. (grown up: dakúq na)
12. I've not been to Perla's house yet.
13. I won't drink coke any more.
14. Dr. Fernandez hasn't arrived yet.
15. She won't deliver the table there since you said it was not to be delivered.
16. It would be better if you came to get it now.
17. This is it (the place we're going to) now. Let's get on!
18. Is Mr. Osmeña still alive? (Say: 'Is Mr. Osmeña dead by now?')
19. We might as well go to sleep; (because) we're tired.
20. What will we have for dinner tonight then (if we won't have the fish I bought)?
(what we have for dinner: súdqan or panihápun)

21. Oh, aren't we going to church?
22. Excuse me, can't we eat first?
23. He has introduced his grandchildren to us already.
24. My, it's raining now.
25. Give it to me for just twenty centavos, will you?
26. Oh, I see. You sell cloth here.
27. (I) can't (call him), Sir, because he left already.
28. Lina, haven't you bought the bananas yet?
29. Hey, boy, just a minute. You forgot something.
30. Please, just listen to him.

II A. Ibutáng ang hústung púrma sa bírbu (active ug passive), ug pilíqa ang hústung púlung nga anáqa sa parentheses. (13 A, 13 B. Cf. also the references for XIV.IB above, p. 570.)

Pananglítan:
a. (Hátag) (si, ni) Mísis Mílir (ang, ug) túbig.

Tubág: Tagáqi si Mísis Mílir ug túbig.
b. (Pahigúp) (ni, si) Mísis Mílir (kanáq, niqánaq)ng sabáw.

Tubág: Ipahígup ni Mísis Mílir kanáng sabáw. Or:
Pahigúpa si Mísis Mílir niqánang sabáw.

1. (Paqinúm) (ni, si) Místir Mílir (ang, ug) búgnawng túbig nga túqas lamísa.
2. Lulíng, (hátag) na ba (ikáw, nímu) (ang, sa) sabáw (ni, si) Mísis Mílir?
3. (Tawág) ba ku (ang, sa) dúktur?
4. Ímu bang (trápu) (kádtu, niqádtu)ng lamísa?
5. Gústu ka bang (hígup) (ang, sa) sabáw?
6. (Sílhig) na ba nímu (ang, sa) sála, Lulíng?
7. (Bílin) lang (ug, ang) básu dínhi sa lamísa.
8. (Híkay) (ka, mu) na ba (ang, sa) panihápun Lulíng?
'Have you fixed dinner yet, Loling?'
9. Nagqingún (si, ni) Mísis Mílir nga labád pa kunú (ang, sa) íyang úlu.
10. (Límpyu) na ba (ka, nímu) (sa, ang) kusína?
11. Kádtung lamisáha muy (butáng) (ka, nímu) (ang, sa) sabáw.
12. (Lútuq) na ba (ka, nímu) (ug, ang) paniqúdtu?
'Have you cooked lunch yet?'
13. (Ánhi) ba (si, ni) Pírla úgmaq?
14. (Kúhaq) na ba (nímu, ka) (ang, ug) trapú?
'Have you gotten the cloth?'

15. Kanáng sabáwng (dalá) (ka, nímu) (hátag) (si, ni) Mísis Mílir.
16. (Kúhaq) ra gud ku (kádtu, niqádtu)ng butílya (sa, ang) lamísa.
17. Maqáyu pang (hígup) (nímu, ka) (kaníng, áning) sabáw.
18. Ngánung (hígdaq) (nímu, ka) pa man diháq?
19. Kínsa man (tu, ádtu)ng (dalá)g sabáw (nímu, ikáw)?
20. (Tánqaw) ra(kádtu, ádtu)ng butílya sa lamísa. (kúhaq) ra!

II B. Hubára ang musunúd nga mga túdling púlung ngádtus Binisayáq. (13B 2)

1. Somebody's calling you, Lena.
2. If somebody calls you, Lena, answer right away.
3. Nobody can watch over my children.
4. I won't go home early if there is somebody to watch the children.
5. If you go out every day, you need somebody to take care of your sick wife.
6. If somebody calls, I'll be very happy.
7. I didn't hear anybody call me.
8. I have somebody looking after the children at home.
9. We didn't tell anybody that Jane was sick.
10. Somebody told the children that we were here.
11. Never tell anybody that I'm ill.
12. Did anybody hear Mrs. Miller call me?
13. Somebody came over and brought you some chicken soup.
14. Are you calling somebody?
15. Somebody has brought me a delicious bowl of chicken soup. (bowl: panáksan)
16. It is difficult if a person is sick all the time.
17. If there's always someone to feed me soup like this, I'll get well in no time at all.

PP-FF Expressions of Manner (9C, 14A)

Step I. (With the words mikalít, mukalít, gikalít, and kalitún.)

'He went out suddenly.'

1. a. Mikalít siyág gawás.
   b. Migawás siyág kalít.

2. a. Mikalít siyág táguq.
   b. Mitáguq siyág kalít.

3. a. Mikalít silág línya.
   b. Milínya silág kalít.

4. a. Mikalít siyág língkud.
   b. Milíngkud siyág kalít.

5. a. Mikalít silág bánhaq.
   b. Mibánhaq silág kalít.

6. a. Mikalít siyág tawág.
   b. Mitawág siyág kalít.

7. a. Gikalít níyag lábay ang láta.
   b. Gilábay níyag kalít ang láta.

8. a. Gikalít níyag inúm ang túbig.
   b. Giqinúm níyag kalít ang túbig.

9. a. Gikalít níyag páhid ang sípqun.
   b. Gipáhid níyag kalít ang sípqun.

10. a. Gikalít siyág dakúp ni Lítu.
    b. Gidakúp siyág kalít ni Lítu.

11. a. Kalitún níyag pápas ang blákburd.
    b. Papásun níyag kalít ang blákburd.

12. a. Kalitún níyag ítsa ang láta.
    b. Iqítsa níyag kalít ang láta.

13. a. Gikalít nílag tánqaw ang ritrátu.
    b. Gitánqaw nílag kalít ang ritrátu.

14. a. Gikalít níyag hígup ang sabáw.
    b. Gihígup níyag kalít ang sabáw.

15. a. Kalitún siyág pangutána.
    b. Pangutánqun siyág kalít.

16. a. Gikalít siyág lábay ug batú.
    b. Gilabáyan siyág kalít ug batú.

Step I a. (With ug maqáyu and giqáyu or ayúhun)

'He held on well.'

17. a. Mikupút siyág maqáyu.
    b. Giqáyu níyag kupút.

18. a. Mubántay siyág maqáyu.
    b. Ayúhun níyag bántay.

19. a. Milútuq siyág maqáyu.
    b. Giqáyu níyag lútuq.

20. a. Miqiháp siyág maqáyu.
    b. Giqáyu níyag iháp.

21. a. Mibántay siyág maqáyu.
    b. Giqáyu níyag bántay.

22. a. Mulútuq siyág maqáyu.
    b. Ayúhun níyag lútuq.

23. a. Mulakáw siyág maqáyu.
    b. Ayúhun níyag lakáw.

24. a. Mikáqun siyág maqáyu.
    b. Giqáyu níyag káqun.

25. a. Misulát siyág maqáyu.
    b. Giqáyu níyag sulát.

26. a. Muqiháp siyág maqáyu.
    b. Ayúhun níyag iháp.

27. a. Mangítaq siyág maqáyu.
    b. Ayúhun níyag pangítaq.

28. a. Misúkliq siyág maqáyu.
    b. Giqáyu níyag súkliq.

29. a. Mitánqaw siyág maqáyu.
    b. Giqáyu níyag tánqaw.

30. a. Mutánqaw siyág maqáyu.
    b. Ayúhun níyag tánqaw.

31. a. Nangutána siyág maqáyu.
    b. Giqáyu níyag pangutána.

32. a. Migúnit siyág maqáyu.
    b. Giqáyu níyag gúnit.

33. a. Mulíngkud siyág maqáyu.
    b. Ayúhun níyag língkud.

34. a. Milabá siyág maqáyu.
    b. Giqáyu níyag labá.

35. a. Misúlti siyág maqáyu.
    b. Giqáyu níyag súlti.

36. a. Miqinúm siyág maqáyu.
    b. Giqáyu níyag inúm.

Step II. (With giqáyu and ayúhun)

1. a. Giqáyu ku siyág tagád.
   b. Gitagád ku siyág maqáyu.

2. a. Giqáyu mu ba siyág túdluq?
   b. Gitudlúqan mu ba siyág maqáyu?

3. a. Giqáyu kug límpyu ang bányu.
   b. Gilimpyuhán kug maqáyu ang bányu.

4. a. Giqáyu níyag lútuq ang ságing.
   b. Gilútuq níyag maqáyu ang ságing.

5. a. Waláq níya ayúhag bántay ang bátaq.
   b. Waláq níya bantayig maqáyu ang bátaq.

6. a. Waláq níya ayúhag tubág si Dyiin.
   b. Waláq níya tubagág maqáyu si Dyiin.

7. a. Giqáyu níyag híkay ang ílang paniqúdtu.
   b. Gihíkay níyag maqáyu ang ílang paniqúdtu.

8. a. Ayúhag báhin ang túrta.
   b. Bahínag maqáyu ang túrta.

9. a. Giqáyu níyag kupút ang bag.
   b. Gikúptan níyag maqáyu ang bag.

10. a. Ayúhun níyag sulúd ang kwárta sa bag.
    b. Isulúd níyag maqáyu ang kwárta sa bag.

11. a. Giqáyu níyag irís ang blákburd.
    b. Giqirís níyag maqáyu ang blákburd.

12. a. Ayúhun kug sílhig ang salúg.
    b. Silhígan kug maqáyu ang salúg.

13. a. Giqáyu kug butáng ang támbal sa lamísa.
    b. Gibutáng kug maqáyu ang támbal sa lamísa.

14. a. Giqáyu kug táguq ang kwárta.
    b. Gitáguq kug maqáyu ang kwárta.

15. a. Giqáyu kug dalá ang mga líbru.
    b. Gidalá kug maqáyu ang mga líbru.

16. a. Ayúha intáwug labá ang ákung sinínaq.
    b. Lábhi intáwug maqáyu ang ákung sinínaq.

Step III. Various verbs meaning 'do in a certain way.'

Actives:

1. a. Mihínay siyág lakáw.
   b. Milakáw siyág hínay.

2. a. Mikusúg ug ulán.
   b. Miqulán ug kusúg.

3. a. Magdalíq siyág káqun.
   b. Mukáqun siyág dalíq.

4. a. Miqinánay siyág bángun.
   b. Mibángun siyág inánay.

5. a. Mukalít siyág tíndug.
   b. Mutíndug siyág kalít.

6. a. Nagdalíq silág gúlaq.
   b. Migúlaq silág dalíq.

7. a. Diq na silá magdúgayg puyúq dínhi.
   b. Diq na silá magpuyúg dúgay dínhi.

8. a. Mikalít siyág lúksu.
   b. Milúksu siyág kalít.

Passives:

9. a. Giqinánay níyag inúm ang túbig.
   b. Giqinúm níyag inánay ang túbig.

10. a. Nakúsgan níyag lábay ang láta.
    b. Nalábay níyag kusúg ang láta.

11. a. Kúsgun níyag ítsa ang batú.
    b. Iqítsa níyag kusúg ang batú.

12. a. Giqinánay nákug irís ang blákburd.
    b. Giqirís nákug inánay ang blákburd.

13. a. Nindútag búhat ang ímung trabáhu.
    b. Buhátag níndut ang ímung trabáhu.

14. a. Ayúhag sílhig tung iskína.
    b. Silhígig maqáyu tung iskína.

15. a. Ayúha pa tug límpyu.
    b. Limpyuhí pa tug maqáyu.

16. a. Ayúhun kug pakáqun ang bátaq.
    b. Pakánqun kug maqáyu ang bátaq.

Mixed actives and passives:

17. a. Ayúha nínyug pamínaw ang istúrya.
    b. Pamináwa nínyug maqáyu ang istúrya.

18. a. Kúsgag lábay ang láta.
    b. Ilábayg kusúg ang láta.

19. a. Tingálig mukalít lag ulán.
    b. Tingálig muqulán lag kalít.

20. a. Diq ku magdúgay ug huwát nímu.
    b. Diq ku maghuwát ug dúgay nímu.

21. a. Paghínayg súlti.
    b. Pagsúltig hínay.

22. a. Magdalíq tag lakáw.
    b. Maglakáw tag dalíq.

23. a. Ayúhun kug húgas ring pínggan.
    b. Hugásan kug maqáyu ring pínggan.

24. a. Gikalitán siyág lúksu ni Lítu.
    b. Giluksuqán siyág kalít ni Lítu.

25. a. Miqinánay siyág língiq.
    b. Milíngiq siyág inánay.

III. (Expression of Manner) Hubára ang Inínglis nga anáqa sa parentheses sa musunúd nga mga túdling púlung. Úsba ang pagkabutáng sa mga púlung kun gikinahánglan, ug púnqig linkers. (14 A, 9 C)

Pananglítan:

a. Milúksu siyá (suddenly).

Tubág: Milúksu siyág kalít.

b. Mubinisayáq ka man lagí (well).

Tubág: Maqáyu ka man lagíng mubinisayáq.

c. Panílhig intáwun (well).

Tubág: Ayúha intáwug panílhig. or
Panílhig intáwug maqáyu. or
Panílhig intáwun pagqáyu.

1. Uh! Háqin na ba si Lína nga waq man ni mutubág (immediately).
2. Ngánung midúqul ka man (for a long time)?
3. Sus, díqay iskína, waq silhígi (well).
4. Gihumán ni Lína ang pagsílhig sa suqúk arún siyá makapanghúgas sa mga pínggan (fast or right away).
5. Magsultisúlti ta dínhis sála (for a short time).
6. Únyaq kádtu dídtu ímu úntaq tung trapúhan (well).
7. Hásta tung túqa dídtu limpyúhi (well).
8. Misakít ang ákung úlu (suddenly).
9. Gihígup níya ang sabáw kay ínit pa (gradually). (gradually: inánay).
10. Mibákud si Mísis Mílir arún tanqáwun ang ági sa mutsátsa (slowly). (mibákud 'got up')
11. Gilútuq níya ang kik (delicious). (delicious: lamíq)
12. Muhígup si Mísis Mílir básta sabáw sa manúk (fast).
13. Mipaqúliq si Místir Mílir gikans trabáhu (hurriedly).
14. Midágan man gud si Kíkuy maqúng waq hisákpi (fast).
15. Ug giqítsa ni Lítu ang láta (suddenly).
16. Si Mísis Mílir musúlti (fast).
17. Musúlti si Místir Mílir (softly). (softly: hínay)

PP-GG Change the verbs to accidental passive with hi- . . .-an/hi- . . .-i. (14 E)

Step I. (Actives only)

'Lena understood what I said.'

1. a. Nakasabút si Línas ákung gisúlti.
   b. Hisábtan ni Lína ang ákung gisúlti.

2. a. Nakadúqaw siyáng Mísis Mílir.
   b. Hiduqawán níyas Mísis Mílir.

3. a. Nakadakúp siyás bátaq.
   b. Hidákpan níya ang bátaq.

4. a. Nakakitáq ku níyas kusína.
   b. Hikítqan ku siyás kusína.

5. a. Nakaqabút ku níyang nagbásas líbru.
   b. Hiqábtan ku siyáng nagbásas líbru.

6. a. Mitawág siyás íyang mutsátsa.
   b. Hitáwgan níya ang íyang mutsátsa.

7. a. Miqági siyás baláy.
   b. Hiqagiqán níya ang baláy.

8. a. Nakalímpyu na siyás abugúng suqúk.
   b. Hilimpyuhán na níya ang abugúng suqúk.

9. a. Mibisíta siyáng Mísis Mílir.
   b. Hibisitahán níyas Mísis Mílir.

10. a. Nakalimút siyá ni Mísis Abáya.
    b. Hikalímtan níyas Mísis Abáya.

11. a. Nakabíyaq siyág líbrus baláy.
    b. Hibiyaqán níya ang líbrus baláy.

12. a. Nakasílhig siyág papíl sa kwártu.
    b. Hisilhigán níya ang papíl sa kwártu.

13. a. Mihátag kug sabáw níya.
    b. Hitagaqán ku siyág sabáw.

14. a. Nakasaká na siyás baláy.
    b. Hisákqan na níya ang baláy.

15. a. Misílhig na siyás suqúk.
    b. Hisilhigán na níya ang suqúk.

16. a. Nakahátag siLág gása nákuq.
    b. Hitagaqán ku nílag gása.

17. a. Nakalíngkud siyás pínggan.
    b. Hilingkurán níya ang pínggan.

18. a. Nakabíyaq siyág bag.
    b. Hibiyaqán níya ang bag.

19. a. Nakasabáw siyás ísdang gilútuq.
    b. Hisábwan níya ang ísdang gilútuq.

20. a. Nakagústu siyás sabáw.
    b. Higustuhán níya ang sabáw.

21. a. Nakadúqaw si Mísis Abáyas masakitún.
    b. Hiduqawán ni Mísis Abáya ang masakitún.

22. a. Mitrápu si Línas mga sílya.
    b. Hitrapuhán ni Lína ang mga sílya.

23. a. Nakasúlti siyá ni Lína ug díliq maqáyu.
    b. Hisultihán níya si Línag díliq maqáyu.

24. a. Nakaqinúm siyás ákung gátas.
    b. Hiqímnan níya ang ákung gátas.

25. a. Mipalít siyág líbru nákuq.
    b. Hipalitán ku níyag líbru.

26. a. Nakadúbli siyág plíti sa dráybir.
    b. Hidublihán níyag plíti ang dráybir.

27. a. Mibáyad siyás láqing babáyi.
    b. Hibáyran níya ang láqing babáyi.

28. a. Nakaqihíq ang irúq sa kwártu.
    b. Hiqihiqán sa irúq ang kwártu.

29. a. Nakapamínaw siyás ílang istúrya.
    b. Hipaminawán níya ang ílang istúrya.

30. a. Miplíti ang táwu nákuq.
    b. Hiplitihán ku sa táwu.

31. a. Mibíyaq siyás íyang amígu.
    b. Hibiyaqán níya ang íyang amígu.

Step II. (Actives and passives)

'I saw him in the church.'

1. a. Nakítaq ku siyás simbahán.
   b. Hikítqan ku siyás simbahán.

2. a. Natúmba ang káhuy kaníya.
   b. Hitumbahán siyá sa káhuy.

3. a. Nakadúqaw siyág pamílya.
   b. Hiduqawán níya ang pamílya.

4. a. Nakaqági na silá ning dalána.
   b. Hiqagiqán na níla ning dalána.

5. a. Nadungúg sa mutsátsa ang tawág ni Mísis Mílir.
   b. Hidúnggan sa mutsátsa ang tawág ni Mísis Mílir.

6. a. Nakatulúg na silá íning tihirása.
   b. Hikatúlgan na níla ning tihirása.

7. a. Nahátag níya ang sabáw ni Mísis Mílir.
   b. Hitagaqán níyag sabáw si Mísis Mílir.

8. a. Nakabisíta siyás íyang amíga.
   b. Hibisitahán níya ang íyang amíga.

9. a. Giqagiqán níya ang ílang baláy.
   b. Hiqagiqán níya ang ílang baláy.

10. a. Hátdan níya si Mísis Mílir ug sabáw.
    b. Hihátdan níya si Mísis Mílir ug sabáw.

11. a. Nakalimút siyág tawág ni Lína.
    b. Hikalímtan níyag tawág si Lína.

12. a. Gilábay níya ang batús baláy.
    b. Hilabayán níyag batú ang baláy.

13. a. Nakapalít siyág búlak sa tindáhan.
    b. Hipalitán níyag búlak ang tindáhan.

14. a. Nahátdan níya siyág sabáw.
    b. Hihátdan níya siyág sabáw.

15. a. Nakasaká siyás ílang baláy.
    b. Hisákqan níya ang ílang baláy.

16. a. Nagrábi ang íyang sakít.
    b. Higrabihán siyás sakít.

17. a. Nakaqádtu na silás uspitál.
    b. Hiqadtuqán na níla ang uspitál.

18. a. Nalábay níya ang batú sa pínggan.
    b. Hilabayán níyag batú ang pínggan.

19. a. Gibalígyaq níya ang bag sa babáyi.
    b. Hibaligyaqán níyag bag ang babáyi.

20. a. Nakalíngkud siyás ílang plátu.
    b. Hilingkurán níya ang ílang plátu.

21. a. Nasúlti níya ang tinúqud nákuq.
    b. Hisultihán ku níyas tinúqud.

22. a. Nabiyaqán níya ang ákung bag.
    b. Hibiyaqán níya ang ákung bag.

23. a. Gipútlan níyag tiqíl ang manúk.
    b. Hipútlan níyag tiqíl ang manúk.

24. a. Gikúptan níya ang líbrus bátaq.
    b. Hikúptan níya ang líbrus bátaq.

IV A. Ibutáng ang particles nga man ug ra ba sa línya sa hústung paggáwiq. (Gamíta ang ra ba kun mahímuq.) (14G and subsections)

1. Ngánung dúgay ________ ka?
2. Maqáyu ba nang mga táwus pantalán? Díliq ________.
3. Nagqulán na hinúqun. Bágq ________ning ákung sinínaq.
4. Uy Lulíng pagdalág bir dirí. Waq na ________y bir Nyur.
5. Únsa ________y átung duláqun?
6. Adá tagád ka na ________.
7. Maqáyu na kay sipqunsípqun ________ lang.
8. Muqádtu ba nis Banáwaq? Díliq ________ Sir, kay pára ________ nis Gwadulúpi.

9. Panílhig na Liná. Muqabút ________ si Sinyúra run.
10. Abút na ________ diqáy ta.
11. Tutál kahibáwu na ________ kung muqádtu.
12. Ay sus, mulárga ________ diqáy dáyun.

IV B. (1) Hubára sa Binisayáq ang musunúd nga mga túdling púlung gináwiq ang ra, ra ba, ug man. (14 G)

1. (He's It) because he had paper, Ma'am.
2. Who will throw the can?
3. Who is it that made noise?
4. Ah! that's easy.
5. Twelve (pesos) is the lowest price.
6. The people here at the pier are not of a good sort.
7. Oh my, it's raining, and my dress is new.
8. No. Just me.
9. How old are you, Sir?
10. Oh, what shall we play now?
11. 'Do you want to buy crabs?'—'No! They're too expensive.'
12. Where do we get a jeep to go to Banawa?
13. Where are you going, Miss?
14. Only four-fifty? How cheap!
15. Just cook it. It will die for sure.
16. I already have a helper.
17. That one downstairs, I also like that one.
18. Oh, there they are.
19. Oh! I already went (to the bathroom). I'm done.

(2) Ipunúq sa musunúd nga mga túdling púlung ang man, diqáy, u man diqáy.

1. Sus! alás útsu na ________. Ádtu na lang ku.
2. Kamú ________ng tulúy magpuyúq dínhi?
3. Aa. Ikáw ________ si Mis Wílbi.
4. Mulárga ni dáyun Day.—Ay sus! Mulárga ________ ni dáyun!
5. Ása ________ ku sakáyg díliq dínhi?
6. Siyáy nakadaqúg.—Siyá ________!
7. Ayáwg kalímti pagdalá ang papíl pára ilú.
   Aa uu. Kanáq ________ ákung dádqun.

8. Aa ________? Si Huwán ra ________ ang waláq mahágbung!
9. Ang ímu ________ng sinínaq—diq mu ba ________ palábhan?
10. Kínsay hípi dínhi?—Akú bayáq.—Aa, ikáw________!

IV C. Hubára ning musunúd nga mga túdling púlung ngádtus Binisayáq. (14 D)

Pananglítan: We bought ten cents' worth of bukhay.

Tubág: Namalít mig bálig dyis sintábus nga bukháyuq.

1. Lina drinks a glass of water after eating.
2. I will buy two [pieces] crabs.
3. Lito was given a bottle of coke by Perla.
4. Uncle Tibo drinks a bowl of toddy every morning.
5. Miss Wilby bought a dozen pairs of earrings at the store.
6. She drank a bottle of coke.
7. Uncle Tibo did grow old even though he drank a bowl of toddy every day. (Say: A bowl of toddy every day didn't make Uncle Tibo old.)
8. Drink a glass of water.
9. How many [pieces] crabs can you eat?
10. She bought a dozen pairs of earrings because they were cheap.

V. (Direct passive in direct meaning vs. instrumental passive in direct meaning) Ibutáng ang hústung púrma sa bírbu nga náqa sa sulúd sa parentheses. (14 F)

Pananglítan:

a. Únsa kaháy (tubág) ku níya.

Tubág: Únsa kaháy itubág ku níya.

b. Diq ku na lang tingáli siyá (tubág).

Tubág: Diq ku na lang tingáli siyá tubagún.

1. Únsa kaháy íyang (pangutána) nákuq nga gisigíhan man gyud ku níyag tawág.
'What can he want to ask me, that he keeps calling me?'
2. (Pangutána) ka níya kun diqín ka gíkan gahápun nga gabíqi ka na man kaqáyung niqabút.
'He's going to ask you where you were last night. You came home very late.'
3. Únsay (súguq) níya nímu nga ganíha pa man tung nangítaq nímu?
'What does he want to ask you to do? He's been looking for you for a while.'
4. (Súguq) ku si Huwán paglábay sa basúra.
'I told John to throw the garbage out.'

5. Maqú niy (ingún) ku níya inigqabút níya gíkan sa Bágyu.
   'This is what I'll tell him when he gets back from Baguio.'

6. Maqáyu pa tingáling (ingún) ku siyá nga maqú niy isúlti níya kang Pírla.
   'I should probably tell him that that is what he should say to Perla.'

7. Hulát únaq ha, kay ákung (ingún) ang dúktur nga níqa ka.
   'Wait a second. I'll tell the doctor you're here.'

8. Ísaq pa. (Tawág) nákuq si Pírla arún magkasultihánay mug maqáyu.
   'Wait a second. I'll call Perla . . .'

9. Biság únsa pay (tawág) níya nákuq diq gyud ku masukúq.
   'Whatever name he calls me, I won't get mad.'

10. (Sakáy) na lang nátuq tung Kapitúlyu kay layúq kaqáyu.
    'Let's ride to the Capitol, because it's very far.'

11. (Sakáy) ning batáqa sa traak kay samukán kaqáyu.
    'Make this child wait on the bus. He's a nuisance.'

12. Dúna úntaq kuy (hángyuq) nímu Day, kanáq kun díliq ka masukúq.
    'I have a favor to ask of you—that is, if you won't get mad.'

13. Kun ang ímung (hángyuq) ákung mahímuq, ngánu gung díliq?
    'If I can do what you ask, why shouldn't I?'

14. (Hángyuq) ku úntaq ikáw sa pagbalígyaq áning ákung dalá.
    'I would like to ask you to sell these things I brought.'

15. Nagqingún si Mísis Abilyána nga (ságul) dáqan ang túbig ug kámay sa diq pa ibutáng sa káhaq.
    'Mrs. Abellana said to mix the sugar and the water together before putting them into the frying pan.'

16. Maqú ning lubíha ang (ságul) sa kalamáy. Diq nang usá.
    'This is the coconut to put into the kalamay, not that one.'

17. Diq ku siyá gústung (tubág) kay galágut ku níya.
    'I don't want to answer him, because I'm mad at him.'

18. Kiní na lay (tubág) ku níya arún díliq siyá masukúq.
    'That's the answer I'm going to give him. He won't get mad.'

19. (Pangutána) ku siyá kun únsay íyang gisúlti gahápun.
    'I'll ask him what he said yesterday.'

20. Dúna úntaq kuy (pangutána) nímu Dung. Mahímuq ba?
    'I have something to ask of you, Boy. May I?'

VI A. Ibungát ang mga musunúd nga mga túdling púlung sa hústung paníngug. (423 Statement)

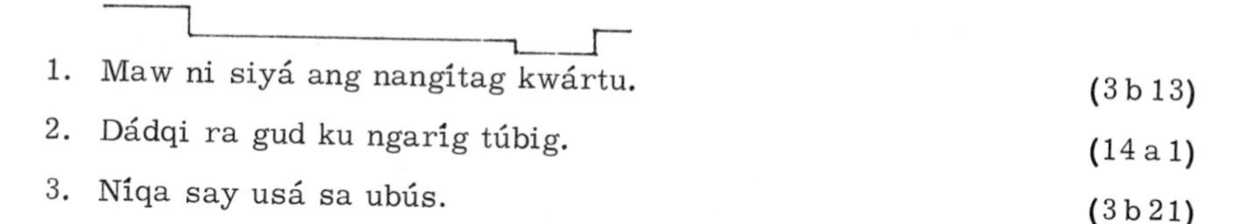

1. Maw ni siyá ang nangítag kwártu. (3 b 13)
2. Dádqi ra gud ku ngaríg túbig. (14 a 1)
3. Níqa say usá sa ubús. (3 b 21)

4. Háqin na ba ning waq man ni mutubág. (14 a 2)
5. Líbri man gung sugáq ug túbig. (3 b 27)
6. Mu ni si Índay. (3 c 4)
7. Maqú diqáy ning Úrmuk (8 c 29)
8. Maqáyu ning higúpun mu sámtang ínit pa. (14 b 35)
9. Sígi na Dung. (12 a 17)
10. Ánhi ta maniqúdtu. (14 b 56)
11. Maqáyu nang magaduqawdúqaw. (14 b 67)

VI B. (324 Question)

1. Náqa ba si Místir Abáya? (1 a 4)
2. Lítu diqáy ímung ngálan? (2 b 24)
3. Maqáyu na bang ímung úlu? (14 a 20)
4. Waláq na ba magsakít? (14 a 21)
5. Diq ka kaháq unyáq samúkans mga bátaq? (3 c 11)
6. Mangádtu na mu? (14 b 55)
7. Waláq diqáy nahabilín sa ínyu? (14 b 61)

VI C. (234 Statement)

1. Dádqi kug túbig. (14 a 3)
2. Uh, salámat. (14 a 8)
3. Uu Nyurá. (14 a 12)
4. Abugún kaqáyu sa suqúk. (14 a 15)
5. Silá man diqáy ning Mísis Abáya. (14 a 25)
6. Dayún Mísis Abáya. (14 a 26)
7. Padayuná lang ngarí. (14 a 29)
8. Gidádqan ta gyud kag sabáw. (14 b 33)
9. Manglíngkud tag kadyút. (14 b 45)
10. Sultisúlti úsaq ta. (14 b 46)

VI D. (243# 234 Statement)

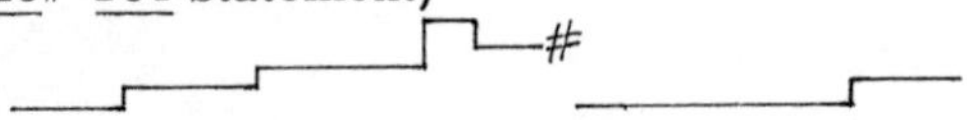

1. Pirú ang ákung hilánat, náqa pay gamáy. (14 a 22)
2. Ug ímu nang kuháqan, bínli lang kug gamáy.

3. Kanáng árka Mam, kanáng mu rag sakayáng dakúq. (13 b 79)
4. Ug naglabád nang ímung úlu, ay lag ánhi úgmaq.
5. Kun muqánhi ka sunúd túqig, iqatúl sa panánggiq.
6. Ug magdalág kaság si Lína, ipabutáng langs lamísa.
7. Masúnug, ug ímung dugáyun ug ínit.

VI E. (243# 423 Statement)

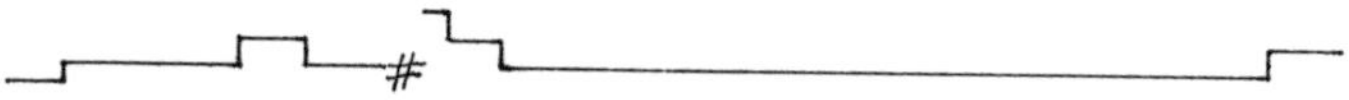

1. Kanáng kawáyan, íla nang ilíbut sa usa ka párti sa dágat. (10 a 10)
2. Ang mga ísdaq nga masúud ánang kurál nga gihímuq, maglisúd na paguwáq. (10 a 13)
3. Kiníng iskináha, ímu untáq ning silhígag maqáyu. (14 a 13)
4. Apán naputúl ang íyang usá ka kamút, kay nabúthan mag dinamíta. (10 a 19)
5. Kádtu dídtu, ímung pangayúhug trápu. (14 a 14)
6. Ug ang ákung bána, maqúy nagtrabáhu dídtu. (10 a 21)
7. Ang ákuq sang mga anák nga laláki, túqa sad gatrabáhu sa kamaqisán. (10 a 22)
8. Inigkahumán nímug límpyu, panghúgas unyáq sa mga pínggan. (14 a 17)
9. Ug dúna say tagaláqing lugár, nga mangánhi arún lang sa pagtábang sa panánggiq. (10 a 33)
10. Kanáng mupulá na nang ílang uháy, maqú na nay hústung tímpu sa pagqáni sa humáy. (10 b 7)

VII A. Pagbása

Pagpanlímpyu pára sa Pigíng

"Kay may pigíng[1] man ta rung Sabadú, kinahánglan manglímpyu kitás baláy. Ang sílung mahímung silhígan lang kay waq na man tay panahún, apán ang sála ayúhun gyug límpyu ug ang mga kahún kuháqun diháq. Únyaq magkáwus tag dághang túbig kay manghúgas tas mga plátu," ingún si Riy.

Dáyun ingún si Buy, "Aw uu, pirú láqin[2] gyuy maníhig, láqin puy manghúgas."

Mitubág pud si Mírli, "Lagí, kay kápuy bayáq kaqáyu básta átuq pang kúskus,[3] kitá pay báyli."[4]

Miqingún pud si Níniq, "Aa, kinahánglan mutábang ang tanáns paglútuq sa paniqúdtu, ug sa ubáng mga pagkáqun."

"Hústu. Nan,[5] kínsa may átung imbitahún? Kitakíta[6] lang diqáy?" mátud pang Líli.

"Túqud nu, kuqán pud, ása[7] man diqáy tag sunáta? Dúna gyud tay sunáta. Syáru pug waláq gyud, biság rádyu na lang," miqingún ang usá.

"Iqí[8] waq gyud tay punugrapúng kahulamán?[9] Ka waláy kaláki pud ánang rádyu. Muqábang na ba lang hinúqug amplipáyir," niqingún pus Ídi.

"Ay na lang, náqa may ákung kahulamán ug radyupúnu. Hulám lang mug pláka," súlti pung Tásyu.

"Aa, sigí, paqúliq na ta. Bálik tag sayú dínhi úgmaq," súlti ni Lulú.

Namaqúliq silá arún makapahúwayg[10] sayú.

1. pigíng 'party'
2. láqin gyuy a láqin puy b 'the person doing a should not be the same as the one doing b'
3. kúskus 'play the guitar'
4. Átuq pang kúskus, kitá pay báyli 'we make the music and we dance'—i.e. 'we fix the dinner, then we eat it'
5. nan 'well anyway . . .'
6. kitakíta 'just us'
7. ása x ug y 'where is x . . . to get y from?'
8. iqí 'hey!' (expressing sudden surprise and disbelief)
9. hulám 'borrow'
10. pahúway 'relax'

VII B. Pagbánsay

(Panlímpyu) pára sa Pigíng

"Kay may pigíng man ta rung Sabadú, kinahánglan (panglímpyu) kitás baláy. Ang sílung mahímung (sílhig) lang kay waq na man tay panahún, apán ang sála (áyu) gyug (límpyu) ug ang mga kahún (kúhaq) diháq. Unyáq (káwus) tag dághang túbig kay (panghúgas) tas mga plátu," (ingún) si Riy.

Dáyun (ingún) si Buy, "Aw uu, pirú láqin gyuy (panílhig), láqin puy (panghúgas)."

(Tubág) pud si Mírli, "Lagi, kay kápuy bayáq kaqáyu básta átuq pang kúskus, kitá pay báyli."

(Ingún) pud si Níniq, "Aa, kinahánglan (tábang) ang tanáns (lútuq) sa paniqúdtu, ug sa ubáng mga pagkáqun."

"Hústu. Nan, kínsa may átung (imbitár)? Kitakíta lang diqáy?" mátud pang Líli.

"Túqud nu, kuqán pud, ása man diqáy tag sunáta? Dúna gyud tay sunáta. Syáru pug waláq gyud, biság rádyu na lang," (ingún) ang usá.

"Iqí waq gyud tay punugrapúng (hulám)? Ka waláy kaláki pud ánang rádyu. (Ábang) na ba lang hinúqug amplipáyir," (ingún) pus Ídi.

"Ay na lang, náqa may ákung (hulám) ug radyupúnu. (Hulám) lang mug pláka," súlti pung Tásyu.

"Aa, sigí, (paqúliq) na ta. (Bálik) tag sayú dínhi úgmaq," súlti ni Lulú.

(Pamaqúliq) silá arún (pahúway)g sayú.

VIII. Sultiqánay: Nagsúlti si Mísis Mílir Ngádtus Íyang Mutsátsa

A: Lulíng! Mariká. Lulíng! Háqin gud ni siyá, waq man mutubág. Lulíing . . .

B: Gitawág ba ku nímu Nyurá?

A: Náqa ka ra man lagí diqáy. Ngánung waq ka man mutubág?

(Waq lang mutíngug ang mutsátsa.)

A: Tanqáwa ra nang salúg (floor). Waq man nímu ayúhag límpyu.

B: Ákuq na nang gilimpyúhag maqáyu, Nyurá. Lisúd kaqáyung pasináwun. (pasináwun 'shine')

A: Aa sigí. Úsbi . . . Ay sag lakáw. Náqa pay ákung ipabúhat nímu.

B: Únsa man Nyurá?

A: Iníti kug kapí ug unyáq . . .

(Milakáw dáyun ang mutsátsa.)

A: Saq pa. Ása gud ka . . . Ngánung mulakáw ka dáyun nga waq pa gániq ku kahumág súlti. Kawáy batásan nímu aq!

B: Aw nákug waq na kay isúlti.

A: Dádqi sad kug paan.

1. Midúqul dáyun si Lúling sa pagtawág ni Mísis Mílir.
2. Nalípay si Mísis Mílir sa trabáhu ni Lúling.
3. Waq níya ayúhag pasínaw ang salúg.
4. Gipaqusáb siyág límpyu sa salúg.
5. Way láqing isúguq si Mísis Mílir.
6. Gústu si Mísis nga hátdan siyág tsa.
7. Milakáw si Lúling sa waq pa mahumág súlti si Mísis Mílir.

A: Lulíng! —Ang ákung kapí diqáy. Ása man tu!

B: Ákuq pang gilimpyuhág úna ang salúg.

A: Waq ba tikáw íngnang pahatúd ku nímug kapí?

B: Ingún kug humág límpyus salúg.

A: Díliq, unáhun tung kapí. Humán, bálik kag límpyu. Diq ka man kasabút sugúqun. Na sigí. Dalíq!

8. Gihátdan dáyun siyág kapí sa waq pa limpyuhí ang sáwug.
9. Nasábtan dáyun ni Lúling ang súguq.
10. Gústu ni Mísis Mílir unáhun paghátag ang kapí úsaq ang paglímpyus salúg.
11. Gipadalíq níya si Lúling.

Ripásu

Nanyánggi[1] si Iyáq Kárya sa Tabuqán[2]

Nína: Iyáq Karyá, manyánggi ka ba run?

Iyáq Kárya: Uu, ngánu man Day?

Nína: Muqubán úntaq ku nímu.

Iyáq Kárya: Únaq pa diqáy. Lúnis túqud run. Ádtu lang ta manyánggi sa Tabuqán kay barátu kaqáyu dídtu básta[3] Lúnis. Tábuq[4] man. Mukúyug lang ka nákuq?

Nína: Uu, sigí. Maqáyu sab kay waq pa gyud ku makaqádtu dídtu. Layúq ba?

Iyáq Kárya: Diq man.

Nína: Taná. Ádtu na ta.

Iyáq Kárya: Uy, tartanílya Dung. Sa Tabuqán mi ha?

(Sa dídtu na silá sa Tabuqán)

Nína: Maw diqáy ning Tabuqán? Dugaydugáy na ku dínhis Sibú, apán karún pa gyud ku makaqánhi dínhi. Dághan man lagí átung mapalít nu? Barátu pa.

Iyáq Kárya: Bítaw.

Nína: Íngnun ku gyud si Manáng, arún káda Lúnis, ánhi ku mupalít.

Iyáq Kárya: Day, Day, tagpíla man ning ímung ísdaq?

Tindíra: Tagsingkwínta ang túhug[5] Yaq.

Iyáq Kárya: Ayáay, kamahál sab! Tanqáwa ra gud Day, gagmátuy[6] kaqáyu, uh.

Tindíra: Uu, sigí. Ihátag ku na lang nag kwarínta. Waq na gániq ku ánay ganánsya.

Iyáq Kárya: Ultimúng prísyu na gyud naq? Diq na naq maqúbsan?[7]

Tindíra: Diq na gyud intáwun Yaq.

Iyáq Kárya: Sigí. Salámat Day ha? Nyaq, kádtung túqang kaság tagpíla man?

Tindíra: Aa, kanáq? Ihátag ku lang naq nímug singkwínta arún diq ta madúgay.

Iyáq Kárya: Pústa kay ákung palitún.

---

* The numbered items in this section are explained in the Notes, page 592.

—oOo—

Iyáq Kárya: Palitá[8] kug kinhasún Day bi. Kanáng duhá ka putús, pilá?

Bátaq: Báynti Iyáq. Kiníng tulú ka putús ihátag ku nímug bayntisíngku.

Iyáq Kárya: Palíhug[9] pagbutáng dirí sa ákung bukág[10] Day. Naglísud[11] na man gud ku pagdáa niqíni.

—oOo—

Íyáq Kárya: Dung, ímu ba ning tanáng tínda dínhi?

Úndung: Uu, Iyáq. Mupalít ka ba?

Iyáq Kárya: Tagáqi kunú[12] kug prísyu niqánang ímung manúk, ságing ug lubí.

Úndung: Kiníng manúk, tagdús písus, báynti ning ságing ug tagdyís ning lubí. Waq na gyud niy hángyuq. Kinaqúbsan[13] na nang prísyu.

Iyáq Kárya: Sigí na lang uy kay nagdalíq ra ba ku kaqáyu. Údtu na. Dálha[14] ning lubí Niná uh, palíhug.

Nína: Kanáng ságing sab bi, ihátag nákuq arún diq ka maglísud[15] kaqáyu.

Iyáq Kárya: Nakapalít ka na bas tanán mung palitúnun?

Nína: Uu, níqa nang tanán Yaq.

Iyáq Kárya: Na halá. Ádtu na ta.

Notes

1.	panyánggi	'go marketing'
2.	Tabuqán	[one of the big markets in Cebu City]
3.	básta	'if (and only if)'
4.	tábuq	'market day'
5.	túhug	'string' (counter for things strung on thread or bamboo)
6.	gagmátuy	'very small' (plural)
7.	maqúbsan	'thing which can be lowered'
8.	palitá	[short for papalitá]
9.	palíhug	'please'
10.	bukág	'basket'
11.	naglísud	[variant of naglisúd; same meaning]
12.	kunú	'please'
13.	kinaqúbsan	'lowest'
14.	dálha	'take' (dialectal form for dádqa)
15.	maglísud	no difference in meaning from maglisúd

Ripásu

Nanyánggi si Iyáq Kárya sa Tabuqán

Nina: Iyáq Karyá, (panyánggi) ka ba run?

Iyáq Kárya: Uu, ngánu man Day?

Nína: (Ubán) úntaq ku nímu.

Iyáq Kárya: Únaq pa diqáy. Lúnis túqud run. Ádtu lang ta (panyánggi) sa Tabuqán kay barátu kaqáyu dídtu básta Lúnis. Tábuq man. (Kúyug) lang ka nákuq?

Nína: Uu, sigí. Maqáyu sab day waq pa gyud ku (ádtu) dídtu. Layúq ba?

Iyáq Kárya: Diq man.

Nína: Taná. Ádtu na ta.

Iyáq Kárya: Uy, tartanílya Dung. Sa Tabuqán mi ha?

(Sa dídtu na silá sa Tabuqán)

Nína: Maw diqáy ning Tabuqán? Dugaydugáy na ku dínhis Sibú, apán karún pa gyud ku (ánhi) dínhi. Dághan man lagí átung (palít) nu? Barátu pa.

Iyáq Kárya: Bítaw.

Nína: (Íngun) ku gyud si Manáng, arún káda Lúnis, ánhi ku (palít).

Iyáq Kárya: Day, Day, tagpíla man ning ímung ísdaq?

Tindíra: Tagsingkwínta ang túhug Yaq.

Iyáq Kárya: Ayáay kamahál sab! Tanqáwa ra gud Day, gagmátuy kaqáyu, uh.

Tindíra: Uu, sigí. (Hátag) ku na lang nag kwarínta. Waq na gániq ku ánay ganánsya.

Iyáq Kárya: Ultimúng prísyu na gyud naq? Diq na naq (ubús)?

Tindíra: Diq na gyud intáwun Yaq.

Iyáq Kárya: Sigí. Salámat Day ha? Nyaq, kádtung túqang kaság tagpíla man?

Tindíra: Aa, kanáq? (Hátag) ku lang naq nímug singkwínta arún diq ta madúgay.

Iyáq Kárya: (Putús) kay ákung (palít).

—oOo—

Iyáq Kárya: (Papalít) kug kinhasún Day bi. Kanáng duhá ka putús, pilá?

Bátaq: Báynti Iyáq. Kiníng tulú ka putús (hátag) ku nímug bayntisíngku.

Iyáq Kárya: Palíhug pagbutáng dirí sa ákung bukág Day. (Lisúd) na man gud ku (pagdáa) niqíni.

—oOo—

Iyáq Kárya: Dung, ímu ba ning tanáng tínda dínhi?

Úndung: Uu, Iyáq. (Palít) ka ba?

Iyáq Kárya: (Hátag) kunú kug prísyu niqánang ímung manúk, ságing ug lubí.

Úndung: Kiníng manúk, tagdús písus, báynti ning ságing ug tagdyís ning lubí. Waq na gyud niy hángyuq. Kinaqúbsan na nang prísyu.

Iyáq Kárya: Sigí na lang uy, kay (dalíq) ra ba ku kaqáyu. Údtu na. (Dalá) ning lubí Niná uh, palíhug.

Nína: Kanáng ságing sab bi, (hátag) nákuq arún diq ka (lisúd) kaqáyu.

Iyáq Kárya: (Palít) ka na bas tanán mung palitúnun?

Nína: Uu, níqa nang tanán Yaq.

Iyáq Kárya: Na halá. Ádtu na ta.

I. Review of Deictics

Ibutáng ang hústung deictic sáma sa túqa, dídtu, dirí, dínhi, dínhaq, ánhaq, díqa, ug ubán pa. (1 A 2)

1. Uy, ________ man diqáy si Mísis Abáya sa sála.
2. Si Mísis Mílir ________ gahígdaq sa higdaqánan.
3. ________ ba si Pírla gahápun?
4. ________ siyá karún sa Kárbun.
5. Sa miqáging tingqinít, si Místir Mílir ______________ sa Pulambatú mubakasyún, diq ba? (tingqinít 'hot season')
6. ________ ka ba manihápun gabíqi sa ámuq Mísis Abáya?
7. ___________ lang dirí, Mísis Abáya, sa ákung kwártu. ___________ ra ku ________ maghígdaq.
8. Liná, ________ ka ba sa siní gahápun sa hápun?
9. ________ ba kaháq ang mutsátsa sa kusína?
10. Ang ákung mga amígu ________ manihápun sa ámuq gabíqi.
11. Tinúqud bang____________ kas Pulambatú mubakasyún sa miqáging tingqinít?
12. Maqáyung búntag ________ Mísis Mílir.
13. Diq ba naq si Mísis Abáya ang ________ sa sála?
14. Uy, ________ man diqáy si Mísis Abáya sa sála.
15. Mahímuq bag ________ ka lang maniqúdtu?
16. Tinúqud bang ________ si Huwán run sa tindáhan?
17. Uy Liná, ________ na ba ang dúktur? 'Has the doctor come yet?'
18. Ánhaq ka ba lang ________ sa sála?
19. Uu, ________ lang úsaq ku _____________ kay magqistúrya pa ming Místir Mílir.

20. Waq bay sílhig ________ sa ímung kwártu?

21. Ang sîlhig ________ sa sála.

22. Ug magkîtaq mu ni Huwán îngnang __________ ku sa pantalán únyang hápun.

23. ___________ ba ___________ si Mísis Abáya matúug sa átuq karúng gabîqi?

24. Dung, _________ lang _________ sa píkas kwártu pakatúlga si Mísis Abáya. (pakatúlga 'have her sleep')

25. Kahibáwu ka bang _________ si Lítu sa uspitál? Gabíqi siyá dádqa ________. 'He was brought there last night.'

PP-V Direct, local, and instrumental (10A) (Change of emphasis, beginning series)

Step I. (Direct passive, real and unreal with potentials: three elements)

a. 'He has written a story.'
b. 'It's a story that he has written.'

1.	a.	Nakasulát siyág istúrya.	(istúrya)
	b.	Istúrya îyang nasulát.	
2.	a.	Makasulát siyág istúrya.	(istúrya)
	b.	Istúrya îyang masulát.	
3.	a.	Makatawág siyág táwu.	(táwu)
	b.	Táwu îyang matawág.	
4.	a.	Nakatawág siyág táwu.	(táwu)
	b.	Táwu îyang natawág.	
5.	a.	Makaqádtu siyá sa siní.	(siní)
	b.	Siní îyang maqádtu.	
6.	a.	Nakaqádtu siyá sa siní.	(siní)
	b.	Siní îyang naqádtu.	
7.	a.	Makaputúl siyág káhuy.	(káhuy)
	b.	Káhuy îyang maputúl.	
8.	a.	Nakaputúl siyág káhuy.	(káhuy)
	b.	Káhuy îyang naputúl.	
9.	a.	Makakúhaq siyág ságing.	(ságing)
	b.	Ságing îyang makúhaq.	
10.	a.	Nakakúhaq siyág ságing.	(ságing)
	b.	Ságing îyang nakúhaq.	
11.	a.	Makasúbay siyás lînya.	(lînya)
	b.	Línya îyang masúbay.	
12.	a.	Nakasúbay siyás lînya.	(lînya)
	b.	Línya îyang nasúbay.	
13.	a.	Makasunúd siyás tartanîlya.	(tartanîlya)
	b.	Tartanîlya îyang masunúd.	

14. a. Nakasunúd siyás tartanílya. (tartanílya)
    b. Tartanílya íyang nasunúd.

15. a. Makadalá siyág sabún. (sabún)
    b. Sabún íyang madalá.

Step II. (Local passive, real and unreal in direct meaning: three elements)

'He rented a house.'

1. a. Miqábang siyág baláy. (baláy)
   b. Baláy íyang giqabángan.

2. a. Muqábang siyág baláy. (baláy)
   b. Baláy íyang abángan.

3. a. Nagqábang siyág baláy. (baláy)
   b. Baláy íyang giqabángan.

4. a. Magqábang siyág baláy. (baláy)
   b. Baláy íyang abángan.

5. a. Milíkuq siyás Burumíyu. (Burumíyu)
   b. Burumíyu íyang gilikúqan.

6. a. Mulíkuq siyás Burumíyu. (Burumíyu)
   b. Burumíyu íyang likúqan.

7. a. Mipuyúq siyás lasáng. (lasáng)
   b. Lasáng íyang gipúyqan.

8. a. Mupuyúq siyás lasáng. (lasáng)
   b. Lasáng íyang púyqan.

9. a. Nagpuyúq siyás lasáng. (lasáng)
   b. Lasáng íyang gipúyqan.

10. a. Magpuyúq siyás lasáng. (lasáng)
    b. Lasáng íyang púyqan.

11. a. Nagpasílung siyás tindáhan. (tindáhan)
    b. Tindáhan íyang gipasilúngan.

12. a. Mupasílung siyás tindáhan. (tindáhan)
    b. Tindáhan íyang pasilúngan.

13. a. Magpasílung siyás tindáhan. (tindáhan)
    b. Tindáhan íyang pasilúngan.

14. a. Nagpasílung siyás tindáhan. (tindáhan)
    b. Tindáhan íyang gipasilúngan.

15. a. Mikanáqug siyás hágdan. (hágdan)
    b. Hágdan íyang gikanaqúgan.

16. a. Mukanáqug siyás hágdan. (hágdan)
    b. Hágdan íyang kanaqúgan.

17. a. Milímpyu siyás kwártu. (kwártu)
    b. Kwártu íyang gilimpyuhán.

18. a. Mulímpyu siyás kwártu. (kwártu)
    b. Kwártu íyang limpyuhán.

19. a. Maglímpyu siyás kwártu. (kwártu)
    b. Kwártu íyang limpyuhán.

20. a. Naglímpyu siyás kwártu. (kwártu)
    b. Kwártu íyang gilimpyuhán.

Step III. (Direct passive, real and unreal direct meaning: three elements)

'He will write a story.'

1. a. Musulát siyág istúrya. (istúrya)
   b. Istúrya íyang sulatún.

2. a. Misulát siyág istúrya. (istúrya)
   b. Istúrya íyang gisulát.

3. a. Magsulát siyág istúrya. (istúrya)
   b. Istúrya íyang sulatún.

4. a. Nagsulát siyág istúrya. (istúrya)
   b. Istúrya íyang gisulát.

5. a. Mitawág siyág táwu. (táwu)
   b. Táwu íyang gitawág.

6. a. Mutawág siyág táwu. (táwu)
   b. Táwu íyang táwgun.

7. a. Magtawág siyág táwu. (táwu)
   b. Táwu íyang táwgun.

8. a. Nagtawág siyág táwu. (táwu)
   b. Táwu íyang gitawág.

9. a. Miqádtu siyás siní. (siní)
   b. Siní íyang giqádtu.

10. a. Muqádtu siyás siní. (siní)
    b. Siní íyang adtúqun.

11. a. Miputúl siyág káhuy. (káhuy)
    b. Káhuy íyang giputúl.

12. a. Muputúl siyág káhuy. (káhuy)
    b. Káhuy íyang pútlun.

13. a. Magputúl siyág káhuy. (káhuy)
    b. Káhuy íyang pútlun.

14. a. Nagputúl siyág káhuy. (káhuy)
    b. Káhuy íyang giputúl.

15. a. Mikúhaq siyág ságing. (ságing)
    b. Ságing íyang gikúhaq.

16. a. Mukúhaq siyág ságing. (ságing)
    b. Ságing íyang kuháqun.

17. a. Magkúhaq siyág ságing. (ságing)
    b. Ságing íyang kuháqun.

18. a. Nagkúhaq siyág ságing. (ságing)
    b. Ságing íyang gikúhaq.

19. a. Misúbay siyás línya. (línya)
    b. Línya íyang gisúbay.

20. a. Musúbay siyás línya. (línya)
    b. Línya íyang subáyun.

Step IV. (Local passive, real and unreal with potentials: three elements)

'He can rent a house.'

1. a. Makaqábang siyág baláy. (baláy)
   b. Baláy íyang {maqabángan / kaqabángan}.

2. a. Nakaqábang siyág baláy. (baláy)
   b. Baláy íyang naqabángan.

3. a. Nakalíkuq siyás Burumíyu. (Burumíyu)
   b. Burumíyu íyang nalikúqan.

4. a. Makalíkuq siyás Burumíyu. (Burumíyu)
   b. Burumíyu íyang {malikúqan / kalikúqan}.

5. a. Nakapuyúq siyás lasáng. (lasáng)
   b. Lasáng íyang napúyqan.

6. a. Makapuyúq siyás lasáng. (lasáng)
   b. Lasáng íyang {mapúyqan / kapúyqan}.

7. a. Makapasílung siyás tindáhan. (tindáhan)
   b. Tindáhan íyang {mapasilúngan / kapasilúngan}.

8. a. Nakapasílung siyás tindáhan. (tindáhan)
   b. Tindáhan íyang napasilúngan.

9. a. Makakanáqug siyás hágdan. (hágdan)
   b. Hágdan íyang {makanaqúgan / kakanaqúgan}.

10. a. Nakakanáqug siyás hágdan. (hágdan)
    b. Hágdan íyang nakanaqúgan.

11. a. Makalímpyu siyás kwártu. (kwártu)
    b. Kwártu íyang {malimpyúhan / kalimpyúhan}.

12. a. Nakalímpyu siyás kwártu. (kwártu)
    b. Kwártu íyang nalimpyúhan.

13. a. Makatrápu siyás lamísa. (lamísa)
    b. Lamísa íyang {matrapúhan / katrapúhan}.

14. a. Nakatrápu siyás lamísa. (lamísa)
    b. Lamísa íyang natrapúhan.

15. a. Makaqubán siyáng Pídru. (Pídru)
    b. Si Pídru íyang {maqubanán / kaqubanán}.

16. a. Nakaqubán siyáng Pídru. (Pídru)
    b. Si Pídru íyang naqubanán.

17. a. Makahúgas siyág pínggan. (pínggan)
    b. Pínggan íyang {mahugásan / kahugásan}.

18. a. Nakahúgas siyág pínggan. (pínggan)
    b. Pínggan íyang nahugásan.

19. a. Makaqádtu siyás siní. (siní)
    b. Siní íyang {maqadtúqan / kaqadtúqan}.

20. a. Nakaqádtu siyás siní. (siní)
    b. Siní íyang naqadtúqan.

Step V. (Instrumental passive in all meanings: three elements)

a. 'He reserved a cot.'
b. 'It was a cot he reserved.'

1. a. Mirisírba siyág tihíras. (tihíras)
   b. Tihíras íyang girisírba.

2. a. Murisírba siyág tihíras. (tihíras)
   b. Tihíras íyang irisírba.

3. a. Magrisírba siyág tihíras. (tihíras)
   b. Tihíras íyang irisírba.

4. a. Nagrisírba siyág tihíras. (tihíras)
   b. Tihíras íyang girisírba.

5. a. Makarisírba siyág tihíras. (tihíras)
   b. Tihíras íyang {ikarisírba / marisírba}.

6. a. Nakarisírba siyág tihíras. (tihíras)
   b. Tihíras íyang {gikarisírba / narisírba}.

7. a. Mupunúq siyág trayntaysíngku. (trayntaysíngku)
   b. Trayntaysíngku íyang ipunúq.

8. a. Mipunúq siyág trayntaysíngku. (trayntaysíngku)
   b. Trayntaysíngku íyang gipunúq.

9. a. Magpunúq siyág trayntaysíngku. (trayntaysíngku)
   b. Trayntaysíngku íyang ipunúq.

10. a. Nagpunúq siyág trayntaysíngku. (trayntaysíngku)
    b. Trayntaysíngku íyang gipunúq.

11. a. Nakapunúq siyág trayntaysíngku. (trayntaysíngku)
    b. Trayntaysíngku íyang {gikapunúq / napunúq}.

12. a. Makapunúq siyág trayntaysíngku. (trayntaysíngku)
    b. Trayntaysíngku íyang {ikapunúq / mapunúq}.

13. a. Mutáguq siyág kwárta. (kwárta)
    b. Kwárta íyang itáguq.

14. a. Nagtáguq siyág kwárta. (kwárta)
    b. Kwárta íyang gitáguq.

15. a. Mitáguq siyág kwárta. (kwárta)
    b. Kwárta íyang gitáguq.

16. a. Magtáguq siyág kwárta. (kwárta)
    b. Kwárta íyang itáguq.

17. a. Muhatúd siyág sinínaq. (sinínaq)
    b. Sinínaq íyang ihatúd.

18. a. Naghatúd siyág sinínaq. (sinínaq)
    b. Sinínaq íyang gihatúd.

19. a. Mihatúd siyág sinínaq. (sinínaq)
    b. Sinínaq íyang gihatúd.

20. a. Maghatúd siyág sinínaq. (sinínaq)
    b. Sinínaq íyang ihatúd.

Step VI. (Instrumental passive in all meanings: four elements)

'He will put (lit. fill) water into the bottle.'

1. a. Mupunúq siyág túbig sa butílya. (túbig)
   b. Túbig íyang ipunús butílya.

2. a. Nagpunúq siyág túbig sa butílya. (túbig)
   b. Túbig íyang gipunús butílya.

3. a. Mipunúq siyág túbig sa butílya. (túbig)
   b. Túbig íyang gipunús butílya.

4. a. Magpunúq siyág túbig sa butílya. (túbig)
   b. Túbig íyang ipunús butílya.

5. a. Mubutáng siyág líbrus lamísa. (líbru)
   b. Líbru íyang ibutáng sa lamísa.

6. a. Nagbutáng siyág líbrus lamísa. (líbru)
   b. Líbru íyang gibutáng sa lamísa.

7. a. Mibutáng siyág líbrus lamísa. (líbru)
   b. Líbru íyang gibutáng sa lamísa.

8. a. Magbutáng siyág líbrus lamísa. (líbru)
   b. Líbru íyang ibutáng sa lamísa.

9. a. Nagtáguq siyág pitákas kwártu. (pitáka)
   b. Pitáka íyang gitágus kwártu.

10. a. Mitáguq siyág pitákas kwártu. (pitáka)
    b. Pitáka íyang gitágus kwártu.

Step VIa. (Subject preposed: four elements)

'The man will answer the truth.'

1. a. Ang táwu mutubág sa tinúqud. (tinúqud)
   b. Tinúqud ang itubág sa táwu.

2. a. Ang táwu nagtubág sa tinúqud. (tinúqud)
   b. Tinúqud ang gitubág sa táwu.

3. a. Ang táwu mitubág sa tinúqud. (tinúqud)
   b. Tinúqud ang gitubág sa táwu.

4. a. Si Pídru mulábay ug batú. (batú)
   b. Batú ang ilábay ni Pídru.

5. a. Si Pídru naglábay ug batú. (batú)
   b. Batú ang gilábay ni Pídru.

6. a. Si Pídru milábay ug batú. (batú)
   b. Batú ang gilábay ni Pídru.

7. a. Si Pídru maglábay ug batú. (batú)
   b. Batú ang ilábay ni Pídru.

Step VII. (Direct passive with four elements)

'He will invite some ladies.'

1. a. Muqimbitár siyág mga babáyi. (mga babáyi)
   b. Mga babáyi íyang imbitahún.

2. a. Miqimbitár siyág mga babáyi. (mga babáyi)
   b. Mga babáyi íyang giqimbitár.

3. a. Magqimbitár siyág mga babáyi. (mga babáyi)
   b. Mga babáyi íyang imbitahún.

4. a. Nagqimbitár siyág mga babáyi. (mga babáyi)
   b. Mga babáyi íyang giqimbitár.

5. a. Makaqimbitár siyág mga babáyi. (mga babáyi)
   b. Mga babáyi íyang maqimbitár.

6. a. Nakaqimbitár siyág mga babáyi. (mga babáyi)
   b. Mga babáyi íyang naqimbitár.

7. a. Mudalá siyág gása párang Pídru. (gása)
   b. Gása íyang dádqun párang Pídru.

8. a. Midalá siyág gása párang Pídru. (gása)
   b. Gása íyang gidalá párang Pídru.

9. a. Magdalá siyág gása párang Pídru. (gása)
   b. Gása íyang dádqun párang Pídru.

10. a. Nagdalá siyág gása párang Pídru. (gása)
    b. Gása íyang gidalá párang Pídru.

11. a. Makadalá siyág gása párang Pídru. (gása)
    b. Gása íyang madalá párang Pídru.

12. a. Nakadalá siyág gása párang Pídru. (gása)
    b. Gása íyang nadalá párang Pídru.

13. a. Mutawág kug táksi párang Máma. (táksi)
    b. Táksi ákung táwgun párang Máma.

14. a. Mitawág kug táksi párang Máma. (táksi)
    b. Táksi ákung gitawág párang Máma.

15. a. Makatawág kug táksi párang Máma. (táksi)
    b. Táksi ákung matawág párang Máma.

Step VIII. (Local passive in all meanings, short agent: four elements)

'He will leave a shirt with Pedro.'

1. a. Mubílin siyág sinínaq ni Pídru. (si Pídru)
   b. Si Pídruy íyang bínlag sinínaq.

2. a. Mibílin siyág sinínaq ni Pídru. (si Pídru)
   b. Si Pídruy íyang gibínlag sinínaq.

3. a. Magbílin siyág sinínaq ni Pídru. (si Pídru)
   b. Si Pídruy íyang bínlag sinínaq.

4. a. Nagbílin siyág sinínaq ni Pídru. (si Pídru)
   b. Si Pídruy íyang gibínlag sinínaq.

5. a. Mutawág siyág tartanílya páras babáyi. (ang babáyi)
   b. Ang babáyiy íyang táwgag tartanílya.

6. a. Mitawág siyág tartanílya páras babáyi. (ang babáyi)
   b. Ang babáyiy íyang gitáwgag tartanílya.

7. a. Nagtawág siyág tartanílya páras babáyi. (ang babáyi)
   b. Ang babáyiy íyang gitáwgag tartanílya.

8. a. Magtawág siyág tartanílya páras babáyi. (ang babáyi)
   b. Ang babáyiy íyang táwgag tartanílya.

9. a. Nakatawág siyág tartanílya páras babáyi. (ang babáyi)
   b. Ang babáyiy íyang natáwgag tartanílya.

10. a. Makatawág siyág tartanílya pára sa babáyi. (ang babáyi)
    b. Ang babáyiy íyang {matáwgag / katáwgag} tartanílya.

11. a. Mutawág siyág tartanílya páras babáyi. (tartanílya)
    b. Tartanílyay íyang táwgun páras babáyi.

12. a. Mitawág siyág tartanílya páras babáyi. (tartanílya)
    b. Tartanílyay íyang gitawág páras babáyi.

13. a. Nagtawág siyág tartanílya páras babáyi. (tartanílya)
    b. Tartanílyay íyang gitawág páras babáyi.

14. a. Magtawág siyág tartanílya páras babáyi. (tartanílya)
    b. Tartanílyay íyang táwgun páras babáyi.

15. a. Nakatawág siyág tartanílya páras babáyi. (tartanílya)
    b. Tartanílyay íyang natawág páras babáyi.

16. a. Makatawág siyág tartanílya páras babáyi. (tartanílya)
    b. Tartanílyay íyang matawág páras babáyi.

Step IX. (Direct, local, and instrumental passives in all meanings)

a. 'I will sweep up the dust from the floor.'
b. 'Dust from the floor is what I am going to sweep.'

1. a. Musílhig kus abúg sa salúg. (abúg sa salúg)
   b. Abúg sa salúg ang ákung silhígun.

2. a. Misílhig kus abúg sa salúg. (abúg sa salúg)
   b. Abúg sa salúg ang ákung gisílhig.

3. a. Misílhig kus abúg sa salúg. (salúg)
   b. Salúg ang ákung gisilhígan sa abúg.

4. a. Musílhig kus abúg sa salúg. (salúg)
   b. Salúg ang ákung silhígan sa abúg.

5. a. Nakasílhig kus abúg sa salúg. (abúg sa salúg)
   b. Abúg sa salúg ang ákung nasílhig.

6. a. Magsílhig kus abúgs salúg. (salúg)
   b. Salúg ákung silhígan sa abúg.

7. a. Mulúkluk kug aríyus bag. (aríyus)
   b. Aríyus ákung ilúkluks bag.

8. a. Milúkluk kug aríyus bag. (aríyus)
   b. Aríyus ákung gilúkluks bag.

9. a. Mutúdluq siyág Binisayás Amirkánu. (Binisayáq)
   b. Binisayáq íyang itúdluq sa Amirkánu.

10. a. Mitúdluq siyág Binisayás Amirkánu. (Binisayáq)
    b. Binisayáq íyang gitúdluq sa Amirkánu.

11. a. Mutúdluq siyág Binisayás Amirkánu. (Amirkánu)
    b. Amirkánu íyang tudlúqag Binisayáq.

12. a. Mitúdluq siyág Binisayás Amirkánu. (Amirkánu)
    b. Amirkánu íyang gitudlúqag Binisayáq.

13. a. Mikawús siyág túbigs láta. (túbig)
    b. Túbig íyang gikawús láta.

14. a. Mukawús siyág túbigs láta. (túbig)
    b. Túbig íyang káwsuns láta.

15. a. Mukawús siyás látag túbig. (láta)
    b. Láta íyang káwsag túbig.

16. a. Mikawús siyás látag túbig. (láta)
    b. Láta íyang gikáwsag túbig.

17. a. Muhatúd siyág sinínas babáyi. (sinínaq)
    b. Sinínaq íyang ihatúds babáyi.

18. a. Mihatúd siyág sinínas babáyi. (sinínaq)
    b. Sinínaq íyang gihatúds babáyi.

19. a. Muhatúd siyás sinínas babáyi. (babáyi)
    b. Babáyi íyang hátdas sinínaq.

20. a. Maghatúd siyág sinínas babáyi. (sinínaq)
    b. Sinínaq íyang ihatúds babáyi.

21. a. Makakawús siyág túbigs láta. (túbig)
    b. Túbig íyang makawús láta.

22. a. Magkawús siyág túbigs láta. (túbig)
    b. Túbig íyang káwsuns láta.

23. a. Magkawús siyás látag túbig. (láta)
    b. Láta íyang káwsag túbig.

24. a. Nagkawús siyás látag túbig. (láta)
    b. Láta íyang gikáwsag túbig.

25. a. Nakakawús siyág túbigs láta. (túbig)
    b. Túbig íyang nakawús láta.

Step X. (Instrumental passive in all meanings)

'He will see the movie with my ticket.'

1. a. Mutánqaw siyág sinís ákung tíkit. (ákung tíkit)
   b. Ákung tíkit íyang itánqawg siní.

2. a. Mitánqaw siyág sinís ákung tíkit. (ákung tíkit)
   b. Ákung tíkit íyang gitánqawg siní.

3. a. Makatánqaw siyág sinís ákung tíkit. (ákung tíkit)
   b. Ákung tíkit íyang ikatánqawg siní.

4. a. Nakatánqaw siyág sinís ákung tíkit. (ákung tíkit)
   b. Ákung tíkit íyang gikatánqawg siní.

5. a. Mupatáy siyág bábuys ákung kutsílyu. (ákung kutsílyu)
   b. Ákung kutsílyu íyang ipatáyg bábuy.

6. a. Mipatáy siyág babúys ákung kutsílyu. (ákung kutsílyu)
   b. Ákung kutsílyu íyang gipatáyg bábuy.

7. a. Magpatáy siyág bábuys ákung kutsílyu. (ákung kutsílyu)
   b. Ákung kutsílyu íyang ipatáyg bábuy.

8. a. Nagpatáy siyág bábuys ákung kutsílyu. (ákung kutsílyu)
   b. Ákung kutsílyu íyang gipatáyg bábuy.

9. a. Makapatáy siyág bábuys ákung kutsílyu. (ákung kutsílyu)
   b. Ákung kutsílyu íyang ikapatáyg bábuy.

10. a. Nakapatáy siyág bábuys ákung kutsílyu. (ákung kutsílyu)
    b. Ákung kutsílyu íyang gikapatáyg bábuy.

11. a. Musúbay siyág línyas ákung lápis. (ákung lápis)
    b. Ákung lápis íyang isúbayg línya.

12. a. Misúbay siyág línyas ákung lápis. (ákung lápis)
    b. Ákung lápis íyang gisúbayg línya.

13. a. Magsúbay siyág línyas ákung lápis. (ákung lápis)
    b. Ákung lápis íyang isúbayg línya.

14. a. Nagsúbay siyág línyas ákung lápis. (ákung lápis)
    b. Ákung lápis íyang gisúbayg línya.

15. a. Makasúbay siyág línyas ákung lápis. (ákung lápis)
    b. Ákung lápis íyang ikasúbayg línya.

16. a. Nakasúbay siyág línyas ákung lápis. (ákung lápis)
    b. Ákung lápis íyang gikasúbayg línya.

17. a. Muqirís kus blákburd áning irísir. (kiníng irísir)
    b. Kiníng irísir ákung iqirís sa blákburd.

18. a. Miqirís kus blákburd áning irísir. (kiníng irísir)
    b. Kiníng irísir ákung giqirís sa blákburd.

19. a. Makaqirís kus blákburd áning irísir. (kiníng irísir)
    b. Kiníng irísir ákung ikaqirís sa blákburd.

20. a. Nakaqirís kus blákburd áning irísir. (kiníng irísir)
    b. Kiníng irísir ákung gikaqirís sa blákburd.

21. a. Mulímpyu siyás ákung sílhig dínhi. (ákung sílhig)
    b. Ákung sílhig íyang ilímpyu dínhi.

22. a. Milímpyu siyás ákung sílhig dínhi. (ákung sílhig)
    b. Ákung sílhig íyang gilímpyu dínhi.

23. a. Maglímpyu siyás ákung sílhig dínhi. (ákung sílhig)
    b. Ákung sílhig íyang ilímpyu dínhi.

24. a. Naglímpyu siyás ákung sílhig dínhi. (ákung sílhig)
    b. Ákung sílhig íyang gilímpyu dínhi.

25. a. Makalímpyu siyás ákung sílhig dínhi. (ákung sílhig)
    b. Ákung sílhig íyang ikalímpyu dínhi.

II. Ibutáng sa lunáq ang túkmang púrmas mga bírbung anáqas sulúd sa parentheses. (4 B, 5 C, 6 A, 8 A, 10 A and their subsections.)

1. Si Pírla ang (lútuq) sa mga kaság gabíqi.
   'It was Perla who cooked the crabs last night.'

2. (Lútuq) mu ba ang Amirkánug pagkáqun?
   'Will you cook some food for the American?'

3. Waláq pa (lútuq) ang súdqan.
   'The dish has not been cooked yet.'

4. (Lútuq) na ba siyá sa kinhasún?
   'Is she cooking the sea shells now?'

5. (Lútuq) na níya ang kánqun pára karúng údtu.
   'She has already cooked the grits for this noon.'

6. (Lútuq) ra gud ku palíhug ug ítlug.
   'Will you please cook an egg for me?'

7. (Súlti) ba nímu siyá sa nahitabúq nákuq gahápun?
   'Have you told him about what happened to me yesterday?'

8. Humán na ba siyá (súlti) nímu?
   'Have you told him yet?'

9. Ámbut lang ug (súlti) na ba níya si Mis Sántus.
   'I am not sure if he has already told Miss Santos.'

10. Ug diq ka (súlti) sa tinúqud mulakáw ku.
    'If you don't tell the truth, I will go away.'

11. Liná, ímu na bang (sílhig) ang sála?
    'Have you swept the living room yet, Lena?'

12. Akú ang (sílhig) sa kusína ganínang búntag.
    'I was the one who swept the kitchen this morning.'

13. (Sílhig) ra gud ku palíhug sa hagdanán.
    'Please do me a favor and sweep the stairs.'

14. (Sílhig) ka u díliq?
    'Are you going to sweep or aren't you?'

15. Ang sabáw (hígup) ni Dyiin.
    'Jane ate the soup.'

16. Páspas kaqáyu siyáng (hígup) ug sabáw. (páspas 'fast')
    'She eats soup very fast.'

17. Gilamiqán si Dyiin nga (hígup) sa sabáw.
    'The soup tasted good to Jane while she was eating it.'

18. Ang masakitún (pahígup) níla ug maqínit nga sabáw.
    'They had the sick person eat hot soup.'

19. (Panágan) mu mga bátaq.
    'Run, children!'

20. (Dágan) silás pagqabút sa ílang maqístra.
    'They ran away when their teacher got there.'

21. (Dágan) ta, ha?
    'Let's run, shall we?'

22. Kinahánglan makamaqú kang (dágan) arún mudaqúg kitá.
    'You have to know how to run so that we can win.'

23. Litú, (lábay) ni Mam ang búla.
    'Lito, throw the ball to the teacher.'

24. Gisáwuq sa bátaq ang (lábay) kung búla.
    'The child caught the ball I threw.'

25. Díliq gyud siyá mapíldi kay maqáyu man siyáng (lábay) sa búla.
    'He won't lose for sure because he throws the ball well.'

26. Plurá, (límpyu)g maqáyu ning átung baláy ha?
    'Flora, clean the house well, will you?'

27. Ngánung waq man nímu ni ayúhag (lîmpyu)?
'Why didn't you do a good job cleaning this?'

28. Tábang mug (panlîmpyu) sa átung baláy mga bátaq.
'Children, help clean up our house.'

29. Kinahánglan kaqáyu nga (lîmpyu) ang tanáng suqúk sa átung baláy.
'It is absolutely necessary that every corner of our house be cleaned.'

30. (Límpyu) úsaq nang mga kaság úsaq nímu lutúqa.
'Clean these crabs before you cook them.'

III A. Pilíqa ang hústung púrma sa bírbung anáqa sa sulúd sa parentheses. (12 C)

Pananglîtan:

a. Miqingún siyá nga (ipahátag, pahatágun) kunú ni nímu kang Mis Kihúti.

Tubág: Miqingún siyá nga ipahátag kunú ni nímu kang Mis Kihúti.

b. Palitún ku nang tanán Yaq, básta ímu kung (ipahángyuq, pahangyúqun).

Tubág: Palitún ku nang tanán Yaq, básta ímu kung pahangyúqun.

1. Kun diq ka muqabút (ipaqádtu, paqadtúqun) man ka nákuq sa ínyu. 'If you don't come, I'll have someone go after you at your place.'

2. Ngánu gung ímu man kung (pahatágun, ipahátag) ug labáws singkwînta?

3. Nyurá, (pahatágun, ipahátag) kunú ning támbal nímu páras labád sa ímung úlu.

4. Uy, Liná, (padádqun, ipadalá) kunú kag usá ka básung túbig ni Mísis Mîlir ngádtus íyang kwártu.

5. Pidrú, íngna si Lína nga (pakantáhun, ipakánta) ku siyá. (kánta 'sing')

6. Uy, Pidrú, (ipatawág, patáwgun) ra gud si Lína. 'Pedro, have someone call Lena.'

7. Liná, ngánung (pabakúrun, ipabákud) pa man ku nímu úsaq ka mudúqul.

8. Kuqán man gud Nyurá, kanáng (pabugnáwun, ipabúgnaw) pa man úntaq nákuq ning túbig kay ínit pa man kaqayu.

9. (Ipahíkay, Pahikáyun) ug dalíq ang átung paniqúdtu kay muqabút na tu run si Ártur.

10. Liná, (ipatánqaw, patanqáwa) ra kang Pídru ang íyang ági. Mu ra gyud ug waq silhígi.

11. Halá, (pasilhígi, pasilhíga) nang iskináha pagqusáb.

12. Pidrú, (palimpyúhun, ipalímpyu) kunú ka pagqusáb kay waq kunú nímu ayúha pagsílhig ang baay.

13. (Ipalîmpyu, Palimpyúhi) dáyun nang mga plátu kay údtu na. 'Have someone clean the dishes because it is late.'

14. Díliq ba diqáy ku nímu (pahumanún, ipahumán) úsaq sa pagpang-lîmpyu?

15. (Padaliqún, Ipadalíq) kunú ka Lindá, kay miqabút na si Místir Mílir.

16. Únsa na, Dyiin, (ipadalá, padádqun) ba ka nákuq sa uspitál? 'How about it, Jane, shall I have someone take you to the hospital?'

17. (Ipaqádtu, Paqadtúqun) lang ang gása sa ka Mísis Abáya.

18. Uu, sigí. Ákuq lang (paqanhíqun, ipaqánhi) ang líbru.

19. Dyiin, (ipalútuq, palutúqun) ku bag ispisyál nga pagkáqun si Lína pára nímu?

20. Aa, (paqímnun, ipaqinúm) lang úsaq ka nákug ínit túbig arún ka paníngtun.

21. Saq pa, kay ákung (pakuháqun, ipakúhaq) ang tírmus. (tírmus 'thermos bottle')

22. Nyur, ákuq bang (ipasaká, pasákqun) si Mísis Abáya?

23. Misís, (palingkúrun, ipalíngkud) saq kunú ka dínhis sála.

24. (Pahigdáqun, Ipahígdaq) lang kunú ka Nyurá.

25. (Ipadáyun, Padayúnun) ba nátuq sa kwártu si Mísis Abáya, Dyiin?

III B. Gamíta ang musunúd sa mga púlung sa mga túdling púlung:

nagquwán	pahíri	higúpun
ihatúd	panglíngkud	manglíngkud
dublíhun	inigkahumán	maghigdaqhígdaq
gikasabútan	kahibáwu	gipatánqaw
mubáyad	magqistúrya	biyáqan
manánghid	nagbánhaq	nahabilín
makabalík	dádqi	makahíkay
makakuqán	gatawág	magaduqawdúqaw
sultíhan	tagáqi	gisúguq
makaqánhi	tanqáwun	muqádtu
pagtanqawtánqaw	ayúha	naghatudhátud
nagtúgun	naqabút	naghígdaq
magkinahánglan	nagsakít	magsakít
makapanghátag	gibisitáqan	manggáwas
nakaqánhi		

IV. Pilíqa ang hústung tubág sa púlung nga náqas sulúd sa parentheses. (I B, 1 C, 3 A 3, 3 B, 5 A 1, 5 D, 6 B, 6 C, 8 C, 9 B 2)

1. Taná, mangádtu (ta, mi)s Pulambatú.

2. Maqáyu dídtus Pulambatú kay mahigaláqun kaqáyu (ang, sa) mga táwu. (mahigaláqun 'friendly')

3. Diq ba nakaqádtu na man (ka, nímu)g kaqusá?

4. Uu bítaw, pirú dúgay na (ku, nákuq)ng waq makabalík ngádtu.

5. Mahímuq na (nímu, ka)ng lutúqun (ang, sa) ságing.

6. Miqingún ra ba tu (si, ang) Pírla nga mukúyug (níya, siyá) kun mangádtu tas Pulambatú.

7. Sigí, sultíhi (siyá, níya) nga mugíkan (kitá, nátuq) inigkahumán (nátuq, kitá)g paniqúdtu.
8. Únsang tráka (ang, sa) sákyan (nátuq, kitá)?
9. Aa, kanáq lang mulárgag alá úna (ang, sa) átung sákyan.
10. Mupaqúliq na ku kay (ákuq, akú) pa ra bang sultíhan (si, ni) Pírla nga manglákaw ta.
11. Uu, sigí. Paqúliq na, arún makaqándam (mu, ka)ng duhá sa (ímu, ínyu)ng dadqunún.
12. Pirlá, mudayún (ka, nímu) bag kúyug (nátuq, námuq) sa Pulambatú?
13. Kun mukúyug (nímu, ka), pamutús na. (pamutús 'pack your bags')
14. Ayáw bayáq pagdugaydúgay, ha, arún (ta, nátuq) makasakáy dáyun.
15. Únsa may (ákuq, akú)ng dádqun Lin?
16. (Ikáw, Nímu) lay magqíguq kun únsay ímung panádqun.
17. Kahínayng mulakáw (si, ni) Dyiin!
18. Ámbi naq, kay (ákuq, akú) nang iqapíl pagdáa. (iqapíl 'include')
19. Taná, (ámuq, átuq)ng hapitún (si, ni) Mis Sántus. (hapitún 'person stopped by for')
20. Maqáyu kay sayú (nínyu, mu)ng miqánhi.
21. Kaníndut (nímu, ka)ng mulútuq uy!
22. (Silá, Níla) man gud si Nánay ang naghíkay sa paniqúdtu maqúng dalíq ra (mi, námuq)ng nakakaqún.
23. (Íla, Silá) pa man gániq ming gipadádqag makáqun sa traak.
24. Pagkaqáyu (silá, níla) nu?
25. Maqáyu bítaw kaqáyu (silá, níla) námuq.

V. Gámqang negative ang musunúd nga mga túdling púlung. (2B, 3C3a, 6A3c, 6B3, 12G3)

1. Gibisitáhan ra ba si Mísis Kapangpángan ni Místir ug Mísis Mílir.
2. Nakadungúg mi nga masakitún ka.
3. Risís na gyud diqáy kay nanggáwas na man ang mga bátaq.
4. Si Kíkuy gyud lagí ang milábayg batú ni Lítu. (batú 'stone')
5. Ákuq lang diqáyng hulatún si Píya.
6. Dayún lang kay makigkítaq man kaháq mung Lítu.
7. Maniqúdtu saq diqáy túqud ta pagqúna, Mísis Abayá.
8. Gústu pa gyung mudúlaq ang mga bátaq.
9. Masakitún pa man kaqáyu si Pídru.
10. Si Mis Sántus nagsúlti nga silhígan sad kunú nímu ang kwártu. 'Miss Santos says that you should sweep the room too.'

11. Miqagí ba kaháq si Lítu ni Kíkuy? 'Didn't Lito come by for Kikoy?'
12. Musakáy lang túqud tag tartanílya arún dalíq ra tang muqabút sa Burumíyu.
13. Búgnaw na kaqáyu ang sabáw apán gústu pa gyud gihápung muhígup si Lítu.
14. Gipadúlaq na kunú ni Píya ang mga bátaq.
15. Musakáy na lang tag tartanílya kay nagqulán na man sab.
16. Kumústa diqáy si Kíkuy, naqáyu na ba?
17. Maniqúdtu na ba lang ta, Misís Abáya?
18. Naglútuq pa si Píya sa átung paniqúdtu.
19. Ákuq ba lang kaháng ibílin kiníng mga pínggan?
20. Kikúy, itawág na lang kug tartanílya.
21. Mihígdaq na lang gyud si Píya kay gihilántan man siyág maqáyu.
22. Miqádtu na man sad diqáy si Pídru ni Mis Sántus.
23. Giqáyu gyud diqáy kaqáyu pagtagád si Mis Sántus ni Mam.
24. Nagtuqún pa man gud ku pagqánhi nílang Mam ug Lítu.
25. Nahibalú na bayáq diqáy si Mis Sántus nga si Kíkuy nangíhiq na sad sa kwártu.

VI. Ibutáng ang hústung púrma sa agent ug recipient. (6 D, 9 A)

		Recipient	Agent
1.	Sultíhan lang ________ ________ ug diq ku makaqánhi úgmaq.	you (sing.)	I
2.	Diq saq ________ mutábang ________g bántay áning tindahan kay labád kaqáyu ang ákung úlu.	you (sing.)	I
3.	Maqáyu man gung mutúdluq ________ ________ sa Sinibwanú.	me	babáyi
4.	Girisirbahán ________g tihíras ________.	Mis Wílbi	he
5.	Ayg kabaláka kay tágdun ________ ________ pagqáyu.	you	I
6.	Kwátru singkwínta ray ________ng ihátag ________.	you (sing.)	I
7.	Mipalít ________ ________g dúlsi gahápun.	me	she
8.	________ ra kunú ang mudalá ________.	ímung bag	he

		Recipient	Agent
9.	Magsuwát gyud ________ ________ dáyun inigqabút nákus Úrmuk.	you (plural)	I
10.	Tagáqan ________ ________g líbru kun mudakuqdakúq na ning ámung tindáhan.	you (sing.)	I
11.	Mupalít ________ ________.	ímung kalamáy	I
12.	Díliq ________ mubáyad ________g mas dakús kasagárang prísyu.	you (sing.)	I
13.	Adúnay ________ng misúgat ________.	you (plural)	táwu
14.	Giqánhi gyud ________ ________ arún pagkúhaq nímu.	you (sing.)	I
15.	Manakáy lang ________ ________.	táksi	we (incl.)
16.	Gidádqag sabáw ________ ________.	Mísis Abáya	Mísis Mílir
17.	Waq ________ bantayíg maqáyu ________.	tindáhan	she
18.	Ihatúd ________ ________ sa Burumíyu.	Mis Wílbi	he
19.	Gipagawás ________ ________ kay risís na man.	mga bátaq	she
20.	Nasákpan ________ ________ kay waq man siyá mutáguq dáyun.	Lítu	abát
21.	Gipápas ________ ________	blákburd	Ánghil
22.	Gitagáqan ________ ________g usá ka básung túbig.	Dyiin	she
23.	Waq dáyun mudúqul ________ ________.	Mísis Mílir	Lína
24.	Giqubanán ________ ________ sa Pulambatú.	Lína	she
25.	Gibisitáqan ________ ________ ganína.	them	Mísis Abáya

VII. Ibutáng and hústung púrma sa bírbu nga anáqa sa sulúd sa parentheses. (11 A, 11 B and their subsections)

Pananglítan: (Kalimút) na ku niqádtung hitabúqa kay dúgay na man tu.
Tubág: Nalímut na ku niqádtung hitabúqa kay dúgay na man tu.

1. (Pangabút) na diqáy ang átung bisíta gíkan sa Úrmuk.
   'So our visitors from Ormoc have already gotten here.'

2. Maqáyu si Tátay (panglútuq)g kaság.
   'Father cooks crabs well.'

3. (Panglíngkud) mi sa sílya sa diháng miqabút silá si Mísis Abáya.
'We were sitting on the chairs when the Abayas got there.'

4. (Kabúhiq) mi sa paníndag kalamáy káda ádlaw.
'We make our living by selling kalamay every day.

5. Waláq gyud mi (kahibalú) nga gihilántan si Dyiin.
'We really didn't know that Jane had a fever.'

6. (Panganáqug) na rung taqudtaqúd ang mga pasahíru kay búntag na man.
(rung taqudtaqúd 'in a little bit')
'The passengers will be getting off in a few minutes because it's morning.'

7. (Panakít) ba ang ímung kamút?
'Do your hands hurt?'

8. (Panglákaw) na mis Mísis kay údtu na.
'My wife and I are going now, because it's already noon.'

9. Ngánung (kabaláka) ka man nákuq nga maqáyu na man ku?
'Why are you worried about me when I'm well again?'

10. Ayáw nig gamítang trapúha kun (pamáhid) ka sa kamút.
'Don't use this rag when you wipe your hands.'

11. (Panánghid) na ming Mísis Mílir nga (pangulíq) na mi.
'We have already asked Mrs. Miller's permission to go home.'

12. (Kahumán) na ba mug dúlaq, mga bátaq?
'Have you finished playing yet, children?'

13. Taná Dung (panghígdaq) na ta kay gabíqi na.
'Come on, Boy, let's go to bed now, for it's getting late.'

14. Si Mísis Abáya (pangumústa) nímu Dyiin.
'Mrs. Abaya sends her regards to you, Jane.'

15. (Panghináqut) ming maqáyu ka dáyun Dyiin.
'We hope that you get well soon, Jane.'

16. Kamú bay (panglútuq) íning kalamáy Dung?
'Were you the ones who cooked this kalamay, Boy?'

17. Dínhi tu si Mísis Mílir (pangítaq) nímu.
'Mrs. Miller was here looking for you.'

18. (Pamúhat) ba sab mug káwuq Nuy?
'Do you also make hats, Sir?'

19. (Kadúgay) mi sa ílang Mísis Ulibár kay nagqistúrya pa mi.
'We stayed late at Mrs. Olivar's because we were telling stories.'

20. Day, mahímu bang (pangutána)?
'May I ask a question, Miss?'

21. Waláq ba (panglímbung) ang bátang gipalitán mug kalamáy?
'Didn't the boy whom you bought kalamay from cheat you?'

22. (Kalúquy) mi níya kay dághan siyág mga bátaq.
'We feel sorry for her because she has many children.'

23. Kinahánglang (pangîhiq) na mu mga bátaq kay humán na ang risís.
'You should go to the bathroom now, children, because recess is over now.'

24. Hígup na Dyiin kay (kabúgnaw) na ring sabáws manúk.

25. Diq ka ba run (paníĺhig) Liná?

VIII. Ibutáng ang hústung púrma sa imperative sa mga bírbung anáqa sa sulúd sa parentheses. (11 C and subsections)

1. (Sílhig) únyaq ning mga kwártu dínhis baláy.
'Sweep the rooms here in the house later.'

2. (Ádtu) mus Pulambatú.
'You go to Pulambato.'

3. (Pangíhiq) na mu, mga bátaq.
'Go to the bathroom now, children.'

4. (Balígyaq) ning mga líbru dídtus atung tindáhan.
'Sell these books in our store.'

5. (Kanáqug) na lang dínhi Day kay kútub ra man mi dínhi.
'Just get off here, Miss, because we don't go any farther.'

6. (Panulúd) na mus átung kwártu.
'Get in the room now.'

7. (Hígup) nang sabáws manúk míntras ínit pa Dyiin.
'Eat that chicken soup while it's hot, Jane.'

8. (Pangutána) ang táwu kun pára Úrmuk ba ning barkúha.
'Ask the man if this boat is for Ormoc.'

9. (Risírba) si Mis Wílbi ug tihíras sa bárku Dung.
'Boy, reserve a cot on the boat for Miss Wilby.'

10. (Hátag) nang sabáws manúk ngádtung Dyiin.
'Give that chicken soup to Jane.'

11. (Pakalíguq) nang mga bátaq Day.
'Give those children a bath, child.'

12. (Tagád) naq silág maqáyu ha?
'Take good care of them, will you?'

13. (Kúyug) nákuq ngádtus Pulambatú.
'Come to Pulambato with me.'

14. (Súlti) únyaq ku kun diq ka na mutábang kanákuq.
'Tell me later if you aren't going to help me any more.'

15. (Padayún) silá Day.
'Let them come in, Miss.'

16. (Panglíngkud) únaq mung Mis Wílbi Pirlá.
'You and Miss Wilby sit down for a moment, Perla.'

17. (Paqánhi) na lang únyaq silá.
'Have them come later.'

18. (Panginúm) úsaq mu, úsaq nátuq súgdi ang átung klási.
'Take a drink before we start our class.'.

19. (Dalá) siyá sa uspitál karún dáyun.
'Take him to the hospital right away.'

20. (Tánqaw) kunú kun límpyu na ba ang íyang sinilhigán.
'Look to see if what she swept is clean now.'

21. (Tubág) dáyun ang mutawág kanímu.
'Answer whoever calls you at once.'

22. (Irís) ang blákburd Litú.
'Clean the blackboard, Lito.'

23. (Pahibalú) únyaq mi kun mulakáw ka na.
'Let us know when you'll be going.'

24. (Dúbli) ang ímung plíti kay ihatúd ku ikáw.
'Pay double fare and I will take you.'

25. Ayáw (límbung) ang ímung mamamálit.
'Don't cheat your customers.'

IX. Ibutáng ang hústung púrma sa únsa. (12B)

1. ________ man naq si Pírla nímu Dung?
'What did you do to Perla, Boy?'

2. Waláq naq siyá nákuq ________.

3. Bísag ________ nímug túdluq si Lítu diq gyung kamaqú.

4. ________ ka man sa Pulambatú Plurá?
'What were you doing in Pulambato, Flora?'

5. ________ man Mam pagbúhat ni Núwa ang árka?

6. Nakahibalú ka bag ________ nímu paglútuq ning kaság Day?

7. ________ man si Dyiin, gihilántan ba?

8. Díliq ni ________ng sabáws manúk sa ímung hilánat. Maqáyu ni.
'This soup will not affect your fever.'

9. ________ tu nímu paglútung manúk Misís nga lamíq man?

10. ________ man ning sabún nímu Plurá? Ímu bang dádqun sa Pulambatú?

11. Ímna lang ning lítsi. Diq lagí ka ________.

12. ________ pa gud si Mísis Ulibár nga diq pa man muqulíq run?

13. ________ mu Litú? Magdúlaq mu?

14. ________ kaháq si Tátay sa basakán nga dúgay mang nakaqulíq?
'What could Dad be doing . . . ?'

15. ________ man nátuq pagdúlaq nang síndul pándul Mam?

16. ________ ba ning mga tartanílya nga diq man ku ihatúd sa Burumíyu?
'What is the matter with these rigs . . . ?'

17. Díliq tingáli ku ________ bísag magpaqulán ku. (magpaqulán 'walk in the rain')
18. ________ man nímu pagqabút dínhi sa ámuq Misís Abáya?
19. ________ man ta sa ka Mísis Mílir Ma?
20. Díliq ka úntaq mahádluk ádtung irúqa. Diq man gud tu ________.
21. ________ gud tung dráybir nga waláq man mutagád nákuq?
22. Waláq gyud núqun ku ________ sa ákung pagsakáy gíkan sa Pulambatú.
23. ________ na gud ka nga waq na man ka mubisíta sa ámuq?
24. Kiníng batáqa ________ man ni nímu Day?
'What did you do to him?'
25. Ngánung midágan ka man gud? Díliq siyá ________ nímu.

X. Hubára ang musunúd nga mga túdling púlung sa Sinibwanú ginámit ang pa ug na. (12 G)

1. I'm going now.
2. Oh! There's no more beer, Sir.
3. Excuse me, when will you move in?
4. Oh, we are already here.
5. I won't get off the boat before it's light.
6. I won't get off the boat while it's still dark.
7. What other things should we bring?
8. Oh, never mind.
9. Come on. We might as well go to the bus station now.
10. He's still in San Remigio.
11. All right, run along now.
12. It's still raining.
13. Have you stayed here long?
14. Not very long yet.
15. If the fare is twenty cents, it's better to walk.
16. Excuse me, don't you need another helper in your store?
17. No, I don't. One helper is enough.
18. I'd better be going for the others.
19. Have you finished yet?
20. Come on, hide again.

XI. Ibutáng ang hústung púrma sa pronoun ug particle ug sa bírbu nga anáqa sa parentheses ginámit ang actives u passives. (4 B, 5 C, 6 A, 8 A, 10 A, 13 A, and their subsections)

1. Kiníng librúha ang (bílin) (níya, siyá) sa tindáhan gahápun.
   'This was the book he left in the store yesterday.'
2. Maqú ba kanáng mga kaságang ímung (dalá) nákuq?
   'Are those the crabs you brought for me?'
3. Si Mísis Abáya ang (ánhi) dínhi úgmaq.
   'Mrs. Abaya is the one coming here tomorrow.'
4. Kiníng iskináha (sílhig) úntaq ug maqáyu.
   'This corner should have been swept well.'
5. Kínsa may (hatúd) ug ínit nga sabáw?
   'Who brought the hot soup?
6. Si Nánay ganína rang (bákud) waláq pa gániq mabúntag.
   'Mama got up long ago, even before it was morning.'
7. Si Dyiin ang (bisíta) níla gahápun.
   'Jane was the one they visited yesterday.'
8. Waláq siyáng kadungúg sa (súlti) (si, ni) Mísis Mílir.
   'He did not hear what Mrs. Miller said.'
9. Ikáw Anghíl ang (irís) sa blákburd karún.
   'Angel, it is your turn to clean the blackboard now.'
10. Kamí si Lítu (piik) na.
    'Lito and I had already "picked" [played the game hammer, scissors, paper].'
11. Kanáng tartanílya bay (tawág) (ka, mu) Mis?
    'Is that the rig you called, Miss?'
12. Kiní lang tubíga ang (húgas). Límpyu man ni.
    'Just use this water for washing. It's clean.'
13. Si Nánay ang (lútuq) áning mga kaság ganíhang búntag.
    'Mother was the one who cooked these crabs this morning.'
14. Únsa may (dúlaq) nínyu mga bátaq sa risís?
    'What did you play during recess, children?'
15. Waq siyáy (dakúp) kay hínay kaqáyu siyáng (dágan).
    'He was not able to catch anybody because he runs very slowly.'
16. Ikáw ba Kikúy ang (líbri) námuq?
    'Kikoy, are you the one who is going to free us?'
17. Únsa man tung (súlti) (ni, si) Mísis Abáya nímu Dyiin?
    'What was it that Mrs. Abaya told you, Jane?'
18. Ang báhin ni Núwa ang (istúrya) sa maqístra.
    'The teacher will tell about Noah now.'
19. Ug way (ítsa) sa láta díliq mi manágan.
    'If nobody throws the can, we will not hide.'

20. Díliq ku (dayún) ug ádtu sa Burumíyu kay ulán.
'I'm not going on to Borromeo because it's raining.'

21. Mulakáw si Dyiin ug way (bisíta) níya úgmaq.
'Jane will go out if nobody visits her tomorrow.'

22. Únsa may (trápu) nímu sa lamísa Liná?
'What did you wipe the table with, Lena?'

23. Únsa guy ínyung (dalíq) nga waq pa man ang traak sa istasyunán?
'What are you hurrying for, when the bus is not at the station yet?'

24. Way (pamínaw) sa íyang istúrya.
'Nobody listened to his story.'

25. Kínsa man tung (ánhi) dínhi gabíqi, si Mísis Mílir ba?

XII. Review of the passives. (4 B, 5 C, 6 A, 8 A, 10 A, 13 A, and their sub-subsections)

Pananglítan: (Dalá) (akú, nákuq) dirí (ug, ang) túbig.
Tubág: Dádqi ku dirig túbig.

1. Liná, (kúhaq) ngádtu (ug, ang) támbal páras labád sa ákung úlu.
2. (Dalá) sab ngarí (ug, ang) inít nga túbig.
3. (Sulúd) sa básu (ang, sa) túbig kay (inúm) (nákuq, akú).
4. Kumústa (ka, nímu), Dyiin. Waq (mu, ka) na ba (lisúd) sa paginháwa? (paginháwa 'breathe')
5. Waq (nímu, ka) na ba (labád) sa úlu?
6. Diq na kaqáyu labád apán (lisúd) gihápun akú sa paginháwa.
7. Únsa man tung (dalá) (nímu, ka) diháq Prid?
8. Nyurá, níqa nay (dalá) (nákuq, akú)ng túbig ug támbal.
9. (Butáng) lang (ánaq, naq) dirí (ang, sa) lamísa.
10. (Bíyaq) ka na lang (námuq, nátuq) diháq.
11. (Pangáqun) na ba (mu, nínyu)?
12. Uu, (butáng) lang (ug, ang) pagkáqun (ang, sa) lamísa kay (ádtu) na mi run.
13. Uná lang ngádtu, Prid, kay (ákuq, akú) pa ning (inúm).
14. Lulíng, (áyu) ra ku (karí, ári)ng higdaqánan.
15. Nyurá, túqa (silá, níla)ng Mísis Abáya sa gawás; (tawág) ka.
16. (Padayún) lang (níla, silá) Liná.
17. Aníqay (dalá) (nákuq, akú)ng sabáw sa manúk pára kang Dyiin.
18. (Palíngkud) úsaq (si, ni) Mísis Abáya, Liná.
19. Úsaq pa, kay (paqari) (nákuq, akú) (si, ni) Dyiin.
20. Dyiin, (bisíta) (ka, nímu) (si, ni) Mísis Abáya.

21. (Dalá) (ka, nímu) sab niyág ínit nga sabáw.

22. (Paqánhi) lang (siyá, níya) sa sulúd sa kwártu.

23. (Pasulúd) na (nákuq, akú) (si, ni) Mísis Abáya, ha?

24. Dyiin, níqay ínit nga sabáw sa manúk nga (lútuq) (nákuq, akú) pára nímu.

25. Sus, ikáw pa man gyud (ang, sa) (pangunáy) sa paghatúd (niqánaq, kanáq).

XIII. Ibutáng ang púlung u mga púlung nga náqas sulúd sa parentheses sa hústung lugár diháq sa túdling púlung. (3 C 3)

Panangltan:	a.	Waq silá dínhi.	(ra ba)
Tubág:		Waq ra ba silá dínhi.	
	b.	Díliq ku magdúgay kay údtu na.	(na lang, man gud)
Tubág:		Díliq na lang ku magdúgay kay údtu na man gud.	

1.	Ngánung waq ku nímu sultíhi nga mibisíta dínhi silá si Místir ug Mísis Mílir?	(man, diqáy)
2.	Masakitún si Mísis Kapangpángan?	(ba diqáy)
3.	Uu. Grábi ang íyang sakít.	(ra ba kunú)
4.	Únyaq, díliq nátuq siyá duqáwun?	(ba lang)
5.	Taná, únsay átung gidugáyan?	(pa man)
6.	Tingáli bayág atrasáwu ta.	(na)
7.	Maqú niy ílang baláy?	(na ba)
8.	Uu, maqú ning baláya.	(na diqáy)
9.	Átung súdluns Mísis Kapangpángan.	(ba lang kaháq)
10.	Níqay ámung daa pára nímu.	(ra ba)
11.	Dághang salámat kanínyu.	(kaqáyu)
12.	Ngánung naghaguqhagúq mug daa niqíni?	(pa man gyud)
13.	Kumústa ang ímung sakít karún?	(na man)
14.	Waq ku maqáyu.	(pa gyud)
15.	Kumústa ang mga bátaq?	(sab diqáy)
16.	Malisúd ning magdaqutdáqut ta.	(lagí)
17.	Waq matagád ang mga bátaq.	(na gyud)
18.	Waq gániq silá makakaqún sukád sa búntag.	(pa man)
19.	Gústu nílang akúy mupakáqun kanila.	(man gud, pa)
20.	Díliq silá mangáqun kun láqing táwu ang mupakáqun.	(ra ba gyud)

XIV Ibutáng ang hústung expression of manner sáma sa dalíq, hínay, dúgay, kusúg, inánay, kalít, maqáyu, ug dáyun sa hústung lugar sa túdling púlung. Butangí ug linkers. (9 C, 14 A)

Pananglítan: Si Mis Wílbi musúlti nag Sinibwanú. (well)
Tubág: Si Mis Wílbi maqáyu nang musúltig Sinibwanú.

1. Nakalárga ang bárku. (long time)
2. Ang traak nga gisákyan ku nakaqabút ra sa Pulambatú. (quickly)
3. Si Lítu mudágan maqúng naqabát. (slow)
4. Muhígup sab ug sabáws manúk si Dyiin. (fast)
5. Nawálaq lang ang íyang kagútum. (suddenly)
6. Silhígi ning salúg. (well)
7. Si Místir Mílir musúlti. (very slowly)
8. Kanáng amíga ni Pírla mubinisayáq. (well)
9. Naglínya ang mga bátaq pagkahumán sa risís. (immediately)
10. Nakamaqú ra siyá sa ámung pinulungán. (nakamaqú 'learned'; pinulungán 'language') (quickly or easily)
11. Mulakáw pa siyá kay waláq pa maqáyu sa hilánat. (slow)
12. Diq na kung kalakáw kay nagquwán na. (hard, fast)
13. Mikusúg ang ulán. (very suddenly)
14. Miqabút ang bárku sa Úrmuk. (long time)
15. Nakakátqun ra si Lítu sa istúrya mahitungúd. ni Núwa. (nakakátqun 'learned') (very fast or easily)
16. Nakasakáy siyá kay waláy misugút nga tartanílya. (a long time)
17. Nanágan silá búsaq waláq mi kadakúp níla. (búsaq 'therefore') (fast)
18. Misakít ang íyang úlu. (suddenly)
19. Nahálin ra ang íyang tíndang kalamáy. (nahálin 'got sold out') (in a short time or easily)
20. Kiníng tráka mudágan. (slow)

XV. Hubára sa Binisayáq ang musunúd nga mga túdling púlung:

Pananglítan: a. 'Has anybody cooked the bananas yet?'
Tubág: Waq pa bay nakalútug ságing? or
May nakalútuq na ba ug ságing? or
Dúna/Náqa na bay nakalútug ságing?

b. 'I didn't see anybody.'
Tubág: Waq kuy nakítaq.

1. Has anybody prepared lunch?
2. I saw somebody speak to my father.
3. Didn't anyone bring bananas?
4. Someone came here yesterday.
5. Nobody answered when I called up.
6. Was there anyone selling kalamay on the boat?
7. Is anybody sick in this house, Mrs. Miller?
8. Will anyone go with me to the boat?
9. I saw somebody waiting for a bus at the station.
10. Somebody left these gifts for your mother.
11. Nobody brought your book back here.
12. Somebody told me that Miss Wilby is here.
13. Did somebody give you these books?
14. I don't need anybody to help me in my store.
15. Is there anybody who knows Mrs. Olivar's house? (knows the house of: katúltul sa)
16. Nobody taught me how to play this game.
17. Somebody's following us.
18. I have nothing to say.
19. Has anybody thrown the can yet?
20. Have you given anybody any of your kalamay?
21. Did anybody drink milk from this glass?
22. Somebody has already reserved this cot.
23. Do you have anybody to give the books to?
24. Did anybody go with you to Pulambato?
25. Do you see anybody?

KEY TO THE EXERCISES

Lesson 1

I. 1. díqa 2. náqa 3. túqa 4. níqa 5. túqa 6. díqa 7. níqa 8. náqa 9. níqa 10. díqa 11. túqa 12. níqa 13. díqa 14. náqa 15. náqa.

II. 1. ánhaq 2. arí 3. ánhi 4. ánhaq 5. ádtu 6. ánhaq 7. ádtu 8. ánhi 9. ánhi 10. arí 11. ádtu 12. ádtu 13. arí 14. ádtu.

III. 1. dirí 2. diháq or dínhaq 3. dídtu 4. dínhi 5. dídtu 6. dirí 7. dínhi 8. diháq or dínhaq 9. dínhi 10. dirí 11. dídtu 12. dínhi 13. dirí 14. diháq or dínhaq 15. dídtu 16. dínhi 17. dídtu 18. diháq or dínhaq 19. dínhi 20. dirí 21. dídtu 22. dídtu 23. dirí 24. dídtu 25. dínhi.

IV. 1. náqa, diháq or dínhaq 2. díqa, dirí 3. náqa, diháq or dínhaq 4. túqa 5. náqa, diháq or dínhaq 6. díqa 7. díqa 8. náqa 9. túqa, dídtu 10. náqa, diháq or dínhaq 11. díqa 12. túqa, dídtu 13. díqa, dirí 14. túqa, dídtu 15. díqa, dirí.

V. 1. kiní (ní) 2. kádtu 3. kirí 4. kanáq (naq) 5. kirí 6. kádtu (tu) 7. kirí 8. kanáq (naq) 9. kanáq 10. kanáq (naq) 11. kirí (ri) 12. kanáq 13. kirí 14. kanáq 15. kirí.

VI. 1. kirí 2. kirí 3. kirí 4. kanáq 5. kirí 6. kirí 7. kanáq 8. kirí 9. kanáq 10. kirí 11. kanáq 12. kirí (kiní) 13. kanáq 14. kirí 15. kanáq.

VII. 1. kamí 2. kamí 3. kamí 4. kitá 5. kamí 6. kitá 7. kamí 8. kitá 9. kamí 10. kitá 11. kitá 12. kamí 13. kitá 14. kamí 15. kamí.

Lesson 2

IA. 1. dirí 2. dídtu 3. dínhi 4. dídtu 5. dínhi.

IB. 1. arí 2. ánhaq 3. ánhi 4. ádtu 5. ánhi 6. ádtu 7. arí 8. ádtu 9. ánhi 10. ánhaq.

IC. 1. níqa 2. níqa 3. díqa 4. náqa 5. túqa 6. díqa 7. túqa 8. náqa.

II. 1. ngádtu 2. ngánhaq 3. ngánhi 4. ngádtu 5. ngánhi 6. ngádtu 7. ngánhi 8. ngarí 9. ngádtu 10. ngádtu 11. ngánhaq 12. ngánhi 13. ngarí 14. ngánhaq 15. ngádtu.

IIIA. 1. háqin 2. diqín 3. ása 4. háqin 5. diqín 6. ása 7. diqín 8. háqin 9. diqín 10. háqin 11. ása 12. ása 13. háqin 14. diqín 15. diqín.

IIIB.
1. Diqín man siyá?
2. Ása man siyá maniqúdtu?
3. Háqin man siyá?
4. Háqin man silá?
5. Ása man mu padúung?
6. Háqin man si Místir Abáya?

7. Háqin man ang baláy ni Ínting.
8. Háqin man si Místir Bílu?
9. Háqin man siyá Dung (Day)?
10. Ása man ta manakáy ug dyip?
11. Ása man mu Bay?
12. Diqín man siyá muqinúm ug kukakúla?
13. Háqin man si Místir Bílu?
14. Diqín man gíkan si Místir Abáya?
15. Háqin man si Ínting?

IV. 1. ánhi 2. díqa, dirí 3. náqa 4. díqa, dirí or ngarí 5. dirí or ngarí 6. náqa, diháq or ngánhaq or dínhaq 7. díqa 8. dídtu or ngádtu 9. náqa 10. túqa, dídtu or ngádtu 11. díqa, dirí or ngarí 12. náqa 13. díqa, díqa, dirí or ngarí 14. ádtu, dídtu or ngádtu 15. arí.

VA. 1. ayáw 2. díliq 3. díliq 4. díliq 5. díliq 6. díliq 7. waláq 8. waláq 9. díliq 10. ayáw 11. waláq 12. ayáw 13. waláq 14. díliq 15. ayáw 16. ayáw 17. díliq 18. waláq 19. ayáw 20. díliq.

VB. 1. díliq 2. ayáw 3. waláq 4. díliq 5. waláq 6. díliq 7. díliq 8. waláq 9. díliq 10. ayáw.

VC. 1. díliq 2. waláq 3. díliq 4. díliq 5. waláq 6. waláq 7. waláq 8. díliq 9. waláq 10. díliq 11. díliq 12. díliq 13. waláq 14. waláq 15. díliq.

VI. 1. baláya 2. dyípa 3. draybíra 4. bíra 5. kanqúna 6. Pirnandísa 7. batáqa or bataqána 8. pána 9. sudqána 10. basúha 11. kutsilyúha 12. litsíha 13. lamisáha 14. platúha 15. Dudúnga.

VII.
1. Ákuq kiní.
2. Ímu ba kiní?
3. Ádtu ku sa baláy ni Huwán.
4. Ádtu ta manihápun sa átuq or ámuq.
5. Ang ákung asáwa túqa sa ka Dúktur Pirnándis or túqa sa ílang Dúktur Pirnándis.
6. Ámuq kanáng baláya.
7. Íla kanáng dyípa.
8. Ákuq kiníng paan or kíning pána.
9. Íla ba nang básu? or nang basúha?
10. Kang Tásyu ning lítsi or ning litsíha.
11. Ang ákung amígu túqa sa ka Místir Gamílu or túqa sa ílang Místir Gamílu.
12. Ímu ba ning kukakúla?
13. Ímu kanáng bir.
14. Ádtu ku maniqúdtu sa ka Místir Abáya or sa ílang Místir Abáya.
15. Kang Dúktur Pirnándis ning dyip.

VIII. 1. kínsa 2. únsa 3. kínsa 4. únsa 5. únsa 6. kínsa 7. únsa.

Lesson 3

IA. 1. kanáq or kiní 2. kiní 3. kanáq 4. kanáq 5. kanáq 6. kiní 7. kiní 8. kanáq 9. kanáq 10. kiní 11. kiní or kirí 12. kanáq 13. kanáq 14. kanáq 15. kiní.

IB. 1. ádtu 2. ádtu 3. dínhi or ngánhi 4. dínhi or ngánhi 5. dídtu or ngádtu

6. ádtu, dídtu 7. ádtu 8. dídtu or ngádtu 9. dídtu or ngádtu 10. dínhi or ngánhi 11. ádtu 12. ánhi, dínhi or ngánhi 13. dínhaq or ngánhaq or diháq 14. dirí or ngarí 15. diháq or dínhaq or ngánhaq 16. náqa, diháq or dínhaq or ngánhaq 17. dínhi or ngánhi 18. níqa, dínhi or ngánhi 19. arí, dirí or ngarí 20. níqa.

IC. Where the answer is ta, kitá is also correct. Where the answer is mi, kamí is also correct.
1. ta 2. ta 3. mi 4. mi, mi 5. mi 6. ta 7. ta 8. ta 9. mi 10. ta 11. mi 12. ta 13. ta 14. mi 15. ta.

ID. 1. ayáw 2. waláq 3. waláq, díliq 4. waláq 5. ayáw 6. díliq 7. díliq 8. ayáw 9. waláq 10. díliq 11. waláq 12. díliq 13. díliq 14. waláq 15. waláq 16. waláq 17. díliq 18. waláq 19. díliq 20. ayáw 21. waláq 22. waláq 23. waláq, díliq 24. waláq 25. díliq.

II. There are other possible translations than the ones given.
1. Way bir dirí.
2. Túqay táwu dídtu.
3. Dúna ba muy bir?
4. Diháy or dínhay nagtawág nímu sa tilipunú.
5. Dúna kuy duhá ka buqúk bátaq.
6. Diháy or dínhay or dínhiy táwung nangítaq nímu.
7. Náqay mga dyip ngañhaq (or diháq or dínhaq) nga padúung sa Banáwaq or Túqay mga dyip dídtu (or ngádtu) nga padúung sa Banáwaq.
8. Nahibáwu kung dúnay kwártung paqabángan sa ínyung baláy.
9. Way dyip páras Banáwaq.
10. Dúna nay dyip karún pirú waláq ganína.
11. Náqay dághang dyip niqánang iskináha.
12. Dúna bay mangá bátaq sa ínyung baláy?
13. Diháy or dínhay bátaq sa ka Dúktur Pirnándis.
14. Dúna say kwártus sílung paqabángan.
15. Dúna bay kwártung paqabángan sa ínyung baláy?

III. 1. Ímnun námuq ang kukakúla.
2. Átung sákyan ang dyip padúung sa Banáwaq.
3. Nagpuyúq sa táqas ang ákung anák.
4. Siyá ang muqábang sa kwártu sa sílung.
5. Siláng duhá ang nangítaq nímu.
6. Íyang abángan ang kwártu nga míngaw.
7. Ikáw ang dádqun níya sa Amiriká.
8. Dyip nga gamáy ang muqádtu sa Banáwaq.
9. Giqubán si Pírla ni Mis Wílbi ngádtu sa Banáwaq.
10. Átung pangitáqun ang láqing dyip.
11. Kiní si Místir Gamílu ang nagtawág nímu ganíha.
12. Íyang asáwa ang gidalá níya ngánhi.
13. Mutawág siyág dyip páras Banáwaq.
14. Kiní siyá ang mubáyad ug kwarínta písus nga ábang.
15. Ikáw ang dádqun níya sa Banáwaq.

IV A. 1. Díliq man ni páras Banáwaq.
2. Gústu man sab kug mangá bátaq.
3. Waq na ra bay dyip páras Kárbun kay údtu na man gud.
4. Maqú ba diqáy kiní si Mis Wílbi?

5. Ákuq na ba lang kaháng abángan ning kwartúha?
6. Díliq na lang mi magdúgay kay údtu na man gud.
7. Pangutánqa ang dráybir kun maqú na ba kiní ang pára sa Banáwaq.
8. Díliq lagí ku muqubán sa Amiriká.
9. Ása man diqáy ta manakáyg dyip?
10. Waq túqud naq siyá muqánhi.
11. Díliq na ra ba gyud mahángyuq ang ábang.
12. Kádtung dyip duqúl sa tindáhan muqádtu ba kaháq sa Banáwaq?
13. Díliq ka ba kaháq samúkan sa mangá bátaq?
14. Pilá may bayranán sa káda búwan?
15. Ikáw ba lang diqáy ang muqábang sa kwártu?

IV B. Other word orders are also possible.

1. Kinahánglan na lang kung muqádtu kay údtu na man.
2. Gústu úntaq kung musakáy ug dyip páras Kárbun.
3. Kinahánglang ang ímung sákyan nga dyip dúna gyuy márkang Banáwaq.
4. Kinahánglan kang mubálhin ngánhi sa primíru sa sunúd nga búlan.
5. Gústu úntaq kung muqábang ug kwártu dínhi.
6. Díliq ku gústung muqinúm ug bir.
7. Díliq silá makaqubán nákuq sa Kárbun.
8. Mahímuq bang muqábang ku niqíning kwártu sa sílung?
9. Ayáw mug sakáy niqánang dyip nga páras Lahúg.
10. Kinahánglan kung dádqun si Lítu sa Amiriká.

IV C.

1. Diq ra ba ni muqádtu sa Kárbun Day.
2. Diq diqáy ka ánhi dínhi maghuwát ug dyip?
3. Diq man gud ku gústug mangá bátaq.
4. Waq ba siyáy mangá anák?
5. Waq ba siyá magpuyúq dídtu sa táqas?
6. Diq ba diqáy kamúng duhá ang muqábang sa kwártu?
7. Ang únang nagqabáng ngánhi waláq siyá magbayád káda búwan.
8. Diq man ku gústu sa kwártus táqas.
9. Diq ba diqáy mahímung mutánqaw sa kwártu karún?
10. Waq ka ba mahibáwu nga dúna kuy kwártung gipaqabángan?
11. Diq ba ni siyá maqú ang nangítag baláy?
12. Waq man tingáli si Mísis Abilyána (diháq).
13. Diq ba kanáq maqú ang baláy ni Mísis Abilyána?
14. Ayáw lang kug huwatá dídtus tindáhan ha?
15. Diq mu mangádtus Banáwaq?

IV D. Other word orders are possible for some of these sentences.

1. Dídtu siyá sa Kárbun gahápun.
2. Kinahánglan nímung báyran ang kwártung giqabángan.
3. Níqa ka man diqáy dínhi.
4. Mahímuq nílang abángan ang baay.
5. Dúna ka man diqáy dalá.
6. Díliq siyá mubáyad sa íyang útang.
7. Íla ba ming dádqun sa lúngsud?
8. Ayáw siyág patanqáwa sa siní.
9. Waláq ku musakáy sa dyip.
10. Ánhaq lang mi manáqug sa iskína.
11. Iyá kang dádqun sa Amiriká.
12. Waq ka na ra bay bir.

13. Mahímuq ba ming mutánqaw sa siní?
14. Waláq ku pangitáqa gahápun.
15. Ánhi mu manihápun karúng gabíqi.

Lesson 4

IA. Unless there is a statement to the contrary, deictics with d may be replaced by deictics with ng. Wherever diháq is used, dínhaq is also possible.
1. dídtu 2. diháq 3. dídtu 4. diháq 5. diháq or dínhi (ngánhaq is not possible) 6. arí, dirí 7. túqa, dídtu, dínhi (ngánhi not possible) 8. diháq 9. diháq or dínhaq, arí, dirí 10. arí or ádtu 11. diháq 12. ánhaq, diháq 13. dínhi 14. dínhi 15. ánhi, dínhi.

IC. Answers must have the following words:
1. waláq na 2. díliq 3. díliq or ayáw lang 4. díliq 5. waláq pa 6. waláq pa 7. waláq pa 8. waláq 9. ayáw na lang 10. díliq 11. díliq na 12. díliq pa 13. ayáw 14. díliq 15. ayáw.

ID. 1. ayáw, díliq 2. díliq, waláq 3. díliq 4. waláq 5. waláq 6. díliq 7. ayáw, waláq 8. díliq, waláq 9. díliq 10. díliq, ayáw 11. ayáw 12. díliq 13. díliq 14. díliq, ayáw 15. díliq.

IE.
1. Díliq mi mangádtu sa Talísay.
2. Kinahánglan nátung tanqáwug makasakáy pa ba ta.
3. Mirlí, díliq ba ta mulárga dáyun?
4. Ánhi ta dínhi mangalíguq or Ánhi ta mangalíguq dínhi.
5. Anúsqa pa ba ta mamaqúliq?
6. Ayáw lag dágan sa taytáyan.
7. Díliq ku naq súking tiguwánga or Díliq ku súkiq nang tiguwánga.
8. Kinahánglan tang mamahúlay dínhis baybáay.
9. Diq na ta kinahánglang pahatúd sa Dyuns Abinyú.
10. Anúsqa ta magkítaq pagqusáb?
11. Gústu kung mubálik dáyun sa Sibú.
12. Ánhi ta magbántayg traak dínhi or Ánhi ta dínhi magbántayg traak.
13. Díliq ba ni muqádtu sa Púquk Bay?
14. Ánhi mu mamahúlay dínhis baybáay.
15. Ayáw lag káqun sa haluqháluq.

IF.
1. Ayáw saq mug sakáy kay waq pay dághang táwu or . . . kay díliq pa dághang táwu.
2. Díliq ba ni muqádtus Yáru?
3. Waláq ka makakitáq niqánang taytáyan?
4. Díliq ta muqági diháq.
5. Díliq ra ba ku mahádluk nga muqági ánang taytayána.
6. Ayáwg lakáw ug kusúg arún diq ka mahúlug.
7. Díliq akúy mudalá sa ímung butáng.
8. Díliq ba ta makapahúlay dínhis balaybálay?
9. Waláq man ku tugnawá karún.
10. Díliq dághan ganínag mangá táwu.
11. Waláq ba muqulán ganína?
12. Waláq ba mabasáq si Mírli sa ulán?
13. Díliq mudirítsu sa Sibú kiníng tráka.
14. Waláq pa ba ni muqádtus Tángki Bay?

15. Díliq pa ta musakáy kay dirítsu man nis Sibú.

II. 1. nadúgay, makasakáy 2. mapunúq, madúgay 3. magdalíq 4. mipaqúliq 5. namahúway 6. nangalíguq, namaqúliq 7. nangutána, malíguq 8. nanglákaw 9. nakakaqún 10. mupaqúliq 11. nagpaqingún 12. nagdalá 13. malíguq 14. nabasáq, nagqulán 15. muqági 16. nagqabáng, nagbayád 17. nahibáwu 18. makahángyuq 19. magpíliq 20. nagpuyúq 21. nadúgay 22. nagpaqábut 23. mubálik 24. mutánqaw 25. nakalárga, napunúq.

Lesson 5

IA. Wherever there is a deictic with d, a deictic with ng also occurs unless there is a statement to the contrary. Wherever there is a short form of the pronoun, a long form is also possible.
1. dínhi 2. dínhi 3. diháq or dínhaq 4. ánhaq, dínhaq 5. kanáq, dínhi 6. kanáq 7. dínhi 8. dirí 9. kanáq, kanáq, dínhi 10. dínhi 11. kanáq, náqa 12. kiní, ni or kirí, ri 13. kanáq 14. dídtu 15. dídtu, kiní.

IC(1). The answers must contain the following:
1. díliq 2. waláq 3. ayáw 4. díliq 5. díliq 6. díliq 7. díliq 8. waláq 9. díliq 10. díliq 11. waláq 12. ayáw 13. waláq 14. waláq 15. díliq.

IC(2).
1. Díliq ka ba muqádtu sa Pulambatú úgmaq?
2. Waq ba magqigutqigút kanáng taytáyan?
3. Díliq na ba ku magkúhaq ug bir pára nímu?
4. Díliq ba ta manakáy sa bísag únsang dyip?
5. Díliq ba ang sa táqas nga kwártuy ímung abángan?
6. Díliq ka ba muqinúm ug tubáq káda ádlaw?
7. Díliq ka ba muqádtu sa íla ka Iyúq Tibúq?
8. Waláq pa bay mihángyuq pagpangasáwa nímu?
9. Díliq ba níndut ang ínyung baláy?
10. Díliq ka ba gústung ibílin dínhi sa ka Dúktur Pirnándis?
11. Waláq na ba tay kukakúla dínhi?
12. Díliq na ba lang ku magqunál nímu?
13. Waláq ba mu manakáy sa dyip nga padúung sa Lahúg?
14. Waláq ka ba magpuyúq dínhis ka Mísis Abilyána?
15. Díliq ka ba mubálik dáyun ngánhis Pulambatú?

ID. 1. waláq 2. díliq 3. ayáw, díliq 4. waláq 5. díliq 6. ayáw, díliq 7. díliq, waláq 8. waláq 9. díliq 10. ayáw 11. díliq 12. ayáw 13. díliq 14. waláq 15. waláq.

IE.
1. Díliq ku mangutána?
2. Kinahánglan na ba tang musakáy ug muqádtu tas Banáwaq?
3. Miss Wílbi, gústu ba mung mangádtus Banáwaq?
4. Díliq man diqáy ka tigúwang kaqáyu or Díliq man diqáy ka kaqáyu tigúwang.
5. Díliq ra ba ku kaqiháp sa ákung mga apú.
6. Ánhi lang ta maghuwát ug dyip.
7. Dídtu lang mu pangítag láqin Day, or Pangítaq lang mug láqin dídtu Day, or Pangítaq lang mu dídtug láqin Day.
8. Máqu ba ni ang kwártu ni Mis Wílbi?
9. Anúsqa ka muqábang sa usá ka kwártu?
10. Díliq kaháq ka samúkan únyaq sa mga bátaq?
11. Díliq ba ni pára sa Kárbun Day?

12. Kinahánglan gyud naq silá nákung maqílhan.
13. Ánhi na lang mi matúug.
14. Gústu kung mubálik dáyun sa Sibú.
15. Kanúsqa ka ba mubálik sa Amiriká?

IF.
1. Waq ra ba muqádtu si Mis Wílbi sa ílang Mis Sántus sa Pulambatú.
2. Diq lang nátuq táwgun kanáng tigúwang.
3. Diq man nákuq kaqúban kiní si Mis Wílbi, Nuy Tibúq.
4. Diq ra ba si Nuy Tibúq ang labíng tigúwang táwu sa lúngsud.
5. Diq pa man ku dúgay dínhis Pilipínas.
6. Diq man tingáli si Nuy Tibúq kanáng nagpaduluúng ngánhi.
7. Karún, diq pa gyud ka makabinisayáq.
8. Waq pa gyud kay mga apú Iyúq.
9. Inigbálik nímu ayáw bayáq pagdalág rigálu ha?
10. Waláq gayúd mangítaq si Mis Wílbi ug baláy.
11. Díliq ba mahímung mangutána Iyúq?
12. Ayáw lang nínyug subáya kanáng dálan Piláyis.
13. Waláq may mga dyip ngánhang padúung sa Banáwaq.
14. Díliq lang ku musugút ug náqay muhángyuq.
15. Waq ra bay mga lubí sa ámung dápit.

IIA.
1. Kamíngaw diqáy dínhi sa Pulambatú uy!
2. Kaníndut niqíning kwártu sa sílung!
3. Kadághan túqud sa dyip dínhi!
4. Kadághan na sa ímung mga apú!
5. Kadúgay na diqáy nímu dínhi sa Pilipínas!
6. Kadyútay lang diqáy sa ságing dídtu sa ínyu nu!
7. Kaqignuránti ni Lítu!
8. Kasayún ra niqánaq!
9. Katigúwang na diqáy nímu!
10. Kamíngaw dídtu sa ka Mísis Abilyána!
11. Kalayúq ádtung Púquk kaligúqan!
12. Kalisúd sa agiqánan paqingún sa Púquk!
13. Kabahúq niqíning dapíta!
14. Kalamíq diqáy sa haluqháluq!
15. Kadalíq nílang nahumág kalíguq.

IIB.
1. Dakúq kiníng ínyung tindáhan.
2. Dághan kanáq siyág mga anák.
3. Níndut kiníng mga ságing.
4. Dyútay ang mga Amirkánu dínhi sa Pilipínas.
5. Sayún kiníng pagtulúnqang sagqulúhun.
6. Tigúwang kanáq si Nuy Tibúq.
7. Ignuránti kiníng ímung apú Nuy Tibúq.
8. Hílum ngádtu sa lúngsud ni Pírla.
9. Míngaw ngádtu sa ámung lugár.
10. Dúgay siyáng muqabút gíkan sa ámuq.

IIIA.
1. Dághan na bag anák si Pírla?
2. Níndut gyug baláy ang ákung kaqúban.
3. Dyútay kug kwárta páras ábang.
4. Gamáy siyág baay dídtus Sibú.
5. Dághan man diqáy ug apú si Nuy Tibúq.
6. Buqútan ug anák si Místir Abáya?

7. Dághan ba ug dyip nga muqági dínhi?
8. Mga sabaqán ba mug mga bátaq dínhi?
9. Maqáyu ug higála si Pírla.
10. Míngaw ug kwártu dídtus sílung.
11. Díliq pa ba ka dághag kaqíla?
12. Díliq ku dátug amahán.
13. Dakúq bag baay si Dúktur Pirnándis?
14. Díliq silá dághag ságing sa íla.
15. Dághan kug buluhatún sa tindáhan.

III B. The following give just one possible answer:
1. Dúna na ba lay dyútayng ságing dídtu sa ínyu?
2. Dúna ba muy dághang mga bátaq dínhi?
3. Dúna na diqáy kay dakúng idád?
4. Dúna bay níndut nga tíngug si Pírla?
5. Dúna diqáy kay dághang mga higála dínhi?
6. Waláq ka bay dakúng tíngug?
7. Dúnay dakúng baláy si Iyúq Tibúq sa Pulambatú.
8. Dúna siyáy dághan kaqáyung mga apú.
9. Dúnay gamáy rang simbahán ang Pulambatú.
10. Dúna ra ba gamáyng kwártu dínhi sa ámuq.
11. Dúnay mga maqáyung kwártu dídtu sa táqas.
12. Dúnay níndut nga simbahán dídtu sa íla ka Pírla.
13. Dúnay dyútay rang Amirikánu dínhi sa Sibú.
14. Waláy dághang lubí dídtu sa ámuq.
15. Ngánung dúna ka may dághang gása?

IV. 1. nagsáqad, manihápun 2. mangutána, musakáy, muqádtu 3. makahapít, mibálik 4. manakáy 5. nagqiháp 6. mahímuq, musakáy 7. mamálhin 8. nagdalá 9. muqádtu 10. magtawág, muqádtu 11. mubálik 12. magdalíq, muqabút 13. mangádtu 14. nagtawág 15. musakáy.

V A. 1. muqábang 2. magbántay 3. mutánqaw 4. muhatúd 5. magsígi 6. muláqag 7. nagkaqún 8. mibálik 9. nagqigutqigút 10. milakáw 11. magdalá 12. mupaqúliq 13. nagqulán 14. mupuyúq 15. muqádtu.

V B. 1. mukáqun 2. musúbay 3. makahatúd 4. makasaká 5. muhúnung 6. magbántay 7. makalíngkud 8. muqabút, makasakáy 9. mubáyad 10. makasakáy 11. makaqánhi 12. makahatúd 13. makapangutána, magpuyúq 14. makasakáy 15. makahumán.

VI A. 1. sa 2. si, níya 3. ku 4. siyá, ug 5. kanáq, ádtu 6. kamú, silá 7. niqíni 8. silá, ug 9. si, siyá 10. sa 11. kamú, kamí 12. si 13. kanímu, ka 14. akú, kang Huwán 15. si.

VI B. 1. kamú 2. nímu 3. kamú 4. níya 5. si 6. nímu.

VII A. Where the long form of the pronoun is given, the short form is also possible.
1. ka, nímu 2. kamú 3. kitá 4. kamú 5. íni, nákuq 6. ka, námuq 7. kitá 8. akú 9. si 10. kamí 11. niqíni 12. niqánaq 13. ni Mis Wílbi 14. ni Iyúq 15. ni Huwán <u>or</u> kang Huwán.

VII B. Where the long forms are given the short forms are also possible.
1. ínyu 2. kiní 3. íya 4. íla 5. ni Pilár, kanáq 6. ínyu 7. siyá 8. átuq. 9. kitá 10. ikáw (ka <u>is not possible</u>).

Lesson 6

IA. 1. níqa 2. ánhi 3. díqa 4. dídtu 5. ánhi 6. ánhi 7. dínhi or ngánhi 8. níqa 9. túqa, dídtu 10. ngánhaq or diháq or dínhaq 11. dínhi 12. dínhi 13. dídtu 14. ánhi 15. ánhi.

IB. Where the long forms are given, the short forms are also possible.
1. kiní 2. kiní 3. kiní 4. kádtu 5. niqánaq, kirí 6. kanáq 7. kanáq 8. kirí 9. kanáq 10. niqánaq 11. kádtu 12. kádtu, kádtu or kanáq, kanáq 13. kádtu or kanáq 14. kádtu or kanáq 15. kanáq or kádtu.

IC. The answers should have the following words:
1. waláq 2. díliq 3. díliq 4. waláq 5. ayáw 6. waláq 7. waláq 8. ayáw 9. ayáw 10. díliq 11. díliq 12. waláq 13. díliq 14. waláq 15. díliq.

ID.
1. Gústu úntaq kung musúud ánang tindáhan sa mga aláhas nga kinhasún.
2. Díliq na lang nátuq pangutánqun ang Ínsik kun mahímu ba nig dyis.
3. Gústu úntaq kung mupalít niqánang kaság pirú diq na man kaqáyu lábqas.
4. Kinahánglan gyud kung mangítag sinsíyu dirí arún ákung mapalít nang kaság.
5. Gústu úntaq kung mupalít ug usá ka dusína niqíning mga aríyus.
6. Aa, maqú ba kiní ang dyíp páras Mabúlu?
7. Kinahánglan kung musakáy dáyun páras Mabúlu.
8. Maqú man gud kanáq ang muqádtus Mabúlu.
9. Kinahánglan kung mubálik dáyun sa Sibú kay dághan pa ra ba kug buhatúnun sa tindáhan.
10. Gústu úntaq kung muqádtus ínyu pirú giqimbitár man ku ni Pírla ngádtus íla.
11. Gústu úntaq nákung (or Gustu ku úntang) ipaqilaqíla nímu ang ákung anák.
12. Mahímu kung muhapít sa ínyu gíkan sa íla Pírla.
13. Gústu man gud úntaq nákung ipaqilaqíla kanímu ang ákung mga bátaq ug ákung mga apú.
14. Díliq kaqáyu hílum run ngánhis ámuq.
15. Ádtu na lang ta manihápun sa ka Nuy Tibúq.

IE.
1. Díliq ba mahímung dyis písus na lang ni?
2. Díliq na man ka makahángyuq.
3. Díliq nákuq (or ku) siyá pangutánqun.
4. Díliq gyud tingáli ni madalág dyis Mis.
5. Díliq ku musúud dínhi.
6. Waláq na kuy láqin niqáning báynti.
7. Díliq ra ba ni muqádtus Lahúg Mis.
8. Ayáwg lakáw diháq sa píkas kay waláq diháq ang mga dyip páras Mabúlu.
9. Ayáwg tanqáwa nang (or Ayáw nag tanqáwang) nagbalígyaq diháq káluq.
10. Waláq kuy ikasinsíyu niqánang ímung kwárta Mis.
11. Díliq naq mamatáy ug lutúqun.
12. Díliq na naq silá búhiq Day.
13. Díliq na lang ni nákuq (or ku na lang ni) ipamalígyaq.
14. Ayáwg lakáw Mis.
15. Ayáw nag bálik ngarí Mis.

IIA. 1. mubisíta 2. makasakáy 3. makaqádtu, maglútuq 4. makasáqad, manihápun 5. nakaqádtu 6. mupalít 7. nagháng yuq 8. nagdalá 9. nagbalígyaq 10. nangutána 11. naglútuq 12. mupalít 13. muqádtu 14. nagmatá 15. makasakáy.

IIB. 1. nagqingún, makaqádtu 2. musúlti 3. muqábang 4. magpíliq 5. nagsakáy 6. mupíliq 7. mipalít 8. makabalígyaq, makapaqúliq 9. maglútuq 10. mupaqúliq 11. muqádtu 12. maglútuq 13. nagdalá 14. nakasakáy 15. mitánqaw.

IIIA. 1. lutúqa 2. palitún 3. gikúhaq 4. táwgun 5. gidalá 6. lutúqa 7. dádqa 8. gipangutána 9. táwgun 10. giputús 11. gipangutána 12. gipalít 13. giqinúm 14. dádqun 15. bisitáqun or bisitáhun 16. imbitahá 17. palitá 18. gikúhaq 19. gitawág 20. giháng yuq.

IIIB. 1. nadalá or gidalá 2. giqimbitár 3. makúhaq 4. nalútuq or gilútuq 5. madalá 6. nadalá 7. gipalít or napalít 8. tanqáwa, tanqáwun 9. palitún, giputús or naputús 10. bisitáhun or bisitáqun 11. madungúg 12. nakúhaq or gikúhaq 13. íngna 14. nadungúg 15. mapalít 16. maháng yuq 17. pangutánqa or mapangutána 18. balhína 19. huwatún 20. mabúhat.

IV A. Long forms of the pronouns are not given when their usage is not common. Answers in parentheses are less common.
1. ta, ka or ka, nákuq 2. siyá, nákuq or nákuq, siyá 3. ta, níya 4. ku, nímu 5. siyá, nákuq (nákuq, siyá) or ku, siyá 6. ka, níla 7. silá, níya 8. ka, námuq 9. ka, níla 10. siyá, námuq (námuq, siyá) 11. siyá, nínyu (nínyu, siyá) 12. ku, nínyu 13. ta, níla 14. ta, níla 15. mu, námuq 16. ta, níla 17. ka, níla 18. ka, níya 19. mi, níya 20. silá, nátuq.

IV B. 1. si 2. níya 3. ikáw 4. si 5. ang 6. nínyu 7. kamí 8. kiní 9. silá 10. siyá 11. ang 12. ang, ni 13. námuq 14. kádtu 15. nátuq 16. kamú 17. silá 18. íla 19. sa 20. akú.

IV C.
1. Ámuq lang dádqun si Lítu sa Amiriká.
2. Ibílin lang nákuq (or ku lang) ning ákung amígu sa tindáhan.
3. Íla gyud kunúng adtúqun si Místir Abáya.
4. Íya pang tanqáwun ug makalakáw ba siyá.
5. Imbitahún ra ba siyá námuq sa písta.
6. Súgtun na lang nákuq (or ku na lang) si Huwán.
7. Ínyu bang palitún ang gibalígyaq?
8. Gilútuq ba níla ang kaság?
9. Ámuq ka lagíng báyran sa giqútang ni Husí.
10. Huwatún diqáy nínyu ang dyip.
11. Ámung úsbun ang púrma sa baay.
12. Maqáyu pag íla lang himúqun ang kurtína.
13. Ímu diqáyng giqiháp ang sinsíyu?
14. Ang ínyung kinhasún hikalímtan.
15. Nalímtan níya ang káluq sa dyip.
16. Ámung huwatúng muqabút siyá.
17. Gikúhaq níla ang mga síya sa kwártu.
18. Ákuq na ba kahángl lutúqun ang súdqan?
19. Balíkun gyud níya ang nalímtan níya.
20. Ámung abángan ang tindáhan ug barátu ra.

IV D. 1. Waláq námuq humaná ang ámung trabáhu.

2. Ayáwg kánqa ang súdqan nga gibílin nímu.
3. Díliq níla dádqun ang mga kaság sa Kárbun.
4. Ayáw na lag kalímti ang nahitabúq gabíqi.
5. Waláq mi imbitahá ni Pírla sa ílang lúngsud.
6. Waláq tay bisíta karúng búntag.
7. Díliq silá muqádtu (or muqádtu silá) si Nuy Tibúq ug si Pírla sa Pulambatú sunúd túqig.
8. Waláq ba nímu palitá ang mga aríyus nga gibalígyaq?
9. Díliq ba mahímung mangutána?
10. Díliq ba dághag dyip átbang sa tindáhan?
11. Díliq lang nákuq silá ibílin dínhi.
12. Díliq na lang námuq ibalígyaq ang bir.
13. Díliq ka ba muqinúm ug kukakúla?
14. Waláq kuháqa ni Husí ang mga síya gíkan sa kwártu.
15. Díliq ming tanán manáqug sa Banáwaq.

Lesson 7

I. Where deictics with d are given, those with ng are also possible unless there is a special comment.
1. níqa, dínhi 2. dínhi 3. ása 4. níqa, dínhi 5. arí, dirí 6. diqín 7. háqin, níqa or náqa 8. háqin 9. túqa or náqa 10. dirí 11. níqa or náqa 12. díqa 13. arí, dirí 14. níqa 15. ádtu or ánhaq 16. náqa 17. túqa 18. dínhi 19. níqa, dínhi or náqa, diháq (dínhaq) 20. túqa or náqa 21. ása, ádtu 22. dídtu (ngádtu not possible) 23. dínhi (ngánhi not possible) 24. náqa, túqa 25. dirí.

II. 1. kamí 2. kitá 3. kamí, kamí 4. kamí 5. kitá 6. kamí 7. kamí 8. kamí 9. kitá 10. kamí 11. námuq 12. ámuq 13. kitá 14. kamí 15. ámuq.

III. 1. kanáq or kiní 2. kirí 3. kanáq 4. kádtu or kanáq 5. kiní 6. kirí 7. kanáq 8. kanáq 9. kanáq.

IV. The answers must contain the following words:
1. díliq 2. waláq 3. waláq 4. waláq 5. díliq 6. waláq 7. ayáw 8. díliq 9. díliq 10. waláq 11. waláq 12. díliq 13. ayáw 14. ayáw 15. waláq.

V. 1. dapíta 2. kwartúha 3. lugára 4. tindahána 5. urása 6. baláya 7. dána 8. tiguwánga 9. iskináha 10. batáqa or bataqána.

VI. These are only suggested translations. Other answers are possible.
1. Dúna kuy mga bisítang muqabút.
2. Dúnay dághang mga dyip diháq sa iskína.
3. Dúna ka bay kaság gipamalígyaq?
4. Dúna bay dághang kwártu sa ínyung baay?
5. Dúna bay kasílyas dínhi?
6. Dínhay or Diháy miqádtu sa ínyung lúngsud sa miqáging simána.
7. May níndut bang baay si Huwán?
8. Dínhay or Diháy mga táwu sa dálan gahápun.
9. Nahibáwu kang dúna kuy mga líbru sa baay.
10. Dúna siyáy upát ka buqúk apú.
11. Nahibáwu kung dúna siláy gipamalígyang káwuq.
12. May mga aláhas niqádtung tindahána dídtu.

13. Waq nay kaság nga gibalígyaq.
14. Nahibáwu kung waq siyáy bána.
15. Dúna bay mga kwártung paqabángan sa baay ni Pírla?
16. Dínhiy or Diháy táwung nangítaq nímu.
17. Dínhaq ka bay dághang mga amígu sa Amiriká?
18. Waq siyáy mga bátaq sa baay.
19. Dúna ka bay mga igsúqung nagpuyúq sa Mabúlu?
20. Dínhaq or Diháq bay dághang mga táwu sa Kárbun ganínang búntag?

VII.
1. Kalamíq kaqáyu sa súdqan nga gilútuq ni Pírla!
2. Kamíngaw gyud sa ámung lugár ug tímpung bakasyún!
3. Kaníndut tanqáwun sa mga aríyus nga gipalít ni Mis Wílbi!
4. Kalábqas pa sa mga kaság nga gibalígyaq dínhis Sibú.
5. Kamahál diqáy sa mga balígyaq dínhis Sibú!
6. Kagamáy ra diqáy sa baay níla sa lúngsud!
7. Kalayúq sa ámung baay sa sinihán!
8. Kadalíq ra níyang mibálik gíkan sa simbahán!
9. Kadághan gyud nímug apú!
10. Kamahál diqáy nímung mubalígyaq.

VIII A. 1. muqabút 2. palitá 3. malútuq 4. pangitáqun 5. makasakáy, muqági 6. mibálik 7. mamalígyaq 8. makaqági 9. muhátag 10. mubálik 11. makalútuq 12. mubálik 13. nakalíngkud 14. palitún 15. buhátun 16. naputús 17. musugút 18. makapangutána 19. makaqánhaq 20. kuháqa 21. muhátag 22. balhínun 23. maglíngkud 24. musugút 25. makabisíta.

VIII B. 1. miqabút 2. nakasakáy 3. maputús 4. maglútuq 5. naglakáw 6. muqinúm 7. mulakáw 8. nakahátag 9. muhúnung 10. makaqánhi 11. nakabisíta 12. naghulát 13. naglakáw 14. makabálik 15. miqánhi, mutábang.

VIII C. 1. palitún 2. gatawág or nagtawág 3. nangítaq 4. lutúqun 5. dádqun 6. nakítaq 7. maghuwát or huwát 8. bisitáhun 9. mubálik 10. kuháqa 11. muqádtu 12. mubálik 13. gikúhaq or nakúhaq, gipalít 14. makítaq 15. mangutána 16. kánqa 17. himúqun 18. mangutána, palitún 19. tanqáqun 20. gipangítaq.

IX. Where the long forms are given, the short forms are also possible.
1. níya 2. ínyu 3. kitá 4. níya 5. ímu 6. kamú, ínyu 7. kiní 8. átuq 9. ínyu 10. ímu 11. kaníya 12. kitá, ámuq 13. níla 14. kaníya 15. nínyu 16. námuq 17. íla 18. kanámuq 19. nínyu 20. níla.

XA. Some of the following may have several other possible word orders.
1. Gústu úntaq ming manáqug dínhi.
2. Mahímuq ba ming muqádtu sa ínyung baláy karún?
3. Kinahánglan nag nímung humanún karún.
4. Kinahánglan dínhi ka lang Pirlá, ha?
5. Dung, díliq ka námuq dádqun sa Amiriká.
6. Gústu na lang úntaq kung muqádtu kay hápun na man.
7. Gústu ka bang muqinúm ug bir?
8. Mahímuq na ba ni nákung lutúqun?
9. Mahímuq ku na bang ihátag ning sulát níya?
10. Gústu untáq nákung ánhi matúlug sa ínyu karún.
11. Díliq ku na lang ni dádqun.

12. Gústu na lang nákung lutúqun ning kaság, _or_ Gústu na lang ni lutúqun nákung kaság.
13. Mahímuq na ba kung makalakáw?
14. Kinahánglan nátuq kiníng ibálhin arún díliq mahúgaw.
15. Díliq lang ku muhulát nímu.
16. Gústu kung mupalít ug sapátus úgmaq.
17. Ayáw na lang siyág táwga karún.
18. Kinahánglan gayúng ikáw ang muqádtu.
19. Mahímuq ba akúng makasulúd.
20. Gústu na lang kung mubáyad.

XB.
1. Díliq ba mahímug dyis na lang ang dusína sa aríyus?
2. Waq man ku nímu táwga. Waq ba kuy hikalímtan?
3. Ayáw nag buháta run dáyun.
4. Kádtung dyip nga túqas tumúy, díliq ba tu maqúng padulúng sa Mabúlu?
5. Ayáw na lang nag palitá Day.
6. Díliq ba búhiq nang (_or_ naq búhing) kaság mu Yaq?
7. Ayáw saq lutúqa nang (_or_ saq naq lutúqang) kaság.
8. Waq ka bay ikasinsíyus dyis písus?
9. Díliq ba mahímung tanqáwun ku ang mga aríyus?
10. Ayáw ra gug tanqáwa nang (_or_ gud nag tanqáwang) kaság Day.
11. Waláq dáyun siyá mutánqaw sa kaság.
12. Díliq úntaq ku gústung makaganánsyag dyútay.
13. Dung, ayáw rag pasákya si Huwán sa ímung dyip ug ayáw siyág ihatúd sa Mabúlu.
14. Waláq man muqánhi si Mis Wílbi kagahápun.
15. Díliq ba balígyaq nang (_or_ ba naq balígyang) kaság Nang?

XC. 1. ákuq, silá 2. ka, námuq 3. nákuq _or_ ku, si Lítu 4. siyá, nímu _or_ nímu, siyá 5. ku, nímu 6. ta, siní 7. nímu, siyá _or_ siyá, nímu 8. siyá, nímu 9. silá, kwártu 10. kamí, nínyu 11. nákuq, silá _or_ silá, nákuq 12. silá, nímu 13. ta, ságing 14. ku, siyá 15. nátuq, si Mísis Abilyána 16. si Índay, námuq _or_ námuq, si Índay 17. nátuq, ang ságing 18. ámuq, ang kwártu 19. námuq, ang kaság 20. nákuq _or_ ku, ang bátaq.

Lesson 8

IA. Potential forms are also possible answers besides some of these, but they are not listed.
1. girisirbahán 2. kúptan 3. bantayí 4. giqábtan 5. gisákyan 6. báyri 7. gibaligyáqan 8. bisitáhan 9. gihátdan 10. lingkúri 11. dagánan 12. sákyi 13. gisaqáran 14. súdlan 15. súdli 16. bisitáhan 17. ubaní 18. gilutúqan 19. suklíqan 20. balhínan 21. gipalitán 22. bisitáhi 23. hibaluqí 24. dulhúgan 25. dádqi.

IB. 1. palitá 2. palití 3. palitán 4. gidalá 5. dádqi 6. dádqan 7. gidalá 8. kuháqa 9. kuháqan 10. kuháqun 11. gibálhin 12. balhínan 13. giqubanán 14. ubaní 15. girisírba 16. risirbáhi 17. gipangítaq 18. pangitáqi 19. gipangitáqan 20. gipangítaq 21. subáya 22. subáyun 23. ípha _or_ ihapá 24. íphan _or_ ihapán 25. giqíphan _or_ giqihapán.

IC. 1. nagdalá 2. gidalá 3. midágan 4. nagdagán 5. dagáni 6. mibálhin

7. balhínan 8. gibálhin 9. muhatúd 10. gihátdan 11. hátdi 12. magtawág 13. táwgun 14. nagtawág 15. táwga, nagbántay 16. bantayán 17. abángi 18. giqabángan 19. nagqabáng, nagbayád 20. báyri 21. muqági 22. giqagíqan 24. naglútuq 25. lutúqun.

II. 1. níya, ang, siyá 2. si, ug, níya 3. siyá, ug, ni 4. siyá, sa 5. si, sa, siyá 6. si, sa, siyá 7. siyá, sa, ni 8. si, sa 9. siyá, ni, sa 10. ang, níya, si 11. si, ang, níya 12. siyá, sa, ni 13. ni, sa, níya 14. sa, ni, sa, níya 15. si, sa, siyá 16. si, níya 17. siyá, ni, sa 18. si, sa, níya 19. níya, ang, ni 20. ang, ni, níya.

Lesson 9

IA. 1. gihulatán 2. sákyi 3. giqagíqan 4. pangitáqan 5. sákyan 6. paqabángan 7. giqadtúqan 8. pangutánqan 9. himúqan 10. gibáyran 11. báyri 12. gihátdan 13. samúki 14. gisaqáran 15. púyqan 16. ubaní 17. giqíphan 18. gipalitán 19. gibalíkan 20. suklíqi.

IB. The potentials are possible in some cases, but they are not listed here. 1. gisákyan 2. bantayí 3. bantayán 4. kánqan 5. dádqi 6. subáya, gipangítaq, tanqáwa 7. gilaqáyan 8. gisáktan 9. pangutánqun 10. ubanán 11. adtúqun or adtúqan 12. kaligúqan 13. pilíqun 14. sákyan 15. limbúngi 16. sultíhi 17. gisulatán 18. kánqun 19. kuyúgi 20. giqukupahán.

IC. 1. gipalitán 2. pústa, palitún 3. kuháqi 4. mutánqaw 5. pangutánqun, magbalígyaq or nagbalígyaq, gipalitán 6. suklíqi, nagdalíq 7. pangitáqa, tagáqan (hatágan) 8. muqági 9. muqánhi 10. midágan, nagdalá 11. mudirítsu 12. pangitáqun 13. nagqingún or niqingún, muqubán 14. buhíqi 15. giqítus 16. mubinisayáq 17. mulárga 18. nagkáwus 19. mubáyad or báyad.

ID. 1. níya, sa 2. siyá, ang, sa 3. níya, si, sa 4. ang 5. sa, ni 6. ni, sa 7. ug, ang 8. ang, sa, ni 9. níya, ang, ni 10. níya, níya 11. níya, ang, ang 12. siyá, ug 13. siyá, sa 14. siyá, sa, ni 15. siyá, ug 16. siyá, sa 17. siyá, sa, níya 18. níya, ang, ni 19. siyá 20. siyá, sa, ni.

IIA. 1. ku, ni Lítu 2. ka, nákuq or ta, ka or tiká(w) 3. ka, nákuq or ta, ka or tiká(w) 4. ta, níya 5. nákuq or ku, si Ínting 6. ka, nákuq or ta, ka or tiká(w) 7. ku, ni Mis Wílbi 8. ka, nákuq or ta, ka or tiká(w) 9. ka, nákuq or ta, ka or tiká(w) 10. ka, nákuq or ta, ka 11. ka, nákuq or ta, ka or tiká(w) 12. ku, nímu or ku, nínyu 13. ta, ka or ka, nákuq 14. nákuq or ku, ang dálan 15. mu, nákuq or ta, mu 16. ku, nímu 17. ku, nímu 18. ku, ni Pírla 19. ka, nákuq or ta, ka or ta, mu 20. ka, námuq 21. ka, nákuq or ta, ka or tiká(w). 22. ku, níya 23. siyá, nákuq or ku, siyá or nákuq, siyá 24. ka, nákuq or ta, ka or tiká(w) 25. ku, ni Pírla.

IIB. 1. inigpalít 2. inigqabút 3. inigsulúd 4. inigsúgud 5. inighúnung 6. inigkanáqug 7. inigpangutána 8. inig- is not possible. 9. inigqánhaq 10. inig- is not possible 11. inigpadulúng 12. inigqádtu 13. inig- is not possible 14. inigqági 15. inigqiháp.

III. 1. Maqáyu kang musúltig Binisayáq or Maqáyu kang mubinisayáq.
2. Kiníng dyip hináyng mudágan or Hínayng mudágan kiníng dyip.
3. Maqáyu siyáng mulútuq.

4. Si Huwán kusúg mudágan or Kusúg mudágan si Huwán.
5. Kusúg siyáng mudágan.
6. Kahínay nímung mulakáw!
7. Kamaqáyu níyang mulútuq!
8. Maqáyu siyáng mutagád sa íyang mga anák.

Lesson 10

IA. Potential forms are also possible answers besides some of these, but they are not listed here.
1. gihatúd 2. isakáy 3. gisulúd 4. ihatúd 5. ibáyad 6. ipalít 7. gisúkliq 8. ibalígyaq 9. ilútuq 10. ibalígyaq 11. isuwát 12. ikanáqug 13. gibutáng 14. ipangutána 15. isáqad 16. iqubán 17. gisulúd 18. iputúl 19. ikalíguq 20. ikatábang 21. gihatúd 22. isaká 23. gihátag 24. ibalígyaq 25. iqábang 26. ihuwát 27. ihángyuq 28. ilikúq 29. ikatábang 30. itawág.

IB. 1. gikaqún or gikáqun 2. gikánqan 3. kánqi 4. táwgun 5. táwga 6. isáqad 7. gisaqáran 8. gidalá 9. gidádqan 10. gibalígyaq 11. gibaligyáqan 12. pangitáqa 13. pangitáqan 14. pangitáqan 15. ibáyad 16. ibáyad 17. gibáyran 18. isulúd 19. giqábang 20. abángan 21. abángi 22. pangutánqun 23. gipangutánqan 24. gibisíta or gibisitáqan (gibisitáhan) 25. bisitáha (bisitáqa) or bisitáhi (bisitáqi) 26. ibutáng 27. butangán 28. ibutáng 29. isuwát 30. gisuwatán.

Lesson 11

I. 1. musúud 2. misúud or nakasúud 3. isúud 4. mupalít 5. gipalít 6. gipalitán 7. makahátag 8. natagáqan or gitagáqan (gihatágan, nahatágan) 9. tagáqi (hatági) or katagáqi or matagáqi 10. gitawág 11. itawág 12. nagtawág 13. nagtawág 14. tanqáwun 15. matánqaw or tanqáwa 16. gitánqaw 17. tanqáwa 18. musakáy or makasakáy 19. gisákyan or nasákyan 20. giqukupahán or naqukupahán 21. maqukupahí or ukupahí 22. muqukupár 23. ibutáng or mabutáng (ika-) 24. gibutáng or nabutáng (gika-) 25. nagbutáng.

II. 1. nakapangaqún or nangáqun 2. ipanghatúd 3. nabúhiq 4. manglútuq 5. ipamutáng 6. manáqug or mukanáqug 7. ipanghátag 8. mamálhin 9. mangábang 10. manínda 11. namatáy or mamatáy 12. malíguq 13. mangasáwa, nangimbitár 14. nangítaq 15. mamalít 16. nanlíngkud or nanglíngkud 17. mamutús 18. mangádtu 19. nangúhaq 20. mamisíta 21. nahibalú 22. manulúd 23. mangabút 24. mamuyúq 25. mahádluk or nahádluk.

III. 1. ikúhaq 2. ipanghatúd 3. dádqa (dálha) 4. káwsi or ikáwus 5. isakáy 6. tanqáwa 7. ibutáng, isulúd 8. ihatúd 9. pangitáqi or ipangítaq 10. buháta 11. balhína or ibálhin 12. huwatá 13. ihúnung 14. lutúqa 15. pústa 16. suklíqi 17. ipangutána 18. tagáqi 19. ubaní 20. ípha (ihapá) 21. kalímti 22. ipalít or palití 23. irisírba, risirbahí 24. buhíqi 25. kúpti.

IV. 1. nakadungúg 2. makakitáq 3. nakítaq or nakítqan 4. madungúg 5. makítaq 6. makadungúg 7. nakítaq or nakítqan 8. madungúg 9. makítaq 10. makakitáq.

Lesson 12

IA (1). 1. táwgun 2. madalá or dádqa 3. dádqun 4. tanqáwa 5. giqingún or naqingún 6. palitún 7. dádqun 8. gitawág 9. gidúbli 10. gikinahánglan or kinahanglánun.

IA (2). 1. nabáyran or gibáyran 2. gitagáqan 3. suklíqi 4. limbúngan 5. dublíhan or madublíhan (ka-) 6. tagáqi or matagáqi (ka-) 7. tabángan or matabángan (ka-) 8. palití 9. palitán 10. gibaligyáqan.

IA (3). 1. ilíbut 2. gibáyad or gikabáyad (na-) 3. ihátag or ikahátag (ma-) 4. ipalít 5. iplíti 6. ikanáqug 7. gibalígyaq 8. gisúlti 9. gipangutána 10. ibántay.

IB. 1. sákyan 2. iplíti or ikaplíti (ma-) 3. isakáy 4. plitíhi 5. gidalá or nadalá 6. dádqan, giläbdan 7. idalá, dádqun 8. kanaqúgan 9. ikanáqug 10. palitún 11. ipalít, palitá 12. gipalít, gipalít 13. tagáqi, gitagáqan or natagáqan 14. ihátag 15. gibáyran 16. báyri or kabáyri (ma-), ibáyad or ikabáyad (ma-) 17. tanqáwun 18. gitánqaw 19. gitanqáwan 20. itánqaw.

IC. 1. muqádtu 2. magdalá 3. pagdalá 4. dádqi 5. naghátag 6. ihátag 7. tagáqi 8. ihatúd 9. hátdi 10. muhatúd 11. bantayí 12. nagbántay 13. palitún 14. mupalít or makapalít 15. musakáy or makasakáy 16. misakáy 17. gisákyan 18. musúlti or magsúlti 19. sultíhi 20. nagsúlti.

ID. 1. kanáqug 2. tagáqi (hatági) 3. hátdi 4. kanáqug 5. lakáw 6. sultíhi 7. ánhi 8. panánghid 9. katúlug or panqatúluq 10. ubán 11. palití 12. pangutánqa 13. tabángi 14. tabángi 15. pagtuqún or tuqún 16. kanáqug 17. tanqáwa 18. ibalígyaq 19. sultíhi 20. saká.

II. 1. unsáqun 2. giqúnsa 3. giqúnsa 4. magqúnsa 5. naqúnsa 6. naqúnsa 7. giqúnsa 8. naqúnsa 9. magqúnsa 10. magqúnsa 11. giqúnsa 12. unsáqun 13. magqúnsa 14. naqúnsa 15. unsáqa 16. unsáqun 17. unsáqun 18. nagqúnsa 19. unsáqun 20. mangúnsa.

IIIA. 1. ipahátag 2. gipapalít 3. pasákya 4. pasákyun 5. pasultíhun 6. paplitíhun 7. paqanhíqun 8. gipahatúd 9. paqubanún 10. pabalíka 11. pasilhígun 12. ipahátag 13. papalitún 14. papananghíra 15. ipatánqaw 16. gipahulát, paqadtúqa 17. pasákyun 18. ipapalít 19. palákwa 20. paqubanún.

IV. 1. siláng mupalít 2. pagsílhig or níyag sílhig 3. nímug trápu or pagtrápu 4. bang mulímpyu 5. Pírlang muqádtu 6. pagbisíta or Wílbig bisíta 7. siyáng muqádtu 8. bang mutánqaw 9. nílag lútuq or paglútuq 10. bang muhígup 11. kug bisíta or pagbisíta 12. (nga) mubálik 13. siláng musakáy 14. nímug lútuq or paglútuq 15. (nga) muqádtu.

V. The following sentences give one way of translating the English.

1. Ayáw na kug tanqáwa.
2. Níqa na ta.
3. Maqáyu pag mulakáw na lang ku
4. Maqáyu pag mupaqúliq na lang ku.
5. Waq pay nangutána nákuq.
6. Sígi na. Pasákya na ku.
7. Bísag tigúlang na siyá, muqinúm pa gihápúun siyág usá ka húngut tubáq káda ádlaw.
8. Diháq or Dídtu na siyás Sibú sa waq pay gíra.

9. Taná. Manakáy na ta!
10. Gíkan pa si Máma sa San Rimihiyú.
11. Nabalígyaq na ba nímu ang tanáng káwuq?
12. Ang Hulú sákup sa Pilipínas; ang Tawitáwi sákup pa gihápun sa Pilipínas; apán ang Burníyu, díliq na naq sákup sa Pilipínas.
13. Kiní muqádtu sa Úrmuk, ug kanáq pa sad. Apán kádtung túqa dídtu, diliq na.
14. Waq pa gyud ku makakitáq ug basakán.
15. Mangítaq tag dyip. Diq na ku kalakáw.
16. Katúug na diháq.
17. Mas dakúq pa siyá kay kanákuq.
18. Isáq pa. Karún ka pa muqabút.
19. Ayáwg kanáqug sámtang waq pay háyag.
20. Sa 1956 dídtu pa ku sa Pránsya, apán sa 1959, dínhi na ku sa Pilipínas.
21. Waq pa ku kakaqún ug kinílaw.
22. Isáq pa. Diq pa ba ni Banáwaq?
23. Uu. Maqú na ni kay náqa ang baay ni Dúktur Pirnándis.
24. Sa waq pa ku sa Sibú, waq ku kaqilá níya.
25. Dúna pa kay láqing palitún?
26. Maqáyu pang musakáy ka na lang run nga háyag pa.
27. Wánqay (Waq nay) bir Nyur.
28. Uy! Údtu na. Waq na tingáliy dyip. Magtáksi na lang ta.
29. Ay nag súlti. Katúug na.
30. 'Págnga na naq.' — 'Ang rádyu?' — 'Uu, únsa pa man?'
31. Upát pa lang ku ka ádlaw dínhi.
32. Dúgay ka na ba dínhi?
33. Díqa or Níqa pay láqing dyip. Pangutánqun nátug mulárga na ba siyá.

VIA(1). Some of the sentences below may be expressed in several other ways.

1. Ma, diq pa kunú muqádtus Burumíyu si Mis Wílbi.
2. Waq na si Mis Wílbi dídtu sa kusína.
3. Waq pa siyá manáqug kay diq na siyá musakáy sa tartanílya.
4. Waq pa ba makasakáy si Mis Wílbi Day?
5. Waq na siyá maghulát ug tartanílya páras Burumíyu.
6. Dung, diq ka na ba muqágis tiyánggi?
7. Karúng panahúna, diq na kaqáyu lisúd pagpangítag tartanílya.
8. Waq na magpahuwát si Pírla kang Mis Wílbi.
9. Diq pa ku muqádtu kay waq pay tartanílya.
10. Day, diq pa ku muqádtu, kay diq na ku muhapít sa tindáhan.
11. Uy, waq pa man diqáy makasakáy si Pírla.
12. Diq pa ta manlákaw Day kay diq pa man údtu.
13. Waq na man diqáy magsakít ning ákung úlu.
14. Diq pa ba ni ínyung tindáhan Day?
15. Waq ka na bay palitúng líbru Day?

VIA(2).

1. Muqubán pa ku nímu ngádtus tindáhan.
2. Mulakáw na ku run kay dúna na may tartanílya.
3. Nagqingún ang dráybir nga makahuwát pa siyá nímu.
4. Makasakáy na siyág tartanílya kay dúna na may miqági.
5. Ikáw ba tung nagsúlti nákuq nga makaqádtu ka nas Lahúg.
6. Day, dúna pa ba mu dínhiy líbru.
7. Dung, makasakáy pa ba mi sa ímung tartanílya?

8. Anáaq, makalakáw na man diqáy ku kay natagáqan na man ku níyag sinsílyu.
9. Uy, kabayád na man diqáy ku sa kutsíru.
10. Níqa pa ba dínhi tung líbrung ákung gitanqawtánqaw ganíha?
11. Magkinahánglan ka pa ba sa ákung tábang karún Mis?
12. May nabaligyáqan ka na bag líbru karún Day?
13. Musakáy na mu Day? Makahulát pa man ku nínyu.
14. Pírla, may nakítqan pa ba gyud kang láqing tartanílya?
15. Mupalít pa kug líbru dínhi uy.

VIB. The answers should contain the following words:
1. waq pa 2. waq pa 3. waq pa 4. waq na 5. diq na 6. diq na 7. waq pa 8. waq na 9. diq pa 10. waq pa 11. waq pa 12. diq na 13. waq pa 14. waq pa 15. waq na.

VIIA.
1. Kadúgay or Pagkadúgay or Dugáya nimung miqabút!
2. Kalabád or Pagkalabád or Labára sa ákung úlu!
3. Kasakít or Pagkasakít or Sakíta sa ákung tiyán ganína!
4. Kadalíng or Pagkadalíng or Dalíqang nahumán sa ákung trabáhu!
5. Kadághan or Pagkadághan or Daghána íning ímung líbrung balígyaq!
6. Kaníndut or Pagkaníndut or Nindúta íning balígyaq nínyung panáptun!
7. Kamaqáyu or Pagkamaqáyu nímung musinibuwanú!
8. Kasayúp or Pagkasayúp or Sayúpa sa ímung gibúhat!
9. Kasámuk or Pagkasámuk or Samúka íning dapíta!
10. Kaqarangqaráng or Pagkaqarangqaráng na karún nímung musúltig Sinibuwanú.
11. Kasayún or Pagkasayún or Sayúna ra diqáy ánang buhátun!
12. Kalayúq or Pagkalayúq or Layúqa diqáy sa Pulambatú!
13. Kagamáy or Pagkagamáy or Gamáya ra sa ámung ganánsya sa tindáhan!
14. Kadakúq or Pagkadakúq or Dakúqa sa baláy ni Mísis Abilyána!
15. Kadághan or Pagkadághan or Daghána ánang kaság nga ímung gipalít!

VIIB. 1. ka, ni 2. ku 3. nímu, niqánaq, ku 4. nákuq, ang 5. si 6. siyá 7. nínyu 8. ka 9. ni 10. ku, nínyu 11. silá, nátuq 12. nímu, ang, nímu 13. siyá 14. silá 15. niqádtu 16. kamí 17. nákuq 18. ang 19. si 20. ang, ang.

Lesson 13

IA. 1. maqinúm 2. ímnum 3. giqinúm or naqinúm 4. tanqáwun 5. gitánqaw 6. ilímpyu 7. gilimpyúhan 8. limpyúhi 9. ipalít 10. napalitán or mapalitán (ka-) or gipalitán or palitán 11. palitún, dádqun 12. tagáqan or matagáqan (ka-) (also hatágan, etc.) 13. gihátag or gikahátag (na-) 14. tagáqan or matagáqan or katagáqan 15. ihátag or ikahátag (ma-) 16. gipáhid 17. pahíran or mapahíran (ka-) 18. pahíran 19. hulatá or mahulát 20. hulatá.

IB. 1. muqánhi 2. nakaqádtu 3. nakapangíhiq or nangíhiq 4. nalíbri, dákpun 5. magbáklay, iplíti 6. magbalígyaq 7. mabáyran (ka-) 8. mubáyad 9. ibáyad or ikabáyad (ma-) 10. muqinúm, gipalít 11. ímnun 12. nakaqinúm 13. katagúqan (ma-) 14. kalusán or ikalús 15. nagkalús 16. magqistúrya 17. ikaqistúrya (ma-) or iqistúrya 18. makahígup, maglútuq 19. muqirís or makaqirís 20. irisá.

IC. 1. sulúd 2. pagdúwaq or dúwaq 3. panánghid 4. hugási 5. panglímpyu 6. pagbántay 7. inúm 8. katúlug 9. hígdaq or panghígdaq 10. línya or paglínya 11. tágda 12. hulatá 13. irisírba 14. sugáta 15. púnqi.

ID. 1. ipasílhig 2. paqirisún 3. palabáyun 4. paqímnun 5. pabakláyun 6. patabángun 7. pagáwsun 8. ipagawás 9. palutúqun 10. pabaligyáqun 11. pasákyun 12. ipabalígyaq 13. pasúdlun 14. ipaqánhi 15. ipahulát 16. ipadalíq 17. pakalusún, palimpyúhun 18. patabángun 19. ipaqistúrya. 20. ipatánqaw.

IE. 1. ni 2. ni 3. ang, ang 4. ang, ni 5. sa, si 6. ang, ug 7. si 8. ni 9. ug, ang 10. ni 11. nímu, ni, ang 12. si, sa 13. silá 14. níya, ang, ug, sa 15. ug, si, siyá.

IF. Other translations are possible besides these given here.

1. Mas dakúq pa sa sakayán ang árka ni Núwa.
2. Waq pa muqabút ang túrnu ni Ánghil pagqirís sa blákburd.
3. Mam, humán na ang ámung dúwaq.
4. Waq pa ku kakitáq ug ritrátu sa árka.
5. Nakakitáq na ka Pidrú?
6. Maqáyu pa tingálig paqímnun ta kag túbig sa diq pa ta musúgud sa klási.
7. Mam. Makapaqúliq na ku run Mam?
8. Naqáyu na ba ang labád sa úlu ni Dyiin?
9. Waq pa muhúnung ang ulán.
10. Gidádqan ka na bag túbig ni Lína?
11. Magsuwát pa ku níya.
12. Ayaw na lag bisíta nákuq kung waq diháq ang ímung mga mutsátsa.
13. Nakadungúg ka na bag istúrya báhin ni Núwa ug ang íyang árka?
14. Ngítngit pa naq inigqabút mu dídtu.
15. Waq na bay láqing dúlaq nga átung madúlaq?
16. Waq nay láqing bárkung muqádtu sa Úrmuk gawás niqíni.
17. Nakaqádtu na kug dághang mga lugár, apán nílang tanán, gústu gyud ku sa Pulambatú.
18. Waq pa gyud silá makapíldi námuq.
19. Waq ku pa maqistúrya nínyu ang istúrya ni Núwa, nu?
20. Makapaqúliq na mu mga bátaq.
21. Nangláakaw na lang mi ngádtu sa Burumíyu kay waq mi kasakáy dínhi.
22. Naghulát pa mi níla dínhi.
23. Waq na ra bay áyskrim.
24. Mangáqun na ta.
25. Ngánung diq na man lang ta manakáy dínhi, bísag dághan kaqáyung mga táwung naghulát.
26. Humán na ba mung tanág pangíhiq?
27. Humán na ming tanán Mam.
28. Mas taqás pa si Ánghil kang Lína.
29. Karún pa gyud ku muqabút gíkan sa Pulambatú, Liná.
30. Ngánung waq pa nímu silá pasúdla.

IG. Other translations are possible besides those given here.

1. Kwátru písus na lang ang plíti karún.
2. Uh, síngku singkwínta diqáy? Nákug kwátru singkwínta lang.
3. Isáq pa diqáy, Amirkána ka nu?
4. Ikáw lay dalá sa bag.
5. Subáya lang ang Piláqis Strit.
6. Uy! Hápun na man diqáy.
7. Ásu man diqáy tag dyip padúung sa Kárbun?

8. Láqin pa diqáy átuq, magdúgay ka ba dínhis Sibú?
9. Kamú diqáyng duhá ang magdúwag síndul pándul?
10. Ikáw na lay mamalít.
11. Kínsa man diqáy mulútuq sa mga kaság.
12. Tagbáynti na lang ang buqúk sa kaság.
13. Sakáy na lag láqing dyip.
14. Uy, lutúq na man diqáy ang mga kaság.
15. Únsa man diqáy íyang gipalít?
16. Ádtu na lang mi
17. Diq ba diqáy naq mabalígyag dyis?
18. Magkítaq na lang ta sunúd simána.
19. Maqú diqáy ning Úrmuk.
20. Aa, waq na diqáy dyip. Manglákaw na lang ta.
21. Diq ku man mabalígyag dyis; gibalígyaq ku na lag síngku.
22. Akú diqáy. Waq man ku nímu tagáqi.

II A. 1. ku makaqiháp 2. gidáa lang naq 3. nagpaqábut 4. maqílhan ku silá 5. magbúhat nyaq kug pilípig. 6. sangágun naq nímu 7. gibúhat ni níla 8. ila nang ilábay 9. mudágan siyá bálik ngarí 10. muqutúng naq siyá 11. gipatíndug níla kanáng 12. nakakitáq ka bítaw ánang 13. ka mang musúltig 14. mubántay sa.

II B. 1. gipatánqaw, nímu 2. iqistúrya, ku (nákuq) 3. duláqun 4. mu, magduláq or makaduláq 5. matánqaw or tanqáwun 6. mutawág or magtawág, nákuq, íngna. 7. ímu, gipadágan 8. mudágan 9. mupalít 10. magbánhaq, ku, magqistúrya, nínyu 11. gisúlti, nímu 12. pasultíhun, níya 13. manánghid 14. manánghid, níya (kaníya) 15. si, muqirís.

III. Other translations are possible besides those given here.
1. Dúna bay naglábayg búla nákuq?
2. Dúnay miqánhi pagbisíta ni Dyiin.
3. May nagtúktuk sa pultahán.
4. Kung dúnay muqánhi, íngna nga waq ku dínhi.
5. Dúnay nagtábang nákuq pagdúmdum sa Pulambatú.
6. May nagtawág sa maqístra.
7. Dúnay nagtawág nímu.
8. Dúna bay miqánhi?
9. Waláy mitábang nákuq pagsílhig sa salúg.
10. Way namínaw sa ímung istúrya.
11. Dúnay namínaw pagqáyu sa ákung istúrya.
12. Waq gyud kuy nadungúg nga nagtawág nákuq.
13. Dúna bay nagbántay sa mga bátaq sa gawás?
14. Dúnay nagqingún nákung nagkinahánglan kag tábang.
15. Dúna bay nakakitáng Ánghil.
16. Dúna bay nagtawág?
17. Bísag únsa lang, mahímuq.
18. Básig dúnay mutawág nímu.
19. Dúnay nagkinahánglan sa ímung tábang sa Pulambatú.
20. Ug dúnay gústung muqinúm, paqariqá lang.

IV A. 1. ihátag, ni 2. ihátag, kanáng 3. muhátag, ni, sa 4. kuháqa 5. mudalá or dalá, niqánang 6. ibílin, naq 7. kuháqa, naq, nínyu 8. kuháqun, námuq, námuq, kinahanglána 9. nínyu, kuháqun, ang 10. manggáwas, ta 11. ínyung, butangán, sa 12. ang, mugawás, muqirís or magqirís, sa 13. muqirís, niqánang 14. irisá 15. manggáwas 16. magdúwaq, kitá 17. manggáwas, si 18. naqirís _or_ giqirís, nákuq, ang, manggáwas 19. lakáw _or_ manglákaw, ta 20. ibutáng, nang 21. kamí, mudúwaq _or_ magdúwaq 22. pagdúwaq, mu 23. mulábay 24. milábay, akú, mulábay 25. táguq.

IV B.
1. Dínhi silá magdúlag síndul pándul.
2. Kanúsqa gyud silá makadúlag usáb?
3. Dídtu ni Ánghil ibutáng ang irísir.
4. Únyaq ra silá makagústus ílang dúlaq.
5. Úgmaq pud mudúlag apil si Mis Sántus.
6. Diháq níya masákpi siÚsting.
7. Kanúsqa man gud mudágan silá si Nínig si Kíkuy.
8. Diháq dákpa si Kíkuy.
9. Dínhi níla ibutáng ang ílang dalá.
10. Inigkataqudtaqúd ra siya makahibáwu sa dúlaq.
11. Dínhaq si Pídru makaqinúm ug túbig.
12. Sa sunúd ádlaw na lang si Mis Wílbi magqistúrya.
13. Diháq ku makakitág ritrátus árka.
14. Kanúsqa ba silá huwatá ni Mis Wílbi?
15. Inigkahumán mangínum ug túbig ang mga bátaq.
16. Únyaq pa silá magdúlaq sa gawás.
17. Kásqa ra ku magqistúrya nínyu.
18. Kanúsqa na man pud ka makaqistúrya?
19. Dínhi si Lítu maghuwát níla.
20. Kanúsqa silá magdúlag usáb?
21. Diháq si Mis Wílbi magtíndug duqúl sa blákburd.
22. Dínhi ibutáng ni Nína ang líbru.
23. Diqín man ni Mam hikítqi ang mga ilagáq?
24. Sa Byírnis magdalá si Lítug líbru.
25. Karún dáyun magdúlaq siláng tanán.

Lesson 14

IA. 1. dádqi 2. gidalá 3. dádqa 4. tanqáwun 5. tanqáwa 6. gitánqaw 7. ayúha 8. ayúha 9. giqáyu 10. gisilhígag 11. gisilhigán _or_ nasilhigán 12. isílhig 13. limpyúhi 14. gilimpyúhan 15. ilímpyu.

IB. 1. naghatudhátud 2. maghatúd 3. ímna 4. miqinúm _or_ nakaqinúm 5. biyáqan 6. mibíyaq 7. gidaliqán 8. nagdalíq 9. muqádtu 10. mangádtu 11. maniqúdtu 12. naniqúdtu 13. lutúqi _or_ ilútuq 14. lutúqún 15. gipatánqaw 16. muhíkay _or_ makahíkay 17. hikáyun 18. mutubág 19. tubagá 20. itubág _or_ ikatubág (ma-).

IC. 1. ang 2. si, ang 3. ikáw, kamí 4. ang, sa 5. ang, sa 6. sa, átuq 7. ku, ug 8. ka, nga 9. ang, ímu 10. tu, sa 11. sa 12. nga 13. ang 14. kamú, sa 15. kádtu.

ID. Other translations are possible besides those given here.
1. Pangutánqun ku na lang gyud si Tátay.
2. Tagsíngku písus ang dusína. Apán tagáqan ta kag ispísyal prays, tris písus lang.
3. Si Lína na lay palimpyúha sa kwártu.
4. Dyútay lang ang dyip dínhi. Ádtu na lang ta sa Hwán Lúna ug ádtu ta dídtu maghuwát.

5. Ayáw na lang. Mubálik na lang mi úgmaq.
6. Waq na man siláy gamáy. Dakúq na lay átung palitún.
7. Uh, údtu na man diqáy. Ádtu na lang ku.
8. Aa, maqú diqáy ning baayng púyqan nínyung duhá?
9. Únsa man diqáy ímung gústung kánqun?
10. Isáq pa. Díliq ba ka apú ni Místir Abáya?
11. Dágkuq nang mga anák ni Iyúq Tibúq.
12. Waq pa ku kaqádtus baláy ni Pírla.
13. Diq na ku muqinúm ug kuuk.
14. Waq pa muqabút si Dúktur Pirnándis.
15. Diq na lang níya ihatúd ang lamísa dídtu kay nagqingún man kaháq ka nga ayáw na lang.
16. Maqáyu pag kuháqun na lang tu nínyu run.
17. Maqú na ni. Sakáy na ta.
18. Patáy na ba si Místir Usmínya?
19. Mangatúlug na lang ta kay gikapúy man ta.
20. Únsa man diqáy átung panihápun rung gabíqi?
21. Uh, diq ba diqáy ta manímba?
22. Isáq pa, diq ba diqáy ta makapangáqun úsaq?
23. Gipaqilaqíla na níya ang íyang mga apú námuq.
24. Ginúqu ku, nagquwán na man.
25. Ihátag na lang naq nákug báynti sintábus, ha?
26. Aa, nagbalígyaq ka diqáyg mga panáptun dínhi.
27. Diq na mahímuq Nyur, kay milakáw na man siyá.
28. Liná, waq pa ba diqáy nímu palitá ang ságing?
29. Huy Dung, isáq pa kadiyút. Dúna kay nalímtan.
30. Pamínaw lang gániq níya.

IIA. The potential forms are also possible in many cases although they are not listed here.
1. ipaqinúm, ni, ang or paqímna, si, ug 2. gitagáqan, nímu, sa, si or gihátag, nímu, ang, ni 3. magtawág, sa 4. gitrapúhan, kádtu 5. muhígup, sa 6. gisilhígan, ang 7. ibílin, ang 8. gihíkay, mu, ang 9. si, ang 10. gilimpyúhan, nímu, ang 11. butangán, nímu, sa 12. gilútuq, nímu, ang 13. ánhi or muqánhi, si 14. gikúhaq, nímu, ang 15. gidalá, nímu, ihátag, ni 16. ikúhaq, niqádtu, sa 17. higúpun, nímu, kaníng 18. naghígdaq, ka or muhígdaq, ka 19. tu, nagdalá, nímu 20. tanqáwa, kádtu, kuháqa.

IIB. Other translations are also possible besides those given here.
1. Náqay nagtawág nímu Lína.
2. Kun dúnay magtawág nímu Lína, tubagá dáyun.
3. Way makabántay sa ákung mga bátaq.
4. Diq ku mupaqúlig sayú kun dúnay magbántay sa mga bátaq.
5. Kun mulakáw ka káda ádlaw, kinahánglan kang dúnay magbántay sa ímung masakitúng asáwa.
6. Kun dúnay mutawág, malípay gyud ku.
7. Waq kuy nadungúg nga nagtawág nákuq.
8. Dúna kuy nagbántays mga bátaq sa baláy.
9. Waq námuq isúlti kang bisán kínsa nga nasakít si Dyiin.
10. Dúnay nagsúlti sa mga bátaq nga dínhi mi.
11. Ayáw gyug súlti kang bísan kínsa nga nagdaqút ku.

12. Dúna bay nakadungúg ni Mísis Mílir nga nagtawág nákuq?
13. Dúnay miqánhi paghatúd ug sabáws manúk pára nímu.
14. Dúna kay gitawág?
15. Dúnay nagdáa nákug (usá ka panáksang) lamiqáng sabáws manúk.
16. Lisúd ning kanúnayng magdaqutdáqut.
17. Kun dúnay magpakáqun nákug sabáw ingún kalamíq niqíni mamaqáyu gyud ku dáyun.

III. Other answers besides those given are possible.
1. Uh! Háqin na ba si Lína nga waq man dáyun ni mutubág.
2. Ngánung dúgay ka mang midúqul.
3. Sus, díqay iskína, waq silhígig maqáyu.
4. Gihumán dáyun ni Lína ang pagsílhig sa suqúk arún siyá makapang-húgas sa mga pínggan.
5. Magsultisúlti ta dínhis sálag kadiyút.
6. Únyaq, kádtu dídtu ímu úntaq tung trapúhag maqáyu.
7. Hásta tung túqa dídtu limpyúhig maqáyu or limpyúhi pagqáyu.
8. Misakít ang ákung úlug kalít.
9. Gihígup níyag inánay ang sabáw kay ínit pa.
10. Mibákud ug hínay si Mísis Mílir arún tanqáwun ang ági sa mutsátsa.
11. Gilútuq níya ang kik ug lamíq.
12. Kusúg muhígup si Mísis Mílir básta sabáws manúk.
13. Mipaqúlig dalíq si Místir Mílir gíkan sa trabáhu.
14. Midágan man gud ug kusúg si Kíkuy, maqúng waq hisákpi.
15. Giqítsa ni Lítu ang látag kalít.
16. Kusúg musúlti si Mísis Mílir.
17. Hínayng musúlti si Místir Mílir.

IV A. 1. man 2. ra ba 3. ra ba 4. ra ba 5. man 6. man 7. man 8. ra ba, man 9. ra ba 10. man 11. man 12. man.

IV B(1). The following give one possible answer.
1. Kay papíl man ang íya Mam.
2. Kínsa may mulábay sa láta?
3. Kínsa man tung nagbánhaq?
4. Ah, sayún ra naq.
5. Dúsi ra ang ultimúng prísyu.
6. Láqin ra bang mga táwu dínhis pantalán.
7. Sus, nagquwán na hinúqun. Bágqu ra ba ning ákung sinínaq.
8. Díliq. Akú ra.
9. Pilá may idád mu Nyúr?
10. Uh, únsa na may duwáqun nátuq?
11. 'Gústu ka bang mupalít ug kaság?' 'Díliq, mahál ra kaqáyu.'
12. Ása man ta musakáyg dyip ug muqádtu ta sa Banáwaq.
13. Ása ka man padúung Mis?
14. Kwátru singkwínta ra? Kabarátu!
15. Lutúqa. Mamatáy or matáy ra bítaw naq.
16. Dúna na man kuy katábang.
17. Kanáng náqas sílung, gústu man ku ánaq.
18. Uh, túqa ra silá.
19. Uh, nangíhiq na man ku. Humán na ku.

IV B(2). 1. man diqáy 2. diqáy 3. diqáy 4. man diqáy 5. man diqáy 6. diqáy 7. diqáy 8. diqáy, man diqáy 9. diqáy, diqáy 10. diqáy.

IV C. Other translations are possible besides those given here.

1. Muqinúm si Lína ug usá ka básung túbig káda humág káqun.
2. Mupalít kug duhá ka buqúk kaság Nang.
3. Gitagáqan si Lítu ug usá ka butílyang kuuk ni Pírla.
4. Muqinúm si Iyúq Tibúq ug usá ka húngut tubáq káda ádlaw.
5. Mipalít si Mis Wílbig usá ka dusínang aríyus sa tindáhan.
6. Miqinúm siyág usá ka butílyang kuuk.
7. Waq makapatigúwang ni Iyúq Tibúq ang usá ka húngut nga tubáq káda ádlaw.
8. Inúm ug usá ka básung túbig.
9. Pilá ka buqúk kaság ang ímung makáqun?
10. Mipalít siyág usá ka dusínang aríyus kay barátu man.

V. 1. ipangutána 2. pangutánqun 3. isúguq 4. gisúguq 5. iqingún 6. íngnun 7. íngnun 8. táwgun 9. itawág 10. sákyun 11. isakáy 12. ihángyuq 13. ihángyuq 14. hangyúqun 15. sagúlun 16. iságul 17. tubagún 18. itubág 19. pangutánqun 20. ipangutána.

Lesson 15

I. Wherever a deictic with ng is given, a deictic with d is also possible.
1. níqa 2. túqa 3. dínhi 4. túqa 5. dídtu 6. dínhi 7. arí, díqa, ngarí 8. dídtu 9. túqa 10. dínhi 11. dídtu 12. diháq 13. náqa or túqa 14. náqa or túqa 15. ánhi 16. túqa or ádtu 17. níqa 18. diháq 19. arí, ngarí 20. ngánhi 21. túqa or náqa 22. túqa or ádtu 23. ánhi, ngánhi 24. ánhaq, ngánhaq 25. túqa, ngádtu.

II. 1. naglútuq 2. lutúqan or ilútuq 3. malútuq or lutúqa 4. naglútuq or galútuq 5. nalútuq or gilútuq 6. lutúqi or ilútuq 7. gisultíhan or nasultíhan 8. sultíhi 9. gisultíhan or nasultíhan 10. musúlti 11. nasilhígan or gisilhígan 12. nagsílhig 13. isílhig 14. musílhig 15. gihígup 16. muhígup 17. naghígup 18. gipahígup 19. panágan 20. midágan or nanágan 21. mudágan or manágan 22. mudágan 23. ilábay 24. gilábay 25. mulábay 26. limpyúhi 27. límpyu 28. panlímpyu 29. malimpyúhan (ka-) or limpyúhan 30. limpyúhi.

III A. 1. ipaqádtu 2. pahatágun or patagáqun 3. ipahátag 4. padádqun 5. pakantáhun 6. ipatawág 7. pabakúrun 8. pabugnáwun 9. ipahíkay 10. ipatánqaw 11. pasilhígi 12. palimpyúhun 13. palimpyúhi 14. pahumanún 15. padaliqún 16. ipadalá 17. ipaqádtu 18. ipaqánhi 19. palutúqun 20. paqímnun 21. ipakúhaq 22. pasákqun 23. palingkúrun 24. pahigdáqun 25. padayunún.

IV. 1. ta 2. ang 3. ka 4. ku 5. nímu, ang 6. si, siyá 7. siyá, kitá, nátuq 8. ang, nátuq 9. ang 10. ákuq, si 11. mu, ínyu 12. ka, námuq 13. ka 14. ta 15. ákuq 16. ikáw 17. ni 18. ákuq 19. átuq, si 20. mu 21. nímu 22. silá, mi 23. íla 24. níla 25. silá.

V. 1. Waq ra ba bisitáhi si Mísis Kapangpángan ni Místir ug Mísis Mílir.
2. Waq mi makadungúg nga masakitún ka.
3. Diq pa gyud diqáy risís kay waq pa man manggáwas ang mga bátaq.
4. Diq lagí gyud si Kíkuy ang milábayg batú ni Lítu.
5. Diq ku lang diqáy hulatún si Píya.
6. Ayáw lag dayún kay diq man kaháq mu makigkítang Lítu.
7. Diq saq diqáy túqud ta maniqúdtu pagqúna, Mísis Abayá.

8. Diq na gyud gústung mudúlaq ang mga bátaq.
9. Diq na man kaqáyu masakitún si Pídru.
10. Waq magsúlti si Mis Sántus nga silhígan sad kunú nímu ang kwártu.
11. Waq ba kaháq si Lítu muqagí ni Kíkuy?
12. Díliq lang túqud ta musakáyg tartanílya arún diq ta muqabút ug dalíq sa Burumíyu.
13. Diq pa kaqáyu búgnaw ang sabáw apán diq pa gyud gihápun gústung muhígup si Lítu.
14. Waq pa kunú paduláqa ni Píya ang mga bátaq.
15. Diq na lang ta musakáyg tartanílya kay waq pa man sab magqulán.
16. Kumústa diqáy si Kíkuy, waq pa ba maqáyu?
17. Diq na ba lang ta maniqúdtu, Mísis Abáya?
18. Waq pa maglútuq si Píya sa átung paniqúdtu.
19. Diq ku ba lang kaháq ibílin kiníng mga pínggan?
20. Kíkuy, ayáw na lang kug itawág ug tartanílya.
21. Waq na lang gyud muhígdaq si Píya kay waq man siyá hilántig maqáyu.
22. Waq pa man sad diqáy muqádtu si Pídru ni Mis Sántus.
23. Waq gyud diqáy ayúha kaqáyu pagtagád si Mis Sántus ni Mam.
24. Waq na man gud ku magtuqún pagqánhi nílang Mam ug Lítu.
25. Waq pa bayáq diqáy mahibalú si Mis Sántus nga nangíhiq na sad si Kíkuy sa kwártu.

VI. 1. tiká or tikáw or ta, ka or ka, nákuq 2. ku, nímu 3. nákuq, ang babáyi or ang babáyi, nákuq 4. níya, si Mis Wílbi 5. tikáw or tiká or ta, ka or ka, nákuq 6. ákuq, nímu 7. siyá, nákuq 8. siyá, sa ímung bag 9. ku, nínyu 10. tiká or tikáw or ta, ka or ka, nákuq 11. ku, sa ímung kalamáy 12. ku, nímu 13. táwu, nínyu 14. tiká or tikáw or ta, ka or ka, nákuq 15. ta, ug táksi 16. ni Mísis Mílir, si Mísis Abáya or si Mísis Abáya, ni Mísis Mílir 17. níya, ang tindáhan 18. níya, si Mis Wílbi or si Mis Wílbi, níya 19. níya, ang mga bátaq or ang mga bátaq, níya 20. sa abát, si Lítu or si Lítu, sa abát 21. ang blákburd, ni Ánghil or ni Ánghil, ang blákburd. 22. si Dyin, níya 23. si Lína, ni Mísis Mílir or ni Mísis Mílir, si Lína 24. níya, si Lína or si Lína, níya 25. síla, ni Mísis Abáya.

VII. 1. nangabút 2. manglútuq 3. nanglíngkud 4. nabúhiq 5. mahibalú 6. manganáqug 7. nanakít 8. manglákaw 9. nabaláka 10. mamáhid 11. nanánghid, mamaqúliq 12. nahumán 13. manghígdaq 14. nangumústa 15. nanghináqut 16. nanglútuq 17. nangítaq 18. mamúhat or namúhat 19. nadúgay 20. mangutána 21. manglímbung 22. nalúquy 23. mangíhiq 24. mabúgnaw 25. maníilhig.

VIII. 1. silhígi 2. pangádtu 3. pangíhiq 4. ibalígyaq 5. kanáqug 6. panulúd 7. higúpa 8. pangutánqa 9. irisírba or risirbáhi 10. ihátag 11. pakaligúqa 12. tágda 13. kúyug 14. sultíhi 15. padayuná 16. panglíngkud 17. paqanhíqa 18. panginúm 19. dádqa 20. tanqáwa 21. tubagá 22. irisá 23. pahibaluqá or pahibálqa 24. dublíha 25. limbúngi.

IX. 1. giqúnsa 2. unsáqa 3. unsáqun 4. nagqúnsa 5. giqúnsa 6. unsáqun 7. naqúnsa 8. makaqúnsa 9. giqúnsa 10. unsáqun 11. maqúnsa 12. magqúnsa 13. magqúnsa 14. nagqúnsa 15. unsáqun 16. naqúnsa 17. maqúnsa 18. giqúnsa 19. magqúnsa 20. mangúnsa 21. naqúnsa 22. maqúnsa 23. naqúnsa 24. giqúnsa 25. mangúnsa or makaqúnsa.

X. Other translations are possible besides those given here.

1. Ádtu na ku.
2. Uh, waq na ra bay bir Nyur.
3. Isáq pa, anúsqa pa man mu mamálhin?
4. Uh, níqa na ta.
5. Diq pa ku manáqug sa bárku sámtang diq pa háyag.
6. Diq ku manáqug sa bárku sámtang ngítngit pa.
7. Únsa pa may ubáng dádqun nátuq?
8. Aa, ayáw na lang.
9. Taná. May pang muqádtu na lang ta sa istasyunán karún.
10. Túqa pa siyá sa San Rimihiyú.
11. Na sigí, lakáw na mu.
12. Nagqulán pa.
13. Dúgay ka na ba dínhi?
14. Diq pa dúgay.
15. Kun báynti ang plíti, may pag maglakáw.
16. Isáq pa, waq ka ba magkinahánglan pag katábang sa ímung tindáhan?
17. Waláq na. Íguq nang usá ka buqúk.
18. Maqáyu pag adtúqun ku na ang ubán.
19. Humán ka na ba?
20. Sígi. Táguq na sab.

XI. 1. gibílin, níya 2. gidalá 3. muqánhi 4. gisilhígan or silhígan 5. naghatúd 6. mibákud 7. gibisitáhan 8. gisúlti, ni. 9. muqirís 10. nagpíik or nakapiík 11. gitawág, mu 12. ihúgas 13. naglútuq 14. gidúlaq 15. nadakúp or nadákpan, mudágan 16. mulíbri or maglíbri 17. gisúlti, ni 18. iqistúrya 19. muqítsa 20. mudayún 21. mubisíta 22. gitrápu 23. gidaliqán or daliqán 24. namínaw 25. miqánhi.

XII. 1. kuháqa, ang or pagkúhaq (kúhaq), ug 2. dádqa, ang or pagdalá (dalá), ug 3. isulúd, ang, ímnum, nákuq 4. ka, ka, maglisúd 5. ka, lábdi 6. naglisúd 7. gidalá, nímu 8. gidalá, nákuq 9. ibutáng, naq, sa 10. biyáqan, námuq 11. mangáqun or nangáqun, mu 12. ibutáng, ang or pagbutáng, ug, sa, muqádtu 13. ákuq, ímnun 14. iqáyu, ári 15. silá, gitawág 16. padayuná, silá 17. gidalá, nákuq 18. palingkúra, si 19. paqariqún, nákuq, si 20. gibisíta or gibisitáhan (gibisitáqan), ka, ni 21. gidádqan, ka 22. paqanhíqa, siyá 23. pasúdlun, nákuq, si 24. gilútuq, nákuq 25. ang, nangunáy, niqánaq.

XIII.

1. Ngánung waq man ku nímu sultíhi nga mibisíta diqáy dínhi silá si Místir ug Mísis Mílir?
2. Masakitún ba diqáy si Mísis Kapangpángan?
3. Uu. Grábi ra ba kunú ang íyang sakít.
4. Únyaq, díliq ba lang nátuq siyá duqáwun?
5. Taná, únsa pa may átung gidugáyan?
6. Tingáli bayág atrasáwu na ta.
7. Maqú na ba niy ílang baláy?
8. Uu, maqú na diqáy ning baláya.
9. Átuq na ba lang kaháng súdlun si Mísis Kapangpángan?
10. Níqa ra bay ámung dáa pára nímu.
11. Dághan kaqáyung salámat kanínyu.
12. Ngánung naghaguqhagúq pa man gyud mug daa niqíni?
13. Kumústa na man ang ímung sakít karún?
14. Waq pa gyud ku maqáyu.
15. Kumústa sab diqáy ang mga bátaq?

16. Malisúd lagí ning magdaqutdáqut ta.
17. Waq na gyud matagád ang mga bátaq.
18. Waq pa man gániq silá makakaqún sukád sa búntag.
19. Gústu man gud nílang akú pay mupakáqun kaníla.
20. Díliq ra ba gyud silá mangáqun kun láqing táwu ang mupakáqun.

XIV. Other translations are possible.

1. Dúgayng nakalárga ang barku.
2. Ang traak nga gisákyan ku dalíq rang nakaqabút sa Pulambatú.
3. Si Litu hínayng mudágan maqúng naqabát.
4. Kusúg sab muhígup ug sabáws manúk si Dyiin.
5. Nawaláq lag kalít ang íyang kagútum.
6. Silhígig maqayu ning salúg.
7. Hínayng musúlti si Místir Mílir.
8. Kanáng amíga ni Pírla maqáyung mubinisayáq.
9. Naglínya dáyun ang mga bátaq pagkahumán sa risís.
10. Dalíq ra siyáng nakamaqú sa ámung pinulungán.
11. Hínay pa siyáng mulakáw kay waláq pa maqáyu sa hilánat.
12. Diq na kung kalakáwg kusúg kay nagquwán na.
13. Kalít nga mikusúg ang ulán.
14. Dúgayng miqabút ang bárkus Úrmuk.
15. Nakakátqun rag dalíq si Lítu sa istúrya mahitungúd ni Núwa.
16. Dúgay siyáng nakasakáy kay waláy misugút nga tartanílya.
17. Kusúg siláng nanágan, búsaq waláq mi kadakúp níla.
18. Kalít nga misakít ang íyang úlu.
19. Dalíq rang nahálin ang íyang tíndang kalamáy.
20. Kiníng tráka hínayng mudágun.

XV. Other translations are possible besides these given here.

1. Dúna na bay nagqándam ug paniqúdtu?
2. Dúna kuy nakítqang nakigsúlti sa ákung tátay.
3. Waq bay nagdáag ságing?
4. Dúnay miqánhi dínhi gahápun.
5. Way mitubág sa pagtawág nákuq.
6. Dínhaq bay nagbalígyag kalamáy sa bárku?
7. Dúna bay nagdaqút íning baláya, Mísis Mílir?
8. Náqa bay muqubán nákuq sa bárku?
9. Dúna kuy nakítqang naghulát ng traak sa istasyunán.
10. Dúnay nagbílin íning mga gása pára sa ímung nánay.
11. Way nagqúliq sa ímung líbru ngánhi.
12. Dúnay nagqingún nákuq nga níqa si Mis Wílbi dínhi.
13. Dúna bay naghátag nímu niqíning mga líbru?
14. Waq ku magkinahánglan ug mutábang nákuq sa tindáhan.
15. Dúna bay katúltul sa baay ni Mísis Ulibár?
16. Way nagtúdluq nákuq pagdúlaq íning duláqa.
17. May nagsunúd nátuq.
18. Waláq kuy ikasúlti.
19. Dúna na bay naglábay sa láta?
20. Dúna ka na bay natagáqan sa ímung kalamáy?
21. Dúna bay miqinúm ug gátas íning basúha?
22. Dúna nay nagrisírba íning tihirása.
23. May tagáqan ka ba íning mga líbru?
24. Dúna bay miqubán nímu ngádtus Pulambatú?
25. May makítaq or nakítaq ka ba?

CEBUANO-ENGLISH GLOSSARY

The items in this Glossary appear in normal English alphabetical order, except that ng is treated as a single letter following n.

All vocabulary items appearing in the Basic Sentences of Part I are included, together with references to the first occurrence of each separate meaning for each item. (References consisting of numbers and letters are to lesson number, part (a, b, or c), and sentence number.) Certain forms not appearing in the Basic Sentences are listed also, to clarify forms that do occur; for example, under balígyaq 'sell,' pamalígyaq 'sell [to plural recipients]' is introduced in order to clarify gipamalígyaq, namalígyaq, and mamalígyaq. For words that have appeared only in secondary meanings, primary meanings are introduced here. (Forms derived from Basic-Sentence vocabulary but appearing only in the Exercises are not shown separately, since their meanings can be inferred from their grammatical make-up.)

The following abbreviations and conventions are used.

Adj.	Adjective [see 5 B].
CN	Common noun or name of a place.
Dat.	Dative [1 A 1, B 1 5 D 2].
Final	Used at end of sentence.
Gen.	Genitive [1 A 1 B 1 5 A 1].
Initial	Used at beginning of sentence.
N	Personal name.
Nom.	Nominative [1 A 1, B 1].
Numeral	A number of Cebuano origin linked with ka to the word it modifies.
Number	A number of Spanish origin not linked with ka and used for money, dates, time, and ages.
Q	Qualifier (postpositive, prepositive or other word modifying predicate). [3 C 2 , 3 C 3 a]
V	Verb (a word which contains one of the active or passive affixes. [6 A, 12 A])
Title	Word used immediately before a name and itself preceded by si, ni, ka, or kang.
Voc.	Vocative (special form of a name or title used in direct address).
*	Forms marked with an asterisk (*) occur only with affixes.
[ ]-	Cebuano/items enclosed in brackets are affixes; hyphens represent base to which the affix is attached.
[ ]- (→)	Right arrow after a bracketed affix indicates that stress shifts to final vowel in completed form.
[ ]- (←)	Left arrow after a bracketed affix indicates that stress shifts to next-to-last vowel.

-N-   -N- represents nasalization of initial consonant of base, as follows:
p or b becomes m
t, d, or s becomes n
k becomes ng
Other consonants remain unchanged but the prefix before them ends in n or ng.
[See 4 E.]

~   Represents the root as listed at the beginning of the item.

Dialectal   Forms marked dialectal are not in general use throughout the entire Cebuano-speaking area.

Forms having an l which is sometimes dropped (see the comment to 2 a 9 p. 40) are listed with the l. Any l between two a's, two u's, or a u and an a may be dropped unless there is a specific statement to the contrary.

Because of the multiplicity of English tense forms and phrases, any Cebuano verb form has a number of English equivalents. Verb forms are therefore glossed in a single simple form. Cebuano active forms are translated in a simple active form: mukáqun, mikáqun, magkaqún, nagkaqún, makakaqún, and nakakaqún are all glossed simply 'eat.' Direct passive forms are glossed 'thing [verb]ed' (e.g. gikáqun, kánqun, kánqa 'thing eaten'); local passives are glossed 'person for whom [verb]ed,' 'thing [verb]ed,' or 'place of [verb]ing,' depending on the meaning appropriate for the root; and instrumental passives are glossed 'thing with which [verb]ed' or 'thing [verb]ed,' whichever is appropriate.

Forms consisting of affixed roots are indented under the root. A form with a single affix comes directly under the root:

káqun V eat

maka- (→) eat [read makakaqún]

Forms having more than one affix are indented under the first affix, as:

káqun V eat

pa- V feed [read pakáqun]

pag- feed [read pagpakáqun (pag- + pa-káqun)]

A

aa Q [initial] (1) [pause before starting to speak] 1 a 7, 14; 2 a 2, b 9; 3 a 8, 10, 17, 19, 28, b 6, c 6, 12, 28, 35 and passim; (2) [precedes a response that indicates foregoing was unimportant, mistaken, a poor idea, etc.] 3 b 23; 4 a 25, b 37, 44, 50; 10 b 6, 19; 11 c 23; (3) [begins a statement that recalls a fact or concedes a point] 3 a 2, 27, c 15; 13 a 16, 40; 14 b 44, 64; (4) [pause before a question which means 'is that so?' or a statement which means 'so that is the way it is?'; cf. aw] 3 a 24, 35, b 10, 17; 5 a 9, 34, b 43; 6 a 20, b 43, 57; 8 a 26, b 28, c 29; 10 a 16; 11 b 8, 25, c 20; 12 b 41, 50, 52; 13 b 63, 83, 86; (5) [before exclamation] 13 b 70

ábang V rent
mu- rent 3 b 7, c 3, 7
nag- rent 3 b 26
-an person from whom rented 3 a 2
pa- V rent out
-an thing rented out 3 b 15, 19

abát CN the one who is It (in games) 13 a 17, 32

Abáya N [surname] 1 a 1, 4, 12, 25;

2 b 33; 14 a 25, 26, 27, 28, 31, b 44, 47
ábi Q [followed by Gen.][Gen.] thought (took for granted) 8 c 24
Abilyána N [surname] 3 a 1, 41, b 4
abúg CN dust
-un Adj. dusty 14 a 15
abút V (1) arrive; (2) attain
abút [= mi-, ni-] arrive 8 c 20; 9 b 19
pag- (1) arrive 4 b 51; 5 a 14
inig- (1) upon arriving, when [Gen.] arrives 3 a 23, 25; 4 a 28; 8 a 19
ning- [= mi-] arrive 9 c 2
mu- (1) arrive 2 b 11
maka- (2) reach 9 b 17
ma- [-un unreal nonpotential] (1) place gotten to 11 b 23
hi- V (1) happen to arrive
na- [= nahi-] (1) arrive 8 c 19; 14 a 19
*ábut
pa- V wait for (something to happen)
nag- wait 5 b 49
adá Q [= adáa] [initial] what the heck (exclamation dismissing something as unimportant) 14 b 39
adáa Q [= adá] [initial] what the heck (exclamation dismissing something as unimportant) 4 b 59
adíqa [short form díqa] (1) is here (near speaker, far from hearer) [1 A 2, 1 A 2 a, 3 A 1]; (2) is there (toward speaker but away from hearer)
ádlaw CN (1) day 5 a 16, b 56, 57; 8 c 11; 11 a 17; (2) daytime 5 b 42
-a (←) (1) particular day 4 b 36
karúng adláwa today 12 b 29
ádtu (1) [short for niqádtu or naqádtu; see kádtu]; (2) [short for kaniqádtu; see kaniqádtu]
ádtu there (future—far from speaker and hearer) [1 A 2, 1 A 2 c] 4 a 7, 20; 9 b 16, c 5; V go, come (to a place far from speaker and hearer) 5 b 50; 10 a 1
ádtu [= mu-] go 1 a 18, 25; 2 a 12, b 30, 34; 3 c 19, 20; 4 a 2, 15, b 46, 50; 6 a 15, 26, b 51, 53; 8 a 32; 9 a 20; 10 a 2, 23; 12 a 12, 15, b 34, c 61, 66; 14 b 53, 73
pag- go 3 a 7
mi- go 5 a 1; 9 a 1
mu- go 3 a 16, c 26, 29; 4 a 2, 16; 6 b 55, 56; 8 c 26; 9 a 18; 14 b 59
naka- go 9 a 19
maka- go 5 b 52; 11 c 15
adtúqan place gone to 9 b 5
paN- V go (several agents)
maN- go 3 a 5, 17; 14 b 55
adúna [existential] there is, was, were; [subject] has, have, had [short form dúna: 3 A 1, 3 A 2 b]
ági V go by, pass by, go through, pass through; CN thing accomplished 14 a 9
ági [= mu-] go over 4 a 27
mu- go over, by 3 c 28; 4 a 31, b 42
paN- V pass by (several agents)
maN- pass 3 a 27
pa- CN way, means (of doing something) 10 a 9
akú I [1 B] 4 a 32 and passim
ku [Nom.] 1 a 15 and passim
nákuq [Gen.] 6 a 32 and passim
nákuq ug I thought [short for gipakaqingún nákuq ug] 12 a 26, b 41, c 57
ku [Gen.: 6 D 1]
kanákuq [Dat.] 8 a 33 and passim
nákuq [Dat.] 3 b 23 and passim
ákuq [preposed Gen.] 3 b 6 and passim
ákuq na 'May I have [subject]?'
aláhas CN jewelry [not without l] 6 a 1
alás Q [precedes numbers in time of day except úna 'one'] [not without l] 8 a 19; 14 b 57
áli V block
alí CN obstruction 10 a 14
álsa V lift, raise, pick up
alsáhun thing to be picked up 11 c 21
ámbi Q [followed by nominative] [short form bi] give me, let me have 4 a 32; 6 b 36, 44
bi 8 b 24
amígu CN male friend 1 a 9, 16
Amiriká CN America 2 b 13, 22; 5 b 37, 42
Amirikána CN [= Amirkána] American (female) 5 a 25; 8 a 25
Amirkána CN [= Amirikána] American (female) 5 a 26; 6 a 7; 8 b 4, c 4; 12 b 45
ámuq [preposed Gen.] our [see kamí]
anáaq Q [initial] expression of surprise: (1) at something pleasant 6 a 2; 10 b 4; (2) at something which causes worry 6 a 17; 8 a 5
anák CN son, daughter 3 c 9; 5 a 19, 20; 9 c 19, 20; 10 a 22, 32; 11 a 16

ánaq [Gen. of kanáq]
anáqa [short form náqa] (1) is there [1 A 2, 1 A 2 a, 3 A 1]; (2) there is [3 A 2 a, 3 A 2 b]
ándam V prepare something or oneself
  pag- prepare 11 a 16
ánhaq there (far from first person, near second person; or near something remote in time but just referred to) [1 A 2, 1 A 2 c] 3 a 25; V go (to place far from speaker but near hearer)
  ánhaq [= mu-] go 2 a 6
ánhi here (future, near first and second persons) [1 A 2, 1 A 2 c] 2 b 31; 3 a 38, 40, c 22; 12 b 43; 14 b 56, 58; V come here
  ~lang, ~ra will get off here 9 b 13, 14; 12 a 4
  pag- come 2 b 17
  naka- come 14 a 32
  maka- come 12 b 32, c 56
  gi- [-un unreal] person who somebody has come to pick up 8 c 25
  paN- V come here (plural agents)
  maN- come here 10 a 33
áni this (near speaker and hearer) [see kaní]
áni V harvest (usually said only of rice) [cf. sánggiq]; CN harvest 10 b 14, 16
  pag- harvest 10 b 7, 8, 15
  maka- harvest 11 a 14
  aníhun thing harvested 10 b 5
  ma- thing harvested 10 b 6
  paN- V harvest; CN action of harvesting 11 a 1, 21
  maN- harvest 10 b 24, 25
aníndut Adj. (1) beautiful; (2) nice to hear, taste, touch, etc. [short form níndut]
  níndut (1) 4 a 21, 23; 10 b 25; 13 b 73; (2) 4 b 60; 8 b 22
    nindúta [exclamatory] (2) how nice! 11 a 11
    ka- [exclamatory] (1) how beautiful! 5 a 1; 6 a 2; 10 b 4; (2) how nice! 13 b 70
aníqa is here [short form níqa] [1 A 2, 1 A 2 a, 3 A 1]
  níqa 3 b 5 and passim
antígu V know how to [base used alone only as short for naqantígu]
  ka- V know how to
  ma- know how to 11 b 44
ántus V suffer, undergo or endure pain [cf. sakít]
  mag- suffer 11 a 28
Ántuy N [man's name; nickname for Huwán] 11 c 3
anúsqa when? (with tenses expressed by unreal) [4 D]
ang [short form ng] (1) [subject marker] [1 E 1, 3 B 1] 3 a 19 and passim; (2) [preceding predicate] [3 B 1]
ángay Q [prepositive] ought to [verb], [verb] is the proper thing to do 9 a 1
angáy CN suitableness 4 a 22
Ánghil N [man's name] 13 b 61, 63
apán Q [= píru] [initial] but, on the contrary 10 a 19; 11 a 24
apú CN grandchild 5 a 21, 24, b 53
  paN- V have grandchildren
  naN- have grandchildren 5 a 24
aq Q [final] [particle used with exclamations contradicting hearer's impression] 5 a 18
aráng V fit, be the right size
  arangqaráng Adj. fairly well, quite good
    ma- Adj. fairly well 12 b 53
arí here (near first person and far from second person) [1 A 2, 1 A 2 c]; V go (1) to place far from second person and near first person; (2) (in the direction of speaker farther from the hearer)
  arí [= mu-] (2) go 11 a 22, c 26; 14 b 43, 44
  ~na ku, ~na mi I am (we are) on my (our) way now (on saying good-bye) 1 a 20
ári [short for niqári] this (near speaker but not near person spoken to) [see karí]
aríyus CN earrings 6 a 2
árka CN ark 13 b 72, 74, 78, 79, 81
arún Q [initial] in order to, so that [with infinitive] 8 c 25; [with verb or sentence] 4 a 33; 5 b 53; 8 c 9, 10; 9 a 1, 29, c 16; 10 a 28; 12 b 31
ása (1) where? (for unreal tense meanings) [2 A 2] 4 a 15; 6 b 49; 12 a 2, 10; (2) which (of several)? [3 D] 4 a 16
asáwa CN wife 2 b 13
  paN- V take a wife
  maN- marry 5 b 45

asyínda CN plantation 11 a 26
atúbang V face
-an CN place facing 6 b 51
atúl V cause something to coincide
i- thing made to come at the same time as something else 10 b 24
atúp CN roof 11 b 33
átuq [preposed Gen.] our [see kitá]
atúqa [short form túqa] is there [1 A 2, 1 A 2 a, 3 A 1]
túqa 4 a 19 and passim
aw Q [initial] (1) [precedes a sentence or question meaning 'Is that so?' and shows surprise [cf. aa (4)] 14 b 60; (2) [pause word before starting to speak] 3 b 26, c 18; (3) [particle preceding a predetermined answer] of course 5 a 26, b 46; 8 a 34; 9 a 7; 14 b 67; (4) [particle used upon remembering something] 9 b 16, c 6
ay Q (1) [initial] [expression dismissing what follows as unimportant] 11 b 2, c 11, 17; (2) [initial] [preceding an exclamation] 9 a 23; (3) [initial] I wish I could (expression of frustrated helplessness) 12 c 58, 63; (4) [final] [expression used when pointing to something the hearer should see] 3 a 9; 13 b 48, 53, 87; (5) [initial—short for ayáw—see ayáw]
ayáw Q [initial] do not (imperative) [2 B, 3 E 1] [ay short form]
~lang (1) never mind (polite refusal) 4 b 62; 8 a 12, c 32; 9 c 12; (2) don't! (it's a small thing to ask) 9 b 15, c 14
~na lang never mind (polite refusal) 1 a 14; 9 a 16, c 7
~úsaq, ~únaq don't just yet
ay 8 a 28
áyskrim CN ice cream 4 b 59
*áyu very, to a high degree
ka- Q [postpositive] very [short form kaqáy] 1 a 24; 2 b 18, 32; 3 a 15; 4 a 19, 21, 23, 28, etc.
kaqáy 4 a 6, 17
áyu V do well
pag- well 8 a 28; 11 b 30
ayúha thing done well 14 a 10, 16
ka- V get well
ma- get well 14 b 69
paN- V do well (plural recipients)
pangayúhun things done well 14 a 14
ma- Adj. [short forms maqáy, máyu] (1) nice, good, well 1 a 8; 3 b 31, c 15, 18; 5 a 5, b 55; 8 a 9, 32, b 1, 6, c 6, 16, 28; 9 a 27, c 16; 10 b 8; 11 c 24; 12 b 47, 51; 14 a 13, 20, 32, b 35, 41, 67
maqáy 3 b 12, c 6
maqáyu kay it's good that 14 a 32
(2) greeting used upon arriving at someone's premises 1 a 1; 3 a 12, b 3; 9 b 21, c 1; 12 b 27, 36; 14 a 23, 30, 31
máyu 3 a 13, b 1, 2, 4;
(3) maqáyung plus a word for a time or season Good [morning, etc.]! (as greeting) 1 a 2, 12; 5 a 5; 9 c 1
máyu 3 b 4
ayuqáyu V be in a good state
pag- be in a good state; good-bye 8 b 2

B

ba Q [postpositive] [1 D 2] (1) [question marker; used in questions with no interrogative] 1 a 4; 2 a 2, 7, 11, 13, b 1, 8; 3 a 14, b 18, c 7, 13; 4 a 11, b 34, 46; 5 a 9; 6 a 8, 10, 23, 30, b 38, 53; 8 a 1, 6, b 11; 9 a 6, 8, 15, 21, b 5, c 10; 10 b 2, 5; 12 a 24, b 38, c 54; 14 a 20, 21; (1 a) [with indirect questions] whether 3 a 34; 4 a 8; 6 b 44; (2) [with interrogatives; indicates impatience or a strong questioning tone] 2 b 3, 14 a 2
únsa ba what do you say? how about it? 9 a 15
ba gud [particle with questions; indicates disbelief] 5 b 47;
(3) [particle asking if the hearer understands] 11 a 5; (4) [in exclamations] though 6 a 35; (5) ra ba (5 a) [particle with a predicate following a first statement: the first statement is good or bad because of predicate] 4 a 3, 4; 5 b 54; 8 a 16; 9 a 9; 12 a 14; 14 b 40; (5 b) [particle with statement of apology] 2 b 27; 3 c 25, 32
bag CN bag (handbag or suitcase) 8 a 11, 14, c 31
bágqu Adj. new 12 a 14
báhin V divide; CN share 10 b 14; Q [followed by Dat.] concerning 13 b 72
bahúq Adj. odorous 4 b 42
báklay V walk from one place to another

báklay (cont.)
mag- walk 9 b 3
bákun V get up
mi- get up 14 a 9
baláka V cause concern [does not occur without 1]
ka- V be concerned about 8 a 22, 28; 9 b 15
balángay CN village (smaller than lúngsud) [does not occur without 1] 10 a 4
baláy CN house, home 3 a 1, 2, 41, b 7, 15; 5 b 50; 9 b 3; 10 a 3; 11 b 24, c 26; 14 a 1
-a (←) particular house 2 b 2
balaybálay CN shack 4 a 28
balhíbu CN (1) body hair; (2) feather 11 b 38, 39
bálhin V move something or oneself from one place to another
mu- move 3 c 16
balígyaq V sell
balígyaq [= nag-] sell 12 b 38
nag- sell 6 b 50; 9 b 25
gi- -an person to whom sold 8 b 7
gi- thing sold 8 b 18
i- thing sold 8 c 10
paN- V sell (plural recipients)
naN- sell 8 b 18
maN- sell 8 c 17
gi- [i- unreal] things sold 6 a 27
-an (→) CN place where things are sold 12 b 39, 41
bálik V return (put, go, or come back) [cf. ulíq] [10 C] 2 b 35; 4 a 9; 6 a 16; 8 c 1; Q [followed by Dat.] back toward 11 b 19
pag- return 10 b 24
ig- [= inig-] when [Gen.] comes back 5 b 61
inig- when [Gen.] comes back 4 a 18
mu- return, come back 5 b 58, 59; 9 a 27; 10 b 23
maka- [= maka- (→)] come back 11 a 1; 12 b 31
balikbálik V (1) keep coming back; (2) good-bye (to departing guests) 1 a 26; 14 b 65, 74
balú I don't know
hi- V know (facts, how to)
ka- V [=naka-, maka-] know (how to) 5 b 60; 9 a 18; 13 b 74, 75, 76
na- know 3 b 15
bána CN husband 9 c 28; 10 a 18, 21
Banáwaq CN Banawa (section of Cebu City) 2 a 7, 9, 11; 3 a 1, 4, 7, 16, 17, 26, 34, 36, 39
bánhaq V make noise
nag- make noise 13 b 85
bánsay Adj. knowing how to do something which requires skill; V train, make skillful
mag- practice 11 b 30
bántay V (1) watch over, take care of; (2) watch for; (3) be careful
mu- (1) take care of 12 b 29; (2) watch for 11 b 10
nag- (1) watch over 9 b 10
mag- (2) watch for 4 a 7; (3) be careful 8 a 17
-an (→) (1) person taken care of 8 a 23
-i (→) (1) thing taken care of 8 a 27, b 1
ma- -an (→) (1) thing taken care of 9 a 29
bányu CN bathroom 9 c 8
banggiqítan Adj. (1) famous (for achievement or supremacy); (2) good in fighting 11 c 4, 9
báqat V tie together into a bundle, raft, etc.
paN- V tie together (plural recipients)
gi- -an things tied together 10 a 7
baqúl CN field for crops 11 a 16
barátu Adj. inexpensive
ka- [exclamatory] how inexpensive! 8 b 9
bárku CN ship, boat 8 a 1, 25
báryu CN barrio (division of a town)
tinyínti dil ~ head of a barrio 9 c 19
basák CN marsh
-an CN rice field 9 b 27
basáq Adj. wet
ka- V get wet
ma- get wet 4 b 54
básin Q (1) hoping something will occur 12 c 65; (2) in case (something happens)
~pa (1) I hope so 3 a 44; (2) lest 14 b 42
básta Q provided that (if and only if) 5 b 41; 9 b 2
básu CN drinking glass 4 b 57; 14 a 5

bátaq Adj. young (at age of child); CN (1) child (boy, girl) 2 b 19; 3 c 11, 12, 13; 8 b 18; 9 b 7, c 13, 17, 22; 11 b 1, 16, 20, 26, 42; 13 a 1, 6, b 43; (2) child, offspring 3 c 10; 5 b 53; 14 b 62
 batánqun Adj. young (not said of a child); CN young man 12 b 36
batú CN stone, rock 13 a 15
Bay Voc. [term of address used by males to other males of the same age] 2 a 8; 4 a 12, 13, b 46, 49
báyad V (1) pay; recompense for service rendered; atone for wrongdoing; (2) pay rent
 báyad [= mu-] (1) pay 4 b 62
 mu- (1) pay 8 c 14; 9 b 2; 12 a 26
 nag- (→) (2) pay rent 3 b 26
 ka- [= maka-] (1) pay 8 c 5
 gi- [i- unreal] (1) money paid out 8 b 31
 pa- V (1) make someone pay
  gi- (1) person made to pay 8 c 2
  pabáyrun (1) person made to pay 8 c 6
 bayranán CN thing paid for 3 b 25, 30; 4 b 61
bayáq Q [postpositive] (1) [with a statement or exclamation] [statement or exclamation] is different from what should be 14 b 37; (2) [with imperatives; gives admonitory tone] make sure . . . ! 5 b 53, 61; 8 c 16
báybay CN beach
 -un CN beach 10 a 1
bayí CN female (animal)
báyi CN female (human)
 babáyi CN female (person) 8 b 4, 31, c 3; 9 b 1, c 17; 12 b 51
báynti [number] twenty 2 b 4; 6 a 23; 12 a 21, 24, 25
 únu ~ one-twenty 6 b 38, 45
 syintu ~ tris one hundred twenty-three 8 c 36
bi Q (1) [initial—short for ámbi—see ámbi] give me; (2) [final] [particle with commands asking to be given or told something] 4 a 32; 8 b 13, 25; 9 c 5
Biblíya CN Bible 13 b 69
biis CN base, starting-place 11 b 23
bílin V leave behind, bequeath [cf. bíyaq]
 i- thing, person left behind
 hi-/ha- (→) V leave behind
 naha- person left behind 14 b 61
bir CN beer 1 a 13; 2 b 26, 27
Bírtu N [man's name; short for Rubírtu, Robert, and other names]
 Birtú Voc. 13 b 78
bísan Q [initial] even, ever [short form bisán]
 ~ug/kun plus [predicate] [predicate] even; any [predicate] whatever 3 b 23; 4 b 35; 9 b 2
 ~na lang not even [predicate] when [predicate] would have been undesirable 8 c 11
Bisayáq Adj. Bisayan
 -in- Adj. Bisayan language; V speak Bisayan
  mu- speak Bisayan 8 b 6
bisíta CN visitor 3 c 1; 9 c 13; V visit
 mi- visit 1 a 1
 mu- visit 9 a 1, c 15
 gibisitáqan person visited [= gibisitáhan] 14 a 23
bítaw Q [postpositive] [particle expressing agreement with foregoing]; (1) [particle affirming what interlocutor exclaimed] 5 a 24, b 55; 9 c 31; (2) [particle with statement saying something conforms with something] 9 c 32; (3) [particle with statement confirming a fact] anyway 6 a 34; 8 a 13; 11 b 31, 42; (4) [particle with statement of unexpected yet not surprising fact] 10 a 18
biyáhi CN trip 8 c 27, 28
bíyaq V leave behind, abandon [cf. bílin]
 -an person left behind 14 b 49
blákburd CN blackboard 13 b 60, 62
búgnaw Adj. cool, cold (food, drinks, weather) [cf. túgnaw] 8 a 9
 ka- V get cold
 ma- get cold 14 b 42
Bugú CN Bogo (town in northern Cebu) 9 b 17
búhat V (1) do work [cf. hímuq]; (2) make, construct; CN (1) work, thing to be done 11 a 25
 mag- (2) make 11 a 2
 gi- [-un unreal] (2) thing constructed 11 a 23
 gi- [i- unreal] (2) thing used to

búhat, gi- (cont.)
make something 11 b 36
-unun CN (1) things to be done 5 b 58
búhiq V (1) go free; (2) release
-i (2) thing let go 8 a 15
búhiq Adj. alive 6 a 31
ka- V live
ma- live 8 c 9
-in- CN life 9 c 24
paN- V earn one's living
naN- earn one's living 10 a 17
maN- earn one's living 11 a 19, 21
bulág V separate from someone or something
mag- (←) part from each other 4 b 63
búlan CN month 3 b 25, 26, c 17; 8 b 3; 10 b 6; 12 b 49
búlang CN cockfight (with gaffs) 11 c 16, 17
-an (→) CN place where cockfights are held 11 c 14, 15
búntag CN morning 1 a 2, 12; 3 a 12, b 4; 5 a 5; 8 a 19; 12 b 27; V be morning
ganíhang ~ this morning (past) 4 b 37
ma- -an (→) be overtaken by morning 8 a 21
ka- V become morning
pag- when morning came 8 c 19
bung [exclamation used in games when It has caught someone] 13 a 27, 39
búngsud CN bamboo fish trap 10 a 8, 9
búqang Adj. fool; CN (1) fool [cf. túntu]; (2) the one who is It in a game 13 a 18
buqúk CN (1) piece 6 a 29; (2) [counter after numerals or numbers] 2 a 14; 3 b 19, c 10; 4 a 13; 5 a 20, 22; 9 c 20, 22; 12 c 58, 62
ti- CN whole (entire) 8 c 11; 9 c 29
buqút CN mind, understanding, will; Q want 9 a 14
-an (←) Adj. good, well-behaved
ka- [exclamatory] how good! 14 b 37
Burumíyu CN Borromeo (name of a street) 12 a 3, 11, 13
burút Adj. bloated
búrut V (1) make bloated; (2) become bloated
mu- (2) get bloated 10 b 11
butáng CN thing, object 4 a 32
butáng V put, set
gi- -an place something was put 11 b 19, 38
-an place something is put 10 a 12
i- thing put 9 c 4, 5
hiN-/haN- V happen to be located
kahímtang CN state, situation, condition 8 c 12; 9 a 13
butú V explode
nabúthan person who had something explode on him 10 a 19

D

da Q [initial] [particle expressing disgust over an unavoidable happening] 12 a 6
dágan V run, move fast; run, function 4 b 53; 13 a 23, 24
mi- run 2 b 20, 21
mu- run 11 b 19
-an distance to be run 11 b 20
dágat CN sea 10 a 10
dághan Adj. much, many 3 a 27, c 28; 4 a 22, 28, b 36, 37; 5 a 23, b 54, 58; 6 a 22
dághang or ~salámat thank you very much 1 a 25; 3 a 28; 8 a 30, c 15
ka- [exclamatory] what a large number! 9 c 21
dakúp V catch (capture) [cf. sakúp]
dákpan [=hidákpan] person who got caught 13 a 39
dakúq Adj. (1) big (in size, extent) 13 b 79, 80; (2) big (in amount) 8 c 6
ka- [exclamatory] (1) how big! 5 a 12; 9 c 30
dakuqdakúq Adj. bigger, rather big; V become bigger
mu- become bigger 12 c 65
dalá V (1) carry; bring, take [cf. hatúd]; (2) take away
dalá [=mu-, mag-] (1) bring, take 4 a 32; 8 a 11, c 31, 32; 9 c 5
pag- (1) bring 2 b 26; 5 b 61
nag- (1) carry 9 c 17; 11 c 2
mag- (1) bring 9 a 6
gi- (1) person or thing brought or taken 3 b 6, 14; 5 a 33
dádqun (1) person or thing brought 2 b 22; 9 a 1, 4, 5; (2) thing taken away 12 c 62

ma- (1) thing brought 9 b 9
gidádqan (1) person to whom brought 14 b 33
dádqi (1) person to whom brought 14 a 1, 3
dálan CN street, trail 3 a 21
dalíq V come here! [cf. mariká] 3 b 8, c 2; 5 a 4; 8 a 24, c 26, 30; 11 a 22; 14 a 11
dalíq Adj. in a hurry, fast 11 a 25; V (1) be in a hurry 4 b 53; (2) do immediately
nag- (1) be in a hurry 1 a 15
mag- (1) be in a hurry 4 b 41
-a (2) thing to be done immediately 14 a 18
-an (1) reason for which one is hurrying 14 b 54
daliqdalíq V do hastily
-in- CN thing done hastily 11 a 25
dapít CN place where something is; Q [followed by dative] at 11 b 39
dápit CN place, region 5 a 27, 28, 31, 32
daq Q [final] (1) [exclamation upon noticing something not known previously] 4 a 4, b 39, 51; (2) [particle used upon recalling something] come to think of it . . . 13 a 40
dáqan Adj. old, of an earlier time; Q in advance 13 b 50, 56
daqúg V win, best (an opponent)
maka- win 11 c 6
naka- win 11 b 16
ka- [= maka-] win 11 c 10
daqút Adj. bad, thin, sickly
dáqut V cause to spoil
ka- V become spoiled
ma- become spoiled 10 b 9
daqutdáqut V be sick most of the time
mag- be sick most of the time 14 b 71
day [see índay]
dayún V go, come into a house 1 a 6; 2 b 7; 3 b 3; 9 b 22; 12 b 37; 14 a 24, 26
pa- V have someone come in
-a person bidden to come in 14 a 29
dáyun Q [postpositive] (1) immediately 5 b 58; 8 a 34; 9 a 21, 22, 23, c 16; 10 a 28; 13 a 23; (2) the next thing 8 b 21
dídtu (1) there (far from speaker, far from hearer) 4 a 19 and passim [1 A 2, 1 A 2 b]; (2) there was [3 A 1]
díguq V bathe, cause someone to be bathed
kalíguq V (1) take a bath; (2) swim
ma- (1) take a bath 9 c 10
paN- V (2) go swimming (several agents)
naN- (2) go swimming 4 a 26
-anan CN (2) place to go swimming 4 a 21, 23
diháq [= dínhaq] (1) (1 a) there (near person spoken to) [1 A 2 b] (1 b) there (not far, but not near [speaker or hearer]) 6 b 50; (2) (2 a) was there (near second person) [3 A 1] (2 b) there was (no locational meaning) [3 A 2 b]
díliq Q (1) [prepositive] [short form diq] no, not (with future or potential verb; with noun, adjective, pronoun, or numeral predicate) [2 B, 12 D] 2 a 8 and passim
~ku I don't want to 4 a 22 and passim
~ta let's not 4 b 4 and passim
~akú not me
~pa not yet, before [12 G 2 a, b, under pa]
~na no longer [12 G 1 b] 5 a 23 and passim;
(2) [initial] [short form diq] therefore diq 14 b 58
dinamíta CN dynamite 10 a 19
dínhaq [= diháq] [1 A 2 b]; (1) there (near second person) 2 a 6 and passim; (1 a) there [place not near either speaker or hearer, but not far off] 6 b 51 and passim; (2) there (at place mentioned previously)
dínhi [1 A 2, 1 A 2 b]; (1) (1 a) here (near speaker and hearer); (1 b) [in narration] here at this time (2) there was here [3 A 1]
taga- CN (1) one who is from this place 4 a 25
diq (1) no [see díliq]; (2) therefore [see díliq]
díqa there is here [see adíqa]
diqáy Q [postpositive] [13 G 2 ff.]
(1) [particle indicating speaker has re-

diqáy (cont.)
ceived new information]; (1 a) [in statements] 1 a 24; 2 b 15; 3 b 5, 10, c 1, 15; 4 b 36; 5 a 13, 18, 34, b 43, 47; 6 a 10, 14, 20, 25, b 57; 8 a 26, b 4, c 20, 23, 29; 9 b 18; 10 a 16; 11 b 8, 25; 12 b 41, 50, 52; 13 a 16, b 83; 14 b 60
man diqáy [14 G 1 e] 4 b 36; 9 a 23, b 12; 12 c 61; 14 a 25;
(1 b) [in questions with no interrogative]so the fact is that . . . 2 b 24; 3 a 24, b 17, c 7; 9 b 10, 14, c 2; 11 c 20; 13 b 86; 14 b 61; (2) [in questions with interrogative] (2 a) [particle indicating deep curiosity] 5 a 10, b 56; 9 b 4; (2 b) if it isn't [predicate] what is it then? 2 a 9; 3 c 27; (3) [particle indicating that the speaker realizes something of which he was unmindful or is making the hearer mindful of something] 9 a 4
ísaq, úsaq pa ~ excuse me (bringing up a new topic) 9 a 4
(4) [particle in statement correcting oneself] 8 b 10
diqín (1) where? (past) [2 A 2] 11 c 10; (2) [place] where [3 D 1]; (3) which one [of several places]? [3 D]
dirí here (near speaker, far from hearer) [1 A 2, 1 A 2 b] 11 a 22 and passim
dirítsu V go directly, go straight (without doing anything else)
dirítsu [= mu-] go directly 4 b 47, 48
mu- go directly 4 b 45
diyút Adj. few [used only in set expressions]
-ay (←) Adj. [cf. gamáy] (1) few 3 b 28; 4 a 21; 5 a 34; 11 a 12; (2) little, small [not common usage] 10 a 20
kadíyut Q [initial, final] for a short time, immediately [short form kadiyút] [= kariyút]
kadiyút 3 b 9, c 2; 14 b 45
dráybir CN driver, chauffeur 2 a 7, 11; 3 a 33
draybír Voc. 8 a 1
Dru Voc. [man's name; short for Pedro] 14 b 53
dúbli V double
dublíhun thing doubled 12 a 18
Dúdung N [man's name; short form Dung] 2 a 5
dúdung [term of address to male children or men of about the same age as or younger than speaker; short form dung]
dung 2 b 19, 22; 3 a 40, c 24, 31 and passim
dúgay Adj. (1) long (time) 5 b 44; 11 a 15; 12 b 48; 14 a 6; (2) long ago 11 a 24; V delay; Q [initial] it was or will be late before . . . 4 a 6
ka- [exclamatory] (1) how late! 4 a 1
-un thing delayed 10 b 8
ka- V take a long time
ma- take a long time 4 a 5; 14 b 68
duhá [numeral] two 2 a 15; 3 b 19, 22, c 7; 5 b 57; 8 c 37; 10 b 6
ika- CN or Numeral second 3 a 42
ka- Q [initial, medial, final] twice, in two [= maka-] 10 b 19
dúktur (1) CN (medical) doctor; (2) Title Dr. (term of address) 2 a 2, 13, b 8, 28, 29
dúlaq V play (a game); CN (1) action of playing 13 b 43; (2) game 11 b 29
dúlaq [= mag-] play 13 a 2
ga- play 11 b 7
gi- game played 11 b 1, 26
-un game played 13 a 3
dúlhug V go down, descend (an incline) 3 a 22
dúlsi CN candy 8 c 9, 13
dulúng V go toward
pa- V [= padúlung] go toward [cf. paqingún] 2 a 7, 9, 11; 3 a 26; 4 a 10
dúmdum V find one's way
hiN- V remember, recollect [cf. hándum]
-an (→) thing remembered 8 c 18
-i (→) thing remembered 8 c 16
Dumínggu CN Sunday 5 a 2
ka- V be Sunday
ma- on Sundays 11 c 11, 13
dúna [see adúna]
dung [short form of dúdung]
dungúg V hear [11 D]
na- thing heard 5 b 36
dupá CN fathom (distance from fingertips to fingertips of outstretched arms) 11 a 19

duq Voc. [= dung] [term of address for male of same age as or younger than speaker] 12 b 37
dúqaw V visit [cf. bisíta]
duqawdúqaw V keep visiting
maga- keep visiting 14 b 67
duqúl Adj. (1) near 14 b 66; (2) near (in time) 14 b 57; CN vicinity [= dúqul] 12 a 4
dus [number] two 13 a 9, 14
dúsi [number] twelve 6 a 9, 14
dusína CN dozen 6 a 5, 6, b 36
Dyiin N Jeanne, Jane (woman's name) 14 a 19, 27, 28, b 68
dyip CN jeep 2 a 9; 3 a 25, 26, 32, c 22, 23, 27, 28; 4 a 9; 6 b 49, 51, 55
-a (←) particular jeep 3 c 24
dyis [number] ten 6 a 8, 10, 12, 19
únu~ one (peso and) ten (centavos) 6 b 45
dyud [see gayúd]
Dyuns Abinyú CN Jones Avenue (name of street) 4 b 49

G

gabíqi CN night, evening 5 b 41; V be night
magabhiqán [= magabínqan] person overtaken by night 4 b 41
gamáy Adj. (1) small (in size) 11 b 5; 12 c 59, 60, 63, 65; (2) small (in amount, distance) 3 a 22; 5 a 31; (3) small (in intensity) 14 a 22 [cf. diyútay]
gágmay Adj. (1) small (plural) 4 a 28; 11 b 39
kinagámyan CN least, smallest 11 b 12
Gamílu N Gamelo (surname) 1 a 10, 11, 22; 2 a 5
gámit CN use; V use
-un thing used 11 b 6
ganánsya CN gain, profit 6 a 14; 12 c 60, 65
ganíha Q [initial, final] [= ganína, kaganíha] (1) a while, a moment ago; (2) before (a recent past time) 12 a 24
ganíha nga [time expression] this morning, evening etc.; this [time of day] just past 4 b 37
gániq Q [= ngániq, gáliq, gáling] (1) [postpositive] even 5 a 23, 24; 10 b 20, 22; 11 a 19; (2) [initial] only (were it not for this one condition, namely . . .) 12 c 56

gása CN gift [cf. rigálu] 9 a 6
gawás CN the outside, exterior (part); V go, come outside
~pa Q (1) [initial] besides 4 a 18; 10 a 6; (2) [followed by Dat.] besides 11 b 10
paN- V (←) go outside (plural)
maN- (←) go outside 13 a 1
gayúd Q [postpositive] [predicate] for sure [short forms gyud, dyud]; (1) [with Adj.] [Adj.] without doubt
gyud 4 b 42, 60; 9 b 1, c 23, 24; 11 c 8
dyud 3 b 28
(2) [with verbs]; (2 a) make it a point to [do]
gyud 5 b 53; 8 a 34, c 25; 11 a 1; 13 a 36, 40; 14 b 33, 38; (2 b) [do] for sure
gyud 8 c 5, 14, 18, 23; 9 a 29
(3) [with waláq, díliq] (3 a) never
gyud 5 a 17; 6 a 10; 8 a 23 b; (3 b) at all
gyud 10 b 22
dyud 5 a 28, b 48
(4) [with CN, pronouns] it is or was [CN, pronoun] for sure
gyud 2 b 2; 5 b 62; 8 b 11; 9 a 4, 11; 11 c 13, 21
maqú~ that is the way it is 5 a 2
(5) [Q] for sure, without a doubt
gyud 9 a 7, 13, c 25; 11 b 30, c 25; 14 b 36
karun pa~ just this minute 2 b 12
(6) [with positive existential predicate or with deictic] there is [predicate] for sure
gyud 5 a 21; 14 b 58
dyud 5 a 19
(7) [with numerals] [numeral] for sure
gyud 6 a 9; 10 b 19; 11 a 14
(8) [in phrases]
na or ra~ at last 9 c 13
gihápun Q [postpositive] still, as before 10 a 26; 11 c 17; 13 a 32, 33
gíkan Q [followed by Dat.] from (a place) 2 b 13; 5 a 33, b 52; 8 b 11; 10 b 15; 13 b 69; 14 a 19; V come from
~pa just come from 9 b 27
-in- -an CN parents 10 a 17
Ginúqu CN (1) Lord; (2) Lord! (exclamation)
Ginúqu ku My Lord! 6 a 18
grábi Adj. serious (of illness); V become worse
mu- become worse 14 b 70
gubáq V break down, render useless
ka- V become broken

gubáq (cont.)
na- become broken 11 a 25
gud [see ugúd]
gúlang Adj. old (of age)
tig- Adj. old (of people) 5 a 8; 10 a 4, 6; CN old man, woman 4 a 29; 5 a 3; 11 c 1
-a a certain old man 4 a 30
ka- [exclamatory] how old! 5 a 13; V become old
ma- become old 5 a 17
guláq V go outside
pag- go outside 10 a 13
mu- go outside 10 a 15
gúnting CN scissors 13 a 12, 15
gústu CN thing desired 3 b 22; 13 a 6; Q want, like 2 b 14; 3 b 16; 9 c 6; 10 b 2, 3; 11 c 25; 13 b 49, 51; V like
gústu [= maka-, naka-] 3 b 24, c 12; 13 a 4
Gútsan CN Go Chan Building 4 a 3, b 50
gyud [see gayúd]

H

ha Q (1) [final] [particle asking whether interlocutor has understood] 9 b 16; 13 a 26; 14 b 65; (1 a) salámat ha? thanks (said sincerely) 2 b 5; 3 a 28; 6 a 26, b 47, 52, 57; 8 c 15; 9 b 20; 14 b 47; (1 b) [to soften a command] 2 b 35; 3 b 9, c 35; (2) [final] [particle asking for agreement] O.K.? 2 b 35; 3 b 9, c 35; 5 b 50, 61; 6 a 13; 8 a 27, 33, b 1, 29; 9 b 13; 12 a 11, b 31, 34, c 62; 13 a 41; 14 b 49, 73; (3) [initial] huh! (particle expressing strong surprise) 5 a 12
hádluk V make afraid
ka- V be afraid of
ma- be afraid of 4 a 31; 9 a 8, 10
háguq V (1) exert effort; (2) waste time
haguqhagúq V trouble oneself to do something
pag- 9 a 17
halá [particle expressing agreement; usually alone or preceded by na] (1) [before commands] go ahead (and do it now) 13 a 1, b 50; (2) all right (acceding to a request) 12 a 19, b 30, 35; (2 a) good-bye (said by the one staying behind after the other has asked permission to go) 14 b 73
háluq V mix liquid and solids
haluqháluq CN a mixture of ice or ice cream and fruit 4 b 56, 58
hándum V remember, think of something or someone from the past [cf. hinúmdum]
-anan CN remembrance 12 c 62
haníg CN something put between two horizontal things to protect one from the other; V put something between two horizontal things for protection
gi- -an thing something is placed on, as a cushion 11 b 37
hángtud Q [initial] until, up to (the time or point of) 11 b 23
hángyuq V (1) request, ask for (with humility); (1 a) propose (marriage); (2) bargain (to lower price); CN (2) offer 6 a 12
mu- (1 a) propose 5 b 46
ma- (2) thing bargained over 3 b 29
hapák V strike, beat (with hand or weapon
hapakhápak V strike continuously
gi- [-un unreal] thing batted continuously 11 b 3
hapít V drop by or in for
mu- drop by 5 b 52
hápit Q [initial] on the verge of 13 b 44
hápun CN afternoon, early evening 2 b 30; 9 c 1; 14 a 23, 30, 31
pani- V take evening meal
mani- take evening meal 2 b 31, 33
háqi [= háqin] (1) where? (2) which (of several)? 11 c 5
háqin [2 A 2, 3 D] (1) where? 2 b 8; 9 c 8; 14 a 2; (2) which (of several)?
hásta Q [followed by subject] including [subject] 14 a 16
hátag V give
maka- give 6 a 6
gi- -an person to whom given [fancy for gitagáqan: 8 A 5]
i- thing given away 8 b 16
paN- V give (plural recipients)
maka- give 12 c 64
hatúd V (1) deliver; (2) take a person somewhere
mu- (2) take to 2 a 13; 4 a 11, 12, b 49
i- (2) person taken somewhere

12 a 11, 13, 16
hatudhátud V (1) bother to bring things
nag- (1) bother to bring 14 b 38
háyag Adj. (1) giving off bright light; (2) light, daylight 8 a 23 b
hayáhay Adj. fresh (said of a breeze or an airy place) 8 a 9
hibalú know [see balú]
hígdaq V lie down
nag- lie 14 a 27
higdaqhígdaq V spend time lying down
mag- lie around 14 b 52
hígup V eat or drink hot liquids
-un thing eaten 14 b 35
híkay V prepare food
maka- prepare 14 b 64
hilánat CN fever 14 a 22
hilú hello [used only in answering telephone] 2 a 1
hílum Adj. silent, quiet 5 a 1
hímu V [=hímuq] do (a nonphysical activity) [cf. búhat]
ma- thing done 6 a 20; Q [followed by nga plus verb] can do [verb] 3 b 18
hímuq V [=hímu] (1) make, construct; make, cause to [do] [cf. búhat]; (2) do (a nonphysical activity); (3) hold (an affair or recurrent event)
gi- [-un unreal] (1) thing made 10 a 13
ma- (1 a) thing done 3 a 15; 6 a 8, 14; 12 a 15; (1 b) Q [followed by nga plus verb] can [verb] 3 a 14, b 18, c 17; 6 a 10, 19; 10 a 15; 12 a 15; (3) affair held 10 a 29, b 16
hináqut I hope
~úntaq I hope 14 b 70, 72
hinúg Adj. ripe 11 a 5
hinúmdum remember [see dúmdum]
hinúqun Q [postpositive] [short form núqun] (1) however, instead 9 a 15, c 8; 10 a 23; 14 b 68
núqun 4 b 41
(2) [predicate] is contrary to desire or expectation 12 a 6; (3) (or, usually, gyud núqun) [particle indicating that predicate is more so than expected] 8 c 5; 9 b 1, c 23; (4) [particle acknowledging a less than satisfactory situation] 9 a 28
húgas V wash
paN- V wash 14 a 17
hulát V wait, wait for, stay inactive until 13 a 28
mag- wait 3 c 22, 34
-un person waited for 9 a 25
hulathúlat V (1) wait for a bit; (2) keep waiting and waiting
nag- (2) keep waiting 9 b 9
mag- (1) wait for a bit 8 a 21
*húlay
pa- V rest
maka- rest 4 b 34
húlug V drop something
ka- V fall
ma- fall 4 a 33
humán V bring to an end [cf. tápus]
~na it is finished 13 b 52, 57; Q [initial] after [do]ing 11 b 19
ka- V be finished
inig- moment [Gen.] is finished 5 b 58; 11 a 7, 10; 13 b 66, 67; 14 a 17
ma- is finished 13 b 44
humáy CN (ground or unground) rice 10 b 7, 9, 17, 24, 25; 11 a 5
-an (→) CN rice fields 10 b 1
-a (←) particular rice fields 10 b 12
ka- -an (→) CN rice fields 11 a 12
húmul V soak in water
ka- V get soaked
ma- get soaked 10 b 11
húnung V (come to a) stop, stop [do]ing [cf. pára]
mu- stop 3 a 25
húngut CN [drinking bowl made from half coconut shell] 5 a 16
hústu Adj. (1) proper, correct 11 b 35; 12 a 25; (2) sufficient, enough 6 b 38; 12 c 58; 13 b 43; Q [initial] right time to do something 10 b 5, 7
Huwán N John (man's name) 1 a 1
~Lúna CN Juan Luna (name of a street in Cebu City) 3 a 25

I

idád CN age 5 a 10, 12
idára particular age 5 a 14
ignuránti Adj. ignorant 2 b 21
igsúqun CN brother, sister [see *súqun]
ígut V creak

ígut (cont.)
igutqígut be rickety, creak continuously
ga- (→) is rickety 4 a 31
iháp V count
maka- count 5 a 23
íhiq CN urine
paN- V urinate 9 c 15; 13 b 50
maN- urinate 9 c 12, 14; 13 b 49, 51
ikáw you (sing.) [1 B 1] 3 c 33 and passim
ka [Nom., short form] 3 c 5 and passim
nímu [Gen.] 4 a 1 and passim
mu [Gen.] [6 D 1]
kanímu [Dat.] 5 b 53 and passim
nímu [Dat.] 14 a 30 and passim
ímu [preposed Gen.] your 5 a 24 and passim
ilá V (1) know as, recognize; (2) be acquainted with
maqílhan (2) persons with whom acquainted 5 b 55; 9 c 16
ilaqíla V get acquainted with
pa- V introduce someone to someone else
i- person introduced to someone 2 b 14; 5 b 53
íla their [see silá, 1 B 1]
ilú CN thing used to clean oneself after using the toilet
papíl pára ~ toilet paper 9 a 3
imbitár V invite
gi- [imbitahún unreal] person invited 5 b 51
ímu [Gen.] your [see ikáw]
iná CN mother [used only in set expressions]
inahán CN mother 8 c 9
Índay N [girl's name] 3 c 4, 9
Indáy Voc. 3 c 5
índay Title [term of address to females of same age as or younger than speaker; short form day]
day 1 a 13; 2 b 4; 3 c 2, 25 and passim
íni [short for niqíni] this (near speaker and hearer) [see kiní, 1 A 1]
ínit Adj. hot, warm 14 b 35, 41
Ínsik CN (1) Chinaman; (2) Chinese store owner 6 a 11
intáwun Q [postpositive] [short form táwun] (1) [particle expressing pity] 5 b 48; 9 b 9, 11, c 29; (2) [particle expressing humility]
táwun (1) 11 a 26, 27 (2) 11 a 21
Ínting N [man's name] 1 a 1
inúm V drink 13 b 47, 56
inúm [= mu-] drink 5 a 16
mu- drink 9 c 6; 13 b 46
ka- [= maka-] drink 13 b 55
ímna thing drunk 14 b 42
ínyu your (plural) [see kamú, 1 B 1]
ingún V say, tell
íngna person told 2 a 6; 6 a 12
gi- [i- unreal] thing said 8 b 12
*ingún
pa- [= padulúng] V go toward Q [followed by Dat.] toward 3 c 24
nag- go toward 11 c 1
íri [short for niqíri] this (near speaker, not near person spoken to) [see kirí, 1 A 1]
irís V erase
pag- 13 b 62
irísir CN eraser 13 b 66
irúq CN dog 4 a 24
-a (→) particular dog 4 a 25
ísaq [= úsaq, únaq]
~pa (1) wait a minute 2 b 10
(2) excuse me (used in asking permission to interrupt a conversation) 5 a 25
ísdaq CN fish 9 b 25; 10 a 13, 14
paN- V fish; CN occupation of fishing 10 a 17
maN- go fishing 10 a 6
mangingísdaq CN fisherman 10 a 5, 18
iskína CN corner 3 a 19, 25; 14 a 10
iskináha particular corner 14 a 1
ispisyál Adj. special 6 a 6; 8 b 27
istasyún CN bus stop
-an CN bus stop 9 a 20
istúrya CN story, tale [cf. sugilánun] 13 b 88 V tell story
isturyáha particular story 13 b 68, 71
mag- tell story 13 b 67, 84
ísug Adj. (1) brave, fierce; (2) fierce fighter 11 c 5
ítsa V toss, throw with little force [cf. lábay] 13 a 22
ítus V boil until water evaporates
gi- [-un unreal] thing boiled 8 b 21
íya his [see siyá, 1 B 1]
iyáq Title [term of address to peas-

ant woman older than speaker] 6 a 28, b 36
iyúq Title [term of address to peasant man older than speaker] 5 a 7, 10

K

ka [particle preceding name or title meaning at (name's) place] 2 a 13 and passim
ka you [see ikáw]
ka [linker between numeral and noun]
káda Q [precedes time nouns] every, each (day, month, etc.) 3 b 25; 5 a 16
kádtu [1 A 1] (1) that (far from hearer and speaker) 11 b 7 and passim; (1 a) that one (who was just here and has gone out now) 3 c 29; (2) that (distant) past time 3 a 2 and passim
tu [short for kádtu]
niqádtu [Gen., Dat.] [in meaning 'formerly' see kaniqádtu]
ádtu [short for niqádtu] 2 a 12 [in meaning 'formerly' see kaniqádtu]
tu [short for niqádtu]
kaganíha [see ganíha]
kaháq Q [postpositive] perhaps; (1) [in questions with ba or no interrogative] by any chance, I wonder if 3 c 11; 4 a 11; 5 b 45; 13 a 37; (2) [in questions with interrogative] can (it) be? 6 a 18
kahímtang CN state, condition, situation [see butáng]
káhuy CN (1) wood, tree; (2) stick, small piece of wood 11 b 3, 6, 7, 10, 15, 17, 19
kalámay CN brown sugar; V put brown sugar in
-an thing into which sugar is put 11 a 8
kalamáy CN [a kind of candy] 8 b 19, 21 [does not occur without l]
Kalámba CN [name of street in Cebu City] 3 c 26 [does not occur without l]
kalíguq take a bath [see díguq]
káluq CN hat 6 b 50
kalús V fetch water
pag- fetch water 9 c 25, 29
mag- fetch water 9 c 27
-an (1) place from which water is fetched; (2) person for whom water is fetched
pa- V cause to fetch water
-an (2) person for whom someone is made to get water 9 c 11
kamí we (exclusive) [1 B, 1 B 2, 13 E] 13 a 8 and passim
mi [short for kamí] 3 a 40 and passim
námuq [Gen.]
kanámuq [Dat.]
námuq [Dat.] 4 b 49
ámuq [preposed Gen.] 4 b 56 and passim
kamú [short form mu] you (plural) [13 E] 5 b 37 and passim
mu [Nom.] 3 b 5 and passim
nínyu [Gen.] 3 a 21 and passim
kanínyu [Dat.]
nínyu [Dat.]
ínyu [preposed Gen.] 3 b 15 and passim
kamút CN (human) hand 9 c 28; 10 a 19
kanákuq me [see akú]
kanámuq us (exclusive) [see kamí]
kanáq (1) that (near hearer, far from speaker) 3 a 21 and passim; (2) that (past time just referred to); (3) that well-known 11 a 4 and passim; (4) ~nga when, at the aforementioned time 10 b 7, 24; 11 c 11
naq [short for kanáq] 3 a 19
niqánaq [Gen., Dat.]
ánaq [short for niqánaq] 10 a 13 and passim
naq [short for niqánaq]
kanáqug V descend [see *náqug]
kanátuq us (inclusive) [see kitá]
kaní [= kiní] (1) this [near speaker and hearer] 10 a 26 and passim; (2) this [in narrations: at the time or place of the story]; (3) kaní nga when (at the aforementioned time)
ni [see kiní]
niqáni [Gen., Dat.] 6 a 2 and passim
áni [short for niqáni]
kaníla them [see silá]
kaniqádtu [short forms niqádtu, ádtu] formerly 11 a 22
niqádtu 9 a 19
kanímu you (sing.) [see ikáw]
kanínyu you (plural) [see kamú]
kaníya him [see siyá]
kanúnay Q [prepositive] always, at all times 5 b 49
kanúsqa when? (all tenses) [4 D] 5 b 59

kang [see si]
kapín Q [followed by Dat.] more than [Dat.] 11 a 24
Kapitúl CN Capitol (place in Cebu City where the capitol building is) 2 a 10, 12
kaqáyu very, to a high degree [see *áyu]
kaqugalíngun CN (1) one's own 3 b 31; (2) oneself 8 a 23 a
káqun V eat
pag- eat; CN food [see also below]
maka- (→) eat 8 c 10
kánqun thing eaten 11 a 10
pa- V feed
pag- feed 9 c 22
paN- V eat (several agents)
naN- eat 4 a 26
ma- CN food 8 c 11
pag- CN food 14 b 59
Karbún CN Carbon (market in Cebu City) 3 c 24, 25, 27, 29, 31
karí [= kirí] (1) this (near speaker, far from hearer); (2) this (on side of speaker, away from hearer)
ri [short for karí, kirí]
niqári [Gen., Dat.]
ári [short for niqári]
ri [short for niqári, niqíri]
Kármin CN Carmen (town north of Cebu City) 9 b 6, 12
karún Q [initial, medial, final] [short form run] (1) now, this time 5 a 11; 8 c 13; 9 a 21; 11 a 26; 12 c 56, 60, 64; 13 a 41; 13 b 88
run (1) 3 a 5, 43, b 16, 18; 5 a 11; 9 b 10; 13 a 3, b 63; 14 b 41
~pa just now 2 b 11, 12
(2) karún nga plus time expression (plus -a) this [time expression]; (2 a) this [time] (now) 12 b 29; (2 b) this [time] (approaching) 3 c 17
run (2 a) 4 b 36
kaság CN type of small sea crab 6 a 27, 28; 9 c 4
kasílyas CN toilet 3 b 31
kastígu CN punishment 11 b 14
kawáyan CN bamboo 10 a 7, 8, 10
kay Q [initial] (1) because 1 a 9, 15; 2 b 13, 30; 3 b 6, 7, 15, 30, 31 and passim; (1 a) tungúd~ because 11 c 18; (1 b) why? why do you say that? 9 b 4; (2) [Adj. plus kay plus sentence] [Adj.] that [sentence] is the case
maqáyu~ it is good that 14 a 32
Kíkuy N [man's name: short for Pransísku and other names]
Kikúy [Voc.] 13 a 39, 42
kilumítru CN kilometer 9 c 25, 26
kinahángan CN need [dialectal for kinahánglan] Q [prepositive] should 9 a 7, 13; 11 b 30
~gyud there is nothing else to do but 9 c 25
kinahánglan CN need [= kinahángan]; Q should, must, is necessary 8 a 21, c 17; 10 b 23; V need
nag- need 12 c 57
mag- need 12 c 54
*kínhas
kinhasún CN seashell 6 a 1
kiní [= kaní] [1 A 1] (1) this (near speaker and person spoken to) 1 a 10 and passim; (2) this (aforementioned, or close in time or space); (3) this place, this situation; (4) kiní nga when (at aforementioned time)
íni nga at this (time)
ni [short for kiní] 14 a 9 and passim
niqíni [Gen., Dat.]
íni [short for niqíni] 4 b 42, 43 and passim
ni [Gen., short for niqíni; Nom., short for kiní]
kínsa who? whose? 2 a 1, 4; 9 c 17, 27; 13 a 19, b 55, 60, 76
~pa who else? 13 b 49
~y ngálan [Gen.] what is [Gen.]'s name? 2 b 19
kínsi [number] fifteen 6 a 6
kínta Q [precedes or follows word it modifies] (1) a certain amount agreed on; (2) let's say for instance so many 11 b 13
kirí [= karí] [1 A 1] (1) this (near speaker but not near hearer); (2) this (on side of speaker away from hearer)
ri [short for kirí]
niqíri [Gen., Dat.]
íri [short for niqíri]
ri [short for niqíri]
kitá [short form ta] we, us (inclusive) [1 B, 1 B 2, 13 E] 13 a 1 and passim
ta [Nom.] 3 a 5 and passim
nátuq [Gen.] 3 a 2 and passim

ta [Gen.: 6 D 1]
ta [Gen. with ka or ikáw: 9 A] I 8 c 33
kánatuq [Dat.]
nátuq [Gen., Dat.]
átuq [preposed Gen.] 4 a 9 and passim
únsa may átuq what would you like? 1 a 3, 22; 4 b 55; 12 b 37 and passim
kítaq V earn
mu- earn 11 a 17
kítaq V see, notice [11 D]
mag- see each other 4 b 64; 8 b 3
naka (→) see 4 a 27; 8 b 18; 11 b 42
ma- thing seen 9 a 13
paN- V look for 2 a 10; 3 c 30
naN- look for 3 a 1, b 13
maN- look for 6 b 44; 13 a 29, 36
hi-/hing- V happen to see
nakítqan [short for nahikítqan or nahakítqan] thing seen 11 b 3
ku (1) [Nom.] [short for akú: see akú]; (2) [Gen.] [short for nákuq: see akú]
kúhaq V (1) get, obtain, take hold of; (2) take out, take away; (3) fetch
pag- (1) take 8 c 25
inig- (2) when [Gen.] is taken 11 a 10
mu- (2) take 10 b 14
mag- (3) fetch 11 a 26
maka- (1) get [= maka- (→)] 11 b 12
-un (1) thing gotten 11 a 5
-a (2) thing taken 10 b 15
ma- (1) thing gotten 11 a 15
-an (1) person for whom gotten 8 c 33
tiN- V strive, aim
paN- V strive
maN- strive 11 b 7
kukakúla CN Coca-Cola 1 a 23
kumústa how is . . . ? 1 a 7, 11; 2 b 16; 3 b 11, c 5; 5 a 7; 8 c 27; 14 a 19
kun Q [initial] if, when (future, habitual) 5 a 32, b 37; 10 b 22, 25; 11 c 21
kúntra CN opponent 11 c 21
kunú Q [postpositive] [short form nu] he said, it is said 9 a 9
nu 3 b 7
kupút V take hold of, hold tightly
kúptan [short for gikúptan] thing held 8 a 14
kuqán Q, CN, V whatchamacallit 1 a 13; 5 b 40; 9 a 2, b 7, 25, c 8, 18; 11 a 4, 18, b 31, 33, 40, c 7, 11; 12 b 40; 13 a 4, 41, b 72
maka- can whatchamacallit 12 b 31
ka- [= maka-] can whatchamacallit 12 c 60
ma- thing that had whatchamacallit happen to it 10 b 10
kurál V fence; CN fence 10 a 13
kusúg Adj. (1) fast 4 a 33; (2) hard, using much force or effort 11 b 20
kutána V ask a question
paN- V ask a question
naN- ask 12 b 47
maN- ask 3 a 8, 10, 14
pangutánqun person asked 4 a 9; 6 a 11, 13
pangutánqa person asked 3 a 9, 32, 34
kútub Q [followed by Dat. or final] to the point as far as [Dat.] in space or time 4 b 50
kutúy V feel hungry
nag- rumble 9 b 8
kúyug V go together with 9 a 17
-an person accompanied 9 a 15
kwarínta [number] forty 3 b 26; 10 b 14
kwártu CN room (part of a house) 3 b 7, 13, 15, 19, c 3, 7, 13; 14 a 27
kwartúha particular room 3 b 31
kwátru [number] four 8 a 19
~singkwínta four-fifty 8 b 7, 8, 15

L

labád Adj. aching (said of the head) 12 b 29; V ache
gilábdan one who has a headache 14 a 1
lábay V throw; CN throw 11 b 18
pag- throw 11 b 6
mu- throw 11 b 11, 20; 13 a 19
nag- throw 11 b 10
gi- -an place thrown 11 b 17
i- thing thrown 11 b 5, 15
labaylábay V throw repeatedly
i- thing thrown repeatedly 11 b 16
labí Q [followed by nga plus adjective] most, more, very 5 a 8; 10 a 4
ilabí na [short form labí na] Q especially: [verb] is likely to happen; [agent] [does] more than others
labí na 10 b 10
lábqas Adj. fresh (of seafood) 6 a 30, 31

lagí Q [postpositive] (1) [in contradictions] [predicate] is so, despite contradictory factors 3 b 5; 4 a 24; 8 b 15, 31; (2) [in statements after a point has been won in an argument]
aw~ of course (as you now agree)! 14 b 67
(3) believe it or not 4 a 23; 9 b 7

Lahúg CN (District of Cebu City) 2 a 8; 6 b 56, 57

lakáw V (1) walk 4 a 33; 11 a 28; (2) go (riding or walking) 6 b 55; 13 b 54; (3) leave, go out or away 9 c 13; CN way to somewhere 8 c 24
mi- (3) go away 3 c 9
ni- (3) go out 2 a 3
mu- (1) walk 4 a 21; 9 c 25; (3) go out 12 b 28

lakí CN (nonhuman) male
laláki CN (human) male 10 a 22

lamíq Adj. delicious, tasty 11 a 10; 14 b 40, 42

lántay CN bamboo bench, bed, or table with slatted top
-a (←) particular bamboo table 4 b 35

lang Q [postpositive] [13 G 1 ff.] [= lámang] (1) let [noun or pronoun predicate] do [verb subject] 3 b 22; 4 b 62; 8 a 13, c 7; (2) [particle indicating that predicate must be done as least undesirable alternative] 1 a 16, 17; 3 c 34, 35; 6 b 39; 9 a 15, b 2; (3) merely; (3 a) [with verbs not in exhortation] [verb] is a little thing to do 4 a 26; 5 a 16, 33; 9 c 12; 10 b 13, 14; 12 b 43, 47; (3 a i) [with abstracts] 9 c 25; (3 b) [with imperative forms or exhortations] [imperative] is a little thing to do; (3 b i) [with imperatives] 2 a 6, 10; 3 a 21, c 30; 4 a 23; 6 b 39; 9 c 5; 12 a 12, 13; 14 a 5, 29; (3 b ii) [with exhortations] 1 a 6; 2 b 31; 4 a 20, 21, b 35, 44; 12 b 37, 42, 44; 14 b 58; (3 b iii) ayáw~ 9 b 15, c 4; (3 b iii a) please don't 9 b 15; (3 b iii b) no, thanks [with refusal; = ayáw na~] 4 b 62; 8 a 12, c 32; 9 c 12; (3 b iv) sígi~; (3 b iv a) never mind 6 a 15; 8 c 21, 34; (3 b iv b) [indicating agreement to let someone do something] 12 b 44; (3 b iv c) oh please! 12 a 5; (3 c) [with nouns or pronouns] merely [= ra: 14 G 2 f.] 1 a 23; 4 b 56; 9 b 6; 10 a 5; 14 b 69
ákuq na~ May I have it? 12 c 62
(3 d) [with numerals, numbers, prices] it is a small [number, etc.] (cf. 4 b) 8 b 27; (3 e) bísan ug [interrogative] [noun] ~ any [noun] whatever 3 b 23; (3 f) arún~ just to [verb] (and nothing else which is better) 10 a 33; (4) na~ [12 G 1 d] (4 a) the least undesirable of available alternatives) 1 a 25; 2 b 30, 34; 3 c 19, 20, 33; 6 a 15; 8 a 32, b 3, c 26; 9 a 27, c 13; 12 c 61, 65; 14 b 59, 73
ayáw na~ [= ayáw~] no, thank you 1 a 14; 9 a 16, c 7
ságdi na~ never mind 2 b 28
salámat na~ thanks anyway 2 b 29, 32
bísan na~ not even X (when X is less than what is desired) 8 c 11
(4 b) the only one from now on, X and only X [= ra which does not occur after na]; (4 b i) [with numbers] only [number], reduced to [number] 3 c 32; 6 a 8;
(5) waláq~, díliq~ [less curt than waláq, díliq) 5 b 60
waláq~y sapayán never mind (I am not offended) 12 c 66
diq na~ no thanks 9 c 7
(6) dínhi, ánhi, or ngánhi~ [= ra] I'll leave (you) here (on this vehicle) 4 b 63; 9 b 14; 12 a 20
arí~ku I'll stay here 14 b 51

láqag V roam (go about aimlessly)
laqág Adj. stray 4 a 25

láqay Adj. tiresome, boring; V be affected by something tiresome
-an one who considers something tiresome 4 b 42

láqin (1) CN other, another, different 3 c 30, 31, 34; 6 a 23; 11 c 26; 12 b 31, c 60; (2) Adj. of a bad type, something not nice 8 a 16
~pay átuq (1) by the way 12 b 45, c 54
taga- CN (1) person from another place 10 a 33
ka- -an CN (1) difference 11 c 16

lárga V leave [cf. gíkan]
mu- leave 9 a 21, 22, 23
ka- [= maka-] leave 4 a 6

láta CN can 13 a 19

layúq Adj. distant (in space or time) 3 c 13, 14; 4 a 17; 9 b 5; CN distant place 11 b 5, 15; Q [followed by Dat.]

far from 11 c 14
-a [exclamatory] how far! 11 a 27
layuqlayúq Adj. a bit far 11 b 20
líbri Adj. (1) free (of charge) 3 b 27; (2) free (in a game) 13 a 31
líbru CN book 8 b 1; 9 a 29; 12 b 40, 42, 44, c 62
líbut V go around, surround; Adj. roundabout, circuitous 12 a 16
i- thing used for surrounding 10 a 10
*líguq
kalíguq take a bath [see díguq]
Liin CN Lane Theater (in Cebu City) 4 b 50, 51
likúq V make a turn (on the road) 3 a 23
límbung V cheat, deceive
paN- cheat, deceive
maN- cheat 8 c 16
límpyu Adj. clean; V make clean 14 a 16, 17
limpyúhi thing cleaned 13 b 66
límut V render unconscious
ka- V forget
hi-/ha- (→) V accidentally forget
pag- forget 8 a 33
hi-/hing- V forget accidentally
hikalímtan thing accidentally forgotten 6 a 18
Lína N [woman's name; short for Ilína and other names]
Liná Voc. 14 a 1, 3, 11
línya CN line; V get in line 13 b 45
língin Adj. round 11 b 34
língkud V sit, sit down 3 b 9
paN- V sit down (plural agents) 13 b 59
maN- sit down 14 b 45
lipák CN slat 10 a 7
líqug CN neck 11 b 39
lisúd Adj. difficult to do, hard to endure 4 a 19; 9 c 23; 11 b 29, 43; V [followed by infinitive] have a hard time
mag- [= mag- (←)] have a hard time 2 b 17, 18; 4 a 18; 10 a 13
ka- [exclamatory] how hard!
pag- how hard! 9 c 24
lisudlisúd Adj. quite difficult 14 b 71
Lítu N [man's name; short for Husilítu and other names] 2 b 24; 13 a 10, b 86
lubí CN coconut, coconut tree 5 a 27, 28
lubúk V pound (with pestle in mortar) 11 a 10
lúbkun [= lúkbun] thing pounded 11 a 7
lugár (1) CN place [cf. lunáq] 4 b 34; 8 a 25; 10 a 33; 11 c 4; (2) CN room, space 3 c 32; (3) Q Shall we call it . . . ? [cf. kínta] 11 b 23
-a (←) (1) particular place 4 a 16, 22, b 42
Lúling N [woman's name; short for Dulúris and other names]
Lulíng Voc. 2 b 25
Lúna N [surname]
Huwán Lúna CN Juan Luna [name of a street in Cebu City] 3 a 25
lunáq CN (1) place [cf. lugár]; (2) piece of land 10 a 20
lungág CN hole 11 b 5, 19
lúngsud CN town (settlement larger than báryu and smaller than dakbayán) 5 a 8, 33
lúquy Adj. having pity, sympathizing [used only in set expressions]
ka- V feel pity for, sympathize with
ma- sympathize with, feel pity 8 c 7
makalulúquy Adj. pitiful 8 c 12
ka- [exclamatory] how pitiful! 6 a 35
lútuq V prepare food
mu- cook 8 c 9
mag- cook 14 b 59
-a thing cooked 6 a 34
luyú CN the place behind, rear, back 9 c 9

M

ma Voc. Ma [short for máma; see máma]
Mabúlu CN Mabolo (part of Cebu City) 6 b 49, 51, 53, 55
Magsáysay N Magsaysay (surname of the third president of the Republic of the Philippines) 11 a 23
mahál Adj. dear, expensive; dear, cherished 9 b 1
ka- [exclamatory] how expensive! 8 b 29
mahalmahál Adj. rather expensive 3 b 28

mam Title [term for addressing female teacher or office-holder] 13 a 2, 4, 8 and passim
máma Title mother [short form ma]
Ma 3 c 1
man Q [postpositive] [1 D 2, 14 G 1]
(1) because 1 a 15; 2 b 30, 33; 3 a 39, b 15, 30; 4 a 31, b 48; 5 a 2, b 44; 6 a 7, b 56; 8 a 2, c 21; 9 a 18, 19; 10 a 5, 14, 19, b 8, 9; 11 a 15, 17, b 13, c 13, 14, 15, 18, 26; 12 a 12, 15, b 43, 47; 14 b 59, 66, 69, 71
~gud because 2 b 13; 3 b 27; 5 b 40; 8 c 4, 8; 10 b 21; 11 c 7, 19; 12 a 14, b 51, c 56, 59
(2) [question particle after interrogatives] 1 a 22; 2 a 9, 14, b 8; 3 a 1, 7, 16, b 25, c 16, 24 27; 4 a 15, 16, b 55, 58, 61; 5 a 10, 14, b 36, 39, 56, 59; 6 a 3, 5, 28, 32, b 49; 8 b 12, 18, 20, 26, 31, c 2; 9 a 1, 5, b 4, 10, c 4, 10, 17, 22, 27; 10 a 7, 29, b 16; 11 a 3, b 1, 26, c 10, 16, 22; 12 a 2, 10, b 37, 46; 13 a 3, b 78; 14 a 6
(3) [particle with statement giving new information after noticing something] 1 a 5, 8; 2 a 3, b 20, 21; 3 a 19, b 12, 24, c 6, 14, 18, 28; 4 a 24, b 36, 37, 38; 6 a 17, 23; 8 a 5, b 15, 31, c 3; 9 a 11; 10 a 18, b 11; 11 c 21; 12 a 16, b 40, c 55, 61; 14 a 2, 22, b 57
~diqáy [particle used with statement resulting from receipt of new information] 1 a 24; 3 b 5, c 1; 8 c 20; 9 a 23, b 12; 12 c 61; 14 a 25
(4) [particle with statement contradicting previous statement or presumption] 2 b 18; 3 c 12; 4 a 31; 5 b 51; 6 b 42; 9 a 10, c 12; 12 a 4, b 39
Tagád ka na~. Don't worry about it. 14 b 39
manáng Title [short form nang] (1) [term for addressing elder sister]; (2) [term for addressing female older than speaker]
nang Voc. (2) Ma'am 9 b 4, 15
manúk CN chicken 11 b 38, c 4, 5, 19, 21, 26; 14 b 34
-a (←) particular chicken 11 c 9
mánuy Title [short form nuy] (1) [term for addressing elder brother]; (2) [term for addressing males older than speaker]
nuy (2) 3 a 12, 28; 4 b 34; 5 a 4, 5, 8, b 40, 48; 6 b 49, 52; 10 a 3; 11 c 3, 22
mangá (1) [plural marker for CN and Adj.] 3 a 25 and passim; (2) [preceding numbers] about, around 5 a 11, b 57; 8 a 19
maqáyu Adj. good [see áyu]
maqís CN corn 10 a 24, 27
ka- -an CN cornfield 10 a 22, 25; 11 a 12
maqú [short forms mu, maw] is, are; was, were (1) [preceding subject in sentences with nominal predicates] 6 b 55; 8 a 1, 2, 25, b 11, 16, c 29; 9 a 11; 13 a 6, b 82, 83 and passim
mu 5 a 9, 18 and passim
(1 a) [with no subject] it's [predicate] which is the one
~bítaw that is so 9 c 31 and passim
~gyud that's the way it is! 5 a 2 and passim
kun~kanáq if that is so . . .
(2) ~kanáq nga, ~kádtu nga for that reason, consequently 8 c 25; 12 b 53 and passim
mu 5 a 17 and passim
(3) ~ra ug it seems
mu 4 b 38; 8 a 5; 13 b 79 and passim
(4) V know how to
ka- [= maka-] know 8 c 24
mariká come here! (said to inferiors) [= umarí ka; cf. dalíq] 2 b 25
márka CN mark, sign 3 a 36; 8 a 2
mas Q more, -er 8 c 6; 9 a 27, c 16
matá CN eye 9 a 13; V wake up or be awake
mag- be awake 5 b 37, 38
matág Q [precedes time nouns] every [day, month, etc.] 3 b 26
matáy V kill (with poison, sickness, or the like) [cf. patáy]
matáy [= ma-] die 6 a 34
ka- V die
ma- die
matáy [exclamation of displeasure] 4 b 38
mátud Q [followed by Gen.] [Gen.] said 8 b 15
may there is; have [3 A 1]
mga [abbreviation for mangá; see mangá]
mi [short for kamí] we (exclusive)
Milíndris N [surname] 9 c 18, 22

Mílir N Miller [surname] 14 a 1, 9, 19, 30, b 48
Mírli N Merlie [woman's name; short form Mirl]
Mirlí Voc. 4 a 1
Mirl 4 b 53
mis Title [term for addressing young unmarried woman of high rank] 3 a 1, b 6, 10, 11, c 3, 4, 13 and passim
mísis Title [term for addressing high-ranking married woman] 3 a 1, 41, b 4 and passim
místir Title [term for addressing a man of high rank] 1 a 1, 4, 10 and passim
misyunáryu CN missionary 8 b 5
mu (1) you (plural) [see kamú]; (2) you (sing.) [see ikáw]; (3) [short for maqú]
mubúq Adj. short 11 b 3, 4, 7, 10, 15
muskitíru CN mosquito net 9 a 2
mutsátsa CN maidservant 14 a 9, b 63
myíntras Q [initial] while
~tántu in the meantime 14 b 43

N

na Q [postpositive] (1) by now [12 G 1 a] 1 a 24; 2 b 30; 4 a 19, b 37; 5 a 10, 11, 12, 13, 24, b 44; 8 a 5, 13, 18, c 19, 20; 9 a 18, 19, b 8, 12, 18, 19, c 2, 3; 10 a 6, 27, b 5, 7, 10, 24, 25; 11 a 10, 24, b 9, c 6, 21; 12 b 48, 53, 55; 14 a 7, 9, b 57; (2) [with negatives] no longer, not any more [12 G 1 b] 2 b 27; 5 a 23; 9 a 24; 10 a 14; 11 a 9; 12 c 58, 61; 14 a 21, 22, b 42, 68; (3) ~lang [12 G 1 d] (3 a) [the predicate is the least undesirable choice] 1 a 25; 2 b 30, 34; 3 c 19, 20, 33; 6 a 15; 8 a 32, b 3, c 11, 26; 9 a 27, c 13; 12 c 61, 65; 14 b 59, 73; (3 b) only [predicate] now (as contrasted with more, earlier) [cf. meaning (4) 3 c 32; 6 a 8; (4) [predicate] now, as contrasted with previously [12 G 1 c]; (4 a) [with CN, pronouns] 3 a 39; 8 a 2; 9 c 29
ákuq~ [subject] may I have [subject]? 12 c 62
(4 b) [with verbs] [verb] now (to initiate the action) 4 b 48, 51; 6 a 19, 20, 26; 9 a 26, c 15; 10 a 2; 12 a 6; 14 a 20, b 42, 55
adtu~ku, mi or arí~ku, mi goodbye (said upon departing) 1 a 18, 20; 3 a 30; 12 b 34, c 66
(4 c) [with adjectives] now 6 b 46
(4 d) do now 9 a 26; 14 b 42
ayáw~ stop [cf. also under meaning (2)] 9 c 14
sígi~ go ahead and . . .! 12 a 17
ayáw~lang no thank you, never mind doing that 1 a 14; 9 a 16, c 7
diq~lang no thanks, [subject] doesn't want 9 c 7
ságdi~lang never mind 2 b 28
salámat~lang thanks anyway 2 b 29, 32
(4 e) [with exhortations] let's [verb] now! 2 a 17; 9 a 20; (4 f) [with interrogative deictics] where is [subject] now? 14 a 2; (4 g) [with nouns or numbers; cf. meaning (3 b)]; (5) na pud, sad, or sab; (5 a) again 14 b 69; (5 b) in turn 11 b 10, 11; (6) [predicate] is not the same as others in the group
díliq or waláq~ [predicate] is not like the other things of the same class 3 b 29
labí or ilabí~ especially 10 b 10
tagád ka~man or guqúl~man nímu never mind! Don't worry about it! 14 b 39
na Q [initial] [particle used upon broaching a new subject] (1) all right, I agree; but only under a certain condition 6 a 21; 13 a 14, 18, 21, b 88; (1 a) all right [to terminate conversation] 3 c 19, 20; 4 b 63; 9 a 27, 28, b 15; 12 b 30, 34, c 66; 14 b 65, 73, 74; (2) [before exhortations or commands to begin an action] let's 8 c 38; [do]! 3 c 33; 9 c 13; (3) [particle used before concluding the conversation] 13 a 32, 41, b 43; (4) [preceding a warning] 13 a 26
nákuq (1) Gen.; (2) Dat. I, me [see akú]
námuq (1) Gen.; (2) Dat. we, us (exclusive) [see kamí]
nánay Title mother 9 b 24
nang [see manáng]
napúluq ten [see púluq]
naq that (near hearer but not speaker); (1) Nom. [short for kanáq]; (2) Gen. [short for niqánaq; see kanáq]
náqa there (near hearer, far from speaker) [see anáqa]
náqay Q it is there [pointing out objects] 11 b 3

*náqug
ka- V go out of the house; go or come down; get off [a vehicle] [10 C] 12 a 12
ma- go down, get off [a vehicle] 3 a 38; 4 a 20; 8 a 23 b, c 21; 9 b 16
nátuq (1) Gen.; (2) Dat. we, us (inclusive) [see kitá]
ni (1) Gen. [particle before names: see si]; (2) Dat. [alternant of kang: see si]; (3) [short form of kiní, kaní: see kiní, kaní]; (4) [short form of niqíni, niqáni: see kiní, kaní]
Nída N [woman's name]
Nidá Voc. 8 c 23
níla (1) Gen.; (2) Dat. they [short for kaníla: see silá]
nímu (1) Gen.; (2) Dat. you [short for kanímu: see ikáw]
níndut Adj. beautiful, pretty [see aníndut]
nínyu (1) Gen.; (2) Dat. you (plural) [short for kanínyu: see kamú]
níqa here (near speaker, far from hearer) [short for aníqa]
niqádtu (1) formerly [see kaniqádtu]; (2) Gen., Dat. [see kádtu]
niqánaq Gen., Dat. [see kanáq]
niqáni Gen., Dat. [see kaní]
niqári Gen., Dat. [see karí]
niqíni Gen., Dat. [see kiní]
niqíri Gen., Dat. [see kirí]
níya he, him; she, her; (1) Gen.;(2) Dat. [short for kaníya: see siyá]
nu [someone] says [see kunú]
nu Q [final] (1) isn't that right? (1 a) [particle asking hearer to agree] 3 a 43; 5 a 25; 8 c 35; (1 b) so it is, isn't it?
túqud~ [exclamation of self-correction] 3 a 37; 12 a 25; 14 b 64;
(2) you know? do you see? 3 a 19; 8 a 19; 9 c 30
nubintayqútsu [number] ninety-eight 5 a 11, 12
nunút V follow along with [cf. kúyug and ubán]
mag- depend upon 10 b 21
núqun Q [see hinúqun]
Núwa N Noah [Biblical name] 13 b 72
nuy [see mánuy]
nyaq [see únyaq]
nyurá Ma'am [see sinyúra]
ng (1) Gen. [alternant of ni, 1 B: see si]; (2) Dat. [alternant of kang: see si]; (3) [alternant of nga: see nga]; (4) [alternant of ang: see ang]
nga Linker [short form: ng after vowels, n, q; zero after consonants other than n, q] (1) [following preposed genitive] (1 a) [preceding passive verb: 6 B 2] 2 a 9, b 10, 14; 6 a 21 and passim; (1 b) [preceding CN: 1 F, 2 E] 1 a 9; 2 b 19 and passim; (2) [following demonstrative pronouns] (2 a) [before noun: 1 F] 1 a 16; 2 b 2 and passim; (2 b) [before deictic] 11 b 6 and passim; (2 c) [before verb] 3 a 2 and passim; (3 a) [between noun and adjective: 1 F] 4 a 23 and passim; (3 b) [between nouns] (3 b i) [with measurements: 14 D] of 10 b 14; (3 c) [between deictic and noun] 10 a 3 and passim; (3 d) [between verb and noun] 3 b 19 and passim; (4) [preceding sentence] (4 a) [after certain verbs: 12 E 3] 12 b 29; (4 b) [following noun qualified by a sentence] 8 c 3 and passim; (5) [linker for qualifier: [3 E, 9 A 1 b] (5 a) [with adjectives of manner: 9 c 1, 14 A] 8 b 6 and passim
ngádtu [1 A 2, 2 A 1] there (place far from speaker and hearer) 5 b 37 and passim
ngálan CN name 2 b 19, 24
ngánhaq [1 A 2, 2 A 1]; (1) there (near hearer) 3 a 19 and passim; (2) at place referred to previously
ngánhi [1 A 2, 2 A 1] here (near speaker and hearer) 4 a 1 and passim
ngánu Q [prepositive] why? 8 a 14, b 31, c 2; 9 b 10, c 10; 12 a 23, b 46; 14 a 6
ngarí [1 A 2, 2 A 1] here (near or toward speaker and far from hearer) 3 b 8 and passim
ngítngit Adj. dark 8 a 20, c 21

P

pa Q [postpositive] [12 G 2] (1) still, yet, until now; (1 a) [with verbs] 12 b 43; 14 b 52; (1 b) [with deictics] 9 b 25; 14 a 22; (1 c) [with adjective] [adjective] until now 8 a 20, c 21; 12 c 63; 14 b 35, 41; (1 d) [with time expression] still 8 a 19; 11 a 23; (1 e) [with measurements] only [measurement] up to now 12 b 49; (1 f) [with negative] not yet 4 a 4; 5 b 47, 48; 8 c 21; 9 b 24; 10 b 6; 11 a 5, 12 c 60, 64; (2)

[with negatives] before 8 a 23 b, c 21; 9 b 17; (3) else, in addition; (3 a) [with CN or pronoun] [CN or pronoun] as well
únsa~ what else? 9 a 5
(3 b) [with verbs] (3 b i) still have [verb] to do 4 a 3; 9 b 3; 12 a 15; 14 b 59; (3 b ii) [verb] when one shouldn't 14 b 38; (3 c) [with imperative forms] [verb] as well 14 a 16; (3 d) [with existential y] there is also [predicate] 11 c 26; 12 a 16
gawás~ besides 4 a 18; 10 a 6; 11 b 10
láqin~y átuq by the way (changing subject) 12 b 45, c 54
(4) [in comparison] more 9 a 27; (5) just now [cf. meaning 1 e]
karún ~ just now 2 b 11, 12
gíkan~ just back from 9 b 27
(6) ísaq~, úsaq~, taym~ excuse me 2 b 10; 3 c 16; 5 a 25, b 35; 6 a 11, 24;
(7) básin~, hináqut~ I hope 3 a 44; 12 c 65; 14 b 70
páhid V wipe [something small] [cf. trápu]
pahíra thing to be wiped 13 b 48
pahúlay V rest [see *húlay]
palít V buy
palít [= mu-] buy 8 b 23; 12 b 42
pag- buy 9 a 24
mu- buy 6 a 5; 8 b 25, c 13
nag- bought 8 b 31
-un thing bought 6 a 19, 21
pa- V cause to buy
-a one allowed to buy 6 b 36
paN- V buy (plural agents or recipients)
naN- go shopping 6 a 1
maN- buy 9 a 26
-unun (←) CN things to buy 9 a 24
pamílya CN family 9 a 1, c 29; 11 a 18
pamínaw V listen 13 b 84, 88
panahún CN (1) time [cf. tímpu] 11 a 1, 23; (2) weather 10 b 21
pananglítan Q for example [see sánglit]
panihápun evening meal [see hápun]
paningúhaq strive after [see kúhaq]
pánit CN (1) skin (animal, human), peel, rind (of fruit or vegetable); (2) leather 11 b 37
pantalán CN pier 8 a 16
pántaw CN kitchen stoop
-an CN kitchen stoop 9 c 5
pangutána ask [see kutána]
pápas V erase
-a thing erased 13 b 65
tig- CN one who has the duty of erasing (the blackboard) 13 b 60
papíl CN paper 9 a 3; 13 a 11
paqági means, way [see ági]
par CN pair 6 a 4
pára Q (1) [followed by Dat.] (1 a) for the sake or benefit of 3 b 23; 8 a 6, 7, b 27; 9 a 3, c 29; 10 a 8; (1 b) in the direction of 2 a 8, 10; 3 a 34, c 27; 6 b 49; 8 a 1; (1 c) as change for [money] 6 b 42; (2) [preceding verb] for the purpose of, in order to 10 a 6; 11 b 40; (2 a) [followed by a noun meaning 'perform an action'] to be used in [doing] 9 a 3
pára V (1) hail a vehicle (2) stop! [cf. húnung] 3 a 40
paríha CN same, similar [cf. sáma]
~ra it's all the same 11 c 17
párti CN part (taken from a whole) [cf. báhin] 10 a 10
pasáhi CN fare [cf. plíti] 8 b 11
patáy V kill (with violence) [cf. matáy]; CN dead person or thing 11 c 21
pag- kill 6 a 32
patyánay V kill each other; CN a fighting to the death 11 c 19
pátid V kick
patíran thing kicked 11 b 41
pátung V put something over something else
i- thing over which something is put 11 b 5
Pidíl Rusáryu CN P. del Rosario (name of a street in Cebu City) 3 a 19
Pídru N Pedro (man's name) [short form Dru] 13 b 53
pik V play 'hammer, paper, scissors' 13 a 7
píkas CN the other (of two adjacent sides or things) 4 a 7, 28; 6 b 55
píkqap CN bus or jeep not running on a schedule 4 a 8
pilá how much? how many? to what extent? 2 a 14, b 3; 3 b 25; 4 b 61; 5 a 10, 22, b 56; 6 a 5; 10 a 29, b 16; 11 b 13
bísag~ any amount whatsoever 9 b 2
tag- (←) how much apiece? 6 a 3, 28; 8 b 26
Piláyis CN Pelaez (name of a street in Cebu City) 3 a 19, 21

pfldi V defeat, make lose (in a contest)
pfldi [= na-] is defeated 13 a 10, 13, 15, 16, 17
ka- V be defeated
na- be defeated 11 b 17
pilípig CN rice crunch 11 a 2, 3, 4
Pilipínas CN the Philippines 5 b 41, 44; 9 a 11
Pilipínu CN Filipino 5 b 45
píliq V choose, pick (out) 4 b 35
mag- choose 3 b 22
-un thing chosen 4 b 45
pínggan CN dish, chinaware 14 a 17
Pírla N Perla (woman's name) 5 b 51
Pirlá Voc. 3 a 1, b 5, c 20, 33; 5 a 1; 8 a 22
Pirnándis N Fernandez (surname) 2 a 2, 13, b 8
píru [short form pirú] Q [initial] but, on the contrary [= apán] 5 b 49, 52; 14 b 65
pirú 3 c 29; 4 b 37; 5 a 29; 8 c 6, 16; 9 a 8, b 2, 26; 11 a 12; 12 b 31; 14 a 22
písu CN one peso 8 b 27, 28
písus CN (1) one peso (2) peso (unit of currency) 3 b 26; 6 a 4, 6, 14
pitú [numeral] seven 11 a 24
piyúr Adj. genuine 11 c 8
plíti V pay the fare; CN fare [cf. pasáhi] 2 b 3; 9 b 1; 12 a 18
Plúra N Flora (woman's name) [short form Plur]
Plurá Voc. 9 a 1, 27
Plur Voc. 9 a 1
prays CN price [= prísyu] 8 b 27
prisidínti Title president 11 a 23
prísyu CN price [= prays] 6 a 6; 8 c 6
ultimúng~ lowest price offered 6 a 9
prútas CN fruit (as part of meal, or snack) 4 b 59
púbri Adj. poor, having little money 8 c 8; 9 a 9; 10 a 5; 11 a 18
pud [see upúd]
pulá Adj. [a shade of red, yellow-orange, or brown]; V be or become red, yellow-orange, brown
mu- become yellow-brown 10 b 7
Pulambatú CN Pulambato (village in northern Cebu) 5 a 1; 9 a 1, 8, 15, 17, b 16; 10 b 14; 11 a 1, 13
púlta CN door, gate
pultahán CN door, doorway 10 a 11, 12, 14
púluq [numeral] ten [= napúluq]
na- [numeral] ten [= púluq]
ka- Q [initial, medial, final] ten times 11 c 6
pulús Q [prepositive] 8 a 5 [not without l]
púntus CN point; unit of credit, scoring, or measuring 11 b 9, 12, 13
punúq Adj. full 4 a 4 V (1) fill (2) add
gipúnqan (2) thing to which something is added 8 b 21
pursíntu CN per cent 10 b 14
pústa wrap [see putús]
púsu CN artesian well 11 a 22
pusúha particular artesian well 11 a 23
Púquk CN Pooc (name of a barrio of Talisay, south of Cebu City) 4 a 16, 17
putús V wrap
pústa thing wrapped 6 a 21
puyúq V dwell in
mag- live 3 c 9; 10 b 12
ga- live 4 a 29
pwírti Q [preceding exclamatory] how (nice, etc.)! 11 a 27

R

ra Q [postpositive] [14 G 2] (1) [with number, numeral, CN, or pronoun predicates] [predicate] and nothing else; (1 a) only [predicate] performs [subject], nothing else than [predicate] 3 c 8; 5 a 18; 8 b 16, c 32; 11 c 13; (1 b) [with number or numeral predicate] no more than [predicate] 5 b 57; 6 a 9, 12; 8 b 15, 29, 31, c 3; 10 b 19, 20; 11 a 14; (2 a) [with adjectives] too [adjective] 11 c 14; (2 b) [with adjectives indicating the smaller, easier, lighter, lesser, etc. of two opposites] very 5 a 15, 31, 34; 6 a 33; 11 a 12, 25; 12 c 59, 60, 65; 14 b 66
hústu~naq that's just right 12 c 58
paríha~ it's all the same 11 c 17
(3) [with deictic predicate] 4 b 50; 11 a 19; 12 a 4
dínhi~ku (mi), ánhi~ku (mi), ngánhi~ku (mi) I (we) get off here 3 a 40; 9 b 13
(4) [with verbs] [verb] is sure to happen 6 a 34; (5) [as imperative softener] 6 b 50; 8 c 1
~gud [as imperative softener] 3 c 2; 5 a 4; 8 a 24; 14 a 1, 11

(6) ~ba (6 a) [particle accompanying advice or warning] 4 a 3, 4; 5 b 54; 8 a 16; 9 a 9; 12 a 14; 14 b 40; (6 b) [particle of apology] 2 b 27; 3 c 25, 32; (7) [with nouns] merely, nothing more than [noun] [cf. lang, 13 G 1 e] 8 c 35; (8) maqú~ug seem 4 b 38; 8 a 5 and passim

rása CN breed, stock
  rasáha particular breed 11 c 22

ri this (near speaker but not hearer) [short for karí, kirí, niqári, niqíri: see karí, kirí]

rigálu CN gift [cf. gása] 5 b 61

risírba V reserve
  girisirbahán person for whom reserved 8 a 25
  gi- [i- unreal] thing reserved 8 a 6, 7

risís CN recess 13 a 1, b 44

ristáwran CN restaurant 4 b 52

ritrátu CN photograph 13 b 81

Riyál Istrít CN Real Street 8 c 36

S

sa [6 B ff.] (1) [preceding specific goal: 5 D 2]; (2) [preceding time qualifier] at, during 2 c 17 and passim; (3) [preceding pag- infinitives: 9 B 2, 12 E 1] 9 c 25 and passim; (4) [preceding place qualifiers] to, from, in, on, at 2 a 7, 13 and passim; (5) [preceding nonqualifying Gen. or Dat.: 6 B ff.] 5 a 1, 9 b 27; (7) [Dat. marker after qualifiers]:
  humán~ after
  kútub~ up to
  gíkan~ from
  tungúd~ on account of

sab also [see usáb]

sabáw soup, broth 14 b 33, 34, 38

sabún CN soap 9 a 2

sábung CN cock sparring, cockfight without gaffs 11 c 25; V pit a rooster without gaffs
  i- thing to be pitted against something else 11 c 27

sabút V understand, grasp the meaning of
  sábut V make an agreement
  gi- -an (1) person agreed with; (2) thing agreed upon
  gika- -an (2) thing agreed upon 11 b 13; 12 a 24

sad also [see usáb]

*ságad
  ságdi [short for paságdi] thing to be disregarded
    ságdi na lang never mind 2 b 28

ságad CN common, usual
  kasagáran CN usual type 8 c 6; 11 a 13

ságing CN banana 5 a 29, 30, 31, 32, 34; 8 c 11

saká V (1) climb, go up [10 C]; (2) go into a house 14 a 27; (3) stay at someone's place; (4) get on a boat
  paN- V (4) get on
  maN- (4) get on 8 a 4, 10
  sakqanán CN (3) place where one stays 3 a 1

sakáy V ride on, get on (animal, boat, vehicle) 4 a 14, 18
  sakáy [= musakáy] get on 3 a 35; 4 b 48
  pag- get on 4 a 19
  mi- get on 9 b 1
  mu- ride, get on 3 a 16, c 33; 4 a 2; 6 b 49
  maka- get on 4 a 8
  sákyan thing ridden 2 a 9; 8 c 35
  pa- V allow to get on
    pasákya person allowed to get on 12 a 9
  paN- V ride, get on (plural agents)
  maN- get on 2 a 17; 3 c 27; 4 b 43; 8 c 34
  -an CN boat [cf. bárku] 13 b 79, 80

sakít Adj. painful; V be painful
  nag- was aching 12 c 56
  mag- ache 14 a 21

sakúp V (1) catch in the act of; (2) catch after chasing [cf. dakúp]
  hi-/hing- V catch
  sákpan [= hisákpan] (2) person caught 13 a 27, 30, 40

sákut mix [something] into [something]
  gisáktan thing into which something is mixed 4 b 59

sála CN living room 14 b 43, 44, 53

salámat thanks, thank you 1 a 19, 25 and passim [not without 1]
  dághang~ thanks a lot 3 a 28; 8 a 30, c 15

salúq catch (something thrown)
  inigka- when [Gen.] has caught 11 b 9

salúq (cont.)
naka- catch 11 b 11
maka- catch 11 b 7
sáma CN same, similar; V be the same
mag- is the same 10 a 30
sámtang Q [initial] while, at the same time as; while, as long as 8 a 23 b; 14 b 35
sámuk V disturb, trouble, create disturbance
-an person who considers something bothersome 3 c 11
San Rimihiyú CN San Remigio (town in northern Cebu) 9 b 25; 10 a 20; 11 c 15
Sansyángku CN [name of a street in Cebu City] 3 a 23, 25
Sántus N [surname] 3 a 1; 5 a 1
sángag V roast in a pan 11 a 7
-un thing roasted 11 a 6
sánggiq V harvest corn (cf. áni]; CN thing harvested 10 a 29
paN- V harvest; CN action of harvesting 10 a 32, 33
maN- harvest 10 a 27
sánghid V (1) ask permission; (2) ask permission to leave
paN- V (2) ask permission to leave
maN- (2) ask permission 12 b 29
sánglit Q [initial] inasmuch as
paN- Q [initial] for example
-an Q [initial] for example 5 b 38; 6 a 5; 11 b 20
sapayán CN [occurs only in set expressions]
waq lay~ it doesn't matter 12 c 66
waláy, way~ you're welcome 1 a 26; 3 a 31; 8 a 31; 14 b 48
sapút V wear, put on clothing; CN clothing [cf. sinínaq]
panáptun CN cloth 12 b 38, 39, 41
saq: see úsaq
sáqa [dialectal for ása, háqin] (1) where?; (2) which one (of several)? 4 b 35
sáqad V promise
naka- promise 2 b 33
saqúp CN tenant 10 b 14
pa- V cause to be worked by tenant
gipasápqan land caused to be worked by tenant 10 b 13
sátung CN (1) [a children's running game] 11 b 2, 3; (2) [word said in playing satung] 11 b 22
sayún Adj. easy 5 a 15; 6 a 33
ka- [exclamatory] how easy! 5 a 18
sayúp Adj. in error
ka- V make a mistake
na- make a mistake 8 b 17
si [particle before names] [Nom.: 1 B, 1 D 1] 1 a 4 and passim
ni [Gen.] 3 a 41 and passim
ng [Gen. after vowel] 3 c 13
kang [Dat.] 8 a 6
ni [short for kang]; ng [short for kang after vowels]
Sibú CN Cebu [= Súgbu] 4 b 45, 47, 48; 5 b 58; 8 b 2, 5
Sibuwánu CN Cebuano (a native of Cebu)
-in- (→) CN Cebuano language 12 b 47, 49, 51
Síbya N [woman's name, short for Yusíbya 'Eusebia'] 13 b 48
sígi V (1) continue, still exist; (2) Q [with infinitive complement] continue [do]ing 11 b 22
nag- (2) continue [do]ing 11 a 1
sigí (1) go ahead and [do as planned] 2 a 16; 3 a 29; 4 a 14, b 35; 9 a 25; (2) good-bye 1 a 19; 2 b 35; 3 c 21, 35; 9 a 27, 28, b 15; 14 b 50, 65, 74; (3) O.K., I agree 3 a 6; 6 a 21, b 40; 8 b 30; 12 a 19; 13 a 5, 7, 14, 18, 21, 34, 35, 42, b 47, 58, 78, 84, 88; (4) come on! 10 a 2; 13 a 2; 14 a 18, b 42; (5) You're welcome. 3 a 29; 6 b 48
sigí lang (1) go ahead and [do as planned] 12 b 44; (2) never mind! 6 a 15; 8 c 21, 34
sígi lang Oh, come on, please! 12 a 5
sigí na Come on! (urging) 12 a 17; 13 a 24
sigurádu Q [prepositive] sure 5 b 62
sigúru Adj. for sure, for certain 2 b 2; V make sure
sigurúqa [= sigurúha] thing to be made sure 5 b 53; 11 a 1
siin CN galvanized-iron roofing sheet 11 b 33
silá they [1 B and 13 E] 5 a 22 and passim
níla [Gen.] 4 b 51 and passim
kaníla [Dat.]

nfla [short for kanfla] 9 b 10 and passim
ífla [preposed Gen.] 5 b 51 and passim (1) home of [2 E 3 (1 b)]
silabí Q that is better than, preferable to having [so-and-so] happen 9 b 3
sílbi V serve, be used; Q [prepositive] that which serves as 11 b 14, 40
sílhig V sweep 14 a 10
-an thing swept 14 a 13
paN- V sweep; CN action of sweeping 14 a 9
silíngan CN neighbor 9 c 15; 10 a 32; 14 a 23
ka- -an (→) CN neighborhood 11 a 18
sílung CN ground floor; cellar 3 b 24
pa- V take shelter
pasílung [= mu-] take shelter 12 b 43
paN- V take shelter [plural agents]
maN- take shelter 4 b 52
simána CN week 10 a 27; 12 b 49
síndul pándul CN [children's game: hide and seek, kick the can] 13 a 4
siní CN moving pictures 14 b 63
sinínaq CN (1) shirt; (2) dress 12 a 14
sinsíyu CN change, small money [= sinsílyu: cf. súkliq] 6 b 42, 43, 44; V make change
ika- money given in change 6 a 23
sintábus CN centavo [monetary unit] 6 a 29
sinyúr Title [term of address for a highly placed man] sir [short form nyur] nyur 2 b 27
sinyúra Title [term of address for a lady of high social position] Ma'am [short form nyúra]
nyúra Ma'am
nyurá Voc. 14 a 4, 7, 12
sínggit V scream 11 b 22
síngku [number] five 6 b 41, 42, 44
~singkwínta five-fifty 8 b 10
singkwínta [number] fifty 6 b 39, 40, 46; 8 b 7, 8, 10, 15, 29, c 2, 14; 11 a 17
sípqun CN nasal discharge 13 b 48
sipqunsípqun CN slight cold 14 b 69
siyá he, she 3 a 43 and passim
níya [Gen.]
kaníya [Dat.]
níya [Dat.; short for kaníya]
íya [preposed Gen.] (1) his
iyáha his 13 a 11, b 62
tag- CN owner 10 b 12
sst CN [exclamation to draw attention] 12 a 1
súbay V follow a trail; follow a model
-a thing to be followed 3 a 21
súbra CN remainder, part left over 4 a 26
sugáq CN lamp, light 3 b 27, 30
súgat V go to meet
mi- meet 8 c 22, 23
Súgbu [= Sibú] CN Cebu 10 b 12
súgid V tell
sugilánun CN story 13 b 69
sugút V agree to [do], accede to a request
mu- agree to 5 b 45, 46
súhul V employ, hire, pay for services; CN pay, salary
i- thing to be paid out 10 b 15
sukád Q [followed by Dat.] since, from [some time] forward 9 c 28
paN- V start from [a certain place]
maN- will start from [a certain point] 11 b 17, 19
súkiq CN steady customer; person steadily patronized 4 a 30
súkliq V make change [cf. sinsíyu]
-i thing for which change is given 6 b 41
sulát V write
pag- write 8 a 33
mag- write 8 a 34
súling V (1) peep, look through small opening; (2) peek, take a quick, sly look
sulingsúling V (2) peek several times
gi- [-un unreal] person peeked at several times 9 c 12
súlti V speak, say, talk [cf. ingún]
mu- speak, tell 12 b 47, 53
nag- talk to each other 9 c 22
sultíhan person told 12 b 32
sultíhi person told 12 b 31
pakig- V make conversation with
gi- -an person talked to 8 b 4
sultisúlti V spend time chatting
sultisúlti [= mag-] pass time chatting 14 b 46
sulúd V go, put inside [10 C] 13 b 58; CN place inside 3 b 8
mi- go inside 2 b 19
ning- go inside 12 b 36

sulúd (cont.)
mu- go inside 6 a 1
hi-/ha- V happen to go inside
ma- [= mahi-/maha-] happen to enter 10 a 13
sunúd V follow, be next; pursue; imitate [cf. nunút] 4 a 23
CN next, following 3 c 17; 8 b 3; 10 a 27, b 24; 12 c 65
sunúy CN rooster 11 c 2, 22
suqúk (1) Adj. out-of-the-way place in the interior of a building or region (2) CN inner corner (of an enclosure) 14 a 15
*súqun
ig- CN brother, sister 10 a 17
súruy V go around from place to place [cf. láqag]
paN- V take a stroll (plural agents)
maN- take a stroll 10 a 1
suruysúruy V stroll around 11 a 1
sus Q [preceding exclamatory] My! (expression of strong emotion) 4 b 42; 5 a 12; 6 a 35; 9 a 23, b 7, c 24; 11 a 11, b 2, c 24; 14 a 10
syíntu [number] one hundred
~báynti tris one hundred twenty-three 8 c 36

T

ta we (inclusive) (1) Nom. [short for kitá]; (2) Gen. [short for nátuq] [see kitá]
tábang V help, assist
pag- help 9 a 12; 10 a 33; 11 a 20
mi- help 10 b 15
mu- help 9 a 14; 12 b 31
pa- V cause to help
-un person made to help 11 a 16
tumatabáng CN helper 12 c 60
ka- CN helper 10 a 32; 12 c 54, 55
tabíq V gossip [cf. súlti]
-an Adj. talkative, fond of talking 9 b 1
tabunúk Adj. fertile land
Tabunúk CN Tabunok (name of village south of Cebu City) 4 a 10
tagád V (1) give notice to; (2) take care of
~ka na man. (2) Nonsense! It's no trouble. 14 b 39
tágdun (2) person taken care of 8 a 28
*tágaq V give [colloquial local passive]
-i person to whom given 6 b 39; 14 a 5
tagqíya owner [see siyá]
táguq Adj. hidden; V (1) be hidden (2) keep, hold
táguq [= mu-] hide 13 a 23
paN- V hide (plural agents) 13 a 34, 42
maN- hide 13 a 37
tahúp V winnow; CN chaff 11 a 10
táksi CN taxi 8 c 33, 34
tákyan CN [plaything of chicken feathers] 11 b 31, 40; V play takyan
nag- play takyan 11 b 28
talá [= taná] let's go! come on! 4 a 7; 9 c 15; 14 b 53
Talísay CN Talisay (name of a place south of Cebu City) 4 a 2, 11, 12, 16
támbuk Adj. fat; V grow fat
mu- grow fat 9 c 32
taná [= talá] let's go! come on! 2 a 16; 3 a 41; 4 a 2, b 41, 48, 51; 8 a 4, 10, c 26, 38; 9 a 20, 26; 10 a 1; 11 c 26
tanán CN (1) all, everything, everyone 9 b 20; 10 b 14; 13 a 31, b 57; (2) all, any whatever 13 b 65
tánqaw V look at
pag- look 14 a 9
mu- look 3 b 16, 18; 10 b 2, 3; 11 c 25
-un person looked at 4 a 8; 6 a 24; 8 b 13, 24; 10 a 24, b 25; 14 a 9
-a thing looked at 6 b 50; 9 c 14, 32; 14 a 15
pa- V cause to see
gi- [-un unreal] person allowed to see 14 b 63
tanqawtánqaw V pass time looking around
pag- 12 b 44
tántu Q [initial] after [do]ing for many times
myíntras~ for the time being, in the meantime 14 b 43
tanúm V plant
maka- plant 10 b 22
gitámnan place planted 11 a 13
katámnan place planted 10 a 28
paN- V plant (plural); CN action of planting 11 a 20
Tángki CN Tangke (name of barrio in Talisay) 4 b 46

tápus V finish, put an end to [cf. humán]
ka- -an CN last, end 11 b 18
taq [see úntaq]
taqás Adj. (1) long (in space) 11 b 6; (2) tall, high
i- (←) CN upstairs [short form táqas] 2 b 9; 3 b 20, c 9; 8 a 8
*taqúd
taqudtaqúd Q [initial] (1) after a while; (2) for some time
pagka- after a short while 9 a 27, b 18; 14 b 54
tartanílya CN two-wheeled passenger rig 8 c 30, 35; 12 a 1, 7
tárung Adj. (1) straight; (2) proper in behavior
ma- (2) proper
-in- (→) in the right way 8 c 17
tátay Title Dad 9 b 26
tawág V (1) call, shout; (1 a) call on the telephone; (2) call, name
nag- (1 a) call 2 a 4
ga- (1) call 14 a 4
gi- (1) person called 6 a 17; (2) person called 11 b 2, c 18
táwgun (1) person called 2 b 10
táwu CN man, person, people 3 a 9; 4 b 36; 5 a 8; 8 a 16, c 16, 22; 9 a 9, 12; 10 a 4, b 15
táwun [short for intáwun: see intáwun]
taym Q [initial] wait
~pa excuse me (interrupting) 5 b 35
*táytay
-an CN bridge 4 a 27
-a particular bridge 4 a 31
Tibúq N [man's name; short for Tibúrsyu and other names] 5 a 4, 5, 8; 10 a 3
tibuqúk CN whole, entire [see buqúk]
tígbak V kill outright
tigbakáy V hold cockfight; CN illegal cockfight 11 c 12, 13, 16, 17, 18
tigúlang Adj. old [see gúlang]
tihíras CN cot 8 a 5, 6, 18
tíkit CN ticket 8 b 7, 12, 15
tíksas CN 'Texas' breed of cock 11 c 7, 23
pagka- CN state of being a Texas cock 11 c 8
tímpu CN during, at the time (something happened) [= tyímpu] [cf. panahún] 10 b 7
tínda V sell (as a livelihood) [cf. balígyaq]
tindáhan CN store, place where things are sold 5 a 8, b 58; 6 a 1, 18; 8 b 1; 9 a 27; 12 b 29, 40, c 54, 59, 60, 63, 65
tíndug V stand up, be standing
pa- V make stand
gi- [-un unreal] thing made to stand 11 b 39, 40
tinyínti dil báryu CN barrio lieutenant, head of barrio 9 c 19
Ting N [man's name; short for Ínting and other names] 1 a 7
tingála V amaze
ka- V be amazed
na- be amazed 8 b 6
tingáli Q [initial] perhaps, probably 3 a 43, b 30; 4 a 10, b 40, 41; 5 a 24, b 52, 57; 6 b 51; 8 a 32
tingúhaq V aim [see kúhaq]
paningúhaq V strive [see kúhaq]
tip CN tip, gratuity 8 a 29
tiyán CN stomach 9 b 8
tiyánggi CN market place 12 a 12
traak CN bus, truck 4 a 2, 4, b 43; 9 a 20
tráka particular bus 4 b 46
trabáhu V work; CN work, job 9 a 11, c 30; 14 a 19
nag- work 10 a 21
ga- work 10 a 22
trápu V wipe [cf. páhid] 14 a 14
tráynta [number] thirty 12 a 22, 23, 26
tag- thirty apiece 6 a 29
trayntaysíngku [number] thirty-five 8 b 31, c 3
tris [number] three 6 a 4; 13 a 9, 14
syíntu báynti~ one twenty-three 8 c 36
trísi [number] thirteen 9 c 20, 22
tsápa CN washer (to protect head of screw) 11 b 31, 32
tu [short for kádtu]
tubág V answer (orally)
mu- answer 14 a 2
tubáq CN coconut-palm-blossom toddy 5 a 16
túbig CN water 3 b 27, 30; 9 c 11, 25, 26, 27; 10 b 11; 11 a 26; 13 b 46; 14 a 1, 3, 5, 7

tubú CN sugar cane 11 a 13, 14, 15, 20, 21
túdluq V teach
mu- teach 12 b 51
túgdun V (accidentally) land, descend to earth
gi- -an place where something comes down 11 b 18
túgnaw Adj. causing someone to feel cold [cf. búgnaw]; V feel cold
gi- [-un unreal] feel cold 4 b 38
túgut V permit, allow [a person] to [do]
pag- CN permission 11 c 18
tulú [numeral] three 12 b 49
ka- [= maka-] Q [initial, medial, final] three times 10 a 31; 11 b 16
túlug V put to sleep
ka- V be asleep
na- sleep 5 b 37
paN- V sleep (plural)
maN- are asleep 5 b 38
túmba V cause [something erect] to fall down
ka- V fall
ma- fall 10 b 10; 11 b 40
tungáq CN (1) middle; (2) one-half 6 b 36
tungaqtúngaq (←) CN middle, center 11 a 22
túngud Q [followed by Dat.] on account of
~kay because 11 c 18
túntu Adj. fool 2 b 21 [cf. búqang]
túnuq CN juice squeezed from coconut meat 8 b 21
túqa [short for atúqa] there
tuqálya CN towel 9 a 2
túqig CN year 10 a 29, b 16, 22; 11 a 14, 24
tuqú CN right (hand), right (direction) 3 a 23
túqud Q [postpositive]; (1) [particle expressing agreement with foregoing explanation] 8 a 3, c 12; (2) [particle expressing sudden awareness] 3 a 27, 37; 14 b 64
hústu ~ nu? That's right, isn't it? 12 a 25
tuqún V study
nag- study 12 b 49
túrnu CN turn, time (in order or rotation) 13 b 62
tutál Q anyway, anyhow 4 b 40; 9 a 11, 18; 14 b 57

U

ubán CN other another (person or thing) 5 a 33; 9 a 5; 11 a 18, b 7; 12 b 44; 13 a 29
ubán V go along with [cf. kúyug]
ka- (←) CN friend, companion 5 a 6
ubús CN (1) place below (another place) 3 b 21; (2) downtown (main part of a town) 12 a 15; Q [followed by Dat.] below 6 a 14
údtu Adj. noon 1 a 24
pani- V eat noon meal; CN dinner, noon meal 5 b 51, 52; 14 b 64
mani- eat noon meal 14 b 56, 57, 58
ug [short form g] [particle showing grammatical relation between two forms] (1) [preceding goals: 5 D 2, 6 C, 8 C 2] 3 b 7 and passim; (1 b) [preceding infinitives: 12 E 1] 4 a 18 and passim; (1 bi) [with adjectives of manner: 9 C 2] 8 b 1 and passim; (1 c) [linker between qualifier and predicate: 3 E 1, 8 D]
ábi, kaqingún~ I thought 8 c 24 and passim
ayáw~ [3 E 1, 8 C] don't!
nákuq~ I thought 12 a 26 and passim
tingáli~ perhaps 4 b 41 and passim
(2) [adjective plus ug plus noun: 5 B] have 5 a 34 and passim; (2 a) [following exclamatory: 5 B 2] 5 a 12 and passim; (3) if, when 5 b 45 and passim; (4) [introducing an indirect question: 4 F]; (5) or; (6) and 3 b 27 and passim
úgmaq Q [initial, medial, final] tomorrow 4 b 64; 12 b 31, 32
ugúd Q [postpositive; short form gud] (1) man gud because 2 b 13; 3 b 27; 5 b 40; 8 c 4, 8; 10 b 21; 11 c 7, 19; 12 a 14, b 51, c 56, 59; (2) [particle accompanying statement of explanation] 3 b 6; 4 b 59; 5 b 41; 11 c 17; 12 b 47; 14 b 71; (3) [particle in exclamations over newly learned facts] 4 a 1; 5 a 12; 9 c 21; (4) [in questions with interrogative or ba] [interrogative] in the world! 5 b 47; 8 a 14, c 2; 12 a 23; (5) ra gud [to soften commands] 3 c 2; 5 a 4; 8 a 24; 14 a 1
uh Q (1) [initial] [exclamation of surprise upon receiving information] 1 a 24; 3 b 3, 5, 8, c 23, 31; 4 a 24; 8 a 14, b 11, 14, 15, 31; 9 b 14, c 2; 12 a 23, b 27,

39; 13 a 15, 30, b 64; 14 a 2, 8, 27; (2) [initial] [exclamation to attract attention] 4 a 27, b 43; 6 a 16; 12 a 21; 13 a 3, 30, b 54, 64; 14 a 7, b 33; (3) [initial] [pause before speaking] 12 a 13; 13 b 52; (4) [final] [particle used to call attention to something] 3 a 32, c 23; 5 a 3; 6 b 41, 46; 8 a 3, 29; 12 a 7; 14 a 15

uháy CN ear of grain 10 b 7

ukupár V occupy
  giqukupahán place occupied 8 a 5

ulán CN rain 10 b 22; 12 c 61 V rain
  ulán [= nag-] rain 12 b 43
  mu- rain 4 b 40, 51
  nag- rain 12 a 6, 14

Ulibár N Olivar (surname) 9 a 1, b 23; 11 a 1

ulíq V [= paqúliq] return home
  pa- (←) V return home 4 b 38
    pag- 9 b 3
    maka- go back home 9 b 2
    paN- V go home (plural agents)
    naN- go home 4 b 37
  umuqúliq CN one who is about to return home 9 b 6

ultimú last
  ~ng prísyu lowest price offered 6 a 9

úlu CN head (part of body) 12 b 29, c 56; 14 a 1, 20

úna CN (1) first (in time); (2) previous one 3 b 26; V do first (before doing something else)
  mag- do (it) first 10 a 1
  uná V [do] before someone else [does]
    mag- go ahead of 1 a 17; 3 c 35

únaq Q [postpositive] [= úsaq] (1) beforehand 8 a 21; (2) for now, for a moment 14 b 49

unáy V belong to, be a part of
  paN- V do by oneself
  maN- do by oneself 9 c 29

úndang V stop (doing something)
  paN- V stop (doing something) (plural agents)
  maN- stop 11 b 13

únsa [12 B] what? 1 a 3, 22; 2 a 9; 4 b 55; 5 b 36, 39; 6 a 18; 8 b 12, 18, 20; 9 a 1, 5; 11 b 26, c 16, 22; 13 a 3, b 68, 71, 74, 78; 14 b 54
  ~ba What do you say? How about it? 9 a 15
  ~y átuq What can I do for you? 12 b 37
  gi- how? what was done with [goal or subject]? 5 a 14
  unsáqun how? what is to be done with [goal or subject]? 3 a 7; 6 a 32; 9 c 22
  na- what happened to [subject]? 14 a 9

unsálan what? [dialectal form of únsa] 4 b 58

únsi [number] eleven 14 b 57

unsingálan what? [short form singálan; dialectal for únsa] 10 a 7; 11 a 3, b 1

úntaq Q [postpositive; short form taq] [particle to qualify something that should be or is desirable] (1) [with requests or suggestions] should, would like to 12 b 28, 29
  hináqut~ I hope 14 b 70, 72
  (2) [in contrary-to-fact conditions] 14 a 13

únu [number] one (used only in set phrases) 6 b 37, 38, 39, 40, 45, 46; 11 a 17; 13 a 9, 14

únyaq Q [short forms unyáq, nyaq] (1) [initial, medial, final] at a later time 2 b 35; 3 c 11; 4 b 54; 5 b 50; 8 a 27; 11 a 2; 14 b 65; (2) [initial] furthermore (in addition) 12 a 16, c 60; 14 a 14, 17; (2 a) then, next, after that 4 a 21, 28, 33; 11 a 14, 25, b 10, 17, 21; (2 b) then, the next thing [in a series] 11 a 6, 8, b 5, 38, 41; (2 c) also, now, next 3 a 7, b 16, c 27; 4 b 59; 5 a 21, b 44; 8 a 20, 33, b 2, c 14

upát [numeral] four 3 c 10; 4 a 13, b 57; 5 a 20
  ka- Q [initial, medial, final] four times 10 a 31

upúd Q [postpositive] [short form gud] (1) also, in addition to; [after negatives] either 2 b 6; 8 c 5; (2) again, for the second time 13 a 42; 14 b 69

úqu [short form uu] yes (answering when called; affirmation; consent) 1 a 19, 21; 2 b 35 and passim

úras CN hour, time 9 a 24

Úrmuk CN Ormoc (city on Leyte) 8 a 1, 2, 19, b 11, c 29

usá (1) [numeral] one 3 b 20, 21, c 3, 32 and passim; (2) CN a certain (unnamed) one 2 b 19; 8 b 4; 9 b 1; 10 a 9,

usá (cont.)
10; 12 b 36; 13 b 69, 81
ka- Q [initial, medial, final]
[= kásqa] once 9 a 19; 11 a 14
usáb V do again 5 b 59 Q [postpositive; short forms sab, sad] [cf. upúd] (1) also, in addition; [after negatives] either 3 b 21, 24, 31, c 18; 4 b 39; 5 a 21, 30 and passim; (2) [predicate] conforms with [something]; [predicate] at the same time as [something] 5 b 38; 11 a 25, b 6, 20; (3 a) [usually preceded by na] again 10 a 28; 13 a 34; (3 b) in turn 11 b 10, 11; 13 a 13; (4) [particle exclaiming over new information] 6 a 35
usáhay Q [initial, medial, final] sometimes 8 c 11; 10 a 31, b 20
úsaq Q [short forms saq, usáq] [= únaq] (1) [initial, followed by sentence] before 10 b 6; 11 b 13; 13 b 46; (2) [postpositive] beforehand 13 a 8, b 46, 47, 50; (3) [postpositive] for now, in the meantime 3 b 9; 9 b 13; 12 b 43; 14 b 43, 46, 51
ayáw~ don't [do] yet! 14 b 56
(4) ~pa (4 a) just a second (wait awhile); (4 b) just a second, I'll be right back 6 a 11, 24; 13 a 28; (4 c) just a second (changing subject) 3 c 16
utsínta [number] eighty
únu~ one-eighty 6 b 37
utúng V hold one's breath
mu- hold breath 11 b 21
uy Q (1) [initial] (1 a) [impolite: to attract attention] hey! 2 b 25; 13 b 48; 14 a 11; (1 b) [exclamation of surprise upon noticing something] 3 c 1; 8 b 4; 12 c 61; 14 b 54; (1 c) [exclamation of delight or worry] 4 b 60; 6 a 2, 17, 27; 8 b 6; (2) [final] (2 a) [particle contradicting hearer's impression] 11 b 43, c 24; (2 a i) [with exclamation] [particle used to intensify predicate] 14 b 37; (2 a ii) [particle with emphatic denial] 13 b 87
díliq ku~ I don't want to! 2 b 23
(2 b) [particle minimizing importance of remark] 11 a 24; (2 c) [with imperatives] go on now, do it!
ayáw úsaq~ ! Don't just yet! 14 b 56
(2 d) [particle indicating surprise upon discovering something] 5 a 1; (3) [final] [particle expressing annoyance] 4 a 17, b 42

W

waláq no, not [short form waq] [2 B] (1) [Q preceding verbs] not [meanings expressed by real: 4 B 2 d, 6 A 3 c, 12 D] 2 b 17, 18 and passim; (2) [negative existential] there is (are, was, were) no . . .; has (had, have) no . . . [3 A 1] 4 a 22 and passim
~na no more 2 b 27; 6 a 14 and passim
wánqa (= waq na) 9 a 24
~y sapayán you're welcome 1 a 26; 3 a 31; 8 a 31
(2 a) [used as predicate alone] is, are, was, were not here, there [3 A 2 b]
Wílbi N Wilby (surname) 3 a 1, b 6 and passim

Y

y [= dialectal, ing: 1 D 1, 3 A 1, 3 B 5] (1) [subject marker: 3 B 5] 3 a 10 and passim; (2) [existential particle: 3 A 1] 3 a 9 and passim
Yáru CN (name of a night club at Talisay, Cebu) 4 a 20
yútaq CN land 10 a 20; 11 a 13, 19

INDEX

Ábi: linking of, 8 D
Abstract form, 9 B; as imperative, 9 B 1 c; as noun, 9 B 1 d; constituting clause, 9 B 1 a; in the infinitive construction, 9 B 1 b, 12 E 1; introduced optionally by sa, 9 B 1 a (2); of bases with ka-, 11 B 6
Accidental action: expressed by accidental passivé, 14 E; expressed by verb with ka-, 11 B 1; expressed by potential, 5 C 3 (4)
Accidental passive, 14 E f.
Action: accidental, 5 C 3 (4), 11 B 1; completed, 5 C 1 (2); durative, 5 C 2; habitual, 5 C 1 (3); perfected, 5 C 3 (3); potential, 5 C 3 (1), (2), 11 B 2; volitional, 5 C 1 (1)
Active verb, 4 A, 5 C, 11 A, B, 12 C; as predicate, 5 D 1; as subject, 5 D 1; compared to direct passive, 6 A 1 a, b, e; contrasted with passive, 13 D ff.; imperative, 11 C 1; meaning of, 6 A 1 e; modifying noun agent, 6 A 1 d; obligatory in certain constructions, 13 B ff.; real, 4 B 1; unreal, 4 B 2, 13 F; when to use, 6 A 1 e
Adjective, 5 B; forming local passive verb, 8 A 4 b; forming other verbs, 14 A 1; meaning manner of action following the verb, 9 C 2; meaning manner of action preceding the verb, 9 C 1; modified by ra, 14 G 2 c; preposed genitive not used in phrase consisting of ~ plus noun, 6 B 1; with pag- added to form an infinitive, 9 C 3
Adúna: as sentence, 3 A 2 b; attracts postpositives, 3 C 3 d; in existential sentences, 3 A 1, 5 B 1
Advice: expressed by ra ba, 14 G 2 g
Affixes, 3 E; active, 4 A; derivative, 11 A; dropping of, 12 C 2, 14 E 1; passive, 12 A
- -a: exclamatory suffix, 12 F; specific noun suffix, 2 C; verb suffix, 6 A, 11 C 2 a, 12 A
- -an: accidental passive, 14 E; local passive, 8 A, 12 A
- (C)ulu-, 14 C 2
- ga-, 4 A, 14 B
- gi-: direct passive, 6 A, 12 A; instrumental passive, 10 A, 12 A
- gi--an, 8 A, 12 A
- gika-, 10 A, 12 A
- gika--an, 11 B
- gikapaN-, 11 A
- gina-, 12 A, A 1
- gina--an, 12 A, A 1
- gipa-: direct passive, 12 C 3, 6, 14 F 2; instrumental passive, 12 C 4, 6, 14 F 2
- gipa--an, 12 C 5, 6
- gipaN-, 11 A
- gipaN--an, 11 A
- hi--an, 14 E 1
- hi--i, 14 E 1
- hing--an, 14 E 1
- hing--i, 14 E 1
- i-, 10 A, 11 C 2, 12 A
- -i, 8 A, 11 C 2, 12 A, 14 E
- ig-, 9 B f.
- iga-, 12 A, A 1
- igka-, 11 B 5
- ika-, 10 A
- ikapaN-, 11 A
- inig-, 9 B f.
- inigka-, 11 B 5
- ipa-, 12 C 5, 6, 14 F 2
- ipaN-, 11 A
- ka-: derivative verb prefix, 11 B ff., C 3; exclamatory affix, 5 A; potential active prefix, 4 A, 5 C 3, 11 C 3
- ka--an: local passive potential, 8 A; local passive of verbs with ka-, 11 B
- ka--i: local passive potential, 8 A; local passive of verbs with ka-, 11 B
- kapa-, 12 C 1
- kapa--an, 12 C 5
- kapa--i, 12 C 5
- kapaN-, 11 A
- kapaN--an, 11 A
- kapaN--i, 11 A
- ma-: active verb affix, 4 A, 11 B; direct passive affix, 6 A, 12 A; instrumental passive affix, 10 A, 12 A
- ma--an, 8 A, 12 A
- ma--i, 8 A, 12 A
- mag-, 4 A, 5 C 2 ff.
- maga-, 4 A, 5 C 2, 14 A
- magpa-, 12 C 1, 2
- maka-, 4 A, 5 C 3 ff.
- makapa-, 12 C 1
- makapaN-, 5 C 4, 11 A
- maN-, 4 A, 5 C 4, 11 A
- manga-, 11 B 5
- mapa-: direct passive, 12 C 3; instru-

mental, 12 C 4
mapa--an, 12 C 5
mapa--i, 12 C 5
mapaN-, 11 A
mapaN--an, 11 A
mapaN--i, 11 A
mi-, 4 A, 5 C 1; replaced by na-, 11 B; replaced by naN-, 5 C 4, 11 A
mu-, 4 A, 5 C 1, 2 b; replaced by ma-, 11 B; replaced by maN-, 5 C 4, 11 A
-N-: added to doubled roots, 14 C (footnote); meaning of, 4 E
na-: active verb affix, 4 A, 11 B; direct passive affix, 6 A, 12 A; instrumental passive affix, 10 A, 12 A
na--an: local passive potential, 8 A; local passive of verb with ka-, 11 B
nag-, 4 A, 5 C 2 ff.
naga-, 4 A, 5 C 2, 14 A
nagpa-, 12 C 1
nagpaN-, 5 C 4
naka-, 4 A, 5 C 3 ff.
nakapa-, 12 C 1
nakapaN-, 5 C 4, 11 A
naN-, 4 A, 5 C 4, 11 A
nanga-, 11 B 5
napa-: direct passive, 12 C 3; instrumental passive, 12 C 4
napa--an, 12 C 5
napaN-, 11 A
napaN--an, 11 A
ni-, 4 A, 5 C 1
pa-, 12 C ff.
pa--a, 12 C 3, 6, 14 F 2
pa--an, 12 C 5, 6
pa--i, 12 C 5, 6
pa--un, 12 C 3, 6, 14 F 2
pag-: abstract former, 9 B f.; added to adjectives forming infinitives, 9 C 3; imperative former, 9 B 1 c, 11 C 1; noun former, 9 B 1 d
pag--a, 11 C 2
pag--i, 11 C 2
paga--a, 12 A, A 1
paga--an, 12 A, A 1
paga--i, 12 A, A 1
paga--un, 12 A, A 1
pagka-: abstract, 9 B f., 11 B; exclamatory affix, 12 F
pagkapaN-, 11 A
pagpaN-, 11 A
pagqi-, 11 C 2
paN-, 4 E, 5 C 4, 11 A ff., 11 C 3
paN--a, 11 A
paN--an, 11 A
paN--i, 11 A
paN--un, 11 A
panga-, 11 B 5
ulu-: see (C)ulu-
-un, 6 A, 12 A
Agent, 5 D 1; as predicate with active verb, 5 D 1; as subject with active verb, 5 D 1; indefinite pronouns as, 13 B 2; of abstract forms, 9 B 1 a ff., of active verbs, 5 D 1, 6 A 1 b; of imperatives, 9 B 1 c, 11 C 1, 2; of passive verbs, 6 A 1 b, B 2, 8 C 1; preceding the verb requiring an active form, 13 B 1; word order of ~ with passive verb, 6 D
Agreement: expressed by mu lang, 13 G 1 f
Amount: how to express, 14 D
And: how '[pronoun] and [name]' is expressed, 13 E
Ang: marking the performer of the action of an active form of a verb, 4 A; marking the subject, 3 B
Anúsqa, 4 D
'Anyone, anybody': see Indefinite pronouns
Apology: expressed by ra ba, 14 G 2 h
Ása, 2 A 2, 3 D
Attraction of postpositives, 3 C 3 a
Ayáw: as prepositive, 3 C 3 a; linking of, 3 E 1, 8 D
Áyu: verbs formed from, 14 A 2

Ba, 1 D 2; ra ba, 14 G 2 g, h
Base, 4 A; alone in place of base plus affix, 12 C 2, 14 E 1; as imperative, 11 C 1; as infinitive, 12 E 1; derived, 11 A; forming local passive verb, 8 A 4 a, b; meaning expressed by, 4 A
'Because': expressed by man, 14 G 1 b
'Become,' 11 B 3
'Belong to,' 2 E, E 1
Benefaction: expressed by instrumental passive, 10 A, A 3; expressed by local passive, 8 A 2

'Can,' 5 C 3 (1), 11 B 2
Causative, 12 C ff.
Clause: complementing a verb, 12 E 3; containing abstract, 9 B 1 a. See also Sentence
'Come': expressed by future deictics, 1 A 2 c; passives of verbs meaning ~, 10 C, 14 F 1
Command: see Imperative
Common noun: see Noun
Comparison: expressed by pa, 12 G 2 b
Complement: 12 E ff. See also Goal
Consonant: dropping of final, 3 F 2
Contraction: of markers, 3 F 2, 3; when affixes are added, 6 A 2
Conveyance: expressed by instrumental passive, 10 A 2
Customary action: expressed by unreal, 4 B 2

Dághan: in special type of sentence, 4 C
Dative, 1 A 1, B, 5 D 2; as goal, 5 D 2, 8 C 2; as recipient of active verb, 6 A 1 b
Deictics, 1 A 2; attracting postpositives, 3 C 3 d; beginning with d, 1 A 2 b, 2 A 1; beginning with ng, 1 A 2 d, 2 A 1; future, 1 A 2 c; in existential sentences, 3 A 1; interrogative, 2 A 2, 3 D ff.; modified by ra, 14 G 2 b; present, 1 A 2 a; with no time meaning, 1 A 2; with time meaning, 1 A 2
Demonstratives, 1 A 1; as predicate, 3 B 4; as subject, 5 D 1; word order of long forms of, 3 C 4
Derivative verb prefix, 11 A
Díliq, 2 B; as prepositive, 3 C 3 a; linking of, 12 D; preposed genitive not used after, 6 B 3
Dínhaq: as a sentence, 3 A 2 b; in meaning of dúna, 3 A 2 a
Diqáy. 1 D 3, 13 G 2 ff.
Diqín, 2 A 2, 3 D f.
Direct meaning: expressed by direct passive, 6 A 1 e; expressed by local passive, 8 A 3
Direct passive, 6 A; affixes 6 A, 12 A; compared to the active, 6 A 1 a, b; contrasted with instrumental passive, 10 C, 14 F ff.; contrasted with local passive, 8 B 3, 10 C; having same meaning as local passive, 8 B 4; imperative, 11 C 2 a; meaning of, 6 A 1 e; modifying a noun recipient, 6 A 1 d; of verbs with pa-, 12 C
'[Do] together': verbs meaning ~ , 14 F 3
Doubled verb roots, 14 C f.
Dropping: of hi-/hing-, 14 E 1; of mag-, 12 C 2; of n, q at the end of a word, 3 F 2; of vowels when affixes are added, 6 A 2
Dúna: see Adúna
Durative, 5 C 2 ff.; compared to the volitional, 5 C 2 a; expressed by naga-, maga-, ga-, 14 B; passive forms, 12 A 1
Dyútay: in special type of sentence, 4 C

Emphasis: expressed by making the verb the subject, 3 B 2
Exclamatory sentences, 5 A, 12 F; compared with statements, 5 B 3; containing ug, 5 B 2; use of genitive in, 5 A 1 a, 6 B 4; with adjective of manner, 9 D
Exhortation: see Hortatory
Existent, 3 A 1; containing a verb obligatorily passive, 13 A 3 f.
Existential sentences, 3 A 1; deictic in, 3 A 1; in which a verb is obligatorily active, 13 B 2; in which a verb is obligatorily passive, 13 A 3; meaning 'have,' 3 A 5, B 1; subject of, 3 A 3

'Few': how expressed, 4 C
Future meaning: expressed by unreal, 4 B 2; of deictics, 1 A 2 c

Genitive, 1 A 1, B 1, 5 A 1; as agent with abstract, 9 B 1 a; as agent with passive verb, 6 A 1 b, c, B 2, 8 C 1, 11 C 2; as thing exclaimed over in exclamatory sentences, 5 A 1, 9 D; in exclamatory sentences, 5 A 1, 6 B 4, 9 D; in expressions of place or time, 6 B 5; indicating possession, 6 B 1; of demonstrative, 1 A 1; preposed, 2 E ff.; preposed ~ in idioms, 2 E 1 ff.; preposed ~ not used in exclamatory sentences, 6 B 4; preposed ~ not used in a phrase consisting of an adjective plus a noun, 6 B 1; preposed ~ not used in a phrase containing a prepositive, 6 B 3; preposed ~ used like other genitives, 6 B, 8 C 1
Giqúnsa: see Únsa
'Go': expressed by future deictics, 1 A 2 c; passives of verbs meaning ~, 10 C, 14 F 1
Goal, 5 D 2; nonspecific, 5 D 2; recipient of active verb, 6 A 1 c; sentences without, 5 D 2; specific, 5 D 2; with abstract forms, 9 B 1 a; with active verbs, 5 D 2, 6 A 1 c; with imperatives, 11 C 1; with passive verbs, 6 C, 8 C 2
Gústu: as prepositive, 3 C 3 a; followed by unreal, 5 C 1 (4); preposed genitive not used after ~, 6 B 3

Habitual action: expressed by unreal, 4 B 2; with passive verbs, 12 A
Háqin, 2 A 2, 3 D
Hátag: local passive of, 8 A 5
'Have': expressed by existential sentences, 3 A 3, 5 B 1; expressed by ug, 5 B ff.
Hortatory meaning: expressed by active verb, 13 D 2; expressed by passive verb, 13 D 3 a; expressed by unreal, 4 B 2 a, 5 C 2 b; with lang, 13 G 1 c
'How [so and so] is/was done,' 9 C ff., 12 B 6, 14 A ff.

'I': expressed by kitá, 9 A
Imperative: active, 9 B 1 c, 11 C 1; active contrasted with passive, 13 D 1; agent of, 9 B 1 c, 11 C 1, 2; modified by lang, 13 G 1 c; modified by na, 12 G 1 c; modified by ra, 14 G 2 d; of derived bases, 11 C 3; passive, 6 A 3 c, 11 C 2 ff.; use

of abstract for, 9 B 1 c; use of subjunctive for, 6 A 3 c
Indefinite pronouns, 13 B 2; how expressed, 13 A 3 a, B 2, C
Indirect question: see Question
Infinitive, 9 B 1 b; complement, 12 E 1, 2; derived from adjective expressing manner, 9 C 3; expressing manner 9 C 3, 14 A 1, 2
Instrumentality: expressed by instrumental passive, 10 A 1
Instrumental passive, 10 A ff.; affixes, 10 A, 12 A; contrasted with the direct passive, 10 C, 14 F ff.; contrasted with the local passive, 10 B, C; expressing benefaction, 10 A 3; expressing conveyance, 10 A 4; expressing time, 10 A 2; imperative, 11 C 2 c; meaning of, 10 A 1; of verbs with pa-, 12 C 4
Interrogative, 3 B; ~ deictics: see Deictics; derived forms of únsa, 12 B ff.; ~ sentences with diqáy, 13 G 2 b; ~ sentences with man, 14 G 1 a
Intonation: page 8

Ka: 'at X's place,' 2 E 1 a; 'you,' 1 B 1
Kamí, 1 B 2
Kang, 1 A 2, 2 E 1
Kanúsqa, 4 D
Kinahánglan: as prepositive, 3 C 3 a; followed by volitional, 5 C 1 (4)
Kitá: expressing first person singular, 9 A; vs. kamí, 1 B 2
Kun or kung, 4 F

'Late': how expressed, 1 E
'Let's': how expressed, 5 C 2 b
Linking, 1 F; of adjective and noun, 1 F; of adjective and verb, 9 C 1; of ayáw, 3 E 1, 8 D; of demonstrative and noun, 1 F; of díliq, waláq, 12 D; of maqáyu and clause complement, 12 E 4; of measurements and amounts, 14 D; of preposed genitive and noun, 1 F; of prepositives, 3 C 3 a, E, 8 D; of verb and clause complement, 12 E 3; with ug, 8 D
Local passive, 8 A ff.; affixes of, 8 A, 12 A; contrasted with direct passive, 8 B 3, 10 C; contrasted with instrumental passive, 10 B, C; expressing meaning 'affected by,' 8 A 4; expressing personal behalf meaning, 8 A 2; expressing place, 8 A 1; formed from an adjective, 8 A 4 b; formed from a noun, 8 A 4 a; having same meaning as direct passive, 8 B 4; imperative, 11 C 2 b; with direct meaning, 8 A 3; of verbs with pa-, 12 C 5
Long forms: obligatory when in predicate construction, 3 B 4; of demonstratives, 1 A 1; of pronouns, 1 B 1; other long forms, 3 F 1
Mahímu(q): as prepositive, 3 C 3 a; followed by unreal, 5 C 1 (4)
Man, 1 D 2, 3, 14 G 1 ff.
Manner: how expressed, 9 C ff., 14 A ff.
'Many': how expressed, 4 C
Maqáyu: complemented by nga plus sentence, 12 E 2
Maqú, 2 D ff.; attracting postpositives, 3 C 3 b; plus ra: linking of, 8 D
Markers: contraction of, 3 F 2. See also Subject marker
May: does not occur as sentence, 3 A 2 b; in existential sentences, 3 A 1, 5 B 1; word order in sentences containing, 3 C 3 d (1)
Measurement: how expressed, 14 D
Metathesis, 6 A 2

n (word ending), dropping of, 3 F 2
-N-, 4 E; added to doubled roots, 14 C (footnote)
Na: 12 G 1 ff.
Náqa: in existential sentences: see Deictics; as sentence, 3 A 2 b; in meaning of dúna, 3 A 2 a
Negative, 2 B; of phrases containing na and pa, 12 G 3; requiring subjunctive, 6 A 3 c; requiring unreal, 4 B 2; with imperatives, 2 B
Nga: see Linking
'No one, nobody': see Indefinite pronouns
Nominative, 1 A 1, B 1; as agent of an active form of a verb, 4 A, 6 A 1 b, c; as recipient of passive verb, 6 A 1 b, c; as subject, 3 B, 5 D 1
Noun: complemented by an infinitive, 12 E 2; composed of an abstract form, 9 B 1 d; formed into a local passive verb, 8 A 4 a; formed into a verb by adding paN-, 11 A 2
'Now, by now': expressed by na, 12 G 1 ff.

Order: see Word order

Pa: 12 G 2 ff.
Particles: see Markers, Postpositives, Subject marker
Passive verb, 6 A; affixes, 12 A; imperative, 11 C 2 ff., 13 D 1; in existential sentences, 13 A 3 f.; goals of, 6 C, 8 C 2; meaning of, 13 D 3; obligatory in certain constructions, 13 A ff.; of causative verbs, 12 C 3, 4, 5, 6; of verbs that are not usually used in the active, 13 D 4; with specific recipients, 13 D 3 b. See also Accidental passive, Direct passive, Instrumental passive and Local passive
Person: first singular expressed by kitá, 9 A

Personal behalf: expressed by instrumental passive, 10 A, A 3; expressed by local passive, 8 A 2
Place: expressed by genitive, 6 B 5; expressed by local passive, 8 A 1
Plural: of agents or recipients expressed by verb with paN-, 11 A 1; of pronouns together with a name or title, 13 E
Possession: expressed by genitive, 6 B 1; with proper names, 2 E, E 1
Postpositives, 3 C 2; attraction of, 3 C 3 ff.; position of, 3 C 2, 3 ff.
Potential, 4 A, 5 C 3 ff.; active meaning, 13 D 2; expressed by ka-, 11 B 2; in passive sentences, 6 A 4; linking of díliq and waláq to, 12 D; meaning ability, 5 C 3 (1); meaning accidental action, 5 C 3 (4); meaning 'have opportunity to,' 5 C 3 (2); meaning 'perfected action,' 5 C 3 (3); meaning of passive ~, 13 D 3 a; obligatory use of, 11 D; unreal ~ refers to past, present or future time, 4 B 2
Predicate, 3 B; consisting of long form, 3 B 4; constituting a sentence, 3 B 3; position of ~ vis-a-vis the subject, 3 C 1; transformation into subject, 3 B 2
Prefixes: see Affixes
Preposed genitive: see Genitive
Prepositive, 3 C 3 a, 3 E; followed by unreal, 4 B 2 b, 5 C 1 (4); followed by volitional forms, 5 C 2 (4); linking of, 3 C 3 a, E
Pronouns: demonstrative: see Demonstratives; long forms of, 3 C 4; personal, 1 B 1; word order of, 3 C 4
Pronunciation, page 7 f.
'Put': passives of verbs meaning ~, 10 C, 14 F 1

q: dropping of, 3 F 2; inserted after vowel, 5 C (2)
Question: indirect, 4 F; with ba, 1 D 2; with diqáy, 13 G 2 b; with man, 1 D 2, 14 G 1 a

Ra, 14 G 2 ff.; ra ba, 14 G 2 g, h
Real: in active sentences, 4 B 1; in passive sentences, 6 A 3 a; meaning of, 4 B 1
Recipient, 6 A 1 b; indefinite pronouns as, 13 A 3 a; of action preceding the verb, requiring passive verb, 13 A 2; of passive verbs, 6 A 1 b; specific ~ requiring passive verb, 13 D 3 b

Sa: as dative marker, 5 D 2, 6 C; as genitive marker, 5 A 1, 6 B, B 5; preceding a word or phrase, marking goal, 5 D 2, 6 C; optionally marking abstract, 9 B 1 a (2); optionally marking infinitive, 9 B 2, 12 E 1
'Say, tell': verbs meaning ~, 14 F 4
Sentence: as complement, 12 E 3; consisting of a predicate alone, 3 B 3; consisting of two subject-like constituents, 3 B 1; containing dághan or dyútay, 4 C. See also Existential and Exclamatory sentences
Short forms: not used in predicate construction, 3 B 4; of demonstratives, 1 A 1; of pronouns, 1 B 1; of words, 3 F 1
'Should': expressed by unreal, 5 C 2 (2)
Si: marking subject, 3 B
'Somebody, someone': see Indefinite pronouns
Statements: contrasted with exclamations, 5 B 3; with diqáy, 13 G 2 a, 14 G 1 e; with man, 14 G 1 c, d
Stress, page 8
Subject, 1 C, 3 A 3, B, 5 D 1 a; consisting of a verb, 3 B 2, 13 D 5; lang with a subject consisting of a verb, 13 G 1 c; position of, 3 C 1; of existential sentence, 3 A 3; transformed into a predicate, 3 B 2; word order of ~ with passive verb, 6 D
Subject marker, 1 C; si, ang, as ~, 1 D 1; y as ~, 1 D 1, 3 B 5
Subjunctive: used after waláq, 6 A 3 c; used after other words, 13 F
Suffixes: see Affixes

*Tágaq: local passive of, 8 A 5
'There are many, few,' 4 C
Tiká, 9 A
Tikáw, 9 A
Time: expressed by genitive, 6 B 5; expressed by instrumental passive, 10 A 4; of deictics, 1 A 2; of existential sentence, 3 A 1
'Together': see '[Do] together'
Transformation: of predicate into subject, 3 B 2

Ug: as a linker, 8 D; introducing indirect questions, 4 F; marking goal, 5 D 2; meaning 'have,' 5 B ff.; preceding an adjective of manner, 9 C 2; preceding an infinitive, 12 E 1
Unreal: active used after certain words, 13 F; after prepositives, 4 B 2 b, 5 C 1 (4); active used in negative sentences, 4 B 2 d; after prepositives in passive sentences, 6 A 3 b; meaning of, 4 B 2 ff.; of instrumental passive meaning time, 10 A 4; preceded by an adjective expressing manner, 9 C 1
Únsa, 3 B; derived forms of, 3 B, 12 B ff.
Unsáqun: see Únsa

Verb: as predicate, 5 D 1; as subject, 3 B 2,

5 D 1; complemented by an infinitive, 12 E 1; complemented by a sentence, 12 E 3, 5; doubled ~, 14 Cf.; expressing manner, followed by infinitive, 14 A 1, 2; formed by adding paN- to a noun, 11 A 2; formed from adjectives, 8 A 4 b, 14 A 1; formed from nouns, 8 A 4 a, 11 A 2; that tends to be used in passive, 13 D 4. See also Active, Affixes, and Passive
Volitional: meaning compared to durative, 5 C 2 a; meaning 'come into the state,' 5 C 1 (3); meaning of, 5 C 1

Waláq, 2 B, 3 A 1; as a prepositive, 3 C 3 a; as a sentence, 3 A 2 b; linking of, 12 D; preposed genitive not used after, 6 B 3; use of subjunctive after, 6 A 3 c
Word order, 3 Cff.; of agent and subject with passive verbs, 6 D
'When': in questions, 4 D; in statements, 9 B 1 f.
'Where,' 2 A 2
'Which of several,' 3 Df.

Y: marking existentials, 3 A 1; marking subjects, 3 B, B 5

Zero: base alone with no affix, 11 C 1, 12 C 2, 14 E 1